MW00826601

THE BLOOD OF MY BLOOD

A Journal of Bible Meditations

By Pastor Oscar L. Destruge

As **"the life of a creature is in the blood" (Leviticus 17:1),** our spiritual life is nourished and sanctified through the Bread of Life.

"Whoever eats this bread will live forever" **(John 6:51).**

Así como ***"la vida del cuerpo está en la sangre" (Levítico 17:11)***, nuestra vida espiritual se alimenta y santifica mediante el Pan de Vida.

"Si alguno come de este pan, vivirá para siempre"
(Juan 6:51).

Όσο ***"η ζωή τής σάρκας είναι στο αίμα·" (ΛΕΥΙΤΙΚΟΝ 17:11),*** η πνευματική μας ζωή τρέφεται και αγιάζεται με τον άρτο της ζωής.

"Αν κάποιος φάει απ' αυτόν τον άρτο, θα ζήσει στον αιώνα"
(ΚΑΤΑ ΙΩΑΝΝΗΝ 6:51).

Epigraph - "I shall pass through this world but once. Any good, therefore, that I can do or any kindness I can show to any human being, let me do it now. Let me not defer it or neglect it, for I shall not pass this way again." **Stephen Grellet**

To my brother
John Norberto Destruge Sandoval
(5/9/1952 - 1/15/2022)
I prayed so many times for you, for guidance to figure out how to help you. Your struggle with mental illness and addiction helped me be more patient and kinder to strangers. In all their faces, I saw your face and the face of Jesus. Today you've been set free from your unrest. Rest in peace querido hermano.

Copyright ©2023 Pastor Oscar L. Destruge

Unless otherwise noted, all scriptures are from the Holy Bible, New International Version®, NIV® Copyright ©1973, 1978, 1984, 2011 by Biblica, Inc.® Used by permission. All rights reserved worldwide.

All Hebrew Bible Word translations are from Baker, W., & Carpenter, E. E. (2003). The complete word study dictionary: Old Testament. AMG Publishers. All Greek Bible Word translations are from Zodhiates, S. (2000). The complete word study dictionary: New Testament (electronic ed.). AMG Publishers.

ISBN:

Cover design by Doug Pashley
Cover photo: shutterstock.com 5 Standard License Download

Common Lectionary - The basis for these meditations is the Bible, based on the Common Lectionary. This edition covers January to November of Year B and December of Year C. Those who established the Common Lectionary devoted much time and prayer to ensure that over the course of three years, we will have read the entire Bible, not in the order of the Bible, but based on the ecclesiastical calendar that we follow (Advent, Christmas, Epiphany, Ordinary Time, Lent, Easter, Pentecost, Ordinary Time). In this way, they offer us a varied daily banquet from the Hebrew Scriptures, Psalms, Gospels, and Epistles, in which sometimes two or three readings come together perfectly.

ABOUT THE PHOTOGRAPHS

I've always been fascinated by snow-capped mountains, sunsets, night skies, colonial architecture, and rivers. Growing up in Quito, Ecuador until age 10, I was surrounded by these. The majestic snow-capped Cotopaxi volcano was always visible from the southern side of our house, the Machángara river ran a hundred meters behind on the western side, and Quito's 360°-night sky, at 2,800 meters high, consistently painted the most amazing constellations. Frequent visits to grandma's house at the center of colonial Quito exposed me to the most beautiful religious and secular structures.

Wherever our travels took us, I made sure to take pictures of such sites which inspire and awaken my curiosity to better know our creator and appreciate His creation, knowing that at a future date, I would use one of the photos in our daily meditations.

I've also asked my friends and family to lend me their photos of sunsets, night skies, mountains, and rivers. I'm delighted to share these with you. All photographs, unless otherwise noted, are from the Destruge-Sandoval / Xanthópoulos-Koktsídis families and friends. Thank you for sharing your pictures.

See photo credits at the end of the book.

ABOUT THE AUTHOR

Pastor Oscar was born in Ecuador and emigrated to the United States at age 10.

Oscar was neither a Christian nor a leader for much of his life. He was a shy, introverted musician who saw an opportunity to acquire quick wealth in real estate. Unfortunately, real estate took a nose-dive in 1987, with it, all his dreams, hopes, and savings. Not only was he in debt, but he was also emotionally and spiritually bankrupt! Anxiety filled him and led to months of sleepless nights.

The Father of Lies made Oscar believe he was a lousy provider, useless as a husband, father, employee, and investor. He pointed to his half-million-dollar life insurance policy as the answer to debt. The M*A*S*H theme song and its soothing refrain, "suicide is painless," kept buzzing around his head.

He almost acted on the lie, believing everyone would be better off without him, but God had better plans! His 8-year-old son, Jean-Paul, had become aware of their financial difficulties and said, "Dad, its ok if we're broke, as long as we're together."

In February 1989, a friend invited Oscar to a three-day spiritual retreat where he experienced an intimate, personal, and transforming encounter with Jesus (you can read the full story in the Closing Remarks at the end of the book). On Saturday, February 25, during an evening prayer chapel, he realized that God and his family loved him despite his faults and failures, and he began accepting and loving himself as he was. Since that three-day retreat in '89, God radically transformed his life. He found peace and joy in his heart and stopped worrying about many things.

Immediately, Oscar became an active Bible study participant and volunteer with the Children's choir. He created a Bible study group in his office, meeting weekly for study and prayer from 1990 through 1998. In 1991 he became a Stephen Minister, where he learned that saying yes to God produces spiritual growth, leadership, self-confidence, discipline, communication skills, and a deep appreciation for the value of time and family.

In 1991, Oscar went on a mission to Nagarote, Nicaragua, and continued pursuing mission work. In 1993 and 1995, he participated in Ecuador's Christian mission with Medical Missions International. As a result, Oscar reconnected with the Hispanic culture and, in 1994, began to work in Norwalk, CT with El Camino United Methodist Church (UMC). He was a counselor for the Billy Graham Evangelical Association and participated in the 1994 New York Central Park campaign.

From 1995-1998 Oscar became more involved in the leadership of El Camino, serving as a worship music leader, lay leader, lay speaker, treasurer, and Bible study teacher. While on a 2004 mission in Bolivia, God called Oscar to become a local pastor, serving the Hispanic communities in Norwalk and Bridgeport through worship, Bible study, social justice, immigration, feeding, and educational programs.

In October 2010, after 35 years of service, Oscar retired from Diversified Investment Advisors as Vice President - Compliance / Spanish Services to dedicate more time to church, community, and missions. Oscar became the Team Leader for Volunteer In Missions, leading groups to Ecuador for construction, medical, and Vacation Bible Study missions. In June 2017, Pastor Oscar retired from the United Methodist Church to dedicate more time to family. He writes daily Bible meditations in English and Spanish on Facebook and YouTube and enjoys racquetball, bicycling, music, and chess.

Family: Pastor Oscar is married to Margarita Xanthopoúlou-Destruge. God has blessed them with two children: Jean-Paul and Sophia, and three grandchildren, Ségolène Sevastí, Salomé Elly, and Lázaro Elías.

ACKNOWLEDGEMENTS

I thank my daughter, Sophia Eleni, who inspired me to embark on this project. After retiring, I told Sophia I missed studying for and writing sermons.

Sophia suggested, "Why don't you write a daily journal and share it with friends and family?"

I doubted that I could write daily for more than a month. I'd run out of things to say! My mind lacks the organization to select essential topics. But God has been faithful, and with each message guides, affirms, and **strengthens you and me to continue being God's messengers of peace, unity, hope, forgiveness, and love.**

Since August 2018, the **members of "Oscar's Bible Meditations group"** (English) and *"Meditaciones Bíblicas de Oscar"* (Spanish) grew to 296 English and 643 Spanish. I'm grateful for their prayers, likes, and comments encouraging me to continue writing. I might have given up if I'd only heard silence. But God spoke loudly through the Bible, their comments, and their presence.

There were days when I couldn't come up with the meditation and thought, *"It's ok to skip one day!"* One such day, I received a message from Luz Nina saying, *"pastor, can you send today's meditation? We have many people in Bolivia and other countries anxiously waiting for your reflections."*

"I do not cease to thank God for you" **(Ephesians 1:16),** my family and friends. You motivate me daily to be a better messenger and imitator of Jesus and my father-in-law/mentor, **Aristoklís Xanthópoulos,** a faithful servant who rests with the Lord. I looked up to him as an example of a Christian man, husband, father, brother, uncle, friend, and all the roles we hold within the family and community structures.

I'm grateful for everyone whose words and acts of kindness inspired me to put together over 1500 meditations in English and Spanish and about one hundred in Greek. I'm forever thankful to **Haroula Konstandinidou,** the best Greek Translator in the industry, who generously volunteered her time and talents to bless our Greek family and friends with accurate translations of our meditations during the Summer of 2019. I also thank my wife**, Margarita**, who allowed me to set aside a few hours per day, even during vacations, to study, meditate, and write to our family, friends, and future generations.

The time I spend with God's Word and you in my heart and prayers has become an essential and nurturing part of my day. It's a time when I feel connected with God, family, friends, and the communities where I've been privileged to live and serve.

If God called me to His presence tomorrow I'd go happily knowing I've fulfilled **my covenant and purpose**. I've had the joy and privilege of transmitting Christian values, hopes, and dreams to friends, family, my children, and the children of their children. I've done this so that together we might **all live according to God's design.**

PREFACE

I'd always wished that the churches where I was appointed would grow, that *"the words of my mouth and the meditations of my heart"* **(Psalm 19:14) would have a greater audience and impact**. God's plan and timing didn't grant me that wish until after retiring as pastor of a traditional church. Today, we have over 900 members in two daily Bible meditation groups. The marvelous thing is that God's Word and presence won't leave us the way we were found. We're no longer what we were because the Lord cleanses and reshapes us daily through God's inspired Holy Word and the fellowship we share.

When I retired as a pastor in 2017, I thought that my days of leading and encouraging others in their faith were behind me. I had no clue that God was preparing to enlarge my ministry in a new way and deepen my relationship with Him, friends, family, and the communities surrounding us and throughout the world. I thank God for granting me a new way to remain connected with Christ and the beloved community! We are truly connected to life-giving power through God's Word and by sharing how we've experienced the transformative moving of God's Holy Spirit in our lives.

When I sit to write, I imagine hundreds of people (present and future generations) ready to hear God's loving word. They include family, friends, friends of friends, and future great-grandchildren, speaking multiple languages (Greek, Spanish, and English). To honor our ancestors from both sides of the family, I've written these meditations in English, Spanish, and some Greek. **This publication is in English, with scripture verses in Spanish and Greek.**

Whatever our preferred language, by God's grace, we're all transforming daily into the image of our Savior. Jesus sacrificed His life so we may continue His ministry in our communities and circles of love and trust. In a way, God granted my wish! Only **God's perfect timing** could accomplish in a brief time what I could not do in sixteen years as pastor of a traditional church with my efforts and strategies.

The following question appears on my screen as I prepare for daily meditations: *"What do I want my children and future generations to know about God and me?"* **About me**, I want you to know that I love you and our family. Although my eyes might have never seen you on this earth, I've prayed for God to increase your faith so that you do not chase after the gods of this world.

About God: God is real, loves you unconditionally, and has good plans for your life. You were wonderfully formed. God doesn't make mistakes or trash! **You are God's masterpiece, created to serve the King.** You must know that nothing can make your parents love you less and that you can trust God and your parents with your greatest regrets and failures because God's Mercy is unconditional and eternal. The Bible is God's love letter to you. Many will tell you that **"all roads lead to God,"** but that is a misguided lie. There is only one road (Jesus) and one God, the creator of the universe. The Lord is jealous, consumes those who reject and disobey Him, but is a loving and protective parent to His children. God purifies us through the fire that never consumes and sanctifies us by His Word.

I'm grateful for the trust and responsibility I've been given to share God's Word with friends and family. I fearfully and meticulously remain faithful to Scripture so that the *"words of my mouth and the meditations of my heart would be pleasing in your sight, Lord, my Rock, and my Redeemer,"* **(Psalm 19:14)** and be a source of strength and encouragement in the faith of friends, family, and my future generations. I pray that God would prevent the enemy from interfering in our continuous search and desire to know God more deeply through God's Holy and Inspired Word. That, my beloved, is my prayer for you.

One afternoon, explaining to a good friend how I chose the title for this journal, I said, *"I wrote it for my children and their children's children who are the blood of my blood."*

She asked, *"but is there another meaning?"*

I answered, "Yes! 'I believe that Jesus tells all of us as children of God: 'You are the *blood of My Blood.*'" We are privileged to live and tell our God stories because Jesus loves us and gave His life for us.

God isn't done with you or me! God answers prayers in God's perfect time and manner. We might not get what we asked for, but we always receive what's required to fulfill our divine purpose. As you meditate on God's Word through this journal remember that You are the **precious blood of Christ's Blood.** May God grant you guidance and joy as you seek God's fruitful will.

INTRODUCTION

When I was an employee in the Corporate world, I dedicated inordinate amounts of time and energy to my job. After the Lord saved me, God taught me the importance of having a **healthy balance** between serving God, family, and work. Many times, even pastors lose the notion of that healthy balance. Well-intentioned clergy give an inordinate priority to the things of the church, convinced that we're doing it *"for the Lord,"* leaving the needs of our families on the sidelines. This often results in high levels of friction in the home, stress, disillusionment, divorce, and sometimes suicide.

I wrote this book to be a positive reminder to friends, readers, family, and my future generations that we all go through periods of depression, questioning life itself. But, no matter our past, what we feel about ourselves, no matter our doubts and fears, we must come to realize that we are of great value to God and our family. By feeding daily on God's affirming and loving statements found throughout the Bible and this journal, we can come out of our depressions and take our place in society with gratitude and humility.

Many people know about God, but fewer know or have personally experienced God's *"agape"* love. Without God's love, protection and guidance, we're easy prey to the enemy's lies which can lead to isolation, low self-esteem, depression, and suicidal thoughts. Everyone needs to know that God is in the business of loving the unlovable, strengthening the weak, enriching the poor in spirit, and putting Humpty Dumpty together again.

I also embarked on this project because there's a growing distrust of the Bible and, more so, of organized religion. **Think about this:** What would happen if we didn't transmit our faith and hope to future generations quickly and intentionally? I believe that we'd fail our children, who would be headed towards a disappointing life lacking purpose, knowledge of God, joy, love of self and neighbor, and hope.

The Bible is quickly losing its credibility, reliability, and authenticity. Skeptics say that it contains noble poetry and some good morals but is full of lies (Mark Twain). Others claim it's filled with contradictions, thereby rejecting its Divine origin. Some say that the Bible **contains** God's Word **and** the words of men, so they cannot trust its direction. The Bible says: *"All Scripture is inspired by God and useful to teach, to reprove, to correct, to instruct in righteousness, so that the man of God may be perfect, equipped for every good work"* (**2 Timothy 3:16-17**).

A recent poll says that ***"18- to 29-year-old Americans are less likely than older respondents to say the Ten Commandments are still important today."***[1] God gave us the commandments for our protection **(Exodus 20:1– 17). Can you imagine a world without laws against robbery and murder?**

Living in obedience to God's laws offers society purpose, direction, peace, joy, and protection. The key is to know and **follow** the rules. We acquire knowledge and understanding through daily **Bible study, prayer, and meditation**. Then, motivated by gratitude for the love, mercy, and compassion God has showered upon us, we practice what we've learned.

Through prayer, the Holy Spirit helps us to gain clarity and purpose. Many brilliant scholars analyze why *the author* of the book, be it Paul, John, Peter, etc., used one word and not a clearer one. In these meditations, you'll notice I've stated that ***"God teaches or says to us"*** through John, Peter, Paul, etc., which is essential to establish God's authorship and maintain the integrity of the Bible. The Lord used imperfect people to record His Holy Word in this beautiful book you and I enjoy reading and studying **(2 Timothy 3:16).**

I was moved by the June 10, 2021 Greek Evangelical meditation that appears in the photo and wanted to share it with you. Following is the English translation.

"Today, if you hear his voice, do not harden your hearts" **(Hebrews 3:15).**

"A crumpled piece of paper was found in an American soldier's coat who was killed in the war. It contained a letter to God. Sometimes, the words of a dying person are most trustworthy.

*'Hear me, my God. I haven't spoken to you before. **I was told that you don't exist**. Last night, however, I looked at your Heavens from the bottom of an artillery bunker and discovered that I had been lied to… But strangely… I had to*

---

[1] *https://www.deseret.com/2018/3/28/20642391/poll-are-the-ten-commandments-still-relevant-today-americans-and-brits-differ-and-millennials-stand.*

come to this awful place to see your face. I love you…This is what I want you to know. In a little while, there will be a horrific battle. Who knows, maybe I'll arrive at your house tonight! We haven't been comrades until now, and I wonder if you'll be waiting for me at the door … **Aghhh, If I had only met you earlier!** *…. Strange… From the moment I met you, I stopped being afraid of dying. Till we meet again!'"*

As God-loving and God-fearing Christians, our task is to **rebuke and correct the lie**. If we do, many will be released from the bondage of fear, doubt, and depression into a life of love, peace, joy, and hope. But if we don't correct the lie, someday it might be our children in a bunker who have lived their entire lives in fear of death, crying out, *"aghhh… If only I'd known you sooner."*

My father-in-law, Aristoklís Xanthópoulos, said, *"Oscar, you don't need to change religion. You need to know God. Many people know about God, but few know God personally."* Bible study, prayer, and meditation will guide you to **know God's** heart, know your own identity (your actual value to God), and discover your life's purpose. I pray that these daily meditations will help you unravel these essential mysteries, my dear friends and family, the *blood of my blood.*

> **"OSCAR, YOU DON'T NEED TO CHANGE RELIGION. YOU NEED TO KNOW GOD. MANY PEOPLE KNOW ABOUT GOD, BUT FEW KNOW GOD PERSONALLY."**

Each meditation takes about 4 minutes to read. Start your day by feeding on God's Word. **Keep a Journal of your studies and time alone with God.** Write small anecdotes of how God intervened in your life to raise you to higher ground. Your children and their children will thank you for passing on your love, faith and treasure through your life's example.

TESTIMONIALS / ENDORSEMENTS / REVIEWS

Generations of trauma, loss, and healing are brought to the present. Oscar shares in an authentic way the histories and legacies of our ancestors that have provided lifelong lessons. A true masterpiece to support in the healing of communities through prayer, meditation, and love.

Erica Sandoval, LCSW, CEO and Founder of Latinx in Social Work
Author of **Latinx/e in Social Work, Vol. I and II**

*****

This book is a celebration of one person's collection of sermons, meditations, and passion-filled interpretations of Judeo-Christian scriptures, the Holy Bible. Penned in a unique and reflective voice with Bible verses translated into English, Spanish, and Greek, this soul-searching anthology beckons a large Christian community.

I've known Oscar Destruge for nearly twenty years. Words have power, and, in his writings, they come from the heart. They're filled with love and a desire to help future generations. He reinforces his messages by example. Oscar has led and served on countless missions, organizations, and boards to serve those in need.

The author's cross-cultural heritage makes him compassionate, inclusive, and open-minded to differing world views and diversity. He knows that humanity is a giant tapestry composed of different cultures and ways of life.

If we are to be like Jesus, which is what this book and Oscar's life's work is about, we must accept and love all sentient beings knowing that every thread, every soul, and every creature in that tapestry contributes to the greater whole. His May 24th entry emphasizes this point beautifully: *"God distributes gifts according to the needs of the church and community for mutual benefit."*

Two ideals set the tone for this singular book; the author's unwavering desire to live and set an example for the higher good of all and the belief that by embodying timeless Christ-conscious truths, we create a peaceful, harmonious, and thriving global community - **Roxana Bowgen, Author Agapanthus Rising.**

*****

Pastor Oscar's meditations welcome you to his family, his love for people, and his faith in God's love, wisdom, and grace. Oscar writes like the person he is; someone who is a steward of God's Word. He writes with thoughtfulness and care because he wants us all to see a life in Christ. And he has done just that.

I first met Oscar at a Christian retreat weekend over thirty years ago. Over the years, we've shared our joys and concerns. We played original songs together in a four-piece contemporary Christian band for nearly a decade. The joy we shared in the music, prayer, and fellowship had much to do with Oscar being in the band.

Pastor Oscar's life is immersed in Christian service and study. With actions, words, and food, he has cared for others. His gentle spirit allows him to witness God's love in ways only he can. His book is filled with inspired meditations. In his prayer for his meditation on February 9th, Oscar writes that, *"despite our inconsistency"* in living God's word, *"you tenderly lead us along the paths of abundant life."* His prayer asks God to grant us *"goodness, faithfulness, and humility."* Amen.

In *"The Blood of my Blood,"* compassionate meditations overflow with love…God's love, wisdom, and grace are at work through Pastor Oscar. His writing is for us all.

David Johnston - Retired President Visual Services, Inc; Photo Journalist; Musician; and Friend

*****

I have known Oscar Destruge since the early days of our walk with our Lord. He is a kind, gentle soul strong in his faith. Oscar's daily devotions are an insightful, thoughtful, and inspirational way to stay connected to your faith on a daily basis. I highly recommend spending a few minutes a day with these devotions. I have no doubt they will soon become part of your daily routine.

Keith Donnelly, Author of *The Christmas Stranger*
www.donaldyoungbloodmysteries.com

*****

I've known Oscar since before I married his good friend Jill Calandrelli almost 30 years ago. Jill was a member of Oscar's Bible study group at work and I thank God that Oscar put in a good word for me back then. Our daughter Emily is Oscar's goddaughter.

A friend in Christ can be closer than a brother, and I'm privileged and blessed to call Oscar my brother in Christ. As iron sharpens iron, Oscar's friendship and life example have helped me to become a better husband, parent, and friend.

This book is an easy read, and life is short. Read it! Learn from it. Use it to dive into God's word and embrace the hope that He offers through His Son, Jesus.

You have a choice to share your faith experience with others. Oscar reminds us through the meditations and prayers in this book that we do not need to be perfect in order to share hope in Christ. The world will always need hope. Thank you, Oscar, for reminding us that hope in Christ must be shared with each generation.

John Monroe - Lifelong friend

*****

I met Pastor Oscar in 2009 when he was the Spiritual Director of a retreat I attended. Ten years later, I had the pleasure of serving on a retreat team with him and learned that he was writing daily meditations online.

Pastor Oscar starts each online meditation with, *"I wish you a blessed day, my beloved friends and family,"* and it is with this audience in mind that he makes scripture extremely relevant to our 21st-century lives. Each meditation includes specific Biblical readings, and Pastor Oscar's close relationship with our Lord is revealed as he interprets and gives meaning to the scriptures. I am constantly in awe of his devotion to God and his dedication to his readers.

I love spiritual music, and his meditations often bring a related hymn to mind. I feel the chorus from the hymn, "Here I Am Lord," describes Pastor Oscar: *"Here I am Lord. Is it I Lord? I have heard you calling in the night. I will go Lord if you lead me. I will hold your people in my heart,"* based on **Isaiah 6:8** and **1 Samuel 3:4**.

I personally give thanks to God for Pastor Oscar and his spirit-led, enlightening meditations! I hope all readers of this compilation will find that his meditations enrich their faith journeys just as they have mine.

Eileen R Doyle, Devoted Reader

*****

I'm excited about Pastor Oscar's publishing of his daily devotionals. His commitment to sharing the Word of God and daily worship through song & scripture in three languages is an amazing undertaking! And his dedication and devotion have been an example to me and many others.

I pray the Lord will bless and use this tool to minister the gospel and the hope that is found in Jesus Christ to many hurting people around the world!

Rev. Johnny Cardamone, Norwalk, CT

*****

I am honored to pen a review of this book written by my dear friend, Pastor Oscar L. Destruge. While both of us have been ministry leaders for a very long time, I best know him as a competitor on the racquetball court. There have been but a handful of occasions our paths have crossed in ministry, hence my fascination to read what he has written. My interest was to see how his heart would be reflected in his writings, as I have known him primarily as a competitor. By his own admission he would acknowledge that while others play racquetball for fun, he plays to win!

The Blood of my Blood is a daily journal of meditations derived from the common lectionary. These have been shared with members of his online study community. The format of the meditations is the inclusion of the assigned Bible reading for that day and Pastor Destruge's explanation and application of that text. Each daily meditation ends with a prayer.

The book is saturated with Scripture. Beyond the occasional reference to some words in their original language, Pastor Destruge offers a very straightforward and down-to-earth explanation. Many times he would reference his own history in shedding light on the text. The appeal of this book is for those believers who take their faith seriously and desire to mature spiritually. It is intertwined with historical references to Oscar's own family, including that of his in-laws. Actually, the term in-laws is a misnomer for him in that he presents the family of his wife as his own family. I am still processing the inclusion of royalty in the family tree of Pastor Destruge!

I am blessed by the commonalities I hold with Oscar. Both of us are immigrants who have adopted the United States as our new homeland. We have a profound love for this country and are grateful for the many blessings of prosperity we have been fortunate to experience. We know that this country is not completely perfect, as no other country is. While others may want to implode America for the "five" things they consider bad about America; Oscar and I unashamedly and unapologetically choose to celebrate the other "ninety-five" things that make America a great land of opportunities and possibilities. We also both believe that the church and the institution of family are crucial for the stability and progress of America. A commitment to both prompts the favor of God.

Having read the **Blood of my Blood**, I was overtaken with a bit of nostalgia. Pastor Destruge lavishly acknowledges his ancestors and current family members for the impact they have had in his life, making him the man he is today. It is providential that his first book is a book of meditations. Less than a year ago, my beloved mother transitioned from time to eternity; from earth to glory. Whenever she would visit me in Connecticut, she made certain to collect her Daily Bread from our display rack at the church. She truly enjoyed reading the daily meditations. Sometimes I have had to mail them to her back home.

May God richly bless those who read this book.

Rev. Dr. Jeffrey A. Ingraham, Pastor of Calvary Baptist Church, Norwalk, CT.
Author, *Preaching The Ten Commandments* (2017);
Major Messages From Minor Prophets (2021)

*****

I found **Blood Of My Blood** *Bible Meditations* by Pastor Oscar Destruge to be very enlightening and inspirational. I especially enjoyed the testimonials shared by Pastor Destruge, which helped bring the scripture to life. This life application helps the reader to realize that God's Word applies to every aspect of their life.

I highly recommend **Blood Of My Blood** *Bible Meditations* and believe that it is a book that will transform lives.

Rev. Dr. Sheldon E. Williams, Pastor of the Co-op City BC, Bronx, NY

*****

I had the opportunity to participate in a clergy Bible Study group while serving a UM Church, a prosperous small parish, in Southern Fairfield county. We were a faithful mixed group, male and female, white and black, younger and older. We came to respect and indeed care for each other so that it became an important spiritual time for all of us.

The contrast in our ministries was what made our commitment and perspective to Scripture also varied. Oscar's was sincerely and deeply and always freshly evangelical. He was serving more marginalized communities in urban settings. A number of us were serving "Gold Coast" congregations. So our sharing was always varied in its context and perspective. We were all honest in our involvement. Oscar was surely the most evangelical of our group and he became a teacher for at least myself after serving as a bureaucrat for over 25 years. I rarely missed a meeting because of how sustaining and renewing the time together was for me, and Oscar was a significant part of that, reminding me of what our ministry was at its best.

These meditations are so heart-felt and faithful to the Word that I'm certain they will reward you with a deepening of your faith and a fresh perspective on the Word of God. Oscar is a remarkable student and leader in God's service.

Rev. Stephen Goldstein, United Methodist, Elder, Retired

*****

The scripture you share with the meditations is always relevant and uplifting. I have found great solace and encouragement, and am challenged to be the best I can be for Christ's sake. Thank you for continuing to share from your heart!

Gail Brown, Devoted Reader and Friend

*****

I do appreciate these daily meditations. They typically speak directly into something that is on my mind and in my heart.

LJ, Devoted Reader, and Friend

*****

DEDICATION
To my wife, Margarita (Mery)

When I was 14, living in the Washington Heights neighborhood of New York City, a Greek/Brazilian family lived one floor above us. They had a beautiful, kind, and humble daughter named Georgía. I was silently in love but too shy to speak to her. I decided in my heart, *"someday, I will marry a Greek woman."* And I did! Lucky me!

God has been more than good to me. First, by choosing me as an adopted child, and second, by guiding both sets of our parents to immigrate to the United States so that we'd meet, fall in love, and spend 47 years (as of November 15th, 2022) creating a Godly home for our children and their children. I am grateful that Mery chose me to be her husband.

Thank you, Mery, for your love, two beautiful children, three precious grandchildren, and for loving and helping my parents and extended family (brothers, aunts, uncles, cousins, etc.). Thank you for your sacrifices and planning to build a nurturing home and family. For all the amazing, but especially the European and South American vacations. All my hopes and childhood dreams are fulfilled in you. I dedicate this book to you with much love, gratitude, and admiration.

To my children and future generations,
The flesh of my flesh, and blood of my blood.

When I retired from my Corporate job with Diversified Investment Advisors in 2010, before I started writing these meditations, I became addicted to racquetball, playing 3-6 hours daily, five days per week. Nothing interrupted my routine until I began to write in August 2018. Sitting here, thinking about you in the year 2122 (100 years from now), reading and meditating on these words motivates me beyond expectations. Thank you for showing interest in learning who we were, and how we lived and loved our Christian call and family.

I'm crazy in love with my son, **Jean-Paul** Xanthópoulos Destruge, and my precious daughter, **Sophia Eleni** Destruge. I've never loved another man as I love and admire you, Jean-Paul. You're an amazing dad, loving, caring, and fun with Ségolène and Salomé. A man that genuinely loves to cook! You have a huge heart, and I love you. I thank God daily for you and pray that God gives you the health, strength, and wisdom to prosper in all you do.

I'm also proud that Jean-Paul carries the Greek maternal surname, **Xanthópoulos**. Papoú Artistoklís didn't have boys to continue the name. Therefore, we gave him Papou's surname as a middle name. I encourage you never to forget where you came from and be proud to carry the Destruge-Xanthópoulos names with honor and dignity.

My **Sophia Eleni**, we're so proud of all the challenges you've faced and surmounted. Mom and I love you very much. On October 12, 1984, God chose mom and me to love and care for our special gift. You are, have been, and will always be my special gift from God. I'm **overjoyed** that Carlos was persistent, and you chose each other as lifelong partners. With Carlos by your side and Lázaro Elías under your loving care, I rest knowing that **you are living the life that we've prayed for you**; a good life and that you are and will be happy and loved.

May God continue to bless you, Jean-Paul and Phoenix, Sophia and Carlos, and may God be at the center of your home forever. I love you with all my heart and strength.

To my future and yet unknown generations (children of Ségolène, Salomé, Lázaro, should they choose to have and be blessed with natural or adopted children), although I may be long gone to my resting place, know that I've prayed for you who, for now, are nameless but carry the Destruge-Xanthópoulos names and/or blood in your veins. I've prayed that through these meditations and the stories of your parents, God would transmit our love, joy, and hope to you. That God would increase your faith so that you do not chase after the gods of this world. I pray that you meditate and study the Bible and this journal and pass them down to your children and their children as a sign of our endless love, prayers, and hope for you. With unfailing love, I dedicate this book to you, the flesh of my flesh and *blood of my blood.*

Abuelito (Grandpa)

Yiayía Mery has always been a strong guiding presence in all our lives. Over 47 years, I've witnessed her care and protectiveness for our home, her parents, sister, cousins, our children and grandchildren, nieces and nephews, and as I've said, even for members of my Sandoval family.

Writing is not her strength, although I'm sure that if you sat with her for a cup of coffee she would share stories, advice, and values by which to ensure that your relationship with each other, as family members who share the same blood and heritage, is one in which you place God and family above all else.

Here are a few words that **Yiayia Mery** shares with you, the *blood of her blood*, from an interview we had on September 18, 2022, in Megály Yiayia Kyriakí's home in Katerini.

1 **What is the most important thing that you want our present and future generations to know about you, your family, or God?** - Togetherness is very important to me. That you never forget our humble but proud beginnings and strive to retain and imitate those character traits. Our ancestors didn't have the survival means, but they persevered. I want you to know that God is real and you should seek to find, know and love God.

2 **Whom do you admire?** I admire my ancestors because they lived hard, horrible lives, particularly during the wars. Their spirit, which trusted and loved God, brought them through.

3 **What inspires you to take action?** When I see unfairness or things not getting done right, I want to jump in and fix the problem. You should be open to helping those in need.

4 **What makes you mad?** It bothers me when I see people that have been brainwashed by propaganda, that don't take the time to review other world views and information. It also bothers me when my advice is pooh-poohed. People often misunderstand my good intentioned advice.

5 **What do you enjoy the most?** Family! Spending time with my grandchildren and children. I love when our children and grandchildren remain connected with each other and with our Greek culture and family here in Greece.

6 **If you could live anywhere, where would you live?** Where my children are! Although presently, I need to be here in Greece with my mother, to care for her.

7 **Which human characteristics and core values do you value most?** I value family, God, security (peace), loyalty, respect, and freedom.

TABLE OF CONTENTS

— JANUARY —
BEGINNINGS -
DESTRUGE / ILLINGWORTH

The **Destruge-Illingworth** family traces its origins back to Ecuador via France and England.

Paternal: My great-great-grandfather, Dr. Colonel Jean-Batiste **Destruge,** was born in 1803 in France and emigrated to Venezuela, where he met and married Rosa Maitín (1827). They had five children: Rosa, **Alcides (my great grandfather)**, Camilo, Ana, and Matilde Destruge. **Dr. Alcides**, born on July 14, 1828, met and married **Carmen Illingworth**, daughter of **John Illingworth Hunt.**

Juan Illingworth Hunt

My great-great-grandfather, Admiral **Juan Illingworth Hunt ,** was born on May 10, 1786, to **Abraham Illingworth** and **Mary Hunt**, in Stockport, Chester, England. Thanks to my great-uncle **Camilo Destruge Illingworth** (Guayaquil, October 20, 1863 – February 26, 1929), who was a distinguished Ecuadorian historian, journalist, and chronicler, we are lucky to have abundant historical records on the life of Admiral Juan Illingworth, the most famous and recognized in the family. **Destruge** and **Illingworth** worked under General Simón Bolivar to liberate South America from Spain's rule, based in Guayaquil, Ecuador.*

In 1819, **General Bolivar commissioned Juan Illingworth to defend and protect the pacific borders along Chile, South America, and appointed him Colonel on October 9, 1821**. On May 24, 1822, he joined forces with Sucre, Bolivar's Chief Lieutenant, to take Quito from Spaniard control and was appointed chief Military and Civic leader of Guayaquil.

Camilo Destruge

While residing in Guayaquil, Juan Illingworth met **Mercedes Décima Villa y Cosío**, daughter of the Spanish merchant Vicente Décima Villa and the **Lady Mercedes Cosío y Villamar**. They had six children; Juana, Carolina, Juan, **Carmen (our great-grandmother)**, Gertrudis, and Vicente.

Carmen and Dr. Alcides had 13 children, including my grandfather, **Federico Carlos Destruge Illingworth**, born in 1877, who died on August 28, 1928.

My paternal grandmother **Amada Clorinda Osorio Maldonado** was born to **Juan Maldonado and Josefina Osorio** in the 1890s. I remember her telling me that her parents were influential citizens in Quito and **President Eloy Alfaro (1842 - 1912)** frequented their home at "La Plaza del Teatro" and cuddled her as a baby. President Eloy Alfaro was assassinated on January 28, 1912, while in prison, where he and his colleagues had been detained. I suppose Abuelita

Amada's father was also imprisoned and had their lands and properties confiscated. As a result, Abuelita Amada was poor.

Federico Destruge Illingworth met **Abuelita Amada Clorinda Osorio Maldonado** in Quito, married and had my dad, **Galo Destruge Maldonado** on June 5, 1925 (died on September 2, 2012). My grandfather Federico had three other children: Carmelina, Alcibiades, and Julia Destruge. Abuelito Galo never met his dad or brothers. On December 31, 2009, we traveled to Cuenca to meet the sixteen nephews from Alcibiades and Julia and nearly 120 grand-nephews who bear the Destruge surname. It was a fantastic family reunion. Abuelito's brothers had passed away a few years earlier.

My dad, Galo Destruge Maldonado, had two sons: **Galo Destruge, Jr**. (1/14/1947 - 10/20/2001) and **Fernando** Mentor Destruge (3/14/1949) with Piedad Ponce. Life situations caused him to separate and start a new family. He met and married my mother, **Lilia María Sandoval Ortega,** with whom he had three children, my brother **John Norberto Destruge** (5/10/1952-1/15/2022), me, Oscar Leopoldo Destruge (July 1, 1954), and my twin (**Juan** Destruge Sandoval) who lived for just a few hours. All of abuelito Galo's children were born in Quito, Ecuador.

*In 2008, the Ecuadorian government ordered that **Admiral Juan Illingworth** be buried in a monument in the Navy Park in Guayaquil, where he was given the full military funeral he deserved.

January 1
HAPPY NEW YEAR
Ecclesiastes 3:1,5b

How fitting that we start the year with **Ecclesiastes 3:1**, *"There is a time for everything, and a season for every activity under the heavens."*

Gratitude is always a good place to start. I'm infinitely grateful to my God for His kindness and mercy toward my family and me. I'm also thankful for the privilege of serving our Lord through these daily Bible meditations: a bridge connecting me through time and space with my future generations, the children, and grandchildren of my children, Jean-Paul and Sophia Destruge. Although my voice does not cooperate with me, I'm grateful for the privilege of singing daily praises to our God. Lastly, my infinite gratitude to each of you, my beloved friends and family, readers and listeners, who immensely encourage this ministry with your presence and feedback.

Many of you know me personally. Others are friends of my friends or family. But know that I'm not merely a voice or presence on social media, but a friend/brother who is praying for you and your future generations.

I pray for you and those who may read or view this spiritual journal in future years, that God grants you His love, joy, peace, hope, gratitude, prosperity, and a sense of purpose. May these meditations be food for your souls and help you face the day's challenges with the certainty that God is by your side and will give you victory in every time and season. Happy day and New Year.

January 2
WISDOM
James 3:17

We begin a new year with the **James 3:17** text, which speaks of Godly Wisdom, acquired through the Bible, revelation from the Holy Spirit, prayer, meditation, and trials and victories.

Everything material is subject to spoilage, but the instruction, intelligence, and Wisdom that come from God, accompany us forever, in all situations, and are never lost, corrupted, or changed. They're as invariable as God's love.

3

Wisdom, Justice, Salvation, and Hope are the inheritance that God has prepared for those who can say, **"I'm a child of God."**

We receive **Wisdom** through secular and spiritual books. But the essential teachings derive from *"each Word that comes from the mouth of God" (Matthew 4:4).* They enter our minds through our eyes or ears, where we analyze them through logic and reasoning, creating seeds of faith.

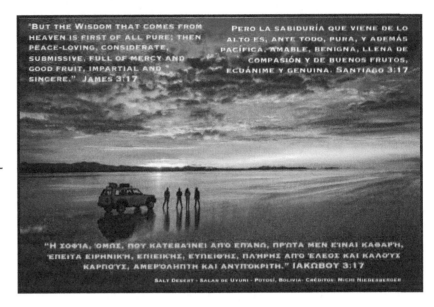

Wisdom flows from the fear of failing loved ones in our duty as parents, uncles, spouses, brothers, etc., and failing to do God's will. It's a gift from God, starting with reverence for all things of God, including following His commandments and seeking justice. **Wisdom** is how we use intelligence, i.e., putting into practice the instructions and revelation that God has given us.

As we begin a new year, God calls us to demonstrate **Godly Wisdom** through our good conduct and *"deeds done in the humility that comes from wisdom"* (James 3:13). The first quality mentioned is **HUMILITY**, in contrast to the *"bitter envy and selfish ambition"* that we find in *"earthly, unspiritual, demonic"* wisdom, which generates *"disorder and every evil practice"* (James 3:14-17).

Earthly wisdom is NOT the desired inheritance for our children and their children's children. We seek wisdom from *"heaven* [which] *is first of all pure; then peace-loving, considerate, submissive, full of mercy and good fruit, impartial and sincere"* (James 3:17).

By instructing our children to practice these qualities of God's Wisdom, they'll experience a harvest of *"peace and righteousness"* that will never rot or spoil in their lives and future generations (James 3:18).

Let us pray: Dear God, open our eyes, ears, and hearts to distinguish between **Godly Wisdom** and wisdom which flow from a human and deceitful heart. Don't let the seeds of knowledge you've sown in our hearts go to waste. We pray in your holy name.

January 3
LET'S SING TO THE LORD A NEW SONG

"Sing to the Lord a new song, for he has done marvelous things; his right hand and his holy arm have worked salvation for him. The Lord has made his salvation known and revealed his righteousness to the nations." Psalm 98:1-2

"Cantad al Señor un cántico nuevo, porque ha hecho maravillas, su diestra y su santo brazo le han dado la victoria. El Señor ha dado a conocer su salvación; a la vista de las naciones ha revelado su justicia". **Salmo 98:1-2 LBLA**

"ΝΑ ΨΑΛΕΤΕ στον Κύριο ένα νέο τραγούδι· επειδή, έκανε θαυμαστά έργα· το δεξί του χέρι, και ο βραχίονάς του ο άγιος, ενέργησαν σ' αυτόν σωτηρία. Ο Κύριος έκανε γνωστή τη σωτηρία του· μπροστά στα έθνη αποκάλυψε τη δικαιοσύνη του." **ΨΑΛΜΟΙ 98:1-2**

When we enter into an intimate relationship with God, everything becomes new, even the songs. *"Therefore, if anyone is in Christ, the new creation has come: The old has gone, the new is here!"* **(2 Corinthians 5:17).**

When musicians court the lady of their dreams, the musician's ideal is to write an original song that captures the magnitude of their love and how dazzled they are by her beauty, tenderness, etc. God composed a song we're unable to understand until we enter a relationship with God, who wants everyone to fully experience the magnitude of the love and sacrifice God has made to win our hearts. I imagine God's song says, *"Yes, this love is so deep, you are my pampered bride, and I want the whole world to know it"* (lyrics by Carlos Vives).

The Bible says that God will put a new song in our mouths and everyone will see, fear, and trust God **(Psalm 40:3).** All the earth will sing it **(Psalm 96:1)** *"in the congregation of saints"* **(Psalm 149:1).**
In heaven, we'll sing the song *"of the Lamb: 'Great and marvelous are your deeds, Lord God Almighty. Just and true are your ways, King of the nations. Who will not fear you, Lord, and bring glory to your name? For you alone are holy. All nations will come and worship before you, for your righteous acts have been revealed'"* **(Revelation 15:3–4).**

Revelation 5:9 says that we'll sing the new song to Jesus, *"And they sang a new song, saying: 'You are worthy to take the scroll and to open its seals, because you were slain, and with your blood you purchased for God persons from every tribe and language and people and nation.'"*

Let us pray: Dear God, *"Great and marvelous are your deeds, Lord God Almighty. Just and true are your ways, King of the nations."* We long to join the heavenly choir that will sing praises in your presence forever and ever. Keep us in your love. We pray in your Holy Name.

January 4
TRUST GOD
Proverbs 3:5-6

Telemarketers use all kinds of tactics and promises to gain our trust so that we'll buy their merchandise or services, such as, *"Believe me!" "I assure you it's 24k gold!"* And when all else fails, they use adulation; *"You'll be the envy of...."*

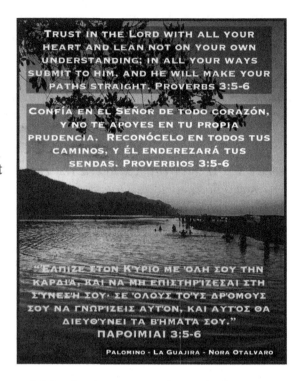

We'll often believe them. Shortly after investing, we realize the product is inferior to what was promised. It is a simple imitation, or instead of helping, it causes damage or illness. Often, we become addicted to such products. We want to but can't quit their use, such as cigarettes, alcohol, or drugs.

Not so with God! Today's verse invites us to **trust in God**, to put our future and hope in the Lord's hands. Faith and trust in God are gifts offered to those who recognize the need to straighten their ways and change their lifestyle because, until now, everything we've tried hasn't solved the situation. **Like the woman with the issue of blood,** many of us have lost time and money with imitations and false healers. But only God offers us a complete makeover, **a new heart, and a fresh start**. All we have to do is **trust in God!**

Today's verse is one of my favorites: *"Trust in the Lord with all your heart, and lean not on your own understanding. In all your ways, acknowledge Him first, and He will make your paths straight"* **(Proverbs 3:5-6). Psalm 55:22** is very similar. *"Cast your cares on the Lord, and he will sustain you; he will never let the righteous be shaken."*

My beloved, we can trust in God's promises. God is faithful and wants the best for His children. Jesus said, *"If you then, though you are evil, know how to give good gifts to your children, how much more will your Father in heaven give the Holy Spirit to those who ask him!"* **(Luke 11:13).** God will never fail us!

Let us pray: Dear God, grant that we may delight ourselves in Your Word and presence. Help us to trust our present and future, including that of our children, in Your miraculous hands so that You can turn our sorrows and anxieties into joy and gladness. Straighten our paths and give us a new heart dedicated to You. We pray in Jesus's name.

January 5
JESUS' GOLDEN RULE
Luke 6:31

Jesus's golden rule is our **divine mandate**. It's the compass that guides our actions, intentions, and words. The GPS (God Positioning System) that leads us along the right path to the heavenly mansion. The Golden Rule is *"Do to others as you would have them do to you"* **(Luke 6:31, Matthew 7:12).**

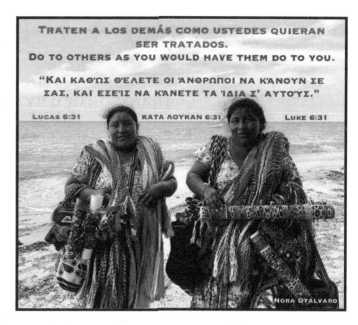

The Christian faith conveys God's deep and inexhaustible love that the world must experience **through our loving service to achieve God's peace.**

LOVE: **Jesus Christ challenges us to love** those around us, including our neighbor and enemy. This includes those passing through our community and individuals who don't share our religious, political, or civic views. Loving them means being kind, treating them as we'd like to be treated.

SERVICE: Unfortunately, many talk about God's love, but **their attitudes don't show that God is the love of their life**. What's the use of seeing a brother cold and not offering a blanket or shelter? Saying God bless you doesn't protect them from the cold. Serving others with disgruntled faces, as if it were an unpleasant chore, shows that we don't intimately know God's love. However, offering a pair of gloves, a wool hat, or a scarf will warm their body and soul, preparing their spirit to draw closer to Jesus, who sent us to serve and love in His Name. The key is to help those in need with love and make them feel important and worthy of God's loving care. It's treating them how we'd like them to treat our children.

Loving service leads us to the God of Peace. Only by applying the golden rule in our relationship with others do we experience *"the peace of God, which transcends all understanding"* **(Philippians 4:7).**

> **Loving service leads us to the God of Peace**. Only by applying the golden rule in our relationship with others do we experience *"the peace of God, which transcends all understanding"* **(Philippians 4:7).**

My beloved, the day is coming when our children will no longer **be taught about war** and will transform weapons of war into agricultural tools **(Isaiah 2:4).** When we live the Golden Rule, people of all religions, races, and languages will know God, work together, and with God's guidance, we'll eradicate war. Then peace will flow like springs in the desert.

Let us pray: Dear God, thank You for the example we have in Jesus Christ and the angels You've placed throughout our lives. They've taught us that it's possible to **live the golden rule**; being at peace with others, loving and serving those who need to know that You are present and active in their lives. May Your presence and blessing fill our souls with Your loving service. We pray in the name of Jesus.

January 6
TRANSFORMED BY GOD'S LIGHT

"See, darkness covers the earth, and thick darkness is over the peoples, but the Lord rises upon you and his glory appears over you." Isaiah 60:2

"La tierra está cubierta de tinieblas, y una densa oscuridad envuelve a las naciones; pero sobre ti brilla el Señor, como la aurora; sobre ti se puede contemplar su gloria". Isaías 60:2

"Επειδή, προσέξτε, σκοτάδι θα σκεπάσει τη γη, και παχύ σκοτάδι τα έθνη· επάνω, όμως, σε σένα θα ανατείλει ο Κύριος, και η δόξα του θα φανερωθεί επάνω σου." ΗΣΑΪΑΣ 60:2

We don't know when, but each day the great day draws near when the Lord will remove the darkness and lead us toward His light to be transformed into His likeness. This verse tells us that when God's light has transformed the church into the likeness of His glory, you and I, the bride of Christ, will change all nations into the likeness of Christ.

Although these verses refer to the Messiah's Light, as representatives of Christ, you and I are called to let our lights shine so that those shipwrecked, surrounded by darkness, can direct their lives toward God's glory and be **transformed by God's light.**

As we enter 2021, the world's condition is cloaked in darkness. Even though science has produced the COVID-19 vaccine, global distribution will take time. Meanwhile, the pandemic continues to attack, tear apart, and claim lives. Millions of families suffer from the highest unemployment experienced in a century. If we don't do something, millions more will suffer from food insecurity, and we'll all continue suffering from isolation.

Isaiah 60 was written to us for times like these, warning that we'll go through seasons when *"thick darkness is over the peoples."* But we're urged not to faint. God calls us to **arise** from our beds of despair with the certainty of **Divine protection**. As proof, we read, *"the Lord rises upon you."* While the rest of the world (the lost sheep, unbelievers, and evildoers) continue in darkness and fear, God tells us that *"his glory appears over you."*

We receive God's light as a gift to rescue, bandage, and bring God's lost sheep back to the fold. Having been **transformed by God's light**, our **purpose and responsibility** are to let our light shine for those who've repented and seek salvation in God's sanctuary, the immovable rock from which the Divine Light emanates.

Once **transformed by God's light,** we have clarity of purpose. We appreciate the value of time and won't waste a minute to shine because every minute we fail to do so is like leaving millions of defenseless souls waiting for their COVID-19 vaccine.

Let us pray: Dear God, thank You for transforming us into messengers of your light. Help us shine and save the eternal future of souls for whom Jesus gave His life, understanding that our task is one of life or death. We pray in Your Holy Name.

January 7
GOD ESTABLISHES AND REMOVES
1 Samuel 3:10

In **1 Samuel** and **Acts 9**, the Lord calls chosen servants by name to be His spokespersons. In Acts, God calls Ananias to heal Saul and **establish** his ministry. *"Go! This man is my chosen instrument to proclaim my name to the Gentiles and their kings and to the people of Israel"* (**Acts 9:15**). In **1 Samuel 3:13**, God calls Samuel to **remove** Eli from the priesthood, along with his entire family, because *"his sons blasphemed God, and he failed to restrain them."*

When we do God's will, keeping and respecting His law and holiness, God **establishes** the servant. It wasn't easy for Samuel to deliver the message of rejection to Eli, but he did it out of reverence for God.

On January 6, 2021, we saw the destruction and assault on the United States Capitol, a sacred place representing our country's heart. My painful reaction was to ask God to *"look to our congress and protect everyone from physical injury, to help us achieve a peaceful transition of power."* God must be sad seeing the anarchy, but just as God removed Eli, God will remove the one who allowed or instigated the people to rise against the pearl of our freedom because, having the power and authority, *"he failed to restrain them."*

To inspire or incite? That is the question. As Christians, we're called to inspire others toward peace, love, unity, kindness, tolerance, honor, respect for humans, and law. Inciting someone to violence has no part in the character of a Christian or a United States citizen.

God **establishes** who will be His **chosen instrument**. I pray to God that President-elect Joe Biden is genuinely a chosen instrument to reunify the country and **establish** peace and cooperation in our joint fight against the pandemic and **hate**. It's not my intention to be political or demonize any group of followers. Instead, I ask that God enlighten us all, that God silence and **remove** from power those who would instigate riots and clashes.

Let us pray: Dear God, *"Speak, for your servant is listening."* Don't let brother rise against brother. We ask You to silence and remove the father of lies from our midst. Grant that in the

9

next four years of leadership Your truth reigns in our hearts and that we act for the country's welfare in general and not for political parties. We pray in Your Holy Name.

January 8
THE BEST PARENTS
1 Timothy 4:12

How beautiful to see fresh snow, free of footprints (as in today's photo). For those who have the privilege of being a parent, nothing pleases us more than to see our children *"dwelling together in unity"* **(Psalm 133:1)** and prospering in their education, professions, and homes.

I heard the following in" Music of Ecuador, HCJB (March 28, 2006)", *"The best parents not only give us life, but they teach us to live."* Following are some instructions for parents which, based on experience, will help your children live in peace and prosper in their homes.

The best parents model a life guided by God's Word.
"How can a young person stay on the path of purity? By living according to your word" **(Psalm 119:9).** There's nothing better than to lie down to rest knowing that we've been good examples for our children and that everything in our lives is pure as snow.

We should instruct our youth to *"Take delight in the Lord, and he will give you the desires of your heart"* **(Psalm 37:4).** They should learn that **God knows their needs**, and as they commune with Him regularly, God will delight in them, supplying the desires of their hearts.

The best parents model a moderated life.
"Similarly, encourage the young men to be self-controlled" **(Titus 2:6).** Risks and adventures are exciting, but whoever walks with **prudence** and acts with **moderation** and **caution**, reaches their destination unharmed and rejoices with their offspring.

The best parents exemplify a life away from evil.
"The highway of the upright avoids evil; those who guard their ways preserve their

10

lives" **(Proverbs 16:17).** God calls us to demonstrate good works. *"In your teaching show integrity, seriousness and soundness of speech that cannot be condemned, so that those who oppose you may be ashamed because they have nothing bad to say about us"* **(Titus 2:7-8).**

The best parents exhibit a thirst for God's kingdom.
"Do not love the world or anything in the world. If anyone loves the world, love for the Father is not in them" **(1 John 2:15).**

Let us pray: Dear God, thank You for teaching us how to instruct our youth so that they arrive unharmed into your presence. Although they might not presently be our imitators, we trust that someday they too will be parents and follow Your guidance and instruction. We pray in Your Holy Name.

January 9
TRANSFORMATIVE INSTRUCTIONS
Luke 5:10

Before looking at our key verse, I draw attention to King David's instruction to his son Solomon before he died. *"Observe what the Lord your God requires: Walk in obedience to him, and keep his decrees and commands, his laws and regulations, as written in the Law of Moses. Do this so that you may prosper in all you do and wherever you go"* **(1 Kings 2:3).**

In **Luke 5,** Jesus instructs Peter to move his fishing boat slightly offshore, transforming it into a pulpit from which to teach the crowds. *"When he had finished speaking, he said to Simon, 'Put out into deep water, and let down the nets for a catch.' Simon answered, 'Master, we've worked hard all night and haven't caught anything. But because you say so, I will let down the nets'"* **(Luke 5:4-5).**

That night they hadn't caught anything because they were counting on luck and human experience. Much of what we do outside God's will won't produce the desired catch. Images of fishers retracting nets full of plastic bottles, tires, etc., come to mind. However, when we follow God's instructions, putting our time and work tools at His disposal, God transforms the mundane *"for divine use"* and prospers everything we do in God's time. **Verse 6** says, *"When they had done so, they caught such a large number of fish that their nets began to break."*

Later, Jesus commissions the fishers with a better and nobler profession, **transforming them into fishers of people.** Jesus called His first disciples in Galilee with these words; *"'Come, follow me,' Jesus said, 'and I will send You out to fish for people'"* **(Matthew 4:19). You and I are also called** fishers of men, women, children, elderly, orphans, homeless, poor, and rich of every race and culture.

Let us pray: Dear God and Savior of souls, thank You for giving us a second chance to transform our words into fishing hooks of love. Please help us surrender with all our possessions, strength, soul, and mind to be Your fishers of souls. We pray in Your Holy Name.

January 10
NO TEARS IN HEAVEN

"God will wipe every tear from their eyes. There will be no more death or mourning or crying or pain, for the old order of things has passed away." Revelation 21:4

"Dios enjugará las lágrimas de los ojos de ellos, y ya no habrá muerte, ni más llanto, ni lamento ni dolor; porque las primeras cosas habrán dejado de existir". Apocalipsis 21:4

"Και ο Θεός θα εξαλείψει κάθε δάκρυ από τα μάτια τους, και ο θάνατος δεν θα υπάρχει πλέον· ούτε πένθος ούτε κραυγή ούτε πόνος δεν θα υπάρχουν πλέον· επειδή, τα πρώτα παρήλθαν." ΑΠΟΚΑΛΥΨΗ ΙΩΑΝΝΟΥ 21:4

I wish you a blessed day, my beloved friends and family worldwide. May God's glorious presence manifest itself today, transforming our lament into joy, gratitude, courage, and purpose to move forward in our struggles.

I love Eric Clapton's song *"Tears in Heaven"*, musically and spiritually. One of its lines says, *"Would you know my name / if I saw you in heaven? / Would it be the same / if I saw you in heaven? / I must be strong / and carry on / 'cause I know I don't belong / here in heaven."*

Clapton wrote this song at the most painful moment of his life - when his child died by accident. Clapton found encouragement and inspiration to move forward with faith in God's promise of preparing a heavenly home where there will be no more death. **Revelation 21:4** says, *"God will wipe every tear from their eyes."*

God willing, none of us should ever have to face a loss of a child. For those who've lost a loved one at a young or mature age, God alleviates the pain through an eternal perspective and hope of being reunited with them and our Creator. There will be tears of joy in that reunion, and *God will wipe away your tears.* We will never again remember our past sufferings nor suffer a sense of loss.

The human perspective focuses on what we lack, e.g., what we've lost. We seek an explanation or look at it as a punishment. Why did this happen to me? Doesn't God love me or hear my prayers? Faith's perspective affirms God's great love, showing us a scene where the end of this short life gives rise to an eternal life where everything is perfect, noble, pure, and full of joy and ever-lasting love.

Let us pray: Dear Heavenly Father, thank You for giving us the hope that we'll meet again with those who today rest from their labors, those who left early, and those who left after a lengthy illness. We pray for those who've lost a child and lack hope of reuniting with their loved ones. Help us to meditate on this and, when necessary, that we may cry with those who today experience such suffering.

> **There will be tears of joy in that reunion, and** *God will wipe away your tears.* **We will never again remember our past sufferings nor suffer a sense of loss.**

January 11
BLESSED FORGIVENESS
Romans 4:8

We haven't always been the best example as a parent, spouse, or Christian. We've all suffered moments we wish hadn't happened. An inappropriate word in a moment of anger or distraction, an action that caused suffering, an indiscretion or addiction that affected the entire family, a broken promise, etc. **Those of us who have felt the crippling weight of sin lifted from our shoulders are blessed for several reasons:**

BLESSED IS THE ONE WHOSE SIN THE LORD WILL NEVER COUNT AGAINST THEM." ROMANS 4:8

"ΜΑΚΆΡΙΟΣ Ο ΆΝΘΡΩΠΟΣ ΣΤΟΝ ΟΠΟΊΟ Ο ΚΎΡΙΟΣ ΔΕΝ ΘΑ ΛΟΓΑΡΙΆΣΕΙ5 Σ' ΑΥΤΌΝ ΑΜΑΡΤΊΑ»." ΠΡΟΣ ΡΩΜΑΙΟΥΣ 4:8

¡DICHOSO AQUÉL A QUIEN EL SEÑOR NO CULPA DE PECADO!» ROMANOS 4:8

KERKYRA (CORFU), GREECE

First, by confessing our offenses to God or neighbor, we've been **forgiven of the penalty** of our trespass. The Bible teaches that *"the wages of sin is death, but the gift of God is eternal life in Christ Jesus our Lord"* **(Romans 6:23).** Having been forgiven, God removes the **penalty** and weight of our guilt. Imagine! God sets aside our punishment, and instead of the death we deserve, we receive eternal life.

Second, we're blessed because, being freed from **our past shame,** we can analyze and place our lives, talents, abilities, and resources to serve God and finally **begin to fulfill our purpose.**

Third, through forgiveness, **God restores our relationship** with the Holy Trinity, and for the first time, we attain the true *"peace of God that transcends all understanding."* Peace is the antidote to *"guard our hearts and minds"* against the enemy's attacks **(Philippians 4:7).** This peace allows us to see our world and situations from God's perspective and *"love our neighbor as ourselves"* **(Mark 12:33).**

Fourth, freed from the guilt and penalty of sin, we learn to *"forgive as we've been forgiven"* **(Matthew 6:9)**. An unforgiven offense, like a virus, steals our joy of living and robs us of the peace and energy that God had planned when He formed us. However, by forgiving others, we acquire wings to fly, *"strength to run without getting weary"* **(Isaiah 40:31)**, and joy to live within the Divine plan.

> An unforgiven offense, like a virus, steals our joy of living and robs us of the peace and energy that God had planned when He formed us.

We're blessed to experience the joy and fullness of living in harmony with God and neighbor by confessing our sins and forgiving others. My beloved, there's nothing in our past that God won't forgive. Likewise, there shouldn't be anything we're not prepared to forgive in God's name.

Let us pray: Dear God, thank You for granting us the joy of being forgiven, of receiving a second opportunity so that our lives may be the best possible example of a parent, spouse, or Christian. Help us to be forgiving like You. We pray in the name of Jesus.

January 12
CONSECRATED FOR WORSHIP

"Whoever makes perfume like it and puts it on anyone other than a priest must be cut off from their people." **Exodus 30:33**

"Cualquiera que componga un aceite semejante, y que lo derrame sobre algún extraño, será expulsado de su pueblo". **Éxodo 30:33**

"όποιος συνθέσει όμοιο μ' αυτό ή όποιος βάλει απ' αυτό σε αλλογενή, θα εξολοθρευτεί από τον λαό του." **ΕΞΟΔΟΣ 30:33**

Things consecrated for God's service and worship are sacred, pure, and require the highest respect and reverence. The Reverend Henry Yordon of the First Congregational Church in Norwalk instructed that the altar is exclusively for placing the Bible, cross, candelabra, and the Holy Sacrament elements, the Eucharist. Musicians sometimes would set the music scores on top, but immediately, remembering the instructions, we'd remove the papers from the altar.

Worship is so important to God that the Lord dedicated a large part of Exodus, instructing us on the worship protocols, including when and where to use the elements. God is loving and kind, but He's also jealous and demands our exclusive love, worship, and obedience to His Word.

When worshiping, we should know and follow God's instructions. Regarding the anointing oil, God said that the oil is restricted to sanctify and consecrate the priests together with *"the tent of meeting, the ark of the covenant law, the table and all its articles, the lampstand and its accessories, the altar of incense"* **(Exodus 30:26-27)**. In **verse 33**, God warns, *"Whoever makes perfume like it and puts it on anyone other than a priest must be cut off from their people."*

Likewise, the **incense** was for exclusive use in worship within the tabernacle. God explicitly forbids pirating His fragrance for personal use outside the tabernacle and repeats the warning, *"Whoever makes incense like it to enjoy its fragrance must be cut off from their people"* **(v.38).**

The fragrance was part of a Divine experience within the tabernacle for the Jewish people. To their olfactory senses, the perfume represented God's presence. **The scent was for drawing near to God, not for personal enjoyment.**

My mother had an altar at home, where she worshiped Jesus every day. I always liked the fragrance when she burned incense, and it's still one of the things that attract me when visiting my friends or family's churches. Its scent brings me back to my mother's room and God's presence.

Let us pray: Dear God, create in us a reverent and respectful attitude toward what you've consecrated for Your exclusive and deserved adoration. We pray in Your Holy Name.

January 13
HEAL US FROM ALL EVIL

"Look, the Lamb of God, who takes away the sin of the world!" **John 1:29**

"Éste es el Cordero de Dios, que quita el pecado del mundo". **Juan 1:29**

"Να, ο Αμνός τού Θεού, ο οποίος σηκώνει την αμαρτία τού κόσμου."
ΚΑΤΑ ΙΩΑΝΝΗΝ 1:29

Given the events of January 6, 2021 in the United States, more than ever, we need the master surgeon to remove the cataracts from our eyes, allowing us to move toward restoring peace and unity. No longer viewing others based on their race or political affiliation, but as members of God's family - reaching out a brotherly hand. We must remember who we are, what, and for whom we're constructing.

John the Baptist saw his cousin Jesus *"coming toward him and said, 'Look, the Lamb of God, who takes away the sin of the world!'"* If asked to apply this phrase to our times, I'm sure John would say, *"'This is the Lamb of God' who removes the cancer of hatred from our hearts. The specialist surgeon who purifies us of selfishness, fanaticism, and all the 'isms' afflicting our society. The psychologist who frees us from racial phobias.'"* All the evils that we suffer today have their origin in sin, disobedience, and rebellion against God.

Who could free us from the evil we've allowed to control our lives, schools, churches, governments, etc.? **The answer is within us.** We can continue to kindle the hostile fire by accusing each other of being the cause of the problem, for being too liberal or conservative. But the answer is within us who **with humble pride, call ourselves Christians**. Remember that Christ dwells in our hearts and perceives our thoughts. Let's **allow the Lamb of God to start mending our hearts** first before trying to repair or change others.

You and I are building a secure bridge so that our children and future generations may live in peace and harmony, caring for one another as they walk **toward God's eternal home**. We want them to be responsible with the gifts and talents they've received and to leave this planet in better shape than when they inherited it. Therefore, through our loving instruction, they must know and accept the Lamb of God in their hearts to guide and inspire them after our days.

Let us pray: Dear God, thank You for sending Jesus, Your humble lamb who built the access bridge to Your heavenly mansion, allowing us to cross from the field of slavery to sin to pastures of freedom, redemption, unity, and eternal life. Heal us and give us Your peace Lord, in the name of Jesus.

January 14
SENTINEL FOR LIFE
Psalm 139:3

Just as my daughter Sophia watches over her newborn child (our precious grandson Lázaro Elías Aristiza-bal), **God is our sentinel for life.** God is always guarding His children, day and night, to ensure that we're nurtured and protected from all evil, including evil that might come from ourselves.

We live in times when the government electronically monitors our every movement, purchase, conversation, photo, or video recording. Sometimes forgetting that big brother is watching, we break the law, e.g., we drive the car faster than allowed or, according to this week's news, use threats and violence to acquire what we think belongs to us. Actions and words have consequences! God is watching. If we've broken God's law, we will pay the fine.

Psalm 139:3 says, *"You discern my going out and my lying down; you are familiar with all my ways."* This affirms God's care, protection, and nurturing for those who've received the adoption as a child of God. We're blessed to have God as our sentinel for life. But adoption also endows us with responsibilities. Our words and actions have the power to rescue, heal, build, bind, infect, and destroy. Sometimes, we forget who we are or even that God is present. We take things into our own hands and won't let God be our sentinel.

During the next 24 hours, before taking action, speaking, or writing something, I invite you to consider the following: God not only watches your ways and is aware of everything you do, but

16

God also knows your heart. *"You have searched me, Lord, and you know me. You know when I sit and when I rise; you perceive my thoughts from afar"* **(Psalm 139:1, 2).** Therefore, ask yourself:

✦ *Would Jesus be pleased to see the way I intend to react?*
✦ *Would I be a good reflection of what Jesus modeled for me?*
✦ *Does what I intend to do move toward peace or division?*
✦ *What would Jesus do or say in my situation?*

Let us pray: Dear God, thank You for being our sentinel for life. Help us immerse ourselves daily in Your Holy Word so that Your Holy Spirit may remind us of who we are and whom we represent. Teach us how to respond to life's situations. Help us to be, for Your little ones, sentinels for life. We pray in Your Holy Name.

January 15
WHEN FEELING UNWORTHY
Acts 13:25

When you feel unworthy of rescue, forgiveness, and restoration, remember, *"For God so loved the world [you] that he gave his one and only Son, that whoever believes in him shall not perish but have eternal life"* **(John 3:16).** Let's analyze how God used the words of three men who said *"I am not worthy"* to speak to us today.

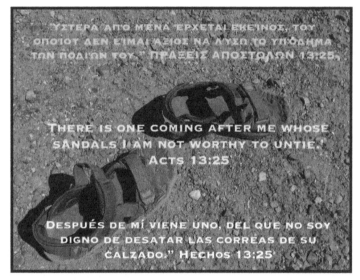

"**I AM NOT WORTHY**" are words of those who humbly acknowledge their position and purpose. They appear ten times in the Bible as modest expressions before the greatness and magnificence of our merciful God, who forgives our failures, heals our ailments, and sends us as messengers of mercy and hope.

GOD FORGIVES OUR FAILURES - A son received the inheritance from his father, wandered off to a distant country, and *"squandered his wealth in wild living"* **(Luke 15:13).** Repentant and destitute, he decided to return to his father. Arriving home, the son cried out, *"Father, I have sinned against heaven and against you. I am no longer worthy to be called your son... make me like one of your hired servants"* **(Luke 15:19, 21).** The father forgave, embraced, and restored him to the position of son and heir.

GOD HEALS OUR AILMENTS - A centurion sent for Jesus to come and heal his servant. As Jesus was coming, the centurion sent a message saying, *"Lord, don't trouble yourself, for **I do***

not deserve to have you come under my roof. That is why I did not even consider myself worthy to come to you. But say the word, and my servant will be healed" **(Matthew 8:8, Luke 7:6–7).**

WE ARE GOD'S MESSENGERS - John the Baptist clarifies his function as servant and messenger: *"I baptize you with water. But one who is more powerful than I will come, the straps of whose sandals I am not worthy to untie. He will baptize you with the Holy Spirit and fire"* **(Luke 3:16, Matthew 3:11, Mark 1:7-8 and John 1:27).**

"Lord, do not trouble yourself, for **I am not worthy** to have you come under my roof; therefore I did not presume to come to you. But only speak the word, and let my servant be healed." **Luke 7:6-7 (NRVSA)**

The Apostle Paul, a highly educated man of prominent position and great possessions, declared: I *"do not even deserve to be called an apostle, because I persecuted the church of God"* **(1 Corinthians 15:9).**

Let us pray: Dear God, despite having failed You so often, despite being **undeserving** of such great love, we thank You for receiving us back as adopted children and heirs of Your Grace. Thank You for healing our wounds and filling our souls with purpose and hope. We pray in Jesus's name.

✝✝✝✝✝✝

January 16
TO KNOW AND BE KNOWN
Matthew 25:12

Jesus recounts that five brides weren't ready to receive the groom. *"Later the others also came. 'Lord, Lord,' they said, 'open the door for us!' But he replied, 'Truly I tell you, I don't know you'"* **(Matthew 25:10B-12).**

God says, *"Before I formed you in the womb I knew you" (Jeremiah 1:5). "You are mine" (Isaiah 43:1).* But the cares of the world and the enemy's lies blind and separate us from God's

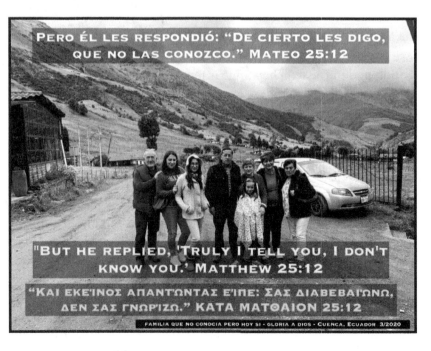

presence. Although we're princes and princesses, we live like **prodigal** beggars.

It's essential to know and to be known by God. I had learned about God but my *eyes were veiled* and lived in spiritual poverty **(Luke 24:16).** My father-in-law said, *"Oscar, many know about God, but few know him."*

KNOWING GOD
Jesus offers keys to knowing God:
1. Diligently studying the Holy Scriptures. *"Then you will know the truth, and the truth will set you free"* **(John 8:32).**
2. Walking prudently along the indicated path. *"I am the way and the truth and the life. No one comes to the Father except through me"* **(John 14:6).**
3. **Through Bible study,** although we haven't seen Him, our soul perceives God's goodness and infinite love for sinners like you and me. *"Anyone who has seen me has seen the Father"* **(John 14:9).**
4. Be prepared to recognize and receive the groom. *"He was in the world, and though the world was made through him, the world <u>did not recognize him</u>"* **(John 1:10).**

BE KNOWN BY GOD
The parable of the ten virgins calls us to be prudent in our relationship with God, know Him intimately, and ensure that God knows us.

Jesus knows us by *"the love of God in our hearts"* **(John 5:42)** and by our good fruits. *"Many will say to me on that day, 'Lord, Lord, did we not prophesy in your name and in your name drive out demons and in your name perform many miracles?' Then I will tell them plainly, 'I never knew you'"* **(Matthew 7:22–23).** However, to those who serve, help, and support the poor and needy, Jesus knows, smiles at them, and opens the door of His heart and kingdom.

Let us pray: Dear God, thank You because at one time we didn't know You or were known by You, but You revealed yourself by Your love and grace, and we humbly call ourselves Your children, Christians in formation. Heal our sick and our land. We pray in Jesus's name.

I had learned about God but my *eyes were veiled* and lived in spiritual poverty **(Luke 24:16).** My father-in-law said, *"Oscar, many know about God, but few know him."*

January 17
FEED MY LAMBS

"'Simon son of John, do you love me more than these?' 'Yes, Lord,' he said, 'you know that I love you.' Jesus said, 'Feed my lambs.'" John 21:15

"'Simón, hijo de Jonás, ¿me amas más que éstos?' Le respondió: 'Sí, Señor; tú sabes que te quiero.' Él le dijo: 'Apacienta mis corderos'". Juan 21:15

"Σίμωνα του Ιωνά, με αγαπάς περισσότερο τούτων; Του λέει: Ναι, Κύριε, εσύ ξέρεις ότι σε αγαπώ. Του λέει: Βόσκε τα αρνιά μου." **ΚΑΤΑ ΙΩΑΝΝΗΝ 21:15**

Reading God's Word has become my daily breakfast, as I learned from my father-in-law Aristoklis Xanthópoulos (**a man of few words and many small actions**). When he lived in our home for extended periods, I was privileged to observe his disciplined custom of reading and writing God's Word and praying to God, which prepared him to **feed God's sheep**.

My father-in-law's mission was to create a hunger and thirst for God's Word in everyone. When he moved back to Greece, **he entrusted me with his work of feeding sheep** by giving away Bibles and sharing the love and peace of God.

In **John 21:15**, Jesus is on a beach preparing breakfast. After eating he asks Peter: *"Simon son of John, do you love me more than these?"* Despite the three times that Peter denied him, Jesus didn't decommission Peter for having failed in a moment of fear and weakness. We've all experienced such moments.

Jesus uses the Greek word "*αγαπάς*" (**do you love me**?), but Peter responds with the term "*φιλώ*," meaning "**to like**" as in friend. Knowing that Peter wasn't yet capable of loving as Christ loves, Jesus changes the question to *"do you like me more than these."* **Jesus accommodates himself to our abilities.** Peter affirms with a yes, and Jesus entrusts him to *"Feed my sheep."*

Regardless of our abilities, God commissioned us to feed His sheep. **To feed His followers and those who have been lost.** Jesus speaks of the heavenly food that leads to eternal life. Not about creating a people dependent on our leftovers but on the first fruits of God's Word. Whoever loves Jesus keeps His Word in their heart and looks for ways to nurture the Kingdom.

I rejoice in the growing number of friends and family accompanying us for this breakfast with God's Word, where we find and make peace with God and neighbor. Jesus said, *"Whoever eats this bread will live forever"* (**John 6:51**).

Let us pray: Dear God, thank You for entrusting us with the care of Your sheep. Grant that, before attempting to feed others, we feed ourselves until we're satisfied with Your true and living Word. We pray in Jesus's name.

January 18
CLEANSED AND RESCUED
2 Corinthians 7:1

One of my favorite illustrations for today's verse comes from a personal anecdote.

Returning from Greece in 2018, twenty days after a heavy rain that flooded many houses, I discovered that my tool shed where I stored my dad's vinyl records had been flooded. The water and mud partially disintegrated the jackets that covered them, and when they dried, they became em bedded in the vinyl records. I trashed the jackets and was sad, thinking that the vinyls were destined to be recycled. They were of such sentimental value that I attempted to **rescue** them. Water, soap, and disinfectant left them **clean**, like new, although without the jackets.

Limpiémonos de toda contaminación de carne y de espíritu, y perfeccionémonos en la santidad y en el temor de Dios. **2 Corintios 7:1**

Let us purify ourselves from everything that contaminates body and spirit, perfecting holiness out of reverence for God. **2 Corinthians 7:1**

Ας καθαρίσουμε τον εαυτό μας από κάθε μολυσμό σάρκας και πνεύματος, εκπληρώνοντας αγιοσύνη με φόβο Θεού. ΠΡΟΣ ΚΟΡΙΝΘΙΟΥΣ Β΄ 7:1

Today's verse **(2 Corinthians 7:1)** calls us to purify ourselves of all evil and filth, recognizing that our lives are like those records and jackets. It doesn't matter how much dirt has become embedded in our exterior. In eternity they're inconsequential. **God values what we've stored in our hearts, and that's worth cleaning and rescuing at all costs.**

"Since we have these promises" refers to our adoption as God's children. As believers, we have the promise and must continually cleanse and disinfect our lives of all evil that adheres to our exterior in the process of rescuing lives that rivers of mud have tossed about.

> **"God values what we've stored in our hearts, and that's worth cleaning and rescuing at all costs!"**

2 Corinthians 6:14-18 warns us to maintain a spiritually healthy distance from unbelievers. *"Do not be yoked together with unbelievers"* who bear the yoke of sin; they're slaves of evil. Therefore, the believer shouldn't bond emotionally or relationally with them. ***The downfall of Solomon, the wisest man in the world, was associating with unbelieving women who inclined his heart to their idols (1 Kings 11:3).*** God doesn't absolve us from rescuing lost lives. But in the rescue process, we ought to maintain a healthy detachment from the unclean.

Verse 17 appears to demand a total **separation** from all that is unclean, including lost and needy sheep. In light of Jesus's testimony, this would be a misinterpretation. Jesus came to cleanse and rescue the lost and entrusted us with continuing His work. We must help along the periphery but not enter into the center of unholiness.

Let us pray: Dear God, thank You for cleansing us of all evil, for the value You place in each life, and for keeping us focused on Your mission and purpose. May we be valuable tools to rescue and cleanse Your lost sheep. We pray in Your Holy Name.

January 19
THE CONSEQUENCES OF LYING
Psalm 86:11

There are seven things that God hates and *"are detestable to him: haughty eyes, a <u>lying</u> tongue, hands that shed innocent blood, a heart that devises wicked schemes, feet that are quick to rush into evil, a false witness who pours out <u>lies</u> and a person who stirs up conflict in the community"* **(Proverbs 6:16–19).**

Lying appears twice, giving importance to what we ought to avoid. Sadly, we've become infected by (or overly tolerant of) lying. The following two verses reveal God's reaction to lies.

King Saul ignored God's instructions, allowing his soldiers to do whatever they wanted. When confronted, he lied to cover up his failure to rule and obey. His excuses;
1. *"The soldiers took sheep and cattle from the plunder, the best of what was devoted to God, in order to sacrifice them to the Lord your God at Gilgal."* And,
2. *"I was afraid of the men and so I gave in to them"* **(1 Samuel 15:21, 24B)**. Disobedience and lying caused God to remove Saul and replace David as King.

Acts 5 records the spouses Ananias and Sapphira accused of *"lying to the Holy Spirit."* No one in the congregation *"claimed that any of their possessions was their own, but they shared everything they had"* **(Acts 4:32)**. The couple sold a piece of land but kept some of the money. Peter said, *"'What made you think of doing such a thing? You have not lied just to human beings but to God.' When Ananias heard this, he fell down and died"* **(Acts 5:4-5)**. The same happened with his wife **(v.10)**.

Samuel's words help us understand what pleases God; *"To obey is better than sacrifice, and to heed is better than the fat of rams"* **(1 Samuel 15:22)**. In **Psalm 33:5**, we read, *"The Lord loves righteousness and justice; the earth is full of his unfailing love."*

The Psalmist cries out, *"Teach me your way, Lord, that I may rely on your faithfulness; give me an undivided heart, that I may fear your name"* **(Psalm 86:11)**. God blesses children whose **hearts are inclined to the truth that God loves and far from the lie that God detests.**

Let us pray: Dear God, show us Your way so that by walking in Your truth, this virus called "**lying**" does not embed itself into our character or position as Your children. We pray in Your Holy Name.

"Sadly, we've become infected and overly tolerant of lying."

"God blesses children whose **hearts are inclined to the truth that God loves and far from the lie that God detests.**"

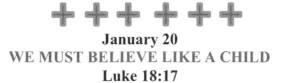

January 20
WE MUST BELIEVE LIKE A CHILD
Luke 18:17

"A child asked his father:
—'Dad, is Satan bigger than me?'
*—'**Yes, my son,' said the father.**'*
—'Is he bigger than you, dad?'
*—'**Yes, my son, he's bigger than me.**'*
--Surprised, the boy thought for a second and asked, 'Is he bigger than Jesus?'
*—'**No, my son,' answered the father, 'Jesus is bigger than him.**'*
The boy, smiling, said,
—'then I'm no longer afraid of him,'
and walked away to continue playing.'"

We must believe like a child to move
forward in our work and delight ourselves without fear. Not only is Jesus greater, but *"The Lord is near to all who call on him...in truth"* **(Psalm 145:18).**

We can't see God, but the Lord is closer than we can imagine. In the best and worst moments of our lives, when we laugh, God laughs with us. When we suffer, God suffers and extends His hand.

God is greater than all the problems we might face. The Lord is near and fights on our behalf. It should be reason enough to remove any fear and courageously face everything that threatens our life, peace, and joy, anything that tries to distract us from our goal, responsibility, or relaxation in God's presence. **But it's not enough to listen.**

We must believe in God's Word **like a child**. We need to believe everything the Lord has said, warned, and promised in God's Word. In my church, we used to pray the following before reading God's Word; *"I believe in the Word of God, the Bible. I **am** what it says I am. I **have** all that*

23

*it says I have. I **can do** what it says I can do. I **confess** that my mind is alert, and my heart is receptive. I am about to **receive** the incorruptible, indestructible, ever-living seed of God's Word. I **will never be the same. In Jesus's name.** Amen."*

Jesus said, *"anyone who will not receive the kingdom of God like a little child will never enter it"* **(Luke 18:17). We must believe like a child** to face everything that prevents us or others from entering the rest and peace God has prepared for His children.

Let us pray: Dear God, increase our faith and humility. Help us believe like a child and trust Your Word and promises. Strengthen us in our weaknesses. Inspire us with Your vision of the kingdom that we can create today. We pray in Jesus's name.

✜ ✜ ✜ ✜ ✜

January 21
FAITH ACTIVATES GOD'S HAND
Psalm 62:6

I believe that **faith activates God's hand** in our favor and that our faith increases by continuously feeding on His Word. Thanks to the intelligence that God has given us, we can learn through repetition.

As infants, we learn our parents' language through the repetition of sounds. By dedicating time to repeating and memorizing words, we learn several languages. Taking time to repeat movements, such as sports or music, we create muscle memory that responds instantly, without thinking. **Writing and repeating phrases and promises from the Bible increases our knowledge of God** and strengthens our **faith** in God's promises and protection.

Psalm 62 is proof that our faith grows through repetition. **Verse 2** says, *"He only is my rock and my salvation; He is my defense; I shall not be <u>greatly</u> moved,"* leaving the possibility of being moved slightly. **Verse 6** is almost the identical repetition except for the removal of "**greatly**" - *"Truly he is my rock and my salvation; he is my fortress, I will not be shaken."* On repetition, the **"I will not be shaken" becomes absolute.**

SÓLO DIOS ES MI SALVACIÓN Y MI ROCA; PORQUE ÉL ES MI REFUGIO, NO RESBALARÉ. SALMOS 62:6

TRULY HE IS MY ROCK AND MY SALVATION; HE IS MY FORTRESS, I WILL NOT BE SHAKEN. PSALM 62:6

"ΑΥΤΟΣ, ΜΟΝΑΧΑ, ΕΙΝΑΙ ΠΕΤΡΑ ΜΟΥ, ΚΑΙ ΣΩΤΗΡΙΑ ΜΟΥ· ΠΡΟΠΥΡΓΙΟ ΜΟΥ· ΔΕΝ ΘΑ ΣΑΛΕΥΤΩ." ΨΑΛΜΟΙ 62:6

SEDONA, AZ - JULIE BOHL

I believe that **faith activates God's hand in our favor**. Our faith grows by feeding on God's Word and regularly repeating His promises. We then act according to the Holy Spirit's guidance, who **moves God's hand** to transform our possibilities into realities. By feeding on God's Word, we discover and accept that the Lord is our only refuge, *"rock, and salvation."*

As Christians and adopted children of God, we have the joy and privilege of repeatedly witnessing to our friends and family how God has been our strong rock, salvation, strong tower, and refuge in times of trials. That thanks to God's faithfulness, **we weren't shaken in our faith and hope.**

Our testimony should include the rewards we've experienced or expect from God. **Verse 12** says, *"You reward everyone according to what they have done."* If we repeatedly do good, God will reward us. But if knowing the good that we must do, we instead do evil; God will also give each one *"according to what they have done."*

Let us pray: Dear God, grant us the discipline to feed daily on Your Holy Word. Increase our faith so that, through our witness, those who seek Your **peace, justice, and freedom** might see Your hand move in their favor. May You be our only *"fortress, rock, and Savior."* We pray in Your Holy Name.

January 22
WAITING AND WATCHING
2 Peter 3:3-4

The tempter and father of lies will use all means to make us doubt God's Word. Jesus said, *"I will not leave you as orphans; I will come to you"* **(John 14:18).** But the devil will use mockery, contempt, and half-lies so that we abandon the way of the Lord and move to his camp. For the most part, the victims are those who haven't yet delved into the study of God's Word.

Today's verse says, *"In the last days scoffers will come, scoffing and following their own evil desires. They will say, 'Where is this 'coming' he promised?'"* Jesus knew that every generation would be afflicted with this type of attack. He tells us what will happen on His day of return. He won't arrive in secret. Anyone with the ability to look up to the heavens will see Him. *"For as lightning that comes from the east is visible even in the west, so will be the coming of the Son of Man"* **(Matthew 24:27).**

WAITING
Jesus warned, *"But about that day or hour no one knows, not even the angels in heaven, nor the Son, but only the Father" (Matthew 24:36).* We patiently wait because God keeps His

promises. Let's remember that a thousand years are like a day for God. In every generation, to win recruits, the tempter has used *"Where is this 'coming' he promised?"* But whoever knows and hopes in God's Word will respond like Jesus when the devil tempted him; *"No, because it is written"* (**Matthew 4:9-10**). And *"in the name of Jesus Christ,"* the devil will flee from our presence.

WATCHING

We shouldn't worry about the day or hour when Jesus will return. We must continue to affirm our Apostolic Creed, *"He ascended into heaven and is seated at the right hand of the Father. From there He will come again to judge the living and the dead."* Meanwhile, we must be **watching** and active in the mission that Jesus entrusted to us (*"feed my sheep"*) because *"the Son of Man will come at an hour when you do not expect him"* (**Luke 12:40**).

Let us pray: Dear God, Your Word says that *"Jesus will return as a thief in the night"* (**1 Thessalonians 5:2**). Help us stay awake, alert, watchful, and active in our work of rescuing, healing, and caring for Your prodigal sheep. We pray in Your Holy Name.

✛ ✛ ✛ ✛ ✛ ✛

January 23
SPEAKING OF REJECTION
Luke 10:16

Rejection leaves a bad taste, be it a job or a courtship. It makes us feel worthless and can lead to depression. We must anticipate that, like our Lord, we'll also be rejected at some point.

Jesus was persecuted, sold for 30 pieces of silver, denied, falsely accused, condemned, and crucified (**Hebrews 4:15**). His rejection opened the door for us to be accepted into God's family.

THE WORLD REJECTS GOD'S WORD claiming that it's full of errors and contradictions. Those who reject the Divine food sentence themselves to a fruitless life, separated from God. You and I can feed on the bread of life from heaven. God transforms us from enemies into His adopted children when we trust His Divine Word.

THE WORLD REJECTS GOD in favor of world philosophies. Of those claiming to know God, the Lord says, *"They claim to know God, but by their actions they deny him. They are detestable, disobedient and unfit for doing anything good"* (**Titus 1:16**).

God frequently complains that the Israelites *"had not obeyed my laws but had rejected my decrees and desecrated my Sabbaths, and their eyes lusted after their parents' idols"* (**Ezekiel 20:24**). We haven't always been faithful or obedient followers.

26

When we reject one of the Lord's statutes, we reject God. God was angry then and is angry now when we disobediently reject God instead of following and loving Him.

There are great blessings for those who receive and accept God as Lord. But there will also be punishment for those who intentionally reject God's Word, love, and friendship.

> There are great blessings for those who receive and accept God as Lord. But there will also be punishment for those who intentionally reject God's Word, love, and friendship.

GOD DOES NOT REJECT ANYONE. We thank God because, despite our repeated rebellions, God is always waiting with outstretched arms, ready to welcome us back as prodigal children. *"God will not despise a broken and contrite heart you"* **(Psalm 51:17).** Although we might be estranged from God, we're not alone, abandoned, or rejected; God walks by our side, encouraging us; *"I myself will tend my sheep and have them lie down, declares the Sovereign Lord"* **(Ezekiel 34:15).**

We must renounce our previous alliance with the evil powers. This means *"giving up ungodliness and worldly desires"* **(Titus 2:12)** and allowing the Holy Spirit to control our instincts, leading us toward the **holiness of the heart**.

Let us pray: Dear God, give us discernment to recognize the wolves in sheep's clothing and reject their corrupt teachings. After tasting Your truth and freedom, please don't allow us to reject Your offer of grace and return to the slavery of sin. We pray in Your Holy Name.

January 24
FOR WHAT SHOULD WE ASK?

*"Ask and it will be given to you; seek and you will find; knock and the door will be opened to you." **Matthew** 7:7*

"Pidan, y se les dará, busquen, y encontrarán, llamen, y se les abrirá". **Mateo 7:7**

"Ζητάτε, και θα σας δοθεί· ψάχνετε, και θα βρείτε· κρούετε, και θα σας ανοιχτεί·" ΚΑΤΑ ΜΑΤΘΑΙΟΝ 7:7

For what should we ask? For a God-pleasing heart! To receive God's blessings, we **must act so that God is pleased with us.** Jesus said: *"The one who sent me is with me; he has not left me alone, for I always do what pleases him"* **(John 8:29).**

God is pleased when we obey Him and our parents, *"for this pleases the Lord"* **(Colossians 3:20).** God is pleased *"When brothers and sisters live together in harmony"* **(Psalm 133:1).** We please God when we *"live a life worthy of the Lord… bearing fruit in every good work, growing in the knowledge of God"* **(Colossians 1:10);** when we don't *"forget to do good and to share with others"* **(Hebrews 13:16).**

Pleasing God has obligations but also **rewards that God is pleased to give us**:
1. *"When the Lord takes pleasure in anyone's way, he causes their enemies to make peace with them"* (**Proverbs 16:7**).
2. *"To the person who pleases him, God gives wisdom, knowledge, and happiness"* (***Ecclesiastes 2:26***).
3. *"Your Father has been pleased to give you the kingdom"* (**Luke 12:32**).

The world entices us to win the lottery, but God invites us to seek the enduring and incorruptible wealth acquired through giving and serving. Because we desire happiness, peace, wisdom, knowledge, joy, security, and God's protection, we ought to *seek first God's kingdom* by serving God and our neighbors.

Jesus promised that God **would supply all our needs.** *"Ask and it will be given to you; seek and you will find; knock and the door will be opened to you. For everyone who asks receives; the one who seeks finds; and to the one who knocks, the door will be opened"* (**Luke 11:9-10**).

Therefore, **strive to inherit the incorruptible treasure found in pleasing God and winning souls for the kingdom**. All material things grow old, fail, become corrupted, or can be stolen/confiscated. But by pleasing God, we create treasures, **here and in heaven**, that will never;
✦ age
✦ fail
✦ become corrupted, rot, or
✦ be stolen.

Let us pray: Dear God, thank You for showing us how to please You and be worthy of Your name. Grant that in our weakness, we may keep our eyes fixed on Jesus and the goal you've lovingly set for us and those you've entrusted us with caring for their souls. We pray in Your Holy Name.

January 25
YOU ARE WORTH A KING'S / QUEEN'S RANSOM
1 Corinthians 7:23

Every day the Lord offers us a new opportunity to start over, repairing or correcting previous mistakes, through the authority of God's Word, which reminds us of our value and purpose.

OUR VALUE - In "***The God Memorandum***," Og Mandino writes, *"Why have you valued yourself in pennies when you are worth a king's ransom? You are not mediocre."* God considers your life valuable and proves it. *"**But God demonstrates his own love for us in this: While we were still sinners, Christ died for us**"* (**Romans 5:8**). The price for your ransom was Jesus's life. Yes! An innocent life in exchange for our lives.

God is the author of our redemption. Because of God's great love and mercy, the Lord extends the free and undeserved gift to all who, by faith, receive Him. The initiative is entirely God's.

"He who created you, Jacob, he who formed you, Israel: 'Do not fear, for I have redeemed you'" **(Isaiah 43:1).** The *"Do not fear"* refers to the enemy's lies, which point to our past or present, hoping to disqualify us from being worthy rescue recipients.

RESCUED THROUGH JESUS CHRIST'S SACRIFICE - God descended into our world in human form in the person of Jesus Christ, who underwent a bloody and painful death to rescue us. *"In whom we have re-*

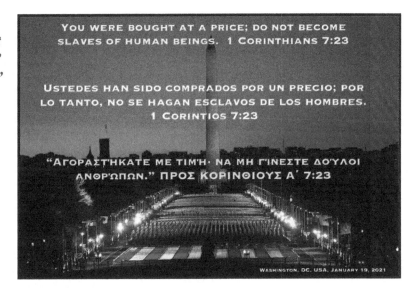

demption, the forgiveness of sins" **(Colossians 1:14).** After living a perfect life, Jesus died on the cross, and on the third day, He rose again. *"And, once made perfect, he became the source of eternal salvation for all who obey him"* **(Hebrews 5:9).**

Never doubt the value that God has placed on your life! You're **"worthy of a king's ransom,"** but the redemption that You enjoy or can enjoy is entirely by God's grace. All we need is to have faith in the person and sacrifice of Jesus Christ. Yet, even our faith is a gift from God so that no one can boast **(Ephesians 2:8-9).** *"And all are justified freely by his grace through the redemption that came by Christ Jesus"* **(Romans 3:24).**

Since Jesus paid for our ransom with His life, let's walk toward the freedom we find in God and distance ourselves from the slavery of sin.

Let us pray: Dear God, thank You for clarifying the value you've placed in our lives. Thank You for Jesus's sacrifice, who paid with His life as a ransom for our freedom. We entrust our children, sick, and planet to Your care, love, and grace. We pray in Jesus's name.

January 26
IT'S USELESS TO FIGHT AGAINST GOD
Acts 5:39

God gave me the joy and confidence to invite over a thousand friends and family to join the Bible Meditation Group. I asked them because I'm convinced that there's no better spiritual food and strength than the Holy Scriptures. **Psalm 127:1** says, *"Unless the Lord builds the house, the builders labor in vain. Unless the Lord watches over the city, the guards stand watch in vain."* I'm convinced that this space where friends and family share spiritual food is the Lord's work and initiative.

In today's verses, the Sanhedrin had ordered Peter and the apostles to stop speaking in Jesus's name. But they flatly refused, saying, *"We must obey God rather than human beings!"* **(Acts 5:29)**. After being jailed and released, they resumed preaching, thus enraging the religious leaders, who sought to kill them.

Gamaliel, a respected Pharisee and Saul's (Apostle Paul) teacher intercedes with wise counsel; *"Leave these men alone! Let them go! For if their purpose or activity is of human origin, it will fail. But if it is from God, you will not be able to stop these men; you will only find yourselves fighting against God."* They all agreed with him **(Acts 5:38-39)**.

Often, the enemy tries to stifle our testimony by stating, for example, that it's **"not politically correct"** to speak of Jesus in mixed circles for fear of offending those of different beliefs. I'm not saying that our only topic of conversation is the gospel of Jesus Christ, but apart from the gospel, there's no topic more vital and of eternal consequence. We can't remain silent because *"if it is from God, no one will be able to stop or destroy it."*

It's useless to fight against God because God will fulfill His purpose. Sometimes we create barriers that prevent us from sharing

> PERO SI ES DE DIOS, NO LO PODRÁN DESTRUIR. ¡NO VAYA A SER QUE USTEDES SE ENCUENTREN LUCHANDO CONTRA DIOS! HECHOS 5:39
>
> BUT IF IT IS FROM GOD, YOU WILL NOT BE ABLE TO STOP THESE MEN; YOU WILL ONLY FIND YOURSELVES FIGHTING AGAINST GOD." ACTS 5:39
>
> "ΑΝ, ΌΜΩΣ, Ε'ΙΝΑΙ ΑΠΌ ΤΟΝ ΘΕΌ, ΔΕΝ ΜΠΟΡΕ'ΙΤΕ ΝΑ ΤΟ ΜΑΤΑΙΏΣΕΤΕ, ΚΑΙ ΠΡΟΣΈΧΕΤΕ Μ'ΗΠΩΣ ΒΡΕΘΕΊΤΕ ΚΑΙ ΘΕΟΜΆΧΟΙ." ΠΡΑΞΕΙΣ ΑΠΟΣΤΟΛΩΝ 5:39
>
> EPHESUS, TURKEY - JULIE BOHL

> We can't remain silent because *"if it is from God, no one will be able to stop or destroy it."*

the good news with friends and family. Low self-esteem or fear of *"what people might say"* can stop us from fulfilling our calling. Today's verse encourages us to press forward because *"if it is from God, no one will be able to stop, destroy,"* silence, or deter it. In **2 Chronicles 13:12**, we find the warning, *"People of Israel, do not fight against the Lord, the God of your ancestors, for you will not succeed."*

Let us pray: Dear God, please engrave in our hearts that it's useless to fight against You. Strengthen our resolve when the enemy tries to silence us, even when fear inclines us to be silent. We pray in Your Holy Name.

January 27
ENDURING WEALTH
Proverbs 8:17

Education and a good work ethic are keys to prosperity. Likewise, a solid **knowledge** of God's Word, coupled with a commitment to follow the Lord's wise counsel, is essential to achieving **enduring wealth**.

One way to gain spiritual Wisdom is by reading the Bible throughout the year. You can read one of the thirty chapters of Proverbs each day during the month and assigned readings from the Old and New Testaments. Repeat every month. Thus, in repetition, you'll create muscle memory.

In Proverbs, we find our heavenly Father's wise and loving direction. Inspired by God's Wisdom, King Solomon wrote these passages, considered pearls and treasures to achieve a life pleasing to God, filled with His blessings.

Proverbs 8 personifies God's Wisdom inviting everyone to search for it as a treasure. *"To you, O people, I call out; I raise my voice to all mankind"* **(v.4).**

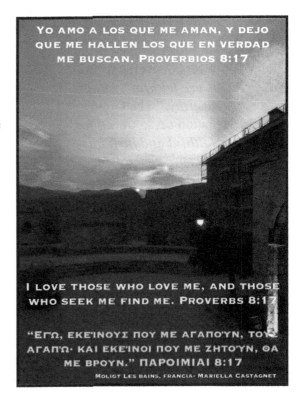

YO AMO A LOS QUE ME AMAN, Y DEJO QUE ME HALLEN LOS QUE EN VERDAD ME BUSCAN. PROVERBIOS 8:17

I LOVE THOSE WHO LOVE ME, AND THOSE WHO SEEK ME FIND ME. PROVERBS 8:17

"ΕΓΩ, ΕΚΕΊΝΟΥΣ ΠΟΥ ΜΕ ΑΓΑΠΟΎΝ, ΤΟΥΣ ΑΓΑΠΏ· ΚΑΙ ΕΚΕΊΝΟΙ ΠΟΥ ΜΕ ΖΗΤΟΎΝ, ΘΑ ΜΕ ΒΡΟΥΝ." ΠΑΡΟΙΜΙΑΙ 8:17

MOLIGT LES BAINS, FRANCIA- MARIELLA CASTAGNET

All material things acquired can be spoiled or lost instantly in this world. But not the education and Wisdom that we've gained from exemplary books and teachers. God's Wisdom tells us, *"Choose my instruction instead of silver, knowledge rather than choice gold, for wisdom is more precious than rubies, and nothing you desire can compare with her"* **(vs. 10-11).** Before silver and gold, let us first seek God's Wisdom.

By reading, studying, and memorizing God's Wisdom, we'll find *"Counsel and sound judgment"* **(v.14)** to face trials and temptations, along with the patience, intelligence, and power that come from God's mouth to instruct our children.

Reading, studying, journaling, memorizing, and putting into practice God's Wisdom, will lead us *"in the way of righteousness, along the paths of justice, bestowing a rich inheritance on those who love me and making their treasuries full"* **(vs. 20-21).**

Therefore, my dear children, friends, and family, let us show respect and fear to God's counsel. Let's seek and learn from them because God, personifying Wisdom, promises, *"With me are riches and honor, enduring wealth and prosperity"* **(v.18).**

Let us pray: Dear God, help us be disciplined in studying and memorizing Your holy counsel so that we do not drift to the right or left. Only then can we become heirs of the **enduring wealth** you've stored for Your children. We pray in Your Holy Name.

Some Bible versions reflect, *"All his precepts are faithful" rather than "trustworthy."* The Good News translation says, *"In all he does he is faithful and just; all his commands are dependable"* (**Psalm 111:7**).

The differences may be puzzling, but it is essential to identify the Hebrew word used in the manuscripts and ensure that the translation uses one of its synonyms. The Hebrew word for faithful, אָמַן (**amman H-539**), has several synonyms, including *"firm, trust or believe, comply, permanent, assurance, truth, faithful, verify."* All these translations are worthy of our confidence.[2]

We're responsible for the spiritual safety of our family. Therefore, we must be confident in whom we place our trust. Today's verse encourages us to trust God's promises, pointing out that *"The works of his hands are faithful and just; all his precepts are trustworthy,"* sure and faithful.

During 33 years of walking with God, I've confirmed in my own life and those who've placed their trust in the Lord that God's works are indeed *"faithful and just."* The promises and commandments that God establishes in His Word are trustworthy because God cannot lie. God never fails and is never late. Therefore, *"his commandments are dependable"* (**Psalm 111:7**).

The result of placing our trust in God's Word is that we're building a spiritual inheritance for our future generations, not on the sands shifted by the philosophies of our times, but on Jesus Christ, the cornerstone, firm, and tested through the centuries. Children and youth are our imitators. They need to know in whom to place their trust and life.

God's Word says, *"blessed is the one who trusts in the Lord, whose confidence is in him"* **(Jeremiah 17:7).**

Let us pray: Dear God, help us seek Your blessing by placing the trust and security of our family in Your precious hands. May our children and future generations continue to build on Your solid rock. We pray in Jesus's name.

---

[2] *(Strong, J. (2002). New comprehensive Strong's concordance: Dictionary (p. 9). Nashville, TN: Caribbean.)*

January 29
HEALTHY FEAR

"The fear of the Lord is the beginning of wisdom; all who follow his precepts have good understanding. To him belongs eternal praise." **Psalm 111:10**

"El principio de la sabiduría es el temor al Señor. Quienes practican esto adquieren entendimiento y alaban al Señor toda su vida". **Salmo 111:10**

"Η αρχή τής σοφίας είναι ο φόβος τού Κυρίου· όλοι εκείνοι που τις εκτελούν, έχουν καλή σύνεση· η αίνεσή του μένει στον αιώνα." **ΨΑΛΜΟΙ 111:10**

Today's verse points to two fundamental and often misunderstood issues. These are (1) Wisdom and (2) *"The fear of the LORD."*

When my son Jean-Paul was less than a year old, my mother-in-law said to me, **"your son must learn to fear you** (*'να μάθει να σε φοβάσαι'*)."** I didn't understand the instruction at the time since it's not my character to make anyone afraid of me, especially my son. But little by little, I learned that it wasn't about creating terror but rather a **healthy fear** so that he'd learn to follow my instructions precisely and instantly when necessary (for example, in case of imminent bodily danger).

The Bible uses several synonyms to refer to fear. Reverence, fright, fear, respect, and honor are the most common. A healthy *"fear of the LORD"* is **"holy fear."** In other words, we should not fear GOD but instead have a **"holy fear."**

This **holy fear** comes from a faith that we have a loving God who has good plans for His children. This faith tells us that God loves us and delights in us, even when we make mistakes, as infants tend to do when learning to walk, eat, talk, etc. A **healthy holy fear** helps us strive to heed God's instruction and please Him in everything within our capacity.

By following and respecting God's instruction, we acquire wisdom, which leads us along paths of peace, life, and justice. **Psalm 111:10** says, *"all who follow his precepts have good understanding. To him belongs eternal praise."* For our future generations, we wish; that instead of being **"politically correct,"** they might be **"biblically faithful."** After all, when we appear before God's throne of judgment, we want God to find us biblically faithful, don't we? The way to ensure this is by having a **healthy holy fear and respect for God's Word** and doing what it asks of us.

Let us pray: Dear God, help us have a healthy respect for Your Holy Word and that, more than anything in this world, may we seek to be faithful to you. Make us instruments of peace and reconciliation with those who seek a more intimate and profound relationship with You and Your church. Let us be slow to judge others and yet quick to judge and correct our walk with you. We pray in the name of Jesus.

CHARACTER

"Whoever can be trusted with very little can also be trusted with much, and whoever is dishonest with very little will also be dishonest with much." **Luke 16:10**

"El que es confiable en lo poco, también lo es en lo mucho; y el que no es confiable en lo poco, tampoco lo es en lo mucho". **Lucas 16:10**

"Ο πιστός στο ελάχιστο, και στο πολύ είναι πιστός· και ο άδικος στο ελάχιστο, και στο πολύ είναι άδικος." **ΚΑΤΑ ΛΟΥΚΑΝ 16:10**

In the office, we had a coffee club. Each member paid $7 per month to enjoy unlimited coffee. A new treasurer took the position, who received the treasury with pennies in petty cash and without an accounting. Within a year of administering it and delivering quarterly reports, the treasurer reported enough money in petty cash to offer members free coffee for two months. The following year, there was enough to forgive a five-month fee. **"Whoever can be trusted with very little can be trusted with much."**

Children are the greatest treasure and responsibility to those who are parents. When selecting daycare, we're diligent in ensuring various things. 1. They don't have a criminal record, 2. they have a license and verifiable experience, and 3. by observing the patience and attention they provide to other children and the hygiene of the center, we can decide if the person/entity is reliable. **He who takes care of what is worth little is of good character and can be trusted with much.**

John Wooden said, *"Character is the way we act when nobody is watching."* Character and honesty are proof of our integrity. The temptation to take something that doesn't belong to us might seem small, but there is one who looks at what we do in secret. God!

God has entrusted the family to our love, support, care, and protection. The way we act at home, how we administer money (ours or someone else's), how we treat our friends and the strangers that we meet, what we do with the 24-hours-a-day that we have life, all these **point to our character and faithfulness.** *"Whoever can be trusted with very little can be trusted with much."*

Let us pray: Dear God, please **form our character** to be excellent examples for our children and those who observe our lives in search of an honorable Christian model. Grant us the wisdom to choose intelligently the people with whom we share the responsibility of raising and instructing our children. At the end of our days, may we hear: *"Come, you who are blessed by my Father; take your inheritance, the kingdom prepared for you since the creation of the world"* *(Matthew 25:34).* Find us faithful, Lord. We pray in Your Holy Name.

January 31
DIVINE SUBMISSION

"Submit yourselves, then, to God. Resist the devil, and he will flee from you." James 4:7

"Por lo tanto, sométanse a Dios; opongan resistencia al diablo, y él huirá de ustedes".
Santiago 4:7

"Υποταχθείτε, λοιπόν, στον Θεό· αντισταθείτε στον διάβολο, και θα φύγει από σας."
ΙΑΚΩΒΟΥ 4:7

Of all the women in the Bible, Ruth's submission and love toward Naomi touch me deeply.

After her sons passed away, Naomi asked her two daughters-in-law to return to their parents' houses. *"But Ruth replied: 'Don't urge me to leave you or to turn back from you. Where you go I will go, and where you stay I will stay. Your people will be my people and your God my God. Where you die I will die, and there I will be buried. May the Lord deal with me, be it ever so severely, if even death separates you and me'" (Ruth 1:16-17).*

These are exemplary words for those who have entrusted our lives to God. Wherever God indicates, we will go, His people will be our people (whoever they are). Where God dwells, we will live and be by His side forever. Nothing will separate us, not even death.

By submitting ourselves to God (knowing and doing His will), we gather the strength to resist the temptation to choose an easy life or momentary pleasures. Using God's Word well, we respond to temptations by crying out, *"No, because it is written" (Matthew 4:10),* and in the name of Jesus Christ, we will make the devil flee from our presence.

> **Wherever God indicates we will go, His people will be our people (whomever they are). Where God dwells, we will live and be by His side forever. Nothing will separate us, not even death.**

Ephesians 4:27 says, *"and do not give the devil a foothold."* With only a small opportunity, a carelessness, or a small innocent indiscretion, the devil can move within us and cause harm for generations. With just a bit of unresolved anger in your heart, the devil can cause division within the home and the church. Ruth didn't give in to temptation but chose love and submission.

Our struggle is not brother against brother *"but against the rulers, against the authorities, against the powers of this dark world and against the spiritual forces of evil in the heavenly realms" Ephesians 6:12.* Therefore, when someone says or does something against us, remember that **the real enemy is the devil**, and choose to respond in love. We can resist the devil's attacks by submitting to God, and the devil will flee.

Let us pray: Dear God, thank You for those who've been an example of submission and service to You. Grant that we may imitate them, so our life may be an example of submission to You for future generations. May our people be their people, and You, our Father, their God, and Father. We pray in the name of Jesus.

February 1
A BLESSED PEOPLE
Numbers 22:12

If you've trusted Jesus Christ as Savior, you have the assurance of adoption into God's family. Adoption and blessing arise from the Abrahamic covenant in which God promised, *"I will bless those who bless you, and whoever curses you I will curse; and all peoples on earth will be blessed through you"* **(Genesis 12:3).**

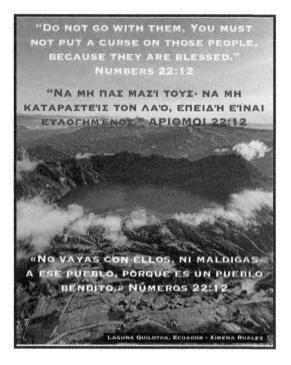

In **Numbers 22:6**, Balak, the Moabite king, calls for Balaam to curse the Israelites camped on the edge of Moab. His request was: *"Now come and put a curse on these people, because they are too powerful for me. Perhaps then I will be able to defeat them and drive them out of the land. For I know that whoever you bless is blessed, and whoever you curse is cursed."*

Balaam consulted with God, who told him, *"Do not go with them. You must not put a curse on those people, because they are blessed"* **(v.12).** Balaam replied to the messengers that God wouldn't allow him to go with them. But Balak sent other messengers offering riches if the prophet came and cursed the Israelites. I love Balaam's answer; *"Even if Balak gave me all the silver and gold in his palace, I could not do anything great or small to go beyond the command of the Lord my God"* **(v.18).**

That should be our response! We can't disobey God's will and guidance; we **can't curse what God has blessed nor call good what God has called evil.** Light can't mix with darkness except to illuminate the path for those seeking to escape from the night. We must obey God in the least of His orders. God promises, *"Now if you obey me fully and keep my covenant, then out of all nations you will be my treasured possession"* **(Exodus 19:5).**

We're a blessed, *treasured* **people.** Let's act with the nobility of character and purity of heart - confident that God will never forsake us. Therefore, we shouldn't fear the world nor give in when they incite us with fear or riches to curse God's people, detract from God's Word, or be the cause of a curse based on our disobedience and lack of faith.

Let us pray: Dear God, help us act as Your children, worthy of being called Your chosen and blessed people. Fill Your people with power and bless us with Your peace so that in everything we do, Your name may be glorified, and we might help others be part of your **blessed people.** We pray in Your Holy Name.

February 2
WORRY-FREE
1 Corinthians 7:32A

We tend to worry and stress about many things. For many, death is the ultimate source of worry. My daughter Sophia shared some thoughts on this topic.

"Death. It's not something that I think about daily, but I'm not one to shy away from the topic either. I grew up with my grandparents speaking about death as if it were some sort of a gift. That... in the end, we all share the same inevitable fate. There was no sugarcoating it in my family – we're all going to die, so live well, be kind and have faith."

Words of wisdom and hope flowing from our children's mouths! **Don't worry**, be happy. Death is inevitable. Live well, be kind and have faith. Thank God for lessons that our children absorb from their grandparents - an excellent source of wisdom that often points you back to what matters, thus removing any anxiety.

When I'm in Greece, I worry about careless drivers who don't respect cyclists (like me), but not so much to lose sleep over it or putting my bicycle away in storage. Instead, I put my ride in God's hands and am attentive to everything and everyone on the road. Thus I can anticipate their move and react safely. Before each ride, as I do with airplane rides, I say, *"Lord, into thy hands I commit my spirit,"* and fall into the most restful nap until my senses tell me that coffee is being served.

Before the Lord saved me (1989), I worried about death and thought life insurance was the answer. Taking financial care of the family was paramount. But the insurance policy didn't relieve me from worrying and losing sleep over many things. *"Anxiety weighs down the heart, but a kind word cheers it up" (Proverbs 12:25).*

The kind words I discovered in the Holy Scriptures removed the worry and replaced it with love, joy, peace, and wonderful, relaxing, restful sleep. *"Do not be anxious about anything, but in every situation, by prayer and petition, with thanksgiving, present your requests to God. And the peace of God, which transcends all understanding, will guard your hearts and your minds in Christ Jesus"* **(Philippians 4:6-7).**

Let us pray: Dear God, help us learn from the faith of our grandparents and be **free from concern** so that we may be happy, live well, and fan the flames of our faith. We pray in the name of Jesus.

February 3
HOPE, TRUST, AND PRAY

"You will seek me and find me when you seek me with all your heart." **Jeremiah 29:13**

"Cuando ustedes me busquen, me hallarán, si me buscan de todo corazón". **Jeremías 29:13**

"Και θα με ζητήσετε, και θα με βρείτε, όταν με εκζητήσετε με όλη σας την καρδιά."
ΙΕΡΕΜΙΑΣ 29:13

We should plan as if we're going to remain on this planet for a lifetime but live as if today is the last day of our lives. We **hope, pray and trust** that this year will be better than the last.

HOPE
In 2021, we hoped that more than 90% of the world's population would be COVID vaccinated. We hope for improved economies and people returning safely to their workplaces. Yet, we should anticipate that we'll experience a combination of blessings and continued struggles. Consider the following; **When trouble arises, who do you hope will come to your rescue?**

When problems and crises arise, we're inclined to seek advice from experts (doctors, lawyers, professionals, neighbors, Google, etc.) before seeking direction from God's Word. Even for pastors, as we prepare Bible study lessons or sermons, we sometimes seek first the insights of well-known pastors and authors, giving them more coverage and attention than God's living Word. Our hope ought to be first in following God's will.

TRUST
When trouble comes, we tend to get unfocused, confused, and unable to decide on the right path. However, when we're at peace, we think clearly. The key to guarding our peace during storms comes from trusting that our life is in God's hands. A favorite Bible passage is **Jeremiah 29:11.** God says: *"'For I know the plans I have for you,' declares the Lord, 'plans to prosper you and not to harm you, plans to give you hope and a future.'"* In whatever situation you might be, you won't lose your peace when you trust that God has good plans for you, that God is in charge, and will guide you through this storm.

PRAY
As we experience God's faithfulness amid challenges, we shift our trust from human knowledge to God's wisdom, from relying on humans to trusting God's plans and establishing a pattern of communication and **prayer** with God. *"'Then you will call on me and come and pray to me, and I will listen to you. You will seek me and find me when you seek me with all your heart. I will be found by you,' declares the Lord, 'and will bring you back from captivity'" (Jeremiah 29:12-14).*

Let us pray: Dear God, in our times of trial, please help us to seek first Your wisdom and guidance, to seek You with all our heart, and find You in the small and big challenges and blessings of our daily life. We pray in Your Holy Name.

February 4
CALLED TO BE FREE
Galatians 5:13

In gratitude for delivering us from the bondage of sin, God calls us back to another kind of bondage, called reciprocity, in which we demonstrate our love for God by loving and serving one another.

God's Word says: *"It is for freedom that Christ has set us free. Stand firm, then, and do not let yourselves be burdened again by a yoke of slavery"* (**Galatians 5:1**).

God delivered us from *slavery to sin* because, under the law, no one could be justified. The law's rituals

lost their effectiveness when Jesus gave His life on the cross as the just and sufficient sacrifice to grant us the much-desired **freedom**. Faith in Jesus's sacrifice opened the bridge once and for all, giving us entrance into God's presence and **positionally** freeing us from the bondage of sin and its temptations.

But it's interesting that having placed our faith in Christ and receiving the freedom from sin and eternal death, in this verse, God calls us to become voluntary servants again, no longer to the law or to sin, but to one another. *"Serve one another humbly in love"* (**Galatians 5:13**).

The word *"serve"* is δουλεύω (**douleúo**); which means to **"be a bondservant to** (involuntarily or voluntarily): *servant, service, serve."* On this side of the cross, we serve each other with gratitude and for the love of God.

It's neither burdensome nor grievous to serve one another when done for love. Households would be happier and more grateful when couples cooperate and help each other. "**Machismo**" robs couples of sweet companionship and reciprocity. That is also true for churches in which the same people often carry different positions and eventually grow weary and discouraged from serving because their service is unidirectional.

Let us pray: Dear God, thank You for calling us to be free from slavery to sin and giving us a family and community that expresses their love and gratitude through mutual service and support. Help us reflect this love and kindness in and outside our homes and churches. We pray in the name of Jesus.

February 5
ME, A LIFEGUARD?
1 Corinthians 9:16

Psalm 147:11 says, *"the Lord delights in those who fear him, who put their hope in his unfailing love."* We honor God when we faithfully carry out our commission, the same one that the Apostle Paul acknowledges in his letter to the Corinthians. Although we may not be apostles or preachers, **God commissions every disciple of Christ to preach the gospel.**

Have you considered that you're a lifesaver? The gospel that saved you is now in your hands. God deposited His love and Word in your heart so that, at the right moment, you may throw your buoy to whomever you see in danger of drowning. The Holy Spirit will guide you to use your buoy, whether in words, actions, prayers, or combinations of these.

Perhaps you've heard the saying, *"Our lives might be the only Bible that people will ever read!"* The Bible is extensive and sometimes difficult to read. Therefore, instead of reading it, people will look at our lives to determine if we're genuinely Christians. In other words, how you and I act affirms what we believe and live. When we extend a helping hand, we're preaching to the world that we believe in a merciful God, full of grace and love, who goes in search of, and rescues lost sheep that were led astray and marginalized by the father of lies.

God commissioned us with the gospel of Jesus Christ, a powerful lifesaver. Through His life and sacrifice, Jesus **did not stop preaching the gospel** in words and actions, thus healing and rescuing many lost sheep. Before ascending to heaven, Jesus **commissioned** us with these words, *"Go into all the world and preach the gospel to all creation"* **(Mark 16:15).**

You might not feel up to the task, saying, **"I'm not a preacher or an evangelist."** But you are a lifesaver **commissioned** by the Holy Spirit, who will help you. Jesus promises each disciple, *"But you will receive power when the Holy Spirit comes on you; and you will be my witnesses in Jerusalem, and in all Judea and Samaria, and to the ends of the earth"* **(Acts 1:8).**

Let us pray: Dear God, bathe us with the power of Your Holy Spirit so that, beginning in our homes and neighborhoods, we may preach the gospel of love with actions and, if necessary, with words. We pray for our COVID patients. Heal them and our planet, Lord. We pray in the name of Jesus.

> God deposited His love and Word in your heart so that, at the right moment, you may throw your buoy to whomever you see in danger of drowning.

February 6
COMPASSION IS ABOVE THE LAW
Matthew 12:12

The Pharisees asked Jesus whether it was lawful to heal on the Sabbath. Jesus compared the value and compassion they showed toward a sheep fallen into a pit on the Sabbath and concluded that 1. **humanity is worth much more than animals** and 2. **compassion is above the law.**

WE'RE WORTH MUCH MORE THAN ANIMALS
Although we're insignificant relative to all creation, God holds us in high esteem. *"what is mankind that you are mindful of them, human beings that you care for them? You made them rulers over the works of your hands; you put everything under their feet"* **(Psalm 8:4,6).**

Jesus repeatedly mentions our superior value over animals, such as sheep, birds, etc. *"Are you not much more valuable than they?"* **(Matthew 6:26).** *"So don't be afraid; you are worth more than many sparrows"* **(Matthew 10:31).**

COMPASSION IS ABOVE THE LAW
The love and compassion we've received from God compel us to care more about our neighbors than about human laws and interpretations.

The Pharisees boasted of their high knowledge and authority over the people. But they forgot the supreme law; *"love our neighbor as ourselves"* *(Luke 10:27).* Worried, they passed by ignoring another human, fallen and bleeding, so as not to break the Sabbath, be late to the tabernacle, or be found "**unclean**" and unable to perform their prestigious rituals in the Sanctuary **(Luke 10:31).** Jesus said, *"do not worry about* [the laws, rituals, politics, the news] your life, what you will eat or drink; or about your body, what you will wear. Is not life more than food, and the body more than clothes?" **(Matthew 6:25).** Instead, seek first the essence and will of God: love and **compassion**.

Jesus was clear that He is *"Lord even of the Sabbath" (Mark 2:27–28).* He has the power to guide us in healing and saving others, even on the Sabbath.

Let us pray: Dear God, thank You for the doctors, nurses, and all first aid personnel who, during these ten months, have worked tirelessly, even on the Sabbath, to heal and save Your people. Bless them and their loved ones. Thank you for the value you've placed in our lives. Help us to be compassionate like You. We pray in Your Holy Name.

February 7
THREE ARE BETTER THAN ONE

"Though one may be overpowered, two can defend themselves. A cord of three strands is not quickly broken." Ecclesiastes 4:12

"Y si alguno prevaleciere contra uno, dos le resistirán; y cordón de tres dobleces no se rompe pronto". Eclesiastés 4:12

"Και αν κάποιος υπερισχύσει ενάντια στον έναν, οι δύο θα του αντιταχθούν· και το τριπλό σχοινί δεν κόβεται γρήγορα." ΕΚΚΛΗΣΙΑΣΤΗΣ 4:12 FPB

A parallel is found in verse **9**: *"Two are better than one because they have a good return for their labor."*

We know that Satan walks around like a roaring lion, looking for someone to devour **(1 Peter 5:8).** In general, the people who fall victim to these assaults are those who choose to walk alone and unprotected. The devil might defeat one lonely unsuspecting soul, but not two or three who are walking with the Lord.

God didn't create us to live alone, to walk the earth without a soul by our side to defend, or to give us a helping hand in times of need or danger.

God is a relational being and created us in His image to have an intimate relationship with us, but He also wants us to love and support each other. Therefore, God said in *Genesis 2:18, "It is not good for man to be alone; I will make him a helper suitable for him."* And God formed the woman, the pinnacle of creation. Glory to God! Note: Some people have received the **gift of singleness** to dedicate their lives to serving God and His people. God has provided a suitable partner for those who haven't received that gift.

We know the saying, "Two minds are better than one." Many times, to get to the bottom of an issue or situation, I ask myself, *"What other question would Margarita ask?"* This helps me think as she thinks and to reach a solution.

Indeed, *"two are better than one, because they get more out of their efforts"* That's true in all relationships, including business, church, and community. Two advise and encourage each other toward success. Three take care of and protect each other. If one falls, the others are there to help them rise.

Within marriage, the apparent benefits are intimacy and family formation, which offers an even more intimate and fruitful relationship. According to God's goodness in granting children to the marriage, the two-chord strand becomes three or four. These alleviate the aging problem of isolation and loneliness. A faithful partner provides help, comfort, and protection in the family, business, or community.

Let us pray: Dear God, help us to be grateful, faithful, and honest in our role as *"suitable partners"* with our spouses as well as with our peers at church, work, and community. We pray in Jesus's name.

February 8
THE FIRST RESURRECTION

"When Elisha reached the house, there was the boy lying dead on his couch." **2 Kings 4:32**

"Cuando Eliseo llegó a la casa, el niño yacía tendido sobre la cama, sin vida". **2 Reyes 4:32**

"Και όταν ο Ελισσαιέ μπήκε μέσα στο σπίτι, νάσου, το παιδί ήταν νεκρό, πλαγιασμένο επάνω στο κρεβάτι του." **Β΄ ΒΑΣΙΛΕΩΝ 4:32**

Today we find the account of **the First Resurrection** in the Bible, which is a shadow of the Resurrection of our Lord Jesus Christ, who opened the heavens for all humanity who have put their faith in Him. I invite you to read **chapter 4 of 2 Kings** to clarify this story's background, our story, and hope.

In gratitude for the Shunammite woman's caring attention, Elisha offers to return her kindness by granting her a wish. After learning that the woman had no children, we read, *"'About this time next year,' Elisha said, 'you will hold a son in your arms'"* **(v.16).** The child was born but then fell ill, died, and the Shunammite woman sent for the prophet Elisha.

"When Elisha reached the house, there was the boy lying dead on his couch. He went in, shut the door on the two of them and prayed to the Lord. Then he got on the bed and lay on the boy, mouth to mouth, eyes to eyes, hands to hands. As he stretched himself out on him, the boy's body grew warm" **(v.32-34).** Then he repeated the process, and the child was resurrected.

It's worth highlighting **verse 33,** *"He went in, shut the door on the two of them and prayed to the Lord."* Elisha resurrected the child, not by his power but through prayer with God. Doing precisely what God directed, the boy's life was restored, and the gift of new life was returned to the Shunammite woman.

The Shunammite represents each believer who puts their faith and hope in the presence and Word of God. God rewards every charitable work toward the poor with the promise of abundant life. The Shunammite received the child, and not even death could deny her the gift of the Resurrection. You and I have the hope that *"nothing can separate us from the love of God in Christ Jesus"* **(Romans 8:39).** His Resurrection defeated the power of death, offering us that, just as Christ rose, we, together with our past and future generations, will also rise to eternal and abundant life.

Let us pray: Dear God, thank You for the promise of the Resurrection to eternal life. There's nothing impossible for You, Lord. In Your hands, we entrust our lives and future. Guide us along the path of justice and goodwill toward those in need. We pray in Your Holy Name.

Elisha resurrected the child, not by his power but through prayer with God. Doing precisely what God directed, the boy's life was restored, and the gift of new life was returned to the Shunammite woman.

✚✚✚ ✚✚✚

February 9
RESTITUTION
Psalm 102:17

Continuing with the Shunammite woman's account, God sent a message through Elisha, warning her to leave soon with all her family to a distant country because seven years of great famine were approaching. She left her land and house and lived in the country of the Philistines. Once the famine ended, *"she came back from the land of the Philistines and went to appeal to the king for her house and land"* **(2 Kings 8:1-3).**

What was this woman's kindness toward Elisha, that God would recompense her and her family? Upon seeing Elisha regularly pass by her house, she invited him to dinner. She then built a room with *"a bed and a table, a chair and a lamp for him"* so that when the prophet came to eat, he'd rest before continuing on his long journeys **(2 Kings 4:10).**

The Shulamite's humble yet generous kindness caught God's attention, who did the following for her:

1. Granted her the birth of the desired child.
2. Resuscitated the child when he died.
3. Warned her before the danger of hunger approached her and her family, and
4. Provided safe guidance back to her land and restored her land, house, and produce.

It's no coincidence that the king was hearing about Elisha's miracles, and wanting to hear more, the resurrected child's mother came forward to ask for restitution of her land. Moved by God's hand, the king ordered the restoration of her house and land and *"all the income from her land from the day she left the country until now"* (**vs. 5-6**).

My beloved, God's **hand is active in the lives of His children**. Our safety lies not in the absence of danger but in God's presence, who promises to be *"a wall of fire around us… and I will be its glory within"* (**Zechariah 2:5**). God *"will respond to the prayer of the destitute; he will not despise their plea"* (**Psalm 102:17**). Even when we're unaware of imminent danger, God sends His angels to free us from evil and **restore** what was ours.

> Our safety lies not in the absence of danger but in God's presence, who promises to be *"a wall of fire around us… and I will be its glory within"* (**Zechariah 2:5**).

Let us pray: Dear God, we're not worthy of so much love and goodness. Despite our inconsistency in following Your statutes and guidance, you tenderly lead us along the paths of abundant life, restoring our faith and life. Grant us the goodness, faithfulness, and humility of the Shunammite woman, so that Your presence and mercy will be our companion and guide. We pray in Your Holy Name.

February 10
EVERYONE WANTED TO TOUCH HIM

"For he had healed many, so that those with diseases were pushing forward to touch him."
Mark 3:10

"Como había sanado a muchos, todos los que tenían plagas querían tocarlo y se lanzaban sobre él". **Marcos 3:10**

"Επειδή, θεράπευσε πολλούς, ώστε, όσοι είχαν αρρώστιες, έπεφταν επάνω του, για να τον αγγίξουν." **ΚΑΤΑ ΜΑΡΚΟΝ 3:10**

We're quick to seek relief from the plagues that afflict our bodies, such as COVID-19, but slow to recognize our need for spiritual healing and purpose.

I've never seen so many deaths of acquaintances as in this pandemic. We long to get close to Jesus and receive His healing touch, which has the power to deliver us from our physical, emotional, and spiritual afflictions. If Jesus were with us physically, all the sick and afflicted would rush to the airports to get to where He is, touch him, and be healed.

"For he had healed many, so that those with diseases were pushing forward to touch him" **(Mark 3:10).** Wherever he went, *"the people all tried to touch him, because power was coming from him and healing them all"* **(Luke 6:19).** Such was the case of the woman who, for many years, suffered from hemorrhages. She stopped suffering the day that Jesus passed through her town, and with faith, she said, *"If I only touch his cloak, I will be healed" (Matthew 9:21).*

The woman's faith activated Jesus's healing power. Those with confidence in this power approached Jesus begging Him to let them *"just touch the edge of his cloak, and all who touched it were healed"* of physical, spiritual, and emotional illnesses (**Matthew 14:36**).

Today more than ever, we need to rekindle our faith to believe in Jesus's power to heal, save, and rescue our lives from the plagues that afflict us - COVID, which as of May 2022 has claimed 6.3 million lives and the spiritual virus called "**unbelief**." Our world has stopped believing in the healing power that Christ entrusted to the church. We haven't been good stewards of this gift, which is why so many don't want to hear about church or Jesus. *"He was in the world, and though the world was made through him, the world did not recognize him"* **(John 1:10).**

As representatives of the body of Jesus Christ (the church), you and I are the manifestations and physical presence of our Lord and His power. If we act with our Lord's humility and authority, the world will again believe in Jesus, and all *"those with diseases will push forward to touch him" (Mark 3:10).*

Let us pray: Dear God, forgive us for the times and ways we've failed to serve You faithfully. Our world needs Your healing touch. Give us clarity of purpose to effectively represent Your grace, love, and healing power. We pray in Jesus's name.

February 11
FRAGRANT AND TRIUMPHANT
2 Corinthians 2:14

Since childhood, I've loved two fragrances; my father's *"Old Spice"* cologne and the "incense" that my mom burned on her altar. Both fill me with a sense of peace, freshness, and the feeling of being ready to face whatever comes.

When we surrender our lives to the Lord, God enables us so that amid any adversity, *"trouble, hardship, persecution, famine, nakedness, danger, sword"* or plagues, we come out **triumphant**, with the **aroma of life** and *"more than conquerors through him who loved us"* (**Romans 8:35-37**).

A stench of death penetrates even through double masks in those who resist God. We know that before his transformative encounter with Jesus, Saul persecuted the church of Christ. Wherever he went, that stench accompanied him. But God triumphed over this adversary, making Saul an aroma of life, a servant, and the most prolific ambassador of Christ's church.

BUT THANKS BE TO GOD, WHO... USES US TO SPREAD THE AROMA OF THE KNOWLEDGE OF HIM EVERYWHERE. 2 CORINTHIANS 2:14

PERO GRACIAS A DIOS, QUE ...POR MEDIO DE NOSOTROS MANIFIESTA EN TODAS PARTES EL AROMA DE SU CONOCIMIENTO. 2 CORINTIOS 2:14

"ΌΜΩΣ, ΕΥΧΑΡΙΣΤΊΑ ΑΝΉΚΕΙ ΣΤΟΝ ΘΕΌ, ΠΟΥ ...ΣΕ ΚΆΘΕ ΤΟΠΟ ΦΑΝΕΡΏΝΕΙ Μ'ΕΣΑ ΑΠ'Ο ΜΑΣ ΤΗΝ ΟΣΜΉ ΤΗΣ ΓΝΏΣΗΣ ΤΟΥ." ΠΡΟΣ ΚΟΡΙΝΘΙΟΥΣ Β' 2:14

ATARDECER NEVADO - NORWALK, CT - FANNY ZAMORA

When we stop fighting against God, surrendering our strength and will to the Creator, through faith and obedience, **God transforms;**

1. Our slavery to freedom,
2. Our sadness into joyful hope,
3. Our adversaries into friends,
4. Our stench of death into the **fragrance of life and knowledge**, and
5. Our blindness into a clear vision.

Like Saint Paul, we've been chosen, saved, healed, and renewed so that we'd obediently become ministers *"of Christ Jesus to the Gentiles. He gave us the priestly duty of proclaiming the gospel of God, so that the Gentiles might become an offering acceptable to God, sanctified by the Holy Spirit"* (**Romans 15:16**). Ephesians 5.2 calls us to walk *"in the way of love, just as Christ loved us and gave himself up for us as a fragrant offering and sacrifice to God."*

My beloved, we **no longer have to be ashamed of our previous life**, of what we were before we perceived the aroma of the knowledge of Jesus. Like Saul, our senses had become used to the stench of death. It followed us everywhere, separating us from each other. But now, through the one who loved us, *"we are a fragrant offering and sacrifice to God."*

Let us pray: Dear God, having enjoyed the sweet fragrance of triumph over sin and death, allow us to press toward the goal you've set for us and our home. Please let us project that **triumphant fragrance of life** to the world. We pray in Your Holy Name.

February 12
DON'T BE ASHAMED

"Christ Jesus came into the world to save sinners—of whom I am the worst."
1 Timothy 1:15B

"Cristo Jesús vino al mundo para salvar a los pecadores, de los cuales yo soy el primero".
1 Timoteo 1:15B

"Ο Ιησούς Χριστός ήρθε στον κόσμο για να σώσει τούς αμαρτωλούς, από τους οποίους πρώτος είμαι εγώ·" Α΄ ΠΡΟΣ ΤΙΜΟΘΕΟΝ 1:15B

Yesterday, we said we **no longer have to be ashamed of our previous life**. But perhaps you're still searching for peace with your past. God tells us in **Isaiah 54:4**, *"Do not be afraid; you will* *not be put to shame. Do not fear disgrace; you will not be humiliated. You will forget the shame of your youth."*

Paul declared the errors of his youth and attributed them to **ignorance and unbelief.** *"I thank Christ Jesus our Lord, who has given me strength, that he considered me trustworthy, appointing me to his service. Even though I was once a blasphemer and a persecutor and a violent man, I was shown mercy because I acted in ignorance and unbelief"* **(1 Timothy 1:12-13).**

DON'T BE ASHAMED. Instead of being silent about what he was and did, Paul used his weaknesses to glorify God, who, instead of rejecting and destroying him, welcomed him as an adopted son. *"Christ Jesus came into the world to save sinners, of whom I am the first"* **(1 Timothy 1:15B).**

DON'T BE ASHAMED to acknowledge your mistakes. The first step to healing and reconciliation with God (and neighbor) is recognizing our error, the damage we caused, and asking forgiveness. I implore you to put aside fear and pride - weapons the enemy uses to distance, divide and conquer. Admitting our mistakes frees us from the weight of guilt but not necessarily from the product of our error. If you recognize your mistake, don't be afraid to seek reconciliation as soon as possible because, otherwise, the weight becomes intolerable.

> **Admitting our mistake frees us from the weight of guilt but not necessarily from the product of our error.**

DON'T BE ASHAMED to tell others about what God did for you. Once forgiven, the Lord strengthens us with His Word, love, and acceptance and places us to work in His mission field. Then we begin telling the world, without fear or shame, what we were and the **spiritual transformation** that God worked in our life. Thus we can sing the best-known hymn on the planet; *"Amazing grace, how sweet the sound, that saved a wretch like me. I once was lost, but now I'm found. Was blind, but now I see."*

Let us pray: Dear God, touch us with Your Holy Spirit to promptly acknowledge our guilt and seek reconciliation. *"Forgive us our debts, as we also forgive our debtors. And lead us not into temptation, but deliver us from evil; for yours is the kingdom, the power and the glory, forever"* **(Matthew 6:12)** We pray in Jesus's name.

February 13
SEE JESUS IN EVERY TEAR

"As he approached Jerusalem and saw the city, he wept over it." **Luke 19:41**

"Ya cerca de la ciudad, Jesús lloró al verla". **Lucas 19:41**

"Και όταν πλησίασε, βλέποντας την πόλη, έκλαψε γι'αυτήν," **ΚΑΤΑ ΛΟΥΚΑΝ 19:41**

Sometimes we're moved to tears by the situation of loved ones, elders, orphans, and widows. God made us in His image, so it shouldn't surprise us that Jesus also weeps at our world's condition.

Entering Jerusalem, Jesus wept *"and said, 'If you, even you, had only known on this day what would bring you peace—but now it is hidden from your eyes'"* **(Luke 19:41).** The Holy City was meant to be God's dwelling place. Knowing that the people would reject Him, and considering the great suffering that Jerusalem would experience, *Jesus wept* because *"they did not realize the moment when God came to visit it"* *(v.44).*

JESUS STILL WEEPS over our people who no longer revere God's Word. Our children no longer learn to pray or read His Word, and Jesus weeps. Driven by addictions, temptations, and vices, husbands who professed love and honor today inflict fear and pain on their wives, and **Jesus weeps** as he sees **how far we've strayed from His command to** *"Love one another as I have loved you"* **(John 13:34).**

We're moved to tears by the condition and lifestyle of some in our surroundings. Our spirit often struggles to rationalize **actions** contrary to God's will. We might even show ourselves as friends, calling their way of life **"acceptable."** But that'd be irresponsible. **Can we justify the actions of one who abuses his wife? No!** Can we justify a drug and alcohol addict's stealing? No! We can and should love them, but we can't qualify their actions as good, healthy, and acceptable to God or society. Hear God's Word: *"Streams of tears flow from my eyes, for your law is not obeyed"* **(Psalm 119:136).**

Jesus wept and still weeps for those who, by disobeying the Divine law, don't *"realize the moment when God came to visit them"* **(Luke 19:44).** We must evaluate how our well-intentioned actions and words invalidate God's Word, **causing Jesus to weep** and further alienating us from God's Truth.

Let us pray: Dear God, forgive us when we cause you to weep. Grant that we may **see Jesus in every tear.** Help us to give **greater** importance to what hurts and offends you. We pray in the name of Jesus Christ.

February 14
LESSONS FROM DAD
Ephesians 5:1

It's almost ten years since dad's departure, I'm still learning from and trying to imitate dad's kind and noble qualities. Dad was very cheerful, social, honest, and affectionate. Although I wasn't his favorite, I always felt loved and appreciated by dad.

I gained his appreciation by striving to please him, to rise to the top at school, university, work, and home. One day, despite his fear of flying, my dad traveled from Quito to the United States exclusively to attend a conference where I was recognized for "excellence in customer service."

I'm not extroverted and cheerful like dad or my brother Fernando. I prefer not to be the center of attention. But God had a good sense of humor in calling me to be a pastor. My response: "Who? Me? But how? I don't like being in front of people; I'm afraid of public speaking. What if I get tongue-tied? People will laugh at me!" Despite the excuses, God placed me in leadership positions at church, work, and community for more than a quarter-century. I survived and learned to overcome my fears.

Things I learned (through God) from my father:
I learned to trust that *"I can do all things in Christ who strengthens me" (Philippians 4:11)*. My dad left everything to offer a better future for his family. He fought against all barriers.

I learned not to fear if people laugh at me and instead look at it as if they're laughing with me. Dad was a comedian!

I also learned that nobody is perfect, and we all deserve a second chance. I learned not to judge others but rather to support them and work instead on my flaws and weaknesses.

I learned that it's proper and necessary to apologize when we're wrong, even to our children. It was a good lesson in humility for me.

Finally, I learned that **there are no favorites**, but one pays more attention to the neediest and modifies the focus as their situation changes.

Thus and even more incredible and perfect is God's love. **God loves everyone the same** but pays more attention to the neediest; the orphans, widows, and the poor. God's arms are far-reaching and can draw us to Him, to hug and place a kiss on our cheeks (like my dad used to do affectionately), saying, *"this is my beloved child in whom I am pleased" (Matthew 3:17)*.

Thank you, Papi, for your love and lessons that I continue learning and imitating. Rest in Peace!

Let us pray: Dear God, may our lives continue to honor our parents and please you. We pray in Jesus's name.

February 15
PAY THE MOST CAREFUL ATTENTION

"We must pay the most careful attention, therefore, to what we have heard so that we do not drift away." **Hebrews 2:1**

"Por tanto, es necesario que prestemos más atención a lo que hemos oído, no sea que nos extraviemos". **Hebreos 2:1**

"Γι' αυτό, εμείς πρέπει να προσέχουμε περισσότερο σε όσα ακούσαμε, για να μη ξεπέσουμε ποτέ." **ΠΡΟΣ ΕΒΡΑΙΟΥΣ 2:1**

The letter to the Hebrews makes it clear that the peace, freedom, hope, and salvation that you and I enjoy *"was first announced by the Lord, was confirmed to us by those who heard him. God also testified to it by signs, wonders and various miracles, and by gifts of the Holy Spirit distributed according to his will" (Hebrews 2:3B-4).*

The Apostles, who personally heard and saw Jesus, conveyed their message through letters that eventually became part of the Holy Scriptures. God preserved and transmitted His Word to us through the centuries so that its unaltered message would reach our ears and hearts.

Today more than ever, we live in the age of the information explosion. If you want to know something about the Bible, search "Google," and you'll find thousands of articles with different and opposing opinions and interpretations. But God calls us so that, amid an abundance of human views, we *"pay the most careful attention, therefore, to what we have heard, so that we do not drift away" (Hebrews 2:1).*

The worst thing that can happen to us is that we stray from God's path. That we pay more attention to science or the world's noise, leaving aside the wisdom, guidance, and love of our heavenly Father, who wants to lead us back to His heavenly Mansion.

God calls us to *"pay the most careful attention"* to His Word; That we become like the Bereans, who *"received the message with great eagerness and examined the Scriptures every day to see if what Paul said was true"* (Acts 17:11). Our primary source of knowledge is the Holy Scriptures. Jesus said about them, *"But the seed falling on good soil refers to someone who hears the Word and understands it. This is the one who produces a crop, yielding a hundred, sixty or thirty times what was sown"* (Matthew 13:23).

Let us pray: Dear God, amid so much noise, please help us *"pay the most attention"* to Your Word. Allow those who receive Your Word, *"which they heard from us, to accept it not as a human word, but as it actually is, Your word, which is indeed at work in all who believe"* (1 Thessalonians 2:13).

February 16
MY REDEEMER LIVES
Job 19:25

Shortly after Valentine's Day, the Lord invites us to study the meaning and importance of **REDEEMER**, which appears in today's reading.

"Redeemer"- from Hebrew, is גָּאַל (*go'el* **gaal**) – *"One who pays a price on behalf of an impoverished relative, in order to effect the release of the relative or his/her property."* The idea of **redemption** appears in several variations in the Hebrew Bible:
1. The repurchase of property sold due to financial hardship **(Leviticus 25:25–34).**
2. The freeing of an Israelite who has sold themselves as an enslaved person to satisfy a debt **(Leviticus 25:47–55).**

51

YO SÉ QUE MI REDENTOR VIVE. JOB 19:25

I KNOW THAT MY REDEEMER LIVES. JOB 19:25

ΕΠΕΙΔΉ, ΞΈΡΩ ΌΤΙ Ο ΛΥΤΡΩΤΉΣ ΜΟΥ ΖΕΙ. ΙΩΒ 19:25

MARGARITA VITERI~ COTOPAXI, ECUADOR

The New Testament uses the term (λυτρόω **lutróo**) about Jesus, whose death comes to represent both *"payment for sin and freedom for the believer."* [3]

I invite you to read the book of Ruth, 4 small yet wonderful chapters filled with **God's redeeming love** as seen through the love of a daughter-in-law for her mother-in-law and through Boaz, who redeems the property of his near-kin and marries Ruth. The offspring of this **redemptive love affair** is part of the lineage of King David and eventually Jesus. **(Ruth 4:13–20; Matthew 1:5; Luke 3:32).**

Job, whom Satan tested, claims God's redemptive power, and despite having lost absolutely everything (friends and family abandoned him, his wife told him to *"curse God and die!"* **(Job 2:9)**, Job remains confident that he *will see God with his own eyes* **(Job 19:27)**. Job knows that he's in an everlasting battle between good and evil. Though his flesh and body may wither away in the struggle, in the end, God will have victory over sin, and Job's resurrected body will be in God's abiding presence.

Let us pray: Dear God, thank You because, through Jesus Christ, **You've redeemed me from being a slave to sin and received me as Your adopted child.** Grant me the faith to say, *"I know that my redeemer lives" (Job 19:25)* because *"He lives in me!"* There's no other kinsman-redeemer apart from Christ. Help me to remain loyal and faithful to Your abiding love. I pray in Jesus's name.

> *Job knows that he's in an everlasting battle between good and evil. Though his flesh and body may wither away in the struggle, in the end, God will have victory over sin, and Job's resurrected body will be in God's abiding presence.*

February 17
MORE THAN DUST IN THE WIND
Isaiah 58:4b

---

[3] *(Parker, N. T., & Balogh, A. L. (2016). Redeemer. The Lexham Bible Dictionary. Bellingham, WA: Lexham Press.)*

Every Ash Wednesday, remembering that we're *"dust and ashes" (Genesis 18:27)*, we approach God in an attitude of **repentance**, penance, and fasting. But if we want God to hear us, we must practice a different fast.

During Lent, we ought to ask: Am I being moved by the world's winds or by God's breath? **Romans 12.2** says, *"Do not conform to the pattern of this world, but be transformed by the renewing of your mind."*

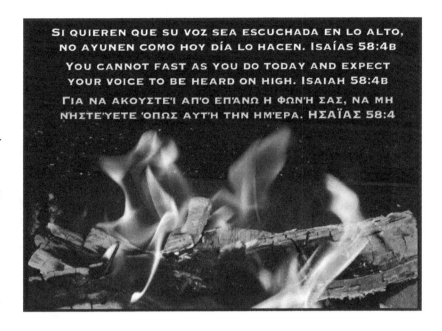

Although **we're dust,** pray that we'd be moved by the breath of the Holy Spirit to produce the fast that God seeks, one that nurtures, protects, and offers help to the poor and needy.
Then, *"your light will break forth like the dawn, and your healing will quickly appear; then your righteousness will go before you, and the glory of the Lord will be your rear guard"* **(Isaiah 58:8).**

God won't permit interference with the world salvation plan. Just as the Lord put Jonah back where he should have been, during our 40 days of Lenten personal reflection, God is putting us where we ought to be so that we might be **more than dust in the wind.**

God placed us in this time and place to announce the good news that even though we're dust in the wind, God's breath will strengthen us to fulfill our purpose. The world needs to know that God's grace, mercy, and love are available by putting our house in order and **living responsibly** toward God and neighbor. If we do this intentionally, we won't be blown like dust in the wind without purpose or destination.

It comforts me to know that God's breath enables us to reach the unattainable and that, despite our temporary condition of being **dust in the wind**, *"God will complete the good work that He began in us"* **(Philippians 1:6).**

My beloved, we're dust, yet loved. We're sinners yet forgiven through **repentance**. And, although imperfect, we're chosen to fulfill the wonderful world salvation plan, beginning in our home.

Everyone needs to hear this truth: God *"raises the poor from the dust and lifts the needy from the ash heap; he seats them with princes and has them inherit a throne of honor"* **(1 Samuel 2.8).**

Let us pray: Dear God, let Your Holy Spirit be the wind beneath our wings to rescue those who've strayed from the path, forgetting their sense of purpose. Strengthen those who think and live as if they were merely **dust in the wind.** We pray in Your Holy Name.

February 18
THE PRAYER OF CONFESSION
1 John 1:9

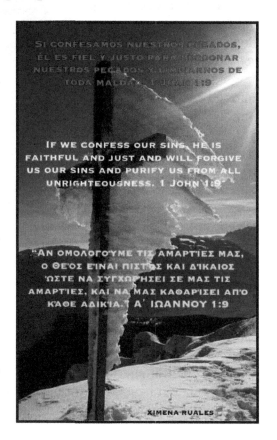

In **Daniel 9**, we find a beautiful example of a **confessional prayer,** not like the ones we do in general **("Father, forgive my sins"),** but explicitly detailing how the people failed to reflect God's faithfulness.

Let's take a look at the form and content of Daniel's **confessional praye**r for his people.

THE ATTITUDE - *"So I turned to the Lord God and pleaded with him in prayer and petition, in fasting, and in sackcloth and ashes. I prayed to the Lord my God and confessed"* ***(Daniel 9:3-4a).***

The way to approach God is with gratitude, reverence, and humility. Jesus gives importance to prayer, indicating that certain demons and diseases come out *"only by prayer"* (some manuscripts include *"and fasting"* **(Mark 9:29).**

THE WORDS - Daniel begins his confession by saying, *"we have sinned and done wrong. We have been wicked and have rebelled; we have turned away from your commands and laws. We have not listened to your servants the prophets, who spoke in your name to our kings, our princes and our ancestors, and to all the people of the land"* **(Daniel 9:5-6).**

His words point to personal sins, listing each one of them so that the Holy Spirit might provide the discernment to correct them, one by one. He also confesses that all the people, beginning with kings, princes, and ancestors, disobeyed God's prophets. We often minimize our confession to God for various reasons before identifying everything that ails us. We must pray calmly, entirely, and without distractions.

Prayer might appear ineffective in light of the natural disasters, diseases, and human conflict that afflict our world. But believe me, God is attentive to every child's plea who approaches Him with a contrite heart and in search of His forgiveness and justice. *"If we confess our sins, he is faithful and just and will forgive us our sins and purify us from all unrighteousness"* **(1 John 1:9).**

Let us pray: Dear God, thank You for being faithful, just, and merciful with us. For offering us the prayer of confession, which allows us entrance into Your presence and reconciles us with you

54

and our neighbor. Please help us search for Your sheep that need to be rescued and healed through confession. We pray in Jesus's name.

February 19
I GIVE YOU THIS CHARGE

"I give you this charge: Preach the word; be prepared in season and out of season; correct, rebuke and encourage—with great patience and careful instruction." **2 Timothy 4:1-2**

"Te encargo … que prediques la palabra; que instes a tiempo y fuera de tiempo; redarguye, reprende, exhorta con toda paciencia y doctrina". **2 Timoteo 4:1-2**

"Εγώ επίσημα σε σένα … να κηρύξεις τον λόγο· να επιμείνεις έγκαιρα, άκαιρα· να ελέγξεις, να επιπλήξεις, να προτρέψεις με κάθε μακροθυμία και διδασκαλία."
Β΄ ΠΡΟΣ ΤΙΜΟΘΕΟΝ 4:1-2

When someone says, *"I give you this charge,"* they consider us suitable and place at our disposal the resources to fulfill the task. Whether small or large, we're responsible for caring for and nurturing what's been placed in our hands while the other person is absent or engaged in other matters.

For example, when they entrust us with the care of their greatest treasures, our grandchildren. Not all grandparents have the joy of living close enough to assume this beautiful task. But it's not only a charge to entertain the grandchildren for a couple of hours but also an opportunity to **transmit values, teachings, and stories of divine and human love.**

> Caring for grandchildren is also an opportunity to **transmit values, teachings, and stories of divine and human love.**

God also charges us with the care of His sheep. Jesus said to Peter, *"Feed my sheep"* **(John 21:15-17).** This charge was successively transferred across generations, and today it applies to us. We show love for Jesus by *"feeding his sheep."*

Through life examples, these daily meditations allow me to continue the charge of *"feeding his sheep."* God charges us to *"Preach the word; be prepared in season and out of season; correct, rebuke and encourage—with great patience and careful instruction"* **(2 Timothy 4:2).**

There's a saying, *"it's easier to preach ten sermons than to live one."* Shepherding requires that we place the sheep's welfare before our own. Today I posted on Facebook, *"I've done my duty"* by receiving the COVID vaccine. I did it mainly for my grandchildren, grand-nephews, family, and friends so that I'd not be a carrier of the virus for them. We're called to preach the good news of God's love, and the best way to do this is by putting the sheep first.

God is pleased when we live what we preach. John Wesley said, *"Preach the gospel, and if necessary, use words."* God has entrusted us with the care and nurturing of His sheep. Let's use **wisely** every opportunity we're given to guard and transmit values, teachings, and stories of divine and human love that feed and strengthen their faith.

Let us pray: Dear God, grant us the grace so that our lives may be an open Bible, that our words be like those of Jesus, sweet as honey and at the same time sharp as a double-edged sword to repel the enemy's attacks. We pray in Your Holy Name.

February 20
SERVE WITH GRATITUDE AND REVERENCE
Psalm 2:11

Our precious granddaughter, Salomé, was five months old in this picture. When she smiles, my heart melts!

Today's meditation has a common thread of **service**; forced, prudent, and voluntary.

FORCED SERVICE: In **Exodus 6:6, God hears the cries of the Israelites**, whom the Egyptians had **enslaved**, and pledges to free His people from **forced labor**. *"Therefore, say to the Israelites: 'I am the Lord, and I will bring you out from under the yoke of the Egyptians. I will free you from being slaves to them, and I will redeem you with an outstretched arm and with mighty acts of judgment."*

We have monitoring equipment around the house to hear when Salomé wakes up from her nap. Likewise, God is everywhere and is attentive to your cries. Call on God, and He will come to comfort, heal, and rescue you from the enemy's heavy **yoke**.

PRUDENT SERVICE: In **Psalm 2:11,** God cautions Kings and rulers of the earth to be **prudent** and *"Serve the Lord with fear and celebrate his rule with trembling."* My wife and I enjoy being Salomé's babysitter three days per week. We serve with gratitude and fear. Gratitude because she is a gift from God. Fear because while she's with us, we're responsible for her emotional and physical care and nutrition, ensuring that nothing harms her physically or emotionally.

God rejoices when we serve the weak, poor, orphans, and widows. If we vow to help them, we're to serve with a healthy level of fear, doing and offering the best at our disposal with gladness because the Spirit of the Lord is guiding our steps.

VOLUNTARY SERVICE: **Hebrews 8:1-2** speaks about Jesus offering himself to be both lamb and priest. *"We do have such a high priest, who sat down at the right hand of the throne of the Majesty in heaven, and who serves in the sanctuary, the true tabernacle set up by the Lord, not* *by a mere human being."* Since we have a high priest interceding for us in heaven, our reasonable response is to serve the Lord in continuing His mission voluntarily - to bring everyone closer to God's love, love of each other, and self.

Let us pray: Dear Lord, give us a heart willing to love and serve one another voluntarily, with gratitude, reverence, and fear of failing you. Help us so that *"whatever we do, we work at it with all our heart, as working for You, and not for human masters"* **(Colossians 3:23).** We pray in Your Holy Name.

February 21
ALL THINGS RESTORED

"Jesus replied, "To be sure, Elijah does come first, and restores all things. Why then is it written that the Son of Man must suffer much and be rejected?" Mark 9:12

"Pero yo os digo que Elías ya vino, y no le reconocieron; más bien, hicieron con él todo lo que quisieron. Así también el Hijo del Hombre ha de padecer de ellos". Marcos 9:12

"Και εκείνος απαντώντας είπε σ' αυτούς: Ο Ηλίας μεν, αφού έρθει πρώτα, αποκαθιστά τα πάντα· και ότι. για τον Υιό τού ανθρώπου είναι γραμμένο ότι, πρέπει να πάθει πολλά, και να εξουθενωθεί." **ΚΑΤΑ ΜΑΡΚΟΝ 9:12 FPB**

The disciples asked Jesus, *"'Why do the teachers of the law say that Elijah must come first?'"* **(Mark 9:11).** Jesus responded with **Mark 9:12** and added that Elijah had already come, *"and they did not recognize him, but have done to him everything they wished. In the same way, the Son of Man is going to suffer at their hands" (Matthew 17:12).*

Our world still suffers the ravages of selfishness, racism, and evil. Things are going from bad to worse. This indicates that John the Baptist and Elijah are not the ones who will restore **ALL things**, but rather **Jesus when he returns the second time. Colossians 1** says, *"For God was pleased to have all his fullness dwell in him, and through him to reconcile to himself all things, whether things on earth or things in heaven, by making peace through his blood, shed on the cross"* **(Colossians 1:19–20).**

John the Baptist testifies that *"The Father loves the Son and has placed everything in his hands" (John 3:35).* Jesus has the power and authority to forgive, sanctify, and **restore all things to their original design,** especially the relationship that was broken in the Garden of Eden. It was necessary for Jesus to suffer the Cross, rise again, and ascend to heaven *"until the time comes for God to restore everything, as he promised long ago through his holy prophets" (Acts 3:21).*

No one knows the day or the hour when Jesus will return. *2 Peter 3:10* says, *"the day of the Lord will come like a thief. The heavens will disappear with a roar; the elements will be destroyed by fire, and the earth and everything done in it will be laid bare."* But whoever trusts in

Christ's restorative work needn't fear because *"in keeping with his promise we are looking forward to a new heaven and a new earth, where righteousness dwells" (2 Peter 3:13).* I believe that God's Kingdom is already within us, guiding our thoughts, words, and actions, restoring and reconciling those things within our abilities.

Let us pray: Dear God, we await the arrival of Your Kingdom, where all things will be new, good, and incorruptible. Restore the areas of our life that need Your touch, and use us to announce that Your Kingdom is at hand. We pray in Your Holy Name.

✝ ✝ ✝ ✝ ✝

February 22
CREATED TO BE BREAD AND CUP
Ephesians 2:10b

God created us to do this good work; that in Jesus's name, we **become the bread and cup of blessing** for those who've lost the strength, faith, and hope of finding the way of Salvation. Like Peter, Jesus commissions us to *"feed my sheep and lambs"* **(John 21:15-17).**

"God's Handiwork."- We were created in, by, and with love. We came to this world because, in love, our earthly parents fulfilled the mandate to *"be fruitful and multiply"* **(Genesis 1:29).** God had a part in our creation by forming us in our mother's womb **(Jeremiah 1:5)** and breathing His Spirit into us so that we might have life **(Job 33:4). Colossians 1:16** says that *"everything was created through him and for him,"* [Jesus]. **You are God's masterpiece!**

"Created in Him"- Regardless of our past, by placing our faith and hope in Jesus's redemptive work, God recreated us, granting us **a second chance to be bread and cup of blessing.** In **John 11:25-26,** Jesus said: *"I am the resurrection and the life. The one who believes in me will live, even though they die, and whoever lives by believing in me will never die. Do you believe this?"* Although we were sentenced to die for our sins, instead, Jesus offered us forgiveness and eternal life.

"To do good works" - For love, God formed us to have an intimate and personal relationship with us, and also that we may be both **bread and cup** for those around us. *"To do all the good we can, in all places, to all peoples, at all times that we can" (John Wesley).* Our works are not to gain salvation but rather to show gratitude for God's grace in our lives.

"To live according to them" - God wants us to know His heart and purpose so that our lives, though imperfect, might be a reflection of His will. The way to discover God's mind and essence

is through the Bible, God's love letter bequeathed to His children so that we may *"tend the sheep"* **and escort them back to the heavenly mansion.**

Let us pray: Dear God, thank You for creating us in, through, and with love. Help us deeply learn Your Word so that we may **be the bread, wine, and shepherds** for Your sheep and live according to Your will. We ask these things in the precious name of our Lord Jesus Christ.

February 23
I WAS BLIND, BUT NOW I SEE
1 Peter 3:15b

During this COVID-19 year, many of us cried out, *"Will the Lord reject forever? Will he never show his favor again?"* **(Psalm 77:7).** Sometimes we've doubted if the Lord is listening. But the psalmist says, *"I will remember the works of the Lord; surely I will remember Thy wonders of old"* **(Psalm 77:10-12).**

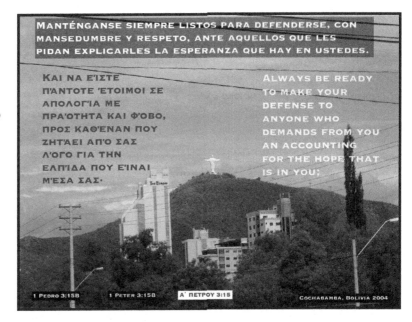

The antidote to doubt, stress, discouragement, and afflictions is to remember what God has done in our lives and always be ready to explain *"with gentleness and respect"* the reason for our hope **(1 Peter 3:15).**

Jesus Christ is my strength and hope. I've learned to value myself through Him, recognizing the great price God paid for my ransom. When I was on the edge of the precipice, Jesus stretched His strong arm, filling me with love, self-esteem, and purpose. **It happened like this:**

The father of lies made me think that I was a lousy provider, useless as a husband, father, employee, or investor, pointing to my half-million dollar life insurance as the answer to my debts. I almost believed that ***"everyone would be better off without me."*** The MASH theme song kept its soothing lyrics buzzing around my head *"suicide is painless!"* October 8, 2008, was to be my last day on this planet, but God had better plans; rescuing and placing me on a secure foundation.

The devil whispers such thoughts to many, but God has the last word. He rescues and heals us so that, in the future, we'd stop listening to the father of lies. Jesus said, *"his sheep follow him because they know his voice. But they will never follow a stranger; in fact, they will run away from him because they do not recognize a stranger's voice"* **(John 10:4–5).**

I'm not ashamed of **almost falling** for the devil's lies. It's part of my testimony, summarized as, *"I was blind, but now I see"* **(John 9:25).** If you've been through such trials, *"In your heart sanctify Christ as Lord" (1 Peter 3:15),* recognizing that sometimes God allows us to cross valleys of the shadow of death to appreciate and value our life and live for God and family.

> **Sometimes God allows us to cross valleys of the shadow of death to appreciate and value our life and live for God and family.**

Let us pray: Dear God, help us always be ready to give a reason for our hope, *"with gentleness and respect,"* and be **attentive to Your voice**. We pray in Your Holy Name.

February 24
FOOD FOR THE SOUL

"Jesus answered, 'It is written: Man shall not live on bread alone, but on every word that comes from the mouth of God.'" **Matthew 4:4**

"Jesús respondió: 'Escrito está: No sólo de pan vive el hombre, sino de toda palabra que sale de la boca de Dios'". **Mateo 4:4**

"Και εκείνος απαντώντας είπε: Είναι γραμμένο: «Μονάχα με ψωμί δεν θα ζήσει ο άνθρωπος, αλλά με κάθε λόγο που βγαίνει από το στόμα τού Θεού»."
ΚΑΤΑ ΜΑΤΘΑΙΟΝ 4:4

On February 18, 2021, we completed the first of three years using the daily lectionary for our Bible Meditations. My gratitude and congratulations to those who've faithfully accompanied me. If God gives us life, we'll have read the entire Bible and tasted all its delicacies at the end of the third year.

Generally, we joyfully share the discovery of a new restaurant with family and friends, saying, **"You have to try that place. They serve the best ... etc."** How wonderful when the recommendation is on target! Everything is the same or better than described. There's nothing like tasting for yourself the delicacies prepared by master chefs for your delight, to make known their talent and culture's cuisine. They hope that you'll recommend them to your friends and family.

Sometimes the least expected places offer the most delicious and unforgettable dishes. The best country hen broth we enjoyed with my son Jean-Paul was returning from Papallacta to Quito under a hut that protected us from the rain, with chicks, roosters, and hens running around the tables looking for fallen corn kernels.

Jesus said, you *"shall not live on bread alone, but on every word that comes from the mouth of God"* **(Matthew 4:4).** God created 66 different restaurants from which we can taste a variety of **food for the soul**. If you like the "tapas" style, I recommend **"Proverbs"**; it serves small but wonderful delicacies. If you enjoy "spicy" food, **"James"** will spice your tongue.

Imagine each Bible book being a restaurant and propose to visit each. Taste their delights, and recommend them to your friends and family whenever you find something in them that satisfies your soul. If you visit us daily, you'll have enjoyed the complete Word of God at the end of three years. Don't worry **if you fall behind; you can always catch up.**

As a car needs fuel, our soul needs God's daily Word. Daily meditations take no more than 5 minutes. But I promise you that you'll be satisfied and thus you can be a source of **bread and cup** to the hungry.

Let us pray: Dear God, thank You for *"every Word that comes from your mouth"* **(Matthew 4:4, Luke 4:4).** Grant us the desire and discipline to study and savor all that you've prepared for us, and thus be prepared to feed Your sheep. We pray in Jesus's name.

February 25
DESPISED
Psalm 22:24

One of my teachers taught me that the Bible is its own dictionary. We can understand the application of *"Despise"* by looking at how the word **H-959 -** בָּזָה *bāzāh* was used in its original Hebrew in different verses and contexts. Its synonyms are *"to hold in contempt or to despise. Disdain or disrespect."*[4]

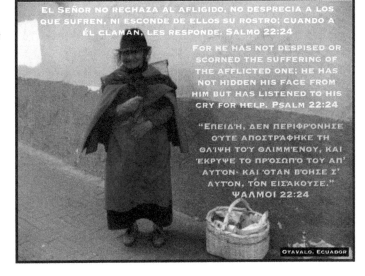

The first Biblical use of *"despise"* appears when Esau *despised* his birthright in exchange for a *"stew of lentils and bread"* **(Genesis 25:34).** The next two are:
1. Seeing David dancing in the streets before God, his wife Michal *"despised him in her heart"* **(2 Samuel 6:16).**
2. God accuses David saying, *"you despised me and took the wife of Uriah the Hittite to be your own"* **(2 Samuel 12:10).**

No matter how close we might be to God, we're prone to despise God's Word and will, yielding to the lust of the flesh. Esau **despised** the spiritual heritage by giving in to hunger. Michal despised love, yielding to shame; David despised righteousness yielding to lust.

---

[4] (Baker, W., & Carpenter, E. E. (2003). In The complete word study dictionary: Old Testament (p. 125). AMG Publishers.)

Thankfully, God hasn't *"despised or scorned the suffering of the afflicted one; he has not hidden his face from him but has listened to his cry for help"* (**Psalm 22:24**). In our anguish, we cried out for the Lord, and this was His response. *"He was <u>despised</u> and rejected by mankind, a man of suffering, and familiar with pain. Like one from whom people hide their faces he was despised, and we held him in low esteem. Surely he took up our pain and bore our suffering, yet we considered him punished by God, stricken by him, and afflicted. But he was pierced for our transgressions, he was crushed for our iniquities; the punishment that brought us peace was on him, and by his wounds we are healed"* (**Isaiah 53:3–5**).

At the cross, we finally receive God's grace and mercy. *"By his wounds,"* we're rescued and placed on the firm rock. Jesus suffered so that all prodigal children may return to the place of honor and eternal peace in the arms of God the Father. Even the vilest sinner can be healed and reconciled through Jesus's suffering and pain.

Let us pray: Dear God, thank You for Your love and mercy that doesn't respond according to our actions and attitudes. Please don't allow us to despise our neighbor, in word or deed, and even worse, to disdain Your Word and will. We pray in the name of Jesus.

✝ ✝ ✝ ✝ ✝

February 26
I WILL BLESS THOSE WHO BLESS YOU
Genesis 16:4

A friend posted on Facebook the phrase, *"You can't treat people like trash and praise God."* If by God's grace, we've risen to a position of prestige or leadership, it's no reason to boast at the expense of others. We can't belittle, disparage, judge, ignore or curse people based on their social/economic class, political affiliation, religion, gender, race, disability, etc., because, by doing so, we'd be breaking the commandment to *"love your neighbor as yourself"* (**Matthew 22:39**). God warns us, *"I will bless those who bless you, and whoever curses you I will curse"* (**Genesis 12:3**).

Today we again encounter a different synonym of *"despise."* This time, the Hebrew word [**H7043**] is קָלַל **Câlal**; a verb *"to be slight, to be trivial, to be swift, curse, despise."* *"Sarai said to Abram, 'You are responsible for the wrong I am suffering. I put my slave in your arms, and now that she knows she is pregnant, she despises me. May the Lord judge between you and me'"* (**Genesis 16:5**).

God wanted to bless the world through Abram, to whom he swore, *"whoever curses you I will curse"* (**Genesis 12:3B**). The result of despising Sarai (synonymous with cursing) was that Hagar had to flee into the desert without shelter and provision. But God instructed her, *"Go back to*

62

your mistress and submit to her" (Genesis 16:9). God hates pride and even more when we, directly or indirectly, curse His chosen ones.

Contempt isn't always expressed verbally or physically. A curse is manifested when, being able to help, we turn our backs on human anguish. Furthermore, we can disguise our disdain as a prayer to God. *"The Pharisee stood by himself and prayed: 'God, I thank you that I am not like other people—robbers, evildoers, adulterers—or even like this tax collector'"* (**Luke 18:11**). Any attitude, thought, or prayer that puts another at physical, spiritual, or emotional risk, has the effect of devaluing or disparaging others directly or indirectly, thus displeasing and causing God to disregard our praise and prayers.

Let us pray: Dear God, don't allow us to use Your Word as a sword to judge, intimidate or condemn others because of their ideologies, affiliations, or who they are. Instead of cursing and despising, help us to **bless and help**. Guide us to defend the dignity of the poor, orphans, and widows around us. We pray in Jesus's name.

February 27
MERCIFUL GOD

"When God saw what they did and how they turned from their evil ways, he relented and did not bring on them the destruction he had threatened." Jonah 3:10

"Y al ver Dios lo que hicieron, y que se habían apartado de su mal camino, también él se arrepintió de hacerles el daño que les había anunciado, y desistió de hacerlo". Jonás 3:10

"Καὶ ὁ Θεός εἶδε τὰ ἔργα τους, ὅτι ἀπέστρεψαν ἀπό τον πονηρό τους δρόμο· καὶ ὁ Θεός μεταμελήθηκε για το κακό, που εἶχε πεῖ νὰ κάνει σ' αὐτούς· καὶ δεν τὸ ἔκανε." ΙΩΝΑΣ 3:10

God is merciful! He's shown us the way of repentance so that we may return to Him with all our hearts and free ourselves from the evil that He's proclaimed for those who rebel against God.

In today's reading, God sends Jonah to Nineveh to proclaim this message: *"Forty more days and Nineveh will be overthrown"* (**Jonah 3:4**). We're used to seeing people with billboards calling us to repentance because **"the end of the world is near."** Most people ignore them. But that didn't happen in Nineveh. *"The Ninevites believed God. A fast was proclaimed, and all of them, from the greatest to the least, put on sackcloth"* (**Jonah 3:5**). Seeing that the people repented and abandoned their evil ways, God relented and did not destroy them.

God is merciful! Exodus 32:14 says: *"Then the Lord relented and did not bring on his people the disaster he had threatened."* Moses intervened on behalf of the people. As a result, God repented and didn't do the evil He'd planned on account of Moses' intervention.

> **Seeing that the people repented and abandoned their evil ways, God relented and did not destroy them.**

God has decreed that the payment for disobedience (sin) is death and without the shedding of blood, there is no forgiveness **(Hebrews 9:22)**. Being just, God cannot ignore His decrees. Therefore, God provided the sacrificial Lamb to redeem us from our sins. **Jesus intervened for us.** Those who've repented of their sins, and turned away from their evil ways, will not be destroyed in the final judgment and will enter into the eternal rest that God has prepared for them.

But one thing is for sure: without repentance, the world is destined for punishment. *"And God sent an angel to destroy Jerusalem. But as the angel was doing so, the Lord saw it and relented concerning the disaster and said to the angel who was destroying the people, 'Enough! Withdraw your hand'"* **(1 Chronicles 21:15)**. **God is merciful** but is also just. God accepts and receives us into the Royal Family when we turn away from sin.

Let us pray: Beloved and **merciful God**, give us a heart that trusts in Your complete, written revelation. Yesterday some of us were anointed with ash on our foreheads as an external sign of our repentance. Anoint our hearts also so that we may stop sinning against you. We pray in Your Holy Name.

February 28
IS IT RIGHT FOR YOU TO BE ANGRY?
Jonah 4:4

Jonah preached that God would destroy Nineveh in forty days. Everyone believed, turned away from their evil ways, and as a result, the Lord relented and did not bring on the disaster He had threatened for that great city.

In **Jonah 4,** we discover why Jonah had fled in the opposite direction, not wanting to preach to those of Nineveh, the capital city of Syria, whom he despised. He said, *"That is what I tried to forestall by fleeing to Tarshish. I knew that you are a gracious and compassionate God, slow to anger and abounding in love, a God who relents from sending calamity" (Jonah 4:2)*. Jonah's anger was so great that he asked God to take his life **(4:3)**. *"But the Lord replied, 'Is it right for you to be angry?'" (4:4)*.

We're not so different from Jonah. God calls us to proclaim peace and love, but instead, we pronounce judgment. The enemy has created political-religious divisions such that we don't allow ourselves the courtesy of listening to each other. Any possible communication is filtered with snubs, suspicions, and accusations.

The United Methodist Church is going through one of the most challenging periods. Since its foundation, the UMC has been a source of joy, nourishment, and leadership in social justice for many. But in the last fifty years, it's been struggling with the full inclusion of LGBTQ. Presently the Church is embarking on an amicable separation, forming a new Traditional Church.

For many, this process is excruciatingly painful since they've invested everything in their local Church, and possibly, as happened to Jonah's vine, which gave him shade, some local churches might wither away. Being human, we look for whom to blame and become angry. God also asks us: *"Is it right for you to be angry?"*

God is *"gracious and compassionate, slow to anger and abounding in love, and repents of evil" (Jonah 4:2)*. Since we're created in God's image, we should reflect these good qualities by praying for each other. Now is not the time to become angry unto death, but to follow the call to love each other and let God be the judge.

Let us pray: Dear God, don't let the enemy sow seeds of anger as he did with Jonah. Help us to follow and live by the golden rule. Bless Your churches with Your Holy Spirit so that Your will may be done in everything. We pray in Your Holy Name.

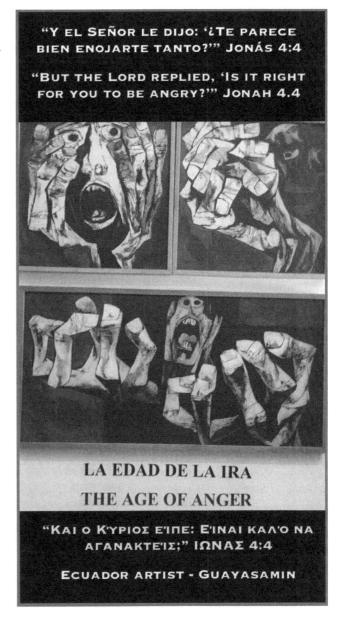

"Y EL SEÑOR LE DIJO: '¿TE PARECE BIEN ENOJARTE TANTO?'" JONÁS 4:4

"BUT THE LORD REPLIED, 'IS IT RIGHT FOR YOU TO BE ANGRY?'" JONAH 4.4

LA EDAD DE LA IRA
THE AGE OF ANGER

"ΚΑΙ Ο ΚΎΡΙΟΣ ΕΊΠΕ: ΕΊΝΑΙ ΚΑΛΌ ΝΑ ΑΓΑΝΑΚΤΕΊΣ;" ΙΩΝΑΣ 4:4

ECUADOR ARTIST - GUAYASAMIN

Now is not the time to become angry unto death, but to follow the call to love each other and let God be the judge.

Two of my weaknesses are bread and figs. Even if I propose to eat only one slice of bread with cheese and figs, I end up eating two or three. That's why I practice cycling and racquetball to enjoy a variety of guilt-free bread. Everyone knows where to buy bread for physical nourishment. But not everyone understands the meaning of or believes in the bread of life that nourishes the soul.

Leviticus 17:11 says, *"The life of a creature is in the blood."* Likewise, spiritual life is nourished and sanctified through the bread of life. When we receive Jesus Christ as King and Lord, He becomes our sustenance. God opens our understanding so that every word that comes out of God's mouth might strengthen our faith, change our way of life, transform us into the likeness of our Savior, and lead us to our eternal dwelling.

Jesus said: *"'For the bread of God is the bread that comes down from heaven and gives life to the world.' 'Sir,' they said, 'always give us this bread.' Then Jesus declared, 'I am the bread of life. Whoever comes to me will never go hungry, and whoever believes in me will never be thirsty. For my Father's will is that everyone who looks to the Son and believes in him shall have eternal life, and I will raise them up at the last day'"* **(John 6:33-35, 40).**

Beloved friends and family, God wills that we'd believe in Jesus Christ and daily nourish ourselves with His Holy Word to resist the enemy's darts. So that through our testimony and teachings, our children and their children's children would have eternal life, feeding daily from the *"Bread of Life."*

Jesus affirms: *"I am the bread of life. Your ancestors ate the manna in the wilderness, yet they died. But here is the bread that comes down from heaven, which anyone may eat and not die. I am the living bread that came down from heaven. Whoever eats this bread will live forever"* **(John 6:48-51A).**

Let us pray: Dear God, thank You for the bread of life. Don't let discouragement or fatigue cause us to put aside feasting on Your Holy Word to another day when we might have more time, when the priorities of work, family, and friends have lessened. Help us to dedicate the first four minutes of each new day to feed on the Bread of Life that you freely offer to all. We pray in Your Holy Name.

✝ ✝ ✝ ✝ ✝

— MARCH —
THE BETTER HALF -
XANTHÓPOULOS FAMILY

XANTHOPOULOS A. 5 BROTHERS -1924 - ARISTOKLIS P. X. BABY ON THE LEFT

Maternal: The Xanthópoulos family traces its origins back to Pontos, Turkey, as written by Papou **Aristoklís P. Xanthópoulos :**

"Savvas Naziroglou was born in Sinope (Sinop), present-day Turkey. After some turmoil, he left Sinope and moved to a region called Vezirkioprou (Veziköprü). He settled in the village named Tsáïkouneï (Tsa-ï-kou-ne-i), where he married (I don't know his wife's name). They moved from Tsaikounei and founded the village of Derekoïyou (Dereköy). They moved there since Dereköy had plenty of water, and he and his children were farmers and water millers. His children grinded the area's wheat.

Savvas (my great-grand father) *had four boys and one girl. Their names were: Lázaros, Yeórgios, **Anastásios** (Anastás), Ioánnis (Yiannis), and Dés-poina.   **Anastásios (Anastas)** was my grandfather. He had seven children, two girls, and five boys. The boys, **Pávlos,** my father, Sávvas, Ionás, Aléxandros (Alekos,) and Vasílios - all born in Turkey. **Pávlos** had three children; Kons-tantínos (Kostas), **Aristoklís,** and Déspoina."*

Though subject to the Ottoman empire, they retained their Greek ethnicity. It wasn't easy to live in Pontos, Turkey, as a Greek Evangelical. They had to choose between keeping their language or their faith. Many chose their faith and lost their use of the Greek language. Eventually, they became refugees and were part of the **1923 Treaty of Lausanne Population Exchange**. They had to give up land and property to return empty-handed to Greece. After a short time, they settled in Sevastí, Central Macedonia, because of its farming advantages.

Uncle Kóstas was born in Turkey and was an ordained minister in the Greek Evangelical Church. **Papou Aristoklis** was born in Thessaloniki. His sister Dés-pina was born in Se-vastí.

Living in Greece post-World War I and during WWII was not easy. Papou Aristoklis was around 18 years old when Germany invaded Greece and forced him to dig trenches, not knowing if one was for himself. God kept him from harm for a reason! He needed to meet and marry my mother-in-law (Petherá) **Kyriaki Koktsidou.**

March 1
SCEPTER OF JUSTICE
Hebrews 1:8

On February 28, 1989, Jesus Christ saved my life and soul from disaster. *"Jesus, the Son of God, became human so that humans might become children of God."* That's what my cousin Fernando said on February 28, 2021, during his father's funeral (my great-uncle José Jorge Ortega Morales,) who rests from his labors, having *"fought the good fight"* **(2 Timothy 4:7).**

God chose **love, humility, and justice as** the standards of His kingdom and our lives. These are the qualities that God wants to sow in those who seek to be called *"children of God"* **(John 1:12).** Uncle Jorge certainly sowed seeds of love and faith in many hearts, which, when they sprout, **create perennial gardens of brotherhood and justice.**

JUSTICE means a just action promoting equality among humanity. Justice gives human beings what they deserve, be it punishment for the oppressor or restitution for the oppressed. The final result is to take us toward peace, שָׁלוֹם **(shalom)**, a harmonious position in which injustices have been corrected and the disadvantaged regain their prosperity and dignity.

Instead of inheriting wealth, God offers us something inherently superior, entrance to heaven, where the **"scepter of justice will be the scepter of His kingdom"** and His reign *"will last for ever and ever"* **(Hebrews 1:8).** However, as a proverbial carrot, the world offers us a **type of justice** that is both temporary and false.

It seems that **justice has been kidnapped**. Actions which decades ago would have united a nation, demanding the most severe punishment; today, the courts dismiss them without applying the law. The people demand justice, but justice evades us, vanishing like the morning dew. The world demands justice in favor of the victims of wars, the exiles; children separated from their families, the marginalized, and the unprotected orphans, widows, immigrants, and the poor. But politicians legislate laws without teeth, power, or results.

Although we can't find true justice here, we know that each unjust person will receive what they deserve when they appear before God, who sees and hears every cry of injustice.

Let us pray: Dear God, thank You for those who sowed seeds of love and justice in us. **Grant the well-deserved rest for those who've fought the good fight**. Please give us the strength to keep fighting until real and eternal justice flows like rivers. We pray in Your Holy Name.

The late Reverend Dr. Robert A. Cook always asked his radio listeners, **"How in the world are you?"** We are in this world, but we *"are not of the world"* **(John 17:14).** At the end of his program, Dr. Cook always said goodbye with these words, *"Walk with the King today, and be a blessing."* The secret of **walking with the King** is knowing that we are His and everything rests in God's hands.

The Greek word for faith is *"πίστις (pístis)."* Today's verse tells us that **pístis (faith)** *"is confidence in what we hope for and assurance about what we do not see" (Hebrews 11:1).* It's trusting that Jesus wants to and can rescue, refine, sharpen, cleanse and restore our lives and world.

Faith is knowing that everything depends on God. The heroes of faith mentioned in **Hebrews 11** placed all their trust in God and His promises. Faith doesn't guarantee that life will be easy. Jesus told us, *"In this world you will have trouble. But take heart! I have overcome the world"* **(John 16:33).** Faith promises that God will walk with us in whatever situation, enabling us to fulfill our purpose and not allow the enemy to touch our soul.

God promised Abram an inheritance countless like the stars of heaven and like the sand in the world. More than 20 years passed, but God didn't forget the promise. **Hebrews 11:11** says: *"And by faith even Sarah, who was past childbearing age, was enabled to bear children because she considered him faithful who had made the promise."* God's blessings and promises come at their due time, not when we want them. Faith grants us the patience to wait for God to fulfill His promises and His perfect work in our lives and family.

Let us pray: Dear God, increase our faith to wait on You and commit ourselves to Your mission of rescuing and healing Your lost sheep, among which we were once counted. We confess our tendency to go astray in search of greener pastures. We need Your faith and guidance to **"Walk today with the King, and be a blessing."** We pray in Your Holy Name.

March 3
CHILDREN OF LIGHT

"Believe in the Light while you have the Light, so that you may become children of Light."
John 12:36

"Mientras tengan la luz, crean en la luz, para que sean hijos de la luz". **Juan 12:36**

"Ενόσω έχετε το φως, πιστεύετε στο φως, για να γίνετε γιοι τού φωτός."
ΚΑΤΑ ΙΩΑΝΝΗΝ 12:36

God wants all creation to believe in the Son, Jesus, *"so that we may be children of light"* and have eternal life.

My beloved, the Light won't be with us forever. When the last soul enters heaven, God will close the door, and there won't be a need for the Light of the Gospel. Then, God will extinguish the Light that today shines in each believer, remove us from this place of storms and pain, and establish us in the eternal home, where God will be our Light.

Whoever fails to believe in the Light while it shines will be left out, navigating without direction or light. That's why our task is so essential, requiring all our resources, gifts, and time, to invite everyone to receive Christ as Savior and thus transform them into *"children of the light."*

It's not enough to believe in the Light to be children of the light. We must publicly confess our faith. Today's Gospel says that *"many even among the leaders believed in him. But because of the Pharisees they would not openly acknowledge their faith for fear they would be put out of the synagogue; for they loved human praise more than praise from God" (John 12:42-43).*

If we're not focused on the Light, the enemy can make us worry more about ***"what people will say."*** Since we're in a life and death struggle, we must place everything aside and continue rowing our boats toward God, who has the power to rescue us. A child of the Light sets themself as a light amid the storms to guide and save those who drift aimlessly in the darkness.

We don't know when the Lord will come back for His people, but while we wait, let's make sure our light shines in the darkness.

Let us pray: Dear God, help us so that, as children of Light, we love Your approval more than that of man, that *we walk like Your children, "having nothing to do with the fruitless deeds of darkness"* **(Ephesians 5:8-10)**, and that we recharge our light directly with Your Word and presence, oh giver of life and hope of the world. We pray in Your Holy Name.

March 4
TIRELESS

"I carried you on eagles' wings and brought you to myself." **Exodus 19:4b**

"Los he traído hasta mí sobre alas de águila". **Éxodo 19:4b**

"και σας σήκωσα σαν επάνω σε φτερούγες αετού, και σας έφερα προς τον εαυτό μου·"
ΕΞΟΔΟΣ 19:4Β

71

Margarita told me, *"your mom is depressed. She needs to distract her mind. Why don't you take her on vacation."* Thus, in June of '91, I had the great joy of traveling to the Holy Land with my mother, RIP. Rheumatoid Arthritis had disabled mom, who suffered much pain in her joints, hands, and feet, and was going through a challenging situation. But nothing would prevent mom from fulfilling her dream of flying to experience Jerusalem.

Mom was determined to continue the journey despite the danger of Scud missiles that began to fall on Tel Aviv. As she disembarked from the plane, she said, *"it has a scent of holiness!"* But what surprised me was that mom was tireless during the 12 days in Israel. She flew *on eagle's wings*, rejuvenated, not feeling any pain or weariness. Early evening, after dinner, we'd go out on our own to revisit the streets of Jerusalem. I'd never seen mom so happy. Then we traveled for two weeks to Margarita's family in Greece, where we enjoyed another time of blessing after blessing. God *"satisfies your desires with good things so that your youth is renewed like the eagle's"* **(Psalm 103:5).**

Isaiah 40:28B says, *"He will not grow tired or weary."* **"Faint,"** which comes from the Hebrew יָעֵף **yaáf,** means to *"tire, to faint, to fatigue, to falter, to give up."* But, God *"gives strength to the weary and increases the power of the weak. Even youths grow tired and weary, and young men stumble and fall; but those who hope in the Lord will renew their strength. They will soar on wings like eagles; they will run and not grow weary, they will walk and not be faint"* **(Isaiah 40:29-31).**

Our **God is tireless**, as His love is inexhaustible. God's also patient and merciful by forgiving our defects. Let's not misunderstand believing that our infrequent transgressions don't hurt God. But God looks at us tenderly through the cleansing blood of Christ, knowing what He is forming in us. God won't leave us the way He found us but will cleanse us from all sin and defects to present us as redeemed and perfect children **with the strength and flight of an eagle.**

Let us pray: Dear God, thank You for Your inexhaustible love and forgiveness. For strengthening us when we feel weak and tired, for redeeming us when we were hopeless, and for the care and protection you promise us and our home. Thank you for that special time with mom. We pray in Jesus's name.

> **God won't leave us the way He found us but will cleanse us from all sin and defects to present us as redeemed and perfect children with the strength and flight of an eagle.**

March 5
SACRED PLACES
Acts 7:33

Every place where we call on the name of the Lord is sacred. Every place where God meets His people is holy and requires our highest reverence and attention.

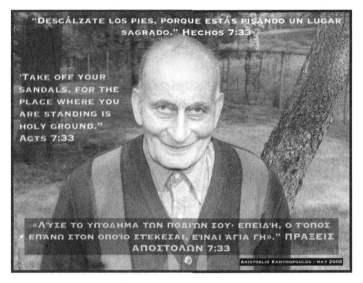

One of the ways we meet God is through prayer. A beautiful custom in our dining room, **learned from my father-in-law, Aristoklís Xanthópoulos,** is that nobody speaks or moves at prayer time; we turn off all background music and the TV while invoking God's presence in gratitude. Thus we silence our feet, hands, mouth, and mind, recognizing that wherever we speak with God, **it's a holy place!**

Sacred places are those where the Lord touches and restores us with His Word; *"Lord, I do not deserve to have you come under my roof. But just say the word, and my servant will be healed"* **(Matthew 8:8).** By invoking God's presence in ordinary places such as our work, home, the stores, markets, public transportation, automobiles, etc., these become sacred places which demand that our feet, minds, ears, and hearts be free from all the world's noise so that we may **listen only to God.**

After killing the Egyptian in defense of one of the Israelites, Moses *"fled to Midian, where he settled as a foreigner"* **(Acts 7:29).** Forty years later, while grazing his father-in-law's sheep, an angel of God appeared to him in the flames of a burning bush in the desert near Mount Sinai to commission him as savior and liberator of His people **(Acts 7:30).** God told Moses, *"Take off your sandals, for the place where you are standing is holy ground"* **(Exodus 3:5, Acts 7:33).** Joshua also heard the same instruction **(Joshua 5:15).**

In the Great Commission, you and I are sent to all the world, to make disciples *"of all nations, baptizing them in the name of the Father and of the Son and of the Holy Spirit, and teaching them to obey everything I have commanded you. And surely I am with you always, to the very end of the age"* **(Matthew 28:19–20).**

Let us pray: Dear God, we believe that Your Holy Spirit dwells in our hearts. Your Word of faith, love, hope, and healing **goes with us every day, everywhere**, empowering us to fulfill our commission. Every place we stand on is a **sacred place** of restoration, love, peace, and hope for the nations. Please help us to live accordingly. We pray in Your Holy Name.

March 6
THE RESULTS OF GOOD FRIENDSHIP
Micah 7:18

On March 2, 2020, we went to Quito Ecuador for what was to be a three-week vacation. God had other plans! The picture shows the view from my uncle Ricardo Sandoval's terrace (RIP). We

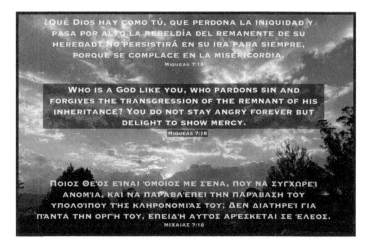

thank uncle Ricardo and aunt Blanca for receiving us in their beautiful home from March 2 to June 8, 2020 when we were unexpectedly quarantined in Ecuador.

Since I can remember, they've had a close-knit friendship with my parents and have lived close by several times for many years. Their good friendship has spread to their children, my cousins, Michelle, Ricky, and Lizeth.

The result of good friendships is a joyful presence in good times and encouragement, support, and shelter in times of need. We've shared joyful moments throughout the years and have supported each other. Friendship with God also offers peace, refuge, and hope in difficult times. Today's verse tells us, *"Who is a God like you, who pardons sin and forgives the transgression of the remnant of his inheritance? You do not stay angry forever but delight to show mercy"* (Micah 7:18).

Although we have a heart inclined to rebellion, God's heart is inclined to mercy and forgiveness. God forgets His anger when we approach His throne of Grace, confessing, and repenting of our sins. Amidst the storms of life, a good friendship with God offers us peace, refuge, and hope for a better tomorrow.

After God, the second most important relationship we should tend to is with the family; spouses, children, grandparents, parents, brothers, uncles, cousins, and then friends. Since we're imperfect beings, without exception, we're susceptible to excessive anger. *"For all have sinned and fall short of the glory of God"* (Romans 3:23). But friendship with God (if we're genuinely friends) drives us to show empathy toward others in their misfortunes and times of need, extend the hand of forgiveness and help, and not persist in our anger.

Let us pray: Dear God, thank You for those who have supported us in times of need. The benefits of Your friendship and Lordship are countless. We need Your presence, love, and friendship. Bless us with hearts inclined to delight ourselves in showing mercy. We pray in Your Holy Name.

March 7
GOD'S EYES OF GOD ARE UPON US
Isaiah 51:4

While driving in Quito, I'm careful not to exceed the speed limits because the eyes of the law are everywhere, capturing images of our actions. In 2017, I learned the hard way when, a month after returning from vacation to the USA, I received a charge on my credit card worth $130 dollars for a speeding violation (along with an image of my rental car).

God's eyes are like surveillance cameras. God records every one of our words, actions, and thoughts. The Lord calls our attention with a loud voice, with signs and wonders. God's Holy Word says that *"Instruction will go out from me; my justice will become a light to the nations"* **(Isaiah 51:4).** Perhaps some might incorrectly think they got away because the law didn't stop them. However, someday we all must give an account of every word, thought, and action before God's tribunal.

Thank God we have a lawyer in heaven who intercedes for us. Those who live under the world's powers will not understand God's Word - they will mock our faith and despise us. But today's Word assures and encourages those who keep the law of God in their hearts; *"Hear me, you who know what is right, you people who have taken my instruction to heart: Do not fear the reproach of mere mortals or be terrified by their insults"* **(Isaiah 51:7).**

It is worth clarifying that by no means are we free to ignore the civil and social laws of our governments. Likewise, because we have a lawyer in heaven, it doesn't allow us to follow the world's customs and commit infractions against God and neighbor.

Let us pray: Dear God, **thank You because Your eyes are always upon us,** caring for, guiding, and protecting us from all evil. Thank you for engraving Your law in our hearts so that we might not sin against you. And thank You for such great love and care, which allows us to walk freely but cautiously, even amid pestilences and viruses. We pray in Jesus's name.

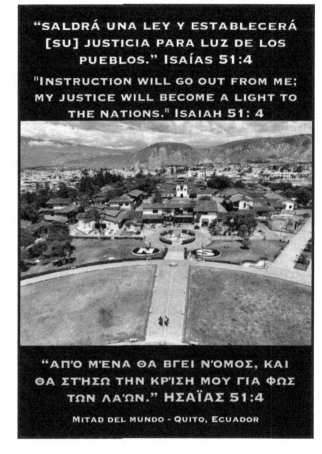

March 8
IN GOD'S TEMPLE
1 Corinthians 3:16

March 14, 2021, marked a year since many churches closed their doors due to COVID-19, and many of us hadn't yet returned to **God's physical temple.**

Technology has benefited our efforts to replicate what we did and felt **during our temple worship time.** However, to some, sharing the **"Holy Eucharist"** by zoom is not the same as receiving the consecrated elements from the priests' hands. Others think that the praises don't compare to live singing. (As a musician, I agree, although I've seen the wonders that music engineers are doing with technology). **And so,** we long to return to the temple and fellowship, to be a vibrant church in our worship of the Lord.

Today's reading presents us with a welcoming image of God's Temple.

Psalm 84:1 declares, *"How lovely is your dwelling place, Lord Almighty!"* In God's courts, we gather to sing praises to the Lord. We find **joy** and **strength** to face each day **(v.4-5).** It's where we go *"from strength to strength"* until we appear before God **(Psalm 84:7).**

> **We long to return to the temple and fellowship, to be a vibrant church in our worship of God.**

1 Kings 6:1 paints for us details of the physical Temple. Its construction was started by King Solomon in the *"fourth year"* of his reign and was completed seven years later **(1 Kings 6:38).** I can't imagine waiting four years to start building something so essential to unify the community and keep it focused on God's goodness and direction.

The letter to the Corinthians affirms that we are *"God's temple and that God's Spirit dwells in our midst"* **(1 Corinthians 3:16, 6:19).** My beloved, the physical temples of this world symbolize the eternal temple that God seeks to create in every heart.

It doesn't matter if we Worship God in person or via Zoom. Wherever and in whatever way we invoke God's name, it becomes a sacred place and occasion where the peace, joy, and praise of the Lord infuse our soul with power, love, and hope to go from heart to heart, sowing seeds that will become Temples of God.

Let us pray: Dear God, thank You for choosing us as Your adopted children, for building Your temple in our hearts. In our worship, whether live or via zoom, may we bring you glory by heeding every Word you've spoken and offering you the best of our lives. We pray in Your Holy Name.

March 9
WASH ME EVERY DAY

"Consecrate yourselves now and consecrate the temple of the Lord, the God of your ancestors. Remove all defilement from the sanctuary." **2 Chronicles 29:5**

"Santifíquense ahora, y santifiquen el templo del Señor, el Dios de sus padres. Saquen del santuario toda impureza". **2 Crónicas 29:5**

"Αγιαστείτε τώρα, και αγιάστε τον ναό τού Κυρίου τού Θεού των πατέρων σας, και βγάλτε έξω την ακαθαρσία από τον άγιο τόπο." **Β΄ ΧΡΟΝΙΚΩΝ 29:5**

Today's reading focuses on **purification**. In one of the first actions taken as king, Hezekiah opened the temple doors and commanded the Levites to sanctify themselves and the temple. **Sanctification** is a cleansing process.

Hezekiah began reigning at age 25. *"He did what was right in the eyes of the Lord, just as his father David had done. He removed the high places, smashed the sacred stones and cut down the Asherah poles. He broke into pieces the bronze snake Moses had made, for up to that time the Israelites had been burning incense to it"* **(2 Kings 18:3–4).** Regardless of their intrinsic value, *"The priests went into the sanctuary of the Lord to purify it. They brought out to the courtyard of the Lord's temple everything unclean that they found in the temple of the Lord" (2 Chronicles 29:16).*

Before using the temple as the center of worship, it must be washed and disinfected of all impurities because God can't be present in places that haven't been sanctified. And yet, *"The Lord has chosen you to stand before him and serve him, to minister before him" (2 Chronicles 29:11).*

As temples of God, the Lord offers to wash our souls through the cleansing blood of Jesus Christ. *"The law requires that nearly everything be cleansed with blood, and without the shedding of blood there is no forgiveness"* **(Hebrews 9:22).** Unlike the priests who entered yearly to offer sacrifices for themselves and the people, Jesus Christ *"appeared once for all at the culmination of the ages to do away with sin by the sacrifice of himself"* **(Hebrews 9:26B).**

The Levites worked for eight continuous days to purify the temple **(2 Chronicles 29:17).** However, our purification is a process that doesn't occur instantaneously but instead progressively and for life. Through daily study of the Word, God washes our minds and hearts so that, together with our family, we may attain the glory of being, although somewhat flawed, **God's temple, consecrated for His service.**

Let us pray: Dear God, nothing I can do will produce the purity of heart you seek from me. Only Your grace and will can cleanse me. I want to be cleaner each day. Give me discernment to identify the unclean things that offend you and the strength of character to cast them out of my life. Renew my spirit Lord, and *"I shall be as white as snow" (Isaiah 1:18).* We pray in Your Holy Name.

March 10
GOD WORKS THROUGH PRAYER

"My house will be called a house of prayer for all nations." **Mark 11:17B**

"Mi casa será llamada casa de oración para todas las naciones". **Marcos 11:17B**

"Ο οίκος μου θα ονομάζεται οίκος προσευχής για όλα τα έθνη." **ΚΑΤΑ ΜΑΡΚΟΝ 11:17B**

During Lent, we evaluate our lives through Bible study and prayer to strengthen our faith and fellowship with God and His people.

The temple was the center of prayer, worship, and sacrifice. It was the life and hope of the people. Seeing the temple's destruction, the prophet Daniel prayed, saying, *"Now, our God, hear the prayers and petitions of your servant. For your sake, Lord, look with favor on your desolate sanctuary"* **(Daniel 9:17).**

When Israel returned from captivity in Babylon, their first communal act was to rebuild the temple and walls. Although resistance had suspended the work for a couple of decades, they resumed the reconstruction and, with God's help, completed it with great joy. Ezra's book teaches us that the physical work is of man, but God directs it in response to prayer.

> **The physical work is of man, but God directs it in response to prayer.**

The temple's rebuilding was ultimately successful because God touched the Assyrian king's heart to *"have compassion"* for the Israelites and support them with the reconstruction **(Ezra 6:22).** Upon completion, *"the priests, the Levites and the rest of the exiles—celebrated the dedication of the house of God with joy"* **(Ezra 6:16).**

Almost five hundred and thirty years later, the priests had allowed God's house to become an open market, forgetting the temple's purpose. *"On reaching Jerusalem, Jesus entered the temple courts and began driving out those who were buying and selling there. He overturned the tables of the money changers and the benches of those selling doves, and would not allow anyone to carry merchandise through the temple courts. And as he taught them, he said, "Is it not written: 'My house will be called a house of prayer for all nations'? But you have made it 'a den of robbers'"* **(Mark 11:15-17).**

The following questions help us identify the walls that we must repair to remain protected against the enemy's attacks on our temples of flesh and blood.
Which doors must we repair or close to prevent sin from infiltrating us?
Which doors must we open for the Holy Spirit to guide us along paths of peace, justice, and love?

Let us pray: Dear God, thank You for teaching us that although the physical work is ours, we can approach you in prayer so that you touch and influence those with the power to support us in strengthening our walls and doors so that our temples of flesh and spirit be restored to Your honor and glory. We pray in Your Holy Name.

March 11
THE BENEFITS OF BEING ADOPTED
Ephesians 1:5

I don't have enough intelligence or time to get into the debated topic of predestination. Still, despite being a privileged person, as a Hispanic immigrant, I know what it feels like to be excluded and rejected as inferior. I remember the desire to belong to the dominant culture, to be part of the winning team. Nothing could satisfy the insatiable desire to belong until, through Jesus's sacrifice, I received **the benefits of adoption.**

As a **child of God,** I no longer feel alone, isolated, excluded, or rejected. I'm part of a vast global family that freely shares God's love, where everyone generously supports each other so that each family member may reach their potential and purpose through God's gifts.

Being a child of God is a great and undeserved privilege with **great benefits**, responsibilities, and expectations. **As a benefit**, Jesus promises His Holy Spirit, who frees us from the bondage of fear and sin and puts us directly in contact with our *"Abba, Father"* **(Romans 8:15).**

Those who at some point have felt alone (i.e., orphans) receive the unbreakable promise from a heavenly Father who offers care, presence, and vigilance. *"I will be a Father to you, and you will be my sons and daughters"* **(2 Corinthians 6:18).**

"You watch over me when I walk and when I rest; You know everything I do!" **(Psalm 139:3).** This verse affirms God's care, protection, and nurturing for those of us whom God has adopted as His children. We're blessed to have God as our Father and personal **sentinel for life**.

But adoption also gives us responsibilities. Our words and actions have the power to rescue, heal, build, bind, infect, and destroy. Sometimes forgetting who we are or even that God is present, we take matters into our own hands and don't act as members of God's family.

Jesus said, *"Blessed are the peacemakers, for they will be called children of God"* (**Matthew 5:9**). As children and representatives of the Highest, we're expected to be peacemakers, lovers of God, neighbors, and peace.

Let us pray: Dear God, thank You for filling the void that existed in our lives. For predestining us to be Your children. Grant that we may be good representatives of Your Holy Family in thought, words, and actions. We pray in the name of our Lord Jesus Christ.

March 12
SEALED

"And you also were included in Christ when you heard the message of truth, the gospel of your salvation. When you believed, you were marked in him with a seal, the promised Holy Spirit." **Ephesians 1:13**

"También ustedes, luego de haber oído la palabra de verdad, que es el evangelio que los lleva a la salvación, y luego de haber creído en él, fueron sellados con el Espíritu Santo de la promesa". **Efesios 1:13**

"στον οποίο και εσείς ελπίσατε, όταν ακούσατε τον λόγο τής αλήθειας, το ευαγγέλιο της σωτηρίας σας· στον οποίο και, καθώς πιστέψατε, σφραγιστήκατε με το Άγιο Πνεύμα τής υπόσχεσης·" **ΠΡΟΣ ΕΦΕΣΙΟΥΣ 1:13**

Today's verse continues with the benefits of adoption, stating that we've been *"marked in him with a seal, the promised Holy Spirit."*

Sealed is an essential word in developing our faith, courage, and hope in our Redeemer. It comes from the Greek, σφραγίζω (**sfragízo**; **G-4972**), which means to *"stamp (with a ring or private mark) for preservation, prevention or security."*

Security - On March 11, 2021, I received my second vaccine, which hopefully gives me 95% protection against COVID-19. I trust that even if I walk through contaminated places, this virus will no longer have the same impact on me. My autoimmune system will have learned to fight effectively against any attack. On August 12, 2022, I contracted COVID-19, and with four vaccines, the symptoms were like a mild cold.

You and I don't have to make appointments or wait in long lines to receive the seal of the promise of the Holy Spirit. We only need to have *"heard the message of truth, the gospel of salvation… and …believed"* in Jesus. Thus, even if our physical body deteriorates on the outside, our soul will always be under the care and complete protection of God's Holy Spirit.

Unlike God's sign on Cain so that no one would kill him (**Genesis 4:15**), our seal of protection is also one of belonging and embodies the promise of presence and blessing. Although we're sinners by nature and deserve death, God *"has qualified us to share in the inheritance of his holy people in the kingdom of light"* (**Colossians 1:12**), sealing us with His Holy Spirit to preserve our souls and bless our homes. Glory to God!

80

Although we live in a body of flesh that opposes the spirit, the invisible seal of promise reminds us of who we are and whom we serve, endowing us with the power to resist evil and do the good expected of one that's been saved and sealed by God's Holy Spirit.

Let us pray: Dear God, we haven't been destroyed by the enemy because of Your love and mercy. Thank you for opening our eyes and ears to hear Your Word of life, which led us to believe in Jesus Christ and receive the seal of Your Holy Spirit. Allow our children and their children to be recipients of Your seal and be faithful followers of Jesus Christ, in whose name we pray.

March 13
A NEW WORLD

"And in Him you too are being built together to become a dwelling in which God lives by his Spirit." Ephesians 2:22

"En Cristo, también ustedes son edificados en unión con él, para que allí habite Dios en el Espíritu". Efesios 2:22

"στον οποίο κι εσείς συνοικοδομείστε σε κατοικητήριο του Θεού διαμέσου τού Πνεύματος."
ΠΡΟΣ ΕΦΕΣΙΟΥΣ 2:22

I thank God for you whenever I remember you in my prayers. Thank you for your support of our ministry. For joining us in this vision of **creating a new and better world**, if not for us, for our children's children. **Can you imagine;**
+ a world where no one goes to sleep hungry?
+ two peoples who've lived in conflict making peace?
+ converting two groups into one?

Exodus 16 and **Ephesians 2** point to such a world. In Exodus, no one suffered from hunger because God sent bread from heaven, commanding: *"'Everyone is to gather as much as they need. Take an omer for each person you have in your tent.' The Israelites did as they were told; some gathered much, some little. And when they measured it by the omer, the one who gathered much did not have too much, and the one who gathered little did not have too little. Everyone had gathered just as much as they needed"* **(Exodus 16:16-18).**

Even though God provides the means of nourishment (earth, sun, water, seed, etc.), we've not yet learned to collect enough, to share the blessings, and as a result, many live hungry, on the brink of extinction. Still, we don't lose hope that one day our world will trust God again for each day's sustenance, and no one will go to sleep hungry.

In **Ephesians**, God promises to make two groups one, breaking down the walls of separation and hostility. Through His sacrifice, Jesus did away with the commandments, allowing grace and love to abound in our hearts **(Ephesians 2:14-16).** In this way, two groups who lived in enmity today live as one, waiting for a new world when God will be in our midst, and there will be no more hunger, disease, pain, wounds, lies, death, betrayals, or crying.

You and I are being edified and strengthened every day through reading and meditating on God's Word. *"In Christ the whole building is joined together and rises to become a holy temple in the Lord. And in Him you too are being built together to become a dwelling in which God lives by his Spirit"* (Ephesians 2:21-22).

Let us pray: Dear God, grant us the privilege of creating, in Your name and with Your help, a new world overflowing in love and obedience. Cleanse our hearts so that we may be a holy temple for You. We pray in Your Holy Name.

March 14
A NECESSARY ENCOUNTER

"Now he had to go through Samaria." John 4:4

"Le era necesario pasar por Samaria". Juan 4:4

"Επρεπε, μάλιστα, να περάσει διαμέσου τής Σαμάρειας." ΚΑΤΑ ΙΩΑΝΝΗΝ 4:4

In Exodus, we find the now liberated but hungry Israelites in the wilderness. God instructed them to collect manna six days a week. They had to gather for two days on the sixth day and thus rest on the seventh day. Yet, some disobeyed by going out to collect on the seventh day **(Exodus 16:28)**. God became angry and complained to Moses, *"How long will you refuse to keep my commands and my instructions?"* **(v.28)**. The reading concludes by reminding us that *"The Israelites ate manna forty years, until they came to a land that was settled"* **(v.35)**.

John 4:1-6 sets the background for the precious encounter between Jesus and the Samaritan woman. Let's read it together:
"Now Jesus learned that the Pharisees had heard that he was gaining and baptizing more disciples than John— although in fact it was not Jesus who baptized, but his disciples. So he left Judea and went back once more to Galilee. Now he had to go through Samaria. So he came to a town in Samaria called Sychar, near the plot of ground Jacob had given to his son Joseph. Jacob's well was there, and Jesus, tired as he was from the journey, sat down by the well. It was about noon."

I've read this passage many times, and what caught my attention today is **verse 4.** *"Now he had to go through Samaria."* Why it was necessary? For one, because the most direct route between Jerusalem and Galilee was through Samaria Samaria was considered enemy territory. However, there was great enmity between the Jews and the Samaritans. A real Jew would not risk his spiritual cleanliness by interacting with the Samaritans. Yet, **for Jesus, it was necessary to go through Samaria** because, listen to this, He had planned a Divine encounter with a Samaritan woman.

> **For Jesus, it was necessary to go through Samaria** because he had planned a Divine encounter with a Samaritan woman.

On March 13, 2020, Margarita, Fanny, and I crossed from north to south of Ecuador for a family reunion. It'd been three years since our last visit, and **it was necessary** to go back to strengthen family ties. God brought us safely along the wide Pan-American Highway until we reached Cuenca, some 455 km away from our base, Quito.

Let us pray: Dear God, thank You for Your love that strengthens family ties. Indeed, *"the distance to a friend's house is never far."* Thank you for narrowing the distances that separated us from Your kingdom. Help us to attend to the necessary encounters to reach Your heavenly mansion. We pray in Your Holy Name.

March 15
OUR GLORIOUS HOPE

"But Christ is faithful as the Son over God's house. And we are his house, if indeed we hold firmly to our confidence and the hope in which we glory." **Hebrews 3:6**

"Cristo, en cambio, como hijo es fiel sobre su casa, que somos nosotros, si mantenemos la confianza firme hasta el fin y nos gloriamos en la esperanza". Hebreos 3:6

"Ο Χριστός, όμως, ως υιός επάνω στον δικό του οίκο· του οποίου εμείς είμαστε ο οίκος, αν μέχρι τέλους κρατήσουμε βέβαιη την παρρησία και το καύχημα της ελπίδας." **ΠΡΟΣ ΕΒΡΑΙΟΥΣ 3:6**

To be the house of God requires perseverance in our faith and hope for the glorious morning when we'll be resurrected to a new life, free of suffering, and pain, where there'll be no more crying, illness, or hostilities.

While we wait, God calls us to **persevere in prayer**, watching with thanksgiving. **Watching** means **staying awake and vigilant**. Jesus said, *"My house will be called a house of prayer"* **(Mark 11:15)**. God's Word says, *"pray without ceasing"* **(1 Thessalonians 5:17)**, in every place, in every situation, for all people and needs.

My prayer list grows daily. There are more requests added than those crossed-off as **"answered."** But that doesn't mean God **isn't listening or answering prayer**. Sometimes God answers yes, sometimes it's **"not yet,"** and sometimes no. While we wait, we're called to continue praying and sharing our **glorious hope** with those who suffer and mourn today.

In times past, we also suffered without hope until God's Divine Word took root in our hearts, filling us with faith, courage, and hope of a glorious tomorrow. Everyone should know that *"if indeed we hold firmly to our confidence"* (Hebrews 3:6), we will glory in His presence, and while we wait, we'll be a **house strengthened by prayer and hope.**

God has endowed us with His love letter (the Bible), which contains the map to reach the heavenly mansion. *"For everything that was written in the past was written to teach us, so that through the endurance taught in the Scriptures and the encouragement they provide we might have hope"* (**Romans 15:4**). The **glorious hope** that you and I share with the poor, suffering, helpless, sick, prisoners, refugees, widows, orphans, etc., are the seeds of love and consolation that God wants to deposit in those lives through your actions, words, and presence.

Let us pray: Dear God, purify us so that in every way, we may be for you and the world, **"a house of prayer"** and hope. May Your **glorious hope** shine in us, spreading seeds of love so that *"all who have this hope in him purify themselves, just as he is pure"* (**1 John 3:3).** We pray in Your Holy Name.

SOMETIMES GOD ANSWERS YES, SOMETIMES IT'S "NOT YET," AND SOMETIMES NO.

March 16
GOD WILL PROVIDE A WAY OUT
1 Corinthians 10:13

The word *"temptation"* (πειρασμός, Peirasmós) in Greek means an adversity, as in **"trial"** or **"temptation."** We all face temptations, they're inevitable. Being tempted is not a sin. We sin when acting upon our temptations.

God will provide a way out, not to avoid it, but to face temptation successfully and stand firm in our faith. God stands by to prevent us from being led astray by temptation. When tempted, faith in God helps us out.

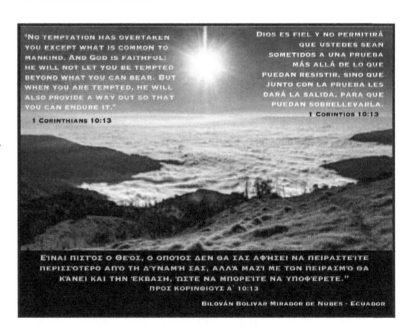

It's important to know that **God does not initiate temptations**. *"For God cannot be tempted by evil, nor does he tempt anyone; but each person is tempted when they are dragged away by their own evil desire and en-*

ticed" **(James 1:13-14)**. God allows trials to purify us or to demonstrate our character and faithfulness in the face of adversity. On the other hand, the devil uses temptation to induce us to sin, as he did with Adam and Eve in the garden or as he tried with Jesus in the desert **(Matthew 4:1)**.

Always remember that **Jesus intercedes for us**. Jesus said to Peter: *"Simon, Simon, Satan has asked to sift all of you as wheat. But I have prayed for you, Simon, that your faith may not fail. And when you have turned back, strengthen your brothers"* **(Luke 22:31-32)**. After Peter denied Jesus, strengthened by prayer and friendship with the Master, Jesus appointed him to *"feed my sheep"* **(John 21:17)**. Jesus also intercedes in each of your trials and temptations so that your faith doesn't fail and to show you how to come out victorious.

The Bible teaches that *"when I am weak, then I am strong"* **(2 Corinthians 12:10)**. But be careful with overly relying on your strength to resist temptation. *"So, if you think you are standing firm, be careful that you don't fall!"* **(1 Corinthians 10:12)**.

Let us pray: Dear Lord, thank You for teaching us how not to fall into temptation. For strengthening our faith to endure temptations and for the promise that, when we've withstood the test, we'll receive the crown of life you promised to those who seek you. We pray in the name of Jesus Christ.

March 17
WHEN WILL OUR SORROWS END?
Isaiah 60:20

Humanity eagerly cries out; Lord, when will you fulfill the promises in **Isaiah 60**?:

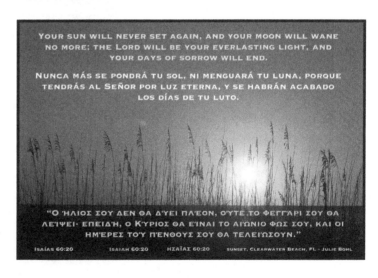

+ *"Although you have been forsaken and hated…I will make you the everlasting pride and the joy of all generations"* **(v.15)**.
+ *"No longer will violence be heard in your land, nor ruin or destruction within your borders"* **(v.18)**.
+ Lord, when will come the day that your Light will be our Light for eternity, and **when will our sorrow end**? **(v.19-20)**.

God answers all these questions, *"I am the Lord; in its time I will do this swiftly"* **(v.22)**. In God's time, our food will be the best of the nations **(v.16)**. Finally, the Lord *"will make peace your governor and well-being your ruler"* **(v.17B)**. We pray that our children and future generations might live amid peace and justice, illumined by God's Light.

Can you visualize it? Imagine your children guided by peace and justice, being *"the everlasting pride and the joy of all generations,"* dwelling free from violence, hunger, and death. Now ask yourself, **what must I do so that my children can enjoy God's light, peace, and justice**?

While we wait for God's perfect time, you and I are bearers of His Light. **Galatians 2:20** says that we *"no longer live, but Christ lives in"* us. Therefore, we are a continuation of that enduring Light of life, and our name is Χριστόφορος (Christopher) which means **bearers of Christ's Light.**

Jesus said: *"I am the light of the world. Whoever follows me will never walk in darkness, but will have the light of life"* **(John 8:12).** By reflecting the Light of life, we bring a piece of God's Kingdom to our world, alleviating and shortening the period of mourning and grief in our environment. What a worthy task!

Let us pray: Dear God, **illuminate the shadows of our lives**, use us to bring Your Light, peace, justice, and hope to the world. Though we walk through valleys of darkness, help us cross them without fear, knowing that You hold our hand, giving us the courage to live for and through you. Transform our mourning into dancing. We pray in Your Holy Name.

March 18
LET'S RESPECT ALL ORDINANCES
Jeremiah 2:7

God accuses us of defiling His land. Honestly, we haven't been good stewards or respected God's ordinances. According to scientists, today, the earth suffers the ravages of our neglect. It's enough to look at the reduced snowcap of the majestic Cotopaxi, Ecuador, to confirm our abandonment and selfishness. The capitalist thirst has turned God's inheritance into something *"detestable."*

As we confront the coronavirus, which spread its claws across our planet with full force and ferocity, God calls us to meditate on how

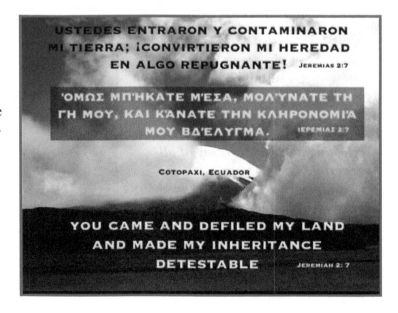

we've contributed to giving wings to this plague and what we can and should do to destroy it. By respecting the ordinances and following all the protocols issued by our health centers with mutual care, we can avoid contributing to the continuation of local and global contamination.

As of 00:01 am, March 28, 2020, throughout Ecuador, we had to obey the curfew and the restriction of movement ordinances that went into effect or face the consequences; up to a $6,000 dollar fine or three years of imprisonment.

God declares that we've strayed from Him and seeks an explanation; *"What fault did your ancestors find in me, that they strayed so far from me? They followed worthless idols and became worthless themselves"* **(Jeremiah 2:5)**. In **Jeremiah 2:13**, God says, *"My people have committed two sins: They have forsaken me, the spring of living water, and have dug their own cisterns, broken cisterns that cannot hold water."*

Abandoning God and polluting His inheritance has a much more significant penalty than our earthly rulers impose. Our inheritance is the land and the children God has given us to raise and instruct in God's righteous ways. If we neglect to educate them on God's ordinances, they will not know what to do or where to go to be under God's safe conduct.

The solution is to return to God, cover ourselves under His mantle of protection, learn His will, and respect and follow all of God's ordinances.

Let us pray: Dear God, just as we fear and are obedient to the ordinances of our cities and countries, help us to be even more diligent in knowing and making known Your decrees to our children and the children of their children. Make us good stewards of Your inheritance. We pray in Your Holy Name.

March 19
SUSCEPTIBLE TO SIN
Hebrews 4:16

More than ever in history, we are susceptible to temptation and need to be washed from the pollutants of the soul. This is due to two factors; 1. The decrease in church attendance and Bible reading at home, and 2. The uncontrolled use and access to technology.

Many people justify their lack of attendance and participation in the church by saying, *"It is not necessary to go to Holy Mass because I have God in my heart and that is enough."* But children do what they observe in their parents. If we don't give importance to the things of God, trust in the Church and the Bible will continue to decline, and our children will pay for the damage they'll inherit.

87

On the other hand, the Internet is a beautiful tool. What used to require time traveling to the library to search through several books, now, in seconds, without leaving our room, we have access to a universe of information. But, technology is a two-edged sword. It can be used for good and evil, sometimes leading to broken marriages due to addiction to chat or porn.

Have hope, my beloved friends and family! The good news is that God understands our temptations. Jesus Christ *"was tempted in every way, just as we are—yet he did not sin"* (**Hebrews 4:15).** He knows that the spirit wants to please God, but the flesh fights against it, seeking its pleasures and desires. God knows our tendency to make mistakes, to give in to the enemy's tricks.

That's why God invites us to approach the throne of grace confidently, to be washed, renewed, and obtain grace when we need help. **Grace happens when God freely gives us the forgiveness and justification we don't deserve instead of the punishment we deserve.**

We cry out to God through confession and repentance, *"Wash away all my iniquity and cleanse me from my sin"* (**Psalm 51:2).** Then, God renews and strengthens our spirit so that we may resist and not fall again as prey to the same temptations.

Let us pray: Thank you, Lord, for allowing us to approach Your throne of grace. Despite our rebelliousness, we don't understand why and how you love us, but such is Your love. Please give us the strength to resist the temptations when they knock at our doors. We pray in the name of Jesus.

March 20
PEER PRESSURE

"I was afraid of the men, and so I gave in to them." **1 Samuel 15:24**

"Tenía miedo de los hombres, así que me rendí ante ellos". **1 Samuel 15:24**

"φοβήθηκα τον λαό, και υπάκουσα στη φωνή τους·" **Α΄ ΣΑΜΟΥΗΛ 15:24**

Have you ever felt pressured to do something wrong or contrary to regulations? When we're in a hurry, we tend to justify our disobedience.

In the early 70s, I was stopped by the police while driving close to 110 MPH near Washington DC. I saw their lights behind me but kept going to reach a service area. I asked my mom if she could "hold it" for another five minutes. She said, "NO!" I pressed the peddle to the floor, but the police stopped me. As my mom ran out of the Van toward the bushes, the officer asked:

"Didn't you see me behind you for the past 5 miles?"
Me: Yes, I did, but I was trying to reach the service station.
Officer: You're required to stop when signaled. Why did you keep running?
Me: My mother made me do it. She has diabetes and couldn't hold it.

Some say, **"The Devil made me do it."** I said, **"My mom made me do it."** Saul gave **"My soldiers made me do it"** as his reason for disregarding God's specific instructions to destroy the Amalekites and everything that belonged to them, including animals **(1 Samuel 15:3). The error**: Saul had spared the life of Agag, their king, along with animals to sacrifice to God. It seemed like a good reason!

Saul recognizes his disobedience: *"I have sinned. I violated the Lord's command and your instructions. I was afraid of the men and so I gave in to them"* **(1 Samuel 15:24).** King Saul succumbed to peer pressure. As a result, God removed His Spirit from Saul and took away his kingship.

How often do you give in to pressure? Has it gone well when you disobeyed? In 1973 I paid $190 for going 110 MPH. In today's dollars, that's about $900. If we're going to err, wouldn't it be better to err on the side of God and not of flawed humans?

Ignoring God's Word is disobedience and rebellion. *"For rebellion is like the sin of divination, and arrogance like the evil of idolatry"* **(1 Samuel 15:23).** God's Word cautions us that *"No immoral, impure or greedy person—such a person is an idolater—has any inheritance in the kingdom of Christ and of God"* **(Ephesians 5:5).** My beloved, our inheritance is at stake!

> **Ignoring God's Word is disobedience and rebellion.**

Let us pray: Dear Lord, please forgive our rebellion and disobedience. Write Your ordinances in our hearts so that we might not err against you. Help us to desire to please You, Lord, above all things present and future. We pray in Your Holy Name.

March 21
THE WORD WAS GOD

"In the beginning was the Word, and the Word was with God, and the Word was God."
John 1:1

"En el principio existía el Verbo, y el Verbo estaba con Dios, y el Verbo era Dios". **Juan 1:1**

"ΣΤΗΝ αρχή ήταν ο Λόγος, και ο Λόγος ήταν προς τον Θεό, και Θεός ήταν ο Λόγος."
ΚΑΤΑ ΙΩΑΝΝΗΝ 1:1

As Christians, we believe in the Holy Trinity. The Bible affirms that the Father, Son, and Holy Spirit are God and God is one.

Some heartfelt and well-meaning people will knock on your door to speak about the new world order that Jehovah God is creating. They will affirm that Jesus was the firstborn in creation, that he is the exact representation of Jehovah, but that he is not one with God. I suggest you welcome them with love and Christian respect and perhaps take time to analyze one of their bases of error.

John 1:1 affirms Jesus's Divinity. The Geneva Bible - 1599, translated from Greek, says in **John 1:1,** *"In the beginning was that Word, and that Word was with God, and that Word was God."*

In the Greek New Testament (1550 Stephanus), **John 1:1** says; *"εν αρχή (in the beginning) ην ο λόγος (was the Word) και ο λόγος (and the Word) ην προς (was "toward" "near" or "with") τον θεόν (the God) και θεός (and God) ην ο λόγος (was the Word)."*

> **The Bible affirms that the Father, Son, and Holy Spirit are God and God is one.**

The New World Bible (Jehovah's Witness, edited by its founder, Charles Taze Russell) says: *"In [the] beginning was the Word, and the Word was with God, and the Word was <u>a god</u>."* There's no justification for ignoring grammar and translation rules and adding the non-existent article "a." Even worse is reducing the last Greek reference of θεος (God in capital letter) to "<u>a god</u>" with a lowercase letter, placing Jesus as one of the many inferior, false gods of the world.

Philippians 2 affirms Jesus's Divinity. *"Therefore God exalted him to the highest place and gave him the name that is above every name, that at the name of Jesus every knee should bow, in heaven and on earth and under the earth, and every tongue acknowledge that Jesus Christ is Lord ("Κύριος"), to the glory of God the Father"* **(v.9–11).** Κύριος means Lord, which means God, supreme authority, owner.

My beloved, always be prepared to give a reason for your hope *"with meekness and reverence"* **(1 Peter 3:15).** It's vital to study God's Word to distinguish between truth and worldly distortions.

Let us pray: Dear God, thank You for allowing us to study Your Word in the original language, for giving us discernment through Your Holy Spirit who has sealed and reserved us to serve you in Your coming Kingdom and this world. We pray in Your Holy Name.

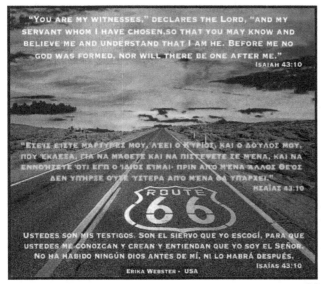

March 22
ONLY GOD CAN SAVE
Isaiah 43:10

God urges us to believe, know, and testify that **apart from God, there is no other who heals and saves (Isaiah 43:11).** 2 Corinthians 3:6 says that God chose and formed us to be witnesses and *"competent as ministers of a new covenant—not of the letter but of the Spirit; for the letter kills, but the Spirit gives life."*

90

Today more than ever, our children, family, and friends, even the strangers in our midst, need to know that we hope in a Savior and Healer who wants to rescue and heal us from our physical and spiritual ailments. They need to know that they're not useless accidents. That God has a noble purpose for their lives, a reason to keep fighting, knowing that in the end, God will give us the crown of victory.

What a great privilege and responsibility to be **chosen**. Chosen (ἐκλεκτός eklektós) means *"select; favorite."* God chose us so that through the revelation of His Holy Word and the inspiration of the Holy Spirit, we might deeply know and believe in God and understand that God is the only Lord and redeemer of our lives. **Isaiah 43:11** says, *"I, even I, am the Lord, and apart from me there is no savior."*

We're privileged because God made us *"ministers"* and *"witnesses,"* not of a strange salvation we've read about but of one we've experienced in flesh and bones. Our testimony is accurate and reliable because we speak of what we know. Like the woman with the issue of blood, we spent much time, energy, and resources on self-help programs and quick fixes, but nothing healed our affliction until we met Jesus, the Savior.

God wants everyone to know, believe, and understand that He alone is Lord, that apart from God, there is no other savior. Our Christian ministry and testimony speak of Jesus, that *"Salvation is found in no one else, for there is no other name under heaven given to mankind by which we must be saved"* **(Acts 4:2).**

Let us pray: Dear God, thank You for revealing that there is salvation only in You. You alone are God, forever and ever. Thank you for choosing us as witnesses and ministers of Your Word of Life. Let us use and share it freely in the way we received it. We pray in Your Holy Name.

March 23
JUDGE, FRIEND, AND GUIDE
Acts 2:21

If we had to appear in court for breaking the law, we should be represented by the best lawyer in the world. Wouldn't it be wonderful if our judge was also our attorney? The good news is that if we've invoked the name of the Lord, in effect, we have Jesus Christ as our advocate before God's tribunal **(1 John 2:1).**

In moments of anguish and fear, we cry out, *"Save us, Lord."* God says: *"Call to me and I will answer you and tell you great and unsearchable things you do not know"* **(Jeremiah 33:3).** On judgment day, we can trust that God, **our judge, friend, and guide,**

will save us. The love of Christ for His sheep is so great that He paid the penalty for our sins, and we'll be found innocent on judgment day. Praise the Lord!

On judgment day, we can trust that God, our judge, friend, and guide, will save us.

God warns us of a fearful day described in **Acts 2:19-20**, *"I will show wonders in the heavens above and signs on the earth below, blood and fire and billows of smoke. The sun will be turned to darkness and the moon to blood before the coming of the great and glorious day of the Lord."*

Jesus also spoke about that day: *"There will be signs in the sun, moon, and stars. On the earth, nations will be in anguish and perplexity at the roaring and tossing of the sea. People will faint from terror, apprehensive of what is coming on the world, for the heavenly bodies will be shaken"* **(Luke 21:25-26)**.

No one knows when that fearful day will come, but despite the announced terror, those who have trusted in the name of the Lord Jesus, placing their lives under the care and direction of the Savior, need not be terrified because God will save them from that horrible day. God says, *"let them foretell what will come. Do not tremble, do not be afraid"* **(Isaiah 44:7-8)**.

Let us pray: Dear God, help us call on the name of the Lord to ensure that we have the best defender in the universe as a **friend, lawyer, and judge.** Strengthen us to effectively share Your message of love, peace, forgiveness, and salvation with Your lost sheep and help them so that our lawyer may also be their lawyer, friend, and guide. We pray in Jesus's name.

March 24
CONDEMNED BY THE WORD
John 12:48

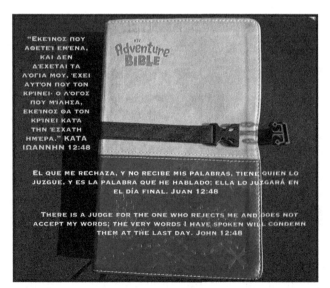

The Bible pictured here is God's complete revelation, lighting the way and instilling the heart with courage and wisdom to choose the path of love, justice, and peace leading to God's home. I don't know which of my children or grandchildren will inherit this youth Bible from my library, but I pray that whoever receives it will treasure its words throughout generations.

Psalm 119:9 says, *"How can a young person stay on the path of purity? By living according to your word."* Unwavering faith in Jesus and His Words, together with gratitude for rescuing us from the bondage of sin, is key to shaping a heart predisposed to **obedience**.

92

Jesus warns us about **obedience**. *"I have come into the world as a light, so that no one who believes in me should stay in darkness. 'If anyone hears my words but does not keep them, I do not judge that person. For I did not come to judge the world, but to save the world'"* (**John 12:46-47**).

I write for two audiences: First, to you, dear friends and family, who encourage me daily with your comments and reactions. Second, to my future generations 20-100 or more years in the future. I write because I wish that you'd believe in Jesus like **papou Aristoklís,** so that you not be seduced by the prince of darkness who will tirelessly seek ways for you to reject God's Word and invitation.

Regarding rejection, Jesus said, *"There is a judge for the one who rejects me and does not accept my words; the very words I have spoken will condemn them at the last day"* (**John 12:48**).

It's no coincidence that you have these words in your hands or screen, tugging at your heart so that you may decide whether to believe the prince of darkness or Jesus Christ, who came to save our world, your world, from eternal damnation.

I encourage you to learn your Bible well. Read it, study it more than any other book, and talk with God so that His Words might be, in your heart, *"the seed that fell on good soil."* So that you may retain it and *"by persevering produce a crop"* in you and your future generations (**Luke 8:15**).

Let's pray together, shall we?: Dear God, thank You for Your Holy Word, which guides and leads us toward Your presence. Thank you for the faith and witness of **papou Aristoklís**. Grant us hearts that are grateful and willing to listen, obey, and share Your precepts. We pray in the name of Jesus.

Believe in Jesus like papou Aristoklís so that you not be seduced by the prince of darkness who will tirelessly seek ways for you to reject God's Word and invitation.

March 25
GOD WITH US

"The virgin will conceive and give birth to a son, and will call him Immanuel." **Isaiah 7:14B**

"La joven concebirá, y dará a luz un hijo, y le pondrá por nombre Emanuel".
Isaías 7:14B

"Δέστε, η παρθένος θα συλλάβει και θα γεννήσει έναν γιο, και το όνομά του θα αποκληθεί Εμμανουήλ." **ΗΣΑΪΑΣ 7:14B**

Today, churches celebrate the Annunciation of the Lord, an occasion in which the Angel Gabriel said to the Virgin Mary, *"Do not be afraid, Mary; you have found favor with God. You will conceive and give birth to a son, and you are to call him Jesus. He will be great and will be called the Son of the Most High. The Lord God will give him the throne of his father David, and he will reign over Jacob's descendants forever; his kingdom will never end"* **(Luke 1:30-33).**

The announcement to Mary represents the fulfillment of God's promise, made four hundred years earlier, to a people shaken by the Syrians' threat who, allied with Ephraim, camped north to conquer them. In that scenario, God promises them- *"The virgin will conceive and give birth to a son, and will call him Immanuel"* **(Isaiah 7:14B).** Because Immanuel means *"God is with us,"* we have the assurance of protection and victory. *"If God is for us, who can be against us?"* **(Romans 8:31).**

In addition to promising us His presence and protection, God clarifies the type of King we'll have through the promised Messiah. He will be a *"righteous branch, a King who will reign wisely and do what is just and right in the land"* **(Jeremiah 23:5).** *"And he will be called Wonderful Counselor, Mighty God, Everlasting Father, Prince of Peace"* **(Isaiah 9:6).**

How wonderful to have a King who practices justice and law, an admirable, wise, mighty counselor, and a prince of peace. You and I are blessed not to live through 400 years of slavery and suffering. The promised Messiah came and fulfilled His purpose of rescuing His sheep.

About His reign, already a reality in our hearts, God tells us, *"Of the greatness of his government and peace there will be no end. He will reign on David's throne and over his kingdom, establishing and upholding it with justice and righteousness from that time on and forever. The zeal of the Lord Almighty will accomplish this"* **(Isaiah 9:7).**

Let us pray: Dear God, thank You for the day in which you wrote in our hearts Your promises, all fulfilled in the person of our King and Savior, the child awaited through centuries who today lives in and is **God with us** every day until the end of time. We pray in the precious name of Jesus.

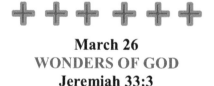

March 26
WONDERS OF GOD
Jeremiah 33:3

Thank you for the privilege of entering into your space to reason a little, explore God's Word, and affirm how God feels about you and me.

In September 2017, my uncle Rodrigo and our wives Margarita, Piedad, and my sister-in-law Fanny visited three great wonders of the world: The Parthenon of Athens, The Basilica of Saint Peter, Rome, and the Island of Santorini, Greece.

In this photo, we see the Santorini crater, where the largest volcanic eruption on our planet occurred. Wikipedia records that *"it was one of the most significant natural phenomena in the*

Aegean Sea during the Bronze Age. The volcanic eruption caused climate change in the eastern Mediterranean area and possibly the entire planet."[5]

When we look at the greatness of the universe, the sun, the moon, the stars, the volcanoes, we think, *"what is mankind that you are mindful of them, human beings that you care for them? You have made them a little lower than the angels and crowned them with glory and honor. You made them rulers over the works of your hands; you put everything under their feet"* **(Psalm 8:4-6).**

Thirty-three years of walking with and studying God's Word have shown me some hidden and **marvelous pearls**.

1. Although relatively small, we are the pinnacle of creation.
2. God created us to have an intimate relationship with God and our neighbors.
3. God will fulfill the purpose for which He created and saved us, and
4. God loves us unconditionally.

You can't imagine the magnitude of God's love for you (it's like a volcanic explosion - immense and incomparable). The only way to appreciate it is by standing at its heart, allowing the Creator of the universe to enter your environment, thoughts, and spirit. This is possible by immersing ourselves in God's Word, putting aside our unbelief, and allowing God to open our eyes to contemplate the greatness of His love and sacrifice to restore the divine image that was disfigured when sin entered the world. Amazed by such great love, we cry out, *"My Lord and my God"* **(John 20:28).**

Let us pray: *"My Lord and my God,"* allow us to call on You today, filled with awe, faith, and hope in Your promises. May we look at the great and small wonders that You've prepared for our delight and salvation, and may we say *"Yes"* to leading others to say **"Yes"** to Your incredible love. We pray in Your Holy Name.

> **1. Although relatively small, we are the pinnacle of creation. 2. God created us to have an intimate relationship with God and our neighbors. 3. God will fulfill the purpose for which He created and saved us. 4. God loves us unconditionally.**

[5] https://es.wikipedia.org/wiki/Erupción_minoica

March 27
GOD'S RIGHTEOUSNESS
Ezekiel 33:12

Our spirit wants to please and obey God, while the flesh, susceptible to temptations, seeks to satisfy its desires. That's why God's Word is sweet to the spirit but bitter to the body.

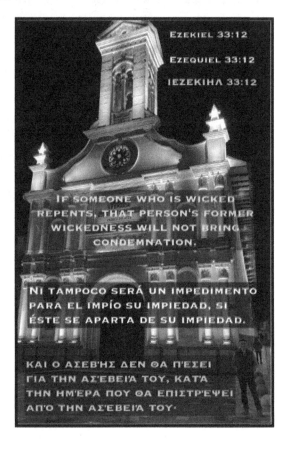

Some say God is good and no longer punishes, while others say God punishes the world because of negligence and disobedience. I believe we experience the consequences of our actions. God **is righteous** and unable to break the ordinances He established to create order in our relationship with the Creator and our neighbor. God's justice abounds in mercy but requires faithfulness and obedience.

Ezekiel 33 points to our struggle with sin and its consequences. **Being righteous, God doesn't want anyone to perish**, but His justice demands that we turn away from our evil ways **(Ezequiel 33:10-11)**. God says that our good works won't save us if we rebel against His Word and will. Being just and merciful, God calls us to separate ourselves from our *"former wickedness"* **(Ezequiel 33:12)**. God wants to save everyone but allows us to choose between obedience and rebellion.

God is righteous, and therefore we cannot sin against God trusting in His mercy. **Verse 13** says that if *"a righteous person …trust in their righteousness and do evil, none of the righteous things that person has done will be remembered; they will die for the evil they have done."*

On the other hand, God adds that if a *"wicked person… turns away from their sin and do what is just and right— if they follow the decrees that give life, and do no evil—that person …will not die"* **(Vs. 14-15)**. We have the example of the criminal condemned to die next to Jesus. This man recognized his sin, confessed, and acted righteously. Jesus assured him, *"Today you will be with me in paradise"* **(Luke 23:43)**.

Good news! No one is so bad to be excluded from God's forgiveness, love and grace if they turn away from evil. On the other hand, no one is righteous enough to be given a free pass to go back to a life of sin and expect entrance into God's kingdom because they trust in God's grace.

Ask yourself: **Am I living in obedience or rebellion to God's Word?**

Let us pray: My Lord and my God, examine my heart and if there's an ounce of rebellion, show me how to become righteous in Your eyes. Since you came to my life, my soul *"hopes in the Lord, for with the Lord is unfailing love and with him is full redemption"* **(Psalm 130:5-7)**. We pray in Jesus's precious name.

96

March 28
GOD WILL TAKE CARE OF YOU

"I am concerned for you and will look on you with favor; you will be plowed and sown."
Ezekiel 36:9

"Como pueden ver, yo estoy en favor de ustedes, y voy a cuidarlos, y ustedes serán cultivados y sembrados". Ezequiel 36:9

"Ἐπειδή, δέστε, εγώ κοιτάζω επάνω σας, και θα στραφώ σε σας, και θα αροτριαστείτε και θα σπαρθείτε." ΙΕΖΕΚΙΗΛ 36:9

God expresses concern for His people and **promises to take care of Israel** as a gardener cares for his garden.

God's relationship with Israel symbolizes His desired and promised relationship with all creation, particularly with those whom God considers His people. This means that God invites you, me, and the whole world to **be part of the new Israel.** When reading the Bible, I often recommend replacing your name in place of those who appear in it. Of course, hold on to the promises of blessings. When it comes to punishments or warnings, seek God's forgiveness and guidance, be obedient to Him and trust that God will take care of your life again.

During COVID lockdown, It was eerie to see our streets and highways previously filled with the movement of people, now empty. Although the coronavirus pandemic continues to afflict us, destroying lives, markets, and economies, God promises that our *"towns will be inhabited and the ruins rebuilt"* **(Ezekiel 36:10).** Yes, beloved friends and family, God will take care of you.

The doctors, nurses, and first responders teams are a group of heroes who've also pledged their lives to care for us. We thank God for them who daily place their health, life, and families at risk to take care of the sick. Today we unite throughout the world to recognize these heroes and heroines, asking that God look on them with favor, to care for them as His beautiful garden, even as they care for us.

These heroes, although fully trained, are going through the worst conditions ever, and just like war-time, they painfully must decide whom to attend first. This causes them unimaginable stress because they've sworn to help everyone, but the lack of resources often leaves them, in some instances, powerless, stressed, and susceptible to contamination.

Let us pray: Dear God, thank You because *"If You are for us, who can be against us?"* **(Romans 8:31).** We ask that you open our minds to understand the Holy Scriptures **(Luke 24:45)** and pour Your Holy Spirit on Your people, especially on the medical and first respondents. Give them wisdom, understanding, the resources needed to care for the sick, and the peace of mind to do their jobs. Watch over them and their beloved families. We pray in Your Holy Name.

MEDIATOR OF A NEW COVENANT
Hebrews 9:15

Following the triumphant entry into Jerusalem, Jesus goes to Lazarus' house, whom he had resurrected. The crowds continue to follow Jesus, along with *"the chief priests [who] made plans to kill Lazarus as well, for on account of him many of the Jews were going over to Jesus and believing in him"* (John 12:10-11).

Knowing that they were looking to kill Him and how he'd die, out of love for us, Jesus went toward the cross without any fear. Verse ten says that they also wanted *"to kill Lazarus."* Those who have an intimate friendship with Jesus can transform many lives but also place their lives and meaningful relationships at risk.

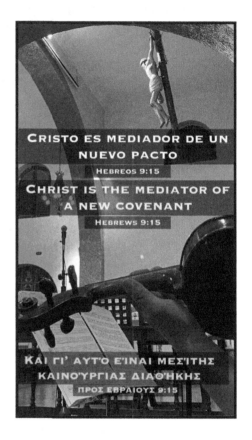

The Hebrew Scriptures contained around 630 laws. Whoever failed in one failed them all. Humans couldn't comply with the law. Without Jesus's sacrifice, we'd still be dead in our sins under the law. Furthermore, the sacrificial system under the old covenant didn't change people's hearts. They repented, sacrificed insignificant animals, and sinned again, repeating the cycle over and over.

Therefore, God sent Jesus so that through His sacrifice, once and for all, Jesus Christ may be *"the mediator of a new covenant, that those who are called may receive the promised eternal inheritance—now that he has died as a ransom to set them free from the sins committed under the first covenant"* (Hebrews 9:15). In this new covenant, there are only two laws; *"Love God"* and *"love your neighbor as yourself"* (Mark 12:33).

Isaiah 42 records that God chose Jesus as the **mediator of this new covenant** to bring *"justice to the nations"* (v.1). *"He will not falter or be discouraged till he establishes justice on earth. In his teaching the islands will put their hope"* (v.4).

As children of the inheritance, our repentance takes on a permanent and tireless commitment to God and the new covenant. With the Holy Spirit's help, each day we become more obedient followers and better lovers of God's Word and presence. No longer destined for death, but heirs with Jesus, **the new and better covenant mediator**.

Let us pray: Dear God, thank You because, seeing our spiritual poverty, you created the new covenant through the sacrifice of our Lord Jesus Christ. Thank you for making us heirs of Your love and grace. At the right time, you called us, and Your Word assures us that you will **deliver us from evil**. Help us be *"a light to the nations"* (Isaiah 42:6) and serve and love you throughout eternity. We pray in the name of Jesus, our only mediator.

March 30
WHY JESUS CAME
John 12:27

From birth to ministry, Jesus's entire purpose in our world was to arrive for the time of passion and suffering, to give His life for His brothers/sisters and friends. Thus, Jesus rescued our souls from the enemy's clutches.

"Now my soul is troubled, and what shall I say? 'Father, save me from this hour'? No, it was for this very reason I came to this hour" **(John 12:27).** Jesus came into our world to save us, and, therefore, He's worthy of our love, faith, praise, imitation, and fidelity. In **John 18:37**, we read, *"You say that I am a king. In fact, the reason I was born and came into the world is to testify to the truth."* Jesus wants us to accept that He died to rescue our lives and, out of gratitude, receive Him into our hearts as our only and sufficient Savior and King.

1 Corinthians 1:30 says, *"It is because of him that you are in Christ Jesus, who has become for us wisdom from God—that is, our righteousness, holiness and redemption."*

Jesus came to be our Wisdom — we're wise if we choose to listen to His instructions and directions, thus avoiding setbacks, pains, and deadly wounds. God calls us to *"have the same mindset as Christ Jesus"* **(Philippians 2:5).**

Jesus came to be our righteousness — neither works nor our social/economic status helps us be found righteous before God. Only through the sacrifice of Jesus Christ can we make peace and friendship with God.

Jesus came to be our holiness — this is the daily spiritual cleansing process (**reading God's Word, meditating, and praying**) that helps us resist temptations and trust in the guidance and strength of the Holy Spirit.

Jesus came to be our redemption — Redeemer is a person who pays the price on behalf of an impoverished relative to effect the liberation of the relative or their property.

Nothing could stop Jesus from rescuing His own; neither the abandonment, insults, accusations, nor death itself. **Jesus came specifically to give His life in exchange for ours (John 12:27).** Now it's our time to **glorify Jesus in our lives**. We were created and rescued for this very reason.

Let us pray: Dear Lord, receive my infinite gratitude for coming specifically to give Your life to rescue mine. Touch our hearts so that with all our senses, we may appreciate what You endured to be our King, our wisdom, our **"righteousness, holiness and redemption."** We pray in Your Holy Name.

> **Jesus came into our world to save us, and, therefore, He's worthy of our love, faith, praise, imitation, and fidelity.**

March 31
THE JOY OF THE LORD
Hebrews 12:2

For over two years, we've been walking through this valley of the shadow of death (COVID-19). It has destructively claimed more American lives than in both world wars. Worldwide, the number of deceased and debilitated is alarming; unemployment, hunger, social isolation, and stress from an uncertain future have increased, **robbing us of the joy of the Lord**. How timely today's verse, in which Jesus didn't focus on the suffering that lay ahead but instead on the joy and certainty of the end game.

Without minimizing the tremendous pain and suffering that God's people are enduring, the best refuge and medicine for such moments is sitting at the Lord's feet to remember who we are and where we're going. Very sure of His identity and mission, and **for the joy of saving the world** from separation from God and eternal death, Jesus mustered the strength by **clinging to the joy of the Lord**.

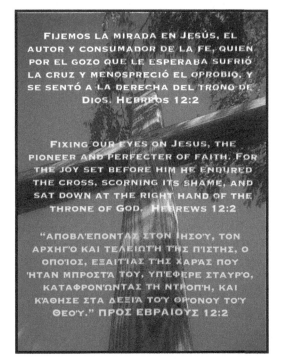

It's my joy to share some favorite verses, which in times of sadness, pain, and confusion, restore **my joy of the Lord.**

"Do not grieve, for the joy of the Lord is your strength" **(Nehemiah 8:10).**

God promises, *"Those who sow with tears will reap with songs of joy"* **(Psalm 126:5).**

Our joy will be perpetual, *"They will enter Zion with singing; everlasting joy will crown their heads. Gladness and joy will overtake them, and sorrow and sighing will flee away"* **(Isaiah 35:10).**

Jesus calls us to cling to Him *"so that my joy may be in you and that your joy may be complete"* **(John 15:11).**

Jesus said to ask in His name, *"and you will receive, and your joy will be complete"* **(John 16:24).**

Jesus Christ prayed to God the Father *"so that they may have the full measure of my joy within them"* **(John 17:13).**

Beloved, Jesus's resurrection was an occasion of *"great joy"* for the women who discovered His empty tomb **(Matthew 28:8).** During Holy Week, it's much more joyful for us to remember that, at the end of the story, the Way, the Truth, and the Life triumphed over chaos, lies, and death.

Let us pray: Dear God, grant us the faith and **joy of the Lord,** to cast all our worries in Your precious hands while You put Your joy and peace in our hearts. We pray in Your Holy Name.

April 1
LOVE ONE ANOTHER

*"A new command I give you: Love one another. As I have loved you, so you must love one another." **John 13:34***

*"Un mandamiento nuevo les doy: Que se amen unos a otros. Así como yo los he amado, ámense también ustedes unos a otros". **Juan 13:34***

*"Σας δίνω μια νέα εντολή, να αγαπάτε ο ένας τον άλλο. Όπως σας αγάπησα εγώ, να αγαπάτε κι εσείς ο ένας τον άλλο." **ΚΑΤΑ ΙΩΑΝΝΝΗΝ 13:34***

Jesus was asked, *"which is the greatest commandment in the Law?"* **(Matthew 22:36).** It was a valid question! The Hebrew scriptures contained around 633 commandments, so it's not unusual for someone who desires some sense of order and priority to want to know *"which is the greatest of all commandments."*

Jesus replied, *"Love the Lord your God with all your heart and with all your soul and with all your mind. This is the first and greatest commandment. And the second is like it: 'Love your neighbor as yourself.' All the Law and the Prophets hang on these two commandments"* **(Matthew 22:37-40).**

Let's clarify: The first and greatest commandment is to love God. The second is to love our neighbor as ourselves. Under this command, believers must love those around them, even if they aren't part of the community but are considered neighbors. This would include those passing by our community who don't necessarily share our religious, political, or civic views. Loving them means being kind and treating them as you'd want to be treated, i.e., applying **the golden rule!**

But now, speaking to the disciples and those gathered around the Passover table, the Lord establishes **a third love commandment for the community of believers:** *"Love one another. As I have loved you."* This commandment applies to the church members who regularly participate in our worship and service. Jesus calls brothers and sisters-in-Christ to *"love one another,"* and is clear about the nature and manner of the love expected of us. He adds, *"As I have loved you."*

The call to love follows the pattern of forgiveness. *"Forgive us our trespasses as we forgive those who trespass against us"* (**Matthew 6:12**). In like manner, love one another *"as I have loved you."* **In what way has Christ loved you? John 3:16** states the form of God's love. **Romans 5:8** proves it: *"But God demonstrates his own love for us in this: While we were still sinners, Christ died for us."*

Let us pray: Dear Lord, grant us the strength to serve, forgive and love as we've been served, loved, and forgiven. That we do not judge or withhold Your grace from anyone seeking to receive sight and be set free from the chains of sin. We pray in Jesus's name.

April 2
OUR MEDIATOR

"He poured out his life unto death, and was numbered with the transgressors. For he bore the sin of many, and made intercession for the transgressors." Isaiah 53:12

"Porque él derramará su vida hasta la muerte y será contado entre los pecadores; llevará sobre sí mismo el pecado de muchos, y orará en favor de los pecadores". Isaías 53:12

"επειδή παρέδωσε σε θάνατο την ψυχή του, και λογαριάστηκε μαζί με ανόμους, και αυτός βάσταξε τις αμαρτίες πολλών, και θα μεσιτεύσει υπέρ των ανόμων." ΗΣΑΪΑΣ 53:12

Today we commemorate the dark day when Jesus Christ, our mediator, freely gave His life on the cross so that you and I might enjoy peace and communion with God and neighbor.

> **Jesus Christ, our mediator, freely gave His life on the cross so that you and I might enjoy peace and communion with God and neighbor.**

Isaiah 53:9 says that despite not having sinned, *"He was assigned a grave with the wicked, and with the rich in his death."* The innocent would die for our rebellions. *"But he was pierced for our transgressions, he was crushed for our iniquities; the punishment that brought us peace was on him, and by his wounds we are healed"* (Isaiah 53:5).

Jesus's ministry was characterized by His dedication and love for the poor and marginalized. Jesus intervened on behalf of humanity so that God wouldn't count our sins against us but rather against Jesus. Even from the cross, with His last ounce of breath, Jesus was thinking and praying for sinners like us. *"Father, forgive them; for they know not what they do"* (**Luke 23:34**).

The Bible teaches that *"there is one God and one mediator between God and mankind, the man Christ Jesus"* (**1 Timothy 2:5**). During His ministry, Jesus mediated between God and humanity on several occasions:

✦ Jesus prayed for our faith: *"I have prayed for you, Simon, that your faith may not fail"* (**Luke 22:32**).

✦ Our mediator prayed so that we wouldn't be alone: *"And I will ask the Father, and he will give you another advocate to help you and be with you forever"* (**John 14:16**).

✦ Jesus prayed and continues to intercede for every one of His sheep that have strayed from the Way. **"I pray for them. I am not praying for the world, but for those you have given me, for they are yours" (John 17:9).**

✦ Jesus is sitting at the right hand of the Father and **"is able to save completely those who come to God through him, because he always lives to intercede for them" (Hebrews 7:25).**

Let us pray: Dear God, thank You for shining your light in our darkness, for sending Jesus, the innocent mediator who *"bore the sin of many,"* and *"always lives to intercede for us."* Please grant that we may also be intercessors for those who suffer today. We pray in Jesus's name.

April 3
GOD NEEDS YOU
Philippians 1:23-24

Saint Paul tells us that his greatest desire was to leave this world and be with Christ. However, God needed him in this world to proclaim the gospel (**Philippians 1:23-24**).

Almighty God can move mountains, constellations, and calm storms with a single word. We're not of the caliber of the Apostles Paul or Peter. So **why would God need us?** It's a question that demands our response and clarity.

First, God created us **to have an intimate and personal relationship** with Him. To be our God, and we'd be God's chosen people.

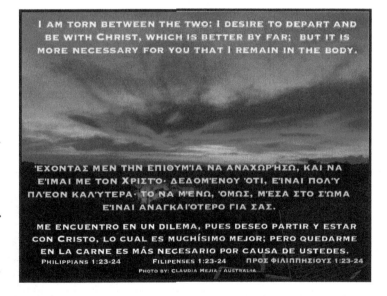

Second, at creation, **God entrusted us with its care (Genesis 1:28, 2:15).** Later on, Jesus came *"to proclaim good news to the poor, to proclaim freedom for the prisoners and recovery of sight for the blind, to set the oppressed free"* (**Luke 4:18**). After His death and ascension into heaven, God formed the church so that we'd **continue Jesus's mission**. As long as the earth exists, there will be poor, sick, and homeless. **God needs us to take care of each other physically, emotionally, and spiritually.**

We want to be in God's presence, to rest from the constant fight against evil and lack of goodness in our environment. But while we're on this earth, **God needs and commissioned you** and me to be active participants in His plan of salvation and restoration. God doesn't want us to be mere spectators. **God needs you** and has *"granted you not only to believe in Jesus but also to suffer for him"* **(Philippians 1:29).**

Amid this terrifying pandemic, those involved in continuing the Lord's good work toward the poor in spirit, sick, needy, widows, orphans, and homeless need courage and confidence in knowing that **God needs them and no evil will come upon them or their families.**

How is your commission and relationship with the Creator going?

Let us pray: Dear God, we need you today more than ever. *"9 Be merciful to me, my eyes grow weak with sorrow, 13 For I hear many whispering, "Terror on every side!" 14 But I trust in you, Lord; I say, "You are my God." 15 My times are in your hands; 16 Let your face shine on your servant; save me in your unfailing love"* **(Psalm 31)**. Grant us the courage to proclaim like Job; *"Though he slay me, yet will I hope in him"* **(Job 13:15)**. We pray in Your Holy Name.

> **As long as the earth exists, there will be poor, sick, and homeless. God needs us to take care of each other physically, emotionally, and spiritually.**

April 4
YOUR FIGHT IS OUR FIGHT
Lamentations 3:55-58

The book of **Lamentations** is attributed to Jeremiah, the Weeping Prophet. It expresses much suffering on account of Jerusalem's destruction. At the same time, it gives us hope in God. It paints the image of an intense *"struggle between faith, fear, and hope, but faith has the last*

word and comes out of the victorious conflict."[6]

In the face of the global pandemic, we strengthen our faith through prayer and study of God's Word because that's our defense and sustenance. Knowing that *God holds me in the palm of His hand* calms me down! However, fearful forecasts, horrifying news about the treatment of the deceased, and the lack of resources, attention, and personnel in hospitals cause us to fear that the virus may knock at our children's door and that they might not be sufficiently protected.

Joseph was placed in an empty cistern, which served as a prison until his brothers sold him as an enslaved person. I imagine that terrified from the bottom of the well, he cried out to God, as **Jeremiah** did. **Verse 55** says, *"I called on your name, Lord, from the depths of the pit."*

Although Joseph's brothers planned to harm him, God never abandoned him but allowed him to suffer momentarily to save the world **(Genesis 50:20).** As the Word says today, God heard Joseph's cry and gave him victory; *"You, Lord, took up my case; you redeemed my life"* **(Lamentations 3:58).**

My beloved, your fight is our fight. When one cries, we all cry. Maybe that's the only good thing we might find about this endless nightmare. That one's lament touches the heart of another human being and that we take the time to treat each other with respect, dignity, and a bit of love. From the bottom of our cisterns, we cry together for God to come to us and tell us: *"Do not fear"* **(Lamentations 3:57).**

Let us pray: Dear God, Creator, Healer, and Savior. You are our only trust and hope. Help us to stir our faith and overcome fear. Jeremiah's fight is our fight between fear, faith, and hope. Show us how to achieve victory, beginning with the protection and well-being of our children, family, and friends. We pray in the name of Jesus, the Lamb of God who takes away the whole world's sins.

April 5
CONFIDENT IN THE RESURRECTION

"'The first man Adam became a living being'; the last Adam, a life-giving spirit."
1 Corinthians 15:45

"'El primer hombre, Adán, se convirtió en un ser con vida'; y el postrer Adán, un espíritu que da vida". **1 Corintios 15:45**

"Ο πρώτος άνθρωπος Αδάμ «έγινε σε ψυχή που ζει»· ο έσχατος Αδάμ έγινε σε πνεύμα που ζωοποιεί." ΠΡΟΣ ΚΟΡΙΝΘΙΟΥΣ Α´ 15:45

---

[6] Henry, M., & Lacueva, F. (1999). *Comentario Bíblico de Matthew Henry* (p. 894). 08224 TERRASSA (Barcelona): Editorial CLIE.

The Lord is risen! Hallelujah! The Resurrection of Christ fills us with the hope that, in the same way, if we live and die in Jesus, we too will rise to a new and abundant life.

What does it mean to live in Christ? Simply that, from the moment God opened our understanding to receive Jesus Christ as Lord and Savior, everything we do from then on (in words, actions, thoughts, and emotions) reflects the essence and character of Jesus. As Saint Paul said, from that moment on, *"I no longer live, but Christ lives in me. The life I now live in the body, I live by faith in the Son of God"* **(Galatians 2:20).**

Being aware of this new reality helps us offer our body and life to Jesus's service to rescue and serve His sheep. Feeding daily on God's Word and repeating *"Christ lives in me"* regularly helps us combat discouragement and fatigue. At such times, we cry out, *"The Lord is my strength and my defense; he has become my salvation"* **(Psalm 118:14).**

Today's verse tells us that Jesus, *"the last Adam,* [is] *a life-giving spirit"* **(1 Corinthians 15:45).** Just as God had the power to breathe life into Adam, *"so he has granted the Son also to have life in himself"* **(John 5:26).**

The Bible records the times that Jesus raised the dead, among whom Lazarus is mainly remembered. In that scenario, Jesus said, *"I am the resurrection and the life. The one who believes in me will live, even though they die; and whoever lives by believing in me will never die. Do you believe this?"* **(John 11:25-26).** Hearing Jesus's voice calling him, *"Lazarus, come out"* **(John 11:43),** the deceased rose and came out of his grave.

My beloved, we don't know when, but Jesus declares, *"Very truly I tell you, a time is coming and has now come when the dead will hear the voice of the Son of God and those who hear will live"* **(John 5:25).**

My beloved, **living for Christ assures our Resurrection to eternal life.**

Let us pray: Dear God, allow our ears and hearts to be tuned to Your voice and guidance so that in the Resurrection, we may hear Jesus's voice and rise with new spiritual bodies, similar to our Savior and Redeemer, in whose name we pray.

April 6
CREATED IN GOD'S IMAGE
Genesis 1:27

Today's verse tells us we're *"created in God's image."* Each of us carries a bit of divine DNA waiting to sprout. Every human being has a deep desire to know and be known by God, *"Emmanuel, which means God is with us"* **(Matthew 1:23).**

God created us in His image and appointed us to be ambassadors. In the words of the great Scottish preacher Peter Marshall, the reason for our existence is *"to present Christ to the people. This is our complete and only business."*

When Jesus was born, there was no place for Him in the Inn. *"He came to his own, and his own did not receive him"* **(John 1:11).** Would the Innkeeper have made room if he'd known that Joseph came from King David's line? He didn't recognize the Royal family. And what about us? **Would we recognize Him if He came to our home? Would you make room for Him?**

I have family throughout the world that I've yet to meet. When I see their photos on Facebook, I see a similarity with my father, mother, grandparents, or uncles. **We carry the same blood**, and I hope to meet them someday. In 2010 we arranged to meet with the Destruge family (around 120 family members that we didn't know of their existence until then). We met through Facebook, and they made room in their homes for my dad, Margarita, and me. It was a wonderful experience. We continue to mutually share our love and emotional and spiritual support to the present day.

Jesus says in **Revelation 3:20**: *"Behold, I stand at the door and knock; If anyone hears my voice and opens the door, I will come in to him and dine with him, and he with me."* Upon hearing these words, would we recognize His voice and that **we are created in His image?** May it not be said of us Christians, *"He came to his own, and his own did not receive him."*

We have two options: To open or close the door. I'm eternally grateful that the Destruge family recognized and made a place for us in their homes and hearts. Every reasonable person would first make a place for God, who offers us adoption within the family, together with hope, peace, reconciliation, and eternal love.

Let us pray: Dear Lord, thank You for creating us in Your image. May our hearts always be predisposed to say to you, *"I have nothing more urgent in my life besides knowing you and Your will for me."* We pray in Jesus's name.

The women worried, *"Who will roll the stone away from the entrance of the tomb?"* (**Mark 16:3**). They didn't know that God had sent His angels to **go ahead of them** to remove the heavy stone. Our concern is, when will God remove this pandemic that has kept us locked up like in tombs? *Who will open the door for us to go out freely and breathe pure air*?

My beloved, we may not see them, but God's angels are removing our present affliction. We worry about many things, forgetting that God has promised always to **go ahead of us**. Being always ahead, the Lord removes obstacles and fights on our behalf. *"The Lord your God, who is going before you, will fight for you"* (**Deuteronomy 1:30**).

God wants us always to remember His promise of presence and protection. *"The Lord himself goes before you and will be with you; he will never leave you nor forsake you. Do not be afraid; do not be discouraged"* (**Deuteronomy 31:8**). We can put fear aside, knowing that **God goes ahead of us,** even now.

Jesus, our Good Shepherd, cares for His sheep with His own life. *"When he has brought out all his own, he goes on ahead of them, and his sheep follow him because they know his voice"* (**John 10:4**). He said he wouldn't lose a sheep because no one can snatch us from His hands (**John 10:28**). **Our job is to know His voice** and trust that our guide is **always ahead** of us.

The Lord's Angel said to the women, *"go quickly and tell his disciples: 'He has risen from the dead and is going ahead of you into Galilee. There you will see him'"* (**Matthew 28:7**). We're also called to *"go quickly"* and tell every little sheep that *"the Lord has risen."* Although we can't see Him, the Spirit of Jesus Christ is **always ahead of us (Mark 16:7).**

Let us pray: Dear God, thank You for **always being ahead** as our guide, presence, protector, sustainer, and defender. Grant us the faith to trust that our life and world are in Your loving hands and no one can snatch us away. Forgive our failures, heal our planet, in Jesus's name.

Nothing is more pleasing than seeing our children sharing and supporting each other. God delights to see the brethren *"living together in unity"* **(Psalm 133:1)**. Therefore, we should strive to fulfill **God's harmonious plan.**

We find the best example of unity in the Holy Trinity, God the Father, God the Son, and God the Holy Spirit. Jesus cooperates fully to fulfill **the harmonious Divine plan** of reconciling the world to God through His sacrifice. Jesus said, *"All I have is yours, and all you have is mine. And glory has come to me through them"* **(John 17:10)**. There's no selfishness in the Godhead; The Father glorifies the Son, and vice-versa.

Jesus implores us to *"be one"* **(John 17:11b)** just as the Holy Deity is one; *"The Lord our God, the Lord is one"* **(Mark 12:29)**. God is one in purpose, essence, justice, and mercy. God is invariable and infinite in love.

The Bible indicates that *"we, though many, form one body, and each member belongs to all the others"* **(Romans 12:5)**. Upon being adopted into God's family through Jesus's sacrifice on the cross, God transforms us spiritually into new creatures with noble goals and new ways of living; *"There is neither Jew nor Gentile, neither slave nor free, nor is there male and female, for you are all one in Christ Jesus"* **(Galatians 3:28)**.

Although we continue to live in bodies of flesh, the Holy Spirit fulfills **the harmonious Divine plan** of making us all of one mind by feeding, strengthening, and cleansing us with God's Word *"until we all reach unity in the faith and in the knowledge of the Son of God and become mature, attaining to the whole measure of the fullness of Christ"* **(Ephesians 4:13)**.

Let us pray: Holy Spirit, feed and strengthen our souls so that we may be one in words, emotions, purpose, and actions, supporting each other as the body of Christ, so that the whole world may reach the adoption into **Your harmonious family**. Make us one. Heal our sick, comfort those who mourn. We pray in Jesus's name.

APRIL 9
A REVEALING GOD
Daniel 2:23

One of the bases of our faith is that *"the Sovereign Lord does nothing without revealing his plan to his servants"* **(Amos 3:7)**. The Bible is the complete revelation of God's harmonious plan for His children to access all the gifts necessary to overcome fear and complete the race.

Jesus reveals a powerful gift that is both a defensive weapon and a building tool. In **Matthew 7:7**, God tells us, *"Ask and it will be given to you; seek and you will find; knock and the door will be opened to you."*

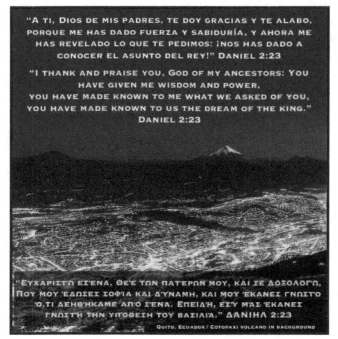

"A TI, Dios de mis padres, te doy gracias y te alabo, porque me has dado fuerza y sabiduría, y ahora me has revelado lo que te pedimos: ¡nos has dado a conocer el asunto del rey!" Daniel 2:23

"I thank and praise you, God of my ancestors: You have given me wisdom and power, you have made known to me what we asked of you, you have made known to us the dream of the king." Daniel 2:23

"ΕΥΧΑΡΙΣΤΏ ΕΣ'ΕΝΑ, ΘΕΈ ΤΩΝ ΠΑΤΈΡΩΝ ΜΟΥ, ΚΑΙ ΣΕ ΔΟΞΟΛΟΓΏ, ΠΟΥ ΜΟΥ 'ΕΔΩΣΕΣ ΣΟΦΊΑ ΚΑΙ Δ'ΥΝΑΜΗ, ΚΑΙ ΜΟΥ 'ΕΚΑΝΕΣ ΓΝΩΣΤΌ Ο,ΤΙ ΔΕΗΘΉΚΑΜΕ ΑΠΌ Σ'ΕΝΑ. ΕΠΕΙΔΉ, ΕΣ'Υ ΜΆΣ 'ΕΚΑΝΕΣ ΓΝΩΣΤΉ ΤΗΝ ΥΠΌΘΕΣΗ ΤΟΥ ΒΑΣΙΛΙΆ." ΔΑΝΙΗΛ 2:23

Quito, Ecuador / Cotopaxi Volcano in Background

Daniel maintained an intimate relationship with God by using prayer to ask for God's gifts of strength, guidance, and wisdom. King Nebuchadnezzar had a disturbing dream, and instead of asking the magicians and soothsayers to interpret it, he asked them to tell him what he dreamt and what it meant **(Daniel 2:6)**. They said it's impossible to know what the king dreamed. The king was angered and ordered them killed, but Daniel intervened, asking for time to consult with God about the dream. Daniel prayed, and God revealed the dream, thus freeing him from death **(Daniel 2:1-20)**.

Faced with threats from the religious leaders, the disciples asked God, *"enable your servants to speak your word with great boldness…After they prayed, the place where they were meeting was shaken. And they were all filled with the Holy Spirit and spoke the word of God boldly"* (Acts 4:29, 31).

Through The Holy Spirit, God promises to reveal *"even the deep things of God"* to every son and daughter who has reached maturity and wisdom **(1 Corinthians 2:6,10)**. You have divine gifts to expand God's kingdom and protect your home from the enemy's threats. Approach God with confidence; ask, seek, and call in the name of the Lord. **God will reveal the way and strengthen you for the task.**

Let us pray: Dear God, reveal Your plan and the gifts you've prepared for me. Let me proclaim Your Word without any fear. *"Stretch out your hand to heal and perform signs and wonders through the name of your holy servant Jesus"* (Acts 4:30). We pray in Jesus's name.

> **The Bible is the complete revelation of God's harmonious plan for His children to access all the gifts necessary to overcome fear and complete the race.**

April 10
WHY CALL THIS A GOOD FRIDAY?
John 19:30

Why Call this a Good Friday? If this were a novel, one would judge it as a literary failure! The Hero is betrayed by one of His closest allies for 30 pieces of silver and dies.

Those who previously shouted, *"Hossana, blessed is he who comes in the name of the Lord,"* were now shouting, *"Crucify him."* How quickly we follow the crowds!

In **John 18:14**, Caiaphas advised the Jewish leaders that *"it would be good if one man died for the people."* Jesus was falsely accused by the religious leaders and judged by the Romans. He was unjustly convicted and executed like a common criminal. *"One [good] man died for the people!"* The disciples lost their leader and disbanded in shame and fear. So, **why call it Good Friday?**

Growing up as a child, Good Friday was a day of mourning. There was no music, joy, or laughter. **There was nothing good** about "Viernes Santo"; we couldn't even go out and play soccer! There seem to be more reasons to call this **Shameful Friday**! But hold on, **the story doesn't end on Friday** with the death of the Hero!

We call this Good Friday because;
✦ Sinless Christ paid the penalty for my past, present, and future transgressions. Jesus said, *"I am the Good Shepherd. I lay down my life for the sheep. No one takes my life from me. I lay it down of my own accord and I take it again"* **(John 10:11,18).**
✦ Jesus is God's good and perfect gift to humanity. On Good Friday, Jesus finished His mission to overcome sin and death. Jesus didn't say I'm done, exhausted, spent. I failed! He said, *"it is finished!"* **I fulfilled the mission!**
✦ Jesus is in command and knows that *"all things work together for good to them that love God,"* even though, on the surface, the battle seems lost **(Romans 8:28).**

My beloved, there's another chapter ahead; **the best is yet to come!** The story goes on to **Resurrection Sunday**, inviting us to make this our story, which continues to play itself out in our communities, shelters, hospitals, street corners, and homes. We're in a relay race where Christ

> Jesus didn't say *"I'm done, exhausted, spent. I failed!"* He said, *"it is finished!"* **I fulfilled the mission!**

has run His course. But your work begins where He left off. This is the most exciting race in the human race.

111

Let us pray: Dear Lord, as we consider this pandemic, the powers of evil want us to feel that we've lost the battle. That evil has overcome good. But Good Friday is followed by Resurrection Sunday when Christ **finished Your excellent work of redemption**. May each day be resurrection day. We pray in Jesus's name.

April 11
WE'LL RISE AGAIN

"So mortals lie down, never to rise. Until the heavens are no more, they shall not awake, nor be roused out of their sleep." **Job 14:12**

"El hombre muere y no vuelve a levantarse; ¡mientras el cielo exista, no se levantará de su sueño"! **Job 14:12**

"έτσι ο άνθρωπος, όταν κοιμηθεί, δεν σηκώνεται· μέχρις ότου δεν υπάρξουν οι ουρανοί, δεν θα ξυπνήσουν, και δεν θα εγερθούν από τον ύπνο τους." **ΙΩΒ 14:12**

Job's reading reflects our struggle between disappointment and hope, life and death.

The disciples had hoped that Jesus would establish a new world order, delivering them from Rome's oppression and the physical, social, and spiritual illnesses related to the daily interaction between opposing cultures. They witnessed the death and burial of Jesus, some from afar, others up close. Their King-elect was dead, and very soon, not even the heap of perfumes and oils could stop the decomposition of the body of Jesus, who died abandoned in the company of evildoers. They wrongly believed in their hearts that *"mortals lie down, never to rise"* **(Job 14:12)**.

The three years of the Master's teachings were drowned out by the blaspheming crowds. Giving in to fear, they forgot Jesus's words that on the third day, He'd rise again. In their minds, Jesus was dead, and there was nothing they could do except return in defeat to their villages, houses, and families because they didn't believe that Jesus would *rise again.*

Our entire world is terrified by a nightmare; we'd like to wake up NOW, free from COVID-19. The enemy wants us to lose hope that **we'll rise again**. He wants us to doubt God's goodness, saying that "If God were good, we'd live for a long time, *without suffering."* The devil offers us riches and delights in exchange for our loyalty, supposedly without suffering.

But Jesus came to suffer and die so that EVERYONE might be free from the weight of sin that plagues us. Jesus repeats His promise to us; *"I am the resurrection and the life; he who believes in Me will live even if he dies, and everyone who lives and believes in Me will never die. Do you believe this?"* **(John 11:25-26)**. Whoever dies believing in Christ **will rise again** when Christ returns for His church. In the world, we'll have many sufferings; as my sister-in-law says, *"When you have to suffer, you suffer."* Jesus said, *"In this world you will have trouble. But take heart! I have overcome the world"* **(John 16:33)**.

Let us pray: Dear God, thank You because, although our eyes might witness death and suffering, You are our inheritance, and in You, we trust forever. Thank you because death is not the end of life but a transition to eternal life in Your presence. **We'll rise again!** We thank and praise you in Jesus's name.

> **Whoever dies believing in Christ will rise again when Christ returns for His church.**

April 12
BELIEVING IN THE IMPOSSIBLE

"If we are thrown into the blazing furnace, the God we serve is able to deliver us from it, and he will deliver us from Your Majesty's hand." Daniel 3:17

"Su Majestad va a ver que nuestro Dios, a quien servimos, puede librarnos de ese ardiente horno de fuego, y también puede librarnos del poder de Su Majestad". **Daniel 3:17**

"Αν είναι έτσι, ο Θεός μας, που εμείς λατρεύουμε, είναι δυνατός να μας ελευθερώσει από το καμίνι τής φωτιάς που καίει· και από το χέρι σου, βασιλιά, θα μας ελευθερώσει." **ΔΑΝΙΗΛ 3:17**

Do you believe that there's anything impossible for God? Daniel's friends, **Shadrach, Meshach, and Abednego**, facing certain death, preferred to believe God would save them from the blazing fire rather than worship a god made by human hands.

King Nebuchadnezzar erected a statue and declared that, at the sound of music, *"Whoever does not fall down and worship will immediately be thrown into a blazing furnace"* **(Daniel 3:6)**. The music sounded, and everyone worshiped the statue except Daniel's friends.

The king asked them, *"Is it true… that you do not serve my gods or worship the image of gold I have set up?"* **(v.14)**. They demonstrated their unshakable faith in God, responding that God can deliver them from the blazing furnace. *"But even if he does not, we want you to know, Your Majesty, that we will not serve your gods or worship the image of gold you have set up"* **(vs. 16-18)**.

Verse 18 demonstrates their loyalty to God, who has indicated the magnitude of His jealousy and whose covenant states that His chosen people should not kneel or worship any god made by human hands. *"The idols of the nations are silver and gold, made by human hands. They have mouths, but cannot speak, eyes, but cannot see. They have ears, but cannot hear, nor is there breath in their mouths"* **(Psalm 135:15-17)**.

Shadrach, Meshach, and Abednego chose to be obedient to God's law, putting their own lives at risk. They believed that **there was nothing impossible for God.** The three were thrown into the fiery furnace, which was so hot that the flames killed the soldiers who threw them in **(v.22)**, but not a hair was burned on the three faithful men **(v.27)**.

Seeing that the three were unharmed, the king called them out of the furnace and declared, *"no other god can save in this way"* **(v.29).** My beloved, if we keep God's law in our hearts and demonstrate that *"with God, all things are possible,"* our friends and neighbors will also confess that our God is the only one who saves.

Let us pray: Dear God, increase our faith so that, like *Shadrach, Meshach, and Abednego*, we may believe in the impossible and be willing to face any human danger, except that of disobeying Your commands. We pray in Your Holy Name.

> **They chose to be obedient to God's law,**
> **putting their own lives at risk.**

April 13
SAVIOR GOD
Daniel 6:16c

Those who have not known the living God try to benefit themselves by falsely accusing and discrediting believers. However, **we serve a God who saves us from persecution.**

In Persia, *"the administrators and the satraps tried to find grounds for charges against Daniel in his conduct of government affairs, but they were unable to do so"* since Daniel was a just man **(Daniel 6:4).** They decided to convince King Darius to establish a law in which *"anyone who prays to any god or human being during the next thirty days, except to you, Your Majesty, shall be thrown into the lions' den."* They lied, saying that *"the royal administrators, prefects, satraps, advisers and governors have ALL agreed that the king should issue"* that edict **(Daniel 6:7-8).** However, Daniel, one of the administrators, wasn't informed of such a law, so it wasn't *"unanimous."*

Misinformed, the king approved that law, and upon hearing it, Daniel opened his windows, and **as was his custom**, he prayed to God fearlessly **(v.10).** The administrators informed the King that Daniel *"pays no attention to you, Your Majesty, or to the decree you put in writing. He still prays three times a day"* to his God **(v.13).**

The king wanted to free him based on Daniel's loyal service and witness, but the rulers objected, stating that the law was irrevocable. Distressed, King Darius ordered Daniel *"be thrown in the lions' den."* However, he said to Daniel: *"May your God, whom you serve continually, rescue you!"* **(v.16).** Daniel's faith awakened King Darius' faith! Very early the next day, the king went to the den and called Daniel, saying, *"Daniel, servant of the living God, has your God, whom you serve continually, been able to rescue you from the lions?"* **(v.20).**

The story has a good ending! God shut the lions' mouths. Karma: The lying administrators and their families were thrown into the pit, and they all died **(v.24).** King Darius wrote a new decree, which is today's prayer:

Let us pray: Dear God, all *"people must fear and reverence the God of Daniel. 'For You are the living God and you endure forever; Your kingdom will not be destroyed, Your dominion will never end. You rescue and save; You perform signs and wonders in the heavens and on the earth. You rescued Daniel from the power of the lions'"* **(vs.26-27).** Lord, have mercy on us; save us from this pandemic. We pray in your Holy Name.

Photo by: https://www.blackartdepot.com/products/daniel-in-the-lions-den-aaron-alan-hicks

---

We serve a God who saves us from persecution.

April 14
PERFECT PEACE
Isaiah 26:3

Perfect and permanent peace; More desired than gold and riches, it's strong like the wind and the waters of a rushing river, porous like the mist, promised by politicians, rulers, and heads of state, but only achievable by submitting to God's Lordship.

Peace evaded me despite the many blessings that God had poured out on my life. I tried to rest at night but couldn't achieve a night of deep and relaxing sleep. The worries of yesterday and tomorrow haunted my mind, causing my pillow to feel like a stone until I got to know intimately the One

who *"keeps in perfect peace those whose minds are steadfast, because they trust in you"* **(Isaiah 26:3).**

God grants us guidance, friendship, and perfect peace when we put all we are, have, and aspire to in His hands. Following are some favorite verses that demonstrate the qualities of God's peace.

115

✦ **It's an undeserved gift from God** - *"I will make a covenant of peace with them"* **(Ezekiel 34:25a).** Knowing that God is with us **gives us strength and peace (Psalm 29:11).**

✦ **God's peace is Abundant** - *"Great peace have those who love your law, and nothing can make them stumble"* **(Psalm 119:165).** The Lord himself will teach us, *"and great will be their peace"* **(Isaiah 54:13).**

✦ **It flows like a river** when we pay attention to God's commandments **(Isaiah 48:18).** God's peace is new every morning, like the river's waters, refreshing to the soul.

✦ **It's Jesus's legacy** - *"Peace I leave with you; my peace I give you. I do not give to you as the world gives. Do not let your hearts be troubled and do not be afraid"* **(John 14:27).**

✦ **It's our help and protection** - *"And the peace of God, which transcends all understanding, will guard your hearts and your minds in Christ Jesus"* **(Philippians 4:7).**

My beloved, the world is constantly attacking our senses, trying to steal our peace and seduce us into wild and aimless living. Put your trust in God, and you'll find peace even amid the worst storm.

Let us pray: Dear God, thank You for granting us Your perfect and eternal peace. *"Lord, you establish peace for us; all that we have accomplished you have done for us"* **(Isaiah 26:12).** We trust that our lives and homes rest safely in Your loving hands even amid this pandemic. But many still don't know you and are terrified of what may come tomorrow. Use us so that they too may know and enjoy **Your perfect, abiding peace**. We pray in Your Holy Name.

> **Perfect and permanent peace…**is only achievable by submitting to God's Lordship.

APRIL 15
GOD OF COVENANTS

"Lord, the great and awesome God, who keeps his covenant of love with those who love him and keep his commandments." **Daniel 9:4b**

"Señor, Dios grande y digno de ser temido, que cumples tu pacto y tu misericordia con los que te aman y cumplen tus mandamientos". **Daniel 9:4b**

"Ω, Κύριε, ο μεγάλος και φοβερός Θεός, που φυλάττει τη διαθήκη και το έλεος σ' εκείνους που τον αγαπούν, και τηρούν τις εντολές του!" **ΔΑΝΙΗΛ 9:4b**

Adam and Eve's sin in the Garden of Eden distorted the perfect relationship that God had planned for humanity. Since then, God activated His plan to re-establish an intimate relationship with us, where God would be our King, and we would be His obedient people. To do so, **God made several covenants with us**.

116

Instead of getting angry over our rebellion, **God made a covenant with Noah** to never again destroy the earth and its inhabitants through a flood **(Genesis 9:11).** The visible sign of the covenant is the rainbow.

The **covenant with Abram** promises to make him *"father of many nations"* **(Genesis 17:4).** The sign of the covenant was the circumcision of every male **(v.10).**

The **covenant with the Israelites** would make Israel God's chosen people of priests and kings; God would provide all their needs, and they would obey the ten commandments **(Exodus 34).**

The Davidic covenant promises to **establish the King's throne forever**. This covenant is between God and King David and his descendants **(2 Samuel 7:16). Jesus fulfills these covenants.** As a descendant of Abraham and David, Jesus was obedient in keeping the whole law, demonstrating that love and a heart dedicated to God can overcome the world's temptations.

Through the blood of Jesus shed on Calvary's cross, the sins of those who've placed their faith in Him are washed away, removing God's anger and punishment. Jesus Christ fulfills the Noah Covenant since God will never again destroy the world because of sin, but rather, God will forgive our trespasses through repentance and faith in Jesus.

In my daily walk and study of God's Word, I've discovered that all of God's promises are reliable. That's why *"In peace I will lie down and sleep, for you alone, Lord, make me dwell in safety"* **(Psalm 4:8).** Indeed, the Lord *"keeps his covenant of love with those who love him and keep his commandments"* **(Daniel 9:4b).**

> **God will never again destroy the world because of sin, but rather, God will forgive our trespasses through repentance and faith in Jesus.**

Let us Pray: Faithful **God of Covenants**; thank You for activating Your Plan to restore our relationship with you. Pour out Your Holy Spirit upon Your people so that we may be faithful and obedient to our part of the covenant. Write Your law in our hearts so that we may obey Your commands. May Your guidance, presence, and protection never be lacking in our house or in that of our children. Forgive our rebellions and heal us, Lord. We pray in Jesus's name.

April 16
HOW ARE MY FLOWERS?
1 John 2:28

Flowers don't grow on their own! They need ongoing nutrition and attention. You're a precious flower in God's garden, and by abiding in Him, you'll receive the daily nourishment needed to grow spiritually.

When my mother-in-law arrived from Greece in 2008, the first thing she did was plant flowers of many colors. For close to a year, she nurtured them, changing their location so that they'd receive

AND NOW, DEAR CHILDREN, CONTINUE IN HIM, SO THAT WHEN HE APPEARS WE MAY BE CONFIDENT AND UNASHAMED BEFORE HIM AT HIS COMING. 1 JOHN 2:28

Y AHORA, HIJITOS, PERMANEZCAN EN ÉL PARA QUE, CUANDO SE MANIFIESTE, TENGAMOS CONFIANZA, Y CUANDO VENGA NO NOS ALEJEMOS DE ÉL AVERGONZADOS. 1 JUAN 2:28

"ΚΑΙ ΤΩΡΑ, ΠΑΙΔΑΚΙΑ, ΝΑ Μ'ΕΝΕΤΕ Σ'ΑΥΤΟΝ· ΩΣΤΕ, ΟΤΑΝ ΦΑΝΕΡΩΘΕΙ, ΝΑ ΈΧΟΥΜΕ ΠΑΡΡΗΣΙΑ ΚΑΙ ΝΑ ΜΗ ΝΤΡΟΠΙΑΣΤΟΥΜΕ ΑΠ' ΑΥΤΟΝ ΚΑΤΑ ΤΗΝ ΠΑΡΟΥΣΙΑ ΤΟΥ." Α' ΙΩΑΝΝΟΥ 2:28

maximum sunlight. But then, she, along with Margarita and my father-in-law, returned to Greece and left me in charge of her flowers. Whenever my mother-in-law called, she'd ask, *"how are my flowers?"* Anticipating this, I made sure to water them at least once a week.

If I hadn't watered my mother-in-law's flowers for some time, they would have withered. It would have been sad to say, *"I'm sorry, but all your flowers died. I forgot, or I didn't have time to water them."* That says three things: 1. I don't appreciate her or consider what's important to her or brings her joy. 2. That I can't be responsible for small things, and 3. I'm not trustworthy. If we're faithful in tending God's garden, we won't feel ashamed; our world will be blessed by the peace and harmony that blooms in each flower because we faithfully watered them with God's love.

If humanity were a garden, God would ask us: **How are my flowers? How would you respond?** You might say, *"How did I wind up being responsible for the garden?"* In my case, nobody else was around to care for it, and my mother-in-law asked me. In God's garden, we became responsible when God adopted us into the family. Upon receiving Jesus, we became gardeners. There are many different flowers in God's garden. God loves each precious flower, and you're one of them. The Lord has granted us the privilege of taking care of EVERYONE of them.

> **There are many different flowers in God's garden. God loves each precious flower, and you're one of them. The Lord has granted us the privilege of taking care of EVERYONE of them.**

When we receive Christ by faith, God transforms us from ordinary people into new creatures with new and noble purposes, some as simple as watering your mother-in-law's flowers. God is knocking on our door and asking us: *How are my flowers?*

Let us pray: Dear God, help us faithfully tend Your garden so that all may grow in knowledge and faith in You. Feed us daily with Your Word and with the Light of the Holy Spirit. We pray in Your Holy Name.

APRIL 17
I'M NO LONGER WHO I WAS
1 Corinthians 15:10

In **1 Corinthians 15**, Saint Paul (formerly called Saul) recalls his previous life and confesses, *"For I... do not even deserve to be called an apostle, because I persecuted the church of God"* **(v.9). Acts 7:58 and 8:3** record how Saul *"began to destroy the church."*
This new man of God must have felt intense remorse for the lives he mistakenly took in God's name. Despite his extensive preparation, he didn't know God at all. However, after his transforming encounter with Jesus, Paul **knew** God's heart and declared, *"But by the grace of God I am what I am, and his grace to me was not without effect"* **(1 Corinthians 15:10).**

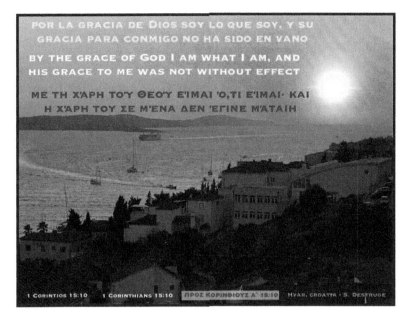

When looking back, some past experiences in our lives cause us remorse, shame, or pain. How can we respond in these cases?

PAIN: If we were offended, God calls us to demonstrate Jesus's humility and grace, who from the cross cried out, *"Father, forgive them because they don't know what they are doing"* **(Luke 23:34).** **Isaiah** prophesied that He would pray for His *"transgressors"* **(53:12).**

REMORSE: If we've offended God or neighbor, we must confess our sin, ask forgiveness, and seek peace, restoring what was lost or discredited.

SHAME: God, who sees and hears all, reveals things we've done in secret. We all have specific memories that cause some embarrassment, i.e., actions that, in God's eyes, weren't the best example for our children. It may have been as small as stealing candy from the store, or big, like misjudging people of different races, lifestyles, economic statuses, an addiction or an extra-marital affair, etc. When the Lord transforms us, we seek forgiveness and the strength and self-discipline not to repeat the sin against God and loved ones.

Not as justification, but God's Word says, *"in all things God works for the good of those who love him, who have been called according to his purpose"* **(Romans 8:28).** Even the pain that we're experiencing today, God can and will use it for good.

Let us pray: Dear God, help us learn from our past and proclaim together with Paul, *"by Your grace I am what I am, and Your grace to me was not without effect" (1 Corinthians 15:10).*

119

I'm no longer who I was, and tomorrow I won't be who I am today because You've promised to complete the *"good work that you began in me"* **(Philippians 1:6).** We pray in Jesus's name.

> *"But by the grace of God I am what I am, and his grace to me was not without effect"* **(1 Corinthians 15:10).**

April 18
PEACE BE WITH YOU
John 20:19

We're going through times in which we've quarantined ourselves in our homes.

The disciples were behind closed doors, traumatized by the crucifixion and fearful of what might happen to them. Even though Mary Magdalene had spoken with the risen Lord and recounted her experience to the disciples **(John 20:14-18),** their doors were closed, and perhaps their hearts were unwilling to continue the work that the Lord began with them.

The locked doors reflect the disciples' fear but also the power of the risen Christ, for whom there are no doors or tombs that can keep Him locked in or out.

Fear might distract us from digging deep into this meditation. Some may think, *"what will happen to our planet, the economy, our life, family, and work? Will we find a similar paying job? How long will we be in quarantine?"*

We don't know what will happen. But I know two things. 1. God has blessed us with gifts of faith and hope to encourage those overcome by fear. 2. God will not abandon us! At times like this, Jesus enters through our locked doors with words of comfort and security: **"Peace be with you."**

We can't see Him, but He is by your side, saying, *"Peace be with you!"* Our task is to be attentive to God's call and ready to obey His voice. Today we have to face that reality! There are many people in pain, scared behind closed doors and hearts. Some haven't been out of their locked houses for long periods, and loneliness weakens their faith and hope.

Either we let fear keep us frozen and locked within our sorrows, or we can honor the work of Jesus Christ, who, with great pain and sacrifice, raised us from our graves and sent us to serve and love our neighbor.

120

God wants us to put into practice the Sacred Scriptures' teachings:

✦ Be strong and continue the good work that the Lord began in and through us.

✦ Be more committed to the eternal things. Bring the good news to the poor, rich, children, elderly, homeless, orphans, and widows of all races, cultures, and lifestyles in our environment through all available means.

Let us pray: Dear God, thank You for speaking a word of Peace and security to our hearts. Help us believe that just as you were present in Jesus's works, Jesus will be present in our faith works. We pray in Your Holy Name.

✚ ✚ ✚ ✚ ✚ ✚

April 19
CALL TO LOVE, JUSTICE, AND COMMITMENT
1 John 3:14

Psalm 150:6 says, *"Let everything that has breath praise the Lord."* The best expression of praise and adoration for God is that His children show one another genuine love, justice, and total dedication.

Analyzing the readings from **1 John 3:10-16,** we can paraphrase **verse 10**: *"This is how we know who the children of God are. Anyone who does what is right and loves their brother and sister is God's child."* Above all, God wants us to be **just** and **love** one another.

Parents experience peace and joy when their children are happy and well accompanied. I thank God for Carlos's great love for my daughter Sophia. I saw it first when he came home to ask for Sophia's hand in marriage, and I've watched and admired it blooming through a decade. With their son Lázaro's birth, that love is multiplied and focused even more on the fruit of their love.

You and I are the fruit of God's love, who expects us to be demonstrative with our love, justice, and commitment. God's call to us is *"that we love one another"* **(1 John 3:11b).**

Without God's love, we're destined for death. However, showing genuine love transports us *"from death to life"* **(1 John 3:14a).** In other words, the seed of life germinates when nourished by love. **Without love, death wins, but death is powerless against love.** When we appreciate Jesus's sacrifice to save and improve our lives, we can say that *"we know what love is: Jesus Christ laid down his life for us"* **(1 John 3:16).**

121

Filled with gratitude for His great sacrifice, we freely and openly demonstrate that there's no more remarkable offering than to *"lay down our lives for our brothers and sisters"* (**1 John 3:16**). Giving one's life for another human being does not necessarily mean dying so that they may live, but rather that we become, in their lives, the constant presence and essence of Christ's love, putting their welfare above our own.

> **Giving one's life for another human being does not necessarily mean dying so that they may live, but rather that we become, in their lives, the constant presence and essence of Christ's love, putting their welfare above our own.**

Let us pray: Dear God, thank You for showing us Your love, justice, and dedication. Help us to be a reflection of Your love for our brothers and sisters in all places and situations. We pray in Jesus's name.

April 20
INTIMACY WITH CHRIST

"For I desire mercy, not sacrifice, and acknowledgment of God rather than burnt offerings."
Hosea 6:6

"Lo que yo quiero es misericordia, y no sacrificio; ¡conocimiento de Dios, más que holocaustos"! Oseas 6:6

"Επειδή, έλεος θέλω, και όχι θυσία· και επίγνωση Θεού περισσότερο, παρά ολοκαυτώματα."
ΩΣΗΕ 6:6 FPB

The true Christian desires to *know Christ intimately* (**Philippians 3:10**).

We Know Christ Intimately Through Faith - We must believe that Jesus is who He says He is, that driven by love, He came into the world to give His life so that through faith, we'd know Him and gain eternal life. St. Paul said: *"I consider everything a loss because of the surpassing worth of knowing Christ Jesus my Lord, for whose sake I have lost all things. I consider them garbage, that I may gain Christ"* (**Philippians 3:8**).

We Know Him Intimately Through Worship - Today's verse tells us: *"For I desire mercy, not sacrifice, and acknowledgment of God rather than burnt offerings"* (**Hosea 6:6**). God doesn't want sacrifices. He wants us to know Him intimately as He is. God reveals himself through the Holy Scriptures, our daily worship, and communion with Him and our neighbor. The best way to know God personally is to **abide continuously in His love and adoration.**

> **The best way to know God personally is to abide continuously in His love and adoration.**

It's taken me 47 years to know my wife's wishes, likes, and dislikes. We learn these through their self-revelation or from our daily life experiences. There's a saying: *"happy wife, happy life."* So true! The key to cultivating love is demonstrating that we know their character, tastes, and desires.

We Know God Intimately Through Obedience - We worship and adore God by knowing God's character and desires and obeying His commandments.

It's impossible to nurture an intimate relationship by doing what hurts or annoys the other person. We can't sing *"Jesus is my long desired friend"* and ignore His commands. *"Jesus wept"* and still weeps when we disobey Him. To declare *"Jesus is my Lord"* and that we enjoy an intimate relationship with Him, we must **do what brings Him joy**. Jesus says: *"You are my friends, if you do what I command"* **(John 15:14).**

We might fool the world, neighbor, or stranger into thinking that we live in obedience to God, but Jesus doesn't look at outward appearances. **Jesus looks inwardly at our hearts.** What God wants from us is *"mercy, not sacrifice, and acknowledgment of God rather than burnt offerings"* **(Hosea 6:6).**

Let us pray: Dear God, we desire to know you intimately and learn to do Your will. We desire to stop conforming to the world's standards but instead to be transformed **(Romans 12:2)** by an intimate knowledge of Your character and Word. Fill us with Your Holy Spirit, we pray in Jesus's name.

✛ ✛ ✛ ✛ ✛ ✛

April 21
GOD WANTS TO HEAL US
Mark 16:18b

There should be no doubt that the gifts given to the disciples, as occurs in a relay race, are also entrusted to the believers in each generation. *"Jesus called his twelve disciples to him and gave them authority to drive out impure spirits and to heal every disease and sickness"* **(Matthew 10:1).**

Today's verse begins with, *"And these signs will accompany those who believe: In my name they will…"* **(Mark 16:17).** God wants to heal us and that we completely heal His world **in Jesus's name.** But healing is incomplete and ineffective if we only focus on physical healing. For healing to be whole, we must seek and pray for physical, mental, spiritual, relational, and social recovery. In this way, if we pray with faith, **in the name of Jesus,** God will completely heal our world, people, and loved ones.

123

With faith and in Jesus's name, the apostles demonstrated the gift of healing, freely and openly; someone's *"father was sick in bed, suffering from fever and dysentery. Paul went in to see him and, after prayer, placed his hands on him and healed him"* (**Acts 28:8**).

Jesus healed the crowds. Wherever He went, the sick were brought to Him so that He would touch and heal them from various diseases (**Luke 4:40**). On one occasion, *"some people brought to him a man who was deaf and could hardly talk, and they begged Jesus to place his hand on him"* (**Mark 7:32**). Jesus performed the miracle on him, and *"the man's ears were opened, his tongue was loosened and he began to speak plainly"* (**Mark 7:35**).

Jesus didn't say, *"stay at home and wait for the sick to come to your doorstep."* Instead, He said, *"Go into all the world and preach the gospel to all creation"* (**Mark 16:15**). My beloved, we're called to go in search of the sick. When we find them, we must pray with faith, believing that God has given us the gift of healing, believing in Jesus's promise, *"Very truly I tell you, whoever believes in me will do the works I have been doing, and they will do even greater things than these"* (**John 14:12**).

Let us pray: Dear God, increase our faith to believe in Your Word and heal the sick around us. Enlighten us to attend to the whole person, not forgetting their emotional, social, and spiritual needs. Today more than ever, our world needs a healing miracle. We pray in Your Holy Name.

For healing to be whole, we must seek and pray for physical, mental, spiritual, relational, and social recovery.

April 22
IN MOMENTS OF FEAR

"Even though I walk through the darkest valley, I will fear no evil, for you are with me; your rod and your staff, they comfort me." **Psalm 23:4**

"Aunque pase por el valle de sombra de muerte, no temeré mal alguno, porque tú estás conmigo; tu vara y tu cayado me infunden aliento". **Salmo 23:4**

"Και μέσα σε κοιλάδα σκιάς θανάτου αν περπατήσω, δεν θα φοβηθώ κακό· επειδή, εσύ είσαι μαζί μου· η ράβδος σου και η βακτηρία σου, αυτές με παρηγορούν." **ΨΑΛΜΟΙ 23:4**

Psalm 23 allows us to place our life in God's hands, in whatever circumstances we find ourselves, because *"the Lord is our Shepherd."*

In times of COVID, we pray that Jesus, our *"Good Shepherd"* (**John 10:11**), keep our loved ones from harm's way. We rest in Jesus's promise to be with us all the days of our lives (**Matthew 28:20**).

Psalm 23 encourages us not to be afraid when we need sustenance, employment, resources, help with utility payments, warm clothing, etc. Because the Lord is our Shepherd, *"Nothing will be lacking"* **(v.1).**

When weary and burdened, tired, stressed, confused, and need spiritual rest, we shouldn't be afraid because our Good Shepherd *"leads us beside quiet waters"* **(v.2).** Jesus says: *"Come to me, all who labor and are tired, I will give you rest"* **(Matthew 11:28).**

When we need comfort and direction, God *"will comfort your soul, will guide you in paths of justice for his name's sake."* Jesus adds: *"Take my yoke upon you and learn from me, for I am gentle and humble in heart, and you will find rest for your souls"* **(Matthew 11:29).**

When facing danger, God's Word encourages us not to fear because *"Even though you walk through the darkest valley, you will fear no evil, for God is with you; His rod and His staff, they comfort you"* **(v.4).**

My beloved, when God closes one door, He opens a better one. And what God closes, no one can re-open, and what God opens, no one can shut. Even death's door is no longer feared because it brings us into God's presence.

Life is filled with circumstances that threaten, worry, pressure, and lead us to fear, but remember, DO NOT FEAR. *"THE LORD IS YOUR SHEPHERD"* AND WILL BE WITH YOU EVERY DAY OF YOUR LIFE.

Let us pray: Dear God, thank You for the safety and peace that Your Word offers us. Thank you because Jesus has prepared a place for us who believe in Him. Increase our faith so that in the most challenging moments, we may affirm, *"I will fear no evil, for you are with me."* We pray in Jesus's name.

April 23
YOUR WORDS MATTER

"But many who heard the message believed; so the number of men who believed grew to about five thousand." **Acts 4:4**

"Pero muchos de los que habían oído sus palabras, creyeron; y contados solamente los varones eran como cinco mil". Hechos 4:4

"Πολλοί, μάλιστα, από εκείνους που άκουσαν τον λόγο πίστεψαν· και ο αριθμός των ανδρών έγινε περίπου 5.000." **ΠΡΑΞΕΙΣ ΑΠΟΣΤΟΛΩΝ 4:4**

"The Words Matter Movement involves being a practitioner of careful, thoughtful and deliberate positive communication… When words are used in the wrong way, it can be devastating."[7]

---

[7] The Words Matter Movement - Operational Excellence Society (opexsociety.org).

It's equally devastating when, for whatever reason, we silence the words that have the power to save lives. If we don't speak, many will be lost. Sometimes clergy ask ourselves, what difference do our ministry and witness make? This question also applies to the lay believer. The answer is not in the difference but in the importance of your testimony within God's plan to rescue His children.

"But many who heard the message believed; so the number of men who believed grew to about five thousand" **(Acts 4:4).** This verse affirms the importance and impact of our words. **Thoughtful and inspired words** rescued more than five thousand souls from the enemy's clutches. In addition to preaching, the apostles met for praise, worship, and offer help to the needy. *"And the Lord added to their number daily those who were being saved"* **(Acts 2:47b).**

Every instrument in a symphony is essential in creating the harmonious melody the composer had in mind when he wrote it, from the smallest to the largest in size and projection. You're crucial to God's symphony. Your words and actions matter. What you say or do in the Lord's name is vital in rescuing the lost sheep, encouraging the disgruntled ones, and lovingly correcting the confused ones who act like goats.

Your words and actions matter.

You may have heard the saying, *"You are the only Bible that some people will read."* This comes from **1 Timothy 4:16**, which says, *"Watch your life and doctrine closely. Persevere in them, because if you do, you will save both yourself and your hearers."* Many observe our lives to see if we act worthy of our name, Christian. Based on your words and actions, many unaware of God's love or who've turned away from God will run back to Him **(Isaiah 55:5).**

Let us pray: Dear God, thank You for reminding us that our words and actions matter in Your rescue plan. Help us put fear aside and speak with courage and joy about what You've done, are doing, and promised to do in our lives. We pray in Jesus's name.

✛ ✛ ✛ ✛ ✛ ✛

April 24
FIRM IN PURPOSE

"You, Lord, give perfect peace to those who keep their purpose firm and put their trust in you." Isaiah 26:3 GNT

"Al de firme propósito guardarás en perfecta paz, porque en ti confía". Isaías 26:3

"Θα φυλάξεις σε τέλεια ειρήνη το πνεύμα που επιστηρίζεται επάνω σε σένα, επειδή, σε σένα έχει το θάρρος του." Ησαίασ 26:3

Today's verse calls to be lifted from its pages to gain free flight in our minds and hearts.

126

"Those who keep their purpose firm" recognize from where their help, inheritance, and daily provision come. Therefore, filled with perfect peace and gratitude, they offer the best of themselves to the Lord. *"What shall I return to the Lord for all his goodness to me?"* **(Psalm 116:12).**

"Those who keep their purpose firm" recognize the price that God paid for their rescue and won't fear any evil that might come their way. They know that *"Precious in the sight of the Lord is the death of his faithful servants"* **(Psalm 116:15).** They recognize God's pain and are moved by those suffering from the early departure of loved ones. Especially for the inability to have a traditional, dignified burial ceremony in COVID times.

"Those who keep their purpose firm" recognize their debt to the Lord for everything they are and have. They pledge, *"I will sacrifice a thank offering to you and call on the name of the Lord"* **(Psalm 116:17).** Their soul is filled with gratitude, praise, and testimonies that seek to fly like butterflies so that everyone might see the transformation that God has done in their lives.

In our greatest need, we cry out to God, who says, *"Come to me, all you who are weary and burdened, and I will give you rest"* **(Matthew 11:28).** Jesus carried our burdens and we've made vows and promises to God. **Those who** *keep their purpose firm* **say**, *"I will fulfill my vows to the Lord in the presence of all his people" (Psalm 116:18).*

God keeps the "firm of purpose" in perfect peace because they trust Him. *"Trust in the Lord forever, for the Lord, the Lord himself, is the Rock eternal"* **(Isaiah 26:4).**

"Those who keep their purpose firm" don't consider it unbearable when God calls us to *"be holy because He is holy"* **(1 Peter 1:16).**

Let us pray: Dear God, grant us **firm hearts that**, filled with gratitude and perfect peace, **trust you and** fulfill the vows made to you and our neighbor. May testimonies of Your beauty, love, and goodness fly from our lips like butterflies of a thousand colors. Help us behave like Your *"obedient children,"* leaving behind our old lifestyles and desires to serve and glorify you. We pray in Your Holy Name.

April 25
AT THE RESURRECTION OF THE RIGHTEOUS

"and you will be blessed. Although they cannot repay you, you will be repaid at the resurrection of the righteous." **Luke 14:14**

"y así serás dichoso. Porque aunque ellos no te puedan devolver la invitación, tu recompensa la recibirás en la resurrección de los justos". **Lucas 14:14**

"Και θα είσαι μακάριος· επειδή, δεν έχουν να σου ανταποδώσουν· δεδομένου ότι, η ανταπόδοση θα γίνει σε σένα κατά την ανάσταση των δικαίων."
ΚΑΤΑ ΛΟΥΚΑΝ 14:14

We don't know when Jesus will return, but when the trumpet sounds on that final day, those who died believing in Jesus will rise and receive new, incorruptible bodies. Those who are alive will be instantly transformed from mortal to immortal. They will shed the corruptible and be clothed with incorruption **(1 Corinthians 15:51-53).**

We generally fear death, even though it's our escort into the arms of our Savior. **At the resurrection of the righteous,** God *"will swallow up death forever"* **(Isaiah 25:8A).** There will be no more diseases, plagues, hunger, lies, suffering, or pain. *"Then the saying that is written will come true: "Death has been swallowed up in victory"* **(1 Corinthians 15:54).**

> **When the trumpet sounds on that final day, those who died believing in Jesus will rise and receive new, incorruptible bodies. Those who are alive will be instantly transformed from mortal to immortal.**

At the resurrection of the righteous, *"The Sovereign Lord will wipe away the tears from all faces; he will remove his people's disgrace from all the earth"* **(Isaiah 25:8B).** I've asked myself, *"If there will be no more death or pain upon reaching heaven, why would it be necessary for God to wipe tears from our faces?"*

Some images come to mind. **At the resurrection of the righteous -**
1. We'll reunite with loved ones who are resting today. There'll be a great gathering and rejoicing that our eyes fill with tears. *God will wipe away every tear.*

2. We will NOT find some loved ones whom we wanted to see in heaven, and we'll cry with sadness. *God will wipe away every tear,* and from then on, there will be no more sadness or pain.

3. We'll appear before God's judgment court. Jesus will defend the righteous, saying, *"He or she belongs to me. Because I was hungry, and he/she fed me."* **(Matthew 25:35).** Surprised, they'll ask, *"Lord, when did we see you hungry and feed you?"* Jesus will answer: *"Truly I tell you, whatever you did for one of the least of these brothers and sisters of mine, you did for me"* **(Matthew 25:40).** We'll weep from joy upon being found innocent, and **God will wipe away all tears.**

Let us pray: Thank you, Lord, because You promise to wipe away our tears. By faith and gratitude for Christ's saving grace, we're moved to help the fallen and needy. Thank you because when we invite them to our tables or circles of friendship and warmth, you promise to reward us *"at the resurrection of the righteous"* **(Luke 14:14).** Praise be to you, Lord.

April 26
MUTUAL RESPECT

"In the same way, you who are younger, submit yourselves to your elders." 1 Peter 5:5a.

"También ustedes, los jóvenes, muestren respeto ante los ancianos, y todos ustedes, practiquen el mutuo respeto". 1 Pedro 5:5a

"ΠΑΡΟΜΟΙΑ, ΟΙ ΝΕΟΤΕΡΟΙ, ΝΑ ΥΠΟΤΑΧΘΕΙΤΕ ΣΤΟΥΣ ΠΡΕΣΒΥΤΕΡΟΥΣ· ΟΛΟΙ, ΜΑΛΙΣΤΑ, ΚΑΘΩΣ ΘΑ ΥΠΟΤΑΣΣΕΣΤΕ Ο ΕΝΑΣ ΣΤΟΝ ΑΛΛΟΝ." Α´ ΠΕΤΡΟΥ 5:5Α

Being that we have a common enemy, today, more than ever, we need to be more understanding and patient and work together respectfully toward the true peace that comes from Christ.

Our homes, churches, and communities need God's healing peace. As today's verse tells, we construct the road of peace by being mutually respectful, submissive, and tolerant. That means respecting others' ideas, beliefs, or practices, even when they're different or contrary to our own.

We all seek *"the way, the truth, and the life"* **(John 14:6).** We need God's enlightenment to learn how to bring the good news of Jesus Christ to the world, beginning in our homes and spreading outward. Yet, it's not an easy task considering that in these times;
1. Our children and youth are losing their trust in God, the church, or both, and
2. They can obtain hundreds of online opposing philosophies on "finding or accessing God."

Against this background, the Spirit of Jesus invites us to consider the words **endure, suffer, cooperate,** and **"respect."**

In 33 years of walking with the Lord, God has led me to sprinkle encounters with individuals of different cultures and beliefs with genuine respect, interest, and curiosity to understand and seek common ground. Initially, some meetings showed resistance, distrust, anger, or even disgust. God transformed those negative feelings into genuine long-term relationships of friendship, peace, and cooperation by showing respect, concern, and kindness.

I consider myself a person inclined toward tradition, somewhat conservative, and continue to struggle with the notion of being more tolerant, that is, of **not judging people's actions beforehand,** leaving God to judge and transform hearts. Who knows, maybe the heart needing transformation might be my own?

Let us pray: Dear Lord, help us seek Your peace through mutual respect. As the song says: *"Let there be peace on earth. And let it begin with me,*[8]*"* in my home, with my children, siblings, friends, family, and foreigners. Lord, heal our sick. Comfort those who mourn. We pray in Jesus's name.

April 27
OUR SADNESS WILL END

"Never again will they hunger; never again will they thirst. The sun will not beat down on them, 'nor any scorching heat." Revelation 7:16

"No volverán a tener hambre ni sed, ni les hará daño el sol ni el calor los molestará".
Apocalipsis 7:16

---

[8] by Jill Jackson-Miller and Sy Miller, 1955

"Δεν θα πεινάσουν πλέον ούτε θα διψάσουν πλέον ούτε θα πέσει επάνω τους ο ήλιος ούτε κανένα καύμα·" **ΑΠΟΚΑΛΥΨΗ ΙΩΑΝΝΟΥ 7:16**

Glory to God, Hallelujah! Come, my beloved friends and family, as **Psalm 95** says, *"Come, let us bow down in worship, let us kneel before the Lord our Maker; for he is our God and we are the people of his pasture, the flock under his care"* **(Vs. 6-7).**

God deserves our gratitude and praise. In **2020-21**, God shepherded us through one of the worst and most fearful valleys. But remember that suffering doesn't last forever. After the storm comes the calm **(Mark 4:39).** We've wept for those God called home and celebrated those who recovered from COVID.

Today's verse encourages us to walk with God because in God's time, *"He will swallow up death forever. The Sovereign Lord will wipe away the tears from all faces; he will remove his people's disgrace from all the earth"* **(Isaiah 25:8).**

Rejoice, my beloved friends and family, *"Come, and let us worship Him!"* Because *"Your sun will never set again, and your moon will wane no more; the Lord will be your everlasting light, and your days of sorrow will end"* **(Isaiah 60:20).**

Let us worship God, my beloved, for the day is coming when *"God will turn our lament into dance"* **(Psalm 30:11).** God says He will end our sadness; *"I will rejoice over Jerusalem and take delight in my people; the sound of weeping and of crying will be heard in it no more"* **(Isaiah 65:19).**

My beloved, nothing is forever. My sister-in-law Fanny joked around, saying, *"when you have to suffer, you must suffer!"* But God assures us that the end of our suffering is near. The glorious day is coming when God will call us into His presence, and *"He will wipe every tear from their eyes. There will be no more death or mourning or crying or pain, for the old order of things has passed away"* **(Revelation 21:4).**

Let us pray: Thank you, Lord, for reminding us that the road ahead is neither long nor impossible and that very soon, **you will end our sadness**. Help us comfort those who mourn and guide Your sheep back to Your pastures. We pray in Your Holy Name.

April 28
DELIGHT YOURSELF IN FORGIVING

"Who is a God like you, who pardons sin and forgives the transgression of the remnant of his inheritance? You do not stay angry forever but delight to show mercy." **Micah 7:18**

"¿Qué otro Dios hay como tú, que perdona la maldad y olvida el pecado del remanente de su pueblo? Tú no guardas el enojo todo el tiempo, porque te deleitas en la misericordia". **Miqueas 7:18**

"Ποιος Θεός είναι όμοιος με σένα, που να συγχωρεί ανομία, και να παραβλέπει την παράβαση του υπολοίπου τής κληρονομιάς του; Δεν διατηρεί για πάντα την οργή του, επειδή αυτός αρέσκεται σε έλεος." **Μιχαίας 7:18**

There's no god like our God, merciful and compassionate, who **delights in forgiving and blessing** His children and the children of their children for a thousand generations. The Bible teaches us that **only God has the power to forgive sins**. *"Who can forgive sins but God alone?"* **(Luke 5:21, Mark 2:7).** On the great and fearsome day, when we all appear before God's Judgment Seat, only Jesus has the absolute power to judge and forgive our many sins, thus deciding our eternal future.

At the same time, God calls us, as far as it's within our capacity, to *"live in peace with all"* **(Romans 12:18).** Therefore, as God's children, we must be quick to listen and **delight ourselves in forgiving others.** Although our forgiveness doesn't determine the eternal future of those who've offended us, it guides us toward a harmonious relationship here on earth.

> As God's children, we must be quick to listen and **delight ourselves in forgiving others.**

We're not gods to judge, but we're called to imitate our heavenly Father as children of God. *"Just as He who called you is Holy, so be holy in all you do"* **(1 Peter 1:15).** We reflect our level of holiness and love for God when we **delight in forgiving our neighbor.**

Yet, it's not enough to forgive. We must also forget, as God does. Though His anger may last for a night, *"God will again have compassion on us; He will tread our sins underfoot and hurl all our iniquities into the depths of the sea"* **(Micah 7:19).** It's challenging to forget without the help of the Holy Spirit, who reminds us that only God can judge - our job is to love and **delight ourselves in forgiving and showing mercy.**

Philippians 4:13 says that **"yes you can"** forgive and forget when you do it in the name and **power of Jesus.** In addition, God tells us in **Revelation 21:7,** *"Those who are victorious will inherit all this, and I will be their God and they will be my children."* **Glory to God!**

Let us pray: Dear God, thank You for reminding us that you're our *"faithful God, keeping Your covenant of love to a thousand generations of those who love you and keep your commandments"* **(Deuteronomy 7:9).** Please help us be faithful imitators who **delight in loving and forgiving our neighbor**, thus demonstrating that we are Your children. We pray in the name of our Lord and Savior, Jesus Christ.

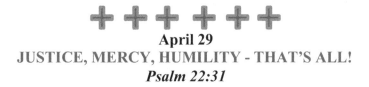

April 29
JUSTICE, MERCY, HUMILITY - THAT'S ALL!
Psalm 22:31

God expects His children to be righteous in their actions, as God is! In **Micah 6:8**, God tells us, *"He has shown you, O mortal, what is good. And what does the Lord require of you? To act justly and to love mercy and to walk humbly with your God."*

Justice, Mercy, and Humility - That's all God expects from His children. It's not a requirement

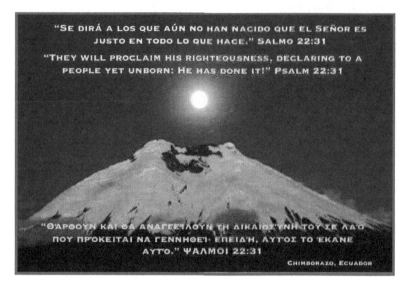

for salvation but rather **a commandment** for those who consider themselves redeemed. God knows the path of life, good and evil, and wants to lead us along the good side. Therefore, we should **strive to be just in all things**.

Justice, Mercy, and Humility are not suggestions but what God requires of His disciples.

Justly (**mišpāṭ**) means a just action that promotes equality among humanity. Justice is giving another person what they deserve as a human being. The final result of justice is to bring us toward peace, a balance that rectifies injustices, and the disadvantaged regain their prosperity and dignity.

"To act justly" is being intentionally aware of our environment's social needs and injustices and fighting to correct them. Unfortunately, we're often too quick to identify the culprit and justify our inaction. For example, *"He chose that kind of life (guilty), and I can't help him until he chooses to change."* God didn't call us to judge but bring healing and hope to a broken world through justice.

"To love mercy" is to show kindness to others freely, voluntarily, and without reciprocity. **Merciful** is being compassionate for the suffering of others and being pious, kind, lenient, and consoling, as in stooping down in kindness to an inferior. Jesus said in **Matthew 5:7,** *"Blessed are the merciful, for they shall obtain mercy."*

"To walk humbly with your God" means living in conscious communion with God, exercising a spirit of humility before Him, and not being proud like the Israelite leaders of whom Jesus said: *"Woe to you, teachers of the law and Pharisees, you hypocrites! You give a tenth of your spices—mint, dill and cumin. But you have neglected the more important matters of the law—justice, mercy and faithfulness"* **(Matthew 23:23). That's all!**

Let us pray: Dear God, grant us merciful hearts like yours and enlighten our minds and hearts to acquire full knowledge of Your character and virtues and be a better reflection of Your Son, Jesus Christ, in whose name we pray.

April 30
UNMUTE GOD
Amos 8:11

If God allows, at the time of publishing this meditation, I'll be flying over the Atlantic, heading for Greece, my second home.

This weekend, in Greece, we celebrate Orthodox Easter. Today, April 30, 2021, is Good Friday, a day of mourning and lament for my Greek family and friends. Two thousand years ago, the people and religious leaders, **with muted receptors**, didn't recognize the Messiah, and due to jealousy and fear, they crucified Him as a criminal.

The prophet Amos speaks of a season on earth when there will be *"a famine of hearing the words of the Lord"* (**Amos 8:11**). From the time of the minor prophets until the birth of Jesus Christ, God had stopped speaking to the people through the prophets. There was a complete silence of almost 400 years from Malachi to the gospels.

We're going through a season of silence, not because God has stopped speaking, but because **many have put God on "mute."** With an abundance of theologies and philosophies, our youth frequently embrace and nurture theologies that superficially appear humane but inherently go against God's Word; and we've said, *"it's okay! Let them explore and decide for themselves."* In a way, our generation has become complicit in silencing God.

> Our youth frequently embrace and nurture theologies that superficially appear humane but inherently go against God's Word; and we've said, *"it's okay! Let them explore and decide for themselves."* **In a way, our generation has become complicit in silencing God.**

God has entrusted us with our youth's spiritual care and nurturing as parents and church elders. We must demonstrate that God's Word is supreme in our homes and feed our children with it to stand firm in the faith when the world presents them with opposing philosophies.

To those who didn't have a humble heart, Jesus spoke *"in parables: 'Though seeing, they do not see; though hearing, they do not hear or understand'"* (**Matthew 13:13**). To those who resist His Word, *"God gave them a spirit of stupor, eyes that could not see and ears that could not hear, to this very day"* (**Romans 11:8**).

My beloved, rest assured that God is still speaking today. **We have to unmute GOD**.

Let us pray: Dear God, grant that our receptors always be in tune with Your signal and that we never allow Your Word to be put on **"mute"** in our homes. Heal our sick and planet. We pray in Jesus's name.

- MAY -
THE SANDOVAL / ORTEGA FAMILY

From my mother Lilia's side, my great-grandfather, **Abel Fernando Ortega** (1882-1959, known as Papá Abel) was the son of José María Ortega and Mamá Jesús Jarri Lasso. Papá Abel and Luz María Nolivos Jarrin had two children: My grandmother, **María Angélica Carlota Ortega (1911- 2004, known as Mamá Carlota)** and **Alfredo** Ortega. Papá Abel also had four children with Rosario Morales Castellano: Jaime Isaac (1921-1979), Lucrecia (1924-2012), Judith (1927), and José Jorge Ortega Morales (1929-2021 - See March 1).

(ALFREDO AND MAMÁ CARLOTA).

My great-grandparents, **Mariano Sandoval Sandoval** and **María Olimpia Sandoval Alban** were cousins, and had three sons, and three daughters: Maria Virginia Sandoval Sandoval (1900-1940), my grandfather, **Leonardo Segundo Aparicio** (1902-3/6/1985), **Mariolimpia**, Laura, Carlos, and José Sandoval Sandoval.

Grand-parents: Around 1927, in Latacunga, Ecuador, Alfredo Ortega married Mariolimpia Sandoval, and Alfredo's sister (Carlota) married Mariolimpia's brother, **Aparicio Sandoval**. My **grandparents**, papá Aparicio and mamá Carlota had 15 children. My mom, **Lilia María Sandoval Ortega** was their first born (September 13, 1928 - 11/15/2008). Her siblings are: Teresa (1930-2001), Susana (1932), Rene (1934-2/22/2010), Sara (1936), Maria de Lourdes (unknown DOB/DOD), Olga (1939), Ricardo Washington (5/10/1941- 4/21/2021), Elsa (3/4/43- 2013), Gloria (1944-7/3/2019), Guadalupe (1947), Eduardo Aparicio (1948) and Rodrigo Mariano (12/23/1951).

MAMÁ CARLOTA & PAPÁ APARICIO

My grandparents weren't wealthy or middle class, but they dressed stylishly because papá Aparicio was a tailor. For two short periods before age 10, my mom and I lived with my grandparents at **"La 5 de Junio"** and **"La Loja."** I remember papá Aparicio teaching me how to hem pants by hand and machine, sew buttons, and iron pants. Tio **Alfredo** was great friends with my dad, and for a short time, we lived near their home in **"La Méjico,"** and we'd get free hair-cuts from him. I've been blessed to have a good relationship with his children and my great-uncle **Jaime's** kids.

Who would have known that approximately 50 years later, two Destruge brothers would marry two Xanthopoúlou sisters? God's plans are always perfect. The result of their union and our unions have created the most amazing, beautiful children. God is good!

May 1
FREEDOM TO SERVE
1 Peter 2:16 ERV

As rescued and redeemed believers, *"we must help the weak, remembering the words the Lord Jesus himself said: 'It is more blessed to give than to receive'"* **(Acts 20:35).** We have complete **freedom to serve** and show our love for God and our neighbors. *"Against love, there is no law"* **(Galatians 5:23).**

Romans 13:1 says, *"Let everyone be subject to the governing authorities, for there is no authority except that which God has established. The authorities that exist have been established by God."*

The question arises; Why do some use their freedom to do evil by passively or openly disobeying the authorities?

We're free to serve, but God's Word says, *"Do not put the Lord your God to the test"* **(Matthew 4:7, Deuteronomy 6:16).** However, we see some churches testing God and disobeying local laws. During the peak of the pandemia, they continue their in-person worship services, with crowds above the maximum number of people, without wearing protective masks.

God calls us to be prudent and considerate - NOT to use our freedom to do evil, but *"to serve God. Show respect for all people. Love your brothers and sisters in God's family. Respect God, and honor the king"* **(1 Peter 2:16-17).**

Before acting or speaking, ask yourself if what you're contemplating;
+ Shows respect and gratitude for God and the authorities?
+ Puts someone's faith, life, or health at risk?

When in doubt, we should do our acts of random kindness for others because it's better *"to give than to receive"* **(Acts 20:35).**

Several nurses in my family have publicly begged everyone to *"Stay home."* Put yourselves in their shoes, and imagine the risk to which doctors, nurses, first responders, and social workers expose themselves when caring for the infected. They risk their health because one of their professional vows says, *"I will prevent disease whenever I can, for prevention is preferable to cure."*

Doctors **use their freedom** and licenses **to serve humanity.** When we act without considering the welfare of others, we disrespect life and become instruments of evil. We must fear God and respect the authorities. Otherwise, our society will continue in chaos.

Let us pray: Dear God, give us prudent hearts that guard and respect the authorities and protect the health and well-being of the masses. Give us humility and gratitude to put our freedom aside and serve you and our neighbor. We pray in Your Holy Name.

May 2
GOD'S LOST SHEEP
Ezekiel 34:11

Today more than ever, we need shepherds to search for **lost sheep** scattered by deception, fear, lack of knowledge, or disenchantment with the church. Everything that God does or causes us to do has its goal of searching **and rescuing His lost sheep.**

Psalm 23 is one of the most precious and treasured psalms. We've engraved it in our hearts for times as these when life's circumstances are overwhelming.

In Ezekiel 34:1-16, God accuses the false shepherds of *"only taking care of themselves"* **(v.1)** and of not taking care of or going in search of lost sheep **(v.3-4)**. God will *"hold accountable"* those who enrich their finances and stomachs instead of strengthening and healing the sheep's wounds **(v.10)**.

Despite the unjust shepherds, God assures, *"I myself will search for my sheep and look after them. As a shepherd looks after his scattered flock when he is with them, so will I look after my sheep. I will rescue them from all the places where they were scattered on a day of clouds and darkness"* **(vs. 11-12)**.

Even if we were lost or distanced from God, we're not abandoned or rejected; God walks beside us, strengthening us by saying, *"I myself will tend my sheep and have them lie down, declares the Sovereign Lord"* **(v.15)**.

In Luke 15:1-7, the Pharisees and scribes murmured against Jesus, saying, *"This man welcomes sinners and eats with them"* **(v.2)**. Jesus responded with the Parable of the lost sheep in which the Good Shepherd leaves the ninety-nine to search for the lost one until he finds it. Then he *"joyfully puts it on his shoulders"* and carries it back home **(vs.5-6)**. Jesus said that *"there will* *be more rejoicing in heaven over one sinner who repents than over ninety-nine righteous persons who do not need to repent" (Luke 15:7).* **Repentance** is the only condition for returning to God's arms.

Though not all are pastors, we've all received the **gift of reconciliation** so that we may go in search of those who've left the fold and live tormented by wolves. **God is counting on your gift of reconciliation to bring the sheep home!**

Let us pray: Dear God, thank You because when we were hurt and suffering, distanced from you, you rescued and healed our wounds. You took us in Your arms and brought us into the warmth of Your eternal home. Grant us hearts like Jesus so that we may go in search of Your suffering lost sheep. We pray in Your Holy Name.

✛ ✛ ✛ ✛ ✛ ✛

May 3
IF GOD TURNED HIS BACK ON US
Psalm 80:19

God cares for us every season, but something about the Sun's rays and warmth fills us with energy and hope. After a long winter quarantined at home, sitting in the sun's warmth on my mother-in-law's balcony in Katerini, Greece, I feel revitalized and restored.

Without the sun's light, the Earth would be covered by an impenetrable layer of ice, and everything would die within a month. Can you imagine what would become of us if God turned His back on us and we didn't have the radiance of His face?

If God turned His back on us, we'd be without sustenance, breath, protection, hope, and life. But, by seeking God's face and will, the Lord promises to rescue us from a mediocre life and place us on heavenly balconies where we can sense the Son's Divine warmth and aroma, leading us back to life and hope.

"ΕΠΙΣΤΡΕΨΕ ΜΑΣ, ΚΥΡΙΕ ΤΩΝ ΔΥΝΑΜΕΩΝ· ΕΠΙΛΑΜΨΕ ΤΟ ΠΡΟΣΩΠΟ ΣΟΥ, ΚΑΙ ΘΑ ΛΥΤΡΩΘΟΥΜΕ." ΨΑΛΜΟΙ 80:19

SEÑOR, DIOS DE LOS EJÉRCITOS, ¡RESTÁURANOS! ¡HAZ RESPLANDECER TU ROSTRO, Y SEREMOS SALVADOS! SALMO 80:19

"RESTORE US, LORD GOD ALMIGHTY; MAKE YOUR FACE SHINE ON US, THAT WE MAY BE SAVED." PSALM 80:19

FLYING OVER SWISS ALPS - APRIL 30, 2021

If God turned His back on us, our lives would lack joy. We'd be between **the sword and a wall,** inclined to disobedience. Only God's face can *"restore to us the joy of salvation"* and give us *"a willing spirit"* to obedience **(Psalm 51:12).**

If God turned His back on us, we'd be physically and emotionally devastated, watching everything we value die. We'd cry heartbroken until death knocked on our door. Our only hope is to seek God's face, crying for mercy. Then, God promises to *"heal, comfort, and lead those who* *mourn"* **(Isaiah 57:18).** Despite our failings, God says, *"Return, faithless people; I will cure you of backsliding"* **(Jeremiah 3:22).** *"I will restore you to health and heal your wounds,"* says He, whose face sustains and rescues us **(Jeremiah 30:17).**

If God turned His back on us, His anger would be noticeable in every aspect of our lives, becoming unbearable. But God's love is so great and merciful that, **if we repent,** the Lord promises to heal our rebellion. *"I will heal their waywardness and love them freely, for my anger has turned away from them"* **(Hosea 14:4).**

Let us pray: Dear God, thank You for **not turning Your back on us,** despite our rebellions. You sent Jesus to show us *"the Way, the Truth, and the Life" (John 14:6),* to teach us to seek Your face and trust Your promises. Thank you because *"You will again have compassion on us; you will tread our sins underfoot and hurl all our iniquities into the depths of the sea"* **(Micah 7:19).** We pray in Your Holy Name.

✚ ✚ ✚ ✚ ✚

May 4
WHEN GOD'S SPIRIT COMES UPON US
Isaiah 32:15

God declares a time of desolation followed by restoration for the people and the earth *when the Spirit of God comes upon us*.

We must understand the level and magnitude of the desolation to appreciate and seek the promised blessing. God declares a season of complete desolation that will fill the people with tears and panic because, in the land that produced fruits, wheat, and flowers, *"thorns and briers will overgrow,"* and the joy will end in all the houses of the happy city **(Isaiah 32:13).**

Desolation doesn't come by chance. It germinates by negligence and disobedience of those in charge of caring for the people and the land. *"The fortress will be abandoned, the noisy city deserted; citadel and watchtower will become a wasteland forever, the delight of donkeys, a pasture for flocks"* **(v.14).** Desolation will continue until *"the Spirit is poured on us from on high"* **(v.15a).**

When the Spirit of God comes upon us, then nature will also be restored. Where there's a king, steward, and an honest and righteous people guided by the Spirit of God, who repent in obedience to God, *"the desert becomes a fertile field, and the fertile field seems like a forest"* **(v.15b).** We will no longer have to advocate for the law, justice, and peace as these will be

139

our standards. *"The Lord's justice will dwell in the desert, his righteousness live in the fertile field. The fruit of that righteousness will be peace; its effect will be quietness and confidence forever"* **(vs.16-17).**

When the Spirit of God comes upon us, we'll finally find true peace and security, and our souls will have eternal rest and joy. Filled with the Holy Spirit, our Good Shepherd will lead us to *"lie down in green pastures, ... beside quiet waters"* **(Psalm 23:2).** The Lord says, *"My people will live in peaceful dwelling places, in secure homes, in undisturbed places of rest"* **(Isaiah 32:18).**

Jesus said, *"The Spirit gives life; the flesh counts for nothing. The words I have spoken to you—they are full of the Spirit and life"* **(John 6:63).** Without God's Spirit, we're nothing but bones with flesh, lifeless, void of joy, destined for desolation.

Let us pray: Dear God, thank You for making us *"competent as ministers of a new covenant ... of the life-giving Spirit"* **(2 Corinthians 3:6).** May Your Holy Spirit be poured out on all the earth's inhabitants. We pray in Jesus's name.

May 5
GOD ANSWERS PRAYER

"Before they call I will answer; while they are still speaking I will hear." Isaiah 65:24

"Antes de que me pidan ayuda, yo les responderé; no habrán terminado de hablar cuando ya los habré escuchado". **Isaías 65:24**

"Και πριν αυτοί κράξουν, εγώ θα αποκρίνομαι· και ενώ αυτοί μιλούν, εγώ θα ακούω."
ΗΣΑΪΑΣ 65:24

When I was an executive in finances, many times, my assistant, Chris Palmer, surprised me by creating something that, at some point, I had said, *"It would be nice if we had ..."* Suddenly, what I had mentioned in passing, Chris had created it. Likewise, in today's verse, God promises, *"Before they call I will answer; while they are still speaking I will hear"* **(Isaiah 65:24).**

This verse appears in the middle of the section titled **"New Heavens and a New Earth,"** in which God describes a new reality for His children; There will be no more weeping or crying, no premature deaths, no memory of the first heaven and earth. There will be joy and gladness. The people will build houses, plant vineyards, and enjoy them. *"They will not labor in vain, nor will they bear children doomed to misfortune; for they will be a people blessed by the Lord, they and their descendants with them. Before they call I will answer; while they are still speaking I will hear"* **(Isaiah 65:17-24).**

I know that God's eyes are on His children, and His ears are attentive to our groans and needs because God answered my spoken and unspoken prayers constantly and better than I'd asked **(1 Peter 3:12a).**

140

The *"New Heavens and a New Earth"* (Isaiah 65:17) may be promises for a future kingdom, but the character and essence of God are eternal and immutable; therefore, we can trust that God's Kingdom is already amid His children and even today, in our prayer space, *"Before we call, God will answer; while we're still speaking, God will hear us"* **(Isaiah 65:24)**.

Jesus adds, *"If you remain in me and my words remain in you, ask whatever you wish, and it will be done for you"* **(John 15:7)**. My beloved, remember that *"The eyes of the Lord are on the righteous, and his ears are attentive to their cry"* **(Psalm 34:15)**.

One way to show our love for God is by knowing His will and, in every situation, just as God does for us, anticipate God's desires, and respond to God's glory.

Let us pray: Dear God, receive our infinite gratitude for Your great love that, without resting, you're aware of our needs, obstacles, and dangers. Thank you for inviting us to ask with gratitude, knowing that you always listen and answer. Increase our faith to share this wonderful gift with Your people. We pray in Jesus's name.

May 6
GOD IS AGAINST ALL PREJUDICE
Acts 10:28b

How wonderful our God, who uses everyday things, such as food, to correct us about **racial and religious prejudices** that go against God's will.

In a vision, God told Peter to eat from a mixture that included animals considered unclean by the Jews. *"'Surely not, Lord!' Peter replied. 'I have never eaten anything impure or unclean'"* **(Acts 10:12-14)**. But God told him, *"Do not call anything impure that God has made clean"* **(v.15)**.

In Jesus's time, Jews and Samaritans despised each other. We find proof in the encounter of Jesus with the Samaritan woman who told him, *"You are a Jew and I am a Samaritan woman. How can you ask me for a drink? (For Jews do not associate with Samaritans"* **(John 4:9)**. Jesus broke that prejudice by speaking with the Samaritan woman and restoring her dignity within the community.

In **Acts 10**, after correcting Peter so that he *"not call anything impure that God has made clean,"* God gave instructions to take Peter to the house of *"Cornelius, a centurion in what was known as the Italian Regiment"* **(Acts 10:1)**. When they arrived, Peter told them: *"You are well

141

aware that it is against our law for a Jew to associate with or visit a Gentile. But God has shown me that I should not call anyone impure or unclean" **(Acts 10:28).**

My beloved, the gospel of Jesus Christ and God's grace were no longer exclusive to the Israelites, so Peter went to Cornelius' house and preached the good news. In **Romans 10:12,** God tells us that among Christians, there should be *"no difference between Jew and Gentile—the same Lord is Lord of all and richly blesses all who call on him."*

God is adamantly against all prejudice and contempt. Jesus warns us, *"For in the same way you judge others, you will be judged, and with the measure you use, it will be measured to you"* **(Matthew 7:2).** Given these passages, I can't understand how some who claim to be Christians can despise people based on race, gender, complexion, religion, political affiliation, etc., ignoring the Divine command to *"not call anyone impure or unclean"* **(Acts 10:28b).**

Let us pray: Dear God, don't allow prejudice and contempt to manifest themselves or be tolerated in our environment. Grant us the courage to correct and reject it when prejudice rears its ugly head in our home, church, and community. We understand that you *"do not show favoritism"* **(Acts 10:34b).** We pray in Your Holy Name.

> Among Christians, there should be *"no difference between Jew and Gentile—the same Lord is Lord of all and richly blesses all who call on him."* **Romans 10:12**

✝ ✝ ✝ ✝ ✝ ✝

May 7
ALL ARE EQUAL IN GOD'S EYES
Acts 10:34b-35

In Ecuador, there's a saying, *"a rooster can't sing any clearer."* Today's verse tells us that **God is impartial.** God's not impressed by the country of our birth, nor by our level of education, the titles or positions we hold, whether we're rich or poor, man or woman, child or old, the color of our skin, etc. **We're all equal in God's eyes.**

Job 34:19 says that God: *"shows no partiality to princes and does not favor the rich over the poor, for they are all the work of his hands?"* But we're unique in how we respond

to God's favor. What pleases and impresses God is how we use what He gave us to **be respectful toward God and act with love and justice toward our neighbor.**

God's justice which we must imitate, is this; God impartially gives His blessing as well as correction **to all**: *"that you may be children of your Father in heaven. He causes his sun to rise on the evil and the good, and sends rain on the righteous and the unrighteous"* (**Matthew 5:45**). We will all give an account for our deeds. We can be sure that God will be impartial and just on judgment day. *"The Lord comes to judge the earth. He will judge the world in righteousness and the peoples with equity"* (**Psalm 98:9**). Meanwhile, God expects us to **be just and impartial,** as exemplified by Him.

God gives us what we deserve without showing favoritism. That's the **justice that we must imitate.** *"Anyone who does wrong will be repaid for their wrongs, and there is no favoritism"* (**Colossians 3:25**). Likewise, whoever has put their trust in redemption through Jesus's blood will be found acceptable to the Lord because they did *"what the Lord commanded"* (**Job 42:9**).

We have a considerable challenge ahead; Yes, great, but not impossible. The Holy Spirit will guide and help us become **better imitators** of our Lord and thus be *"pleasing to God"* (**2 Corinthians 5:9**).

Let us pray: Dear God, thank You for being fair and impartial with us. Help us to be better imitators of our Lord. In the same way, You made us *"accepted in the Beloved"* (**Ephesians 1:6 NKJV),** grant that we may accept everyone into our circle of grace and love, no matter who they are or from where they come. We pray in Your Holy Name.

May 8
GOD TRANSFORMS THE ORDINARY

"Do not come any closer," God said. "Take off your sandals, for the place where you are standing is holy ground." **Exodus 3:5**

"No te acerques. Quítate el calzado de tus pies, porque el lugar donde ahora estás es tierra santa". Éxodo 3:5

"Και είπε: Μη πλησιάσεις εδώ· λύσε τα υποδήματά σου από τα πόδια σου· επειδή, ο τόπος επάνω στον οποίο στέκεσαι, είναι άγια γη." ΕΞΟΔΟΣ 3:5

We can summarize the life of Moses in three stages of 40 years each:

1. A Jew who lived 40 years as the prince of Egypt
Moses, along with every newborn male jew, was destined to die by order of Pharaoh. But, **God transformed a simple basket** and Pharaoh's house into Moses' **refuge and sustenance (Exodus 2:3).** Moses grew up as a prince within Pharaoh's house, and Moses' birth mother received wages from Pharaoh's daughter to raise her own son **(Exodus 2:9).** God is great!

143

2. A prince of Egypt, who lived 40 years as a refugee pastor

At age 40, Moses, the prince of Egypt (who was a Jew), killed an Egyptian soldier in defense of one of his Jewish brothers **(Acts 7:23)**. Upon being discovered, he fled and took refuge in Midian, where his father-in-law Jethro put him in charge of the sheep. **After forty years (Acts 7:30), God appeared to him amid his new daily routine** in the burning bush. Thus, God called and equipped Moses to deliver Israel from slavery.

3. 40 years in the desert as liberator and judge of Israel.

God knows our entire life. Like Moses, our lives are also marked in stages, **"before and after."** For me, 1989, at age 35, began the period when God called me to stand bare-footed on holy ground and start over again, seeking and serving first God's kingdom.

In **Exodus 3**, Moses observed a burning bush that was not consumed, and he drew near to look at it. *"'Do not come any closer,' God said. 'Take off your sandals, for the place where you are standing is holy ground'"* **(Exodus 3:5)**.

God transforms the ordinary into the **Sacred** and requires us to approach Him with fear, permission, an open heart, and bare feet. If you regularly meet God at your kitchen table, that is holy ground. Same with your living room, dining room, and car. Even this space which we share daily, it's Holy Ground.

Beloved friends and family, Moses was 80 years old when God transformed the prince disguised as a pastor into **Israel's deliverer and judge**. It's never too late for God to call and use us for the Kingdom!

Let us pray: Dear God, help us approach every encounter with you with reverence and fear. Give us the courage so that, as princes and princesses, we might leave behind all pretense and excuses and begin to fulfill our purpose. We pray in Your Holy Name.

May 9
SAVED BY FAITH OR OBEDIENCE?

"Very truly I tell you, whoever obeys my word will never see death." John 8:51

"De cierto, de cierto les digo que, el que obedece mi palabra, nunca verá la muerte".
Juan 8:51

"Σας διαβεβαιώνω απόλυτα: Αν κάποιος φυλάξει τον λόγο μου, δεν θα δει θάνατο στον αιώνα." ΚΑΤΑ ΙΩΑΝΝΗΝ 8:51

In **John 8:6**, the Pharisees and scribes appear before Jesus with the adulterous woman to trap Him and *"have a basis for accusing him."* Throughout the chapter, the Pharisees enter into different debates with Jesus, leading to this verse asking for obedience to His word. *"To the Jews who had believed him, Jesus said, 'If you hold to my teaching, you are really my disciples.*

Then you will know the truth, and the truth will set you free'" **(John 8:31-32).**

From what will we be free? Believers in Jesus will be free from death and the bondage of sin and fear. *"Very truly I tell you, whoever obeys my word will never see death"* **(John 8:51).** Jesus also said, *"I am the resurrection and the life. The one who believes in me will live, even though they die; and whoever lives by believing in me will never die. Do you believe this?"* **(John 11:25-26).**

Therefore, the question arises: **Are we saved by faith or obedience?** It's like the question, what came first, the chicken or the egg? Our Christian faith affirms that we're saved by faith. In my experience, obedience without love and faith is fruitless and sterile. Eventually, it dissipates in favor of the flesh and ego. On the other hand, faith, love, and gratitude lead to fruitful obedience.

As Jesus's disciples, our cup overflows with gratitude because God rescued us from a life slipping into the abyss of despair. God raised us to the fullness of life and hope. Our just response for this second opportunity at life here and in eternity is to treasure Jesus's Words (God's Word) in our hearts and **obey them.**

God's Word says, *"And this is love: that we walk in obedience to his commands. As you have heard from the beginning, his command is that you walk in love"* **(2 John 1:6).** My beloved, the entire Bible is God's love letter addressed to you and me to remind us that through mutual love, we demonstrate love and obedience to God and Jesus's Lordship in our lives. In other words, obedience manifests itself in agape love through faith and gratitude.

Let us pray: Lord our God, thank You for **saving us through faith** in Jesus Christ, for encouraging us to walk by faith and with gratitude for Your endless love. *"Our lives are in your hands; deliver us from the hands of our enemies, from those who pursue us. Let your face shine on your servant; save me in your unfailing love"* **(Psalm 31:15-16).** We pray in Your Holy Name.

> **Obedience without love and faith is fruitless and sterile. Eventually, it dissipates in favor of the ego. On the other hand, faith, love, and gratitude lead to fruitful obedience.**

May 10
WAR TACTICS
1 Timothy 6:12

Life is a constant struggle between good and evil, the spirit and the flesh, harmony and conflict, and ultimately, between life and death. The enemy's weapons are many and varied. To be victorious, we must know the enemy's tactics and weapons.

God warns us about the enemy's traps (weapons):

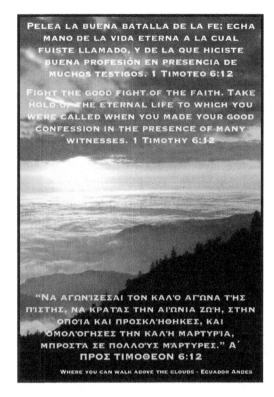

Greed - *"Those who want to get rich fall into temptation and a trap and into many foolish and harmful desires that plunge people into ruin and destruction. For the love of money is a root of all kinds of evil"* (1 Timothy 6:9-10a).

Silver and gold - *"Do not covet the silver and gold on them, and do not take it for yourselves, or you will be ensnared by it"* (Deuteronomy 7:25a).

False gods and Alliances - *"Do not make a covenant with them or with their gods. Do not let them live in your land or they will cause you to sin against me, because the worship of their gods will certainly be a snare to you"* (Exodus 23:32-33).

Idolatry is what most offends the Lord. God said, *"You shall have no other gods before me. 'You shall not make for yourself an image in the form of anything in heaven above or on the earth beneath or in the waters below. You shall not bow down to them or worship them; for I, the Lord your God, am a jealous God'"* (Exodus 20:3-5). Those who worshiped idols fell into ruin (Psalm 106:36).

My beloved, we live in a constant inner battle between the flesh and the spirit. **Ephesians 6:12** says, *"For our struggle is not against flesh and blood, but against the rulers, against the authorities, against the powers of this dark world and against the spiritual forces of evil in the heavenly realms."*

To win, we must remain vigilant, prepared, informed, **fully** consecrated to the Kingdom's cause, and, above all, dependent on the Holy Spirit who fights our battles. Our goal is to 1. train ourselves intensely with the Word and sword of the faith 2. to please God and 3. win the battle.

Let us pray: Dear God, instruct and strengthen us to fight the good fight and be victorious. Please don't allow us to fall under the enemy's traps. Deliver us from all evil, along with our children and future generations. We pray in the name of Jesus Christ.

May 11
A CHARGE TO KEEP
1 Timothy 6:14

In today's verse, God instructs that throughout our lives, as we await the return of our Lord, we *"keep THIS command without spot or blame."*

Since this verse's context doesn't clarify which commandment it refers to, we must study the first letter to Timothy for an answer. **Commandment** appears two other times in the following verses;

1. *"The goal of this command is love, which comes from a pure heart and a good conscience and a sincere faith. Some have departed from these and have turned to meaningless talk. They want to be teachers of the law, but they do not know what they are talking about or what they so confidently affirm"* **(1 Timothy 1:5–7).**

We could assume that the commandment is about loving God above all things. We wouldn't be wrong since verse five says that *"the goal of this is love."* But verse six points to a *"departing"* by *"meaningless talk,"* making us think that it's about "guarding and defending" something. Let's continue our search!

2. *"Timothy, my son, I am giving you this command in keeping with the prophecies once made about you, so that by recalling them you may fight the battle well, holding on to faith and a good conscience, which some have rejected and so have suffered shipwreck with regard to the faith"* **(1 Timothy 1:18-19).** This verse speaks of *"prophecies"* that some rejected and shipwrecked in their faith.

Let's look at the antecedent to verse five. It says, *"As I urged you when I went into Macedonia, stay there in Ephesus so that you may command certain people not to teach false doctrines any longer or to devote themselves to myths and endless genealogies. Such things promote controversial speculations rather than advancing God's work—which is by faith"* **(1 Timothy 1:3–4).** And here we find our answer. The commandment refers to **Timothy's charge to guard and defend the doctrines and teachings of the apostles,** which **for us is the Bible in its entirety.**

My beloved, if you and I, as disciples of Jesus, don't live according to the Bible, then we'd be failing to *"keep this command without spot or blame."* We're to project a life of holiness in which we *"make every effort to be found spotless, blameless and at peace with him"* **(2 Peter 3:14).**

Let us pray: Dear God, help us defend and spread Your Word of Life with love, care, and diligence so that no one in our circle of influence is shipwrecked in their faith. We pray in Jesus's name.

May 12
TEACH THE CHILDREN WELL

"Teach them to your children, talking about them when you sit at home and when you walk along the road, when you lie down and when you get up." Deuteronomy 11:19

"Enséñenselas a sus hijos, y hablen de ellas cuando te encuentres descansando en tu casa, y cuando vayas por el camino, y cuando te acuestes, y cuando te levantes". Deuteronomio 11:19

"και θα τα διδάσκετε στα παιδιά σας, μιλώντας γι' αυτά, όταν κάθεσαι στο σπίτι σου, και όταν περπατάς στον δρόμο, και όταν πλαγιάζεις, και όταν σηκώνεσαι·" **ΔΕΥΤΕΡΟΝΟΜΙΟΝ 11:19**

When our children were young, we read family devotions before dinner. My son Jean-Paul enjoyed reading them and became an avid reader. For a few years, we read the whole Bible together. When we finished reading it the first time, he asked, ***"what do we do now?"*** I responded, ***"we reread it from the beginning."*** And so we did!

As today's verse instructs, we used to read the Bible day and night. We talked about what we'd read. I explained to Jean-Paul what we read; however, I failed to explain how the world would attack the foundations of the faith we'd sown. That friends and university professors would raise doubts with scientific, historical, and philosophical arguments opposed to the Bible, i.e., it's filled with errors and inconsistencies and is therefore unreliable. I didn't teach him how to respond to these arguments.

In part, this daily meditation journal aims to correct that teaching error by speaking to my present and future generations. I don't know how many of my grandchildren and great-grandchildren will be curious enough to read/study these writings (nearly 1,300 meditations to date), but my heart rejoices, believing that one or more will. Also, speaking to my present readers, I don't know the difference that these meditations have made in your life, but if only one or two of you feel strengthened, nourished, encouraged in your faith, and convinced that the Bible is God's complete Word, that your life is filled with peace and hope, then my soul rejoices.

God's Word is like a seed, requiring daily nurturing to take root. But, it's not enough to read the Bible daily, filling the heart with dates, stories, miracles, etc. You also need to feel God's transformative power working in your life. Doing random acts of kindness is a good start. Once you've experienced it, strengthen the roots by anticipating the enemy's tactics and learn to use all the armor that God offers to defend your faith against internal and external attacks.

Let us pray: Dear God, train and prepare us to **teach our children** how to apply Your Word to their lives so that they and their children can defend their faith against the enemy's attacks. Thank you for placing in our hearts the desire to meditate on and share Your Word daily. May Your Word never be lacking in our homes. We pray in Jesus's name.

FULFILLED MESSIANIC PROPHECIES

"Everything must be fulfilled that is written about me in the Law of Moses, the Prophets and the Psalms." Luke 24:44b

"Era necesario que se cumpliera todo lo que está escrito acerca de mí en la ley de Moisés, en los profetas y en los salmos". Lucas 24:44b

"Ότι πρέπει να εκπληρωθούν όλα τα γραμμένα μέσα στον νόμο τού Μωυσή και στους προφήτες και στους ψαλμούς για μένα." ΚΑΤΑ ΛΟΥΚΑΝ 24:44β

Jesus, God's anointed, came to heal, bring the good news of hope to the poor, release the captives, give sight to the blind (like me), and free us from oppression. Jesus astonished the doubtful when, after reading from **Isaiah 61:1-2,** *"He began by saying to them, 'Today this scripture is fulfilled in your hearing'"* **(Luke 4:21).**

If Jesus had fulfilled only one of the dozens of prophecies, it'd be understandable for the skeptical to reject Him. **But He fulfilled at least 60 identifiable prophecies.** Today's verse invites us to study what the prophets and psalms said about the Messiah. Jesus said, *"Everything must be fulfilled that is written about me in the Law of Moses, the Prophets and the Psalms"* **(Luke 24:44b).**

14 Prophecies Jesus Christ Fulfilled		
Prophecies About Jesus	**Hebrew Scripture**	**Fulfilled in New Testament**
1. The Messiah would be born of a virgin and called Emmanuel.	Isaiah 7:14	Matthew 1:22-23 & Luke 1:26-31
2. He would be a refugee in Egypt.	Hosea 11:1	Matthew 2:14-15
3. He'd be rejected by His people.	Psalm 69:8 & Isaiah 53:3	John 1:11 & John 7:5
4. God would declare Him His Son of God	Psalm 2:7	Matthew 3:17
5. Was sent to heal and release the captives.	Isaiah 61:1-2	Luke 4:18-19
6. He'd be betrayed.	Psalm 41:9	Matthew 26:14-16 & Luke 22:47-48
7. He'd be silent before his accusers.	Isaiah 53:7	Mark 15:4-5
8. He'd be crucified along with criminals.	Isaiah 53:12	Matthew 27:38 & Mark 15:27
9. God would forsake Him	Psalm 22:1	Matthew 27:46
10. He'd pray for his enemies.	Psalm 109:4	Luke 23:34
11. Christ would die for our sin	Isaiah 53:5-12	Romans 5:6-8
12. He'd be buried with the rich.	Isaiah 53:9	Matthew 27:57-60
13. God would raise Him from the dead	Psalm 16:10 & Psalm 49:15	Matthew 28:5-7 & Acts 2:24
14. Jesus would ascend to heaven	Psalm 68:18	Mark 16:19 & Luke 24:51

"EVERYTHING MUST BE FULFILLED THAT IS WRITTEN ABOUT ME IN THE LAW OF MOSES, THE PROPHETS AND THE PSALMS." LUKE 24:44B

"ΌΤΙ ΠΡΈΠΕΙ ΝΑ ΕΚΠΛΗΡΩΘΟΎΝ ΌΛΑ ΤΑ ΓΡΑΜΜΈΝΑ ΜΈΣΑ ΣΤΟΝ ΝΌΜΟ ΤΟΎ ΜΩΥΣΉ ΚΑΙ ΣΤΟΥΣ ΠΡΟΦΉΤΕΣ ΚΑΙ ΣΤΟΥΣ ΨΑΛΜΟΎΣ ΓΙΑ ΜΈΝΑ." ΚΑΤΑ ΛΟΥΚΑΝ 24:44Β

ALL the prophecies needed to be fulfilled so that nobody could say **"they're coincidences."** We don't have enough time in 5 minutes (500 words) to study all the prophecies, but I think it's essential to identify the main ones. The above table shows the references to the Hebrew Scriptures and their fulfillment in the New Testament. I hope it helps you continue investigating the 40+ additional prophecies about Jesus, the Messiah, and **why He came to Earth.**

Jesus promised us the Holy Spirit, who would give us the power to understand and apply God's teachings and guidance for our lives and thus become valuable ambassadors of the good news. In doing so, we continue the ministry of Jesus, who came exclusively to save, heal and release the captives such as you and me. *"But you will receive power when the Holy Spirit comes on you; and you will be my witnesses in Jerusalem, and in all Judea and Samaria, and to the ends of the earth"* **(Acts 1:8).**

Let us pray: Dear God, thank You because all the promises and prophecies about our Savior and Redeemer were fulfilled perfectly and entirely in Jesus Christ, in whom we have total physical, spiritual, and emotional health, along with the promise of the Holy Spirit, and in the coming kingdom, Eternal life in Your presence. Open our eyes to understand better and learn more about Your prophecies and promises. Empower us to be Your faithful witnesses and ambassadors *"to the ends of the earth."* We pray in Your holy name.

May 14
THE ALMIGHTY

"Do not be afraid. I am the First and the Last. I am the Living One; I was dead, and now look, I am alive forever and ever!" Revelation 1:17b-18

"No temas. Yo soy el primero y el último, y el que vive. Estuve muerto, pero ahora vivo para siempre". Apocalipsis 1:17b-18a

"Μη φοβάσαι· εγώ είμαι ο πρώτος και ο τελευταίος, και αυτός που ζει, και έγινα νεκρός· και, δες, είμαι ζωντανός στους αιώνες των αιώνων· αμήν·"
ΑΠΟΚΑΛΥΨΗ ΙΩΑΝΝΟΥ 1:17β-18

Almighty God, send Your Holy Spirit upon us so that we may faithfully love and follow you today and always. We pray in the name and spirit of Christ. Amen.
One of the most controversial topics in the early church was **Christ's Divinity**. *"Some viewed Jesus as spirit-filled but still a mere human being who was justified, adopted, and elevated by God to divine messianic sonship through scrupulous obedience to the law."*[9] Some prominent and influential modern sects don't recognize Jesus Christ as God, and one day will knock on your door to convince you that Jehovah is the only God. That's why we must be well informed and confident about the Divinity of Jesus Christ.

"The doctrine of the Divinity of Christ 'affirms that Jesus Christ was not merely an extraordinary human being but the incarnate Son of God, who by nature is coequal and coeternal with God the Father.'"[10]

---

[9] Nah, D. (2018). Jesus 'Divinity. En M. Ward, J. Parks, B. Ellis, & T. Hains (Eds.), *Lexham Survey of Theology*. Bellingham, WA: Lexham Press.
[10] Ibid

150

In **Genesis 17:1**, God (Adonai) appeared to Abram, saying, *"I am God Almighty."* In **Revelation 1:8**, the Lord God says, *"I am the Almighty."* Analyzing this and **verse 18**, we'll verify that **Jesus is equal and coeternal with Almighty God.** In verse **1:8,** Jesus identifies himself as *"The Almighty,"* but also says, *"I am the Alpha and the Omega, who is, and <u>who was</u>, and who is to come."* To clarify, in verse 18, Jesus says, "I am the Living One; <u>I WAS DEAD</u>, and now look, I am alive for ever and ever!"

Has God the Father ever died? No! Jesus Christ died to save all sinners. Jesus died and rose again and lives forever to intercede for us. Upon seeing the risen Christ, by faith, doubting Thomas declared Him, *"My Lord, and my God!"* **(John 20:28).**

These verses should be enough to convince us that **Jesus is eternal God.** The Bible contains multiple statements from Jesus, the disciples, and God himself, affirming that Jesus is *"The Son whom I love"* **(Luke 9:35).**

Let us pray: Dear God, thank You for revealing to us that Jesus Christ is the Alpha and Omega, our beginning and end, Your beloved Son, and at the same time, Jesus is **Almighty God.** Open our understanding to know you better through the doctrine of Christ's Divinity. We pray in Your Holy Name.

May 15
BUILD THE ARK

"Noah was six hundred years old when the floodwaters came on the earth." Genesis 7:6

"Cuando el diluvio de las aguas cayó sobre la tierra, Noé tenía seiscientos años". Génesis 7:6

"Και ο Νώε ήταν 600 χρόνων, όταν έγινε ο κατακλυσμός των νερών επάνω στη γη."
ΓΕΝΕΣΙΣ 7:6

I believe that The Bible is its own dictionary and reference book. For three days, I studied *"how long did it take Noah to build the Ark?"* Some say that it took Noah 120 years to build the Ark based on God's statement, *"My Spirit will not contend with humans forever, for they are mortal; their days will be a hundred and twenty years"* **(Genesis 6:3).** But God did NOT speak to Noah until **verse 13.**

A possible answer appears by **looking at the ages of Noah and his children.** Noah was 500 years old when he began to have children **(Genesis 5:32)** and 600 years old when God told him to go into the Ark **(7:6).** Somewhere between, God instructed Noah to build the Ark.

When God instructed him to build the Ark, **"Noah had three sons" (6:10, 14-16). This is key!** We must ask, **when was the third son born?**

Japheth was the firstborn, followed by Shem, then Ham, the youngest **(Genesis 9:24).** **Genesis 10:21** says that Shem is the brother of the "elder" Japheth and that **at age 100,** he had a son *"two years after the flood" (11:10).* This means that Shem was 97-8 years old when the flood came

151

and that Noah was 502-3 at his birth. We don't know when the youngest, Ham, was born, but Noah fathered the first two children two years apart.

Therefore, **at age 502-3, Noah had three children, and after that, God instructed him to build the Ark.** Thus, 120 years of building the Ark seems incorrect. A more likely answer is any period shorter than 95 years. Isn't it wonderful when the Lord guides us toward truth and clarity?

Can you imagine how Noah felt, knowing that God was planning to **"restart"** the human race in 95 or fewer years as soon as Noah completed the Ark? It's possible that his neighbors mocked and taunted him and his family. Yet, *"Noah did everything just as God commanded him."* *(6:22). "Noah was six hundred years old when the floodwaters came on the earth,"* and God directed him to go into the Ark and his house *(7:6).*

Let us pray: Dear Lord, thank You for guiding us unto truth, hope, and salvation. For assuring us that you can use our gifts at any age. Help us to ignore the world's mockery and keep our eyes fixed on Your instructions so that we can maintain or build new Arks according to Your design to nurture and save the human race, one person at a time. We pray in Your Holy Name.

> *"NOAH DID EVERYTHING JUST AS GOD COMMANDED HIM." (NOAH 6:22).*

May 16
NOT AS THE WORLD GIVES

"Peace I leave with you; my peace I give you. I do not give to you as the world gives. Do not let your hearts be troubled and do not be afraid." **John 14:27**

"La paz les dejo, mi paz les doy; yo no la doy como el mundo la da. No dejen que su corazón se turbe y tenga miedo". **Juan 14:27**

"Ειρήνη αφήνω σε σας, ειρήνη τη δική μου δίνω σε σας· όχι όπως δίνει ο κόσμος, σας δίνω εγώ. Ας μη ταράζεται η καρδιά σας μήτε να δειλιάζει."
ΚΑΤΑ ΙΩΑΝΝΗΝ 14:27

Staying calm during storms can attenuate the intensity of the attack. During quarantine times, we need to create spaces that feed us the peace of Christ, which help us keep our calm in the face of adversity (even COVID). Christ's peace isn't transient nor gives in to fear or continuous remorse for past sins.

Regarding forgiveness, we're generally harder on ourselves than on others. We may have asked God to forgive us but continue unnecessarily to carry the weight of a shameful past. Christ's sacrifice on the cross paid for ALL past, present, and future sins. God says, *"For I will forgive their wickedness and will remember their sins no more"* **(Jeremiah 31:34).** If God has forgiven our sins, **why then do we insist on playing those old tracks of our failures?** Again, the tempter is trying to **steal Christ's peace from us.** Jesus said: *"Do not let your hearts be troubled and do not be afraid"* **(John 14:27).**

We pray for a new era of peace where hostilities and wars cease. Nothing would bring us greater satisfaction than seeing our children inherit a conflict-free planet. But, unless we ALL obediently submit to God and **love our neighbor as ourselves,** forgive as we've been forgiven, there will always be conflicts and hostilities between nations, brother against brother.

And yet, we have hope! The day is coming when our children will no longer *"train for war,"* and weapons of war will be turned into agricultural tools **(Isaiah 2:4).** When we genuinely obey the golden rule, people of all religions, races, and languages will know God, work together for this common cause, and, with God's guidance, will eradicate war and famine from our planet.

Our children and your children's children need to hear from you and me that in this world, they will face adversities and that the way to overcome them is by allowing **the peace of Christ to rule in their hearts.** That peace must begin with them, internally and then outwardly, toward their friends, family, strangers, and even enemies.

Let us pray: Dear God, thank You for giving us the permanent and sincere **peace of Christ, unlike the world's peace.** Grant us love and wisdom to model random acts of love and peace in our circles of influence, thus creating a new and better world for our children. We pray in Jesus's name.

May 17
LIFE STAGES

"Being confident of this, that he who began a good work in you will carry it on to completion until the day of Christ Jesus." Philippians 1:6

"Estoy persuadido de que el que comenzó en ustedes la buena obra, la perfeccionará hasta el día de Jesucristo". Filipenses 1:6

"επειδή, είμαι βέβαιος, ακριβώς σε τούτο, ότι εκείνος που άρχισε σε σας ένα καλό έργο, θα το αποτελειώσει μέχρι την ημέρα τού Ιησού Χριστού."
ΠΡΟΣ ΦΙΛΙΠΠΗΣΙΟΥΣ 1:6

On October 29, 2020, our family celebrated another new birth. Our grandson **Lázaro Elías started a wonderful life stage**, opening new illusions and joys for us. Part of the celebration is the expectation that, with the help of his parents and God's will, Lázaro will learn to eat solids, grow up, walk, run, study, fall in love, and leave home to form his own family. At every stage of his life, we'll celebrate his accomplishments. For now, we enjoy his infancy and beautiful smile, believing that Lázaro will advance through new and beautiful life stages.

Accepting Christ in our hearts is like a new birth, anticipating unique and wonderful post-birth life stages. We can't remain stuck in **the joys of infancy.** We must continue along each step toward maturity and **sanctification.**

Sanctification is a lifelong process in which God transforms us into the image of Jesus Christ. In this process, as newborns, we surrender totally to God, seeking to deepen our faith, hope, and love, giving way to *"a genuine and lasting peace and joy."*[11]

> Accepting Christ in our hearts is like a new birth, anticipating unique and wonderful post-birth life stages. We can't remain stuck in the joys of infancy. We must continue along each step toward maturity and sanctification.

Sanctification is *"the work of God's grace through the Word and Spirit of God,"*[12] which *"moves us toward Christian perfection."* Sanctification must be sought and achievable by every believer. In this stage *"of perfect love, righteousness, and true holiness,"*[13] we express our perfected love (**"agape"**) for God and neighbor. The expression of **sanctification** is the task and requisite for every child born of God.

My beloved, the good news is that **sanctification and agape** are available to every believer at every life stage, even though we may have strayed from God's ways for a season.

Someday, like the prodigal son and many of us in the past, our children and grandchildren will leave their parents' homes and pursue their aspirations. Their parents will always be ready with open arms to welcome them back, be it for an afternoon, a day, or however long it takes to regain strength, hope, and courage. Likewise, God is always ready with open arms to receive us and continue the process of **sanctifying our lives for God's service and praise.**

Let us pray: Dear God, thank You for Your immense love and patience in shaping and restoring our lives and character so that we may be sanctified and found worthy to come into Your presence. Help us love perfectly like you so that Your kingdom may be filled with the sons and daughters for whom Jesus sacrificed His life. We pray in Jesus's name.

May 18
BLAMELESS AND SPOTLESS
Titus 1:7

Our verse dictates the conduct of church officials who, through the **"laying of hands,"** have been charged with leading Christ's church.

These verses clarify the requirements for administering and ordering the houses and things of God. The first, in negative form, says that the person must not be *"overbearing, not quick-tem*

---

[11] John Wesley, La Santidad de Corazón y Vida, Daugherty (p. 26)
[12] De la Disciplina de la Iglesia Metodista Unida – 2004 (¶103, p 73)
[13] Ibid

PORQUE ES
NECESARIO QUE
EL OBISPO, COMO
ADMINISTRADOR
DE DIOS, SEA
IRREPRENSIBLE.
TITO 1:7

"SINCE AN
OVERSEER
MANAGES
GOD'S
HOUSEHOLD,
HE MUST BE
BLAMELESS."
TITUS 1:7

"ΕΠΕΙΔΉ, Ο ΕΠΊΣΚΟΠΟΣ ΠΡΈΠΕΙ ΝΑ ΕΊΝΑΙ
ΧΩΡΊΣ ΚΑΤΗΓΟΡΊΑ, ΩΣ ΟΙΚΟΝΌΜΟΣ ΤΟΎ
ΘΕΟΎ." ΠΡΟΣ ΤΙΤΟΝ 1:7

EGYPT - CARLOS & SOPHIA

pered, not given to drunkenness, not violent, not pursuing dishonest gain" (**Titus 1:7**). I remember a pastor getting so angry that he challenged a brother to *"go outside to settle it in a fistfight."* That pastor didn't last long with us, and unfortunately, we lost some members. On another occasion, while interviewing a pastor candidate, before inquiring about the congregation's needs, the pastor wanted to know, *"How much will you pay me?"* Jesus said that the hireling doesn't care about the sheep (**John 10:13**). What sad examples!

Whoever aspires to shepherd God's sheep or to be a shepherd of shepherds, as administrator and representative of God, they must be *"hospitable, one who loves what is good, who is self-controlled, upright, holy and disciplined. He must hold firmly to the trustworthy message as it has been taught"* (**Titus 1:8-9**). In **1 Timothy 3:2**, God adds, *"Now the overseer is to be above reproach, faithful to his wife, temperate…, respectable…, able to teach."*

God tells us that we should do *"everything without grumbling or arguing, so that you may become blameless and pure, 'children of God without fault in a warped and crooked generation.' Then you will shine among them like stars in the sky"* (**Philippians 2:14-15**).

We're imitators of our church leaders, and during adolescence, our children imitate us. For them to become interested in following us in our private and public life, we must consistently be *"blameless,"* as God describes in **Titus 1:8-9.** My beloved, let us *"make every effort to be found spotless, blameless and at peace with God"* (**2 Peter 3:14**).

Let us pray: Dear God, in Your mercy, we ask that you *"sanctify us through and through. May our whole spirit, soul and body be kept blameless at the coming of our Lord Jesus Christ"* (**1 Thessalonians 5:23**). We pray in Your Holy Name.

May 19
OUR COMFORT AND HOPE
John 16:20

Jesus is our comfort and hope in times of pain. The most significant inheritance we can acquire and gift away is that God couldn't see us suffer, so He sent Jesus Christ to *transform our grief into joy.*

In this world, we'll face temptations, pain, losses, failures, illnesses, etc. We don't know the details of our future, but there will be triumphs and trials ahead. Looking back, we've cried and will

155

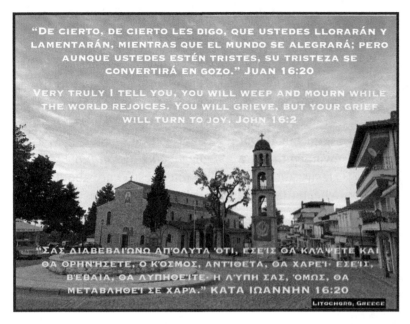

"DE CIERTO, DE CIERTO LES DIGO, QUE USTEDES LLORARÁN Y LAMENTARÁN, MIENTRAS QUE EL MUNDO SE ALEGRARÁ; PERO AUNQUE USTEDES ESTÉN TRISTES, SU TRISTEZA SE CONVERTIRÁ EN GOZO." JUAN 16:20

VERY TRULY I TELL YOU, YOU WILL WEEP AND MOURN WHILE THE WORLD REJOICES. YOU WILL GRIEVE, BUT YOUR GRIEF WILL TURN TO JOY. JOHN 16:2

"ΣΑΣ ΔΙΑΒΕΒΑΙΏΝΩ ΑΠΌΛΥΤΑ ΌΤΙ, ΕΣΕΊΣ ΘΑ ΚΛΆΨΕΤΕ ΚΑΙ ΘΑ ΘΡΗΝΉΣΕΤΕ, Ο ΚΌΣΜΟΣ, ΑΝΤΊΘΕΤΑ, ΘΑ ΧΑΡΕΊ· ΕΣΕΊΣ, ΒΈΒΑΙΑ, ΘΑ ΛΥΠΗΘΕΊΤΕ. Η ΛΎΠΗ ΣΑΣ, ΌΜΩΣ, ΘΑ ΜΕΤΑΒΛΗΘΕΊ ΣΕ ΧΑΡΆ." ΚΑΤΑ ΙΩΑΝΝΗΝ 16:20

LITOCHORO, GREECE

still weep, but not without hope because we trust that in the end, we'll enter our rest victoriously and receive our reward. Jesus said, *"I have told you these things, so that in me you may have peace. In this world you will have trouble. But take heart! I have overcome the world"* **(John 16:33).**

Even though we'll arrive hurt, we'll enter God's kingdom where there'll never again be crying, pain, sickness, malice, or death **(Revelation 21:4).** Jesus said, *"Now is your time of grief, but I will see you again and you will rejoice, and no one will take away your joy"* **(John 16:22).** This is **our comfort and hope**; we'll see the Beloved face to face, and God *will turn our grief into endless joy.*

As we await that day, we'll have dreams, hopes, and aspirations. But, we must flexibly adapt to changes. Only God knows what He proposes to do through and in us. Therefore, when our dreams are truncated, when there's a change in today's plan or the 5-year program, I say, *"if it's you, Lord, guide my steps and heart to do your will."* **The Lord is our comfort and hope**, therefore, we won't concede our joy to changed plans because **God's plans are always good and better.**

My beloved, plans may change, but two things will never change; **God's love and Word,** which guide, encourage, and strengthen us, but are also the measure by which God will judge us. If we're faithful and trust our Savior's direction, we'll reach God's Kingdom where the Lord *"will turn our mourning into gladness; God will give us comfort and joy instead of sorrow"* **(Jeremiah 31:13).**

Let us pray: Dear God, thank You for giving us the faith to trust You and for transforming our tears into joy, our pain into gladness, and our weakness into strength. May Your presence encourage us to move forward with power and love, comforting and guiding Your sheep. We pray in the name of Jesus Christ.

May 20
THE BREATH OF LIFE

"Then the Lord God formed a man from the dust of the ground and breathed into his nostrils the breath of life, and the man became a living being." Genesis 2:7

"Entonces, del polvo de la tierra Dios el Señor formó al hombre, e infundió en su nariz aliento de vida. Así el hombre se convirtió en un ser con vida". **Génesis 2:7**

"Και ο Κύριος ο Θεός έπλασε τον άνθρωπο από χώμα τής γης· και εμφύσησε στα ρουθούνια του πνοή ζωής, και έγινε ο άνθρωπος σε ψυχή που ζει." **ΓΕΝΕΣΙΣ 2:7**

The words *"breath of life"* remind me of when God took Ezekiel to a vast cemetery with bones exposed to the sun and asked him, *"'Can these dead bones live?' Ezekiel replied: 'O Lord God, you know'"* **(Ezekiel 37:3).**

Then God said to him, *"Prophesy over these bones, and say to them, 'O dry bones, hear the word of the Lord. Thus says the Lord God to these bones: Behold, I will cause breath to enter you, and you shall live'"* **(Ezekiel 37:4-5).** Ezekiel did as God commanded, and the dead bones became alive.

The Lord created the heavens and the earth simply by speaking them into existence. However, you and I have a unique place in the creation history. **Genesis 2:7** says, *"And the Lord God formed man of the dust of the ground, and breathed into his nostrils the breath of life; and man became a living being."* Isn't that wonderful? God's hands personally formed us. God breathed the Spirit of life into our nostrils and turned us into living beings.

We may never understand God's work or mind, but the Bible helps us know God's heart and will for us and our planet. First, God created us to have an intimate and personal relationship with Him. Second, God breathed life into us to be kind to each other, sharing and spreading God's love and the Good News of Salvation. Third, to have dominion over His creation. We're here to take care of it for future generations so that there'd always be an equitable distribution of water, air, sunlight and food among all the families of the earth.

Are we taking care of it for our future generations? Let us be responsible stewards of what God has placed in our hands and power. If we are not doing a good job, let's ask ourselves, **What is stopping me?**

> God breathed life into us to be kind to each other, sharing and spreading God's love and the Good News of Salvation. Third, to have dominion over His creation. We're here to take care of it for future generations so that there'd always be an equitable distribution of water, air, sunlight and food among all the families of the earth.

Let us pray: Dear God, pour out Your Holy Spirit so that we may have an intimate and personal relationship with you, serve our neighbors with love and justice, and take care of this beautiful planet that, with due care, has everything needed to sustain us. We pray in Your Holy Name.

May 21
MORE THAN CONQUERORS
1 Corinthians 15:57

This beautiful promise assures us that we have victory through our Lord Jesus Christ, whatever our battles might be. End of story!

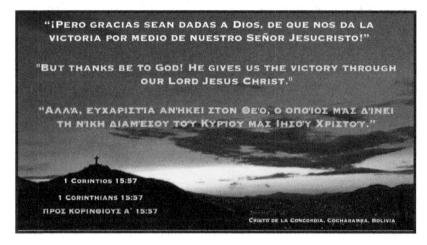

"¡PERO GRACIAS SEAN DADAS A DIOS, DE QUE NOS DA LA VICTORIA POR MEDIO DE NUESTRO SEÑOR JESUCRISTO!"

"BUT THANKS BE TO GOD! HE GIVES US THE VICTORY THROUGH OUR LORD JESUS CHRIST."

"ΑΛΛΆ, ΕΥΧΑΡΙΣΤΊΑ ΑΝΉΚΕΙ ΣΤΟΝ ΘΕΌ, Ο ΟΠΟΊΟΣ ΜΑΣ ΔΊΝΕΙ ΤΗ ΝΊΚΗ ΔΙΑΜΈΣΟΥ ΤΟΥ ΚΥΡΊΟΥ ΜΑΣ ΙΗΣΟΎ ΧΡΙΣΤΟΎ."

1 CORINTIOS 15:57
1 CORINTHIANS 15:57
ΠΡΟΣ ΚΟΡΙΝΘΙΟΥΣ Α΄ 15:57

CRISTO DE LA CONCORDIA, COCHABAMBA, BOLIVIA

It may not be the end of the story as we continue to live in a world full of struggles, sorrows, failures, and strife that inflict pain rather than relief. For some, especially in this period of COVID19, the physical reality might be losing a long battle against a disease. For others, it may be the loss of a loved one, a relationship whose distance widens daily, problems at work or school, or perhaps unemployment or a rebellious child who ignores our guidance. Each weighs heavily on our hearts if we look at the obstacles with physical eyes. However, God's Word gives us hope because we are *"more than conquerors through Him who loved us"* **(Romans 8:37).**

We're victorious because we're not alone in our struggles. Jesus promised to always be with us to the end of time **(Matthew 28:20)**. We're conquerors because the Holy Spirit guides and strengthens us along the triumphant path. Victory is certain because God has surrounded us with angels who offer us words of comfort, hope, and strength to face each battle. We're *more than conquerors* because *"the eyes of the Lord are on those who fear him, on those whose hope is in his unfailing love, to deliver them from death and keep them alive in famine"* **(Psalm 33:18-19)**. God *"gives us the victory through our Lord Jesus Christ"* **(1 Corinthians 15:57)**. With God on your side, you are *more than a conqueror!*

When deciding between two paths, it's good to list the pros and cons and follow the direction dictated by the more extensive list, whether the pros or cons. Even wiser, evaluate the list based on God's victorious Word.

Let us pray: Dear Lord, as we face our challenges, grant us a spirit of victory and trust in Your promises and presence. Open our eyes to recognize that there are more with us than those against us **(2 Kings 6:16)**. Help us believe that *"greater is the One who is in us than the one that is in the world"* **(1 John 4:4)**. Grant us wisdom to decide in favor of the One who gave His life to rescue ours and gave us the victory over sin. We pray in Jesus's name.

May 22
NECESSARY THINGS
Luke 24:46 (NKJV)

Regarding necessities, **Acts 1:8** appeals to our **need** to control this pandemic and overcome it. *"But you will receive power when the Holy Spirit has come upon you."* When we begin caring for each other's well-being, God will give us the **power** to overcome, starting with the fear and anger that brews as we enter the second anniversary of the pandemic.

Psalm 47:6 appeals to our **appetite** for the joy and gladness of life. *"Sing praises to God, sing praises; sing praises to our King, sing praises."* We sing to smooth the waves of fear and stress that daily pound on our doors.

Ephesians 1:17 appeals to our **necessity** for knowledge: that God might give us the *"spirit of wisdom and revelation as we come to know him."*

Ephesians 1:18-19 appeal to our curiosity **about the future**. God will grant that *"you may know what is the hope to which he has called you, what are the riches of his glorious inheritance among the saints, and what is the immeasurable greatness of his power for us who believe, according to the working of his great power."* My beloved, our temporary sufferings here don't compare to the inheritance and eternal joy that God has prepared for us **(Romans 8:18).**

Jesus discloses what *"was necessary"* to happen so that we might have abundant life, even amid tribulations. He said it is necessary *"that repentance and remission of sins should be preached in His name to all nations, beginning at Jerusalem"* **(Luke 24:47).** As God's redeemed children, forgiven and restored to our original position, we must go with power **and authority** to tell of the wonders that God has done in our lives. As a loving parent, God waits with open arms for the return of all children.

If you don't have a spiritual journal for your future generations, I recommend that you start writing one with detailed memories of when the Divine touched your humanity and how God satisfies all your needs.

Let us pray: Dear God, enlighten us to understand and seek what is necessary and indispensable. You know our present sufferings, Lord. With faith and hope in You, we'll cross this valley of the shadow of death and fear, holding on to Your hand and promises. Help us to go as witnesses of Your love and grace everywhere so that where Your Word is preached, Your children would repent, receive forgiveness, and heal their land and people. We pray in Your Holy Name.

May 23
THINGS THAT PLEASE GOD

"The one who sent me is with me; he has not left me alone, for I always do what pleases him."
John 8:29

"Porque el que me envió está conmigo, y no me ha dejado solo, porque yo hago siempre lo que a él le agrada". **Juan 8:29**

"Και εκείνος που με απέστειλε είναι μαζί μου· ο Πατέρας δεν με άφησε μόνον· επειδή, εγώ κάνω πάντοτε τα αρεστά σ' αυτόν."
ΚΑΤΑ ΙΩΑΝΝΗΝ 8:29

Here's a secret! Don't look for happiness outwardly. Everything you need to be happy you already have internally. We achieve happiness by learning and doing **what pleases God.**

For many years I was distanced from God, searching for the elusive happiness. Despite having a beautiful family and all the comforts, I was unhappy, competing with the world for material things. There were years of uneasiness, struggles, and trials until I met our Savior and found happiness by loving God and neighbor. Learning to love and please a spouse is neither easy nor impossible. It requires dedication to understand their thoughts and desires, to think like them, to anticipate what pleases them, and demonstrate love with words, backed by actions.

As Christians, we want to **know what pleases and displeases God.** A wealthy young man asked Jesus, *"What good thing must I do to get eternal life?" (Matthew 19:16).* Jesus said, *"If you want to be perfect, go, sell your possessions and give to the poor, and you will have treasure in heaven. Then come, follow me"* **(Matthew 19:21). Our task is to please God with our actions.** Jesus said, *"The one who sent me is with me; he has not left me alone, for I always do what pleases him"* **(John 8:29). God is pleased when we:**
+ obey our parents in everything **(Colossians 3:20).**
+ live harmoniously with our brothers *"For there the Lord bestows his blessing, even life forevermore"* **(Psalm 133:1, 3b).**
+ *"live a life worthy of the Lord and please him in every way: bearing fruit in every good work, growing in the knowledge of God"* **(Colossians 1:10).**
+ do good and help each other **(Hebrews 13:16).**

Pleasing God requires sacrifice and dedication, but it also offers excellent benefits, such as **things that God likes to do for us**:

> **God is pleased when we:** *"live a life worthy of the Lord and please him in every way: bearing fruit in every good work, growing in the knowledge of God"* **(Colossians 1:10).**

1. *"He causes their enemies to make peace with them"* **(Proverbs 16:7).**
2. *"God gives wisdom, knowledge, and happiness"* **(Ecclesiastes 2:26).**
3. *"Your Father has been pleased to give you the kingdom"* **(Luke 12:32).**

Beloved, while the world tempts us to win the lottery, God proposes that we find true wealth and happiness not in receiving but in **giving, loving, and serving.**

Let us pray: Dear God, give us hearts dedicated to You so that when people look at our lives, they may say that we *"always do what pleases God."* We pray in Your Holy Name.

May 24
THANK GOD FOR DIVERSITY
1 Corinthians 12:7

Each person in the church has a particular utility. **God distributes gifts according to the needs of the church and community for mutual benefit.** The keyword in our text is *"common good."* In the Greek text, συμφέρω (sympherō) means *"to bear together (contribute), i.e., to collect or to conduce"* together.[14]

Thank God for human diversity on our planet. For the variety of food and the assortment of gifts that God has deposited in our communities and churches. Thank God that not everyone has the same gift. For example, not all are musicians, cooks, carpenters, etc. But, most of all, we're grateful because God didn't give the gifts for the benefit of oneself, but so that they collectively benefit the church, spreading the Gospel of Jesus Christ and expanding God's Kingdom on earth.

GOD DISTRIBUTES GIFTS ACCORDING TO THE NEEDS OF THE CHURCH AND COMMUNITY FOR MUTUAL BENEFIT.

The gifts bestowed by the Holy Spirit are diverse and necessary for the churches' ministries. Among them, we find *"a message of wisdom," "of knowledge," "faith," "healing," "miraculous powers," "prophecy," "distinguishing between spirits," "speaking in different kinds of tongues,"* and *"the interpretation of tongues"* **(1 Corinthians 12:8-10).** Other gifts mentioned in **Ephesians 4:11** are, *"that some would be apostles, some prophets, some evangelists, some pastors and teachers."* Finally, **1 Corinthians 13:13** identifies three significant gifts, *"And now faith, hope, and love abide, these three; and the greatest of these is love."*

God calls us to seek, know, identify, abound in the gifts and use them for the edification of the church **(1 Corinthians 14:12)**, but above all, God implores us to seek the greatest of all, *"agape love"* **(1 Corinthians 13:13).** Some might incorrectly say, **"I don't have gifts!"** If you've placed your trust in God, **the Holy Spirit has sealed you with at least one gift!** Your task is to discover

---

[14] Strong, J. (2020). <u>Strong's Talking Greek and Hebrew Dictionary</u>. WORDsearch.

and use it. Every gift is as important as the other. There is no small gift. Even your smile and character are gifts that draw skeptics to Jesus's feet.

Think of something that you do well, that you enjoy doing. Then consider how you could dedicate that gift to the **common good** of the church and community.

Let us pray: Dear God, **thank You for the diversity of people and gifts** that you've placed in our surroundings. Please help me identify, perfect and use my talents for Your kingdom and glory to rescue the little sheep that today suffer and cry without shelter and protection. We pray in Jesus's name.

✠ ✠ ✠ ✠ ✠

May 25
UNITY IS NOT OPTIONAL
Genesis 11:6

We can count on God's support when we act as one voice and heart, in favor of the people or of God's kingdom. But God will resist us when we work for our glory, as He did when the people tried to build the tower of Babel to *"make a name for ourselves"* **(Genesis 11:4).** God divided and confused the languages. But from the beginning, God's plan was unity.

God created us to be part of a spiritual family and for His children to share and grow in knowledge and character. Healthy families are committed to each other's growth and well-being. God's will is that we live in harmonious unity.

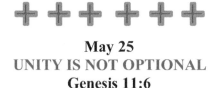

"Y DIJO: ESTA GENTE ES UNA SOLA, Y TODOS ELLOS TIENEN UN SOLO LENGUAJE. YA HAN COMENZADO SU OBRA, Y AHORA NADA LOS HARÁ DESISTIR DE LO QUE HAN PENSADO HACER." GÉNESIS 11:6

"THE LORD SAID, "IF AS ONE PEOPLE SPEAKING THE SAME LANGUAGE THEY HAVE BEGUN TO DO THIS, THEN NOTHING THEY PLAN TO DO WILL BE IMPOSSIBLE FOR THEM." GENESIS 11:6

"ΚΑΙ Ο ΚΎΡΙΟΣ ΕΊΠΕ: Δ'ΕΣΤΕ, ΈΝΑΣ ΛΑΌΣ, ΚΑΙ ΌΛΟΙ ΈΧΟΥΝ ΜΊΑ ΓΛΏΣΣΑ, ΚΑΙ ΆΡΧΙΣΑΝ ΝΑ ΤΟ ΠΡΑΓΜΑΤΟΠΟΙΟΎΝ· ΚΑΙ ΤΏΡΑ ΔΕΝ ΘΑ ΕΜΠΟΔΙΣΤΕΊ Σ' ΑΥΤΟΎΣ ΚΆΘΕ ΤΙ ΠΟΥ ΣΚΟΠΕΎΟΥΝ ΝΑ ΚΆΝΟΥΝ·" ΓΕΝΕΣΙΣ 11:6

MOON OVER KATERINI, GREECE - 5/23/2021 8:42 PM

God does not see a Hispanic, Afro-American, Anglo-Saxon, Catholic or Protestant church. God sees one body, one family, one creation! **Unity is not optional; it's God's will.**

But unity isn't easy. It requires putting self aside and thinking, praying, and planning for the good of God's entire family. Unfortunately, many haven't yet learned to resolve disagreements within the bonds of love.

Unity is God's will for our life and church. Jesus prayed: *"Holy Father, protect them by the power of your name, the name you gave me, so that they may be one as we are one"* **(John 17:11).** We reflect Christian unity through God's love, much like the church in **Acts 4:32**, where *"they shared everything they had."*

162

The first believers gave their hearts and soul to Jesus's Lordship and mission. They lived to serve Christ and were blessed with material possessions to help others. Unless we develop the same mind and purpose, millions will continue to die from hunger, nakedness, thirst, illiteracy, discrimination, loneliness, and dying lost without Christ. Just as the earth is a single planet that protects and feeds its inhabitants, Christ's church is called in unity to be a faithful witness and steward of God's grace and love.

There's strength in unity! When we act as one, we can accomplish the impossible. God said, *"If as one people speaking the same language they have begun to do this, then nothing they plan to do will be impossible for them"* **(Genesis 11:6).**

Let us pray: Dear God, we believe that **Unity is NOT optional.** Please restore the unity you envisioned. May our churches regain their focus on winning souls for Jesus Christ, instructing them in biblical faith, and reaching them through the grace and love of Christ. We pray in Jesus's name.

> God does not see a Hispanic, Afro-American, Anglo-Saxon, Catholic or Protestant church. God sees one body, one family, and one creation. **Unity is not optional; it's God's will.**

May 26
SENT TO HEAL AND LOVE
John 20:21

Today a friend shared the long and often lonely struggle with emotions that stole the joy of life. As believers, we count on those sent by God so that through them, we may receive physical, mental, and spiritual healing. Sin contaminated all creation, and the world could not, and will not, heal itself. God had to send Jesus Christ, our physician, savior, and counselor, to heal and restore our joy.

The Holy Spirit has given understanding and wisdom to pastors specializing in spiritual afflictions and struggles and to doctors specializing in the human body. They, too, are "**God sent.**" God has allowed **doctors** to specialize in the heart, brain, lungs, diseases, etc., and sent them to heal us when our bodies and minds are under stress or attack.

Many live chained by addictions, seduced by worldly attractions. Some good people don't know the power of God to heal and transform their lives through the intervention of the Doctor Par Excellence. Without

163

success, they've tried home remedies, countless prayers, and self-help books to overcome their feelings of defeat, inferiority, or putting aside a lifestyle contrary to God's will. Prayer is powerful, and we must go to God to heal our spirits, but we also trust and go to the medical doctors **sent by** God to heal our bodies and minds.

Jesus proclaimed, *"The Spirit of the Lord is on me, because he has anointed me to proclaim good news to the poor. He has sent me to proclaim freedom for the prisoners and recovery of sight for the blind, to set the oppressed free"* **(Luke 4:18).** You and I, as children of God and disciples of Jesus Christ, are equally "sent." Jesus said, *"As the Father has sent me, I am sending you"* **(John 20:21).**

God poured out the Holy Spirit to infuse us with knowledge, love, tenderness, and power and sent us to work together as a team with doctors, caring for the whole person; mind, spirit, and body. Just as Jesus modeled, doctors and shepherds must act as *"sent children of God"* **(John 10:36).**

Let us pray: Dear Lord, help us heal and love Your people by the power, authority, and wisdom you've given us. Please help us assure them that *"lack of faith"* is not the reason for lingering illnesses or depression. Instead, allow them to trust in the doctors and medicines that, with Your wisdom, we've managed to create. We pray in Jesus's name.

May 27
NO CONDEMNATION
Romans 8:1

How wonderful it is to know, believe, and feel in your heart that despite our past mistakes, God offers us the opportunity to free ourselves from condemnation. *"Come now, let us settle the matter, says the Lord. 'Though your sins are like scarlet, they shall be as white as snow; though they are red as crimson, they shall be like wool'"* **(Isaiah 1:18).**

Jesus, who came to offer us forgiveness, salvation, and freedom, said, *"Very truly I tell you, whoever hears my word and believes him who sent me has eternal life and will not be judged but has crossed over from death to life"* **(John 5:24).** He also said, *"You will know the truth, and the truth will set you free"* **(John 8:32).**

Through hearing the Word and faith in Jesus Christ, we have the freedom to walk with a clear conscience, crossing over from a sentence of *"death to life."* In this way, we can focus on the main task of seeking, healing, and loving the lost sheep while nurturing those who dwell under the shadow of the Almighty.

Whoever has not believed nor felt God's forgiveness carries a hefty load on their shoulders, limiting their ability to run toward the divine goal. Instead of looking up, they're looking back at every corner in case someone discovers their sin. Yet Jesus frees us from such a burden, saying, *"Whoever believes in me is not condemned, but whoever does not believe stands condemned already because they have not believed in the name of God's one and only Son"* **(John 3:18).**

We enjoy the spiritual freedom and clarity to labor in the Lord's vineyard, free from condemnation. God's will is this; that we *"learn to do right; seek justice. Defend the oppressed. Take up the cause of the fatherless; plead the case of the widow"* **(Isaiah 1:17).**

My beloved, if we walk according to the Spirit, not seeking to please the flesh, we have the assurance that *"there is now no condemnation for those who are in Christ Jesus."*

Let us pray: Dear God, thank You for freeing us from the condemnation of sin, for giving us purpose and freedom through Your Word and faith in Jesus Christ. Thank you for depositing seeds of reconciling love and sending us in search of Your lost sheep. Open the gates of heaven for them too. We pray for our sick and those in mourning. Send Your healing and comfort, in Jesus's name.

May 28
RISEN WITH CHRIST
Romans 8:11b

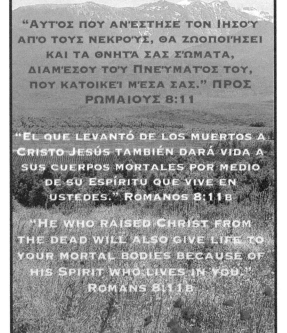

KATERINI FIELDS, MT. OLYMPUS, PIERIA, GREECE

Our text speaks about a future event in which God will *"give life to our mortal bodies."* Those of us who have believed in Jesus Christ, when our mortal bodies have completed the work on earth, we'll sleep, and then the Holy Spirit will awaken us to a new life with new bodies. We anchor our hope in this future promise.

At the same time, speaking spiritually and in past terms, God tells us, *"Since, then, you have been raised with Christ, set your hearts on things above, where Christ is, seated at the right hand of God"* **(Colossians 3:1).** There was a time when I didn't seek the things of God. Like the prodigal son, I turned away from God and wasted the inheritance. I was physically and emotionally dead, but by the grace of our heavenly Father, *"I was lost, and I was found"* **(Luke 15:24).**

165

The spiritual Resurrection represents an unforgettable moment for every believer, when God rescued us from despair, *"from the slimy pit"* (**Psalm 40:2**). For me, it was February 28, 1989. A few months earlier, I was on the edge of a precipice, depressed, feeling like a failure, like I was of no use to family or employer, and overly concerned about financial debt.

When I thought I couldn't take it anymore, the Lord reached out and gave me a second chance to start over, to be a better father and husband, putting God first at home, at work, and in the community. I came to know Jesus Christ as my personal Savior. The Holy Spirit gave me back the joy of living! God *"made us alive with Christ even when we were dead in transgressions"* (**Ephesians 2:5**).

My beloved, having placed our faith and hope in Jesus Christ's sacrifice, we've experienced the Resurrection in our flesh and soul. Through faith, our spirit, which was dead, has *"been raised with Christ."* And one day, we'll shed these fragile and spirit-resistant bodies. God will clothe us with new immortal bodies that perfectly harmonize with our spirit. Remember, God is always waiting with outstretched arms to receive us prodigal children back into the family. Hallelujah!

Let us pray: Dear God, thank You for rescuing and giving us new life and hope through the Resurrection with Christ. Open our understanding to know the Risen Christ better and make Him known through our lives and testimony. We pray in Your Holy Name.

May 29
SPIRIT OF SLAVERY OR ADOPTION?

"The Spirit you received does not make you slaves, so that you live in fear again; rather, the Spirit you received brought about your adoption to sonship. And by him we cry, "Abba, Father." **Romans 8:15**

"Pues ustedes no han recibido un espíritu que los esclavice nuevamente al miedo, sino que han recibido el espíritu de adopción, por el cual clamamos: ¡Abba, Padre"! **Romanos 8:15**

"Δεδομένου ότι, δεν λάβατε πνεύμα δουλείας, ώστε πάλι να φοβάστε, αλλά λάβατε πνεύμα υιοθεσίας, με το οποίο κράζουμε: Αββά, Πατέρα." **ΠΡΟΣ ΡΩΜΑΙΟΥΣ 8:15**

My soul weeps because of Xenophobia, a social problem expressing hatred and fear against people from other cultures and skin tones.

Police are highly trained to de-escalate confrontations and not to use excessive violence. Yet, statistics and videos demonstrate a predominant use of extreme and lethal force against African-Americans like George Floyd. It's as if officers are guaranteed exoneration from hateful assaults that kill or disable such suspects.

In the face of such injustices, Jesus might also tell us, *"I was assaulted, and you did nothing."* And this is where we must ask ourselves whether *"God has given us a spirit of fear or one*

166

of adoption" that recognizes and defends the human value of a brother, a child of God like George Floyd.

Today I exceeded the 500 maximum words of reflection and ask for your indulgence in the face of this social virus that dehumanizes entire cultures. We need to unite and shout, **"Enough!"**

Either we don't understand the United States Constitution or refuse to live by the creed that *"every human being is created in the image of God and is born with the inalienable right to justice, peace, and the freedom"* that great democracies like the USA offer.

Today, after your prayers and dialogue with God, consider going to your doors, windows, balconies, and terraces and shout to God and the world, *"I'm mad, and I'm not going to walk by anymore. Enough with injustice and Xenophobia!"* May we search our hearts and affirm that God has *"given us a spirit not of cowardice but adoption and power."*

Xenophobia won't be eradicated as long as those in Congress have the power and the means to feed us their daily dose of this diabolic poison. My beloved, *you didn't receive a spirit that enslaves you again to fear, but rather the Spirit of adoption,* by which we *"cry, Abba, Father!"* We have the power to eradicate this supremacist virus. Let's ask God to give us clarity and determination to change our countries, starting with our right to vote. **That's our shout of liberty!**

Let us pray: Dear God, perhaps at some point, we were also infected by Xenophobia, but Your love and Spirit of adoption have taught us that we're all Your children, created in Your image. Give us discernment and courage to defend the right of those whose voices are being silenced, to wisely use our vote so that, nowhere on the planet, respect for human-divine dignity is disregarded. Receive Your child, George Floyd, into Your arms and deliver us from this social virus. We pray in Your Holy Name.

May 30
WHEN GOD WEEPS
Matthew 5:4

Matthew 5:4 reminded me of a song that says, *"whether you laugh or cry, I'm with you because I'm a part of you."*[15] **God weeps when we cry.**

Jesus said that he'd be with us *"always even until the end of the world"* **(Matthew 28:20).** If we laugh, God laughs, and if we cry, God cries, **comforts**, and promises to *"wipe our tears"* **(Revelation 21:4).**

---

[15] Los Iracundos - LP "Con Palabras" Track: "Si Lloras, si Ries"

Some believe that God is distant, and because of anger and disillusionment, God has turned His back on humanity. But it's not so. **Jesus knows all of our sufferings and weeps.** The shortest verse in the Bible says, *"Jesus wept"* **(John 11:35)**. Jesus was despised and betrayed by one within the circle of trust. He was denied, slapped, spit on, insulted, ridiculed, falsely accused, whipped, and finally crucified to death for our sake. Jesus accepted this suffering with joy to conquer death and achieve our salvation.

God discerns our thoughts, feels our pain, cries with us, and strengthens our souls. Jesus said that *"in this world we will have afflictions, but that we should be of good cheer because He's over-come the world"* **(John 16:33)**. Through Jesus, we're more than conquerors.

Psalm 33:12 says, *"Blessed is the nation whose God is the Lord, the people he chose for his inheritance."* As sons and daughters of God, we're a chosen nation, a treasured possession, res-cued, redeemed, and restored to continue Christ's work in this world. At our baptism, we were anointed and cleansed, not to live in fear, but to *"proclaim good news to the poor, proclaim freedom for the prisoners and sight for the blind, to set the oppressed free and to proclaim the Year of the Lord's favor"* **(Luke 4.18-19)**. **God weeps when we don't fulfill our purpose.**

As we faithfully go about God's work, *"From heaven, the Lord looks down and sees all man-kind" (Psalm 33:13)*. God weeps at human injustice, knows our struggles, and is near and ready to rescue and dry our tears.

Let us pray: Dear God, thank You because you're not a distant God who doesn't know our feel-ings. Thank you for the faith that the calm will come after the storm and for transforming our la-ment into joy. Since you came into our lives, we're no longer alone or abandoned. On the con-trary, we feel loved in knowing that we have a great cloud of friends and family throughout the world who, together with You, accompany us in our joys and sorrows. We pray in Jesus's mighty name.

May 31
NO SHAME IN STOOPING DOWN
Psalm 113:5-6

I heard about a **young boy** with life-threatening reactions to bee-stings. He was in the car with his mom when suddenly, a bee came in through the half-open window and began to fly around the cabin. The boy became terrified! Without losing control, the mother grabbed the bee. The boy calmed down, but suddenly she released it, which resumed flying around. The boy screamed with fear: *"Mom! Do you want me to die? Why did you let it go?"* The mother calmly said: *"You have nothing to fear, honey. It can't harm you. Look at my hand; see, the stinger is in my hand. It can do you no harm!"*

My beloved friends and family know that Jesus stoops down, inviting us to look closely at the nail prints in His hands and receive comfort knowing that He has paid the price of our rebellion. In Christ, we can remove the word **"fear"** from our vocabulary and **understand** that the Creator of Heaven and Earth, *"who sits enthroned on high, stoops down"* to look upon you and me.

168

The enemy wants us to think that God has much bigger things to worry about than **insignificant, rebellious humans like us**. And we'd be quick to believe the devil if not for God's Word, which assures us that God is aware of and engaged in every aspect of our lives. *"Though the Lord is exalted, he looks kindly on the lowly; though lofty, he sees them from afar"* **(Psalm 138:6).** God lives to *"revive the spirit of the lowly and to revive the heart of the contrite"* **(Isaiah 57:15).** Memorize and recall these verses when you feel like God is distant and unattached. *God is closer than you can imagine!*

There's no shame in stooping down. Jesus mingled with and saved tax collectors and sinners. God sends us also to stoop down to love, protect and restore the lost sheep to their rightful place in God's kingdom. **The Lord counts on you to get closer to the poor, lost and marginalized.**

Let us pray: Dear Lord, help us believe and act knowing that, through Jesus, who **stooped down to us in love,** we can overcome our fears and humble ourselves to love and care for the needy and lonely. We pray in Jesus's name.

✝ ✝ ✝ ✝ ✝ ✝

June 1
THE BENEFITS OF LOVING GOD
1 Corinthians 2:7

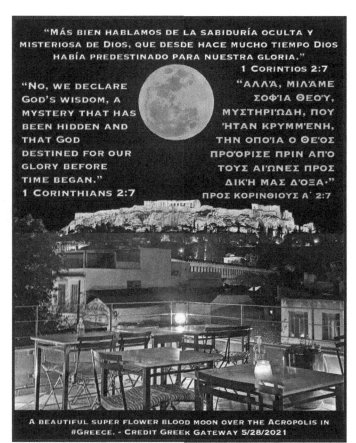

"MÁS BIEN HABLAMOS DE LA SABIDURÍA OCULTA Y MISTERIOSA DE DIOS, QUE DESDE HACE MUCHO TIEMPO DIOS HABÍA PREDESTINADO PARA NUESTRA GLORIA."
1 CORINTIOS 2:7

"NO, WE DECLARE GOD'S WISDOM, A MYSTERY THAT HAS BEEN HIDDEN AND THAT GOD DESTINED FOR OUR GLORY BEFORE TIME BEGAN."
1 CORINTHIANS 2:7

"ΑΛΛΆ, ΜΙΛΆΜΕ ΣΟΦΊΑ ΘΕΟΎ, ΜΥΣΤΗΡΙΏΔΗ, ΠΟΥ ΉΤΑΝ ΚΡΥΜΜΈΝΗ, ΤΗΝ ΟΠΟΊΑ Ο ΘΕΌΣ ΠΡΟΌΡΙΣΕ ΠΡΙΝ ΑΠΌ ΤΟΥΣ ΑΙΏΝΕΣ ΠΡΟΣ ΔΙΚΉ ΜΑΣ ΔΌΞΑ·"
ΠΡΟΣ ΚΟΡΙΝΘΙΟΥΣ Α΄ 2:7

A BEAUTIFUL SUPER FLOWER BLOOD MOON OVER THE ACROPOLIS IN #GREECE. - CREDIT GREEK GATEWAY 5/28/2021

The Bible states, *"How many are your works, Lord! In wisdom you made them all; the earth is full of your creatures"* **(Psalm 104:24A).** Everything God made was good, but disobedience disfigured the perfect harmony between God, humanity, and nature. However, we believe in God's promises. For example, God said, *"'I know the plans I have for you,' declares the Lord, 'plans to prosper you and not to harm you, plans to give you hope and a future'"* **(Jeremiah 29:11).**

Although we don't know all the details of how God will fulfill those plans, we believe that they are good, and we trust the direction and inspiration of His Holy Word, which guides us to our eternal home. The key to partially unfolding God's great mystery lies in the persons of Jesus Christ and the Holy Spirit. Jesus came to show us the Way to the Father, and Jesus sent the Holy Spirit to remind us of *"the Way, the Truth, and Life"* **(John 14:6)** through God's Word.

We cannot understand God's mind with our human minds, but the day is coming when God will *"restore us, that we may live in his presence. Let us acknowledge the Lord; let us press on to acknowledge him. As surely as the sun rises, he will appear; he will come to us like the winter rains, like the spring rains that water the earth"* **(Hosea 6:2b-3)**. One of the *"benefits of loving God"* and His Word is that God reveals Himself and clarifies our path and future.

God's Word says that God has unimaginable things in store for *"those who love him"* **(1 Corinthians 2:9)**. They're things that human eyes and ears haven't seen or conceived, incomprehensible things that the Holy Spirit reveals. Since we claim to love God, we must love and trust His Holy Word as our primary and infallible guide and instruction for life. In it, God reveals Himself and prepares us to understand, in part, the mysteries and promises that God has designed for us children.

Let us pray: Dear God, thank You for opening our ears, eyes, and hearts to know Your will and purpose for our lives. Thank you for revealing *"the Way, the Truth, and the Life"* to us **(John 14:6)**. Please help us be good guides for those who follow our steps and example to reach Your heavenly mansion. We pray in Jesus's name.

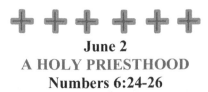

June 2
A HOLY PRIESTHOOD
Numbers 6:24-26

God wanted this blessing to be declared over the *"children of Israel."* To this day, pastors and priests say it over the people when dismissing them from worship.

This verse is a triple blessing and promise:

1. *"The Lord bless you and keep you!"*- declares **goodwill and provision** for those who live under a **covenant** in which God promised to bless and preserve our lives and souls through His omnipresence and power.

2. *"The Lord make his face shine on you and be gracious to you!"* - represents the **presence and mercy** toward God's chosen people. As God's children, we can count on God's intimate presence, guidance, and irreversible salvation: *"Make your face shine on us, that we may be saved"* **(Psalm 80:3).**

"Make His face shine on you" reminds us of Moses' radiant face when he came down from Mount Sinai with the Ten Commandments. God desires to have a face-to-face encounter with every believer who seeks an intimate relationship with God and His people. God offers **mercy** when we make mistakes, whether by word, deed, or omission. Instead of punishing, God will forgive us if we repent from the heart.

3. *"The Lord turn his face toward you and give you peace!"* - *"Turn his face toward you"* represents an act of pleasure and joy toward God's children, similar to when we turn to see our beloved grandchildren or grandnephews attempting to imitate our actions. Whether they fail or succeed, we show joy because they're learning to follow our steps.

"Give you peace" assures us that God is powerful to save, rescue, and heal. Therefore, we can walk with absolute peace by holding God's hand because *"he leads me beside quiet waters"* **(Psalm 23:2).**

My beloved, God calls us to be a *"holy priesthood"* for Him. May we declare this blessing on all of God's people. This is our calling, mission, and purpose.

Let us pray: Dear God, thank You for this undeserved triple blessing. Thank you for calling each believer to *"be a holy priesthood, offering spiritual sacrifices acceptable to God through Jesus Christ"* **(1 Peter 2:5).** Help us at every opportunity to bless our children, family, and friends with this precious triple blessing. We pray in Jesus's name.

June 3
SERVE AND GLORIFY GOD

"Each of you should use whatever gift you have received to serve others, as faithful stewards of God's grace in its various forms." 1 Peter 4:10

"Ponga cada uno al servicio de los demás el don que haya recibido, y sea un buen administrador de la gracia de Dios en sus diferentes manifestaciones". 1 Pedro 4:10

"Κάθε ένας, ανάλογα με το χάρισμα που πήρε, να υπηρετείτε ο ένας τον άλλον σύμφωνα μ' αυτό, ως καλοί οικονόμοι τής πολυειδούς χάρης τού Θεού."
Α΄ ΠΕΤΡΟΥ 4:10

God grants a special gift to each adopted child to **serve and glorify God**. This gift has the power to turn hearts back to God and transform lives and communities.

One of the goals of every human being is to discover their gift. Our instinct is to know the purpose for which we were born in this century and place and to put our gifts to God's and humanity's service. But the enemy opposes such a noble mission.

When my grandmother died in 1968, my father became angry with God and stopped going to church. I took advantage of my father's disillusionment and at age 14 stopped attending church. When Margarita and I got married, it was about the third time I had entered a church in seven years. Very astute, the devil uses anger and disenchantment to distance us from God and prevent us from discovering our purpose.

The enemy also makes us fixate on the failings of others and will use any excuse to distance us from the church or separate us from our partner. For example, an unrequited greeting, a misunderstood comment or a look, turning it into something divisive that, over time, becomes unbearable and irreparable through human eyes. God, however, calls us to give thanks in everything and for everything. Good advice! **Gratitude** heals wounds because it doesn't allow for complaints or grudges.

Thank God I got married into an evangelical Christian family, and fourteen years later, through my father-in-law's example, I learned to love and respect God's Word. In 1989 I discovered my life's purpose; to **serve and glorify God with my gifts** in my life, home, family, community, and with my friends.

When I retired in 2017 as a pastor, I thought that God was done with me. In fact, for over a year, I stopped playing my guitar and writing. Today, by God's grace, I feel complete and grateful for the privilege of continuing to serve and glorify God through daily meditations and this book.

Let us pray: Dear God, thank You for those You have put in our lives to encourage us in Your ways, for their example, patience, and unconditional love. Please help us discover and use the gift you've given us to serve others. We pray in Jesus's name.

> **God grants a special gift to each adopted child to serve and glorify God. This gift has the power to turn hearts back to God and transform lives and communities.**

June 4
A LOVELY OUTFIT
STORED IN HEAVEN
2 Corinthians 5:1

For many, death is most fearsome. My daughter Sophia wrote: "**Death**. *It's not something that I think about daily, but I'm not one to shy away from the topic either. I grew up with my grandparents speaking about death as if it were some sort of a gift. That... in the end, we all share the same inevitable fate. There was no sugarcoating it in*

my family – we're all going to die, so live well, be kind and have faith"[16]

Instead of fearing death, we should view it as a **change of outfit**, with anticipation and joy, like a bride waiting for the day she'll wear her **wedding gown.**

We're here for a short time, with borrowed outfits, useful for our work in this world. But these will be useless in our eternal home. When God has perfected His plans for us, we'll die. Some soften it by saying that we will sleep and have the desired rest and freedom from our labor, pains, sufferings, and anxieties. Afterward, Jesus will awaken us to give us new and incorruptible outfits, which God stores in heaven for now.

"Dear friends, now we are children of God, and what we will be has not yet been made known. But we know that when Christ appears, we shall be like him, for we shall see him as he is" **(1 John 3:2).**

> Instead of fearing death, we should view it as a **change of outfit**, with anticipation and joy, like a bride waiting for the day she'll wear her **wedding gown.**

My beloved, we're "just passing by" this world.
In **Philippians 3:20–21**, God says that *"our citizenship is in heaven. And we eagerly await a Savior from there, the Lord Jesus Christ, who, by the power that enables him to bring everything under his control, will transform our lowly bodies so that they will be like his glorious body."* Jesus will transform our fragile and rebellious outfits into heavenly bodies, perfect like His.

Meanwhile, God sees faithful and helpful ambassadors in us, showing and helping prospective brides to consider and try on the white wedding dresses that will usher all into their heavenly home and citizenship.

Let us pray: Dear God, thank You for the promise of eternal life and citizenship in Your presence. Help us keep our outfits and souls clean and pure; so that when the world sees us, they'll also desire to enjoy **abundant life in eternity**. We pray for the healing of our sick and planet. Cleanse us of all impurity in Jesus's name.

June 5
HAPPY BIRTHDAY IN HEAVEN, DAD

"He said, 'The knowledge of the secrets of the kingdom of God has been given to you, but to others I speak in parables, so that, though seeing, they may not see; though hearing, they may not understand.'" **Luke 8:10**

"Y él les respondió: 'A ustedes se les concede conocer los misterios del reino de Dios, pero a los otros se les habla en parábolas, para que viendo no vean, y oyendo no entiendan'". **Lucas 8:10**

---

[16] The Savvy Travelista. https://thesavvytravelista.blogspot.com/

"Και εκείνος είπε: Σε σας δόθηκε να γνωρίσετε τα μυστήρια της βασιλείας τού Θεού· στους υπόλοιπους, όμως, με παραβολές, για να μη βλέπουν ενώ βλέπουν, και να μη καταλαβαίνουν ενώ ακούν." **ΚΑΤΑ ΛΟΥΚΑΝ 8:10**

On June 5, 1925, 97 years ago, God gave a son to Sergeant Major Federico Destruge Illingworth and Amada Clorinda Maldonado Osorio. They named him Galo Destruge Maldonado. His father passed away when he was barely three years old, and for unknown reasons, my grandmother could not take care of him alone. As a result, my dad grew up in an orphanage, and at age 15, he left there to work and care for his mother and later for his family.

Despite multiple obstacles, he emigrated to the United States to give us a better life. There, God gave new hope and encouragement to the Destruge family. It wasn't easy to leave everything behind, including his mother, but if it weren't for my father, nothing that we have or are would have been possible.

I can only say, **"thank you, Papi."** You lived and fought like everyone else, with courage, leaving us values and teachings that to this day help us face life, sometimes with humor, others with determination. September 2, 2022, will be ten years since his departure. I always remember him with love and gratitude for the good humor and affection that he freely shared with everyone. Happy birthday in heaven, Papi.

Let us pray: Dear God, may Your Holy Spirit grant us keen ears to hear and understand the mysteries, miracles, and promises you have in store for Your children here and in Heaven. We pray in Jesus's name.

June 6
THE GREAT ADVOCATE

"And I will ask the Father, and he will give you another advocate to help you and be with you forever." **John 14:16**

"Y yo rogaré al Padre, y él les dará otro Consolador, para que esté con ustedes para siempre". **Juan 14:16**

"Και εγώ θα παρακαλέσω τον Πατέρα, και θα σας δώσει έναν άλλον Παράκλητο, για να μένει μαζί σας στον αιώνα." **ΚΑΤΑ ΙΩΑΝΝΗΝ 14:16**

The word *"another"* means that there must have been a previous Advocate. Jesus says that while he was in the world, he was our teacher and Advocate. Anticipating His return to heaven, Jesus assures us that God will give us *"another Advocate"* with His same essence. Glory to God!

Jesus promised not to leave us orphans or abandoned **(John 14:18).** Today's verse says that **if we love Him and obey** His commandments **(v.15),** God *"will give you another advocate to help you and be with you forever."*

Therefore, the promise of the Holy Spirit is not unconditional. To receive God's extraordinary power, we must **love Jesus** and demonstrate it through **obedience** to His Word. We all have a special gift that we receive at our baptism as we enter into God's family. **Our task is to discover and fulfill that purpose.**

Speaking with my son about the Bible's complexity, I commented that while it appears complicated and challenging to understand how we're to act and think, it's straightforward. We only have to remember and follow three rules; 1. **Love God**, 2. **Love our neighbor**, and 3. **Love ourselves.** We must express this love with **ALL** our heart, soul, strength, and mind **(Mark 12:30).** All other laws flow from these three.

For Christians, the Bible is God's complete revelation of Jesus Christ, the Lamb of God who takes away the sins and sorrows of the world. The Holy Spirit, **our second Advocate (aka Comforter)**, strengthens and reminds us of all that we've read and learned from God's Word so that we might act, think and speak according to God's will.

I invite you to read **John, chapter 14**. Look carefully at the phrases of comfort and strength that Jesus Christ, our great Advocate and comforter, offers us for times like these:

"1 Do not let your hearts be troubled. You believe in God; believe also in me.
2 I am going there to prepare a place for you.
3 I will come back and take you to be with me.
13 I will do whatever you ask in my name.
15 If you love me, keep my commands.
16 And I will ask the Father, and he will give you another advocate to help you and be with you forever."

Let us pray: Dear God, thank You for being our Advocate, Comforter, and hope. Grant us the power of Your Holy Spirit to love you, understand Your will, and obey Your commandments. We pray in the name of our Great Advocate, Jesus.

> **If you love Jesus and obey** His commandments, God *"will give you another advocate to help you and be with you forever."* **John 14:16**

June 7
THE REASON FOR MY PRAISE
Psalm 108:1

Have you ever considered the **"reason for your praise?"**

Despite the difficulties and sufferings, it's good to sing psalms and praises because God asked us to do so. **Philippians 4:4** says, *"Rejoice in the Lord always. I will say it again: Rejoice!"* We sing praises in good and bad situations because God fills us with hope, and we sow hope in others through them. We rejoice in praising because God *"will transform our mourning into dancing"* **(Psalm 30:11)**, our weakness into strength, and our sickness into the integrity of soul, body, and spirit.

The reason for our praise is that it is medicine for the wounded soul and energy for the tired body. But more importantly, **it's how we transmit our faith from generation to generation.** Although many won't have time to read the Bible, they will pay attention to the praises of your heart which will be engraved in the listeners' minds for days, healing and strengthening their souls.

A reality that some pastors won't admit is that praises are remembered and replayed more often than the pastor's sermon. *"Through Jesus, therefore, let us continually offer to God a sacrifice of praise—the fruit of lips that openly profess his name"* **(Hebrews 13:15).**

Another reason for our praise is that praise satisfies the soul more than a feast and where there is praise, there is the Lord. *"Yet you are holy, enthroned on the praises of Israel"* **(Psalm 22:3).** A Spanish praise song says**,** *"When the Lord's people praise God from their hearts, wonderful things happen; there is healing, liberation, and blessing abound."*

Praises help expand God's kingdom. **Acts 2:47** says, *"praising God and enjoying the favor of all the people. And the Lord added to their number daily those who were being saved."*

There are many reasons for our praise and adoration. God has chosen, healed, acquired, and sanctified us to *"declare the praises of him who called you out of darkness into his wonderful light"* **(1 Peter 2:9).** There's no better way to do this than through praises!

Let us praise: Dear God, great and marvelous are Your works. How could we not sing praises to you? *"My heart, O God, is steadfast; I will sing and make music with all my soul."* Lord, don't allow the trials of this world to silence our lips and hearts of the praises due to Your Holiness, in whose name we pray.

> **Praise** is medicine for the wounded soul and energy for the tired body. But more importantly, **it's how we transmit our faith from generation to generation.**

June 8
YOUR WORKS OF LOVE ARE RECORDED
Revelation 20:12C

During the summer of 2018, I organized more than 19,000 photographs written on various laptops, external drives, and the cloud. I deleted roughly 3,000 duplicates, triplicates, or blurry images, and with the help of google photos, I've sorted them by person, place, and events that have blessed and enriched my life.

I had forgotten some beautiful details that made those moments so special. My memory begins to fail. But thank God for technology which allows us to go back to any particular moment and relive them through photos and videos. To you whose goodness I've recorded in my heart and cloud, thank you for the privilege of serving God together. You've enriched my soul!

Hebrews 6:10 says that *"God is not unjust; he will not forget your work and the love you have shown him as you have helped his people and continue to help them."* This verse represents God's *"gratitude"* for your love toward Him by serving the poor. Whatever you've done, big or small, to restore the dignity of the meek and marginalized, God sees. If we've been kind to one another, God has recorded it in the book of life. How wonderful is that?

In the sacred scriptures, God says: *"Can a mother forget the baby at her breast and have no compassion on the child she has borne? Though she may forget, I will not forget you! See, I have engraved you on the palms of my hands; your walls are ever before me"* **(Isaiah 49:15-16).**

Therefore, dear friends and family, let us not tire of doing good, of sowing seeds of love and hope wherever we see divisions and needs, as this pleases our Creator God. Although the people we serve might not be able to show their gratitude, God's appreciation is enough to feed our souls. On behalf of those who couldn't thank you, I pray that God repays your friendship and kindness.

Let us pray: Dear God, allow our soul to sing, dance, and rejoice, knowing that you've written our names in *the book of life* and on *the palm of your hand.* Heal our sick and planet. We pray in Jesus's name.

Photo: February 13, 2008 at 8:46 a.m. Esthela, Edgar, Dimas (RIP), Cristina, and Naida, serving breakfast from Edgar's truck to the day laborers on the Lowe St Bridge, Norwalk, CT.

June 9
DIVISION WEAKENS
Luke 11:17

There's no doubt that division weakens our resistance. Our world is divided religiously, politically, and socially. The devil has weakened our faith and divided us even within church denominations. The tempter seeks to raise divisions between peoples and families to weaken, divide and conquer. God, however, calls us to the unity of heart, mind, and thought.

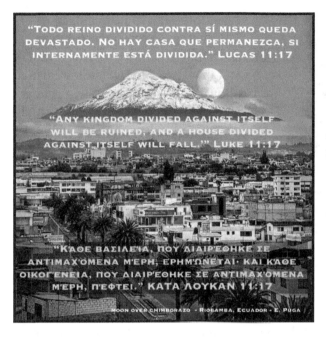

"TODO REINO DIVIDIDO CONTRA SÍ MISMO QUEDA DEVASTADO. NO HAY CASA QUE PERMANEZCA, SI INTERNAMENTE ESTÁ DIVIDIDA." LUCAS 11:17

"ANY KINGDOM DIVIDED AGAINST ITSELF WILL BE RUINED, AND A HOUSE DIVIDED AGAINST ITSELF WILL FALL." LUKE 11:17

"ΚΆΘΕ ΒΑΣΙΛΕΊΑ, ΠΟΥ ΔΙΑΙΡΈΘΗΚΕ ΣΕ ΑΝΤΙΜΑΧΌΜΕΝΑ ΜΈΡΗ, ΕΡΗΜΏΝΕΤΑΙ· ΚΑΙ ΚΆΘΕ ΟΙΚΟΓΈΝΕΙΑ, ΠΟΥ ΔΙΑΙΡΈΘΗΚΕ ΣΕ ΑΝΤΙΜΑΧΌΜΕΝΑ ΜΈΡΗ, ΠΈΦΤΕΙ." ΚΑΤΑ ΛΟΥΚΑΝ 11:17

MOON OVER CHIMBORAZO · RIOBAMBA, ECUADOR · E. PUGA

It's not decorous to have divisions or lawsuits, especially among the body of Christ, the church. In **1 Corinthians 1:10**, we read, *"I appeal to you, brothers and sisters, in the name of our Lord Jesus Christ, that all of you agree with one another in what you say and that there be no divisions among you, but that you be perfectly united in mind and thought."*

As long as there is *"jealousy and quarreling among you, are you not worldly? Are you not acting like mere humans?"* **(1 Corinthians 3:3).** The prince of darkness is dividing us! But God calls us to the unity of heart, mind, and thought. The Bible was given to us to maintain *"the unity of the Spirit through the bond of peace"* **(Ephesians 4:3).** It dictates how to orderly resolve disagreements within the church: *"Whatever happens, conduct yourselves in a manner worthy of the gospel of Christ. Then, whether I come and see you or only hear about you in my absence, I will know that you stand firm in the one Spirit, striving together as one for the faith of the gospel"* **(Philippians 1:27).**

Our behavior within the church, in our homes, and in public must be worthy of the gospel of Christ, steadfast in one spirit, and striving for the faith of the gospel. That's what our children and society expect of us. But most of all, that's what God intends to see in us. *"Finally, all of you, be like-minded, be sympathetic, love one another, be compassionate and humble"* **(1 Peter 3:8).**

Let us pray: Dear God, help us support each other to resist division and maintain unity and peace. May we help each other to perfect ourselves in faith, console each other in our pain and be *"like-minded, sympathetic, love one another, be compassionate and humble."* If we achieve this, we'll live in peace, and You, *"God of peace and love, will be with us forever"* **(2 Corinthians 13:11).** We pray in Jesus's name.

June 10
EVERYTHING SUSTAINED BY HIS POWERFUL WORD

"But we do see Jesus, who was made lower than the angels for a little while, now crowned with glory and honor because he suffered death." Hebrews 2:9

"Jesús, que fue hecho un poco menor que los ángeles, está coronado de gloria y de honra, a causa de la muerte que sufrió". Hebreos 2:9

178

"Αλλά, βλέπουμε τον Ιησού για λίγο ελαττωμένον έναντι των αγγέλων, εξαιτίας τού παθήματος του θανάτου, στεφανωμένον με δόξα και τιμή." ΠΡΟΣ ΕΒΡΑΙΟΥΣ 2:9

My brother Galo Jr. was a watchmaker. When I was around 12 years old, he taught me how to clean and repair mechanical watches. I loved dismantling and putting them back together, leaving them clean and working as they were created, on time and to perfection.

God tells us that He put everything under humanity's *"feet; God left nothing that is not subject to them"* (**Hebrews 2:7-8; Psalm 8:6**). Hebrews 2:8 says, *"Yet at present we do not see everything subject to them."* In other words, we have not accomplished our work of caring for and managing creation.

Concerning the world to come, God tells us, *"But we do see Jesus, who was made lower than the angels for a little while, now crowned with glory and honor because he suffered death"* (**Hebrews 2:9a**).

Jesus, who was fully human, acted on time and perfection, overcoming every obstacle to humbly die for us. *"Therefore God exalted him to the highest place and gave him the name that is above every name, that at the name of Jesus every knee should bow, in heaven and on earth and under the earth, and every tongue acknowledge that Jesus Christ is Lord, to the glory of God the Father"* (**Philippians 2:9-11**).

Jesus is *"far above all rule and authority, power and dominion, and every name that is invoked, not only in the present age but also in the one to come"* (**Ephesians 1:21**). Jesus is *"sustaining all things by his powerful word. After he had provided purification for sins, he sat down at the right hand of the Majesty in heaven"* (**Hebrews 1:3b**).

God created us to function perfectly at His compass and direction. Yet, our world is in disarray because *"we have not yet submitted all things"* under Jesus's feet. He is the master-watchmaker. **Isn't it time to let Him purify and reassemble us to perfection and for His glory?**

> GOD CREATED US TO FUNCTION PERFECTLY AT HIS COMPASS AND DIRECTION. YET, OUR WORLD IS IN DISARRAY BECAUSE *"WE HAVE NOT YET SUBMITTED ALL THINGS"* UNDER JESUS'S FEET.

Let us pray: Dear God, filled with gratitude for rescuing us, we join with those great voices that cry out for eternity: *"Worthy is the Lamb, who was slain, to receive power and wealth and wisdom and strength and honor and glory and praise!"* (**Revelation 5:12**). We pray in Your Holy Name.

NOTE: The book of Hebrews was always complicated for me due to its sophisticated language, contrasts, and comparisons between the law and the superiority of the new dispensation through God's Son, Jesus Christ. From watchmaking and the years working in the finance and Pension Law industry (of which I knew almost nothing at first), I learned to take problems apart, piece by piece and put them back together like clockwork. I learned not to back down from the complicated; instead, to investigate it until God gave me the understanding to explain it in simple terms. This discipline helps in studying the book of Hebrews and the Bible as a whole.

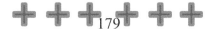

June 11
HOW TO PLEASE GOD

"And without faith it is impossible to please God, because anyone who comes to him must believe that he exists and that he rewards those who earnestly seek him." Hebrews 11:6

"Sin fe es imposible agradar a Dios, porque es necesario que el que se acerca a Dios crea que él existe, y que sabe recompensar a quienes lo buscan". **Hebreos 11:6**

"Χωρίς, μάλιστα, πίστη είναι αδύνατον κάποιος να τον ευαρεστήσει· επειδή, αυτός που προσέρχεται στον Θεό, πρέπει να πιστέψει, ότι είναι, και γίνεται μισθαποδότης σ' αυτούς που τον εκζητούν." **ΠΡΟΣ ΕΒΡΑΙΟΥΣ 11:6**

Hebrews 11 illustrates faith at its best, pointing to individuals like Abel, Enoch, Noah, and Abraham, who pleased God with actions demonstrating great faith, trust, and hope in God. Our challenge: discover **ways to please God.**

First, **we please God by demonstrating our faith**, for *"without faith, it is impossible to please God."* By offering the best of his flock, Abel's sacrifice was pleasing to God. *"Enoch walked with God,"* and his friendship was pleasing to God **(Genesis 5:22, Hebrews 11:5).** Noah believed God and built the ark precisely according to God's specifications. Abraham left everything to go where God indicated. Also, with incredible sorrow, he made all the preparations to sacrifice his only son, trusting that God would resurrect him and provide the sacrificial lamb **(Genesis 22).**

It's not enough to say, *"I believe in God."* Our actions should testify that we *"walk confidently with God."*

Second, **we please God** during our time of prayer and meditation as we approach God's throne daily, **believing that God exists**, that He is real and cares for our well-being and that of our children. It's not enough to believe in God's existence. We must live filled with hope in His presence, sustenance, protection, and direction. My father-in-law used to say, *"It's good to believe, but"* *"even the demons believe, and tremble"* **(James 2:19).** We please God by **doing His will.** And this brings us to the third point.

We please God when we *"earnestly seek him"* with all our hearts. When we're confident that heaven and its rewards and benefits are absolute, and strive to *"seek first God's kingdom"* **(Matthew 6:33).**

Let us pray: Dear God, increase our faith so that our lives, as expressed through words, actions and thoughts, might be pleasing to you and show the world that we **walk confidently holding Your hand.** Thank you for Your tremendous love and all the good you send our way. Heal our sick and our planet. We pray in Jesus's name.

180

June 12
WORDS OF LIFE
Acts 7:38C

A friend sent me a message discrediting a political party. I respectfully asked him, **"please don't send me political propaganda."**
He: "What is the truth, in your opinion, Oscar?"
Me: "I won't enter into political discussions."
He: "Me neither, but Truth is truth."
Me: "'And the Truth will set you free.' That is the only Truth that interests me."
He: "I agree!"
Me: "Thanks! I've saved and gained friendships by not participating in the devil's tactics. I appreciate your understanding, my friend."
He: "God bless, brother."
Me: "Bless you!"

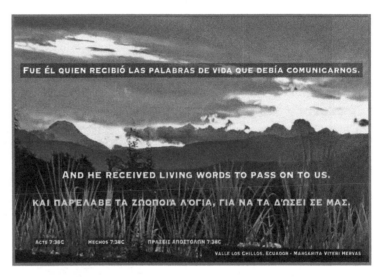

We're bearers of the **Words of Life** in all times, places, and with all people. We can be participants of evil or sowers of seeds of peace, harmony, and hope. The devil wants us to engage in divisive arguments with friends, siblings, spouses, and family. But God calls us to *"love one another"* **(John 11:34).**

Every day **that** we spend five minutes reading God's Words of Life, we receive instructions so that it might go well with us, and we might communicate them to our friends, family, and future generations. The Holy Spirit will remind us of everything we have studied. When sharing them, we ask God that His Word does not return empty but that it be fruitful so that our effort and prayers won't be in vain. As the apostle Paul says;
"Do everything without grumbling or arguing so that you may become blameless and pure, 'children of God without fault in a warped and crooked generation.' Then you will shine among them like stars in the sky as you hold firmly to the word of life. And then I will be able to boast on the day of Christ that I did not run or labor in vain" **(Philippians 2.14-16).**

Today's verse tells us that Moses spoke to God in the desert, and it was he who *"received living words to pass on to us"* **(Acts 7:38).**

What a privilege to be chosen to serve our God by sharing **wonderful words of life** with everyone. The devil seeks to seduce us into divisive fighting, tempting us to abandon the ways of the Lord. Jesus asked the disciples if they also wanted to leave. *"Simon Peter answered him, "Lord, to whom shall we go? You have the words of eternal life. We have come to believe and to know that you are the Holy One of God"* **(John 6:68-69).**

Let us pray: Dear God, help us to feed daily on Your **Words of Life,** to give to those who live far from You so that they may return to their first love, to Your heavenly Mansion. We pray in Jesus's name.

✝ ✝ ✝ ✝ ✝

June 13
GOD MAKE YOUR JOURNEY A SUCCESS
Genesis 24:40A

At the beginning of the pandemic (March 2020), the American Embassy offered humanitarian flights to repatriate us. Still, through various signs, God's angel told us to stay in Ecuador until it's safe to fly. Although we wanted to return home, it was safer and a blessing to remain in Quito.

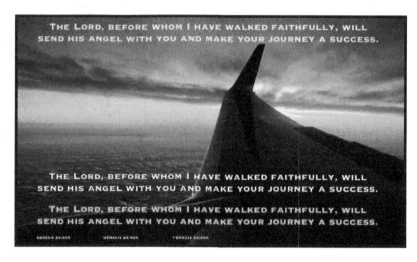

Today we delight in how Abraham obtained a wife for his son Isaac. We first note that Abraham's servant is not identified by name but by his age and responsibility - the oldest of his servants and administrator of his household **(Genesis 24:2). Lesson**: Despite our task's importance, the Lord is the protagonist in our story and all the Bible stories.

Abraham sent his servant to the land of his kindred, saying that *"The Lord, the God of heaven, who brought me out of my father's household —he will send his angel before you so that you can get a wife for my son from there"* **(Genesis 24:7).** Upon arriving at the designated place, the servant entrusted his prosperity to God, *"Lord, God of my master Abraham, make me successful today, and show kindness to my master Abraham"* **(24:12).** He specified the sign by which he'd know that God had granted him success:
"May it be that when I say to a young woman, 'Please let down your jar that I may have a drink,' and she says, 'Drink, and I'll water your camels too'—let her be the one you have chosen for your servant Isaac. By this I will know that you have shown kindness to my master" **(24:14).** God gave the servant success. Isaac married Rebecca, the mother of Esau and Jacob, the patriarch, whose name God changed to Israel. Hallelujah!

This story affirms the key point of **Proverbs 3:5-6;** *"Trust in the Lord with all your heart and lean not on your own understanding; in all your ways submit to him, and he will make your paths straight."* When we trust in the Lord and entrust **ALL** our ways and decisions to God's providence, God's angel will *"go with you and make your journey successful."*

Let us pray: Dear God, we ask that in every decision, both small and large (i.e., whom to marry, where to live, the church where I'll nurture my children, where to retire, when we may return home, etc.), may Your Holy Spirit enlighten us to discern Your voice and direction. **Prosper the way and life** of our children, their children, and those yet to come. We pray in Your Holy Name.

June 14
REBUKE THE LIE
Psalm 53:1

Not only does a fool say, *"There is no God,"* but such a fool attempts to convince everyone else that *"God doesn't exist."* Such was the case of a United States soldier who believed the lie during his entire life. Yet, like the thief on the cross, God revealed Himself on his last day and opened His arms to receive the dying man into paradise.

I was moved by the June 10, 2021, Greek Evangelical meditation (which appears in the photo) and wanted to share it with my beloved friends and family. Following is the translation:

"Today, if you hear his voice, do not harden your hearts" **(Hebrews 3:15).**

"A crumpled piece of paper was found in an American soldier's coat who was killed in the war. It contained a letter to God. Sometimes, the words of a dying person are most authentic.

*'Hear me, my God. I haven't spoken to you before. **I was told that you don't exist**. Last night, however, I looked at your Heavens from the bottom of an artillery bunker and discovered that I had been lied to... But strangely... I had to come to this awful place to see your face. I love you...This is what I want you to know. In a little while, there will be a horrific battle. Who knows, maybe I'll arrive at your house tonight! We haven't been comrades until now, and I wonder if you'll be waiting for me at the door ... **Aghh, If I had only met you earlier!** .... Strange... From the moment I met you, I stopped being afraid of dying. Till we meet again!'"*

As God-loving and God-fearing Christians, our task is to **rebuke and correct the lie**. If we do, many will be released from the bondage of fear into a life of love, peace, joy, and hope. But, if we don't rebuke and correct the lie, someday it might be one of our children in a bunker, who have lived their entire lives in fear of death, crying out, *"aghhh... If only I'd known you sooner."*

Let us pray: Dear Lord, have mercy on us. We pray for our children and their children, who will undoubtedly hear the lie. Reveal yourself to them so that early in their life, they may know you and live and share Your promises joyfully, trusting that you hold their precious lives in Your hand and will welcome them home when they've completed their task in this world. We pray in Jesus's name.

June 15
WHO WILL SEE GOD

"Nothing impure will ever enter it, nor will anyone who does what is shameful or deceitful, but only those whose names are written in the Lamb's book of life." Revelation 21:27

"y no entrará en ella nada que sea impuro, o detestable, o falso, sino solamente los que están inscritos en el libro de la vida del Cordero". Apocalipsis 21:27

"Καὶ μέσα σ' αὐτή δεν θα μπει τίποτε που μολύνει και προξενεί βδέλυγμα, και ψέμα· αλλά, μονάχα οι γραμμένοι μέσα στο βιβλίο τῆς ζωῆς τού Ἀρνίου."
ΑΠΟΚΑΛΥΨΗ ΙΩΑΝΝΟΥ 21:27

Today's verse teaches that nothing impure that the Lamb's Blood hasn't purified will enter into God's Kingdom. *"Only those whose names are written in the Lamb's book of life"* will enter **(Revelation 21:27)**.

Again, we have the theme of the book of life, which invites us to respond to the question, *"How goes it with your heart?"* We must answer it honestly and go through the purification process to find our names in the Lamb's book of life and see God's face.

Moses asked to see God's glory but was only allowed to see His back **(Exodus 33:23)** since *"no one can see God and live"* **(v.20)**. Those who consider ourselves God's adopted children await the day when we'll see God face to face in His kingdom.

To see God's face in His Kingdom, **we must believe in Jesus and live in holiness and peace**. The Greek word for holiness is ἁγιασμός (agiasmós) which also implies **purification** of the heart. Jesus said, *"Blessed are the pure in heart, for they will see God"* **(Matthew 5:8)**.

> To see God's face in His Kingdom, **we must believe in Jesus and live in holiness and peace**.

My beloved, we must allow God's Holy Spirit to guide our desires, actions, words, thoughts, and attitudes. God tells us, *"Make every effort to live in peace with everyone and to be holy; without holiness no one will see the Lord"* **(Hebrews 12:14)**.

It's not easy to be at peace with everyone, especially those who belittle, falsely accuse, or insult us. But remember, what our accusers say has no impact on whether our names appear in the Book of Life. We should say, *"Father, forgive them because they don't know what they are doing"* **(Luke 23:24)**.

We want our names, and those of our children and future generations, to be written in the Book of the Lamb, to see God's face. *"Who may stand in his holy place? The one who has clean hands and a pure heart, who does not trust in an idol or swear by a false god"* **(Psalm 24:3–4)**.

Let us pray: Dear God, we want to see and know you face to face. While we await that day, search our hearts, and if there's anything unpleasant in them, **cleanse us, Lord**. May Your Holy Spirit guide our intentions, actions, and words so that we might please and glorify you in everything, at all times and places. We pray in Your Holy Name.

June 16
TREASURES GAINED BY OBEDIENCE
Luke 6:45

In **1 Samuel 15**, we find Saul, Israel's first King chosen by God, losing his great treasure for disobeying God's instructions. His excuse was, *"I was afraid of the men and so I gave in to them"* **(v.24).** My beloved, it's better to fear God than what man can do.

The Bible teaches that *"no one is good, except God alone"* **(Mark 10:18, Luke 18:19). Psalm 53:3** says, *"Everyone has turned away, all have become corrupt; there is no one who does good, not even one."* Jesus Christ, in

His humanity, demonstrated absolute obedience to God. The fruit of His sacrificial obedience is our Salvation and the church of God, established to spread seeds of love, peace, and hope throughout the world.

Jesus tells us, *"This is to my Father's glory, that you bear much fruit, showing yourselves to be my disciples"* **(John 15:8).** The type of fruit that Jesus expects from our harvest is *"fruit in keeping with repentance"* **(Matthew 3:8).** He also teaches us to judge people, saying, *"By their fruit you will recognize them. Do people pick grapes from thornbushes, or figs from thistles?"* **(Matthew 7:16,20).**

Although no one does completely good, as Jesus showed us, we are created in God's image and carry in our DNA God's seal, which compels us toward obedience, seeking to create treasures in heaven. We've all, at some point, failed God in word, deed, thought, or omission. However, our Creator and Lord expects that we are fruitful through obedience, faith, and repentance.

God placed You and me in this world, time, and place to sow seeds of love, peace, hope, and goodness. Thanks to the **fairly good** people God placed in our path, we've come to trust God and learned to put God first and seek His justice, knowing that God's grace will also give us the fruit of our labor **(Matthew 6:33).**

185

Let us pray: Dear God, thank You for Jesus's life and sacrifice, which showed us the way of sacrifice and obedience. Thank you for the angels you sent to show us the way of truth and life. May we also be good guides and models of fruitful believers for our children and future generations. We pray in Your Holy Name.

June 17
ABANDONED FOR DISOBEDIENCE
1 Samuel 16:14

During the Bible's Old Testament era, we see several examples of God's Spirit abandoning the disobedient. This makes us wonder; will God abandon the believer in Christ who momentarily goes through a period of lack of judgment in which they disobey God's Holy Word?

PRE-JESUS CHRIST DISOBEDIENCE
In the Bible, God abandoned the disobedient without distinguishing between persons. Samson took women who were not from his people. Then, driven by passion, he revealed his source of strength, causing God's power and Spirit to leave him **(Judges 14-16:20)**. Out of fear of the people, King Saul disobeyed God's orders, and the Spirit of God abandoned him **(1 Samuel 16:14)**.

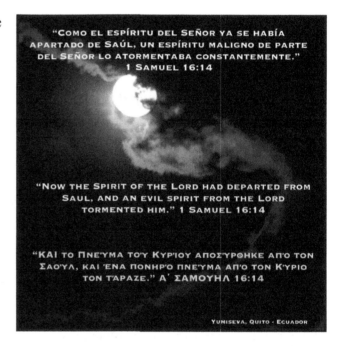

When the Israelites, together with Aaron, the priest, created the golden calf and worshipped it, *"God turned away from them and gave them over to the worship of the sun, moon and stars"* **(Acts 7:42A)**.

The question persists: **Will God abandon the believer in Christ because of disobedience?**

POST-JESUS CHRIST DISOBEDIENCE
It's important to note that before Jesus, God hadn't promised the Holy Spirit indefinitely. However, Jesus promised to send Him to be with the believer *"forever"* **(John 14:16)**. Thus, as genuine disciples of Jesus Christ, our hearts are submissive and obedient to God's will. In which case, God won't abandon us.

Romans 8:38-39 states; *"For I am convinced that neither death nor life, neither angels nor demons, neither the present nor the future, nor any powers, neither height nor depth, nor anything else in all creation, will be able to separate us from the love of God that is in Christ Jesus our Lord."* Though we may abandon the Lord, God will never leave us.

186

It's possible to ***quench the fire of the Holy Spirit*** through our sin of thought, word, action, or omission **(1 Thessalonians 5:19)**. However, that doesn't mean that God's Spirit will abandon us. On the contrary, in times of trial and temptation, the Spirit will always be by our side to show us the way of truth, justice, and love, even the way back to God.

Let us pray: Dear God, thank You for giving us the permanent promise of Your Holy Spirit. We ask for submissive hearts, willing to trust Your Word and do Your will. May our children be assured that you will **never leave or forsake them**. We pray in the name of Jesus Christ, the mediator of this new covenant.

June 18
DEFENDER OF THE POOR
Psalm 9:9

God reveals Himself as the lover and defender of the poor, orphans, widows, and the homeless. The Lord charges us to be His presence, defense, and sustenance for them.

As disciples of Jesus Christ, we cannot forget or ignore this responsibility. God commands justice in favor of the poor, *"Defend the weak and the fatherless; uphold the cause of the poor and the oppressed"* **(Psalm 82:3)**.

Someone might argue, *"We pay taxes. Our government takes care*

of the needy." But the government doesn't have your spiritual gifts to quench spiritual hunger, to give hope and encouragement to the fallen. God gave us skills and resources to share with all those in need and warns us, *"Whoever shuts their ears to the cry of the poor will also cry out and not be answered"* **(Proverbs 21:13)**.

God is the defender of the poor. *"He rescues the life of the needy from the hands of the wicked"* **(Jeremiah 20:13)**. But God does this through the church that Jesus Christ founded to be the needy's physical and spiritual sustenance. You and I are the church of Christ, called to be for the poor, a source of refuge, care, and defense against injustice.

When the Lord saved me, I prayed, *"open my eyes and ears so that I may hear and see the needs of those around me, give me the wisdom to do the right thing."* God allowed me to create a prayer and fellowship group in my office, where I learned to listen and pray for the needs of the people. God also sent me on various mission trips to Nicaragua, Costa Rica, Ecuador, and Bolivia, to help

> **You and I are the church of Christ, called to be for the poor, a source of refuge, care, and defense against injustice.**

the poor and needy physically, mentally, and spiritually. I learned that the spiritual leader serves without forgetting the poor and needy.

God is the defender of the poor. *"You rescue the poor from those too strong for them, the poor and needy from those who rob them"* **(Psalm 35:10).** In Norwalk, I had the privilege of serving the Day Laborers of the Lowe Street Bridge, defending their wage rights, teaching them English, and caring for their physical, emotional, and spiritual health. **God protects the poor through committed people like you.**

Let us pray: Dear God, thank You for the privilege of being Your presence, refuge, and sustenance for the poor and needy in our environment. We ask that our children and future generations be attentive to Your voice, calling them to serve, and in times of personal need, send Your angels to tend to their ailments and supply their necessities. We pray in Jesus's name.

✛ ✛ ✛ ✛ ✛ ✛

JUNE 19
ANGEL OF THE LORD
Acts 5:20

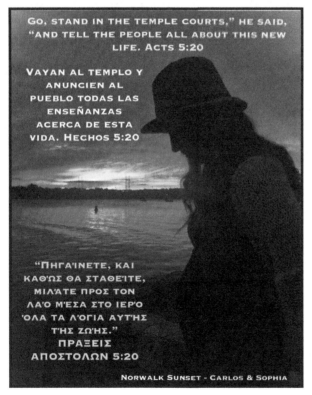

"GO, STAND IN THE TEMPLE COURTS," HE SAID, "AND TELL THE PEOPLE ALL ABOUT THIS NEW LIFE. ACTS 5:20

VAYAN AL TEMPLO Y ANUNCIEN AL PUEBLO TODAS LAS ENSEÑANZAS ACERCA DE ESTA VIDA. HECHOS 5:20

"ΠΗΓΑΊΝΕΤΕ, ΚΑΙ ΚΑΘΏΣ ΘΑ ΣΤΑΘΕΊΤΕ, ΜΙΛΆΤΕ ΠΡΟΣ ΤΟΝ ΛΑΌ ΜΈΣΑ ΣΤΟ ΙΕΡΌ ΌΛΑ ΤΑ ΛΌΓΙΑ ΑΥΤΉΣ ΤΉΣ ΖΩΉΣ." ΠΡΑΞΕΙΣ ΑΠΟΣΤΟΛΩΝ 5:20

NORWALK SUNSET - CARLOS & SOPHIA

The number of believers grew more and more based on the teachings and miracles done by the apostles **(Acts 5:12).** The high priest and the Sadducees, filled with jealousy, put the apostles in prison **(Acts 5:17-18).** At night, an angel of the Lord appeared *"and opened the prison doors ... the angel said to them, 'Go, stand in the temple courts, and tell the people all about this new life.' After hearing this, they entered the temple in the morning and began to teach"* **(vs.20-21).**

Faced with jealousy and opposition from the world, **the Lord's angel will always fulfill** God's purpose. Nothing would stop the apostles from preaching the good news of salvation or healing and setting the captives free. Nothing should deter us from fulfilling what the **angel of the Lord** has entrusted to us, to preach the gospel with actions and, if necessary, with words.

God often sends His **angel** to communicate, defend, and guide us to safety. The **angel of the Lord** instructed Joseph to receive Mary as his wife, even though she was pregnant because the child in her was conceived by God's Holy Spirit **(Matthew 1:20).** The **angel** also warned Joseph and Mary to flee to Egypt to save Jesus's life **(Matthew 2:13).**

But sometimes, the **angel of the Lord** is God Himself, as seen in Moses and the burning bush. *"There the angel of the Lord appeared to him in flames of fire from within a bush... that ...did not burn up. So Moses thought, 'I will go over and see this strange sight—why the bush does not burn up.' When the Lord saw that he had gone over to look, God called to him from within the bush, 'Moses! Moses!' And Moses said, 'Here I am'"* **(Exodus 3:2–4).**

We must pay equal attention since we can't distinguish between God's voice and His angels. Why? Because, even if it were only an angel, he comes with **God's message and authority** to ensure that you, I, our children, and their children's children arrive at our destination safely.

Let us pray: Dear God, thank You for the angels that you've sent throughout our lives. I don't know where I'd be today if it weren't for Your grace, love, and angels, who, at the right time, brought us good news and clear instructions. Please help us pay to attention when you call and to **do Your will**. We pray in Jesus's name.

> "Even if it were only an angel, he comes with God's message and authority to ensure that you, I, our children, and their children's children arrive at our destination safely."

June 20
GOD ANSWERS IMMEDIATELY

"When I am in distress, I call to you, because you answer me." **Psalm 86:7**

"Cuando me encuentro angustiado, te llamo porque tú me respondes". **Salmo 86:7**

"Σε ημέρα θλίψης θα σε επικαλούμαι, επειδή θα με εισακούς." **ΨΑΛΜΟΙ 86:7**

Good thing the Lord doesn't have an answering machine, interactive voice response system, call-waiting, or caller ID! For businesses, these represent practical systems to receive messages, help clients conclude their transactions, or transfer the call to the appropriate representative.

For individuals, these systems are also helpful in receiving messages while we're away or blocking annoying telemarketers. But God doesn't use these systems. Instead, He immediately answers each call personally and, if we're in danger, sends one of His angels to guide us to safety.

Imagine how you'd feel if, when invoking God's name, you'd hear a long list of options; *"To speak in Spanish, press 1. To speak in Italian, press 2. There's a 26-hour wait to speak with God.*

189

If you wish to hold, press 3. To leave a message, wait till the end of this recording, and leave your petition at the sound of the tone."

Although God is possibly answering between 6 and 7 billion calls when your call comes in, God personally answers you; *"My son, my daughter, how good to hear your voice. How are you?"* God's personal, intimate, and immediate attention makes us respond with gratitude and confidence, *"When I am in distress, I call to you, because you answer me"* **(Psalm 86:7).**

God says, *"Call to me and I will answer you"* **(Jeremiah 33:3A).** God will hear your voice and personally answer because God's ear is attentive to the cry of all God's children, especially orphans and widows. *"Do not take advantage of the widow or the fatherless. If you do and they cry out to me, I will certainly hear their cry"* **(Exodus 22:22-23).**

But, also remember that God is jealous and has sworn **not to hear our cry** when we go after other gods. *"Although they cry out to me, I will not listen to them"* **(Jeremiah 11:11B).** If we walk within God's will and guidance, **God will answer our call**! Therefore, it's essential to know God's heart and will and ensure that we act according to the covenant established for God's children.

Let us pray: Dear God, thank You for not blocking our calls and for hearing our cry when we call you. Give us hearts committed to You, with discernment to detect the world's hypocrisy so as not to fall into idolatry, temptations, or displease you in word, deed, omission, or thought. We pray in Your Holy Name.

June 21
JESUS CAME TO FULFILL THE LAW
Psalm 119:126

Is it true that our generation has *"broken"* God's law? The Hebrew word in our text is פָּרַר (pārar); its synonyms include *"break, violate, frustrate: void, undo, impede, infringe, invalidate, belittle, lose."*

Some versions of the Spanish Bibles say, *"they have broken, dissipated, disobeyed, violated, forgotten, invalidated your law."* Jesus said, *"Do not think that I have come to abolish the Law or the Prophets; I have not come to abolish them but to fulfill them"* **(Matthew 5:17).** Jesus came to fulfill all the prophecies about Him and save the world from its sins, since *"without the shedding of blood, there is no forgiveness"* **(Hebrews 9:22).**

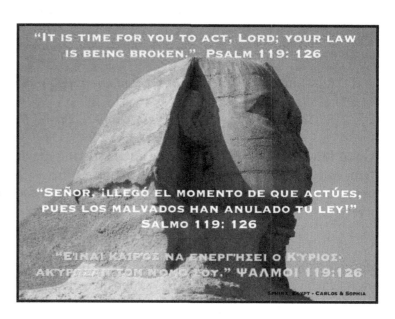

With the arrival, death, and resurrection of Jesus Christ and the Temple's destruction, ceremonial laws (sacrifices) were annulled. On the cross, Jesus Christ became the *"Lamb of God who takes away the sin of the world"* (**John 1:29**). God also showed Peter that He abolished the dietary laws which separated God's people from others. God said, *"Do not call anything impure that God has made clean"* (**Acts 10:15**).

The Israelites could no longer call non-Jews impure because *"there is neither Jew nor Gentile, neither slave nor free, nor is there male and female, for you are all one in Christ Jesus"* (**Galatians 3:28, Colossians 3:11**). Jesus turned the world upside down. He eliminated repaying evil with evil in favor of *"turning the other cheek"* (**Matthew 5:39**). He taught us to *"forgive our debtors"* (**Matthew 6:12**), that the last shall be first (**Mark 9:35**), that the least is greater (**Luke 7:28**), and that the *poor are blessed* (**Matthew 5:3**).

But Jesus did not and will not change God's moral commandments. The fact that God declared, *"Do not call anything impure that God has made clean,"* does not mean that everything that God has called abominable is now good. What God has called impure, only God has the power to change. Our governments can create laws contrary to God's morality, but that doesn't mean that Christians must submit to human laws which nullify God's law (**Acts 4:19**).

Let us pray: Dear God, we pray for clarity to discern between good and evil and compassion to be slow to judge those who today lead a lifestyle contrary to Your Holy Word because, in times past, we were also enemies of Your kingdom. Thank you for purifying us through the sacrifice of Jesus Christ, in whose name we pray.

June 22
IN LOVE WITH JESUS AND HIS WORD

"And because I consider all your precepts right, I hate every wrong path." Psalm 119:128

"Yo estimo la rectitud y pureza de tus mandamientos; por eso me he alejado de la senda de mentira". Salmo 119:128

"Γι' αυτό, γνώρισα ορθές όλες τις εντολές σου για κάθε πράγμα· και μίσησα κάθε δρόμο ψευτιάς." ΨΑΛΜΟΙ 119:128

I was six years old when my mother took me to the movies. We saw *"King of Kings,"* and I met the eternal lover of my life. Seeing the purity of His sacrificial life, I **fell in love with Jesus and His Word.** I **fell in love again with Jesus and His Word** at age 10, when my father gave my mother a Bible. I read it regularly and rediscovered the *purity and righteousness* of His love and Words.

At age 14, as teenagers do, I stopped attending church until 19 years of age. In my first job, I met Marie who insisted that we go to mass. She said, *"God gives us 168 hours of life every week, and He only asks us to give Him back one hour. Can't you do that for God? And if not, do it for me. But I tell you, my grandmother will like it very much if I tell her that you're going to church with me."*

Later on, I met Margarita, got married, and five years later had our first child. I started playing bass guitar in the church choir every Sunday with my brothers. It was nothing more than an artistic commitment. I no longer felt in love with Jesus. I had walked away from God, but God didn't forget me. Jesus, the good shepherd, left the 99 sheep and came in search of that child who felt His love and calling at age six.

> *"God gives us 168 hours of life every week, and He only asks us to give Him back one hour. Can't you do that for God? And if not, do it for me. But I tell you, my grandmother will like it very much if I tell her that you're going to church with me."* **Marie Frangipane**

At age 35, in the most challenging time of my life, God opened my eyes and showed me the greatness of His love and how much Jesus suffered so that I could return to my first love. In 1989, **I fell in love again with the one who was so important in my mother's life.** Thus began an unshakable regimen of study, prayer, and worship that, for 33 years, has filled my life with purpose, joy, peace, hope, and love. Since then, even during trials, I've enjoyed all the flavors and fragrances that life offers when we **walk in love with Jesus and His Holy Word.**

Let us pray: Dear God, thank You for touching my heart, causing that, *"The law from your mouth be more precious to me than thousands of pieces of silver and gold"* **(Psalm 119:72).** Thank you for forgiving my failures and healing my ailments. May our testimony lead others to fall in love with You and Your Word. We pray in Jesus's name.

June 23
GOD HAS POWER OVER STORMS
Mark 6:51

In **Psalm 107:28-30**, we find the verses parallel to our text. *"In their trouble they cried to Adonai, and he rescued them from their distress. He silenced the storm and stilled its waves, and they rejoiced as the sea grew calm. Then he brought them safely to their desired port"* **(Complete Jewish Bible).**

In **Mark 4:37-39,** we find the disciples terrified because *"a furious squall came up, and the waves broke over the boat, so that it was nearly swamped. Jesus was in the stern, sleeping on a cushion. The disciples woke him and said to him, 'Teacher, don't you care if we drown?' He got up, rebuked the wind and said to the waves, 'Quiet! Be still!' Then the wind died down and it was completely calm."*

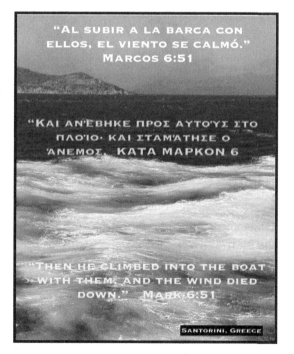

When the Lord Jesus enters our lives, His Word and presence calm our storms, filling us with peace, joy, and hope that we'll arrive unharmed at our safe harbor with Him as captain of our boat.

Yes, my beloved, the Creator of the universe and Savior of our lives, wants and can silence our physical, mental, and spiritual storms. Some storms are natural and beyond our control — we can only entrust ourselves to God's mercy. Others are initiated by the devil so that we'd abandon our first love and go in search of personal power and glory. Some of the devil's lies include, *"God does not exist. Have you ever seen Him? Even if he existed, you wouldn't be in this situation if He loved you. I can save you from this storm if you serve me."*

I implore you not to pay attention to those lies. God exists, loves you, and has good plans for your life. God has absolute power over nature, and in the name of Jesus, you can cast out negative thoughts, entrusting your life to the one who has authority over the universe. **Psalm 65:7** says the Lord *"stilled the roaring of the seas, the roaring of their waves, and the turmoil of the nations."*

Let us pray: *"Lord, guide my ship to Your safe and peaceful harbor because, in the fierceness of the storms, my boat could sink! Direct my course and give me courage, give me confidence, and serenity"* (Author unknown). Calm the winds of our storms. Increase our faith to resist fear. Increase our love for you and our neighbor. We pray in Jesus's name.

JUNE 24
JOY IN TRIBULATIONS
2 Corinthians 7:4b

Perhaps we haven't achieved what we wanted. Possibly some plans were truncated due to changes or unexpected events, causing our present to be quite different from what we dreamed of. In such moments, we trust that God's good plans will give us victory in any situation. For this reason, although we may seem *"sorrowful, yet always rejoicing; poor, yet making many rich; having nothing, and yet possessing everything"* **(2 Corinthians 6:10).**

Thankfully, I believe that few of us have been jailed because of our faith in Jesus. However, throughout history, many have suffered and rejoiced to *"participate in the sufferings of Christ"* **(1 Peter 4:12).**

193

The Apostles expected the multitudes to welcome the Salvation message with joy, but, on the contrary, Peter and John were imprisoned for teaching in Jesus's name. *"They ...had them flogged. Then they ordered them not to speak in the name of Jesus, and let them go. The apostles left the Sanhedrin, rejoicing because they had been counted worthy of suffering disgrace for the Name"* **(Acts 5:40-41).** Likewise, Paul and Silas were flogged and thrown in jail. Despite seeing their dreams crumble, in the isolation of their prison, they prayed and sang *"hymns to God, and the other prisoners were listening to them"* **(Acts 16:25).**

Jesus said, *"In this world you will have trouble. But take heart! I have overcome the world"* **(John 16:33).** Having a high level of trust in God, His power, dominion, and fidelity allows us to remain joyful in our suffering, knowing that God will open the door of victory, glory, and rejoicing. *"For our light and momentary troubles are achieving for us an eternal glory that far outweighs them all"* **(2 Corinthians 4:17).**

I'd always dreamed that in retirement, I'd live three months in Ecuador, three months in Greece, and the rest of the time in the USA. In 2020, without planning, this dream came true. Because of COVID, we lived in Ecuador for three months, and although we were in quarantine, for me, it was a time of joy, gladness, and spiritual restoration. **Praises of the People** and **Morning Praise** videos began as a result of the quarantine.

Let us pray: Dear God, Thank you for placing angels around to support us in our times of trouble. Increase our faith to know that even amid trials, you are by our side, that you have power over our storms and will help us be Your faithful and joyful servants. We pray in Jesus's name.

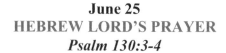

June 25
HEBREW LORD'S PRAYER
Psalm 130:3-4

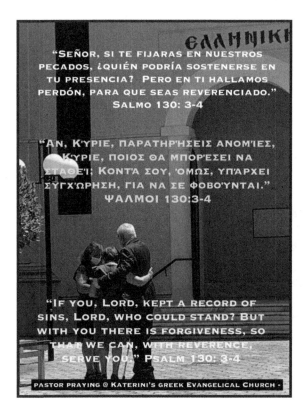

PASTOR PRAYING @ KATERINI'S GREEK EVANGELICAL CHURCH

Psalm 130, a Hebrew prayer similar to The Lord's Prayer, contains repentance, confession, hope, and trust in God.

REPENTANCE - *"Out of the depths I cry to you, Lord; Lord, hear my voice. Let your ears be attentive to my cry for mercy"* **(v.1-2).** The Lord closes His ears to the cry of the wicked who have rejected God's protection. Appealing to His mercy, we pray that God wouldn't leave us, that His ears be attentive to our cries. Even if we've momentarily abandoned Him, God will never forsake us.

CONFESSION - *"If you, Lord, kept a record of sins, Lord, who could stand? But with you there is forgiveness, so that we can, with reverence, serve you"* **(v.3-4).** Our thoughts can take us to the depths of despair or the heights of bliss. Some incorrectly think that God won't forgive their sins. By feeding daily on God's Word, we learn that *"If we confess our sins, he is faithful and just and will forgive us our sins and purify us from all unrighteousness"* **(1 John 1:9).** If God is our Lord, we can count on His love, mercy, forgiveness, correction, restoration and fly again like eagles.

HOPE - *"I wait for the Lord, my whole being waits, and in his word I put my hope. I wait for the Lord more than watchmen wait for the morning, more than watchmen wait for the morning"* **(v.5-6).** We must approach God's throne with hope and confidence in His promises; with gratitude and without fear because God has invited us to cast our burdens on Him.

TRUST - *"Israel, put your hope in the Lord, for with the Lord is unfailing love and with him is full redemption. He himself will redeem Israel from all their sins"* **(v.7-8).** God calls us to fully trust in the Lord and His Word. Jesus Christ is the only one who can save us from our sins and a destiny of being wholly separated from God. He's the Savior and Mediator who grants us entrance to the heavenly mansion.

> *We must approach God's throne with hope and confidence in His promises; with gratitude and without fear because God has invited us to cast our burdens on Him.*

Let us pray: Dear God, thank You for another week of life and sustenance in Your presence. For Your Word and Holy Spirit, who daily calls us to recognize our failures and submit ourselves to Your correction and direction. You're our only hope Lord. Heal our planet and our sick. We pray in Jesus's name.

June 26
LISTEN, FORGIVE, JUDGE, AND ACT
2 Chronicles 20:9

Our key verse is a call to prayer, the most potent weapon to overcome our afflictions. It invites us to imitate God, who, with love and justice, LISTENS, FORGIVES, JUDGES, and ACTS in response to our repentant hearts. It also calls us to imitate the faith of our ancestors.

This verse was proclaimed by King Jehoshaphat and is a repetition of the prayer of his great-great-grandfather, King Solomon, when he dedicated the first

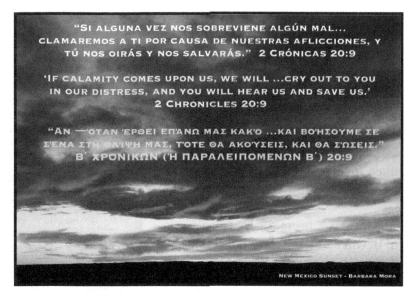

"SI ALGUNA VEZ NOS SOBREVIENE ALGÚN MAL... CLAMAREMOS A TI POR CAUSA DE NUESTRAS AFLICCIONES, Y TÚ NOS OIRÁS Y NOS SALVARÁS." 2 CRÓNICAS 20:9

'IF CALAMITY COMES UPON US, WE WILL ...CRY OUT TO YOU IN OUR DISTRESS, AND YOU WILL HEAR US AND SAVE US.' 2 CHRONICLES 20:9

"ΑΝ —'ΟΤΑΝ 'ΕΡΘΕΙ ΕΠ'ΑΝΩ ΜΑΣ ΚΑΚ'Ο ...ΚΑΙ ΒΟΉΣΟΥΜΕ ΣΕ Σ'ΕΝΑ ΣΤΗ ΘΛΙΨΗ ΜΑΣ, Τ'ΟΤΕ ΘΑ ΑΚΟΎΣΕΙΣ, ΚΑΙ ΘΑ Σ'ΩΣΕΙΣ." Β΄ ΧΡΟΝΙΚΩΝ ('Η ΠΑΡΑΛΕΙΠΟΜΕΝΩΝ Β΄) 20:9

NEW MEXICO SUNSET - BARBARA MORA

Temple (**1 Kings 8**). God affirms the call to prayer and repentance, saying, *"if my people, who are called by my name, will humble themselves and pray and seek my face and turn from their wicked ways, then I will hear from heaven, and I will forgive their sin and will heal their land"* (**2 Chronicles 7:14**).

The response to King Solomon's prayer is; * *"when they turn back to you and praise your name, HEAR from heaven, FORGIVE, JUDGE and ACT"* (**v.46**).

"31 When anyone wrongs their neighbor*
33 When your people Israel have been defeated*
35 When the heavens are shut up and there is no rain*
37 When famine or plague comes to the land… or when an enemy besieges them in any of their cities, whatever disaster or disease may come*
41 As for the foreigner who … has come from a distant land because of your name*
44 When your people go to war against their enemies, wherever you send them*
46 When they sin against you—for there is no one who does not sin)"*
(**1 Kings 8.31,33,35,37,41,44,46**).

Before speaking, listen carefully to what is said and what is not said. Before we refuse to forgive, remember how many times we've been forgiven. Before judging and acting, let's ask ourselves, **"what would Jesus do or say?"** What did our great-grandfather do or say in this situation?

Let us pray: Dear God, *"we have no power to face this vast army that is attacking us. We do not know what to do, but our eyes are on you"* (**2 Chronicles 20:12**). Thank you for teaching us how to turn back from our evil ways, to seek Your face, and know that filled with compassion, you'll hear our cry, forgive our rebellions, judge against our adversaries, and act to give us Your peace and justice. Please help us judge and act according to Your loving grace, imitating our ancestors' faith. We pray in Your Holy Name.

JUNE 27
REBUKE THE SINNER. FORGIVE THE REPENTANT
Luke 17:3

As Christians, we're responsible for our brothers, sisters, and the lost sheep. If we discover someone in sin or committing an **offense**, we must **rebuke** them. If they **repent**, we must **forgive** and support them so they don't fall back into the enemy's camp.

As Christian disciples, Jesus warns us to **beware of sin**. As with tribulations, there will always be *"stumbles."* As long as the prince of darkness rules the earth, *"Things that cause people to*

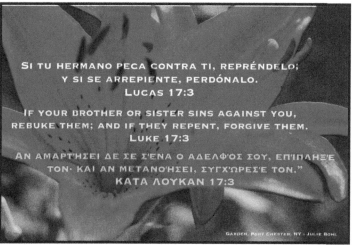

SI TU HERMANO PECA CONTRA TI, REPRÉNDELO;
Y SI SE ARREPIENTE, PERDÓNALO.
LUCAS 17:3

IF YOUR BROTHER OR SISTER SINS AGAINST YOU,
REBUKE THEM; AND IF THEY REPENT, FORGIVE THEM.
LUKE 17:3

ΑΝ ΑΜΑΡΤΉΣΕΙ ΔΕ ΣΕ Σ'ΕΝΑ Ο ΑΔΕΛΦ'ΟΣ ΣΟΥ, ΕΠ'ΙΠΛΗΞΈ
ΤΟΝ. ΚΑΙ ΑΝ ΜΕΤΑΝΟΉΣΕΙ, ΣΥΓΧ'ΩΡΕΣ'Ε ΤΟΝ."
ΚΑΤΑ ΛΟΥΚΑΝ 17:3

GARDEN, PORT CHESTER, NY - JULIE BOHL

196

stumble are bound to come, but woe to anyone through whom they come" **(Luke 17:1).** Jesus cautions us to make sure we're not the cause of stumbling and division. Our lifestyle, words, and actions must be consistent with Jesus's teachings and example. Otherwise, it'd *"be better for them to be thrown into the sea with a millstone tied around their neck than to cause one of these little ones to stumble"* **(Luke 17:2).**

"So watch yourselves," Jesus says. He illustrates how the enemy uses us to cause little ones to stumble in their faith through our anger, rage, judgment, and **failure to rebuke error and forgive the repentant**. *"If your brother or sister sins against you, rebuke them"* **(Luke 17:3).** Failure to rebuke is also a cause for stumbling. So, what's the Christian way of rebuking? Jesus is our example!

> The enemy uses us to cause little ones to stumble in their faith through our anger, rage, judgment, and **failure to rebuke error and forgive the repentant**.

Before correcting a brother, ask yourself; **How would Jesus rebuke him**? I think that Jesus, with eyes of love, said to the adulterous woman, *"neither do I condemn you. Go now and leave your life of sin"* **(John 8:11).** If, instead, we rebuke with accusations like, **"You're never going to be ...** or "**you're not good enough ...**", we're accusing, judging, and being a stumbling block for someone for whom Jesus gave His life. *"Leave your life of sin"* are words of love and a lifeline for those who find themselves shipwrecked in a sea of sin.

"And if he repents, forgive him." We're commissioned to build up the fallen and the lost sheep. If they repent, we must forgive them, even if they sinned multiple times on the same day. If we cling to society's modus operandi of pretending, **"I forgive, but I don't forget,"** our unconscious will take control of our words and actions, causing us to become stumbling blocks because of our lack of genuine forgiveness.

Let us pray: Dear God, Holy Spirit, give us words of love to rebuke those who've fallen into sin and Your grace to forgive whole-heartedly those who repent. We pray in the name of Jesus, our compassionate teacher and Savior.

June 28
ONLY IN YOU, I TRUST, LORD!

"The Lord is my rock, my fortress and my deliverer; my God is my rock, in whom I take refuge, my shield and the horn of my salvation, my stronghold." Psalm 18:2

"Mi Señor y Dios, tú eres mi roca, mi defensor, ¡mi libertador! Tú eres mi fuerza y mi escudo, mi poderosa salvación, mi alto refugio. ¡En ti confío"! Salmo 18:2

"Ο Κύριος είναι πέτρα μου, και φρούριό μου, και ελευθερωτής μου· Θεός μου, βράχος μου· σ' αυτόν θα ελπίζω· η ασπίδα μου, και το στήριγμα11 της σωτηρίας μου· ψηλός πύργος μου." ΨΑΛΜΟΙ 18:2

Although life, in general, is difficult, in times of COVID, this pilgrimage has become even more complicated. We continue to pray for our sick and say goodbye to loved ones who left too soon. Although masks are no longer required outdoors in many places, many choose not to get vaccinated against COVID-19. Thus, not all are protected. Who knows if we've passed this valley of shadows of death or if a new contamination wave looms on the horizon?

Because the Lord is our God, amid threats, dangers, and uncertainties, we confidently cry out, *"my God is my rock, in whom I take refuge, my shield and the horn of my salvation, my stronghold"* **(Psalm 18:2).** We trust because only *"God is our refuge and strength, an ever-present help in trouble"* **(Psalm 46:1).**

Knowing that Saul was looking to kill him, David remained hidden in the desert. His friend *"Jonathan went to David at Horesh and helped him find strength in God"* **(1 Samuel 23:16).** *"David stayed in the wilderness strongholds and in the hills of the Desert of Ziph. Day after day Saul searched for him, but God did not give David into his hands"* **(1 Samuel 23:14).**

It's comforting to know that, although many seek to harm us, the Lord will prevent them from finding us because our life is hidden in God, our defender, savior, strength, and shield. Likewise, if we've received the COVID vaccine, we're more confident that the virus will not affect us as much as if we weren't immunized.

In our surroundings, there are many hiding in deserts, without protection or encouragement, unaware of the help, defense, and security that God offers. Others don't believe in God or the COVID vaccine and remain unprotected. They all need to hear, know, and be encouraged to trust God so that they may be delivered and rescued from this valley of the shadow of death.

Let us pray: Dear God, thank You for being *"my rock, my fortress and my deliverer; my God is my rock, in whom I take refuge, my shield and the horn of my salvation, my stronghold."* Give us boldness and wisdom to encourage all those hiding and unprotected to trust in Your safety and protection. We pray in Jesus's name.

June 29
DIVINE EARS

"In my distress I called to the Lord; I cried to my God for help. From his temple he heard my voice; my cry came before him, into his ears." Psalm 18:6

"Pero en mi angustia, Señor, a ti clamé; a ti, mi Dios, pedí ayuda, y desde tu templo me escuchaste; ¡mis gemidos llegaron a tus oídos"! Salmo 18:6

"Στη στενοχώρια μου επικαλέστηκα τον Κύριο και αναβόησα στον Θεό μου. Από τον ναό του άκουσε τη φωνή μου και η κραυγή μου ήρθε μπροστά του, έφτασε στ' αυτιά του."
ΨΑΛΜΟΙ 18:6

Prayer to God is a frank, open heart-to-heart conversation. God knows everything on our minds and hearts and wants to hear it from our lips because this is how we demonstrate our faith and trust in God. Don't be afraid to approach God, *"For the eyes of the Lord are on the righteous and his ears are attentive to their prayer"* **(1 Peter 3:12).**

It's comforting to know that *"The eyes of the Lord are on the righteous, and his ears are attentive to their cry"* **(Psalm 34:15).** A medicine for times of trial and danger is to trust that *"Surely the arm of the Lord is not too short to save, nor his ear too dull to hear"* **(Isaiah 59:1).**

Many ask me for prayer, saying, *"Pastor, you're closer to God; pray for me. I don't know how to pray."* Or they say, *"I think God is not listening to me."* **Clarification**: God is attentive to everything that happens in the world and your life! There's no detail so big or small of which God is not informed. **Isaiah 65:24,** a precious promise to memorize, says, *"Before they call I will answer; while they are still speaking I will hear."*

God is attentive to the requests of all His children. Each one is special, precious, and loved, yet we're all equal before God. God hears all of our prayers. Some, God answers according to our expectations. Others, God tells us, *"Yes, but not now."* In other prayers, God answers in a way that we cannot understand, and for others, He says **"no."** We must trust that God's will is always right, good, and loving.

I've met many day laborers whom their bosses deceived. Some worked one day, others two weeks, and weren't paid their wages. Some were taken to work at distant places and left by the road to return on their own and without pay. **James 5:4** warns, *"The cries of the harvesters have reached the ears of the Lord Almighty."*

Let us pray: Dear God, thank You for assuring us that You hear all of our prayers. Grant us the patience to wait for you to act in Your time and Your way. Give us ears to listen to our neighbor, without judging and with love. We pray in Jesus's name.

June 30
FAITH - GIFT AND COMMANDMENT

"If you can'? said Jesus. 'Everything is possible for one who believes.'" **Mark 9:23**

"Jesús le dijo: '¿Cómo que "si puedes"? Para quien cree, todo es posible'". **Marcos 9:23**

"Και ο Ιησούς είπε σ' αυτόν, το: Αν μπορείς να πιστέψεις, όλα είναι δυνατά σ' αυτόν που πιστεύει." **ΚΑΤΑ ΜΑΡΚΟΝ 9:23**

I'm pleased to share some of my favorite verses on Faith as a gift and a commandment. *"And this is his command: to believe in the name of his Son, Jesus Christ, and to love one another as he commanded us"* **(1 John 3:23).** God saved us *"through faith—and this is not from yourselves, it is the gift of God"* **(Ephesians 2:8).**

FAITH PRODUCES VICTORY, AUTHORITY, HEALING, and OBEDIENCE -
"Have faith in the Lord your God and you will be upheld; have faith in his prophets and you will be successful" **(2 Chronicles 20:20).** Jesus said that whoever has faith in God *"and does*

not doubt in their heart but believes that what they say will happen, it will be done for them" (**Mark 11:23**). *"Don't be afraid; just believe, and she will be healed"* (**Luke 8:50**). God's command is *"to believe in the one he has sent"* (**John 6:29**).

FAITH AS A DEFENSIVE WEAPON - *"In addition to all this, take up the shield of faith, with which you can extinguish all the flaming arrows of the evil one"* (**Ephesians 6:16**). Christians must *"be sober, putting on faith and love as a breastplate, and the hope of salvation as a helmet"* (**1 Thessalonians 5:8**). God calls us to *"hold on to faith and a good conscience, which some have rejected and so have suffered shipwreck with regard to the faith"* (**1 Timothy 1:19**).

SINCERE FAITH PLEASES AND REWARDS - *"And without faith it is impossible to please God, because anyone who comes to him must believe that he exists and that he rewards those who earnestly seek him"* (**Hebrews 11:6**).

THE PRAYER OF FAITH PRODUCES WISDOM AND HOPE - *"If any of you lacks wisdom, you should ask God, who gives generously to all without finding fault, and it will be given to you. But when you ask, you must believe and not doubt, because the one who doubts is like a wave of the sea, blown and tossed by the wind"* (**James 1:5-6**).

Let us pray: Dear God, thank You for this special moment in which we can savor the sweetness of Your love through these verses that strengthen our faith and hope. Help us share these seeds of love and faith with courage and devotion, first in our homes and then with Your lost and defenseless sheep. We pray in Jesus's name.

- JULY -
GOD, THE MASTER CONDUCTOR
(How we met)

On November 15, 2021, my Sophia Eleni Destruge wrote the following for our 46th wedding anniversary:

"Three life-changing events happened today. My Yiayia was brought into this world 90 years ago today; though we won't celebrate until April, it's a day that made my mom possible.

My Abuelita left this world 13 years ago today; her loving soul gave life to my father.

*My parents said **"I do"** 46 years ago today. They were born worlds away. The odds were against them ever meeting, but because of these matriarchs' difficult decision to leave their countries - love found its way to Queens, NY! Through so many turns of events and obstacles, you've built something beautiful and made everything possible in our world. Thank you! Happy Anniversary - I love you!"*

Nothing happens by chance. I believe that, like a master conductor, God directed every decision, big and small, so that we'd meet. When my in-laws immigrated to the United States on May 7, 1970, they had job offers and were supposed to live in Philadelphia. But unexpected last-minute phone calls were made, and the family stayed in Queens, New York. In 1973, my brother Fernando lived in Canada. After various unsatisfying jobs, he came to the USA and went to work at Bulova Watch Company in Queens, where he met Fanny Xanthopoúlou. He asked her out to see our band playing one Friday evening, but Fanny was not allowed to go out alone; her younger sister, Margarita accompanied her that night. That's how we met on March 8, 1974, at the "Long Island Hofbrau," Elmhurst, NY. Our first date was to the NYC Greek Independence Day Parade on March 24. That's how our story began. The best is yet to come! ***"All things work together for good to them that love God"*** **(Romans 8:28).**

July 1
WHEN IN DOUBT, CONSULT WITH GOD
2 Samuel 2:1

Life is about decisions. Every day, we make decisions; small ones like what to eat, what to wear, whom to meet for coffee, sports, and fitness, with whom we chat, go for a walk or visit, etc. Then, we have significant decisions impacting the rest of our lives, like whom to marry, family size, where to live, career choices, higher education, rent or buy, and finally, the **Mt. Everest of decisions; trusting God with our future**. **It's good to consult with God in all decisions.**

Where to live is a significant decision considering the proximity to family (grandchildren, children, elderly parents). Family support is always vital. Now that we're retired, we struggle to care for elderly parents and desire to be near our children and grandchildren. So, accommodating and supporting each other in our responsibilities and desires is key to a peaceful and joyful life. Saint Paul says, *"I've learned to be content in whatever situation I may be"* **(Philippians 4:11)**.

All of the above decisions affect our lives here. But the decision we struggle with most is the one that impacts our life here and into eternity (putting our trust in God). Why? Because it requires that we stop conforming to the world's demands **(Romans 12:2)** and trust God's promises. We struggle because it means sacrificing time (which we could allocate to other pleasures) to study, pray, witness, congregate with equal-minded believers, and serve the poor and needy.

In this struggle, pastors and missionaries often face the decision first to serve God, ignoring the needs of their young families. They're not easy decisions! No one likes to feel like they're second in your life. Yet and still, we can't offer genuine love to our loved ones without putting God first in our hearts and homes.

Let us pray: Dear God, thank You for another year of life in Your presence. For my family, for their support and sacrifice during our service to Your Kingdom. Guide us to make the right choices according to Your guidance and grant us time to nourish our family with the love and attention they deserve and desire. We pray in Your Holy Name.

July 2
POWER AND AUTHORITY

"So even if I boast somewhat freely about the authority the Lord gave us for building you up rather than tearing you down, I will not be ashamed of it." **2 Corinthians 10:8**

"No me avergüenza el jactarme una vez más de nuestra autoridad, la cual el Señor nos dio para la edificación de ustedes, y no para su destrucción". **2 Corintios 10:8**

"Επειδή, και αν καυχηθώ κάτι περισσότερο, για την εξουσία μας, που ο Κύριος μας έδωσε για οικοδομή, και όχι για καθαίρεσή σας, δεν θα ντροπιαστώ·" **ΠΡΟΣ ΚΟΡΙΝΘΙΟΥΣ Β΄ 10:8**

I used to be ashamed of my inability to hold a conversation until I came to know God and myself. I learned that knowing how to listen is of equal value as knowing how to speak. My granddaughter Salomé is very similar to me in her shy character. She's observant, hears everything, and has a beautiful smile. Listening is a gift. The power and authority God gives us are gifts we can't hide under the shadow of shyness.

As brothers and sisters in Christ, we have the power and authority to build up the community that makes up the family of God. Only God knows who's in the family, including those who are lost from the *"way, the truth and the life"* **(John 14:6).** Without prejudging their condition, God calls us to share the Gospel with all, to build, expand, and nourish the body for which Jesus Christ gave His life.

Despite being a shy person, in 2004, the Methodist Church commissioned me as pastor of El Camino in Norwalk, CT. I entered the Methodist church in '93, offering my services as a musician. When I hold the guitar, my shyness goes away. Amid the praises, God taught me to speak and encourage the community. Thus, God removed shyness and low self-esteem, replacing them with power and authority to edify.

I was afraid to share my faith openly for a long time, not wanting to offend anyone or feel like I was forcing my faith and beliefs on friends and family. However, we were commissioned with the Gospel to share it openly with everyone in and out of season. We urgently share it because it deals with life and death, hope and despair, love and heartbreak, justice and injustice, protection and abandonment.

I invited all my friends and family to participate in the Bible Meditation groups because *"even if I boast somewhat freely about the authority the Lord gave us for building you up rather than tearing you down, I will not be ashamed of it"* (**2 Corinthians 10:8**).

Let us pray: Dear God, thank You for the great privilege and honor of being bearers of Your good news. Thank you for replacing shyness with power and authority to heal, rescue, build up, and guide Your people to the heavenly mansion. We pray in the name of Jesus.

Our generation is losing the **good customs** our parents struggled to sow in us. For example, greet everyone by shaking hands, hugging, or kissing upon entering a place. Now it's fashionable to give a general "hello" wave to everyone and from afar. And this was before Covid19 required social distancing.

Another **bonding** custom was for the family to dine together. Now, each family member eats at different times and places - such as in the living room or bedroom.

Another custom we've lost is businesses no longer close on the Sabbath. They work seven days a week without setting aside time for the family or God. Children no longer learn about the value of worshiping and serving God one day a week. Worship interferes with sports and other prevailing activities.

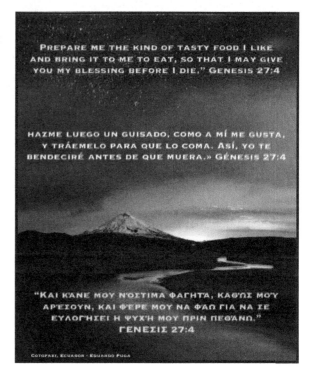

Another critical custom that's being lost, today's theme, is regularly **asking for the parents' blessing** when leaving home. My grandmother lived with us for as long as I can remember. If my parents weren't home, we'd ask Grandma for a blessing when going to school. My father had three jobs, and we would see him at lunch and Sundays. So my mom or grandma were the ones who sent us off to school. **"Mom, grandma, may I have your blessing?"** And making the sign of the cross on our forehead, mom or Grandma Amada hugged and sent us with God's protection and blessings.

The parents' blessing is powerful! Our words have the power to sanctify, protect, prophesy, bless, or curse. **Psalm 45** declares a blessing. *"The city of Tyre will come with a gift, people of wealth will seek your favor"* **(v.12).**

In today's verse, Isaac prepares to bless his firstborn son, Esau. Although we're getting ahead of the assigned reading, the story details how Jacob goes about stealing the blessing from his brother. The point is that the blessings we declare on earth are ratified in heaven. When Isaac realizes he'd been tricked into blessing the younger son with the firstborn's power and authority, he's saddened because he cannot undo the blessing. The older brother must serve the younger.

We live in difficult times. KN95 masks are excellent and necessary to protect each other from Covid19. Still, a parent's blessing will protect and save their children's souls from spiritual attacks and pave the way for spiritual prosperity.

Let us pray: Dear God, help us recover the good customs our parents taught us and bless our children daily. We pray in Your Holy Name.

July 4
BLESSED ARE THOSE WHO HEAR
Luke 10:23B-24

Continuing yesterday's theme, blessed are those who hear their parents' blessings daily. Many have desired to hear what you grew up hearing. Perhaps their parents lost the custom or didn't believe their blessings had power over their children's lives.

Being blind, Isaac couldn't see that it was Jacob who, with the clothes and scent of his brother, claimed to be Esau. Isaac declared this powerful and unbreakable blessing on Jacob: *"May nations serve you and peoples bow down to you. Be lord over your brothers, and may the sons of your mother bow down to you. May those who curse you be cursed and those who bless you be blessed" (Genesis 27:29).*

We're called to bless Jacob's generations, whom God renamed Israel. We must bless our children, family, and friends with the knowledge and testimony of what God has done in our lives so that they may recount your stories and grow in faith. Jesus said in **Luke 10:23-24**, *"Blessed are the eyes that see what you see. For I tell you that many prophets and kings wanted to see what you see but did not see it, and to hear what you hear but did not hear it."*

By God's grace, we've read and heard the words that Jesus recorded for our and future generations. **We're blessed because in the daily hearing of God's Words;**

1. We draw closer to God's heart. We no longer only know "**about**" God, but who is God, His power and authority in the cosmos and our lives. **We know God.**
2. We discover that we're **adopted children of God. We have identity and authority.**
3. We're discovering new and glorious blessings God has prepared for His children. **We're blessed.**
4. We learn not to live in **fear of the law** but rather grateful and obediently live freely in God's grace and will. **We've freedom.**
5. We accept that God formed us **"as we are,"** that, unlike the world's accusations, we're of great value to God, to His kingdom and realm. **We have self-esteem.**
6. We glorify God by helping those who seek the Door to enter and receive God's blessings. Our life in Christ has direction and meaning. **We have a purpose**.

We could continue listing the blessings enjoyed because we've heard and kept God's Word. But I invite you to make your list and share it with your family and friends if you wish.

Let us pray: Dear Lord, thank You for all Your blessings. Please help us know you more, walk with you, and recount Your deeds so the world may be filled with Your glory. We pray in Your Holy Name.

July 5
LET'S SERVE THE KING
2 Samuel 5:1

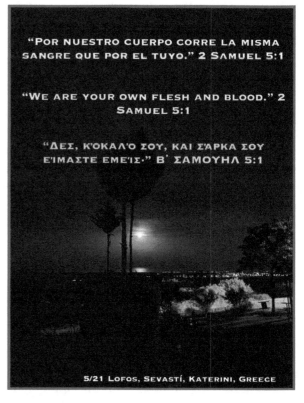

"POR NUESTRO CUERPO CORRE LA MISMA SANGRE QUE POR EL TUYO." 2 SAMUEL 5:1

"WE ARE YOUR OWN FLESH AND BLOOD." 2 SAMUEL 5:1

"ΔΕΣ, Κ'ΟΚΑΛ'Ο ΣΟΥ, ΚΑΙ Σ'ΑΡΚΑ ΣΟΥ Ε'ΙΜΑΣΤΕ ΕΜΕ'ΙΣ·" Β' ΣΑΜΟΥΗΛ 5:1

5/21 LOFOS, SEVASTÍ, KATERINI, GREECE

To God, we are all equal, loved, and gifted to serve the *"King of kings and Lord of lords"* **(Revelation 19:16)** by rescuing and unifying the lost sheep through the Gospel of Jesus Christ.

When David was named King of Israel and Judah, the Israelite people declared their fidelity and loyalty to the new King with these words: *"We are your own flesh and blood. In the past, while Saul was king over us, you were the one who led Israel on their military campaigns. And the Lord said to you, 'You will shepherd my people Israel, and you will become their ruler'"* **(2 Samuel 5:1-2).** They recognized the great triumphs David had over his enemies. They accepted God's will, declaring him the future king of Israel, and admitted that they are of the same blood; sons of Jacob, Isaac, Abram, Adam, and adopted sons of God.

By God's grace, we share the exact source of life, the breath of the Spirit of God that flows in our veins, giving life to our bones and flesh. This same Spirit *"testifies with our spirit that we are God's children"* **(Romans 8:16),** calling us to accept the great triumphs and victories that Jesus achieved over death and sin. The same Spirit helps us do God's will (to love one another) since we are brothers in Christ, enabling us to seek, know, and serve our King and God.

After loving God, our second greatest service to the King is to *"love our neighbor as ourselves"* **(Mark 12:30-31).** We must show love not only with those who share our same blood but also the same "breath" that quickens our bones and flesh. How good it would be if we treated everyone with love, respect, and dignity as if they were *"bones of my bones and flesh of my flesh"* **(Genesis 2:23).**

Let us pray: Dear God, help us to triumph over sin and death, to see our neighbor as You see us, as children and brothers in Christ. Through our service to the King and love of neighbor, we may rescue those souls that today are isolated and desperate in the midst of this world's storms. We pray in the name of Jesus.

July 6
BE PATIENT
James 5:7

Today's theme is **patience**; Ύπομονή (hupomoneê - **(G5281))**, which means *"resistance or joyful endurance (or hopeful) constancy: patience, perseverance."* The New International Version uses **perseverance**, and one uses *"persevere with patience."*

To **persevere with patience** is to persist amid discouragement, enduring pain, fatigue, and suffering, filling our hearts and rejoicing in hope, knowing that in the end, we'll be found worthy of presenting the fruit of our love and faith.

In **James 1:4,** we read: *"Let perseverance finish its work so that you may be mature and complete, not lacking anything."* And this is perfection; **love**. As a pregnant woman patiently awaits the birth of her child, the fruit of her womb, our faith produces **the fruit of love** that God wishes to give to the world through you and me.

Love is the most potent force in the world. *"(Love) always protects, always trusts, always hopes, always perseveres. Love never fails"* **(1 Corinthians 13:7–8a).** No desert wide enough or mountain high enough can stop us when motivated by love.

Speaking of mountains, I attempted several times to climb to the Cotopaxi Volcano refuge. The first time, I failed to ascend even fifty meters. My heart seemed to explode. My watch's crystal shattered from the high pressure at four thousand meters altitude. The second time I surpassed the fifty meters, but not by much.

But the third time was different. My son went ahead at a fast pace, and I lost sight of him behind a hill. I didn't know what kind of danger was on the other

side. The love and concern for my son gave me the strength and endurance to climb, although my chest seemed to explode. With persevering patience, I arrived at the shelter and happily found my son at 4,800 meters altitude.

God's love for you is like that; perseveringly patient. Despite our condition and attitude inclined toward sin and temptation, God welcomes us with patient love, knowing that in His time, God will remove all impurity and resistance to the flow of His love.

Let us pray: Dear God, we've never known anyone like you who loves us with the patience and perseverance of an expectant mother, waiting to show the world the joy and treasure of her life. Thank you for such great love and patience. Help us to act with persevering patience and love toward our neighbor, *"so that when we've done your will, we may receive what you've promised"* **(Hebrews 10:36)**. We pray in the name of Jesus.

To persevere with patience is to persist amid discouragement, enduring pain, fatigue, and suffering, filling our hearts and rejoicing in hope, knowing that in the end, we'll be found worthy of presenting the fruit of our love and faith.

July 7
MIRRORS OF THE SOUL
John 7:7

When we have inflammation or a pimple on our faces, we hate the mirror because it reveals the truth. The Bible is our soul's mirror which shows our spiritual condition. It contains blessings for those who seek God and do His will and curses for those who break His covenant of love and reject His offer of forgiveness.

Jesus says that the world *"hates me because I testify that its works are evil"* **(John 7:7)**. *"The world"* means unbelievers or those who've rejected God's offer of peace and forgiveness through the sacrifice of Jesus Christ. Those in the world hate for their sin to be revealed. When God's Word proves the *"evil"* of their works, they feel resentment and antipathy toward the revealer of their bad deeds. They scoff at the Bible as old-fashioned and Jesus as a madman. Jesus was, is, and will be hated by the world *"without reason"* **(John 15:25)**.

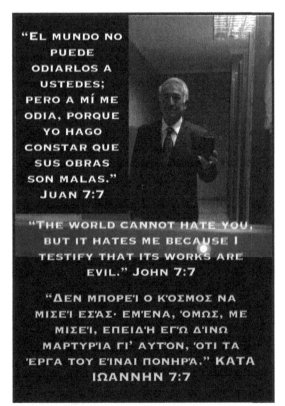

Two thousand years ago, the religious leaders *"were furious and began to discuss with one another what they might do to Jesus"* **(Luke 6:11)**. Then *"they shouted, 'Crucify! Crucify!'"* **(John 19:6)**. Their hatred of Jesus Christ was so intense that they killed him because He revealed their evil works to the world.

208

The Bible declares that the world will hate us because of His name (Luke 21:17). *"Do not be surprised, my brothers and sisters, if the world hates you"* **(1 John 3:13).** According to God's Word, as God's adopted children, we're the soul's mirrors when we reflect an upright, just, humble, and loving life through words and actions. Jesus said, *"Blessed are you when people hate you, when they exclude you and insult you and reject your name as evil, because of the Son of Man"* **(Luke 6:22, Matthew 24:9).**

It's comforting to know that though despised for a moment, God expects us to continue being the soul's mirror and conscience for His lost sheep. Not by accusations or contempt but by the love and care we show in healing them from their momentary disfigurements and afflictions.

Let us pray: Dear God, thank You for sending Jesus Christ as our Savior and Healer; for sending Your Holy Spirit as our soul's mirror and guide. Thank you for revealing Your Word, the way, the truth, and the life. Grant that we may be good mirrors and reflectors of Your eternal and unconditional love in all times and places.

> According to God's Word, as God's adopted children, we're the soul's mirrors when we reflect an upright, just, humble, and loving life through words and actions.

July 8
MYSTERY AND BLESSING
Colossians 2:2

Reading and rereading **Colossians 2:1**, I closed my eyes and perceived God's voice saying, *"I want you to know how hard I am contending for you and for those [in the world], and for all who have not met me personally."* We believe that God's Word is faithful, authentic, and infallible. That *"All Scripture is God-breathed"* **(2 Timothy 3:16).** Therefore, it's not wrong to read the verse that way.

The struggle and sacrifices that God made so that we can approach God's throne of

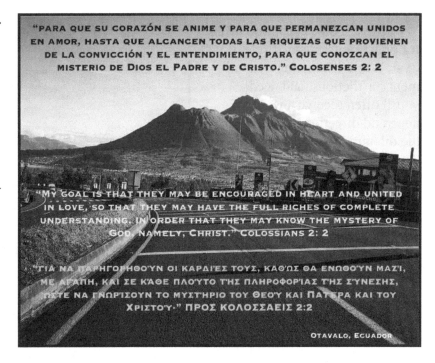

"PARA QUE SU CORAZÓN SE ANIME Y PARA QUE PERMANEZCAN UNIDOS EN AMOR, HASTA QUE ALCANCEN TODAS LAS RIQUEZAS QUE PROVIENEN DE LA CONVICCIÓN Y EL ENTENDIMIENTO, PARA QUE CONOZCAN EL MISTERIO DE DIOS EL PADRE Y DE CRISTO." COLOSENSES 2: 2

"MY GOAL IS THAT THEY MAY BE ENCOURAGED IN HEART AND UNITED IN LOVE, SO THAT THEY MAY HAVE THE FULL RICHES OF COMPLETE UNDERSTANDING, IN ORDER THAT THEY MAY KNOW THE MYSTERY OF GOD, NAMELY, CHRIST." COLOSSIANS 2: 2

"ΓΙΑ ΝΑ ΠΑΡΗΓΟΡΗΘΟΎΝ ΟΙ ΚΑΡΔΙΈΣ ΤΟΥΣ, ΚΑΘΏΣ ΘΑ ΕΝΩΘΟΎΝ ΜΑΖΊ, ΜΕ ΑΓΆΠΗ, ΚΑΙ ΣΕ ΚΆΘΕ ΠΛΟΎΤΟ ΤΗΣ ΠΛΗΡΟΦΟΡΊΑΣ ΤΗΣ ΣΎΝΕΣΗΣ, ΏΣΤΕ ΝΑ ΓΝΩΡΊΣΟΥΝ ΤΟ ΜΥΣΤΉΡΙΟ ΤΟΥ ΘΕΟΎ ΚΑΙ ΠΑΤΈΡΑ ΚΑΙ ΤΟΥ ΧΡΙΣΤΟΎ·" ΠΡΟΣ ΚΟΛΟΣΣΑΕΙΣ 2:2

OTAVALO, ECUADOR

grace have not been easy. We enter our sacred prayer space without fear, free from the shame of our past because God has cleansed us of all impurity through the blood of Jesus Christ. The great mystery and blessing are that, despite our continuous rebellions, God's love for creation is unshakeable.

Between the mystery and the blessing, we find Jesus Christ, who built the bridge with His immense sacrificial love, granting us access to reach God's bosom. *"For we are the temple of the living God. As God has said: 'I will live with them and walk among them, and I will be their God, and they will be my people'"* **(2 Corinthians 6:16).** *"The Lord confides in those who fear him; he makes his covenant known to them"* **(Psalm 25:14).** The divine covenant has always been *"I will be their God, and they will be my chosen people"* **(Jeremiah 32:38).**

For lack of faith and being wrapped up in themselves, the great mystery of God was hidden from the religious leaders in Jesus's time. But to us, *"God has chosen to make known among the Gentiles the glorious riches of this mystery, which is Christ in you, the hope of glory"* **(Colossians 1:27).** The great mystery of the ages and Milena is *"Christ in you."* Hallelujah!

Let us pray: Dear God, thank You for revealing Your great mystery of love and salvation. *"Beyond all question, the mystery from which true godliness springs is great: He appeared in the flesh, was vindicated by the Spirit, was seen by angels, was preached among the nations, was believed on in the world, was taken up in glory"* **(1 Timothy 3:16).** Thank you for Your Word. We pray in the name of Jesus.

July 9
PRAY FOR ME
Colossians 4:3

My beloved, don't be afraid to ask for prayer within your circle of trust. While expressing your ailments, afflictions, and needs, you'll often receive a word of hope and direction to overcome the dilemma. It also shows confidence and strengthens the bonds of friendship.

I'm pleased that when someone asks for prayer in this Bible Meditation Group, many members respond. I also rejoice in hearing that "God answered the prayer."

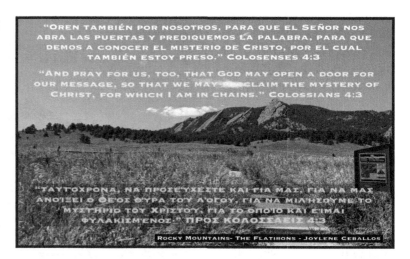

One of my prayers is **Colossians 4:3**, *"And pray for us, too, that God may open a door for our message, so that we may proclaim the mystery of Christ."* As a retired pastor, I no longer have a

210

pulpit other than these daily meditation letters dedicated to my children, grandchildren, future generations, and you, my beloved friends and family.

God gave me the vision to publish these meditations in a book and gift it to every member of my family and future generations. Every day I dedicate a couple of hours to this project *"So that we may proclaim the mystery of Christ, for which I am"* utterly grateful to God for this time in Greece, retired, and far from my racquetball addiction. Thus, I can dedicate the needed time to edit this journal. I ask for your prayers so that I may press undistracted toward that goal.

Likewise, *"Pray also for me, that whenever I speak* [write]*, words may be given me so that I will fearlessly make known the mystery of the gospel"* **(Ephesians 6:19).**

Lastly, I have not been a perfect person. I've failed perhaps more times than I know, but humbly I learned to ask forgiveness, trusting that I serve a God who loves, forgives, and will not allow anything to separate me from His love. *"Pray for us. We are sure that we have a clear conscience and desire to live honorably in every way"* **(Hebrews 13:18).**

Let us pray: Dear God, thank You for the gift of prayer and intercession, knowing that Your ears are attentive to our cry. Thank you for our family and friends who support us by interceding for our ailments and afflictions. Grant that we may be faithful intercessors for them. When my future generations read this book, I pray that they pay more attention to Your Words Lord, which are in *"quotes,"* and that they think and act accordingly. We pray in Jesus's name.

July 10
PREACH THE GOSPEL
Romans 15:20-21

My entire family, except my grandma, emigrated to the United States in February 1964. In the process of writing letters to grandma, I discovered that written words flowed smoother and freer. At age ten, God began training and encouraging me to write.

In 1968, grandma passed away, and my letter-writing days seemed to be over. I exchanged letters for a brief time with my girlfriends. By age 18, my writing days seemed to be over until around age 25, when I became part of a "correspondence team" at Mutual of New York. Although the letters were business-like, I enjoyed personalizing them.

Ten years later, while writing Technical Training Manuals, Jesus Christ became my Lord and Savior. I developed the *"ambition to preach the gospel*

THOSE WHO WERE NOT TOLD ABOUT HIM WILL SEE, AND THOSE WHO HAVE NOT HEARD WILL UNDERSTAND.
AQUELLOS A QUIENES NUNCA LES FUE ANUNCIADO ACERCA DE ÉL, VERÁN; Y LOS QUE NUNCA HAN OÍDO DE ÉL, ENTENDERÁN.

"ΕΚΕΊΝΟΙ ΠΡΟΣ ΤΟΥΣ ΟΠΟΊΟΥΣ ΔΕΝ ΑΝΑΓΓΕΛΘΗΚΕ ΓΙ' ΑΥΤΌΝ, ΘΑ ΔΟΥΝ· ΚΑΙ ΕΚΕΊΝΟΙ ΠΟΥ ΔΕΝ ΆΚΟΥΣΑΝ, ΘΑ ΚΑΤΑΛΆΒΟΥΝ."
ROMANS 15:21
ROMANOS 15:21
ΠΡΟΣ ΡΩΜΑΙΟΥΣ 15:21

MARCO ISLAND, FL., RACHEL CASTILLO

211

where Christ was unknown" and started a Fellowship and Prayer group in the office that met once weekly for lunch.

Many joined the group. Some knew God, but for various reasons, had become disillusioned with church, God, or both. Weekly preparations to guide the discussion required research and writing. When I retired from my corporate job, my coworkers asked, "what will you be doing? I answered, 'I'm going to be a pastor,' but in my mind, I meant a **'writer.'"**

So here I am, retired from writing weekly sermons and still having the time of my life, meditating with you daily on God's Word. Never knowing what I'll write about until opening up the daily lectionary. There's always a verse that says, **"pick me!"** So here we are! You and I have been picked for this formidable, fearsome task of *"preaching the gospel where Christ was not known…[so that] those who were not told about him will see, and those who have not heard will understand"* **(Romans 15:20-21).**

God's been preparing us with personal, intimate experiences so we'd always be prepared to preach the word. To *"correct, rebuke and encourage-with great patience and careful instruction" (2 Timothy 4:2).* It's a formidable and fearsome task because our children will be exposed to the world's philosophies and must be well-founded in Jesus who is *"the Way, Truth, and Life"* **(John 14:6).**

Let us pray: Dear Lord, You've given us unique gifts to help those who don't know you yet to hear and see Your love in action, to help those who've wandered away from the Truth to return home to you. Please help us to use our gifts for Your kingdom. We pray in Jesus's name.

July 11
BEARERS OF THE LIGHT
John 12:46

The Word of God, of Jesus, everything we find in the Holy Scriptures *"is a lamp for my feet, a light on my path"* **(Psalms 119:105).**

God has given us all the instructions to navigate the sea of trials, deceits, and sin without being shipwrecked and reach our destination safely. Like a lighthouse on a foggy coastline, God's Word lights our way, pointing out the dangers and our safe harbor.

Before knowing the Light, we walked through life as sleepwalkers, in darkness, without perceiving the Light and God's direction, putting not only our lives in danger of falling into sin but also those who observe and follow our lead.

I've experienced the densest fogs in Ecuador and have managed to reach my destination by following trucks with many bright lights. There's no light more brilliant than of Jesus! Thank God, we're no longer children of darkness but of the Light. With Christ by our side, we are confident that His *"light shines in the darkness, and the darkness has not overcome it"* **(John 1:5).**

Meanwhile, you and I are **bearers of the Light** that brings hope and life to those who struggle in darkness. Today more than ever, in the face of this global pandemic, we need to ensure that all nations might see and come to His Light. By *"all nations,"* I mean people from different countries, languages, and races within your sphere of contact and influence. I'm talking about your neighbors, family, friends, etc. You don't have to travel the world to let your Light shine for them.

You might respond like Moses, *"I have never been eloquent... I am slow of speech and tongue" (Exodus 4:10).* Don't worry! I did the same too! But, trust that God has called you to deliver a life or death message. You are the Lord's messenger - deliver the news and let God do the rest. **The Holy Spirit will cast out all fear** and enable you to fulfill your mission of being **a bearer of the Light of Christ.**

We are always **bearers of the Light** of Christ, everywhere, with all people. Not only when we feel inspired. Our message is this: Jesus *"came into the world as a light, so that no one who believes in Him should stay in darkness"* **(John 12:46).**

Let us pray: Dear God, thank You for sending Your Light into our lives. Lead us toward the Light and peace we find only in Your Way and presence. Help us walk as children of Your Light and be useful instruments of Light, hope, and love in our environments. We pray in Your Holy Name.

July 12
THE ARK OF THE COVENANT
2 Samuel 6:11

My beloved, when two or three gather in Jesus's name to praise and glorify Him, God is present pouring out blessing and healing upon the gathering **(Matthew 18:20).** The Ark of the Covenant represents God's presence and protection for faithful followers.

Today I learned that *"The ark was a type of Christ in that it*

was a figure of the manifestation of divine justice (gold) in man."[17] The sacred chest stored the ten commandment stones (God's Word). God commanded, *"Take this Book of the Law and place it beside the ark of the covenant of the Lord your God. There it will remain as a witness against you"* **(Deuteronomy 31:26).**

In the desert, the Ark of the Lord *"went before them during those three days to find them a place to rest"* **(Numbers 10:33).** God's presence was guiding, parting the waters of the Jordan River **(Joshua 3:17),** and protecting the people against the enemies, giving them victory in Jericho and other battles. **(Joshua 3:11, 6:11, 1 Samuel 4:6-8).**

When the people obeyed God's instructions, they were blessed, protected, and made victorious. But when they disobeyed, the consequences were drastic. *"When they came to the threshing floor of Nakon, Uzzah reached out and took hold of the ark of God, because the oxen stumbled. The Lord's anger burned against Uzzah because of his irreverent act; therefore God struck him down, and he died there beside the ark of God"* **(2 Samuel 6:6-7).**

The poor man, wanting to prevent the ark from falling on the ground, paid with his life for disobeying the Divine instruction that no stranger should approach it **(Numbers 1:51).** We're incapable of understanding God's mind. But God doesn't ask us to understand Him so much as to obey Him to the letter. Whoever honorably treasures God's Word in their heart is blessed along with *his entire household.*

Let us pray: Dear God, help us to approach Your presence with reverent obedience. *"Now be pleased to bless the house of your servant, that it may continue forever in your sight; for you, Sovereign Lord, have spoken, and with your blessing the house of your servant will be blessed forever"* **(2 Samuel 7:29).** We pray in Jesus's name.

> **The Ark of the Covenant represents God's presence and protection for faithful followers.**

July 13
GOD GUARDS HIS CHOSEN PEOPLE

"But when the son of Paul's sister heard of this plot, he went into the barracks and told Paul."
Acts 23:16

"Pero el hijo de la hermana de Pablo se enteró de la emboscada, y fue a la fortaleza y entró para darle aviso a Pablo". **Hechos 23:16**

"Ακούγοντας, όμως, την ενέδρα ο γιος τής αδελφής τού Παύλου, πήγε, και μπαίνοντας στο φρούριο, το ανήγγειλε στον Παύλο." ΠΡΑΞΕΙΣ ΑΠΟΣΤΟΛΩΝ 23:16

---

[17]Ventura, S. V. (1985). In *Nuevo diccionario biblico ilustrado* (p. 71). TERRASSA (Barcelona): Editorial CLIE.

In **Acts 23**, we see how God works to protect Paul, His chosen one, to bring the gospel to the nations. *"The next morning some Jews formed a conspiracy and bound themselves with an oath not to eat or drink until they had killed Paul"* (**Acts 23:12**). But Paul's nephew divinely and timely *"heard of this plot"* and warned Paul, a man of faith and prayer, who surely consulted with God and managed to avoid death.

The promises of protection and safety were not just for the heroes of the Bible but for everyone throughout time. This promise applies to your life and future generations. *"I am with you and will watch over you wherever you go, and I will bring you back to this land. I will not leave you until I have done what I have promised you"* (**Genesis 28:15**). Spiritually, the promised land is the Kingdom of Heaven.

Jesus prayed for our physical, spiritual, emotional, and social care: *"Holy Father, protect them by the power of your name, the name you gave me, so that they may be one as we are one"* (**John 17:11B**). Paul prayed, *"And the peace of God, which transcends all understanding, will guard your hearts and your minds in Christ Jesus"* (**Philippians 4:7**). God wants to see unity and obedience operating in us. *"Since you have kept my command to endure patiently, I will also keep you from the hour of trial that is going to come on the whole world to test the inhabitants of the earth"* (**Revelation 3:10**).

God has cared for His chosen ones, even before we knew Him. This is called **Prevenient Grace**, God's favor which operated in our lives even before we were born, taking care of our parents and grandparents so that the fruit of their love might flourish and fulfill the purpose for which God created and breathed His Spirit of Life into us. Through faith, we *"are shielded by God's power until the coming of the salvation that is ready to be revealed in the last time"* (**1 Peter 1:5**).

Let us pray: Dear God, *"Summon your power; show us your strength, our God, as you have done before" (Psalm 68:28).* Allow that we might remember Your promises of eternal presence and protection for us and our home during trials and struggles. We pray in Jesus's name.

July 14
DANCING IS FORBIDDEN
Luke 7:32

Margarita tells me that at age 17, her mother was helping serve appetizers at a wedding reception when the music started playing, and one of her cousins pulled her into the dance circle. My mother-in-law froze! She didn't dance! However, someone reported this to her church council, which accused my mother-in-law of **"dancing"** and demanded repentance. In the 1940s, Evangelicals' pleasures like dancing were sinful, though not for Orthodox Christians.

Today's reading from **2 Samuel** highlights David's wife's reaction upon seeing *"King David leaping and dancing before the Lord, she despised him in her heart."* David expressed joy and gladness because he'd been named King and brought back the Ark of the Lord to Jerusalem. All the people rejoiced, except David's wife, for whom David's leaping and dancing were distasteful.

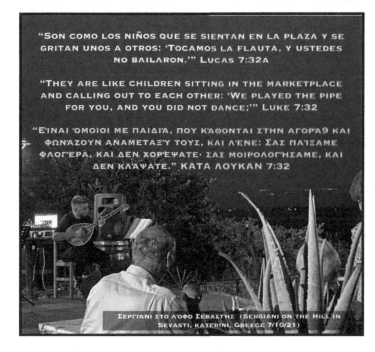

"SON COMO LOS NIÑOS QUE SE SIENTAN EN LA PLAZA Y SE GRITAN UNOS A OTROS: 'TOCAMOS LA FLAUTA, Y USTEDES NO BAILARON.'" LUCAS 7:32A

"THEY ARE LIKE CHILDREN SITTING IN THE MARKETPLACE AND CALLING OUT TO EACH OTHER: 'WE PLAYED THE PIPE FOR YOU, AND YOU DID NOT DANCE;'" LUKE 7:32

"ΕΊΝΑΙ ΌΜΟΙΟΙ ΜΕ ΠΑΙΔΙΆ, ΠΟΥ ΚΆΘΟΝΤΑΙ ΣΤΗΝ ΑΓΟΡΆ9 ΚΑΙ ΦΩΝΆΖΟΥΝ ΑΝΑΜΕΤΑΞΎ ΤΟΥΣ, ΚΑΙ ΛΈΝΕ: ΣΑΣ ΠΑΊΞΑΜΕ ΦΛΟΓΈΡΑ, ΚΑΙ ΔΕΝ ΧΟΡΈΨΑΤΕ· ΣΑΣ ΜΟΙΡΟΛΟΓΉΣΑΜΕ, ΚΑΙ ΔΕΝ ΚΛΆΨΑΤΕ." ΚΑΤΑ ΛΟΥΚΑΝ 7:32

ΣΕΡΓΙΆΝΙ ΣΤΟ ΛΌΦΟ ΣΕΒΑΣΤΉΣ (SERGIANI ON THE HILL IN SEVASTI, KATERINI, GREECE 7/10/21)

When David arrived at his house, Michal scolded him, *"How the king of Israel has distinguished himself today, going around half-naked in full view of the slave girls of his servants as any vulgar fellow would! David said to Michal, 'It was before the Lord, who chose me rather than your father or anyone from his house when he appointed me ruler over the Lord's people Israel—I will celebrate before the Lord"* **(2 Samuel 6:20b-21a).**

In my early years as a new child of God, I learned that we could do anything, *"but not everything is beneficial. 'I have the right to do anything'—but not everything is constructive"* **(1 Corinthians 10:23).**

It's worth clarifying that everything is allowed and beneficial when working with love and altruism for God and His people. Before we act or speak, we must ask ourselves if what we're about to do or say is **"allowed in the Bible."** God never forbade dancing. He approved of it in David, but He cursed the reaction of David's wife since **contempt** is a form of curse. God promised to bless those who bless us and to condemn those who curse us **(Genesis 12:3).** As a result, *"Michal daughter of Saul had no children to the day of her death"* **(2 Samuel 6:23).**

Let us pray: Dear God, help us to be clear about what pleases you, and, whatever Your Spirit leads us to do, that we do it with joy and gladness for Your glory and honor. Help us not to judge expressions of praise that differ from ours. We pray in Jesus's name.

July 15
CREATOR GOD
Colossians 1:16

Children are a manifestation or embodiment of their parents. They're as close to a reflection of them. On the other hand, Christ is the true and perfect manifestation of God the Creator and Redeemer.

Through today's verse, we get a glimpse of the means and purpose of creation. We see the repetition that *"all things were created,"* which establishes that absolutely everything in creation exists thanks to Jesus Christ, the incarnate Word. Without Him, nothing would exist.

"TODO FUE CREADO POR MEDIO DE ÉL Y PARA ÉL." COLOSENSES 1:16

"ALL THINGS HAVE BEEN CREATED THROUGH HIM AND FOR HIM." COLOSSIANS 1:16

"ΤΑ ΠΑΝΤΑ ΚΤΙΣΤΗΚΑΝ ΔΙΑΜΕΣΟΥ ΑΥΤΟΥ ΚΑΙ ΓΙ' ΑΥΤΩΝ." ΠΡΟΣ ΚΟΛΟΣΣΑΕΙΣ 1:16

MY SON, JEAN-PAUL DESTRUGE'S BEAUTIFUL FAMILY

The verse says, "*in him all things were created... all things have been created through him and for him*" (Colossians 1:16).

"*In Him*" means that in Jesus, creation has life, order, and meaning. He is the source of life, sustenance, and hope.
"*By Him*" means that God's Word (the Logos, Jesus) is the instrument and guide of all creation.
"*For Him,*" tells us that Jesus is the purpose of our very existence, which is to glorify God.

I've adopted my mother's habit of calling everyone "**my**" (as in my beloved friends and family). It's an endearing term. If we're true to today's verse, the reality is that nothing is truly ours. We tend to say, "*this is my son,*" when we should say, "*this is the son that God gave me.*"

God's Word affirms that all things (including our life and children) were created by Him, for Him, and have their existence in Him. We must ask ourselves, "*Am I truly living FOR HIM?*" It's never too late to start! Let's consider ways in which we could:
1 Know God better,
2 Be a better manifestation of God in our daily life, and
3 Live for Him.

Let us pray: Dear God, thank You for the gift of life, for placing us at the center of a loving and nurturing family that strives to reflect Your love and presence through its actions, gestures, and words. Thank you for the children and grandchildren who fill our lives with love and the joy of living. Heal our sick. Comfort those who mourn through hope and faith in Your Word. We pray in Jesus's name.

In the picture, the son (Jean-Paul, with his wife Phoenix, and children, Ségolène and Salomé) that God gave to me, with whom I am well pleased. I love saying, Αγόρυμου! (*"my boy"*).

Consider ways in which you could:
1 Know God better,
2 Be a better manifestation of God in your daily life, and
3 Live for God.

God has great blessings in store in this and the life to come for those who seek Him with heart and soul. God is merciful, but our time is not unlimited. God established our time in history *"so that they would seek him and perhaps reach out for him and find him, though he is not far from any one of us"* **(Acts 17:26-27).**

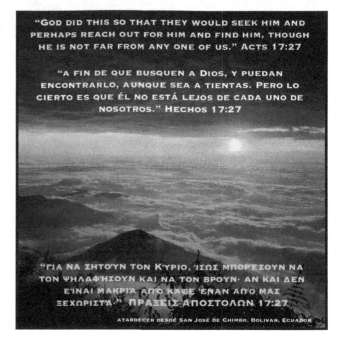

In **Isaiah 55:6**, we read, *"Seek the Lord while he may be found; call on him while he is near."* In other words, seek God while we live since it'll be too late after death. God will be found if we seek Him with all our hearts **(Jeremiah 29:13)** and will fill us with His strength **(Psalm 105:4).**

The Holy Spirit keeps us alive with the breath of life so that we may seek God. For, without God, our life was hopeless suffering. But now, God promised to be our sustenance, protector, joy, and love. *"For in him we live and move and have our being"* **(Acts 17:28A).** However, we must do our part in this covenant of love: seek, reach out, know God, and **follow His instructions**. If we lovingly do this, we will be blessed.

The Bible says, *"Blessed are those who keep his statutes and seek him with all their heart"* **(Psalm 119:2).** God calls us to seek him *"with all your heart and with all your soul. When you are in distress and all these things have happened to you, then in later days you will return to the Lord your God and obey him. For the Lord your God is a merciful God; he will not abandon or destroy you or forget the covenant with your ancestors, which he confirmed to them by oath"* **(Deuteronomy 4:29-31).**

The Lord is closer than we imagine. Jesus said, *"For everyone who asks receives; the one who seeks finds; and to the one who knocks, the door will be opened"* **(Luke 11:10).**

Let us pray: Dear God, thank You for opening our ears to Your voice and hearts to Your eternal love. We pray for our future generations that, as you softened our hearts to seek you, you also do with them through Your Word and angels who are bearers of Your loving presence. We pray in Jesus's name.

July 17
FORMED, CHOSEN, AND HELPED
Isaiah 44:2

Today's beautiful verse affirms us! Although addressed to the Patriarch Jacob, every word in the Bible is addressed to present and future generations of Abraham, by blood or adoption. By adoption, we can personalize and read it this way: *"This is what the Lord says— he who made you, who formed you in the womb, and who will help you: Do not be afraid, [Henry], my servant… whom I have chosen."*

Three verbs stand out in this verse; **formed, chosen,** and **helped**.

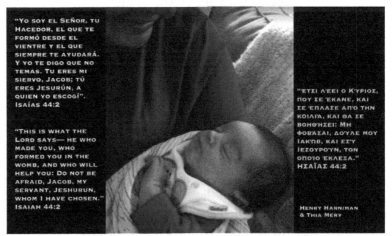

FORMED - My granddaughter Ségoléne wrote a song saying that her parents had created her. Actually, it was God's masterful hand that formed her, using her parents as brushes to produce a masterpiece. God knows every part of our being and discerns our thoughts and feelings. Possibly, for some reason, you might not have a healthy self-esteem. The father of lies has tried to convince you that your life is of little use. You don't know how to speak, everything you touch fails, and your family would be better off without you. **LIE!** Engrave in your mind that you were wonderfully formed. Fear not! God doesn't make mistakes or trash! **You are God's masterpiece, created to serve the King.**

CHOSEN - Don't be afraid because God says, *"I chose you."* You are not an accident or the result of bad luck. Among all the nations, God chose Abram to bless him so that *"all families on earth would be blessed"* **(Genesis 12:3).** God chose to continue that blessing through Isaac, Jacob, and Jesus Christ (lineage of Jacob), and now, God decided to bless you and for you to be a blessing. Jesus said, *"You did not choose me, but I chose you and appointed you so that you might go and bear fruit"* **(John 15:16).**

Our verse says, *"Jacob, my servant, Jeshurun, whom I have chosen."* In Hebrew, this endearing appellation of Israel means **"upright; a symbolic name for Israel"** *(יְשֻׁרוּם Yeshurún H-3484)."* God gives us this name to reflect the righteousness with which He formed us and what's expected from His chosen ones.

HELPED - Fear not! We're not alone, abandoned, helpless, or destitute. God says, *"So do not fear, for I am with you; do not be dismayed, for I am your God. I will strengthen you and help you; I will uphold you with my righteous right hand"* **(Isaiah 41:10).**

Let us pray: Dear God, thank You for affirming our identity, that we are **FORMED, CHOSEN, AND HELPED** personally by You. Thank you because you've promised to be with us *"always, to the very end of the age"* (**Matthew 28:20**). We pray in Jesus's name.

> You were wonderfully formed. Fear not! God doesn't make mistakes or trash! **You are God's masterpiece, created to serve the King.**

July 18
GOD FIGHTS FOR HIS PEOPLE
Exodus 14:14

Today's verse is part of Israel's deliverance from the yoke of the Egyptians. After the ten plagues, Pharaoh allowed the people to leave to worship God in the desert. More than 600,000 men came out, not counting women and children.

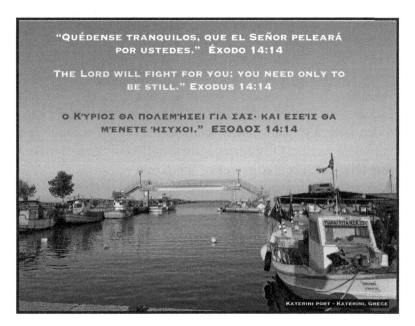

By day, God went *"ahead of them in a pillar of cloud to guide them on their way and by night in a pillar of fire"* to light their way (**Exodus 13:21**). Pharaoh regretted letting them go and pursued them. The people were camped by the Red Sea and had no escape route. Seeing that Pharaoh's armies were approaching and in great fear, they murmured against Moses, *"It would have been better for us to serve the Egyptians than to die in the desert!"* (**Exodus 14:12**).

Then Moses proclaims: *"Do not be afraid. Stand firm and you will see the deliverance the Lord will bring you today. The Egyptians you see today you will never see again. The Lord will fight for you; you need only to be still"* (**Exodus 14:13–14**). I invite you to read **Exodus** chapter **14** to refresh your mind about how God disposed of Israel's enemy, separating the waters of the Red Sea. It's a beautiful story.

The same story repeats itself. There are still people between the sea and walls, with no apparent way to escape from human conflicts. The enemy is Satan, and the world's conflicts are; the pandemic, drugs, alcohol, domestic violence, illicit sex, human trafficking, the obligation to emigrate from countries filled with violence, kidnappings, rapes, and homicides. Facing these conflicts, we're incapable of fighting and defeating them with our strength.

220

But the Spirit reminds us to trust in God. *"The Lord will fight for you"* (**Exodus 14:14**). Then, you will finally have peace and hope in your soul. Past things will be left behind. All things will be new.

Remember that God fights for His people. David was not the one who defeated Goliath, the giant. David said, *"The Lord who rescued me from the paw of the lion and the paw of the bear will rescue me from the hand of this Philistine"* (**1 Samuel 17:37**). To Goliath, he said, *"This day the Lord will deliver you into my hands, and I'll strike you down"* (**1 Samuel 17:46**).

Let us pray: Dear God, grant us the faith to know that in any situation that we find ourselves, in front of walls, seas, pandemics, or giants, you will fight for us, and in the end, you'll give us the victory over everything that endangers the souls of Your children. We pray in the name of Jesus.

July 19
PRAY FOR YOUR PASTORS

"Have confidence in your leaders and submit to their authority, because they keep watch over you as those who must give an account. Do this so that their work will be a joy, not a burden, for that would be of no benefit to you." **Hebrews 13:17**

"Obedezcan a sus pastores, y respétenlos. Ellos cuidan de ustedes porque saben que tienen que rendir cuentas a Dios. Así ellos cuidarán de ustedes con alegría, y sin quejarse; de lo contrario, no será provechoso para us-tedes". Hebreos 13:17

"Να πείθεστε στους προεστώτες σας, και να υπακούτε· επειδή, αυτοί αγρυπνούν για τις ψυχές σας, ως έχοντας να δώσουν λόγο· για να το κάνουν αυτό με χαρά, και χωρίς να στενάζουν· επειδή, αυτό δεν σας ωφελεί." ΠΡΟΣ ΕΒΡΑΙΟΥΣ 13:17

Pastors rarely hear gratitude. More often, they're the recipients of complaints. To prevent burnout or depression, they need your prayers, support, and respect for the decisions they might make after prayerful consideration. And, if the pastor becomes depressed, remember that they're human; don't accuse them of *"having little faith"* or to *"live what you preach."* Your prayers and love will be the balm to help them emerge victorious from such a test.

The enemy attempts to discourage us from loving and serving in God's name - blaming us either for the quality of service we render to those in need or even for the very poverty of those who've fallen into a life of worldly vices and temptations.

Sometimes at the food pantry where I volunteered as a receptionist, clients unhappy with their situation would take out their frustration on the volunteers. This can discourage God's servants, who also need your prayers.

Sometimes, however, God pleasantly surprises us. One day, a lady came into the pantry and asked me, *"Are you the priest who gave away bread in Bridgeport?"* *"Yes! I am,"* I replied. She hugged me with a big smile and tears and said, *"I don't know if you remember, you prayed for my health, and I'm fine. The bread and your prayers helped me more than you can imagine."*

Pastors *"keep watch over you as those who must give an account."* Pray for them *"so that their work will be a joy, not a burden"* **(Hebrews 13:17).**

Let us pray: Dear God, don't permit the complaints of the disgruntled to rob us of the joy of serving and loving the needy. Thank you for those who support us in the ministry through their prayers and spiritual and physical support. We pray in the name of Jesus.

✝ ✝ ✝ ✝ ✝

July 20
A SECURE AND STRONG CONNECTION
Acts 20:32

It's difficult to communicate without wifi! One of our primary concerns is keeping the mobile phone charged with a solid and secure connection. Everywhere I go, I look for a strong signal to send or receive messages. In **September 2018**, while walking with cousin Effie (we attended her wedding), she offered me her *"hotspot"* to connect to the internet. While I was close to her, I had a secure and robust connection. But if I distanced myself from her, I lost the signal.

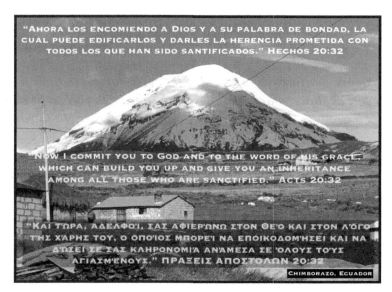

The same happens with God. As we walk close to God, meditating on His Word, we have a secure and robust link. But when distanced, we lose the connection and run the risk of being useless ambassadors, susceptible to Satan's attacks, who wants to separate us from God permanently. That's why our time with God is the medicine and strength necessary to reach our victorious destination, along with our friends, family, and future generations.

We were entrusted with God's Word to *"build you up and give an inheritance"* to the whole world. *"And how can anyone preach unless they are sent? As it is written: 'How beautiful are the feet of those who bring good news!'"* **(Romans 10:15).**

Nowadays, we share the Gospel primarily online. In social networks, greetings and images with good news, preaching, and praise abound, while in churches, the pews are increasingly empty. An average of 12 would come to hear the good news in my church — on special days, 25 would arrive. Now, through social media, you, my friends, and my family have exceeded this attendance more than 20 times. Yet, to carry our message of peace and reconciliation, a secure and robust connection and a well-charged battery are essential.

"I commit you to God and to the word of his grace, which can build you up and give you an inheritance" **(Acts 20:32).** Seek a strong and secure connection with God. Meditate on His Word, attend and support your local church and pray for your pastor.

Let us pray: Dear God, Thank you for reconciling us through Your Son's sacrifice. May this spiritual breakfast be a double recharge for our spirit and a solid and unbreakable connection to you. Give us the courage to go through our neighborhoods and social media, delivering Your *"message of reconciliation"* **(2 Corinthians 5:19).** We pray in Jesus's name.

✚ ✚ ✚ ✚ ✚

July 21
GOD'S GRACE IN ACTION
2 Samuel 9:11B **(ASV)**

One of my favorite illustrations of God's Grace comes from the life of Mephibosheth, found in **2 Samuel 9:1-13.**

Jonathan and David established a covenant in which David would show kindness to Jonathan's descendants as long as he lived. When the Philistines killed King Saul, they proceeded to kill Saul's lifeline. But a quick-thinking maid picked up Jonathan's son and ran to hide him. In the commotion, she dropped him, and the boy became lame and lived in hiding **(2 Samuel 4:4).**

Years later, King David remembered the covenant and asked: *"Is there no one still left of the house of Saul to whom I can show God's kindness?"* (God's grace in action!) *Ziba answered, "There is still a son of Jonathan."*

"Where is he?" the King asked. Ziba answered, *"He is at the house of Makir son of Ammiel in Lo Debar"* (which means barren, pasture-less). *"So King David had him brought from Lo Debar… When Mephibosheth (meaning shame, from God's mouth) came to David, he bowed down to pay him honor. David said, 'Mephibosheth!' 'Your servant,' he replied. 'Don't be afraid,' David said to him, 'for I will surely show you kindness for the sake of your father, Jonathan. I will restore to you all the land that belonged to your grandfather Saul, and you will always eat at my table.'*

"AS FOR MEPHIBOSHETH, SAID THE KING, HE SHALL EAT AT MY TABLE, AS ONE OF THE KING'S SONS." (2 SAMUEL 9:11B -ASV)

"Mefiboset, dijo el rey, comerá a mi mesa, como uno de los hijos del rey." (2 Samuel 9:11)

"ΚΑΙ Ο ΜΕΜΦΙΒΟΣΘΈ, ΕΊΠΕ Ο ΒΑΣΙΛΙΆΣ, ΘΑ ΤΡΏΕΙ ΕΠΆΝΩ ΣΤΟ ΤΡΑΠΈΖΙ ΜΟΥ, ΣΑΝ ΈΝΑΣ ΑΠΌ ΤΟΥΣ ΓΙΟΥΣ ΤΟΥ ΒΑΣΙΛΙΆ." Β' ΣΑΜΟΥΗΛ 9:11Β

Mephibosheth bowed down and said, 'What is your servant, that you should notice a dead dog like me?'… And Mephibosheth lived in Jerusalem, because he always ate at the King's table, and he was crippled in both feet" **(2 Samuel 9:4-8,13).**

Sometimes, we're like Mephibosheth, living a life of shame, hiding in barren places, in fear for our life. But, by God's Grace, without merit or effort, we're granted the gift of a new and abundant life, with angels to watch over us, and a place **at the King's table, as one of the King's sons and daughters.** That, my friends, is an image of God's grace in action, made available through Jesus Christ, to you and me, from Calvary's cross.

Let us pray: Dear God, how can we ever repay you for such love and grace other than to praise and serve you. Help us to pay forward the love you've showered upon us. We pray in Jesus's name.

> **Sometimes, we're like Mephibosheth, living a life of shame, hiding in barren places, in fear for our life. But, by God's Grace, without merit or effort, we're granted the gift of a new and abundant life**

July 22
LACK OF KNOWLEDGE

"We continually ask God to fill you with the knowledge of his will through all the wisdom and understanding that the Spirit gives." **Colossians 1:9**

"No cesamos de orar por ustedes y de pedir que Dios los llene del conocimiento de su voluntad en toda sabiduría e inteligencia espiritual". **Colosenses 1:9**

"Δεν παύουμε να προσευχόμαστε για σας, και να δεόμαστε να γίνετε πλήρεις από την επίγνωση του θελήματός του με κάθε σοφία και πνευματική σύνεση·" **ΠΡΟΣ ΚΟΛΟΣΣΑΕΙΣ 1:9**

Lack of knowledge causes stumbling. Amid trials, it's good to know that we can consult, thank, and entrust our lives and minds to God's hands.

Whom to consult: We turn to seek God's help, direction, and peace before the start of the day and when we lie down to rest.

In 2020, we never imagined governments closing their borders and suspending international flights. I thank God for my uncle Ricardo and aunt Blanca, who offered us safe refuge, affection, and companionship in their home at the start of the pandemic. We shared and cared for each other during our time of quarantine.

Gratitude: There's always something for which to give thanks. I thank God for you, always asking that *"God fills us with the knowledge of his will through all the wisdom and understanding that the Spirit gives"* **(Colossians 1:9)**. The Bible says, *"my people are destroyed from lack of* *knowledge"* **(Hosea 4:6).** Thankfully, filled with wisdom, gratitude, and purpose, we're ambassadors of God's love and power so that the hope of a new day may flow like a waterfall. Consider: **What are you thankful for today?**

Guard your mind: Each day, we're bombarded with messages, tweets, etc., attempting to steal our peace. Jesus offers you *"His Peace."* Our Bible Meditation Group aims to nurture and strengthen the mind and heart, to help each other face today's challenges. Now more than ever, we must guard our minds by trusting in God's Word, seeking Godly knowledge, guidance, and encouragement in His presence and promises.

Trust God: Feeding daily on God's Word, trust your life and that of your children into God's hands, praying for guidance so that we *"may live a life worthy of the Lord and please him in every way: bearing fruit in every good work, growing in the knowledge of God"* **(Colossians 1:10).** We don't know what the future holds, but God is powerful, and *"no one can snatch us from God's hand"* **(John 10:29).**

Let us pray: Dear God, thank You for *"rescuing us from the dominion of darkness and bringing us into your loving Son's kingdom"* **(Colossians 9:13).** Grant us wisdom, knowledge, and prudence to obey Your ordinances. Give us the courage to overcome our fears, shake off the dust, and lift each other. We pray in Your Holy Name.

> **Now more than ever, we need to guard our minds by trusting in God's Word, seeking Godly knowledge, guidance and encouragement in His presence and promises.**

July 23
THE PEACE OF CHRIST

"Let the peace of Christ rule in your hearts … since … you were called to peace. And be thankful." Colossians 3:15

"Que en el corazón de ustedes gobierne la paz de Cristo, a la cual fueron llamados en un solo cuerpo. Y sean agradecidos". Colosenses 3:15

"Και η ειρήνη τού Θεού ας βασιλεύει στις καρδιές σας, στην οποία και προσκληθήκατε σε ένα σώμα· και να γίνεστε ευγνώμονες." ΠΡΟΣ ΚΟΛΟΣΣΑΕΙΣ 3:15

We all want peace of mind, safety in our neighborhoods, security in our homes and communities, jobs, strength in our economy, confidence in our health system, and our leaders and bosses. Today's focus is on gratitude and allowing the *"peace of Christ to rule in our hearts"* **(Colossians 3:15).**

God calls us to be at peace and thankful **for all things (Ephesians 5:20).** When things go well, it's easy to give thanks. But we rarely give thanks amid trials. That's the challenging part. How can we give thanks when it hurts physically, emotionally, or financially? But let me tell you that praise and gratitude, like medicine, work marvelously.

I discovered this healing medicine in the book *"The Power of Praise"* by Merlin Carothers and was surprised at the results from the moment I applied it. It was snowing. We were visiting my cousin Michelle an hour from home. When we left her house, we found that a thief had broken the window in our car and stolen my expensive radio. We nearly froze, returning home with a broken window.

The following day at breakfast with our children, as was our custom, we gave thanks for food, family, and health, but also for God's protection and guidance for the "thief"; that God would touch his heart, make him stop stealing, and help him out of whatever situation led him to steal. In essence, we forgave the thief and stopped feeling pain for such an assault on our property and safety. Gratitude fills us with peace and gives us back the joy of life. **What are you grateful for today?**

Let us pray: Dear God, thank You because when nourished by Your Word, our first reaction is to thank You in all things. Thank you for all the good, noble, peaceful, and reliable people you've placed around us who give us a taste of Your Kingdom's blessings. For each reader or listener of this book, I pray that you grant them Your peace and abundant joy, regardless of the circumstances they may face. We pray in Your Holy Name.

✛ ✛ ✛ ✛ ✛ ✛

July 24
STICK TO THE PLAN
Psalm 105:5

Sometimes, we've experienced shallow and intermittent Wifi signals, followed by complete silence. I compare this to the devil's strategy, which aims to prevent us from communicating with our Commanding General for instructions, encouragement, and reinforcements.

God has created lines of communication so that at any given place or time, we'd be able to connect directly with Him and be assured that we're not alone in the battle, that no matter how outnumbered we might appear, God will tell us, *"Don't be afraid! Those who are with us are more than those who are with them"* **(2 Kings 6:16)**. God constantly reminds us to *"stick to the plan and follow the map to the pick-up point."*

The guide map is filled with action verbs to direct our steps, such as *"praise, proclaim, make known, sing, tell, glory in his holy name, rejoice, look to the Lord and his strength, seek his face, and remember."* As we do these amid battles, we gain courage and strength, knowing that we represent the most powerful being in the Universe, who stands by our side with legions of angels to defeat all enemies we encounter in our walk with the Lord.

Right now, our greatest common enemy might appear to be COVID-19, but in reality, it's often ourselves who, amid battles, do things our way. While the Lord commands us to **stick to the plan**, we carelessly allow our spiritual battery to reach a 2% level or intentionally shut off the connection because we're unable to listen to two voices at the same time; God's and our free will telling us *"you're intelligent, your way is quicker! You have free will."*

God is telling us not to forget the *"wonders he has done, his miracles, and the judgments he pronounced"* (**Psalm 105:5**). As God has been with you in the past, God is by your side now and will be in the future battles. Have faith! Don't give up on your partnership with God. Reactivate your communication line, recharge your spiritual battery and face the enemy, assured that you're never outnumbered.

Let us pray: Dear Lord, in every battle, though we can't see you, give us a sign that you're standing beside us. Help us not to fear the strength of our opponent because you're more powerful than any foe or weapon. Help us to meticulously **stick to Your** guidebook, giving praise and remembering how you've delivered us in the past. We pray in Your Holy Name.

✛ ✛ ✛ ✛ ✛

July 25
SIGNS
Matthew 12:38

Yesterday we prayed, *"give us a <u>sign</u> that you are by our side."* Today, the Pharisees ask Jesus to give them *"a sign."*

Jesus responded sharply, *"A wicked and adulterous generation asks for a sign!"* (**Matthew 12:39**). Are we wicked asking for a sign? **No!** Jesus answered thus because the Pharisees accused Him of working miracles through demons (**Matthew 12:24**). They asked for a sign that He comes from God. However, Nicodemus said, *"Rabbi, we know that you are a teacher who has come from God. For no one could perform the signs you are doing if God were not with him"* (**John 3:2**).

We prayed for **a sign,** not to verify Jesus's identity but to affirm God's everlasting presence. Abram asked for a **sign**, and God pointed to the stars saying, *"so shall your descendants be"* (**Genesis 15:2-5**). Moses asked for signs to show Pharaoh that he came in God's name. The ten plagues demonstrated God's power to deliver

227

His people **(Deuteronomy 6.21).** Asking for **signs** is not an indication of wickedness and **adultery**.

In the Hebrew Bible, *"adulterous generation"* pointed to those who worshiped false gods. In the Greek Testament, God extends this definition in **James 4:4,** saying, *"You adulterous people, don't you know that friendship with the world means enmity against God? Therefore, anyone who chooses to be a friend of the world becomes an enemy of God."* When we place world philosophies over God's Word, we're committing **adultery**. A **sign of infidelity** is when we intentionally disobey God's plan or teach others to doubt the Bible. For example, alluding that it contains errors, and contradictions, that not every word in the Bible comes from God, but instead includes the human prejudices and mistakes of those who wrote it. That's what they teach in some seminars. God save us from such adultery!

> **When we place world philosophies over God's Word, we're committing adultery.**

God says, *"Like newborn babies, crave <u>pure</u> (uncontaminated) spiritual milk, so that by it you may grow up in your salvation"* **(1 Peter 2:2).**

Jesus's many miracles are **signs** of His divine essence, power, and authority. Jesus affirmed to John the Baptist that he was not mistaken because *"The blind receive sight, the lame walk, those who have leprosy are cleansed, the deaf hear, the dead are raised, and the good news is proclaimed to the poor"* **(Matthew 11:5).**

Let us pray: Dear God, thank You for giving us, without having asked but certainly in need of it, the most excellent **sign** of Your deep love, **Jesus's empty cross,** which represents His sacrificial death for our sins and His resurrection. Thank you for the regenerative power that works in us who were blind, and now we see, deaf, and now we're attentive to Your voice, lame and now marathoners of Your gospel. We pray in Your Holy Name.

July 26
I CAN DO ALL THINGS THROUGH CHRIST
Philippians 4:13 **(NKJV)**

When I think that I can't do something or can't go further, I turn to **Philippians 4:13,** my source of strength: *"I can do all things through Christ who strengthens me."* When doubt and fear try to rob you of your power, I invite you to say out loud, *"My heart rejoices in the Lord; in the Lord my strength is lifted high"* **(1 Samuel 2:1).** Also, repeat **Philippians 4:13.**

228

During my early years as a baby Christian, my faith was like that of a child. Every day, through Bible study, my faith and trust in God grew. My motto has been, *"God said it, I believe it!"* Since I met the Lord, I've received the power and determination to carry greater responsibilities at work, church, and community.

When I started my first job, I had a very insignificant function. I worked in the reprographics department. My job was to collate and staple documents. Thirty-five years later, having demonstrated various skills and aptitudes, I retired as Vice President, in the top 5% of a population of 20,000 employees. To God be the glory! The most significant advancements occurred after 1989 when Christ became my Savior and guide. Since then, I gained the self-confidence to speak publicly and express my opinions. I believed in myself for the first time, but even more, I knew that *"I can do all things through Christ who strengthens me"* **(Philippians 4:13)**.

When I retired, the company president gave this testimony: *"Few people really make a difference in companies as Oscar has. He's demonstrated a passion and commitment to helping the Spanish-speaking people, which eventually helped our company accomplish what seemed impossible within the industry"* (**Peter Kunkel**, President, Diversified Investment Advisors).

I was introverted and afraid to speak in public or be the center of attention. Sometimes I don't understand how I overcame such fears and gained these achievements, except that I surpassed them by believing and repeating **Philippians 4:13**, *"I can do all things through Christ who strengthens me,"* and by trusting the Holy Spirit and God's Word.

Let us pray: Dear God, we wholly trust in Your power and authority over all creation. Transform our weaknesses into power. Help us to believe that we *"can do all things through Christ who strengthens us"* **(Philippians 4:13)** and that You have commissioned us to heal and bring the good news to the whole world. We pray in Your Holy Name.

July 27
FORGIVENESS AND BLESSINGS

"After the time of mourning was over, David had her brought to his house, and she became his wife and bore him a son. But the thing David had done displeased the Lord."
2 Samuel 11:27

"pero después de que ella guardó el luto David mandó por ella y la hizo su esposa, y ella le dio un hijo. Pero esta acción de David no le agradó al Señor". 2 Samuel 11:27

"Και όταν πέρασε το πένθος, ο Δαβίδ έστειλε και την πήρε στο σπίτι του· και έγινε γυναίκα του, και του γέννησε έναν γιο. Το πράγμα, όμως, που έπραξε ο Δαβίδ, φάνηκε κακό στα μάτια τού Κυρίου." Β΄ ΣΑΜΟΥΗΛ 11:27

We know King David as a man after God's own heart (**Acts 13:22**), yet, he was a sinner, adulterer, and murderer. David had his general Urias killed to cover up his adultery with Bathsheba, Uriah's wife (**2 Samuel 11**).

Through the prophet Nathan, God accused David saying, *"'Out of your own household I am going to bring calamity on you. Before your very eyes I will take your wives and give them to one who is close to you, and he will sleep with your wives in broad daylight. You did it in secret, but I will do this thing in broad daylight before all Israel.' Then David said to Nathan, 'I have sinned against the Lord.' Nathan replied, 'The Lord has taken away your sin. You are not going to die. But because by doing this you have shown utter contempt for the Lord, the son born to you will die'"* **(2 Samuel 12:11–14).**

God's judgment on David shows that disobedience causes God to become angry and apply the consequences of the law. We suffer because our actions have consequences. But through repentance, we also find God's forgiveness and blessing.

> **We suffer because our actions have consequences. But through repentance, we also find God's forgiveness and blessing.**

David sincerely repented of his sins, cried out to God, and was justified because, despite his sins, God made a covenant to bless the world through David's line. After the child's death, *"David comforted his wife Bathsheba, and he went to her and made love to her. She gave birth to a son, and they named him Solomon. The Lord loved him"* **(2 Samuel 12:24).** The question for us is; do I please God with my life? God is willing to listen to and forgive anything that needs to be corrected.

Let us pray: Dear God, help us understand that even godly people can fall into temptation. Deliver us from laziness and temptation. Cover us with Your Holy Spirit to not ruin what you have built in our lives by grace. We pray in Jesus's name.

✚ ✚ ✚ ✚ ✚ ✚

July 28
GIVE THEM SOMETHING TO EAT
Mark 6:37

We'll have plenty of time in Heaven to rest and rejoice in God's presence. But, while we live in this world, where material and spiritual food distribution doesn't reach all the poor, God tells us, **"You give them something to eat."**

"Because so many people were coming and going that they did not even have a chance to eat, [Jesus] said to them, 'Come with me by yourselves to a quiet place and get some rest'" **(Mark 6:31).**

230

The intention was to rest and regain strength in a desolate place. But the crowds followed them, and Jesus had compassion on them, *"So he began teaching them many things. By this time it was late in the day, so his disciples came to him. 'This is a remote place,' they said, 'and it's already very late. Send the people away so that they can go to the surrounding countryside and villages and buy themselves something to eat.' But he answered, 'You give them something to eat'"* **(Mark 6:34-37).**

God loves the world and wants us to feed them physically and spiritually. Although the disciples wanted to be alone with Jesus to eat, rest, and learn, mercy called them to stay on duty and do God's work amid exhaustion. Jesus said, *"my food is to do the will of him who sent me and to finish his work"* **(John 4:34).** One of my favorite scenes is the dialogue between Jesus and Peter, *"Simon son of John, do you love me more than these? 'Yes, Lord,' he said, 'you know that I love you.' Jesus said, 'Feed my lambs'"* **(John 21:15).**

The world desperately needs the spiritual food that you and I have tasted. God's will is that the whole world listens to His voice, that they return to His arms, and believe in His beloved Son and thus gain a place in the Lord's banquet. Jesus asks us, *"do you love me more than these?"* [If you love me,]' **Feed my lambs.'"** **(John 21:15).**

Let's pray: Dear God, sometimes we feel too tired to keep going. But Your love and mercy urge us to put our weariness aside to serve and love our neighbor. Thank you for reminding us that feeding our neighbors is the best way to reflect our love for you. We pray for our sick and planet. Heal us, Lord, in the name of Jesus.

July 29
WHEN WE FALL INTO IDOLATRY
Exodus 32:26B

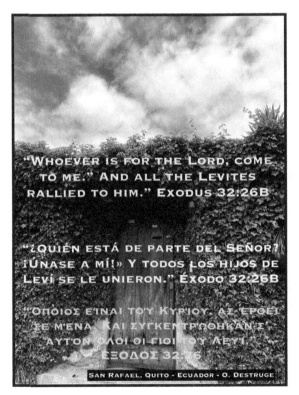

In the desert, the Israelites worshiped a golden calf, enraging God so much that He wanted to destroy them **(Exodus 32:10).** But Moses interceded, pleading with God on behalf of the people. When Moses came down from the mountain and observed the people worshiping the calf, *"his anger burned and he threw the tablets out of his hands, breaking them to pieces at the foot of the mountain"* **(Exodus 32:19).** Then he destroyed the calf and asked, *"Whoever is for the Lord, come to me." And all the Levites rallied to him"* **(v.26).**

It must have been challenging for Moses to execute God's punishment. Moses 'prayer helped so that God did not destroy the people. But their idolatry brought severe consequences. Following Divine instructions, *"that day about three thousand of the people died"* by the sword **(Exodus 32:28).**

Moses 'question also extends to us. *"Whoever is for the Lord, come to me."* Jesus said, *"No one can serve two masters. Either you will hate the one and love the other, or you will be devoted to the one and despise the other. You cannot serve both God and money"* **(Matthew 6:24).** Joshua offered the same choice to the people: *"Choose for yourselves this day whom you will serve, whether the gods your ancestors served beyond the Euphrates, or the gods of the Amorites, in whose land you are living. But as for me and my household, we will serve the Lord"* **(Joshua 24:15).**

We also have our gods of gold, silver, and valuable things that incline us to place God and family in second or third place. This saddens God very much, but thankfully, Jesus Christ intercedes for us daily, I imagine, saying*: "Father, don't look at their faults, look at my wounds and the blood that I shed to buy them. 'Father, forgive them, for they do not know what they are doing'"* **(Luke 23:34).**

Let us pray: Dear God, don't look at the hardness of our hearts, nor our spiritual condition today, but rather through Your beloved Son's sacrifice to make us worthy of receiving, along with our house, incorruptible bodies, totally committed to You. Increase our faith and courage. Help us rescue those who don't believe and comfort those who fear judgment day. We pray in Jesus's name.

July 30
SPIRITUAL POWER
Joshua 23:10

Among Joshua'su'as final instructions, we're instructed to trust God's Word and power: *"Now I am about to go the way of all the earth. You know with all your heart and soul that not one of all the good promises the Lord your God gave you has failed. Every promise has been fulfilled; not one has failed"* **(Joshua 23:14).**

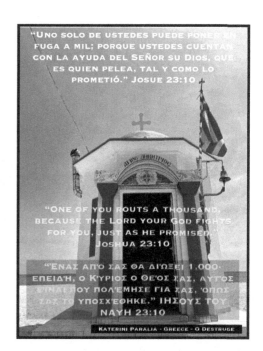

God has given us the power to resist the enemy. *"For the Spirit God gave us does not make us timid, but gives us power, love and self-discipline"* **(2 Timothy 1:7).** God has given us a spirit *"with justice and might"* to defend the poor and the weak, to denounce rebellion and sin around us **(Micah 3:8).**

Divine Power fills our lives with healing abilities. *"God did extraordinary miracles through Paul, so that even handkerchiefs and aprons that had touched him were taken to the sick, and their illnesses were cured and the evil spirits left them"* **(Acts 19:11-12).** *"Jesus returned to Galilee in the power of the Spirit,* *and news about him spread through the whole countryside"* **(Luke 4:14).** Jesus healed the sick, raised the dead, and restored the dignity of the poor and isolated.

Divine Power fills our life with purpose, enabling us to be God's witnesses. *"With great power the apostles continued to testify to the resurrection of the Lord Jesus. And God's grace was so powerfully at work in them all"* **(Acts 4:33).** The gift of God is more powerful than physical forces; it can move mountains and calm storms. God's power does not work through armies or the sword, *"but by his Spirit"* **(Zechariah 4:6).**

Beloved, this power dwells in you, who by faith have believed in God, in His Word, in Jesus Christ and His promises. Let us seek and stir this power in our homes, churches, and communities. Thus, we will overcome the forces of darkness and leave our children a better world.

Let us pray: Dear God, according to the riches of Your glory, pour out the power of Your Holy Spirit so that we may do Your will here on earth. Increase our faith and courage so we may build communities of love guided by Your Holy Word. Heal our sick and planet, Lord. We pray in the name of Jesus.

✝ ✝ ✝ ✝ ✝

July 31
GOD WILL NOT FAIL YOU
Isaiah 41:10

We should trust and be grateful for God's excellent, unshakable promise to Jacob and us. Paraphrasing **Isaiah 41:10,** God promises to *"always help you in all your obligations, commitments, and responsibilities toward your home, family, and community. I will be your strength. I will help and support you in the most difficult moments of your life."* God will not fail with any of His promises!

But the enemy comes with lies, trying to distance us from God and His promises. Satan whispers in our hearts that *"everything we touch fails, that we're alone, that things won't change. That, if God were with you, your son/daughter wouldn't have strayed and fallen into drugs. God doesn't exist or isn't interested in you. God has bigger things to fix. Therefore, enjoy the short life and take care of yourself."*

"NO TENGAS MIEDO, QUE YO ESTOY CONTIGO; NO TE DESANIMES, QUE YO SOY TU DIOS. YO SOY QUIEN TE DA FUERZAS, Y SIEMPRE TE AYUDARÉ; SIEMPRE TE SOSTENDRÉ CON MI JUSTICIERA MANO DERECHA." ISAÍAS 41:10

"SO DO NOT FEAR, FOR I AM WITH YOU; DO NOT BE DISMAYED, FOR I AM YOUR GOD. I WILL STRENGTHEN YOU AND HELP YOU; I WILL UPHOLD YOU WITH MY RIGHTEOUS RIGHT HAND." (ISAIAH 41:10)

"ΝΑ ΜΗ ΦΟΒΑΣΑΙ, ΕΠΕΙΔΉ, ΕΓΏ ΕΊΜΑΙ ΜΑΖΊ ΣΟΥ· ΝΑ ΜΗ ΤΡΟΜΆΖΕΙΣ· ΕΠΕΙΔΉ, ΕΓΏ ΕΊΜΑΙ Ο ΘΕΌΣ ΣΟΥ· ΣΕ ΕΝΊΣΧΥΣΑ· ΜΆΛΙΣΤΑ, ΣΕ ΒΟΉΘΗΣΑ· ΜΆΛΙΣΤΑ, ΣΕ ΥΠΕΡΑΣΠΊΣΤΗΚΑ ΜΕ ΤΟ ΔΕΞΊ ΧΈΡΙ ΤΗΣ ΔΙΚΑΙΟΣΎΝΗΣ ΜΟΥ." ΗΣΑΪΑΣ 41:10

IMBABURA, ECUADOR - EDUARDO PUGA

You may have sensed one or more of these lies and strayed from God's path for a time. Don't lose hope. **God's promises are unshakable**, and He's always waiting, like the prodigal child's father, for us to come to our senses, repent, and return to God's loving embrace.

In the year 2,000, I listened to the enemy and turned away from God and church. I was convinced that God hadn't kept His promise. That my house and I were of no interest to God. Two years later, after one of the worst periods in my life, like the prodigal son, I returned to God, repentant, saying, *"I'm not going to negotiate with you anymore, Lord. My home and family are in your hands. Do according to Your will. As for me, I will return to take care of your church without any conditions."* God received me without reproach and healed my wounds!

God's prevenient grace is taking care of us, even if we don't sense or know God. The devil is the father of lies, but *"God is not human, that he should lie, not a human being, that he should change his mind. Does he speak and then not act? Does he promise and not fulfill?"* **(Numbers 23:19).** God will fulfill His promises, although not in the time and form that we want, but always in what's best for us and His kingdom.

Let us pray: Dear God, thank You for Your unconditional love, which receives us as we are. For Your Holy Spirit, who reveals our rebellion and leads us back to Your loving embrace. For Your Son's sacrifice which cleanses and transforms us into new creatures who seek to know and do Your will. Increase our faith to trust Your promises, knowing that you **never fail** or abandon us. We pray in Your Holy Name.

August 1
ASK WITH FAITH
Matthew 7:7-8

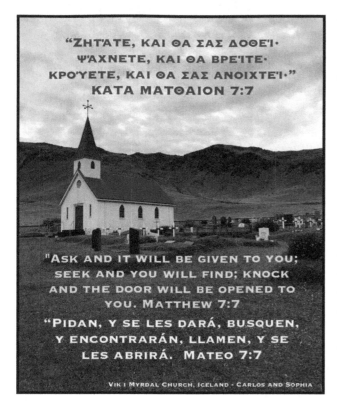

Today's verse reminds me of the story of blind Bartimaeus in **Mark 10:47**: *"When he heard that it was Jesus of Nazareth, he began to shout, 'Jesus, Son of David, have mercy on me!'"* I love Bartimaeus' story because it's my story, and maybe yours. Until we meet the Lord, we're isolated along the way, blinded by fear, anger, lies, phobias, racial, religious, political divisions, jealousy, denial, desires, temptations, etc.
Bartimaeus wasn't on "the road of success" but along the poor's path, like some of us, begging;

✦   for a stroke of luck,
✦   for a second chance,
✦   for a job,
✦   for an opportunity to demonstrate our skills,
✦   for a light to guide us out of a long and fearful tunnel,

✦ to find a doctor who can heal our spiritual blindness and COVID-19, which afflicts our planet.

Upon hearing that Jesus was passing by, Bartimaeus shouted out, **asking**, *"Jesus, Son of David, have mercy on me!"* **(Mark 10:47).** Bartimaeus may have heard Jesus preaching on the Mount of Olives, *"Ask and it will be given to you; seek and you will find; knock and the door will be opened to you"* **(Matthew 7:7).** Therefore, with faith, Bartimaeus asked for mercy.

But people on the sidelines (the poor, lame, homeless, undocumented) are to be *"seen, but not heard."* They've no voice or vote. Therefore, *"Many rebuked him and told him to be quiet, but he shouted all the more"* **(Mark 10:48).** We often remain silent for fear of politically offending others. Yet, we need healing. Don't be afraid to **ask** with all your might and faith. Jesus won't demand that you be silent. On the contrary, His ear is attentive to the cry and **requests** of His sheep.

Jesus asked the disciples to bring Bartimaeus and said, *"What do you want me to do for you?"* That's a question for us also. **What do you want Jesus to do for you today?** Bartimaeus answered: *"'Rabbi, I want to see.' 'Go,' said Jesus, 'your faith has healed you.' Immediately he received his sight and followed Jesus along the road"* (v.51-52).

Jesus tells us, *"Ask and it will be given to you"* **(Matthew 7:7)** and reminds us that *"Our faith will heal us."* So, think about these two questions: ***What do you want Jesus to do for you today? What part of your life needs healing, forgiveness, renewal, and restoration?***

Let us pray: Dear God, grant us voices to **ask with faith** that our Savior heal our souls, lives, and our planet from this virus. We want to see Your face, Lord. We pray in the name of Jesus.

August 2
RENEWED BY THE HOLY SPIRIT

"and be renewed in the spirit of your mind" **Ephesians 4:23**

"renuévense en el espíritu de su mente" **Efesios 4:23**

"και να ανανεώνεστε στο πνεύμα τού νου σας" ΠΡΟΣ ΕΦΕΣΙΟΥΣ 4:23

When I was commissioned as pastor in 2004, I understood that it was for life. And so it is! In 2009, I no longer had the strength to handle two jobs and retired from my secular job to devote more time to the ministry. So God renewed my strength and spirit.

It's not easy being a pastor, but there's no better job. I enjoyed the best moments serving God in this capacity. To dedicate more time to the family and accompany my wife in caring for my mother-in-law, who lives here in Greece, in June 2017, I chose to retire as pastor of the church.

I no longer administer a church, but the role of pastor continues through a larger online community. And although on our exterior, we show wear and tear (evident by hair loss, gray hair, wrinkles, and joint pains), I press forward to serve God. Every day, God is renewing and forming us into the image of our Savior. God is in the business of **TRANSFORMING AND RENEWING.**

Thanks to my daughter Sophia and many of you who encouraged me to write these daily meditations, I now enjoy studying God's Word daily and ministering with you to our friends and family worldwide. When we live in the Word, God molds us, renews our interior, and enables us to face every struggle.

"Though outwardly we are wasting away, yet inwardly we are being renewed day by day" (**2 Corinthians 4:16).** Every day, I am more confident that *"our present sufferings are not worth comparing with the glory that will be revealed in us"* **(Romans 8:18).** Every day, renewed by the Holy Spirit, I know that those *"who hope in the Lord will renew their strength. They will soar on wings like eagles; they will run and not grow weary, they will walk and not be faint"* **(Isaiah 40:31).**

Let us pray: Dear God, our young people will face pain, weakness, weariness, trials, and afflictions. Please give them the faith to claim that they will be more than conquerors in Christ and that the Holy Spirit has given them the power to overcome everything that opposes Your will. Give them clarity of purpose to enjoy time with their loved ones and share their gifts in the community. We pray in the name of Jesus.

August 3
SPIRITUAL AMBITION

"Now eagerly desire the greater gifts. And yet I will show you the most excellent way."
1 Corinthians 12:31

"Ustedes deben procurar los mejores dones. Pero yo les muestro un camino aun más excelente". 1 Corintios 12:31

"Να ζητάτε δε με ζήλο τα μεγαλύτερα χαρίσματα· και επιπλέον σας δείχνω έναν δρόμο που σε υπερβολικό βαθμός υπερέχει." ΠΡΟΣ ΚΟΡΙΝΘΙΟΥΣ Α΄ 12:31

Life became sweeter when I discovered my life's purpose and used God's gifts to fulfill it. There are infinite gifts, but all are equally useful for God to rescue, heal and restore lives for His kingdom and praise. In God's service, you can be a musician, poet, teacher, nurse, etc.

Through the first letter to the Corinthians, God tells us in **chapter 12** that His universal church consists of members with various gifts, among whom we find *"first of all apostles, second prophets, third teachers, then miracles, then gifts of healing, of helping, of guidance, and of different kinds of tongues"* **(1 Corinthians 12:28).**

236

"First of all" implies a hierarchy, where the apostolate takes the lead. Every organization requires a leader dedicated to its mission and goal. But that doesn't mean that the other gifts and members are less important. Second, are the prophets, God's messengers sent to proclaim the good news to the world. Third, those who teach God's Word and will so that the members are of one mind. *"Do your best to present yourself to God as one approved, a worker who does not need to be ashamed and who correctly handles the word of truth"* **(2 Timothy 2:15).**

In fourth place are those who take care of the body of Christ, that is, of the members and people around us, doing miracles, healing, and helping in the community. Finally, are the administrators and those with the gift of speaking in divine tongues.

There are many gifts and positions, all equally important. *"Now eagerly desire the greater gifts. And yet I will show you the most excellent way"* **(v.31),** love, which appears in **chapter 13.** That is, we can be apostles, but with love. We can be prophets, teachers, etc., but we wouldn't be effective in our mission without love. *"Follow the way of love and eagerly desire gifts of the Spirit, especially prophecy"* **(1 Corinthians 14:1).**

Let us pray: Dear God, help us refine, stir and abound in spiritual gifts for Your service and worship. When we're confused or tired, teach us the most excellent way of Your love. We pray in the name of Jesus.

> **Life became sweeter when I discovered my life's purpose and used God's gifts to fulfill it.**

August 4
RESCUED THROUGH PRAISE

"Those who sacrifice thank offerings honor me, and to the blameless I will show my salvation." **Psalm 50:23**

"El que me ofrece alabanzas, me honra; al que enmiende su camino, yo lo salvaré". **Salmo 50:23**

"Εκείνος που προσφέρει θυσία αίνεσης, αυτός με δοξάζει· και σ' εκείνον που βάζει τον δρόμο του σε ευθύτητα, θα δείξω τη σωτηρία τού Θεού." **ΨΑΛΜΟΙ 50:23**

A sister in Christ shared how she dealt with anxiety. She needed to pay an amount five times greater than her weekly income. Otherwise, she'd lose her business. God cared for her needs through praise and thanksgiving.

She recalled how Jesus dealt with the hunger of the crowd that had followed Him into the desert. He asked the disciples how much food they had. They responded, *"Seven loaves and some fish."* Certainly insufficient to feed 4,000 men. Jesus took the loaves and fishes, looked up to heaven, gave thanks, blessed them, and gave them to the disciples for distribution. *"The people ate and were satisfied. Afterward the disciples picked up seven basketfuls of broken pieces that were left over"* **(Mark 8:8).**

The Holy Spirit led my friend to pray as stated in **Philippians 4:6** *"Do not be anxious about anything, but in every situation, by prayer and petition, with thanksgiving, present your requests to God."* She didn't understand why she should give thanks for something that hadn't happened yet- she was still missing $16,500 of the $17,000 debt. Nevertheless, she presented her request with thanksgiving, believing that God would save her, and she experienced peace, knowing that God would provide a way out.

On the day the payment was due, her husband announced that a client had decided to pay off the entire balance owed instead of monthly payments. They received $20,000, paid their debt, and had leftovers, as in the multiplication of the loaves.

In **Psalm 50**, we read, *"Those who sacrifice thank offerings honor me, and to the blameless I will show my salvation"* **(v.23). When we fall into anxiety and fear, the best medicine is to sing praises to God, knowing that God will make a way in the deserts and save us from any danger or disaster.** The Lord comes to our rescue, transforming doubt and fear into consolation and joy.

Let us pray: Dear God, thank You for saving us from disasters and necessities. Grant us wisdom to thank and praise you for what you're about to do in and through our lives. Transform our doubts and fears into comfort, joy, and praise. We pray in Jesus's name.

August 5
THE BIBLE
Romans 15:4

When my parents returned from New York to Quito, Ecuador, in 1991, until my father learned to use the internet, our main form of communication was through letters. My parents are now resting in the arms of God since 2008 and 2012, but among their things, I conserve their letters which still speak to me. The love that they express and their content are unmistakable and **fill me with gratitude, hope, and encouragement.** Even if I didn't have eyes to see their unique handwriting, I could distinguish

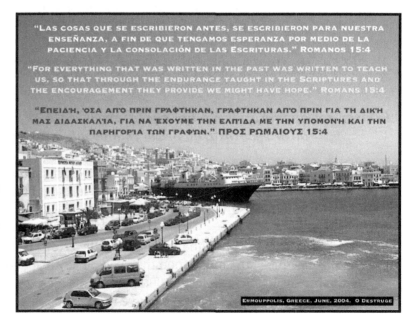

"LAS COSAS QUE SE ESCRIBIERON ANTES, SE ESCRIBIERON PARA NUESTRA ENSEÑANZA, A FIN DE QUE TENGAMOS ESPERANZA POR MEDIO DE LA PACIENCIA Y LA CONSOLACIÓN DE LAS ESCRITURAS." ROMANOS 15:4

"FOR EVERYTHING THAT WAS WRITTEN IN THE PAST WAS WRITTEN TO TEACH US, SO THAT THROUGH THE ENDURANCE TAUGHT IN THE SCRIPTURES AND THE ENCOURAGEMENT THEY PROVIDE WE MIGHT HAVE HOPE." ROMANS 15:4

"ΕΠΕΙΔΗ, ΟΣΑ ΑΠΟ ΠΡΙΝ ΓΡΑΦΤΗΚΑΝ, ΓΡΑΦΤΗΚΑΝ ΑΠΟ ΠΡΙΝ ΓΙΑ ΤΗ ΔΙΚΗ ΜΑΣ ΔΙΔΑΣΚΑΛΙΑ, ΓΙΑ ΝΑ ΕΧΟΥΜΕ ΤΗΝ ΕΛΠΙΔΑ ΜΕ ΤΗΝ ΥΠΟΜΟΝΗ ΚΑΙ ΤΗΝ ΠΑΡΗΓΟΡΙΑ ΤΩΝ ΓΡΑΦΩΝ." ΠΡΟΣ ΡΩΜΑΙΟΥΣ 15:4

ERMOUPPOLIS, GREECE, JUNE, 2004. O DESTRUGE

their voices if someone else were to read them to me.

These daily meditations strengthen and encourage us in hope, but the difference is that what is highlighted in quotation marks represents **God's Word**. The rest are my thoughts, anecdotes, experiences, and reflections that flow through study and prayer.

Faith in God assures us that *"All Scripture is God-breathed and is useful for teaching, rebuking, correcting and training in righteousness, so that the servant of God may be thoroughly equipped for every good work"* **(2 Timothy 3:16-17).** God wants us to arrive in the promised land with our faith intact and undamaged. The Bible is God's letter of love, guidance, instruction, and promise for God's people, to fill us with hope, courage, and consolation.

God knows that this world is full of selfishness, evil, and violence and that His love letter would fill us with the hope that one day good will conquer evil. And that after a short season of trials and tribulations, we'll arrive in the promised land, where there will be no more death, disease, or lies because nothing evil or harmful can enter **God's heavenly Kingdom.**

On that day, our Lord will welcome us to the heavenly mansion which He went to prepare for His brothers and friends. Then, reunited with our loved ones, there will be great joy! That's the hope that the Bible offers us.

That is why God tells us, *"continue in what you have learned and have become convinced of, because you know those from whom you learned it, and how from infancy you have known the Holy Scriptures, which are able to make you wise for salvation through faith in Christ Jesus"* **(2 Timothy 3:14-15).** My beloved, these things were *"written to teach us,"* so that we may have hope.

Let us pray: Dear God of *"endurance and encouragement grant us the same attitude of mind toward each other that Christ Jesus had, so that with one mind and one voice we may glorify the God and Father of our Lord Jesus Christ"* **(Romans 15:5–6).** Increase our faith to persist in what we've learned and to recognize our Savior's voice. We pray in Jesus's name.

> **God wants us to arrive in the promised land with our faith intact and undamaged. The Bible is God's letter of love, guidance, instruction, and promise for God's people, to fill us with hope, courage, and consolation.**

August 6
THE DAY OF REST

"Let us not become weary in doing good, for at the proper time we will reap a harvest if we do not give up." Galatians 6:9

"No nos cansemos, pues, de hacer el bien; porque a su tiempo cosecharemos, si no nos desanimamos". **Gálatas 6:9**

"Και ας μη αποκάμνουμε πράττοντας το καλό· επειδή, αν δεν αποκάμνουμε, θα θερίσουμε στον κατάλληλο καιρό." **ΠΡΟΣ ΓΑΛΑΤΑΣ 6:9**

Unlike our God, who does not get tired or faint, our bodies have limited energy, and in addition to food and water, they need to rest to regain strength. That's why God established the day of **"rest."** The Hebrew term is *"שַׁבָּת shabbát (H7676): - rest, sabbath."*

"Six days you shall labor and do all your work, but the seventh day is a sabbath to the Lord your God. On it you shall not do any work, neither you, nor your son or daughter, nor your male or female servant, nor your animals, nor any foreigner residing in your towns" **(Exodus 20:9-10).** Before Jesus's resurrection, the Sabbath was Saturday. However, from the first day of the resurrection, Jesus's disciples gathered to praise God and share bread on the new Sabbath, the first day of the week - Sunday **(Acts 20:7).**

My father-in-law honored the Sabbath (Sunday) and didn't do any work except doing good. This included visiting the sick and lonely, attending church in the morning and evening, reading the Bible, singing with his hymnal, and sharing the good news of love and hope with whoever would listen.

God urges us to work the six days and rest from all work, except doing good; that we demonstrate God's love by saving and healing lives. That's why for centuries, everyone rested on the Sabbath, except for doctors, police officers, firefighters, first responders, and certain pharmacists. Christian believers rested and praised God during the *"Day of the Lord"* (*Κυριακή* - kyriakí).

The Lord's Day is also a time when we attend church meetings and assemblies to worship God and learn from God's Word as a family.

> **God urges us to work the six days and rest from all work, except doing good; that we demonstrate God's love by saving and healing lives.**

Let us pray: Dear God, in this and every weekend, grant us a peaceful rest from our work so that we may recharge our physical and spiritual strength. Give us the courage to combat the attacks and distractions that try to separate us from Your love and our loved ones. Strengthen the bonds of love and family. We pray in Jesus's name.

August 7
FAITH INSTRUCTORS
Acts 18:25

When people talk about one of my or their children's children, I hope they'd say they *"had been instructed in the way of the Lord."*

My son understood scripture well when he left home for college. He still does! As a seminarian, I've seen that universities and seminaries expose us to different ideologies which test the faith

240

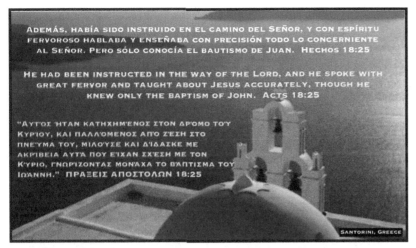

ADEMÁS, HABÍA SIDO INSTRUIDO EN EL CAMINO DEL SEÑOR, Y CON ESPÍRITU FERVOROSO HABLABA Y ENSEÑABA CON PRECISIÓN TODO LO CONCERNIENTE AL SEÑOR. PERO SÓLO CONOCÍA EL BAUTISMO DE JUAN. HECHOS 18:25

HE HAD BEEN INSTRUCTED IN THE WAY OF THE LORD, AND HE SPOKE WITH GREAT FERVOR AND TAUGHT ABOUT JESUS ACCURATELY, THOUGH HE KNEW ONLY THE BAPTISM OF JOHN. ACTS 18:25

"ΑΥΤΟΣ ΗΤΑΝ ΚΑΤΗΧΗΜΈΝΟΣ ΣΤΟΝ ΔΡΟΜΟ ΤΟΥ ΚΥΡΙΟΥ, ΚΑΙ ΠΑΛΛΟΜΕΝΟΣ ΑΠΌ ΖΈΣΗ ΣΤΟ ΠΝΕΎΜΑ ΤΟΥ, ΜΙΛΟΎΣΕ ΚΑΙ ΔΊΔΑΣΚΕ ΜΕ ΑΚΡΊΒΕΙΑ ΑΥΤΆ ΠΟΥ ΕΊΧΑΝ ΣΧΈΣΗ ΜΕ ΤΟΝ ΚΎΡΙΟ, ΓΝΩΡΊΖΟΝΤΑΣ ΜΟΝΆΧΑ ΤΟ ΒΆΠΤΙΣΜΑ ΤΟΥ ΙΩΆΝΝΗ." ΠΡΑΞΕΙΣ ΑΠΟΣΤΟΛΩΝ 18:25

SANTORINI, GREECE

that our parents taught us. That's why the home's religious instruction and faith formation is so important. We cannot raise our children without this foundation. *"Start children off on the way they should go, and even when they are old they will not turn from it"* (Proverbs 22:6).

The **faith formation** responsibility falls mainly on parents, to whom God instructs,

"These commandments that I give you today are to be on your hearts. Impress them on your children. Talk about them when you sit at home and when you walk along the road, when you lie down and when you get up" (Deuteronomy 6:6–7).

Ever since my son was seven years old, we studied the Bible daily and exchanged observations. Dinner was a time to **strengthen and form the faith** through family meditations. My father-in-law dreamed that one of his grandchildren would someday be a pastor. When my son graduated from college with a major in history and philosophy, my father-in-law was very proud but added that he would have liked it even more **"if he were a pastor."**

We can't choose careers for our children, but we must sow the seeds of faith and **mold their values** and character to resemble our Lord Jesus Christ. We must instruct them to be strong enough to resist and refute world philosophies. I always taught my son that **"an untested faith is not faith."** It's good to learn about other cultures and religions, but we must **remain firm** and precise regarding the Lord.

I also hope that those who have spoken with me in person or through our online Bible Meditation medium, when they remember me, they'd say that *"I had been instructed in the way of the Lord, and spoke with great fervor and taught about Jesus accurately!"*

Let us pray: Dear God, help us to accept the challenge of being our children's primary **faith instructor** through our example. Grant us, and our children, Your Holy Spirit. Teach us precisely what we must keep in our hearts so as not to fall victim to, and be able to refute, the world's philosophies. We pray in Your Holy Name.

August 8
GOD STILL SPEAKS IN DREAMS AND VISIONS
Genesis 37:9

Some Bible teachers believe that God no longer speaks to us through dreams or other forms of revelation. They say that once the Bible was completed, God sealed the book. No one should add to or subtract from what is written therein because to the one who adds, *"God will add the plagues that are written in this book."* And whoever takes away from it, God *"will take away his part of the tree of life"* **(Revelation 22:18-19).**

But then, how are we to understand this verse? *"Your sons and daughters will prophesy, your old men will dream dreams, your young men will see visions"* **(Joel 2:28).**

During the past 33 years, God hasn't given me any **new** revelation apart from the Bible. I'd be afraid to receive something that adds to or takes away from the Bible. But countless times, through prayer and dreams, God has shown me the Way, clarified the meaning and purpose of my life, and awakened me with a message, sermon, or answers to my questions.

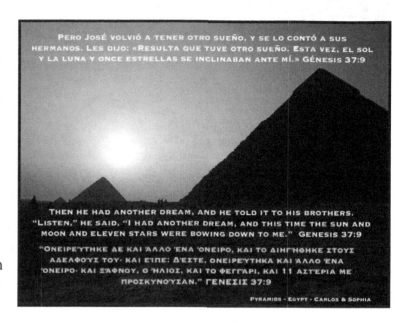

PERO JOSÉ VOLVIÓ A TENER OTRO SUEÑO, Y SE LO CONTÓ A SUS HERMANOS. LES DIJO: «RESULTA QUE TUVE OTRO SUEÑO. ESTA VEZ, EL SOL Y LA LUNA Y ONCE ESTRELLAS SE INCLINABAN ANTE MÍ.» GÉNESIS 37:9

THEN HE HAD ANOTHER DREAM, AND HE TOLD IT TO HIS BROTHERS. "LISTEN," HE SAID, "I HAD ANOTHER DREAM, AND THIS TIME THE SUN AND MOON AND ELEVEN STARS WERE BOWING DOWN TO ME." GENESIS 37:9

"ΟΝΕΙΡΕΎΤΗΚΕ ΔΕ ΚΑΙ ἌΛΛΟ ἝΝΑ ὌΝΕΙΡΟ, ΚΑΙ ΤΟ ΔΙΗΓΉΘΗΚΕ ΣΤΟΥΣ ΑΔΕΛΦΟΎΣ ΤΟΥ· ΚΑΙ ΕἾΠΕ: Δ'ΕΣΤΕ, ΟΝΕΙΡΕΎΤΗΚΑ ΚΑΙ ἌΛΛΟ ἝΝΑ ὌΝΕΙΡΟ· ΚΑΙ Σ'ΑΦΝΟΥ, Ο ἭΛΙΟΣ, ΚΑΙ ΤΟ ΦΕΓΓΆΡΙ, ΚΑΙ 11 ΑΣΤΈΡΙΑ ΜΕ ΠΡΟΣΚΥΝΟΎΣΑΝ." ΓΕΝΕΣΙΣ 37:9

PYRAMIDS - EGYPT - CARLOS & SOPHIA

I know that **God still speaks**, instructs, and corrects us through dreams and gives us visions to accomplish the work that lies ahead. Sometimes it's a necessary tool, an encouraging word to strengthen the fallen, a vision of where a lost item or person lies, or from whom we must ask forgiveness. **God still speaks to His children** through the Bible, dreams, and visions.

> **God still speaks, instructs, and corrects us through dreams and gives us visions to accomplish the work that lies ahead.**

Joseph was known as *"the dreamer."* He dreamed that *"the sun and moon and eleven stars were bowing down to me. When he told his father as well as his brothers, his father rebuked him and said, 'What is this dream you had? Will your mother and I and your brothers actually come and bow down to the ground before you?'"* **(Genesis 37:9-10).**

His brothers despised him for it and sold him as a slave to Egypt. God also gave Joseph the gift of interpreting dreams. With humility and firmness in his faith, Joseph ascended to power using this gift. He clarified that God allowed the harm that his brothers intended to do, *"but God intended it for good to accomplish what is now being done, the saving of many lives. So then, don't be afraid. I will provide for you and your children."* **(Genesis 50:20-21).**

Let us pray: Dear God, thank You for not leaving us in silence, without clarity or hope, especially when COVID-19 threatens our freedom and lives worldwide. Please speak to us through Your Word, dreams, and visions to fulfill Your purpose and be useful instruments in Your Kingdom. We pray in Your Holy Name.

✝ ✝ ✝ ✝ ✝ ✝

False promises! Who hasn't fallen victim to false promises? People go to the polls to place politicians in power because, knowing our needs, as to a bride, they promise to bring down the moon and the stars for us. God doesn't want us to fall victim to false pledges intended to separate us from His love and kingdom.

"See to it that no one takes you captive through hollow and deceptive philosophy, which depends on human tradition and the elemental spiritual forces of this world rather than on Christ" **(Colossians 2:8).** Many will come with worldly philosophies and false promises, such as: *"'All this I will give you,' [the devil] said, 'if you will bow down and worship me'"* **(Matthew 4:9)**, **"live and let live,"** or **"God accepts us just as we are,"** meaning that there's no need to change our lifestyle. God accepts us just as we are but will not leave us incomplete, disfigured, and maimed because we've innocently trusted in false promises.

We need a change of heart and mind. *"Do not be carried away by all kinds of strange teachings"* **(Hebrews 13:9a),** such as words and doctrines opposed to the Bible. We'd have a complete social disorder if we trusted such false promises. Imagine our world if it weren't a sin or crime to steal, rape, kill, etc. Given these conditions, we cannot say *"live and let live."* We're witnessing a radical change in which its become customary to lie and give false testimony. We must lovingly resist this and all kinds of disorders threatening our faith and society.

> "QUE NADIE LOS ENGAÑE CON PALABRAS VANAS, PORQUE POR ESTAS COSAS VIENE LA IRA DE DIOS SOBRE AQUELLOS QUE NO LO OBEDECEN." EFESIOS 5:6
>
> "LET NO ONE DECEIVE YOU WITH EMPTY WORDS, FOR BECAUSE OF SUCH THINGS GOD'S WRATH COMES ON THOSE WHO ARE DISOBEDIENT." EPHESIANS 5:6
>
> "ΚΑΝΈΝΑΣ ΑΣ ΜΗ ΣΑΣ ΑΠΑΤΑ ΜΕ ΜΆΤΑΙΑ ΛΌΓΙΑ· ΕΠΕΙΔΉ, ΓΙ' ΑΥΤΑ ΈΡΧΕΤΑΙ Η ΟΡΓΉ ΤΟΥ ΘΕΟΥ ΕΠΆΝΩ ΣΤΟΥΣ ΓΙΟΥΣ ΤΗΣ ΑΠΕΊΘΕΙΑΣ." ΠΡΟΣ ΕΦΕΣΙΟΥΣ 5:6

> **God accepts us just as we are but will not leave us incomplete, disfigured, and maimed because we've innocently trusted in false promises.**

Jesus tells us, *"If you love me, keep my commands"* **(John 14:15).** We can achieve a world free of disorder, conflict, and evil by obeying His commandments and placing ourselves in the hands of the Divine Potter to remold us according to His design.

Some politicians offer us false guarantees to gain temporary power for themselves. Jesus offers us reliable promises, guaranteed by His life that was poured out on Calvary, so that, along with forgiveness, we may earn Divine power and treasures in heaven.

Let us pray: Dear God, may our lives glorify Your name and bring back all the lost sheep of the world. Give us hearts and ears attentive and obedient to Your Voice and Word to distinguish false promises and not fall under their hypnotic power. We pray in Your Holy Name.

✛ ✛ ✛ ✛ ✛ ✛

August 10
REFUGE AND SHIELD
Psalm 57:1

In my quest to better understand God's heart, I've learned that God's love for us is immense, undeserved, eternal, unchanging, and equal for everyone. I think it's incredible that the Almighty chose to be with us, for us, and in us.

For us: Romans 8:31 says, *"If God is for us, who can be against us?"*

With us: Matthew 1:23 affirms that God is **WITH** us. *"The virgin will conceive and give birth to a son, and they will call him Immanuel,"* which means *"God with us"* (**Matthew 1:23 and Isaiah 8:8**).

In us: *"The one who keeps God's commands lives in him, and he in them. And this is how we know that he lives in us: We know it by the Spirit he gave us"* (**1 John 3:24**).

These verses strengthen and deepen our faith. If we believe that God is for, with, and in us, then by faith, in all situations, we'll remain confident and immovable in our resolve to trust and stay under the shadow of God's wings, under the direction of our God, teacher, protector, strength, and shield.

Psalm 46:1–3 says, *"God is our refuge and strength, an ever-present help in trouble. Therefore we will not fear, though the earth give way and the mountains fall into the heart of the sea, though its waters roar and foam and the mountains quake with their surging."*

Since God is committed to being **for** us, **with** us, and **in** us, we should not fear any evil that might come. And if God is with us, as a shield and strength, we can cry out, *"who can be against us?"* (**Romans 8:31**).

Let us pray: Dear God, give us the faith and security of knowing that you are for, with, and in us (including our children and their children). We place our life, future, and hope in Your mighty, loving hands, confident that You'll rescue us from all trials and tribulations. We trust you'll sustain and strengthen our soul so we do not faint - even if the earth trembles. Put a song in our hearts to help us move forward confidently and humbly, holding Your hand. We pray in Jesus's name.

SERVING WITH GREAT LOVE
John 6:35

My mother-in-law, wife, sister-in-law, and daughter (just as my mother did) feel great love and joy when serving guests at their table, offering the best of their cuisine. They're equally glad whether feeding one or ten, but their happiness increases when we ask for seconds. We do this because 1. It was genuinely delicious, 2. we're still hungry, or 3. we believe we won't taste something as good for a while.

Jesus said to the crowds: *"In a little while you will see me no more"* **(John 16:16A)**. Some years ago, preparing to return to the United States, I decided to enjoy everything that my mother-in-law placed in front of me because 1. it pleases her, and 2. because I know that I won't taste her delicacies for a while.

The crowds were hungry and eager to taste everything that Jesus offered them. They had never tasted such satisfying bread and wanted seconds. Jesus said: *"you are looking for me, not because you saw the signs I performed but because you ate the loaves and had your fill"* **(John 6:26).**

The Divine road has taken us to many encounters, each with a unique purpose and mission. Whether in Greece, Ecuador, the United States, Bolivia, Costa Rica, Nicaragua, or wherever we meet friends or family, some of the best moments have been sharing a meal with beloved friends or family. To each of you, we say, *"May God repay your kindness."* We've felt God's love. You served each dish with love, sacrifice, and care. But, by far, the best moments have been when we've shared bread from the local bakery and God's Word and presence.

Mother Teresa said, *"Not all of us can do great things. But we can do small things with great love"*, and *"If you can't feed a hundred people, then feed just one."* God fed us to feed others. The key to happiness is to serve God with great love.

Let us pray: Dear God, thank You for inviting us to Your table, where bread and spiritual drink fill and strengthen us forever. Fill us with Your Holy Spirit to feed others with great love and power. We ask in Jesus's name.

> *"Not all of us can do great things. But we can do small things with great love."* **Mother Teresa**

✚ ✚ ✚ ✚ ✚

August 12
RADIANT FACES
Acts 6:15

If you knew **Aristoklis Xanthópoulos** (RIP), you'd agree that my grandson Lázaro Elías and Fanny Destruge in today's photograph bear his joyful twinkle in their eyes; a radiance about them that makes you smile and rejoice with them. Those who knew him well were attracted by his angelic peaceful joy, similar to what we read about Stephen in today's verse. *"His face was like the face of an angel."*

We gain radiant joy by seeking to know God, His Kingdom, and Wisdom through the Holy Scriptures. **Ecclesiastes 8:1** says, *"Who is like the wise? Who knows the explanation of things? A person's wisdom brightens their face and changes its hard appearance."*

As we search the scriptures, God's love brings us out of the depths of fear and hiding and into joyful hope. Whatever our condition before experiencing God's loving grace, the Lord replaces it with love, peace, joy, and a sense of purpose. From that moment on, we want to tell the world about our new-found love.

> **As we search the scriptures, God's love brings us out of the depths of fear and hiding and into joyful hope.**

But fear and doubt may set in - *"What if they laugh at me? What if they reject and kick me out of the house or circle of trust?"* All of us experience some level of inadequacy and doubt. Most of the disciples chosen by Jesus were simple, uneducated individuals. Yet, God transformed the world through their faith. *"Now Stephen, a man full of God's grace and power, performed great wonders and signs among the people" (Acts 6:8).*

The Bible refers to various individuals whose radiant faces encouraged their followers to achieve mighty victories over fear, enemies, and doubt. Moses 'face radiated whenever he was in God's presence **(Exodus 34:30).** Jesus took three of His disciples up the mountain and was transfigured. *"His face shone like the sun, and his clothes became as white as the light"* **(Matthew 17:2).** After the resurrection, we read that Jesus's *"appearance was like lightning, and his clothes were white as snow"* **(Matthew 28:3).**

My beloved friends and family, you who are the blood of my blood, know that God will do great things in and through us if we let Him.

Let us pray: Dear Lord, please grant us the faith, joy, and boldness to transform our world, starting with our circle of trust, into believers and followers of Your Kingdom. Make Your face shine upon us so that others may trust in Your presence and promises. We pray in Jesus's name.

August 13
DIVISIONS AND OBSTACLES
Romans 16:17

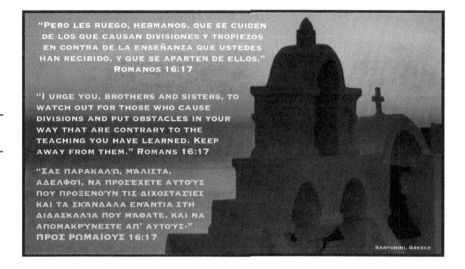

Two important verbs appear in this text - *"watch out"* and *"keep away."* God calls us to watch out and separate ourselves from those who *"cause divisions and put obstacles in your way that are contrary to the teaching you have learned,"* not from those who at the moment practice evil because they're unaware of God's love and forgiveness. We're called to go in search of the lost sheep. Jesus set the example by eating and sharing the good news with sinners, whom He liberated, transformed, and renewed by God's saving power.

Today's verse tells us to be vigilant and distance ourselves from those who claim to be Christians but whose actions and words go against the Bible's teachings. **1 Corinthians 5:11** says, *"But now I am writing to you that you must not associate with anyone who claims to be a brother or sister but is sexually immoral or greedy, an idolater or slanderer, a drunkard or swindler. Do not even eat with such people."* In

> We're called to go in search of the lost sheep. Jesus set the example by eating and sharing the good news with sinners, whom He liberated, transformed, and renewed by God's saving power.

this verse, the focus is on *"anyone who claims to be a brother or sister"* (**Christians**) but whose fruits and actions show that they are not.

Children of light can't coexist with the children of darkness who've heard and rejected God's teachings, preferring to follow and teach the doctrines of the world. God's Word says in **2 Thessalonians 3:6**, *"In the name of the Lord Jesus Christ, we command you, brothers and sisters, to keep away from every believer who is idle and disruptive and does not live according to the teaching you received from us."*

The practical application for us is to pay close attention to those who come into our fellowship, identifying themselves as fellow believers. We shouldn't place them in leadership positions or as teachers over our little ones until they've demonstrated the fruit of the Spirit through their moderate living, consistent with the Bible's teachings.

Let us pray: Dear God, thank You for directing us to watch out and separate ourselves from those who *"cause divisions and put obstacles in"* the teachings found in Your Holy Word. Enlighten us, Lord, to clearly distinguish between those who need rescuing and those who selfishly seek to destroy the foundation of our faith. We pray in Jesus's name.

August 14
KNOWLEDGE AND INTELLIGENCE FROM GOD
Genesis 41:38

Wisdom is how we use intelligence, e.g., acting on the instructions and revelation that God has given us. After communicating the interpretation of Pharaoh's dream, Joseph wisely laid out a well-detailed strategy to save Egypt when the famine arrived. Joseph said, *"And now let Pharaoh look for a discerning and wise man and put him in charge of the land of Egypt"* **(Genesis 41:33).**

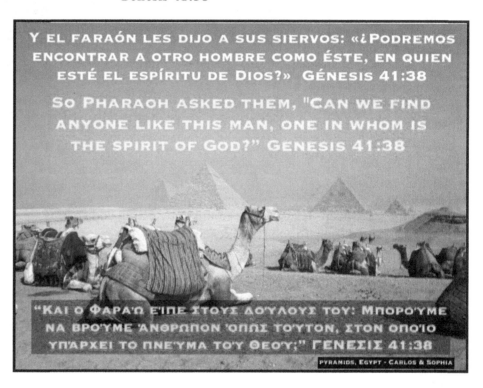

Pharaoh was impressed with Joseph's plan and character and said to his servants, *"'Can we find anyone like this man, one in whom is the spirit of God?'" Then Pharaoh said to Joseph, 'Since God has made all this known to you, there is no one so discerning and wise as you. You shall be in charge of my palace, and all my people are to submit to your orders. Only with respect to the throne will I be greater than you.'"* **(Genesis 41:38-40).** The Spirit of God interpreted Pharaoh's dream and gave it to Joseph for Pharaoh's ears. He also gave Joseph the peace and clarity to formulate a detailed plan to please Pharaoh and save the world from hunger. **Thus, an imprisoned enslaved person rose to the second position in Egypt.**

When I worked at Diversified Investment Advisors, I asked my boss if he'd recommend me for the position of **"Technical Consultant."** The function allocated much time and resources to analyzing pension and finance laws and contracts. My boss said he didn't see the qualities necessary for that position in me. I was sad but also motivated to develop and polish the skills I already possessed; the love of reading, analytical, and writing.

A few years later, God saved me, and the Holy Spirit began His work of empowering and renewing me. To make the anecdote brief, I applied for the position of *"Technical Consultant,"* and based on my written opinions, **God helped me to be promoted** to Senior Technical Consultant, then to Director of Technical Services, and finally, to Vice President of Technical Services and Spanish.

Diversified's president, Peter Kunkel (R.I.P.), often quoted the interpretations that the Spirit of God gave me, and for a brief time, I reported directly to him on Spanish Services. I did not save lives, but I have testimonies of individuals and families who achieved their American dream based on the opinions, strategies, and recommendations God's Spirit gave me to help His people *"save and invest wisely for retirement."*

Let us pray: Dear God, we need Your knowledge and intelligence. Grant us Joseph's humility to recognize that it's not me but Your Holy Spirit who works in me. That, apart from You, we are nothing. We pray in Your Holy Name.

August 15
JOSEPH WEPT

"He turned away from them and began to weep." Genesis 42:24a

"¡José se apartó de ellos, y lloró"! Génesis 42:24a

"Και όταν αποσύρθηκε από κοντά τους έκλαψε·" ΓΕΝΕΣΙΣ 42:24

The shortest verse in the Bible says, *"Jesus wept"* **(John 11:35).** Joseph is a type of Jesus; that is, he's a shadow of what is to come. Today's verse is another typology pointing to Jesus. With deep love and anguish, Jesus wept at the rejection of His people, the agony of Calvary's cross, the temporary separation from God, and His deep love for the world.

In today's verse, Joseph's brothers *"bowed down to the ground,"* fulfilling the prophetic dream that Joseph had as a teenager **(v.6).** The brothers went to buy wheat and did not recognize Joseph, but he did and put them to the test, accusing them of being spies, and putting them in prison. After three days, Joseph declared that one would remain imprisoned while the nine would return home with food and return with Benjamin, the younger brother.

The brothers said to each other, *"Surely we are being punished because of our brother* [Joseph]. *We saw how distressed he was when he pleaded with us for his life, but we would not listen; that's why this distress has come on us"* **(Genesis 42:21).** Joseph felt pain for his brothers' suffering, and turning away from them, *"he wept"* **(v.24).**

Having the power to do so, **Joseph didn't repay evil with evil**. On the contrary, he commanded each brother's sacks to be filled with wheat, and their money returned. Besides, he ordered *"to give them provisions for the journey"* **(v.25B).** Joseph sent them back home to feed his father and brothers. But Simeon remained imprisoned.

Like Jesus, **Joseph wept,** remembering his brothers' betrayal who sold him into slavery. Joseph wept at the anguish they felt for having sinned against him. He cried about the years of separation from his family and his deep love for the brothers. They'd planned to harm him, but in his heart, Joseph knew that God had allowed this to rescue the world. Joseph had forgiven his brothers, and it was time to fulfill God's purpose.

We, too, have sinned against God and His people. We deserve our punishment, but when we repent, God's deep love forgives, heals, and sends us with provisions for the journey ahead. We've also wept at the disappointment and rejection from loved ones. But God's deep love prompts us to **forgive as we've been forgiven, to love as we've been loved.**

Let us pray: Dear Lord, thank You for Your abiding, deep love that forgives and loves despite our failures. Forgive us when our actions, words, or thoughts cause You to weep. We pray in the name of Jesus.

> We've also wept at the disappointment and rejection from loved ones. But God's deep love prompts us to **forgive as we've been forgiven, to love as we've been loved.**

August 16
DEALING WITH GROWING PAINS

"It would not be right for us to neglect the ministry of the word of God in order to wait on tables." Acts 6:2B

"No está bien que desatendamos la proclamación de la palabra de Dios por atender a las mesas". Hechos 6:2B

"Δεν είναι πρέπον να αφήσουμε εμείς τον λόγο τού Θεού, και να υπηρετούμε σε τραπέζια." **ΠΡΑΞΕΙΣ ΑΠΟΣΤΟΛΩΝ 6:2B**

Growth is good, but along with it comes increased obligations. In **Acts 2:41-42,** we read, *"Those who accepted his message were baptized, and about three thousand were added to their number that day. They devoted themselves to the apostles 'teaching and to fellowship, to the breaking of bread and to prayer."* Thus, there was a great joy both in heaven and among the disciples. With just one sermon inspired by the Holy Spirit, the number of disciples increased from twelve, plus some followers, to more than three thousand. *"And the Lord added to their number daily those who were being saved"* (Acts 2:47).

But along with the joy, they had to deal with growing pains. Among the thousands added, there was a mix of languages, Jewish-Hebrew, Aramaic, and Greek. The twelve apostles became involved in the food distribution program to the needy, and apparently, a complaint arose from the new Jewish-Greek believers that Greek widows were being neglected **(Acts 6:1).**

Rather than seek blame, the apostles implemented solutions, stating that *"It would not be right for us to neglect the ministry of the word of God in order to wait on tables"* (**v.2**). For this reason, they asked the others to *"choose seven men from among you who are known to be full of the Spirit and wisdom. We will turn this responsibility over to them and will give our attention to prayer and the ministry of the word"* (**Acts 6:3-4**).

Christians have to deal with growing pains, attending to two equally essential responsibilities, feeding the people with God's Word and feeding the poor with physical food. We cannot be effective in doing one at the expense of the other. We must be organized and intentional in approaching these two vital church ministries without neglecting them. As the community grows through the preaching of the gospel, the poor, orphans, and widows who need our support with food and physical care will also arrive seeking help.

Let us pray: Dear God, thank You for the great privilege of being bearers of Your physical and spiritual sustenance. Help us pray and proclaim Your Word of hope and feed and care for the poor among us. We pray in the name of Jesus.

✝ ✝ ✝ ✝ ✝ ✝

August 17
GOD IS WITH YOU
Acts 7:9

God was with Joseph, freeing him from all the plots, accusations, and sufferings. As with Joseph, God is with you and all those who serve and walk blamelessly with God. (**Psalm 101:6**).

Speaking of suffering, a grandfather was teaching his grandson about his life and said, *"Inside me, there is a terrible fight between two wolves. One is bad - full of lust, gluttony, greed, laziness, anger, envy, and pride. The other is good - full of joy, peace, love, hope, serenity, humility, kindness, benevolence, empathy, generosity, truth, compassion, and faith. The same fight exists within you and in each person. The grandson asked: 'Which wolf will win?' The grandfather replied: 'Whichever you feed the most, my son?' (American Indian Proverb)."*

251

We live in a spiritual struggle to be won by the wolf we feed the most. Every day the spirit struggles to reflect God's image, while the flesh struggles to satisfy its cravings! Many years ago, during Lent, I gave up eating bread (which I love so much). I remember how my desire to eat bread grew with each passing day. By day 20, I counted the days left before I could satisfy my craving.

Easter Sunday arrived, and giving in to my excessive desire for bread, I ate and began to gain weight. It wasn't much, maybe 2 kilos per year. But in 10 years, I had gained 20 kilos of excess luggage. More than a diet, I needed a lifestyle change - to crucify the desires of the flesh.

I've suffered from excess weight all my life. In 2007, my highest weight was 103.41 kilos (228 pounds). I took inventory of my life and prayed for God to help me feed the good wolf. For a year, repeating *"I can do all things through Christ who strengthens me" (Philippians 4:13)*, God helped me resist temptation and change my habits, giving me back control of my life.

We're prone to attacks that attempt to separate us from God's love, from family and friends. But God calls us to be strong and courageous because, at all times, God is with those who serve and walk blamelessly with Him.

Let us pray: Dear God, thank You because despite what the enemy tries against us, You are always with us, freeing us from all evil. Please help us to overcome doubt and temptation. We pray in Jesus's name.

August 18
WE ARE GOD'S TEMPLE

"You did well to have it in your heart to build a temple for my Name." 1 Kings 8:18

"Es muy bueno tu deseo sincero de construir un templo donde se honre mi nombre".
1 Reyes 8:18

"Επειδή ήρθε στην καρδιά σου να κτίσεις οίκο στο όνομά μου, καλώς μεν έκανες που το συνέλαβες στην καρδιά σου·" **Α΄ ΒΑΣΙΛΕΩΝ 8:18**

King David had intended to build a temple for God, but the Lord never asked for a physical temple to be constructed for him. However, he was pleased with Solomon's sincere desire to do so. God doesn't want temples of stone, cedar, and marble, but rather, that our hearts to be temples where God's name is honored.

The letter to the Corinthians affirms that we are *"God's temple and that God's Spirit dwells in your midst?"* **(1 Corinthians 3:16, 6:19)**. You *"are the temple of the living God" (2 Corinthians 6:16).* Being God's temple identifies who we are and to whom we belong.

One of the Greek customs is that when asked to identify yourself (usually in a government office or in small towns), instead of asking **"What's your name?"** they ask, *"whose are you?"* **(Ποιανού είσαι;)** The real question behind this cultural phraseology is, *"who is your father?"*

The Bible clarifies to whom we belong. *"Do you not know that your bodies are temples of the Holy Spirit, who is in you, whom you have received from God? You are not your own" (1 Corinthians 6:19).* God is our Father and Creator, who's given us a body to be God's temple. It's our body, but spiritually Jesus bought it at a great price. So it's no longer ours but belonging to God. We're the temple's caretakers.

Likewise, as Christian parents, we recognize that our children belong to God (although they're the *blood of our blood*). God has entrusted us to care for and raise them until they're old enough to care for themselves. Just as we are caregivers for our children, God is our caregiver and provider.

If today we're asked, *"whose are you?"* may we proudly and humbly say, *"I'm a child of God."*

Let us pray: Dear God, thank You for helping us to recognize that we're Your beloved children, that our life and all that we are and have come from Your grace and love. May we offer our lives and bodies as Your temple to glorify and praise You, and through them, may all the world return under Your protection and kingdom. We pray in Jesus's name.

August 19
IN THE SPIRIT OF UNITY
1 Thessalonians 5:10

There's always one in the family who lives in the spirit of unity. Among Jacob's twelve sons, Judah was the rational and sentimental one. My mother, the first of twelve, was very sentimental. She enjoyed seeing the family united, always looking to create pleasant moments, and that, despite the distance, her children would maintain close family relationships.

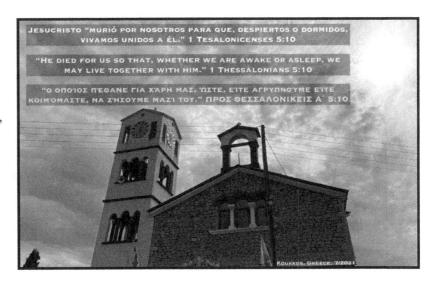

As a teenager, I was lucky to enjoy some summers in Ecuador with my uncles and cousins. We shared unforgettable moments and novelties of youth. In Ecuador, I experienced the first earthquake, the death of my grandmother Amada Maldonado. I climbed Cruz Loma, serenaded young ladies until dawn, and felt the joy of first love and the sadness of seeing it vanish. The family was always by my side, united, supporting, and watching over me in the joys, triumphs, and fears.

Although I didn't know God as I do today, I recognize that the Lord was by my side at all times, watching, strengthening, and calling me to cultivate the spirit of unity in Christ 24/7 (awake or asleep). This is our duty as He made the ultimate sacrifice so that our hearts would be His temples.

Jesus said, *"In this world you will have trouble. But take heart! I have overcome the world"* **(John 16:33).** Amid the disagreements, setbacks, and struggles we experience within our circles of influence (such as family, church, and friends), the Spirit of Christ reminds us who we are and for whom we work. The Spirit gives us a booster of love, patience, and faith at critical moments and maintains us united in and through Christ.

To stay in union and harmony, we must *"be sober, putting on faith and love as a breastplate, and the hope of salvation as a helmet. For God did not appoint us to suffer wrath but to receive salvation through our Lord Jesus Christ"* **(1 Thessalonians 5:8-9).**

Let us pray: Dear God, thank You for the gifts of faith, hope, salvation, and unity of spirit. Thank you for the family, friends, and Christian brothers and sisters who've supported us in times of distress. Give us wisdom, patience, love, and hearts inclined to edify and encourage those who've suffered attacks on their soul and spirit. We pray in Jesus's name.

✚ ✚ ✚ ✚ ✚

August 20
BLESSED AMID TRIALS
Psalm 84:5

"Consider it pure joy, my brothers and sisters, whenever you face trials of many kinds" **(James 1:2).** How blessed are those who love their work and would do it even without being paid! For them, each trial is an opportunity to hone their talents.

Some invest significant amounts of money, time, and effort to train with the best in their field. How many wouldn't want to train with Messi (soccer), Jordan (Basketball), Serena Williams (Tennis), or Ali (Boxing)? Athletes spend seven to ten hours a day learning strategies and techniques and strengthening their bodies to build endurance and muscle memory. They start their training knowing it won't be easy to train with champions who demand commitment, effort, fatigue, and pain.

254

Spiritually, we have as trainers the greats of the faith, among whom Jesus is Captain of captains. Those *"whose hearts are set on pilgrimage"* with the Lord anticipate that walking as Christ did won't be easy. Jesus warns us that we will have trials, rejections, and betrayals.

And yet, we're happy because *"The Lord is our trainer."* Every step I take with Him strengthens my spiritual muscles and prepares me for the subsequent encounter, knowing that God will patiently guide and support me to overcome all trials. *"You know that the testing of your faith produces perseverance. Let perseverance finish its work so that you may be mature and complete, not lacking anything" (James 1:3–4).*

My beloved, our walk with God would be so much easier if there weren't trials. But without testing our faith, you and I would be unable to face even the smallest tests. Much less the big ones to come. Without surpassing the hardship of training, we couldn't give witness and hope to those entering the race, including our children, family, and friends.

Let us pray: Dear God, we are truly blessed because you have chosen us to train under the direction of Jesus and the Holy Spirit. May we follow the example of the greats of faith who, trusting in Your Holy Word, overcame trials and the evil that surrounded them. Grant us the patience and discipline to continue training; thus, we'll be perfect and complete without anything lacking. We pray in Your Holy Name.

> **Without surpassing the hardship of training, we couldn't give witness and hope to those just entering the race, including our children, family, and friends.**

August 21
PREPARE YOUR TESTIMONY
Psalm 124:1

Today's verse reminds me of a Spanish praise song, *"Where would I have been if you hadn't reached out to save me? Where would I be today if you hadn't forgiven me? I'd have a deep void in this heart of mine. Wandering aimlessly and without your guide, If it weren't for your grace and love. I would be like a bird wounded and dying on the ground. I would be like a deer panting for water in the desert. If it weren't for your grace and your love."*

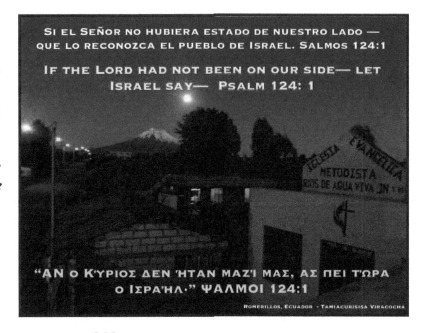

255

There's power in **remembering** God's Word and presence. As His children, we're called to meditate on His mercies, to tell and retell His mighty works, wonders, and favors to our children, family, and friends. We're called to identify ourselves as the people of God. In this way, we stir our faith. Therefore, **it's essential to prepare our testimony.** The Bible says that we must *"always be prepared to give an answer to everyone who asks you to give the reason for the hope that you have"* **(1 Peter 3:15).**

In 1989, I started the good habit of writing in my spiritual journal what God did for me, reflecting on *"how my life was like 'before' and 'after Christ.'"* Much of what I've shared in sermons, Bible studies, and meditations come from my journals, where I've stored experiences and triumphs with Christ and my failures when I tried to do things on my strength and wisdom. As memory begins to fail, it's invigorating to read these writings, which rekindle the faith. Sometimes, like a photograph or video, it causes me to relive the experiences, concluding with a *"thank you, Lord. Where would I be if it hadn't been for your grace and love?"*

It's never too late to start. I urge you to write and **prepare your testimony**, to revive your faith and that of our children and their children, and to leave a spiritual legacy that, like education, will never be lost. Jesus says, *"Do not store up for yourselves treasures on earth, where moths and vermin destroy, and where thieves break in and steal. But store up for yourselves treasures in heaven, where moths and vermin do not destroy, and where thieves do not break in and steal"* **(Matthew 6:19-20).**

Let us pray: Dear God, if it hadn't been for You, we would have fallen into the clutches of our enemies. But, *"Praise be to You Lord, who has not let us be torn by their teeth. We've escaped like a bird from the fowler's snare; the snare has been broken, and we've escaped. Our help is in the name of the Lord, the Maker of heaven and earth"* **(Psalm 124:6-8).** Thank you for being our shield, defender, and protector. For everything you've done, thank you, in Jesus 'name.

August 22
ANNIVERSARY PRAYER

"Be careful," Jesus said to them. "Be on your guard against the yeast of the Pharisees and Sadducees." **Matthew 16:6**

"Jesús les dijo: 'Abran los ojos y cuídense de la levadura de los fariseos y de los saduceos'". **Mateo 16:6**

"Και ο Ιησούς είπε σ' αυτούς: Βλέπετε και προσέχετε από τη ζύμη των Φαρισαίων και των Σαδδουκαίων." ΚΑΤΑ ΜΑΤΘΑΙΟΝ 16:6

On August 22, 2021, we celebrated the **third anniversary of daily meditations**. I thank God for you, asking that God open our eyes and free us from the teachings of the Pharisees and Sadducees of our times.

You and I intentionally spend four to five minutes reading these daily meditations to feed and strengthen our minds and hearts, to help us meet the daily challenges through God's Word. Our purpose is to glorify God and **leave a spiritual legacy for our children and future generations.**

We've had incredible growth, reaching almost nine hundred members, with an average of 250 daily readers. I don't pray for the group to grow for the sake of growth. Instead, I pray that we become doers of God's Word **(James 1:22).** May God's teachings flow among friends and family so that God's name may be glorified in and through us. May our children see in us, men and women, committed to God, home, family, and community.

I also pray that we are delivered from the perverse teachings of the Pharisees and Sadducees of our times. Jesus said, *"And you experts in the law, woe to you, because you load people down with burdens they can hardly carry, and you yourselves will not lift one finger to help them"* **(Luke 11:46).** Though no longer called Pharisees or Sadducees, they do impose regulations which they ignore.

Jesus also said, *"Woe to you, teachers of the law and Pharisees, you hypocrites! You shut the door of the kingdom of heaven in people's faces. You yourselves do not enter, nor will you let those enter who are trying to"* **(Matthew 23:13).** John the Baptist declared them a *"generation of vipers"* **(Matthew 3:7).** Their teachings are dangerous, and we must be careful of them.

Let us pray: Dear God, as we enter our fourth year, I pray that we not give in to the teachings of the Pharisees and Sadducees but instead keep our eyes fixed on Jesus, the cross, and Your Word. May we always use it to discern Your direction. Grant us discernment to recognize wolves in sheep's clothing and reject their corrupt teachings. Thank you, Lord, for all the friends and family accompanying us daily. In times of trial and pandemic, save us from all evil. We pray in Jesus's name.

August 23
MUTUALLY SUBMISSIVE
Ephesians 5:21

Our text calls us to be mutually submissive. Submission in Greek is ὑποτάσσω **(Ipotásso G-5293)**, whose synonyms include *"subordinate, obey, low, submitted, subject, and submissive."* **As followers of Christ, God calls us to cultivate mutual submission among a wide list of relationships**, driven by the fear of God and our reverential gratitude for Jesus's great sacrifice on the cross.

257

Submission is a word that in many circles leaves an unpleasant taste, implying the dominance and control of a superior being over another supposedly inferior, of less value. Examples of submission make us think of slavery. But within the body of Christ, that inference does not fly since, in God's eyes, we're all of equal value.

> AS FOLLOWERS OF CHRIST, GOD CALLS US TO CULTIVATE MUTUAL SUBMISSION AMONG A WIDE LIST OF RELATIONSHIPS.

Jesus is the supreme example of submission. **Philippians 2:5-8** says, **"In your relationships with one another, have the same mindset as Christ Jesus:** *Who, being in very nature God, did not consider equality with God something to be used to his own advantage; rather, he made himself nothing by taking the very nature of a servant, being made in human likeness. And being found in appearance as a man, he humbled himself by becoming obedient to death—even death on a cross!"*

Jesus became submissive to God's will so that humanity might have the opportunity to be rescued and destined for a grand reunion in heaven, together with our loved ones who slept with the faith that, on the final day, they will awaken in the Resurrection to eternal life.

The relationships in which we are to be willingly submissive, kind, and gentle to one another include spouses, children to parents, parents to children, servants to masters, blood brothers, and brothers in Christ. We should all serve each other as if we were serving Jesus. If we do this, we honor the life that Jesus sacrificed and glorify His name.

Let us pray: Dear God, thank You for sending Jesus Christ, who gave us the example of submission. Just as Jesus loved the church, giving His life for her, may we faithfully love and serve one another so that Your will may be fulfilled in our lives, children, and communities. Grant us submissive hearts. Lord, heal our sick and planet. We pray in the name of Jesus.

August 24
CONFIDENT IN GOD'S PROMISES

"If you follow my decrees, observe my laws and keep all my commands and obey them, I will fulfill through you the promise I gave to David your father." 1 Kings 6:12

"yo cumpliré la promesa que le hice a tu padre David, siempre y cuando tú obedezcas mis estatutos y mis decretos, y pongas en práctica mis mandamientos". 1 Reyes 6:12

"Αν περπατάς στα διατάγματά μου, και εκτελείς τις κρίσεις μου, και τηρείς όλες τις εντολές μου, περπατώντας σ' αυτές, τότε θα κάνω βέβαιον τον λόγο μου μαζί σου, που μίλησα στον Δαβίδ τον πατέρα σου·" Α΄ ΒΑΣΙΛΕΩΝ 6:12

We must know our past to understand the present, and, trusting in the promises made to our ancestors, we can, with joy and confidence, forge the path toward a bright future.

"I will fulfill through you the promise I gave to David your father" refers to the Davidic covenant found in **2 Samuel 7:12-16**, in which God promises, *"You shall never fail to have a successor to sit before me on the throne of Israel, if only your descendants are careful in all they do to walk before me faithfully as you have done"* (**1 Kings 8:25**).

King Solomon was the wisest man in the world, but he wasn't perfect. He was enticed by riches, fame, power, and sensuality. Since there wasn't a single king who acted justly, God descended from heaven in human form to fulfill the Davidic promise. *"'The days are coming,' declares the Lord, 'when I will raise up for David a righteous Branch, a King who will reign wisely and do what is just and right in the land'"* (*Jeremiah 23:5*).

David's descendant is Jesus Christ, announced through the prophet Isaiah. *"For to us a child is born, to us a son is given, and the government will be on his shoulders. And he will be called Wonderful Counselor, Mighty God, Everlasting Father, Prince of Peace. Of the greatness of his government and peace there will be no end. He will reign on David's throne and over his kingdom, establishing and upholding it with justice and righteousness from that time on and forever"* (**Isaiah 9:6-7**).

God doesn't want temples other than our hearts to place His throne. But His reign, love, and protection under the Davidic covenant are conditional. There will never be a lack of a righteous King in our hearts, *"if you follow my decrees, observe my laws and keep all my commands and obey them"* (*1 Kings 6:12*).

Let us pray: Dear God, thank You for Your love and mercy, which despite our failures, offer us the opportunity to return under Your kingdom and covenant. Grant us and our offspring an unwavering desire to know and obey Your statutes, decrees, and commandments. *"Grace to all who love our Lord Jesus Christ with an undying love"* (**Ephesians 6:24**). We pray in Your Holy Name.

August 25
CHOSEN
John 15:16

I came to the United States in the winter of 1964, where Stickball was a strange, new game for me. The street was filled with youngsters playing it during the spring and summer. At first, being shy and not speaking English, the boys didn't invite me to play on their team. I practiced alone and learned to hit the ball very well. From the first time I hit a "home run," they began to select me, and eventually, along with my best friend Santiago Lopez, I became captain, in charge of choosing the players.

Colossians 3:12 says, *"Therefore, as God's chosen ones, holy and beloved, clothe yourselves with tender mercy, kindness, humility, meekness, and patience."* This verse points to three realities: We are 1. chosen by God, 2. set apart by and for God (saints), and 3. loved by God.

Chosen: ἐκλεκτός (G-1588 eklektós) means *select; favorite, chosen*. It's a great relief and privilege to be chosen to be part of God's team and family. **Matthew 22:14** says, *"For many are invited, but few are chosen."* Jesus also said, *"You did not choose me, but I chose you"* **(John 15:16)**.

Holy: ἅγιος (G-40 ágios) means *"sacred, pure, moral, blameless, consecrated,"* set aside for exclusive use in God's service. Practicing the imitation of Christ daily, we learn to *"Be holy, because I am holy"* **(1 Peter 1:16)**, to love others, and be good, humble, kind, and patient. The world needs such people on God's team.

Too many timid souls are still not chosen to be part of God's family simply because they speak another language, act, or appear different from the majority. The Lord initiated our sanctification so that we'd be team players and help those who seek to purify their souls and lives.

Loved: Rest assured that we are loved! *"God demonstrates his own love for us in this: While we were still sinners, Christ died for us" (Romans 5:8).* Our love is but a reaction to God's love **(1 John 4:19)**.

Let us pray: Dear God, thank You for choosing, sanctifying, and loving us to fulfill Your plan to be part of Your family. Please help us to promote mercy, kindness, humility, meekness, and patience in our environment. Show us whom to invite to join our faith communities and teach us to be patient and lovingly share the hope and joy of being chosen. We pray in Jesus's name.

August 26
DON'T GIVE UP!
James 1:2

We tend to give up when we're at a disadvantage or under severe stress. But God calls us to persevere, not give up under trials, knowing that God will give us victory. God calls us not to give up *"because you know that the testing of your faith produces perseverance. Let perseverance finish its work so that you may be mature and complete, not lacking anything"* **(James 1:3-4)**.

The mark of a persistent person is that they never give up simply because things don't go their way. Tomas Edison didn't give up. He made thousands of attempts to invent the light bulb, meaning he failed thousands of times, but didn't give up until he was successful.

Jesus appreciated people who refused to give up. God is constantly telling us, *"Don't give up." "Be strong and courageous. Do not be afraid; do not be discouraged, for the Lord your God will be with you wherever you go" (Joshua 1:9).*

In **Luke 18:1-8**, Jesus tells the parable of a persistent woman who didn't give up. This woman appeared before a judge whom neither feared God nor cared about people. He believed himself to be above all. But he wasn't strong enough to resist the persistency of this poor woman. She didn't have power or wealth, but she was persistent and didn't give up. Like a drop of water falling on a rock, she insisted on receiving justice, and her persistence prevailed.

Jesus uses this parable to encourage us not to give up on our struggles and to use the power of prayer. Prayer is not simply saying a few words and thinking that we've left it in the Lord's hands. It is walking in faith, trusting that God will do His part and show us our part. Jesus said that if we have faith, we can do even greater things **(John 14:12).**

Let us pray: Dear God, remind us that you are always with us. Teach us not to give in under the weight of trials and to be persistent in our prayers. That we can't fill the void in our lives by repeating other people's prayers and that prayer is presenting ourselves before You to speak and hear Your voice whispering in our hearts- *"Don't give up! I'm with you."* We pray in Your Holy Name.

August 27
RESISTING TEMPTATION

"When tempted, no one should say, 'God is tempting me.' For God cannot be tempted by evil, nor does he tempt anyone." James 1:13

"Cuando alguien sea tentado, no diga que ha sido tentado por Dios, porque Dios no tienta a nadie, ni tampoco el mal puede tentar a Dios". Santiago 1:13

"Κανένας, όταν πειράζεται, ας μη λέει ότι: Από τον Θεό πειράζομαι· επειδή, ο Θεός είναι απείραστος κακών, και αυτός δεν πειράζει κανέναν." ΙΑΚΩΒΟΥ 1:13

261

When we've done something wrong, our natural reaction is to deny it or point the blame elsewhere. For example, **"Wife:** Did you eat any of the pastries? **Me:** It wasn't me. Ségolène wanted one!"

We learn and improve on the art of deflection from childhood, and it extends generations back to Adam and Eve when Satan tempted Eve into eating the forbidden fruit. Eve blamed the serpent, and Adam blamed Eve and God by saying, *"The woman you put here with me—she gave me some fruit from the tree, and I ate it"* **(Genesis 3:12).** God cursed all three and removed them from the Garden of Eden. And so, today, we are surrounded by all kinds of temptations and the need to 1. accept our guilt and 2. equip ourselves to resist temptation.

Lying complicates our reality, so we can no longer distinguish between truth and lies. When lies are discovered, trust and dreams are shattered, and everyone suffers the consequences. So how do you undo years of perfecting the art of deviation? By confessing our sins and seeking forgiveness from God and those we've hurt. Also, forgiving others as God has forgiven us. With this weight removed, the light shines again through the window of our soul, renewing our faith and hope.

How to resist the power of temptation? The law of physics states that two things cannot occupy the same space. If we fill ourselves with good, evil has no place. God has provided a powerful resistance for His people: the Holy Spirit. *"Be filled with the Spirit, speaking to one another with psalms, hymns, and songs from the Spirit. Sing and make music from your heart to the Lord"* **(Ephesians 5:18B-19).** During the day, I'm always listening to praise hymns. Also, meditating on God's Word helps us to resist temptation, filling our minds and homes with God's presence.

Finally, God's Word says: *"Submit yourselves, then, to God. Resist the devil, and he will flee from you" (James 4:7).*

Let us pray: Dear God, grant us victory over temptations. Please help us to confess and resist temptations and accept our guilt. Only by making peace with you, we'll achieve perfect harmony in Your presence. We pray in the name of Jesus.

August 28
GOD DESCENDED FROM HIS THRONE
Exodus 3:17

After reaching the summit of Mount Olympus, hiking 17 kilometers, with sweaty feet, tired, and without water, the most beautiful view in the distance, facing the peak called **"The Throne,"** was our refuge Chrístos Kákkalos (see red arrow in the photo). There we lodged, refreshed, ate, and slept. The refuge was for us like a land flowing with milk and honey.

In Exodus 3:7-8, God said, *"I have indeed seen the misery of my people in Egypt. I have heard them crying out because of their slave drivers, and I am concerned about their suffering. So I*

"ME HE PROPUESTO SACARLOS DE LA AFLICCIÓN DE EGIPTO Y LLEVARLOS A ...UNA TIERRA QUE FLUYE LECHE Y MIEL." ÉXODO 3:17

"I HAVE PROMISED TO BRING YOU UP OUT OF YOUR MISERY IN EGYPT INTO ...A LAND FLOWING WITH MILK AND HONEY." EXODUS 3:17

"ΚΑΙ Ε'ΙΠΑ: ΘΑ ΣΑΣ ΑΝΕΒΆΣΩ ΑΠΌ ΤΗΝ ΤΑΛΑΙΠΩΡΊΑ ΤΩΝ ΑΙΓΥΠΤΊΩΝ, ΣΤΗ ... ΓΗ ΠΟΥ ΡΈΕΙ ΓΆΛΑ ΚΑΙ Μ'ΕΛΙ-" ΕΞΟΔΟΣ 3:17

THRONOS, MT. OLYMPUS · OUR REFUGE · FROM PROFITIS ILIAS, PIERIA, GREECE· O DESTRUGE

have come down to rescue them from the hand of the Egyptians and to bring them up out of that land into a good and spacious land, a land flowing with milk and honey."

God descended from His heavenly throne to meet Moses and transform him into the deliverer, guide, and judge of God's afflicted people. Rest assured, just as God heard Israel's *"cry because of their oppressors,"* God hears your cry, knows your sufferings, and has **come down from His throne** because of you.

God cares about our welfare, rescue, and freedom from the affliction that we're going through, especially with COVID-19. Like never before, we've experienced, to name a few; illness, death, isolation, unemployment, hunger, thirst, uncertainty, fear, frustration, loneliness, discrimination, etc. **God promises to lead us to a land flowing with milk and honey,** where you and your loved ones will find rest, nourishment, provision, and protection.

To Israel, God promised, *"And I will make the Egyptians favorably disposed toward this people, so that when you leave you will not go empty-handed"* **(Exodus 3:21).** The following day on Mt. Olympus, we had coffee with bread, cheese, and honey and began the descent with 1.5 liters of water and electrolytes. Our guide ensured we had enough energy and supplies for the 7 hours of descent. **God ensured that Jacob's descendants had sustenance and protection for forty years in the desert.**

God cares about every detail of our lives to ensure that, as sons or daughters, we can safely enter and exit, ascend and descend wherever we are sent to seek, find, and lead God's sheep who roam around deserts and mountains without guidance and protection, **back to God's throne of grace and love**.

Let us pray: Dear God, thank You for giving us so much love and care. Thank you **for descending from Your throne**, for stripping yourself of Your divinity to rescue and free us from all affliction. Help us to be useful, **grateful** guides for Your people. We pray in the name of Jesus.

> Just as God heard Israel's *"cry because of their oppressors,"* God hears your cry, knows your sufferings, and has **come down from His throne**, because of you.

✚ ✚ ✚ ✚ ✚ ✚

August 29
HEALED BY HIS BLOOD
Matthew 8:17B

Three days before climbing Olympus, my friend Giorgios invited me for a 10-kilometer hike to break in my new boots. Halfway through, I felt pain between my left foot's third and fourth toes. Taking off my boot and sock, I found a bleeding blister. We stopped the hike and went home, fearing that if my toe weren't taken care of and healed, I'd lose out on fulfilling my dream of climbing Mount Olympus. Friday evening, I prayed, believing that Jesus' blood would heal me.

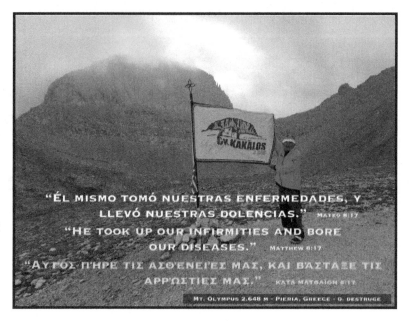

I used several creams, but the blister was still tender by Monday morning, though not bleeding. I placed cream and cotton between my toes and went out, praying it wouldn't bruise again during the ascent or descent. Forty-five minutes into the hike, I felt pain and prayed, *"Lord, there's nothing impossible for you. We have two children accompanying their dad to climb Olympus for the first time. Don't let my injury cause the hike to be canceled or delayed. Please put a new layer of skin between my toes and remove the pain. In the name of Jesus, our healer. Amen."*

Immediately, the pain was gone. During the next 9 hours of walking, I thanked God for His love and care, for allowing me to ascend 16 kilometers without discomfort instead of returning home as happened three days ago. Our verse reminds us, *"He took up our infirmities and bore our diseases."* The most dreadful disease that can befall us is rebellious sin.

The Bible says that we're all injured by sin, that there is no one righteous who understands or seeks God. *"All have turned away, they have together become worthless; there is no one who does good, not even one"* **(Romans 3:10–12).** It also clarifies that *"the wages of sin is death"* **(Romans 6:23a).** In other words, we were all contaminated by sin and condemned to pay for our rebellion with our lives (i.e., to be separated from God forever.) God has provided the medicine for our illness and condemnation, *"but the gift of God is eternal life in Christ Jesus our Lord"* *(Romans 6:23B).*

My beloved, the medicine for our ailment is faith, love, and hope in Jesus Christ's redemptive work. If we don't treat it immediately and repeatedly, we'll lose out on the dream of ascending to God's kingdom and dwelling in the presence of the Lord, our peace and rest. Sin often doesn't

264

hurt like a wound, but it has much more severe results than a bodily injury which heals with time.

Let us pray: Dear God, help us immediately to recognize when sin attempts to hurt or disable us in our race. May our children and their seed know that there's healing through the blood of Jesus, in whose name we pray.

August 30
WISE COUNSEL

"Until I come, devote yourself to the public reading of Scripture, to preaching and to teaching." 2 Timothy 4:13

"Mientras llego, ocúpate en la lectura, la exhortación y la enseñanza". 2 Timoteo 4:13

"Καθώς θάρχεσαι, φέρε το χοντρό επανωφόρι, που άφησα στον κάρπο, στην Τω άδα, και τα Βιβλία, μάλιστα τις μεμβράνες." Β΄ ΠΡΟΣ ΤΙΜΟΘΕΟΝ 4:13

God wants to prosper our journey, that things turn out well for us, and that we have peace. Therefore, God advises that we devote ourselves to **reading, preaching, and teaching**. God has provided the instructions and the means to understand it. *"The statutes of the Lord are trustworthy, making wise the simple"* (**Psalm 19:7**).

Some parts are challenging to understand, requiring help to move forward. One day, Lisa, a work associate, told me that she had enjoyed reading Genesis and Exodus but was stuck and discouraged in the book of Numbers. She didn't understand the importance of the census, which included complicated names and the number of people according to family.

My first instinct was to pray for wisdom to encourage Lisa not to stop reading the Bible I had gifted her. Following was the answer God gave me for Lisa. *"You are important to God. In heaven, there's the book of life, a record very similar to the census we see in Numbers, where your name appears. The book of Numbers affirms that God knows each person by name. Your name and presence at this time are important to God."* Lisa left my office smiling!

God has prescribed ways to understand His word through;
Our Daily reading: *"devote yourself to the public reading of Scripture, to preaching and to teaching"* (1 Timothy 4:13).

The Diligent study: *"Do your best to present yourself to God as one approved, a worker who does not need to be ashamed and who correctly handles the word of truth"* (**2 Timothy 2:15**).

Reflective meditation: *"Keep this Book of the Law always on your lips; meditate on it day and night, so that you may be careful to do everything written in it. Then you will be prosperous and successful"* (**Joshua 1:8**).

Our mind is incapable of understanding God's mind. Therefore, the Holy Spirit helps us understand the scriptures: *"But the Advocate, the Holy Spirit, whom the Father will send in my name, will teach you all things and will remind you of everything I have said to you"* (**John 14:26**).

Let us pray: Dear God, fill us with Your Holy Spirit to help us follow Your wise counsel, to engage in the reading, exhortation, and teaching of Your Word so that we have nothing of which to be ashamed. We pray in the name of Jesus.

✝ ✝ ✝ ✝ ✝ ✝

August 31
HEALED BY HIS WOUNDS
1 Peter 2:24

At age 14 (1968), observing the anguish of two important people in my life, I asked God to allow me to enter into their physical-emotional condition for a moment. At that time, I didn't know what **"empathy"** meant, but with all my heart, I was looking for the ability to identify with and share their feelings, perhaps to help them find a solution. Empathy is a noble character trait, but it is not the same as substitution, which takes the culprit's place, as Jesus did.

Isaiah 53:5 says that despite not having sinned, the innocent would take our guilt and die for our transgressions. *"But he was pierced for our transgressions, he was crushed for our iniquities;* **the punishment that brought us peace was on him, and by his wounds we are healed."** In **Matthew 8:17**, we read, *"He took up our infirmities and bore our diseases."*

If you've seen the movie *"The Passion of the Christ,"* you can appreciate the horrific punishment and suffering that Jesus endured as our substitute to pay for our ransom. He bore our ailments so we wouldn't have to live eternally separated from God's love and presence.

Jesus not only showed empathy but took action to show His love. Thanks to Jesus's substitutionary sacrifice, you and I are privileged to have been rescued, forgiven, and healed of our spiritual illnesses and pains, granting us entrance into God's kingdom. **1 Peter 3:18A** says, *"For Christ also suffered once for sins, the righteous for the unrighteous, to bring you to God."*

Jesus's substitutionary sacrifice *"redeemed us from the curse of the law by becoming a curse for us" (Galatians 3:13A)*. Thanks to God's immense love, you and I consider ourselves God's adopted children, rescued at a great price and for reciprocal service. God expects us to show empathy and be the substitutionary sacrifice that Jesus taught us. *"So that we might die to sins and live for righteousness"* **(1 Peter 2:24).**

Let us pray: Dear God, how can we thank You for saving and healing us from our ailments? Teach us to empathize with those who suffer and strive to cure this world's illnesses, beginning in our communities. We pray in Jesus's name.

> **God expects us to show empathy and be the substitutionary sacrifice that Jesus taught us.**

- SEPTEMBER -
THE KOKTSIDIS FAMILY

Beautiful hearts, children, and smiles also run in the
Koktsidis family. **Yiayia Anatolí** was also born in Turkey
(10/20/1904-10/1992) and, at age 19, was part of the 1923
Treaty of Lausanne Population Exchange. She had chosen to
retain her faith and therefore didn't speak much Greek when
she arrived in Sevastí. Turkish was her primary language.

Yiayiá Anatolí

Yiayiá Anatolí was living in Gyiánana when **Elefthérios P.
Koktsidis** (1906-11/10/1944), who had been living in an orphanage since the Exchange, was released at age 18. He was
alone in the Village, and we don't know if he met Yiayiá
Anatolí or if the townspeople arranged for them to meet and
marry. They had seven children, four of whom lived: Pavlos
(1/7/1926-1/12/2007), yiayia **Kyriakí (4/20/1932)**, An-
dromáxi (3/14/1934- 2/15/2013), and Joseíf (11/20/1939 -
5/26/2015). Papou Eleftherios was killed in WWII, on November 4 or 10, 1944, in the battle of Kilkis.

Thio Pavlos emigrated to Germany in 1959. His sister fol-
lowed for a couple of years. The work was good, but Papou
Aristoklís missed his daughters too much and returned to
Katerini. On May 1, 1969, Thio Pavlos emigrated to the
United States, and one year later, he invited his sister
Kyriakí to join him with the family. The Koktsidis and
Xanthópoulos families lived together for a year. By the time
I met them in 1974, they lived separately in Astoria, Queens.

Elefthérios P. Koktsidis

When our niece Carolyn was born, Yiayía Anatolí flew to
NY. I was warmly greeted by her smile and gentleness when I met her. Thio **Joseíf** had
the same joyful, warm smile as Yiayía Anatolí and Yiayía Kyriakí Koktsidis.

I'm grateful for all the experiences, exchanges, arranged or non-arranged marriages, and
the invitation to **"follow a brother."** These events led to a choice encounter of young
souls born decades later on different Continents and for whom God had destined to bless
and multiply the bloodline of the Destruge-Sandoval / Xanthopoúlou-Koktsidis families.

September 1
BETWEEN THE LAW AND TRADITION
Mark 7:9

Today's Gospel reading raises some questions;

✦ How can I distinguish between God's commandments and human tradition?

✦ In whom should I place my trust and the future of the family?

These are vital questions that we must carefully and prayerfully analyze.

Jesus accused the religious leaders of having invalidated God's law by giving preference and authority to their traditions that, in the final analysis, filled their chests and pockets.

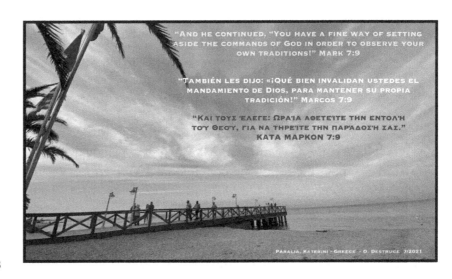

God's law demands, *"Honor your father and mother"* (Exodus 20:12). Yet, the Pharisees and scribes created traditions that appeared to be the absolute fulfillment of the law but evaded God's commandments. Whoever didn't want to honor his parents, i.e., taking care of them in their old age, could pledge whatever was destined for the elderly parents 'care to God (to the congregation and, therefore, to the leaders 'pockets). Jesus concludes by saying to them, *"then you no longer let them do anything for their father or mother"* (Mark 7:12).

When we find ourselves between God's law and human tradition, God's law must prevail. Jesus said that what comes from God is uncontaminated, while what comes from human tradition *"defiles them"* (Mark 7:15).

How can I distinguish between God's commandments and human tradition? God's commandments appear in the Bible. These are immutable. *"For truly I tell you, until heaven and earth disappear, not the smallest letter, not the least stroke of a pen, will by any means disappear from the Law until everything is accomplished"* (Matthew 5:18). Traditions have changed throughout the centuries, depending on who controls church doctrine and on the ignorance of its followers regarding the Holy Scriptures. We cannot blindly follow human philosophies that change with the winds of time.

Consider two critical questions: Which human traditions in our time invalidate God's Word? What should I do if I had to choose between God's law and human conventions?

Let us pray: Dear God, help me so that whenever I have to choose between Your law and tradition, my answer is *"I will follow what God has commanded in His Word."* Give us Your divine wisdom to know and trust Your Holy Word. We pray in Your Holy Name.

September 2
CULTIVATING A HEALTHY FEAR OF GOD

"The fear of the Lord is the beginning of knowledge, but fools despise wisdom and instruction." Proverbs 1:7

"El temor del SEÑOR es el principio de la sabiduría; los necios desprecian la sabiduría y la instrucción". Proverbios 1:7

"Αρχή σοφίας είναι ο φόβος τού Κυρίου· οι άφρονες καταφρονούν τη σοφία και τη διδασκαλία." ΠΑΡΟΙΜΙΑΙ 1:7

Today's theme is **the fear of God**. After extensive analysis by King Solomon (the wisest man in the world), he pens the following conclusion, *"Now all has been heard; here is the conclusion of the matter: Fear God and keep his commandments, for this is the duty of all mankind"* **(Ecclesiastes 12:13).**

The greatest commandment is to love God above all things. Love, gratitude, and wisdom create in us the desire to know in depth the wishes and desires of our loved ones, to do everything that pleases them and avoid everything that hurts them.

It has taken me 46 years to know my wife's wants, likes, and dislikes. We learn these through their self-revelation or our experiences. Many know the saying, **"happy wife, happy life."** It's true! The key is cultivating love by showing that we understand their character, tastes, and requests. The same is true in our relationship with God.

Gratitude allows us to remember what we were before and what we are and have today by God's grace. This creates in us the desire to daily read, study, and scrutinize God's revelation, to know Him better and, with reverent fear, obey God's commandments without any variation or doubt. When we guard God's Word in our hearts and are mindful of it during the day, it becomes easier to please God by keeping His commandments.

Divine wisdom helps us to study and understand the Bible. Along with faith, it helps us believe and trust God and His promises. But, reading the Bible once in a while or listening to it once a week from the pulpit is not enough to transform our rebellious and selfish hearts into reverent, tender hearts dedicated to God's service. Just as we nourish our bodies daily, feeding daily on God's Word is essential to cultivating a healthy fear of God and our spiritual growth.

The Bible says, *"The fear of the Lord is the beginning of knowledge, but fools despise wisdom and instruction"* **(Proverbs 1:7).**

Let us pray: Dear God, grant us wisdom and hearts that are grateful and surrendered to You so that we reverently keep Your commandments and freely demonstrate our love for You and our neighbor. We pray in the name of Jesus.

THE FORMATION OF JUSTICE

"For it is not those who hear the law who are righteous in God's sight, but it is those who obey the law who will be declared righteous." Romans 2:13

"Porque Dios no considera justos a los que simplemente oyen la ley sino a los que la obedecen". Romanos 2:13

"για τον λόγο ότι, δεν είναι δίκαιοι μπροστά στον Θεό οι ακροατές τού νόμου, αλλά οι εκτελεστές τού νόμου θα δικαιωθούν." ΠΡΟΣ ΡΩΜΑΙΟΥΣ 2:13

Those who've been victims of injustice yearn for vindication, not only for ourselves but for all whom we see suffering under its yoke. But any initiative on our strength is bound to fail. The formation and permanence of justice require the intervention and help of the Holy Spirit.

When the Holy Spirit dwells in our hearts, justice begins to germinate within us, seeking to repair the damages in our lives and to show solidarity with the pain and suffering of others. Particularly with individuals who cannot defend themselves due to a lack of knowledge, resources, and social or economic status.

The formation of a creature of God, one of just and noble character, germinates from listening, believing, and doing God's will. *"Consequently, faith comes from hearing the message, and the message is heard through the word about Christ" (Romans 10:17).* That's why Jesus said, *"Not everyone who says to me, 'Lord, Lord,' will enter the kingdom of heaven, but only the one who does the will of my Father who is in heaven" (Matthew 7:21).*

The Holy Spirit sows seeds of faith that help us to believe in and remember God's instructions, leading us to *"do the will of"* God. There are three good things that God demands and expects of us, *"To act justly and to love mercy and to walk humbly with your God" (Micah 6:8).* Jesus said, *"Now that you know these things, you will be blessed if you do them" (John 13:17).*

That's how justice is born and formed in our hearts. The rest is listening and doing God's will when the Holy Spirit prompts us to pray and act as God's children and family. *"For whoever does the will of my Father in heaven is my brother and sister and mother" (Matthew 12:50).*

Change doesn't happen overnight. Therefore, I invite you to copy and pray this prayer with me during the next seven days; *"Dear God, open my eyes, ears, and understanding to detect the injustices in my environment in all the ways and faces that are manifested. Grant me the love and wisdom to face them and do my part in helping the defenseless and weak to repair injustices. I ask this Jesus's name."*

Now, keep your antennas on alert and show the world that your love of justice and righteousness are the compass of your life.

September 4
GOD'S WORD
Romans 10:17

My father-in-law (Papoú [grandpa in Greek] Aristoklís Xanthoupoulos) was a faithful believer in Jesus Christ, and I'm sure he prayed, even as I now do, that our sons and daughters and future generations would find joy, love, peace, and prosperity in their homes by making God the center of their homes.

He also gave me the treasure map to guide me through the tough times, distractions, and impediments to faith and happiness. Without a word, Papou put the Bible in my hand and allowed it to speak and guide me directly. Years later, he told me that many *"know about God, but few really know who God is"* and that I *"don't have to change religion, but rather get to know God personally and to seek His counsel."*

I didn't read the Bible regularly, except when things got difficult. Most of my bibles are filled with hundreds of highlights and notes. But the Bible papou gave me has only one verse highlighted - **Ephesians 5:31** *"For this reason a man will leave his father and mother and be united to his wife, and the two will become one flesh."* Married life is not easy, so we need power, love, and direction from above to stay faithful to the vows, *"till-death-do-us-part."* This verse became my strength and hope through many sleepless nights.

My father-in-law understood the power of scripture to speak to the heart. **Romans 10:14** reads: *"And how can they believe in the one of whom they have not heard? And how can they hear without someone preaching to them?"* **Verse 17** adds, *"faith comes from hearing the message, and the message is heard through the word about Christ."*

Some years ago, I had the privilege of giving a Bible to my son-in-law, Carlos Aristizabal (Sophia's husband), announcing that, in our family, its a tradition that the father of the family welcomes a new member to the family by giving a Bible to the son-in-law so that it can be their guide and encouragement in good times and bad. I pray to God that this tradition continues through the generations and that all of my children and yours know God personally.

Let us pray: Dear God, thank You for sowing Your seeds of faith through Your Word. Today, we unite worldwide, praying that our children and their children allow You to be the center of their homes so that they can resist attacks, and impediments to love and happiness, and walk victoriously toward Your kingdom, holding the hand of their spouse. We pray in the name of Jesus.

September 5
BEWARE OF THOSE WHO KILL THE PROPHETS
Matthew 23:34

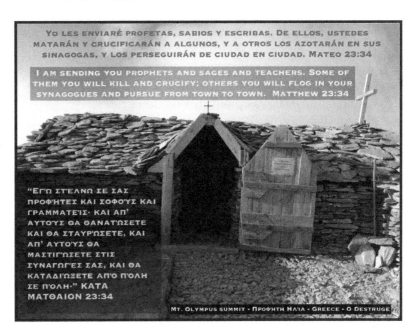

Today's photo shows the chapel "Prophet Elijah" at the summit of Mount Olympus. Whoever doesn't love nature, the pure air of the mountains, destroys it selfishly by leaving garbage on their way up and down. I've seen photos of abandoned mattresses and empty water bottles, which could easily have been disposed of at the mountain's parking lot. They're only interested in taking a picture at the top to say that they *"conquered the mountain"* and going down *"light."* Even in the mountains, everyone must carry their cross.

Whoever doesn't know and love God seeks first to protect their position and salary from people who admire their eloquence. They envy the prophets God sends to guide His people down the dangerous slopes. Instead of receiving them joyfully and heeding their instructions, they kill them, ignoring and nullifying the power of a prophet's words. They position themselves as the true prophets and apostles, presuming to know the way to the mansion. But the path is mysterious and treacherous, instantly surrounded with mist, leaving many stranded, lost, and easy prey for ferocious beasts that kill the unprotected.

Jesus warns us to beware of such guides. Speaking of them, he says, *"You snakes! You brood of vipers! How will you escape being condemned to hell? Therefore I am sending you prophets and sages and teachers. Some of them you will kill and crucify; others you will flog in your synagogues and pursue from town to town"* **(Matthew 23:33-34).**

It shouldn't surprise us that, in our desire to seek and rescue the lost sheep in the mountains and valleys, we'll encounter wolves that resist our message (God's unaltered Word). They will chase us from city to city, or, by lying to people, they'll convince the innocent ones to ignore God's Word because it's full of errors and inconsistencies—posing themselves as the only ones that

273

know the way. Let's be careful and **ensure our children don't fall to the deception of wolves that kill God's Living Word.**

Let us pray: Dear God, knowing that this is the treatment that awaits us, strengthen us so that we don't grow weary or stop searching for Your lost sheep. You rescued, healed, and prepared us for this purpose. You've revealed the path that leads to Your kingdom. Please don't allow even one of Your sheep to fall prey to **those who kill Your prophets.** We pray in Your Holy Name.

September 6
GET RID OF THE EXCESS BAGGAGE
Hebrews 12:1

It's challenging to run with excess baggage! I once tried jogging with 10-pound weights (4.53 kg) on each ankle. It was painful! I couldn't run but a short distance. In 2007, I weighed 228 pounds (104 kg) and managed to jog 100 meters with great pain. My heart was beating excessively high, and I was short of breath. After shedding 60 pounds (27kg) in 2008, I gradually managed to jog 5 miles (8km) in 48 minutes with a bit of training. The point is that excess weight (in this case, sin) prevents us from completing our race and reaching the goal.

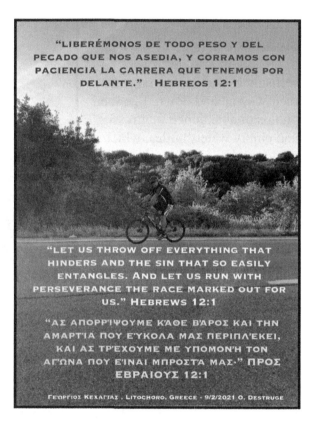

Previously we've analyzed the error of carrying the shame and weight of past sins. Today we explore the benefits of getting rid of all excess baggage since we're in a race to win the crown of life. Our goal is to return to the arms of our Creator and Savior, Jesus Christ. Whoever runs must do so with patience, diligence, and carrying the minimum weight. We must free ourselves from the sins that kept us immobile and useless prisoners for God's work.

Let's not be mistaken; sin is an offense that hurts God and will not allow us to enter eternal rest. God is good and forgives sins that we've sincerely confessed and repented of. But if we persist in them, it's an indication that we're not really under the Lordship of God but of the prince of darkness.

The only way to reach our goal is by shedding ourselves of sin, running the race of life with our eyes fixed on Jesus Christ as our example and inspiration. When we feed daily on God's Word and are in constant prayer with our coach (the Holy Spirit), there's nothing that you and God can't accomplish! Trust me!

Let us pray: Dear God, help us keep our eyes fixed on Jesus, *"the pioneer and perfecter of faith" (Hebrews 12:2).* Please help us to free ourselves from the weight of sin and to run the road ahead patiently. We pray in Jesus's name.

September 7
DISCIPLINE HURTS BUT HEALS
Hebrews 12:11

This verse reminds me of the precious praise song by Alex Campos, **"Al taller del maestro" (TO THE MASTER'S WORKSHOP),** whose lyrics say: *"I come to the Master's workshop because He will heal me. He will take me in His arms and heal every wound. The Master's tools will repair my soul. Though they hurt, the hammer in His hand and much fire, they'll heal."*

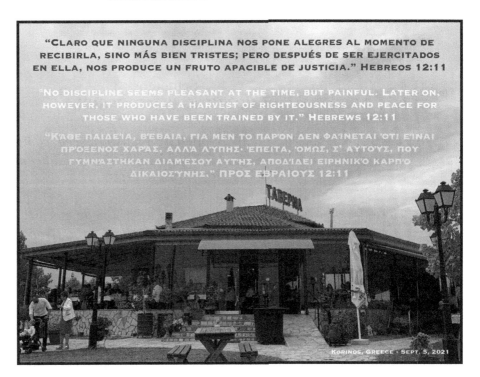

God's discipline sometimes feels like a hammer or fire, but it's a loving discipline that corrects, helps, and seeks to save the eternal, our soul, even though for a moment it might afflict the body and spirit.

Discipline, from the Greek word **παιδεία** (paideía), means *"tutoring, education or training; disciplinary correction: to instruct."*

Whoever loves their children will educate and train them in the essential things of life so that when they become independent and they can put into practice the lessons we've given them with love and sometimes with pain; lessons about character, values, ethics, honesty, generosity, courtesy, reverence for God and love toward others, etc. All these distinguish us from the rest of creation. Because of these **human-divine qualities**, God saw His creation as *"good."*

No parent enjoys disciplining their children. I really think it hurts us more than them. Even in corporations, no boss longs for the time to discipline their employees, but it's done to achieve the goal for which it exists. As humans, our goal is to produce fruit that leads to eternal life.

When we deviate from God's path, God corrects us with love and sorrow. *"As a man disciplines his son, so the Lord your God disciplines you"* **(Deuteronomy 8:5).**

"Even though it hurts (discipline), it will help to know and understand God, to know that we don't deserve anything," except that because God is omniscient and loving, He knows the path of life and for the love of Jesus, our Savior, God will lead us safely through it.

Let us pray: Dear God, as you were with our ancestors, accompany us every day of our lives. Help and guide us when we need to discipline our children, not to avoid it, but give us the wisdom to correct them with love, respect, and dignity. We pray in Jesus's name.

September 8
NOTHING IS IMPOSSIBLE

"Truly I tell you, if you have faith as small as a mustard seed, you can say to this mountain, 'Move from here to there,' and it will move. Nothing will be impossible for you."
Matthew 17:20

"'De cierto les digo, que si tuvieran fe como un grano de mostaza, le dirían a este monte: 'Quítate de allí y vete a otro lugar', y el monte les obedecería. ¡Nada sería imposible para ustedes'"! **Mateo 17:20**

"Σας διαβεβαιώνω: Αν έχετε πίστη σαν κόκκον σιναπιού, θα πείτε σ' αυτό το βουνό: Πήγαινε από εδώ εκεί, και θα πάει, και δεν θα είναι σε σας τίποτε αδύνατο·"
ΚΑΤΑ ΜΑΤΘΑΙΟΝ 17:20

In Jesus's time, impossible things included: the blind seeing, the mute speaking, the deaf hearing, and the dead coming back to life. But Jesus came and did all these things in the presence of many witnesses. And He said that we would do even greater things. Indeed, **for God, and with God's power,** nothing is impossible **(Matthew 19:26).** The only impossible thing is for God to lie **(Hebrews 6:18).**

Jesus proclaimed: *"'The Spirit of the Lord is on me, because he has anointed me to proclaim good news to the poor. He has sent me to proclaim freedom for the prisoners and recovery of sight for the blind, to set the oppressed free'" (Luke 4:18).* Jesus entrusted His ministry to His disciples, the church, to us! *"Jesus said: 'Peace be with you! As the Father has sent me, I am sending you'"* **(John 20:21).**

Sadly, every Christian has been *"sent,"* but few have responded. Many continue to live imprisoned by vices and addictions, by the seductions and attractions of this world. They haven't fully experienced God's power and authority and think that overcoming their temptations is impossible. They've failed many times to abandon a sinful lifestyle. Yes, it's impossible for humans, but with God by our side, nothing is impossible!

Think about the impossible dreams we've achieved, things that 300 years ago, humanity thought utterly impossible. We would list hearing aids, organ transplants, the blind seeing, the iPhone, Internet, electricity, radio, television, flying airplanes, GPS, travel to the moon, etc. We haven't revived the dead (some things are still reserved only for God). But whether we have authority over demons, we have! And we're witnesses that **the same power of Christ, which healed the blind and opened the ears of the deaf, still operates in us to set our captives free.**

> **The same power of Christ which healed the blind and opened the ears of the deaf still operates in us to set our captives free.**

Let us pray: Dear God, thank You for choosing us as instruments to release the captives in our midst. Grant us hearts like yours to look at Your children with compassion and proclaim that, in Jesus's name, they are free from their chains. We pray in Jesus's name.

September 9
FAITH THAT ENSURES SALVATION

"Abraham reasoned that God could even raise the dead." **Hebrews 11:19**

"Y es que Abrahán sabía que Dios tiene poder incluso para levantar a los muertos". Hebreos 11:19

"κάνοντας τον συλλογισμό ότι ο Θεός μπορεί να τον σηκώσει και από τους νεκρούς·" **ΠΡΟΣ ΕΒΡΑΙΟΥΣ 11:19**

The level of trust we have in God's presence and power determines the action that God takes. The level of love, trust, and gratitude we show toward our creator activates God's hand to ensure our salvation and that of our children.

Through Abraham's faith, God saved Isaac's life and descendants. God had promised that in Isaac, his offspring would be as countless as the sand **(Hebrews 11:12).** But God tested Abraham by asking him to sacrifice his only son, Isaac. Abraham demonstrated his great faith *"that God could even raise the dead."* That's why Abraham said to his servants, *"Stay here with the donkey while I and the boy go over there. We will worship and then we will come back to you"* **(Genesis 22:5).**

Spiritually, Isaac was a type of Christ, chosen to demonstrate the extremes God would go to save us when we show great faith and trust in Him. God's love and faith in humanity are so great that He sacrificed His only Son, Jesus Christ, *"that everyone who believes may have eternal life in him" (John 3:15).* Through Jesus's faithfulness and obedience, God provided the substitutionary lamb to save the entire world.

"Jesus said to her, "I am the resurrection and the life. The one who believes in me will live, even though they die" **(John 11:25).** This is one of the foundations of our faith. We will all die

277

one day, but by placing our faith in Jesus Christ, we have the assurance that we will live again on the Resurrection. *"Whoever believes in the Son has eternal life"* **(John 3:36, 5:24).**

We demonstrate great faith when we believe in God's Word and promises. Believing in His Word means trusting that God's hand will fulfill His promise even when things seem impossible. One of the promises that helped strengthen my faith during my honeymoon with God was, *"I will be with you; I will never leave you nor forsake you"* **(Joshua 1:5).**

Let us pray: Dear God, we want to ensure our salvation and that of our descendants. When we fall into trials, increase our faith to believe in Your love, power, presence, goodness, mercy, and faithfulness. Don't let us fall *"into temptation, but deliver us from evil. For yours is the kingdom, and the power, and the glory, forever. Amen"* *(Matthew 6:13).*

✝ ✝ ✝ ✝ ✝

September 10
SAVED BY FAITH OR WORKS?
James 2:26

Jesus said, *"Not everyone who says to me, 'Lord, Lord,' will enter the kingdom of heaven, but only the one who does the will of my Father who is in heaven"* **(Matthew 7:21).** God teaches us that we're justified by grace, through faith, since *"no one will be declared righteous in God's sight by the works of the law"* **(Romans 3:20).** Meanwhile, God's Word declares, *"For it is not those who hear the law who are righteous in God's sight, but it is those who obey the law who will be declared righteous"* **(Romans 2:13).**

Are we saved by faith or by works? This is one of the most contentious issues in the New Testament. Looking at it briefly, it appears to signal a disagreement between salvation by faith or by works. **James 2:14** says, *"What good is it, my brothers and sisters, if someone claims to have faith but has no deeds? Can such faith save them?"*

Faith is indispensable for salvation, but not that **feigned faith** that offers nothing to alleviate the need of a hungry or naked human being **(James 2:15-16).** God tells us, *"In the same way, faith*

"PUES ASÍ COMO EL CUERPO ESTÁ MUERTO SI NO TIENE ESPÍRITU, TAMBIÉN LA FE ESTÁ MUERTA SI NO TIENE OBRAS." SANTIAGO 2:26

"AS THE BODY WITHOUT THE SPIRIT IS DEAD, SO FAITH WITHOUT DEEDS IS DEAD." JAMES 2:26

"ΕΠΕΙΔΉ, ΌΠΩΣ ΤΟ ΣΏΜΑ ΧΩΡΊΣ ΠΝΕΎΜΑ ΕΊΝΑΙ ΝΕΚΡΌ, ΈΤΣΙ ΚΑΙ Η ΠΊΣΤΗ ΧΩΡΊΣ ΤΑ ΈΡΓΑ ΕΊΝΑΙ ΝΕΚΡΉ." ΙΑΚΩΒΟΥ 2:26

PANECILLO, QUITO, ECUADOR

278

by itself, if it is not accompanied by action, is dead" (James 2:17) and does not serve God's purpose.

"For it is by grace you have been saved, through faith—and this is not from yourselves, it is the gift of God— not by works, so that no one can boast" **(Ephesians 2:8-9)**. Here, we find a reconciling answer. Faith saves, not works! **However, faith in Christ means** we receive life *"to do good works" (v.10).*

James 1:22 calls us to *"be not only hearers of the Word, but also doers."* Filled with gratitude for having saved us, we put ourselves at God's service to be the hands, feet, mouth, and tenderness of Christ.

Let us pray: Dear God, thank You because our salvation was entirely Your initiative, motivated by Your grace and love through faith in Jesus Christ. Jesus purchased us to perform good works in His name. Help us not to neglect our purpose and commissioning. Thank you for the confidence you've placed in us. We entrust our children and future generations to Your care, love, and grace. We pray in Jesus's name.

September 11
TELL MY PEOPLE TO MARCH
Exodus 14:15

There is a time for everything, *"A time to cry and a time to laugh"* **(Ecclesiastes 3:4).** Time to say hello and time to say goodbye. Everything has its time. On September 11, 2020, we headed back home. We didn't know what awaited us on the journey, but we were accompanied by God, our Father, Brother, and friend, who promised to be with us every day until the end of the world.

Today's reading tells us about the Israelites' fear - threatened by Pharaoh's armies who pursued them from behind and blocked in by the sea ahead. They certainly imagined death.

Then the Lord said to Moses, *"Why are you crying out to me? Tell the Israelites to move on"* **(Exodus 14:15).** God hadn't yet divided the sea for the people to march forward and escape from Egypt's approaching armies. Indeed, the people would have thought, *"How can Moses ask us to go ahead if there is no way, and only death awaits us behind?"*

The same happens to us. God instructs teachers and pastors to tell the people to march and not stop to look to their right or left. On the mountain top, our guide gives the exact instructions. On our left, we have an abyss, and to the right, a rock to which we cling with two feet and two hands. If we look at the abyss, fear might immobilize us, but if we look at the guide and march forward, clinging to our Eternal Rock, the Lord, we can cross *"through valleys of the shadow of death"* and say, *"I will fear no evil because You are with me"* **(Psalm 23:4).**

With that faith and hope, we presented ourselves at the airport, unafraid, knowing that our Lord called us to Katerini, Greece, for His purpose, for a time, and now God sends us back home so that His will may be done, wherever God sends us.

Due to COVID-19, Summer 2020 was entirely different than any summer ever experienced. It has been the most intense, fearsome, and unforgettable of all the years we've lived. But God has placed His hope and mandate in our hearts; *"Tell my people to march,"* to march and not stop, because, at the end of this journey, God waits for us with open arms and will welcome us.

Let us pray: Dear God, we long to hear your welcome greeting: *"Well done, good and faithful servant! You have been faithful with a few things; I will put you in charge of many things. Come and share your master's happiness!"* **(Matthew 25:21).** Help us to march on without stopping, helping the weak and the fallen so that together we may reach Your Holy mansion. We pray in the name of Jesus.

> **God has placed His hope and mandate in our hearts;** *"Tell my people to march,"* **to march and not stop, because, at the end of this journey, God waits for us with open arms and will welcome us.**

✚ ✚ ✚ ✚ ✚ ✚

September 12
HOW TO FORGIVE
Matthew 6:14

Most of us know how to judge, but few know how to forgive. God wants us to learn **to forgive.**

Is there anything in your past or present that you think God won't forgive if you approach Him with a repentant heart? The Bible teaches that all sins are forgivable when we trust in the sacrifice of Jesus Christ, except one: *"blasphemy against the Spirit shall not be forgiven"* **(Matthew 12:31).**

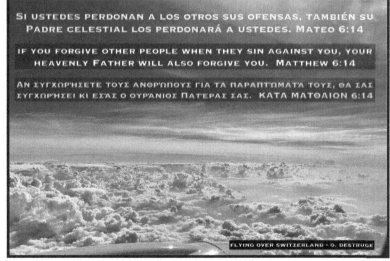

SI USTEDES PERDONAN A LOS OTROS SUS OFENSAS, TAMBIÉN SU PADRE CELESTIAL LOS PERDONARÁ A USTEDES. MATEO 6:14

IF YOU FORGIVE OTHER PEOPLE WHEN THEY SIN AGAINST YOU, YOUR HEAVENLY FATHER WILL ALSO FORGIVE YOU. MATTHEW 6:14

ΑΝ ΣΥΓΧΩΡΉΣΕΤΕ ΤΟΥΣ ΑΝΘΡΏΠΟΥΣ ΓΙΑ ΤΑ ΠΑΡΑΠΤΏΜΑΤΆ ΤΟΥΣ, ΘΑ ΣΑΣ ΣΥΓΧΩΡΉΣΕΙ ΚΙ ΕΣΆΣ Ο ΟΥΡΆΝΙΟΣ ΠΑΤΕΡΑΣ ΣΑΣ. ΚΑΤΑ ΜΑΤΘΑΙΟΝ 6:14

FLYING OVER SWITZERLAND - O. DESTRUGE

Forgive yourself: One of the issues we face as pastors and counselors is people continuing to carry the burden of past sins that have been confessed and which God has forgiven as if they have to complete some penitence to fully activate God's forgiveness. That's a lie of the enemy. *"The blood of Jesus Christ washes us from ALL sin"* **(1 John 1:7).**

There's no need to carry the remorse of the past. Although, if we've defrauded or caused a loss to someone, as new creatures in Christ, we look to restore or make amends for the harm we caused. If possible, make amends, but move forward free of the guilt and excess baggage.

> **Forgive yourself: One of the issues we face as pastors and counselors is people continuing to carry the burden of past sins that have been confessed and which God has forgiven as if they have to complete some penitence to FULLY activate God's forgiveness.**

Forgive as God forgives: *"I will forgive their iniquity, and their sin will I remember no more" (Jeremiah 31:34).* Now if someone has stolen from the church treasury, forgive them, seek restitution, but don't allow them to remain in the same function. We forgive and forget but act responsibly toward the things of God.

Whom shall we forgive? Everyone! Forgiveness is available to the entire world, regardless of what we've done or failed to do: *"Behold, the Lamb of God, that taketh away the sin of <u>the world</u>!"* **(John 1:29).**

Forgive with great love. Without **abundant love**, it's impossible to forgive as God forgives us. God doesn't give us what we deserve but what we don't deserve. God says, *"as far as the east is from the west, so far has he removed our transgressions from us"* **(Psalm 103:12).**

And so, we ask the question again: **Is there anything in people's past or present that God cannot forgive?** The answer is No! Everything is forgivable. It's joyful to receive forgiveness. But it's not as easy to apply God's forgiving grace to others. If we forgive those who offend us, God will forgive us. This also means that God will not forgive our transgressions if we are unforgiving.

Let us pray: Dear God, grant us a forgiving heart and spirit, one that loves and forgives as you do. One which seeks to restore instead of being in the right. Help us to be ambassadors of Your good news wherever we may go today. We pray in Jesus's name.

September 13
HUMILITY THAT IS PLEASING TO GOD
Proverbs 22:4

The Oxford Dictionary defines humility as *"Having or showing a modest or low estimate of one's importance."* The humble person knows who they are, whose they are, and whom they represent. The lowly in heart recognize their place as a creature of God, created to love and serve the Creator. The humble person isn't prideful and doesn't seek recognition for anything they have done to help God or others.

I consider my father-in-law, **Aristoklís Xanthópoulos**, to be a very humble man. All who knew him would agree that he was an unassuming, hardworking man of God who visited the sick, led the church choir, gave out bibles to strangers, preached, prayed, and read the Bible at least twice a day, and welcomed strangers, including me.

I met him at age 21 when Margarita and I married. We didn't speak very much, partly because he didn't speak English and I hardly understood Greek. But years later, I discovered that he spoke not with words, but through actions, by being an example with his loving and forgiving heart (someday I'll write more about that).

"The fear of the Lord" **(Proverbs 22:4)** means knowing our place with God, demonstrating love and respect toward God and His Word. Believing that *"All things have been created through him and for him"* **(Colossians 1:16)**. And so, we humble ourselves before God so that He might lift us.

The benefits of being humble and fearing the Lord are *"riches and honor and life"* **(Proverbs 22:4)**. If God gives us riches in this world, it's so that we may be good administrators and help the poor and needy. My father-in-law was satisfied with what he had and never forgot the poor and orphans. This is the humility that pleases God.

Jesus cautions us: *"But store up for yourselves treasures in heaven, where moths and vermin do not destroy, and where thieves do not break in and steal. For where your treasure is, there your heart will be also"* **(Matthew 6:20-21)**.

Meditate on these two questions:
✦ Where is your treasure?
✦ What humility lessons are you creating for your children and future generations to imitate?

Let us pray: Dear God, thank You for those who have been our examples of humility. Touch and inspire us to also leave a noble legacy for our children, family, neighbors, and friends. We pray in Your Holy Name.

September 14
RAISED WITH CHRIST
Colossians 3:1

Let's recall the resurrection of Lazarus, brother of Martha and Mary and good friend of Jesus. Lazarus had been dead for four days when Jesus came to comfort the family. Upon seeing Jesus, his sister Martha said: *"Lord, 'if you had been here, my brother would not have died. But I know that even now God will give you whatever you ask.' Jesus said to her, 'Your brother will rise again.' Martha answered, 'I know he will rise again in the resurrection at the last day.'*

Jesus said to her, 'I am the resurrection and the life. The one who believes in me will live, even though they die; and whoever lives by believing in me will never die. Do you believe this?'" (John 11:21-26).

That was the first text I ever preached when Joseph F. Barclay (husband of our colleague Eunice) was fatally injured in a car accident. We accompanied her to the hospital and were informed that Joseph was brain dead. As a leader of our office Prayer and Fellowship group, Eunice asked me to speak some words to the family. I remember saying something along these lines. *"We don't understand why bad things happen, but as believers in Christ's promises, we have the assurance that Joseph will be resurrected and that one day there'll be a great reunion in the Lord's mansion. We suffer when losing a loved one, but at the same time, we thank God for allowing us to have known and shared time with our loved ones. It's preferable to have spent even one day in their presence than never to have known them."*

Today I spent several hours meditating on the gift I received from my parents, Galo and Lilia. All the good things I have in life exist because they sacrificed their dreams to ensure my brother and I had an opportunity to have a better life. If they had not emigrated to the United States, I wouldn't have met Margarita, and I wouldn't have the family with whom I enjoy God's love and presence, looking heavenward for the promises that await us.

Let us pray: Dear God, help us remember that we have a counselor in heaven, interceding for us every time we fail. Send the Holy Spirit to remind us who we are, to whom we belong, and where we're going. Thank you because, like Lazarus, You raised us with Christ; therefore, we look toward heaven for that great re-encounter.

✦ ✦ ✦ ✦ ✦ ✦

THE MISUNDERSTOOD TRUTH
John 7:34

Matthew 7:7-8 says, *"Seek and you will find... 8 For everyone who...seeks finds."* This is true when we seek wholeheartedly to discover God's will. Those who reject or doubt the power, authority, and Word of Jesus are prone to misunderstanding the truths and promises that can save even the vilest sinner, but those with hardened hearts, no matter how hard they seek the truth, will not find it. In Jesus's time, the Pharisees, Sadducees, and scribes sought Jesus, not to believe and follow him but to kill him. To such, Jesus declared, *"You will look for me, but you will not find me; and where I am, you cannot come"* **(John 7:34).**

Today I share some verses in which the Jews misunderstood Jesus's words and couldn't treasure the truths that illumine us today.

THE TEMPLE OF THE BODY OF CHRIST, CONFUSED WITH THE EARTHLY TEMPLE - *"They replied, "It has taken forty-six years to build this temple, and you are going to raise it in three days?"* **(John 2:20).**

THE WATER OF LIFE, CONFUSED WITH PHYSICAL WATER - *"The woman said to him, "Sir, give me this water so that I won't get thirsty and have to keep coming here to draw water'"* **(John 4:15).**

CHRIST'S DEPARTURE, CONFUSED WITH SUICIDE - *"This made the Jews ask, "Will he kill himself? Is that why he says, "Where I go, you cannot come?"'"* **(John 8:22).**

SPIRITUAL SLAVERY, CONFUSED WITH PHYSICAL SLAVERY - *"They answered him, "We are Abraham's descendants and have never been slaves of anyone. How can you say that we shall be set free?'"* **(John 8:33).**

THE NEW BIRTH, CONFUSED WITH THE PHYSICAL BIRTH - *"How can someone be born when they are old? Nicodemus asked. "Surely they cannot enter a second time into their mother's womb to be born!'"* **(John 3:4).**

The difference between the unbelieving Jews is that they will not find the truth no matter how much they seek it. Nicodemus, however, was willing to listen and believe in Jesus's Words. He came to know the Way, the Truth, and the Life because the Holy Spirit opened his heart and ears to give him understanding, wisdom, and salvation.

Let us pray: Dear God, when our ears are covered, our eyes blindfolded, and our hearts hardened, causing us to misunderstand Your Word, touch us with Your Holy Spirit. He heals and frees us from our chains, offering salvation for us and our homes. Heal our sick and planet. We pray in Jesus's name.

> **Those who reject or doubt the power, authority, and Word of Jesus are prone to misunderstanding the truths and promises that can save even the vilest sinner.**

✝ ✝ ✝ ✝ ✝ ✝

September 16
BLESSED
Psalm 1:1

The Beatitudes are promised to those who keep God's Word and propose to live according to God's standards, not the world's.

"When Scott Daniel Warren was arrested in 2019 after allegedly providing food, water, beds, and clean clothes to undocumented immigrants near Arizona's Sonoran Desert, the question was whether he had broken the law or upheld it."[18] The government accused Warren of being a criminal and subjected him to up to twenty years in prison. On the other hand, we can see Warren as blessed because he was ready to give his life against injustice.

I respect social activists who fight against injustice in any way it presents itself. I admire those who courageously put aside their political ideologies to be faithful to our Lord Jesus's call. Martin Luther King gave his life to achieve the civil rights of African Americans in this country. Cesar Chavez fought hard for Hispanic peasants against labor injustices. **We're called to fight for justice.**

Today, those who suffer persecution worldwide are undocumented immigrants and refugees. Many of them are honest, hardworking,

---

[18] https://www.washingtonpost.com/nation/2019/06/12/scott-warren-year-sentence-hung-jury-aiding-migrants/

struggling people seeking the welfare of their families. Perhaps today, God invites us to remove our political hearts and ask ourselves, what would Jesus do with this crowd? I think that with love, He would teach them by saying, *"Blessed is the one who does not walk in step with the wicked or stand in the way that sinners take or sit in the company of mockers"* **(Psalm 1:1).**

Immigration impacts every area of our lives. But God's love calls us to a solution that guards the dignity of every human being. We're called to love our neighbors, including enemies, and to pray for them, just as Jesus did from the cross.

What does God expect of us as members of His family?: *"Do justice, Love mercy, and Walk humbly with your God"* **(Micah 6:8).**

Let us pray: Dear God, help us look with Your eyes at the injustice that flows among our people, which grows like a tsunami wave, destroying everything in its path. Give us the courage and **blessedness** to fight together against injustice because if we stay with our arms crossed, tomorrow it will knock at our children's doors. We pray in Your Holy Name.

September 17
IRREVOCABLE
Romans 11:29

"For God's gifts and His call are irrevocable." Two questions arise from this verse; 1. Which are the irrevocable gifts? 2. What is God's irrevocable calling?

THE IRREVOCABLE GIFTS -
The gifts and privileges promised to the Israelites include; *"Theirs is the adoption to sonship; theirs the divine glory, the covenants, the receiving of the law, the temple worship and the promises"* **(Romans 9:4).** The gifts promised to all humanity are found in *Ecclesiastes 5:19; "When God gives someone wealth and possessions, and the ability to enjoy them, to accept their lot and be happy in their toil—this is a gift of God."*

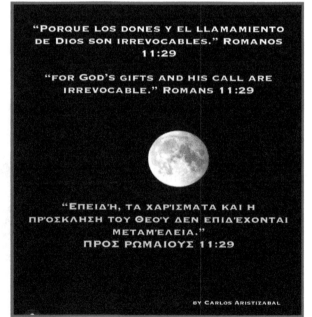

Jesus Christ is God's gift, promised to all humanity: *"Jesus answered her, 'If you knew the gift of God and who it is that asks you for a drink, you would have asked him and he would have given you living water'"* **(John 4:10).** *"For it is by grace you have been saved, through faith—and this is not from yourselves, it is the gift of God"* **(Ephesians 2:8).**

GOD'S IRREVOCABLE CALL

Greater than faith and hope are the gift and commandment of love **(1 Corinthians 13:13)**. That's because it's a Divine quality that God has grafted into us to renew and transform the lives of those around us. Through Jesus Christ and the Holy Spirit, each believer receives their share of love, grace, faith, mercy, and other unique gifts to minister to the body of Christ and to the lost sheep **(1 Corinthians 7:7)**. Just as God is eternal, *"love never fails,"* is irrevocable, and is greater than all gifts **(1 Corinthians 13:8)**.

To help us fulfill our calling, the Holy Spirit empowers every adopted child with His power, guidance, presence, and fruit of the Spirit **(Acts 8:20)**. God calls us to *"fan into flame the gift of God"* **(2 Timothy 1:6)** through Bible study, worship, fellowship, and our service to God. If we stop feeding and fanning them, despite being irrevocable, we can cool down and stop serving God in the Great Commission to save the world through the Gospel of Jesus Christ.

Let us pray: Dear God, thank You that *"your gifts and calling"* in our lives *"are irrevocable."* Grant that the covenants of love and service we make toward You, our family, church, and community may be unshakable and irrevocable, as are Your love and mercy. We pray in Jesus's name.

> **Just as God is eternal, *"love never fails,"* is irrevocable, and is greater than all gifts (1 Corinthians 13:8).**

✝ ✝ ✝ ✝ ✝ ✝

September 18
GOD SATISFIES HUNGER
Exodus 16:12

Precisely 30 days after being freed from Egypt's yoke, the Israelites arrived in the desert of Sin, and again they lost their patience and gratitude. They murmured against Moses, saying, *"If only we had died by the Lord's hand in Egypt! There we sat around pots of meat and ate all the food we wanted, but you have brought us out into this desert to starve this entire assembly to death"* (Exodus 16:3).

"AT TWILIGHT YOU WILL EAT MEAT, AND IN THE MORNING YOU WILL BE FILLED WITH BREAD. THEN YOU WILL KNOW THAT I AM THE LORD YOUR GOD." EXODUS 16:2

"AL CAER LA TARDE COMERÁN CARNE, Y POR LA MAÑANA SE SACIARÁN DE PAN. ASÍ SABRÁN QUE YO SOY EL SEÑOR SU DIOS." ÉXODO 16:12

"ΤΗΝ ΕΣΠΈΡΑ ΘΑ ΦΆΤΕ ΚΡΈΑΣ, ΚΑΙ ΤΟ ΠΡΩΪ ΘΑ ΧΟΡΤΆΣΕΤΕ ΑΠΌ ΨΩΜΊ, ΚΑΙ ΘΑ ΓΝΩΡΊΣΕΤΕ, ΌΤΙ ΕΓΩ ΕΊΜΑΙ Ο ΚΎΡΙΟΣ Ο ΘΕΌΣ ΣΑΣ." ΕΞΟΔΟΣ 16:12

CHIVIQUI, TUMBACO, ECUADOR - EDUARDO PUGA

God satisfied their hunger. *"The Lord said to Moses, 'I have heard the grumbling of the Israelites. Tell them, 'At twilight you will eat meat, and in the morning you will be filled with bread. Then you will know that I am the Lord your God'"* **(Exodus 16:11-12)**.

During 40 years of wandering through the desert, the people never lacked meat, bread, or water. Even the clothing and sandals didn't wear out until after they reached the promised land **(Deuteronomy 29:5).** We can trust that, while we walk with God, we won't lack anything. God will give us enough to survive and overcome. **Exodus 16:18** says, *"the one who gathered much did not have too much, and the one who gathered little did not have too little. Everyone had gathered just as much as they needed."*

In our times, there are disoriented sheep that have strayed from the flock, who, being princes and princesses, live as if they were orphans. We pray that bread and quail come down from heaven to satisfy their hunger. They're sheep that need milk for their children. We don't lose faith that *"The Lord will provide"* (**"Jehovah yir-eh"** is what Abram called the place where God provided the sacrificial lamb, thus saving the life of his son Isaac.) **In the desert, God provided for all the needs of the people.**

The day will come, and it's near, when we'll be in the Lord's presence and, *"Never again will they hunger; never again will they thirst. The sun will not beat down on them, nor any scorching heat. For the Lamb at the center of the throne will be their shepherd; 'he will lead them to springs of living water. And God will wipe away every tear from their eyes"* (**Revelation 7:16-17).**

Because **GOD SATISFIES HUNGER**, you and I are God's eyes and ears, sent in search of those who cry on account of thirst, hunger, bread, or cold, so that through the power and unity of God's family, **those who gather little will lack nothing.**

Let us pray: Dear God, use us to satisfy the hunger in our environment and lead the hungry toward the bread of life. We pray in Your Holy Name.

September 19
COST AND REWARD OF FOLLOWING JESUS
Matthew 19:29

Today we're invited to meditate on **the cost and reward of being Jesus's disciples.**

THE COST:
To the rich young man, Jesus said that he lacked one thing to enter the kingdom of heaven: *"go sell everything you have and give to the poor, and you will have treasure in heaven. Then come, follow me"* (**Mark 10:21**). Jesus adds that we must love God above our parents, brothers, children, or our own life. **(Matthew 10:37).**

Anything worth having requires sacrifice. The greatest thing we can achieve, our salvation, costs us nothing, but Jesus paid a high price so that we'd be called *"children of God."* It cost Jesus 33 years of living on earth as a humbled and despised man and dying so that you and I could live without fear. Therefore, *"Don't be afraid; you are worth more than many sparrows"* (**Matthew 10:31).**

We're called to follow and do God's will, *"not looking to your own interests but each of you to the interests of the others"* (**Philippians 2:4**).

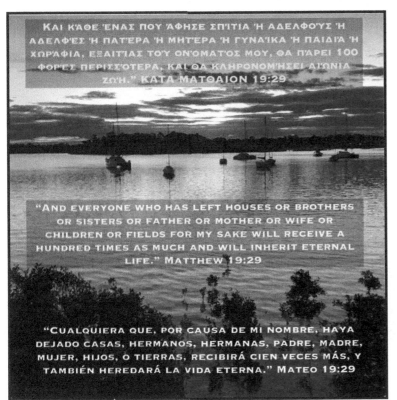

The best gift we can give another human being is of our time. Ask any elderly, *"what do you want most of all?"* Many will answer: *"A call or visit from my children!"* We need the warmth of another human being to sustain and fan the fire of life. The same is true with God, church, or any other entity that needs your time, commitment, presence, and participation.

THE REWARD:
Jesus points to the reward that we'll find when, with pain and sacrifice, we put God's kingdom first. *"Truly I tell you: no one who has left home or brothers or sisters or mother or father or children or fields for me and the gospel will fail to receive a hundred times as much in this present age: homes, brothers, sisters, mothers, children, and fields—along with persecutions—and in the age to come eternal life"* (**Mark 10:29-30**).

We want our children to love God! Let's set an example by **putting God above everything**, giving Him the best of our time, money, and talents. Not from what's left over but from the time, money, and skills you lack. Do so, and you'll see how God blesses, replenishes, and multiplies what you've dedicated to Him, the church, or His lost and needy sheep.

Let us pray: Dear God, help us organize our lives, resources, and calendar, so that we may be exemplary Christians for our children, family, friends, and all who observe our lives to decide whether or not to return to Your fold. Let us be a reflection of Your light and love. We pray in Your Holy Name.

> **The greatest thing we can achieve, our salvation, costs us nothing, but Jesus paid a high price so that we'd be called "children of God."**

September 20
WE CAN DRAW CLOSE TO GOD WITH CONFIDENCE
James 4:8

We can approach God with complete confidence because God has called us to return to His house and presence. God's heart and arms are always open to welcome us back, no matter how far or why we've wandered from His side.

One of my favorite praises that we sang in El Camino and La Gracia churches, where I pastored, was "Draw near to Jesus." You can listen to 1 minute of it (in Spanish) on YouTube via this link

https://www.youtube.com/watch?v=gRLVfy3MrtI

"Draw near to Jesus, your best friend, and you'll live in the light because He's promised to take you in His arms and light the way. He'll walk by your side and always be with you. He's par excellence, the Divine Physician that heals your ailments and listens to your moans. He holds you in His bosom and removes your pain. He'll carry you in His arms because He's filled with love."

Today's verse tells us that, as our heart seeks and draws closer to God, He will reveal Himself, showing us the way, and for each step we take toward Him, God will also draw near to us. This reminds me of the prodigal son who departed from his father's home and squandered his inheritance. Hungry and destitute, the young man repented and decided to return home. While still a distance away, his father ran to meet and welcome him with a great hug and kiss.

This image reflects the love of our Heavenly Father, who will not reject a repentant heart. But we must purify our hearts and minds to draw nearer to God. The wonderful news is that the Holy Spirit cleanses and renews our hearts and minds so that we might be received back into God's circle of love. That's why we can confidently approach God without fear of our past.

Let us pray: Thank you, Lord, for pouring such great love upon us. For being the best friend in this world, who lights our way when we're lost. When all have abandoned us, You're the constant strength and presence. Thank you for healing our ailments, and because even when we've failed and returned repentant, you run to greet and welcome us back with a brotherly hug. We pray in Your Holy Name.

290

September 21
TWO IS BETTER THAN ONE ALONE
Ecclesiastes 4:12

During the summer of 2021, I stopped cycling for long periods. Some months I rode my bike only a couple of times, compared to years ago when I rode up to five times a week. But thank God, this year, the enthusiasm returned with my friend Georgios and the visit of my son-in-law, Carlos Aristizabal, who loves cycling.

Carlos is a fan of major cycling tournaments like the Tour de France. Upon arriving in Katerini, Greece, he bought a bike, and we shared a few trips. Cycling alone is not as enjoyable as with another person or group. When my friend Georgios or Carlos asks me to **"go cycling,"** I immediately say, **"let's go!"**

Today's verse tells us that two or three is better than one. God didn't create us to be and do things alone. Individualism and divisions contribute to personal and community weakness. Loneliness discourages the soul and, in many cases, brings different progressive diseases that advance if we don't put the brakes on them with a positive attitude and faith.

Fellowship helps society, filling us with joy and hope, accomplishing more than we could individually. Two acting together are better than one discouraged soul; They can support each other when needed. God calls us to interact as the body of Christ, as a team. There is no such thing as

291

lonely Christians. As a team, we acquire the resources and adequate strength by forming a robust three-stranded rope.

"Though one may be overpowered, two can defend themselves" (v.12). The enemy is cunning, attacking the weak and unsuspecting. That's why Jesus sent His disciples *"two by two"* to support and defend each other. *"Two are better than one, because they have a good return for their labor" (v.9).* Everything we do together or in a community is more successful than when done individually. Therefore, my beloved, I implore you to promote camaraderie and mutual support with two or more like-minded people.

Let us pray: Dear God, thank You for forming and calling us to be part of a family in which we lift each other in times of weakness and danger through bonds of love and unbreakable support. May our witness of mutual support be the lever to guide Your lost sheep back to Your fold. We pray in the name of our Lord Jesus Christ.

Photo: 4 generations; My daughter, Sophia, her grandmother, Kyriaki, Margarita, and my grandson Lázaro Elías.

> **INDIVIDUALISM AND DIVISIONS CONTRIBUTE TO PERSONAL AND COMMUNITY WEAKNESS. LONELINESS DISCOURAGES THE SOUL AND, IN MANY CASES, BRINGS DIFFERENT PROGRESSIVE DISEASES.**

"CONOCERÁN LA VERDAD, Y LA VERDAD LOS HARÁ LIBRES."
JUAN 8:32

"YOU WILL KNOW THE TRUTH, AND THE TRUTH WILL SET YOU FREE."
JOHN 8:32

"ΚΑΙ ΘΑ ΓΝΩΡΊΣΕΤΕ ΤΗΝ ΑΛΉΘΕΙΑ, ΚΑΙ Η ΑΛΉΘΕΙΑ ΘΑ ΣΑΣ ΕΛΕΥΘΕΡΏΣΕΙ."
ΚΆΤΑ ΙΩΆΝΝΗΝ 8:32

SCHLOSS BURG CASTLE, SOLINGEN, GERMANY - 9/5/2018 - O, DESTRUGE

September 22
I'M FREE
John 8:32

Meditating on this verse, I asked myself: **From how many things have I been liberated?**

On September 30, 2009, at 4:50 p.m., I left my corporate office for the last time and felt freed of the burden of six-day workweeks and countless hours stuck in traffic. I thank God for 35 years of uninterrupted work, for the friends I made, and for the insight received from talented individuals who helped me make wise decisions about retirement. It was always my goal to retire at 55. I was blessed to fulfill my family's financial responsibilities and be freed from this burden. Therefore, when I left the office, I jumped for joy shouting, *"I'm free!"*

292

I have also been freed from the fear of public speaking and the fear of death. I now believe that death is not the enemy but rather a friend who escorts us into the arms of our Savior. And so, we come to the essence of true and absolute freedom. *"Then you will know the truth, and the truth will set you free"* **(John 8:32).**

My absolute freedom date was February 28, 1989. Some call it the new birth, but I call it a second chance. Without getting into details, a few months before, I was literally on the edge of the precipice, depressed, feeling like I was no use to family or my employer. I was too focused on my financial debts. Just when I thought I couldn't take it anymore, the Lord reached out and rescued me. God gave me a second chance to start over, to be a better husband and father by putting God first at home, at work, and in the community. I came to know Jesus Christ as my personal Savior. Jesus not only freed me from fears, doubts, and low self-esteem but also alleviated my attraction to sin and material things. Today, I am a restoration work in progress.

I could go on and on, but instead, I invite you to think about it and perhaps share with your loved ones a way in which God has set you free.

Let us pray: Dear God, thank You for the different and many ways in which you've rescued and freed us from danger and evil. More than anything in the world, we pray that as you've done with us, you save and accompany our children and future generations. We pray in Jesus's name.

September 23
WHEN HUMAN LAWS CONTRADICT GOD'S WORD
Acts 4:19

Since the fall of Adam and Eve, we've been engaged in an internal spiritual struggle. The renewed soul desires to be obedient to God, but *"the flesh is weak"* and selfish **(Matthew 26:41).** The devil takes advantage of our condition by opposing everything and everyone who seeks to know and obey God. Therefore, it is essential to plan how to respond when human laws contradict God's Word.

In our times, many people, including large groups of Christians, disobey or ignore God's laws **(to love and obey God, love your neighbor as yourself)**, giving more importance and reverence to human laws and civil regulations. For example, many are more faithful to political ideologies that sow hatred and division, degrading the dignity and character of opposing groups, and marking them as **"devils"** and enemies of God.

Today more than ever, the church faces divisions and disputes regarding the holiness God demands of His disciples. *"Be holy, because I am holy"* **(1 Peter 1:16).** Some argue that **"God loves and accepts everyone, just as we are."** Amen! God's character is to love, guide, and rescue His creation. Gd does receive us as we are. But His love is so great that day after day, through His Word, patience, and presence, God cleanses us of all evil, preparing us to be received as the bride of Christ. To the woman found in adultery, Jesus said, *"Then neither do I condemn you… Go now and leave your life of sin" (John 8:11).* God never leaves us the way He found us.

God calls us to love and obedience. He doesn't condemn us ahead of time nor gives us the punishment we deserve, but rather the grace and love we do NOT deserve. On the other hand, the devil confuses us with half-truths, enticing us toward disobedience to separate us from God's love and care.

Emboldened by the Holy Spirit, Peter and John said, *"We must obey God rather than human beings!"* **(Acts 5:29).**

Let us pray: Dear God, when we encounter laws and philosophies that contradict Your Word, grant us hearts predisposed to believe and obey Your Holy Word. Help us always to live by the two greatest commandments; to love You and our neighbor as ourselves. We pray in Jesus's name.

✠ ✠ ✠ ✠ ✠ ✠

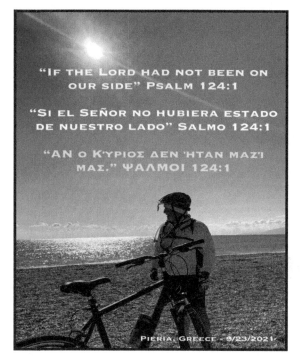

September 24
IF IT HADN'T BEEN FOR THE LORD
Psalm 124:1

Have you ever thought, **"what would have been of me if the Lord hadn't rescued me?"** This question leads us to respond with gratitude and praise. Think about it. At some point in your life, God intervened by extending His love and justice to save, heal or rescue you or a loved one from physical, material, or spiritual disaster.

There's power in God's Word and presence! We're called to meditate on God's mercies, to retell His mighty works, wonders, and favors to our children, family, and friends. That's how we stir our faith. Therefore, **it's essential to prepare our testimony.** The Bible says that we must *"*always be prepared to give an answer to everyone who asks you to give the reason for the hope that you have*" (1 Peter 3:15).

In 1989, I started the good habit of writing in my spiritual journal about what God did for me, reflecting on **what my life was like before and after Christ.** The stories I've shared in sermons, Bible studies, and these meditations come from my journals, which store experiences, triumphs with Christ, and failures. As memory begins to fail, it's invigorating to read these journals and rekindle the faith. I often conclude the readings with, **"Thank you, Lord! Where would I be if it hadn't been for your grace and love?"**

It's never too late to start. I urge you to write and **prepare your testimony.** By leaving a spiritual legacy that will never be lost, you'll revive your faith and that of our children and their children for generations. Jesus said, *"Do not store up for yourselves treasures on earth, where moths and vermin destroy, and where thieves break in and steal. But store up for yourselves treasures in heaven, where moths and vermin do not destroy, and where thieves do not break in and steal"* (Matthew 6:19-20).

Let us pray: Dear God, I would have fallen into the enemy's clutches if it hadn't been for You. But, *"Praise be to You Lord, who has not let us be torn by their teeth. We've escaped like a bird from the fowler's snare; the snare has been broken, and we've escaped. Our help is in the name of the Lord, the Maker of heaven and earth"* (Psalm 124:6-8). Thank you for being our shield, defender, and protector. For everything you've done, thank you, in Jesus's name.

September 25
THERE'S POWER IN THE BLOOD OF JESUS
Acts 13:39

What the devil attempts to destroy, the blood of Jesus is powerful to restore! **The blood of Jesus is powerful enough to grant us a second opportunity to start over.** We desire the best for our family. However, we're human and haven't always been the best example as parents, spouses, or even Christians. We've all suffered moments that we wish hadn't happened or could take back. Maybe a harsh word, uncontrolled anger, an action, indiscretion, or addiction that affected the entire family, an unkept promise, etc., etc.

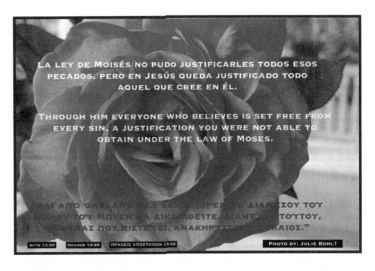

King David was a man after God's heart **(Acts 13:22).** However, he was a sinner, an adulterer who murdered his general Uriah to cover the adultery he committed with Bathsheba, Uriah's wife **(2 Samuel 11).** David repented of his sins, cried out to God, and was justified because, despite his sins, God had plans to bless the entire world through David's line. *"Blessed is he whose iniquities are forgiven, and whose sins are covered!"* **(Romans 4:7).**

In the line of Jesus, we also find Rahab, the harlot, who helped the Israelites to conquer the city of Jericho. Her life was saved, along with everyone in her house **(Joshua 6:25).** In short, we see that sin in the lives of the elect doesn't cancel God's forgiveness and justification, nor the purpose that God had planned for their lives. God wants us to repent from a life led astray by poor choices or manipulated by bad company and the philosophies of our times.

Repenting doesn't mean making a 360-degree turn, but rather a 180-degree turn. The wonderful thing about forgiveness is that God forgets (covers) our sins, and nothing, not even our rebellion and temporary estrangement from God's ways, can *"separate us from the love of God in Jesus Christ"* **(Romans 8:39).**

What is necessary is *"to believe in Jesus,"* repent, and have a heart committed to God. There's nothing better than seeing broken relationships heal through the mutual offering of God's love and forgiveness. Decades later, I rejoice to witness how God has transformed them into exemplary couples and families whose children and grandchildren feel blessed to have their love, instruction, and presence.

What the devil attempts to destroy, the blood of Jesus is powerful to restore!

Let us pray: Thank you, Lord, for granting us the joy of being forgiven, of receiving a second chance so that our lives may be the best possible example of a father, mother, brother, uncle, son/daughter, spouse, and Christian. Create in us a heart committed to You. We pray in the name of Jesus.

September 26
ALL AUTHORITY

"'By what authority are you doing these things?' they asked. 'And who gave you authority to do this?'" Mark 11:28

"Y le preguntaron: '¿Con qué autoridad haces todo esto? ¿Quién te dio autoridad para hacerlo?'" Marcos 11:28

*"Και του λένε: Με ποια εξουσία τα κάνεις αυτά; Και ποιος σου έδωσε αυτή την εξουσία για να τα κάνεις;" **ΚΑΤΑ ΜΑΡΚΟΝ 11:28***

If you think that your life doesn't have much impact and influence, think again: God offers you the power and full authority of the Holy Spirit to save, heal and restore the hope of His people who fight against unseen spirits and diseases.

The Bible teaches that Jesus has all authority over creation. *"The people were amazed at his teaching, because he taught them as one who had authority, not as the teachers of the law"* **(Mark 1:22, Matthew 7:29, Luke 4:32).**

Meanwhile, the congregation's scribes, chief priests, and elders confront Jesus, asking him, *"By what authority are you doing these things?"* Jesus did many things - He healed the sick, raised the dead, cast out demons, preached God's Word, and in their last encounter in the temple, Jesus cast out those *"who were buying and selling there"* **(Mark 11:15).** There is great rejoicing when we hear that one of our own has been healed. The religious leaders should have been grateful rather than enraged. But, Jesus's fame had grown so much that the leaders feared losing their power and authority and sought every means to catch, prosecute, or preferably kill Him **(Mark 11:18).**

We're privileged to have God's infallible Word, in which Jesus declares the source of His authority. *"For as the Father has life in himself, so he has granted the Son also to have life in himself. And he has given him authority to judge because he is the Son of Man"* **(John 5:26–27).**

Jesus commissioned His disciples, including you and me, in this way: *"Jesus called his twelve disciples to him and gave them authority to drive out impure spirits and to heal every disease and sickness"* **(Matthew 10:1–2, Mark 3:15,6:7, Luke 9:1).** His last words before ascending to heaven were: *"But you will receive power when the Holy Spirit comes on you; and you will be my witnesses in Jerusalem, and in all Judea and Samaria, and to the ends of the earth"* **(Acts 1:8).**

Let us pray: Dear God, transform our weaknesses into power. Help our unbelief so that we may believe that we *"can do all things through Christ who strengthens us"* **(Philippians 4:13)** and that we've been empowered to bring healing and good news to the whole world. We pray in Your Holy Name.

God offers you the power and full authority of the Holy Spirit to save, heal and restore the hope of His people who fight against unseen spirits and diseases.

September 27
PERSONAL SACRIFICE FOR SUCH A TIME AS THIS
Esther 4:16

We find several biblical characters who, knowing that God has given them positions of power and leadership for *"such a time as this"* **(Esther 4:14),** placed the welfare of others ahead of their own lives. One is Queen Esther, who was willing to die to save her Jewish people. Although **no one could approach the King without an invitation, Esther** said, *"I will go to the king, even though it is against the law. And if I perish, I perish"* **(Esther 4:16).**

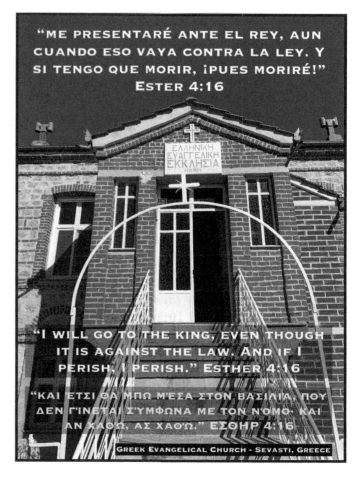

Another biblical character was Moses. **Only Moses could approach God's presence**. He's a type of Christ who was raised as a prince but became a shepherd. When God was going to punish the people for their disobedience, Moses interceded, asking God to *"forgive their sin—but if not, then blot me out of the book you have written" (Exodus 32:32).* Esther and Moses were obediently faithful. They were willing to sacrifice their lives for the joy of liberating their people. **By faith, Moses rejected the benefits of being a prince of Pharaoh** and *"chose to be mistreated along with the people of God rather than to enjoy the fleeting pleasures of sin"* **(Hebrews 11:24-25).**

Things in God's Kingdom are upside down! To win, we must be willing to lose. The cross of Christ is the most excellent example of the reverse sense of God's Kingdom, in which to die is to live, and to seek to live is to die. *"For whoever wants to save their life will lose it, but whoever loses their life for me will save it"* **(Luke 9:24).**

Like Moses and Queen Esther, God calls us *"for such a time as this,"* offering us faith to trust in His promises. Meditating on His Word, we recognize that all the riches of this world cannot compare to the reward God has prepared for those who submit to **personal sacrifice** to please God by defending the weak and poor and rescuing God's lost sheep.

Let us pray: Beloved God, you created us and gave us gifts and power *"for such a time as this."* Grant us the faith of the greats of the Bible, like Moses and Esther, who didn't consider their own lives but trusted that Your plans and designs were good, leading to the glorious beginning of a new life. We pray in Your Holy Name.

September 28
THE PROMISE OF ETERNAL LIFE
1 John 2:25

Through the Holy Scriptures, God has promised to be our guide, defender, protector, sustainer, redeemer, deliverer, and hope during storms. If we live by faith, clinging to His promises and obeying His will, God will always be our God, and we'll be His chosen people to enjoy God's eternal presence, peace, and joy.

No matter how large or intense our storm or enemy might be, the Lord will deliver us from all evil to fulfill the promise of eternal life for His children. By faith, we already have eternal life, which will be manifested when Jesus Christ returns for His church. *"Dear friends, now we are children of God, and what we will be has not yet been made known. But we know that when Christ appears, we shall be like him, for we shall see him as he is. All who have this hope in him purify themselves, just as he is pure"* (1 John 3:2–3).

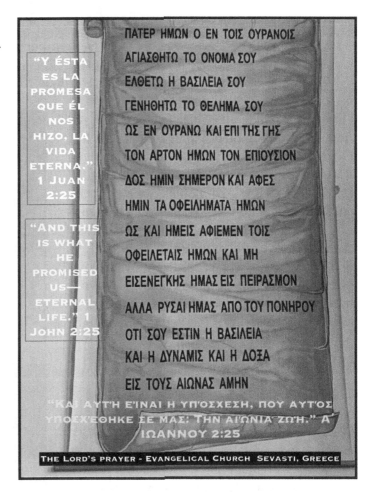

How can we know that we already have eternal life? First, *"The Spirit himself testifies with our spirit that we are God's children" (Romans 8:16).* If we know God's heart and strive to do His will, we can trust that God has transformed us into new creatures destined for eternal life. Jesus said to Nicodemus, *"the Son of Man must be lifted up, that everyone who believes may have eternal life in him" (John 3:14-15).*

Two thousand years ago, Jesus was raised on Calvary's cross so that everyone could achieve eternal life by believing in Him and His sacrifice. It's still necessary for Jesus's name to be lifted to save the world. But there's a sacrifice we must make to inherit eternal life. I love Jesus's promise, *"And everyone who has left houses or brothers or sisters or father or mother or wife or children or fields for my sake will receive a hundred times as much and will inherit eternal life"* (Matthew 19:29).

No matter how great or painful our sacrifice might be, Jesus promises that we *"will receive a hundred times as much and will inherit eternal life"* (Matthew 19:29). Glory to God!

299

Let us pray: Dear God, thank You for Your promise of eternal life. Grant us the faith to trust Your Holy Word and Jesus Christ, *"the pioneer and perfecter of faith"* (**Hebrews 12:2**). We pray in Your Holy Name.

September 29
SPEAKING ABOUT STUMBLING BLOCKS
Matthew 18:7

During this pandemic, we're facing a long period of stumbling blocks that put our faith to the test. Frequent quarantines have limited our freedom to leave the house, to see and hug loved ones. In these 24 months, we've experienced financial, job, status, physical, and emotional losses. We've seen businesses fail, marriages dissolved, relationships broken, and dreams cut short. We've said goodbye to loved ones who departed early. These events have irreversibly transformed our lives. They've struck us to the core of our being and compelled us in search of a safe harbor to renew our faith in God.

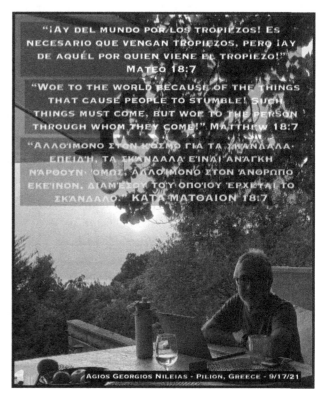

Today's verse tells us, *"Such things must come."* We can't avoid the trials and tribulations in this world that predominantly fight against God's will, that resist the desires of the Spirit. As Christians and leaders in our homes and communities, God calls us to be the humble reflection of Jesus Christ. Meek as a child and willing to put the welfare of others before ours. Although we are the minority in this world, in God's kingdom, which transcends time and distance, there are more who are with us than those against us (**2 Kings 6:16**). Also, *"the one who is in you is greater than the one who is in the world"* *(1 John 4:4).*

My beloved, let us not be afraid of trials and stumbling blocks. *"Such things must come."* Job said, *"Shall we accept good from God, and not trouble?"* (**Job 2:10**). Trials strengthen our faith. They prepare us for the next battle. But let us be careful that our life and testimony are not a cause for stumbling. Jesus said, *"but woe to the person through whom they come!"* The *"woe to the person"* is not an expression of compassion but eminent punishment.

I've said previously that I am afraid of two verses; today's verse and *"I never knew you. Away from me, you evildoers!" (Matthew 7:23).*

Let us pray: Dear God, put Your Spirit in us so that we may never, not in word, deed, or thought, be a stumbling block for those who believe in You. Grant that we may be a constant source of encouragement and hope for those struggling with this pandemic's repercussions. Lord, heal our sick, physically and emotionally. We pray in Jesus's name.

September 30
SPECIAL, BUT EQUALLY LOVED
Galatians 3:28

Upon being adopted into God's family through faith in Jesus's sacrifice on Calvary's cross, God spiritually transforms all believers into new creatures. By faith, we become children of God, like grandchildren, each special but all equally loved. From that moment on, our cultural and social heritage ceases to be important; *"There is neither Jew nor Gentile, neither slave nor free, nor is there male and female, for you are all one in Christ Jesus" (Galatians 3:28).*

Previously, the Israelites were exclusively God's chosen people. God said, *"you are a people holy to the Lord your God. Out of all the peoples on the face of the earth, the Lord has chosen you to be his treasured possession" (Deuteronomy 14:2).* To them belonged the promises, protection, provision, and salvation. The only thing God expected of them in that covenant was their exclusive love, faithfulness, and obedience to God.

Since it was impossible for the people to keep the covenant faithfully, God opened the doors of exclusivity, sending Jesus Christ as the mediator of the new covenant of grace. Thus, God extended the promises, protection, provision, and salvation to the whole world without *"showing partiality"* to persons **(Deuteronomy 10:17)**. As beneficiaries of this new covenant, we recognize that *"there is no Gentile or Jew, circumcised or uncircumcised, barbarian, Scythian, slave or free, but Christ is all, and is in all" (Colossians 3:11).*

Colossians 3:12 says, *"Therefore, as God's chosen people, holy and dearly loved, clothe yourselves with compassion, kindness, humility, gentleness and patience."* We must accept that, as chosen individuals, we are genuinely privileged and unique, but all equally loved. Our titles and responsibilities no longer matter.

Let us also remember that God offers the new covenant to everyone so *"that everyone who believes may have eternal life in him"* **(John 3:15).** The fact that some don't yet believe in God or

301

Jesus Christ doesn't make them less valuable or loved than us, nor excluded from hearing the gospel's invitation.

Let us pray: Dear God, thank You for choosing us to be Your beloved people. Increase our faithfulness that we may be worthy of this call. Please help us share the good news with everyone we meet on our way. We pray in Jesus's name.

October 1
WATERS OF PEACE AND LIFE
Romans 8:6

Bodies of water (rivers, waterfalls, lakes) and gardens lead me to higher levels of peace. Water reminds us of our baptism, and gardens remind us of the brevity and beauty of life.

I took this photo in the Luxembourg Gardens, Paris. The rain couldn't stop us from walking through the streets of my ancestors. I felt peace and gratitude, enjoying this great metropolis's history, beauty, and culinary art and anticipating our return home the following day. Our peace is heightened knowing that we'll return to our Heavenly Father's mansion at the end of our days. This security germinates from our baptismal waters, which welcome us to God's family.

At our baptism, our parents or we renounced the spiritual forces of evil, the evil powers of the world, to satisfy the flesh (to be slaves of sin) and repented of our sins. Through water and the Holy Spirit, God cleansed us from past and present evil and infused us with Divine power to resist corruption, injustice, and oppression in all their manifestations. Confessing Jesus Christ as our Savior, we trusted His loving grace and promised to follow and serve our Lord.

I've joyfully renewed my baptismal vows several times at a family camp in Quinipet, Long Island, on the Atlantic beach. Baptism and its renewal are mountain-top moments when the Holy Spirit lifts us to a higher place, increasing our faith and gratitude, filling us with peace, and helping us to see everything beautiful and full of life, like the gardens of Luxembourg.

Recalling our baptismal waters fills us with joy, love, and hope. It gives us the strength to **engage in the things of the Spirit** and stop living *"in the realm of the flesh" (Romans 8:9).* Jesus said: *"Whoever believes in me, as Scripture has said, rivers of living water will flow from within them" (John 7:38).*

Let us pray: Dear God, thank You for cleansing us with Your waters of life so that we may be sources of life for those who do not yet know you but seek you. Help us care for the things of the

Spirit that represent life and peace for our family and future generations who will believe in You through our faithfulness. We pray in Jesus's name.

✝ ✝ ✝ ✝ ✝ ✝

October 2
MURMURING IS FORBID-DEN
Philippians 2:14

The word *"murmured"* (**grumbling**) appears 44 times in the Bible. It's most often found in **Exodus** when, in the desert, the Israelites repeatedly murmured against God and Moses for lack of water, meat, and bread.

We're a peculiar people, not unlike the Israelites in the desert. We quickly forget what God did to free us. Instead of being grateful, we show ingratitude and impatience. In the congregation, we unanimously claim loyalty, saying, *"We will do everything the Lord has said"* (**Exodus 19:8**). But in our hearts, we murmur about everything that is lacking, that ails or bothers us, such as the heat, cold, rain, snow, the economy, storms, catastrophes, etc., as if God finds pleasure in our sufferings or discomfort.

We're peculiar in that we dislike being told what to do, how, and when to do it. We'll do them when and how we please. However, we murmur and argue about the slightest things when made to feel obligated.

But God calls us to love and serve one another. *"Do everything without grumbling or arguing"* **(v.14)**. *"Everything"* means <u>whatever</u> is necessary to continue the ministry that Christ entrusted to us as individuals and as a church. Upon becoming a part of God's church through baptism, we were anointed with power and authority *"to proclaim good news to the poor. He has sent me to proclaim freedom for the prisoners and recovery of sight for the blind, to set the oppressed free"* **(Luke 4:18).**

Let us unanimously do everything necessary to fulfill this mandate, *"without grumbling or arguing so that we may be blameless and pure, children of God without fault in a warped and crooked generation. Then you will shine among them like stars in the sky"* **(Philippians 2:14-16).**

The devil wants us to look out for our interests, to fight for our rights, titles, and positions of respect and admiration. However, if we do this, we won't reflect Christ's character, who was **blameless, simple, and pure**, thus causing the lost sheep to stay where they are instead of entering a henhouse of grumbling and strife.

Only by **clinging to God's Word**, guided by the Holy Spirit, can we *"shine among them like stars in the sky"* and rescue the lost sheep that roam the world, shivering, without shelter, food, and direction, threatened by wolves dressed in sheep's clothing.

Let us pray: Dear God, remove from us the spirit of murmuring and contention so that we may shine like lights in the darkness of our world. We pray in Your Holy Name.

> **Guided by the Holy Spirit, can we** *"shine among them like stars in the sky"* **and rescue the lost sheep.**

October 3
REST, RECHARGE, AND REFRESH
Exodus 23:12

Thank you for praying for my mother-in-law, who was in poor health at the beginning of summer 2020. Thank God she recovered her strength day by day. When she came home from the hospital, she was weak and couldn't walk or speak. To complicate matters, she came down with the flu, making it difficult for her to breathe and speak. So, she mostly slept.

Part of the therapy was encouraging her to become active. A month later, somewhat recovered; she began knitting a blanket for my daughter Sophia's baby. With two weeks before our return to the USA, there wasn't much time to complete it. Knitting motivated her to push herself. Every day she got up early and went to bed late. But, Sunday came and she didn't knit at all, waiting for the start of the new day to resume her task. Why? Because Sunday, **"Κυριακή"** means **"Lord's Day,"** it's a day to **REST, RECHARGE, AND REFRESH.**

In **Exodus 23:12** God tells us, *"You are to do your work for six days, but on the seventh day you are to refrain from work so that your ox and donkey may rest, and so the son of your maidservant and the alien may be refreshed."* Since I met my in-laws, I learned to honor the **Lord's Day**. They never did any labor that day, dedicating it to reading God's Word, singing hymns at home, visiting the sick, and attending Sunday worship.

More than a good custom, **Honoring the Lord's Day** is a commandment from a loving and protecting God. We weren't created to work seven days a week without taking time to rest and regain strength. In these verses, we rediscover God's care and love for the poor and foreigners. *"You are to sow your land and gather its crops for six years, but you are to let it rest the seventh year, leaving it unplanted. The poor of your people may eat from it, and the wild animals* *may eat what they leave"* **(Exodus 23:10-11).** The earth also requires its rest, and the poor and stranger find their refreshment and sustenance in that rest.

Let us pray: Dear God, thank You for setting aside one day of the week for us to rest, recharge our physical and spiritual strength, and offer refreshments to the poor and foreigner among us. Help us to honor Your day again. We pray in Jesus's name.

October 4
INTIMACY IS A GIFT FROM GOD
1 Corinthians 7:5A

God formed us to have an intimate relationship with God and each other.

The most significant expression of human intimacy with God occurs in our prayer time and our individual and communal worship. It's when we love God *"with all our heart, with all our understanding and with all our strength"* **(Mark 12:33).** It's our total surrender to God's will.

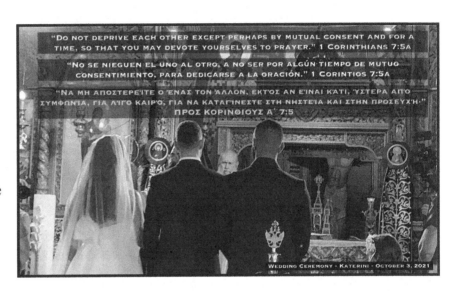

The most significant expression of God's intimacy toward humanity took place on Calvary's Cross, where God *"did not spare his own Son, but gave him up for us all"* **(Romans 8:32a).** Only by approaching the cross can we understand the depth of God's love, grace, and mercy toward all of creation. It's a total surrender that doesn't deprive us of anything to generate due reciprocity.

Whoever has experienced the crucifixion and Resurrection of Christ no longer lives for himself but for God. Through the resurrection, Christ fills us with a new and better view of life. The intimacy we enjoy with God prompts us to put our **"ego"** aside and live by faith in and for the Son of God.

The most significant expression of human intimacy toward others occurs within the family. First in the marriage union, where each swears love *"till death do us apart."* Its benefits are lifelong physical and emotional intimacy and the formation of the family (the children), which gives us even more intimate and beautiful relationships. Children then receive the most sublime and intimate human love and pass it on to their families.

305

Intimacy in the home never dies or ceases to be. As we age, we learn that love transcends trials and barriers, and over the years, it takes on different and better forms of expression, which fill us with gratitude for this precious gift called agape love. Our verse reminds us to *"not deprive each other"* of God's gift of intimacy **(1 Corinthians 7:5).**

Let us pray: Dear God, thank You for the gift of intimacy we relish with you and the family. Grant that we may sow intimate seeds of love with all whom you place in our path so that they might also come to know the greatness of Your love, grace, and mercy. We pray in Jesus's name.

October 5
AN INTIMATE'S BETRAYAL HURTS MORE
Psalm 55:13

We must read **verse 12** to understand our text. *"If an enemy were insulting me, I could endure it; if a foe were rising against me, I could hide. But it is you, a man like myself, my companion, my close friend."*

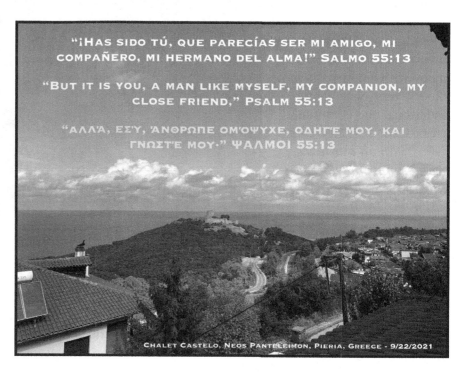

We're not surprised by an enemy attack. Many countries have their border's armed forces prepared against such attacks. But among intimates, we tend to lower our defenses. Therefore, when an intimate takes advantage of our friendship and trust, it usually hurts more than an enemy attack, possibly causing us to lose faith in humanity or in our community.

The devil is the eternal enemy of friendship, family, and everything representing peace, unity, harmony, and fidelity toward God and neighbor. Often, the devil doesn't act directly against us but instead uses those within our circle of intimacy to inflict harm. Such was the case with Jesus and Judas, one of His disciples.

Traditionally, on *Holy Thursday*, we read about Judas's betrayal in the garden of Gethsemane. *"While he was still speaking, Judas, one of the Twelve, arrived. With him was a large crowd armed with swords and clubs, sent from the chief priests and the elders of the people. Now the betrayer had arranged a signal with them: 'The one I kiss is the man; arrest him.'*

306

Going at once to Jesus, Judas said, "Greetings, Rabbi! "and kissed him" (**Matthew 26:47-49, Mark 14:44,45**).

Our text points to this scene of betrayal by one who seemed like a close friend and companion. **Psalm 55:14** adds, *"with whom I once enjoyed sweet fellowship at the house of God."* This is the human condition. While we live in this world, no matter how close we are to God, the devil will seek whomever he can, from the spiritually strongest to the weakest, one close to us, to attack and prevent us from reaching our destination.

Let us pray: Dear God, help us not lose our trust in humanity because of the evil of a few. When the enemy comes against us, grant us to live in peace, knowing that Your plans for our lives and families are good. Give us hearts like yours, willing to suffer for the sake of the gospel of our Lord Jesus Christ, in whose name we pray.

> **While we live in this world, no matter how close we are to God, the devil will seek whomever he can, from the spiritually strongest to the weakest, one close to us, to attack and prevent us from reaching our destination.**

✠ ✠ ✠ ✠ ✠

October 6
ADULTERY - BETRAYAL BY AN INTIMATE
Matthew 5:27

Yesterday we said that the enemy *uses those within our circle of intimacy to inflict harm*. Adul-

tery is one of the ways the enemy has destroyed the peace, love, and trust within many homes. Whomever the devil is using to commit this offense often justifies their actions by thinking that *"what others don't know won't hurt them."* Eventually, everything that is done in secret comes to the surface. For the most part, adultery culminates in divorce, in the breakdown of the home, causing psychological trauma to the children.

Today's verse is about the moral law against adultery. In psychology, the attraction to the forbidden points to our curiosity for the unknown. We see its first case in Eve tasting the forbidden fruit. In the ten commandments, God gave us moral rules to cooperatively prosper as members of society. Cooperation implies a high level of trust that everyone will abide by the laws and statutes, respecting and protecting each other's property and life. Without morality, society disintegrates.

As humans, God gave us a conscience that directs us to act justly, especially concerning God's social laws (Do not kill, steal, lie, commit adultery, and honor our parents). If we do good, we'll be rewarded, and if we do evil, we'll receive just punishment for putting society's well-being at risk.

In our society, adultery is not illegal, nor considered a crime, although it is externally frowned upon by society. God's law is more severe than social law. *"If a man commits adultery with another man's wife—with the wife of his neighbor—both the adulterer and the adulteress are to be put to death" (Leviticus 20:10).* With few exceptions, this religious law is not enforced in our society, although spiritually, whoever practices disobedience is considered spiritually dead.

Jesus said in **Matthew 5:28,** *"But I tell you that anyone who looks at a woman lustfully has already committed adultery with her in his heart."*

Let us pray: Dear God, Your Word says that the *"wrongdoers will not inherit the kingdom of God" (1 Corinthians 6:9).* We long to be found faithful and worthy to enter Your Kingdom. Don't let our wondering eyes disqualify us from the path you've prepared for us. Cleanse our hearts and minds, and deliver us from all evil, Lord. We pray in Jesus's name.

October 7
TRUSTING IN HIS REDEMPTIVE WORK
Psalm 22:1

On Good Friday, Christians commemorate the passion and death of our Lord on the cross. The offer of redemption occurred two thousand years ago when Christ cried out, *"It is finished"* **(John 19:30),** and *"gave up his Spirit"* **(Matthew 27:50).** Our redemption takes effect from the moment we put our faith in the redemptive work of Jesus Christ.

Before dying, Jesus cried out, *"My God, my God, why have you forsaken me?"* **(Mark 15:34, Psalm 22:1).** Through self-sacrifice and abandonment, Jesus glorified God by *"finishing the work that God gave Him to do" (John 17:4).*

In moments of anguish, we cry out with the Psalmist; *"I call on the Lord in my distress, and he answers me"* **(Psalm 120:1).** You might be experiencing times of suffering, guilt, loneliness, or abandonment. No matter how great or small your anguish, remember that the Lord identifies with you. Speaking of Jesus, **Isaiah 53:3** says, *"He was despised and rejected by mankind, a man of suffering, and familiar with pain."* Of us, Jesus said: *"In this world you will have trouble. But take heart! I have overcome the world" (John 16:33).*

Through suffering and trials, we come to believe that there is a Sovereign being who understands the depths of our sorrowing hearts and will never abandon us. God! We can turn to the Lord in times of need. Through suffering and trials, our faith and hope in the redemptive work of Jesus Christ are reborn.

On the cross, Jesus defeated the powers of darkness, crying out *"it is finished,"* (τελέω (teleo) in Greek - **G5055**), which means *"to finish, that is; complete, execute, conclude, discharge (a debt): pay, satisfy, finish, consummate."* My beloved, Jesus completed His redemptive work on the cross. There's nothing else we can do to earn forgiveness for our past and present sins except to believe. Having trusted in Jesus Christ, the Holy Spirit reveals our current sins so that through confession and repentance, we may receive forgiveness from our beloved Redeemer.

Let us pray: Dear God, we don't want to repeat the failures of our ancestors or ours. Increase our faith to believe with all our heart that you fully completed Your redemptive work on the cross and that there's nothing else we can do but believe and worship Your Son Jesus, in whose name we pray.

October 8
LÁZARO ELÍAS ARISTIZABAL
Psalm 22:10

Lázaro Elías Aristizabal - my heart and grandson, bone of my bones and flesh of my flesh **(Genesis 2:23).** What a beautiful and happy child! You are a gift from God in our life. We didn't know when, but we were eagerly awaiting your arrival. For almost ten years, we silently prayed that God would send you to our circle of love, the Aristizabal-Destruge family. Before you were born, you were already under God's love, care, and protection.

On March 17, 2020, we were in quarantine in Cuenca, Ecuador, when your parents, Carlos Andres and Sophia Eleni, called us by video to announce that you were already in your mother's womb. We listened to your heartbeat and rejoiced. It was the best birthday present for yiayía Mery.

309

Every month your parents sent us photos of your growth progress in your mommy's womb. The time in quarantine became more bearable and joyous, knowing that you would soon arrive. You were born on October 29, 2020, and on October 31, you finally arrived at your home, and we were able to hold you in our arms, Lázaro Elías, the fulfillment of our prayers.

In September 2021, with your parents, you came to Katerini, Greece, to visit us and meet your great-grandmother (Megaly Yiayia Kikí). What a great joy! At the end of October, by God's will, we'll celebrate your birthday, giving thanks for each day and experience we've enjoyed with you. You are a precious gift from God.

My beloved friends and family, each of you is equally precious and loved by God and by your blood and spiritual family. Many prayed to God for you and continue to plead for your life, health, and prosperity. **Psalm 22:10** says, *"From birth I was cast on you; from my mother's womb you have been my God."* The day of your birth was one of celebration, rejoicing, and gratitude for the gift of a new life, full of hope and joy.

Let us pray: Dear God, thank You for affirming that we were not an unwanted accident. Don't allow anyone, including ourselves, to minimize our value and importance in Your family or the depth of love You and our loved ones feel for us. Help us to freely express our love for those you've placed in our circle of intimacy. We pray in Jesus's name.

✝ ✝ ✝ ✝ ✝ ✝

October 9
IT IS WRITTEN!
James 4:7

When Jesus was in the desert, *"After fasting forty days and forty nights, he was hungry. The tempter came to him and said, 'If you are the Son of God, tell these stones to become bread.' Jesus answered, 'It is written: 'Man shall not live on bread alone, but on every word that comes from the mouth of God.''"* (**Matthew 4:2-4**). Jesus resisted the devil three times with the words: *"It is written"* (**vs. 7,10**).

SUBMIT
Today, while meditating, the following admonition appeared three times from different sources: *'There is a rule of physics that two things cannot occupy the same space simultaneously. For example, we couldn't add anything to a 10-ounce cup full of coffee until we reduce or consume its content. It's the same with our minds. When God's*

Word remains in us, our minds are filled with all the good that flows from Him." By submitting ourselves daily to God's Word, we can resist temptations by saying, *"No! Because it is written."*

DRAW NEAR

The mind and spirit are controlled by what's closest to our hearts. *"Come near to God and he will come near to you"* **(James 4:8).** To resist the devil, our hearts must be more attached to God than to the world. Thus, we can respond, *"No, because it is written."* Suppose the mind is empty or distant from the things of God. In that case, the enemy can quickly enter and fill our minds with backbiting, doubts, disbelief, anger, and rebellion, causing physical, emotional, and spiritual catastrophes. But we have hope; if we live and act as God's chosen children, even if we've fallen into temptation, Christ will knock on our door, allowing us to return and again **draw near to God**. Then all the demons will flee because God's Word is powerful enough to **purify and sanctify our minds, home, and communities.**

HUMBLE YOURSELVES

James 4:10 also helps us resist the enemy's temptations. *"Humble yourselves before the Lord, and he will lift you up."* When we put God and His Word over our will and others' welfare over our own, God is pleased and strengthens us to resist the devil and fulfill our goal. Asking forgiveness for our mistakes turns our previous weakness into divine strength and resistance. *"It is written"* are words that become a shield and repellent when we **SUBMIT, DRAW NEAR,** and **HUMBLE OURSELVES** before God.

Let us pray: Dear God, thank You for these powerful words. Help us fill our minds with Your Divine Direction and thus resist temptations by answering, *"No, because 'it is written.'"* We pray in Jesus's name.

October 10
CONFESSION
Psalm 106:6

WE HAVE SINNED, EVEN AS OUR ANCESTORS DID; WE HAVE DONE WRONG AND ACTED WICKEDLY. PSALM 106:6

PECAMOS NOSOTROS, COMO NUESTROS PADRES; HICIMOS MALDAD, COMETIMOS IMPIEDAD. SALMOS 106:6

ΑΜΑΡΤΉΣΑΜΕ, ΜΑΖΊ ΜΕ ΤΟΥΣ ΠΑΤΈΡΕΣ ΜΑΣ· ΑΝΟΜΉΣΑΜΕ, ΑΣΕΒΉΣΑΜΕ. ΨΑΛΜΟΙ 106:6

SHEFFIELD ISLAND HARBOR, NORWALK, CT, USA- O DESTRUGE

Confession is good for the soul. The first step toward wholeness is recognizing that we need healing. God has designed laws and signs to warn the world and us individually when something's wrong with us, physically, emotionally, spiritually, or morally.

Perhaps *"global warming"* signifies our physical world is in danger. Many years ago, I didn't follow the recycling protocols. Now I understand that we're responsible for leaving our future generations a healthy planet with clean rivers, beaches, and air. I try doing my

311

part to heal our world by recycling responsibly **and watching my emission footprint.**

In times of COVID-19, we act responsibly by wearing masks and maintaining social distancing. Our planet and its people are in danger because, until August 2022 worldwide, we've exceeded 6.4 million deaths and 604 million infected. Those who understand this danger protect their family and neighbors through the responsible use of masks and following World Health protocols.

Spiritually, God's Word dictates whether our thoughts, actions, and words are wholesome. The psalmist confesses his sin to God; *"We have sinned, even as our ancestors did; we have done wrong and acted wickedly"* **(Psalm 106:6)**. We're no different or better than our parents, but we aspire not to make the same mistakes. We need a healer to free us from this disease of open rebellion against God.

In the desert, God was enraged and wanted to destroy Israel because they worshiped a golden calf. But Moses intervened, and God regretted what He planned to do **(Psalm 106:19-23)**. We also have our gods of gold, silver, and valuable things that incline us to put God and family in second place. This saddens God very much, but we give thanks to Jesus, who **daily intercedes** for us, I imagine, saying, *"Father, don't look at their faults; look at my wounds and the blood that I shed to redeem them. 'Forgive them, Father, because they don't know what they're doing"* **(Luke 23:34).**

Let us pray: Dear God, help us confess our sinful condition, return to Your ways, and *act justly and do what's right.* Thank you for not looking at our present situation but at what we'll be when, by Your grace and love, you'll have completed **purifying and perfecting us to enter into Your presence**. Bring our youth back to Your fold so that our children's children may have hope for a better future in Your presence. We pray in Your Holy Name.

> **The first step toward wholeness is recognizing that we need healing. God has designed laws and signs to warn the world and us individually when something's wrong with us, physically, emotionally, spiritually, or morally.**

October 11
SAVED BY ASSOCIATION OR IMITATION?
Revelation 7:10

God offers salvation for us personally and for our families. **Acts 16:31 says,** *"Believe in the Lord Jesus, and you will be saved—you and your household."* How is that possible? Is it by association or imitation?

Take Noah, for example. We don't know much about his family except that *"Noah found favor in the eyes of the Lord"* **(Genesis 6:8)** and that his wife and children were saved from the flood.

Was it by association only, or did Noah's faith rub off on them, making them worthy of being saved?

I have seen, time and again, God's promise fulfilled. *"You and your household"* will be saved. Whether by association or imitation, the fact is that God's promises are faithful because *"God cannot lie"* (**Hebrews 6:18**). *"The Lord is not slow in keeping his promise, as some understand slowness. Instead he is patient with you, not wanting anyone to perish, but everyone to come to repentance"* (**2 Peter 3:9**).

The more we associate with people of faith, the more we aspire to reach their level of faith and spirituality. We want to have what they have. At first, we imitate their actions and words (their way of praying or their habits of reading the Bible) until these become our discipline and, finally, we think and act like them. Then we experience that warmth in our hearts affirming that we are beloved children of God, whether by association or imitation.

God has blessed me with humble and helpful mentors who've demonstrated a peaceful and gentle way of living with and for Christ. God *"wants all people to be saved and to come to a knowledge of the truth" (1 Timothy 2:4).* Therefore, God has provided various ways and models for receiving salvation, including imitation, association, faith, and grace, so that everyone *"who calls on the name of the Lord will be saved"* (**Acts 2:21**). Thus, God fulfills His Word, *"And all people will see God's salvation"* (**Luke 3:6**).

> **The more we associate with people of faith, the more we aspire to reach their level of faith and spirituality.**

Let us pray: Dear God, grant that at all times, our children may surround themselves with such examples or guide those who seek safety and salvation from the coming tribulations. Help them believe that Your Son Jesus Christ wants to be the Lord and Savior of their lives. We pray in Jesus's name.

October 12
WISDOM IS BORN FROM FEAR
Job 28:28

Job 28:12 asks, *"But where can wisdom be found? Where does understanding dwell?"* Wisdom is born from the fear of failing our loved ones in our duty as parents, uncles, spouses, brothers, etc., and failing God in doing His will. Wisdom comes from God.

Lovingly and patiently, we teach our children to know and obey our voice and trust that we have good wishes for them. We teach them the difference between good, evil, and dangerous; to show respect and fear of the forces

"EL TEMOR DEL SEÑOR ES LA SABIDURÍA. QUIEN SE APARTA DEL MAL ES INTELIGENTE." JOB 28:28

"THE FEAR OF THE LORD—THAT IS WISDOM, AND TO SHUN EVIL IS UNDERSTANDING." JOB 28:28

"ΚΑΙ ΣΤΟΝ ΆΝΘΡΩΠΟ ΕΊΠΕ: ΠΡΌΣΕΞΕ, Ο ΦΌΒΟΣ ΤΟΎ ΚΥΡΊΟΥ, ΑΥΤΌΣ ΕΊΝΑΙ Η ΣΟΦΊΑ, ΚΑΙ Η ΑΠΟΧΉ ΑΠΌ ΤΟ ΚΑΚΌ, ΣΎΝΕΣΗ." ΙΩΒ 28:28

PARALIA, KATERINI, GREECE - O. DESTRUGE OCTOBER 11, 2021

that can cause injuries or death, such as fire, electricity, turbulent waters, streets, and highways.

Some of these lessons include respecting traffic rules and the rules of the house, beaches, or pools. For example; Don't swim without the presence of a lifeguard. Don't cross the street without a known adult. Don't talk to strangers or enter their cars. Likewise, God has shown us what is right, intelligent, and evil. *"The fear of the Lord is the beginning of wisdom, and knowledge of the Holy One is understanding" (Proverbs 9:10).* God leads us toward all that is good, wise, and honorable. God's Word is faithful and true.

The Bible teaches us what is offensive and dangerous to the soul. God wrote it so that we'd find the courage and spiritual guidance to resist temptations and obey God's social order rules. These help us arrive at the celestial mansion less bruised. God says in *Proverbs 3:13-14,16, "Blessed are those who find wisdom, those who gain understanding, for she is more profitable than silver and yields better returns than gold. 16 Long life is in her right hand; in her left hand are riches and honor."*

Therefore, **should we trust in human or Divine wisdom?** We'd be wise to follow God because *"the foolishness of God is wiser than human wisdom, and the weakness of God is stronger than human strength"* (1 Corinthians 1:25).

> The Bible teaches us what is offensive and dangerous to the soul. God wrote it so that we'd find the courage and spiritual guidance to resist temptations and obey God's social order rules.

Let us pray: Dear God, we pray for young parents; grant them wisdom to instruct their children to choose rightly between good and evil. We pray for our children that the example of our lives may inspire them to, instead of trusting human wisdom, they would seek Your instruction and guidance. We pray in the name of Jesus.

✝ ✝ ✝ ✝ ✝

The devil caused a division between God and creation and among human beings through lies and deception. **Isaiah 59:2** says, *"But your iniquities have separated you from your God; your sins have hidden his face from you, so that he will not hear."*

God cannot be amid impurities, which is why the Lord placed a vast, impenetrable chasm between impurity and the holy, between humanity and God. Since then, we've looked for ways to cross that chasm, to live in peace with God and humanity. But our attempts have not achieved the holiness and justice that God demands of His people. Therefore, Jesus Christ came into the world to pay for our sins and purify us from the evil that separated us.

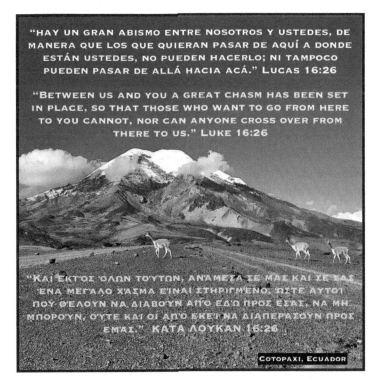

"HAY UN GRAN ABISMO ENTRE NOSOTROS Y USTEDES, DE MANERA QUE LOS QUE QUIERAN PASAR DE AQUÍ A DONDE ESTÁN USTEDES, NO PUEDEN HACERLO; NI TAMPOCO PUEDEN PASAR DE ALLÁ HACIA ACÁ." LUCAS 16:26

"BETWEEN US AND YOU A GREAT CHASM HAS BEEN SET IN PLACE, SO THAT THOSE WHO WANT TO GO FROM HERE TO YOU CANNOT, NOR CAN ANYONE CROSS OVER FROM THERE TO US." LUKE 16:26

"ΚΑΙ ΕΚΤΟΣ ΟΛΩΝ ΤΟΥΤΩΝ, ΑΝΑΜΕΣΑ ΣΕ ΜΑΣ ΚΑΙ ΣΕ ΣΑΣ ΕΝΑ ΜΕΓΑΛΟ ΧΑΣΜΑ ΕΙΝΑΙ ΣΤΗΡΙΓΜΕΝΟ. ΩΣΤΕ ΑΥΤΟΙ ΠΟΥ ΘΕΛΟΥΝ ΝΑ ΔΙΑΒΟΥΝ ΑΠΟ ΕΔΩ ΠΡΟΣ ΕΣΑΣ, ΝΑ ΜΗ ΜΠΟΡΟΥΝ, ΟΥΤΕ ΚΑΙ ΟΙ ΑΠΟ ΕΚΕΙ ΝΑ ΔΙΑΠΕΡΑΣΟΥΝ ΠΡΟΣ ΕΜΑΣ." ΚΑΤΑ ΛΟΥΚΑΝ 16:26

COTOPAXI, ECUADOR

Jesus tells the parable of the rich man and the beggar Lazarus, both of whom die. Lazarus was taken to consolation near Abraham, while the rich man descended into Hades, where he was perpetually tormented. The rich one asked Abraham to *"'send Lazarus to dip the tip of his finger in water and cool my tongue, because I am in agony in this fire. 'But Abraham replied, 'Son, remember that in your lifetime you received your good things, while Lazarus received bad things, but now he is comforted here and you are in agony. And besides all this, between us and you a great chasm has been set in place, so that those who want to go from here to you cannot, nor can anyone cross over from there to us'"* **(Luke 16:24-26).**

My beloved, the bridge to God will be removed on the last day when God judges our works. Until then, whoever has trusted in Jesus will ascend into God's arms. Sadly, many still live apart from God, and if we remain unconcerned, they will not enter into God's joy and rest.

Let us pray: Dear God, thank You for sending Jesus Christ, who is the Way and the bridge that connects us to Your kingdom. We pray for those who refuse Your offer of salvation. Enlighten us to reach them with Your message of love and reconciliation. We pray in Jesus's name.

October 14
GLORIFYING GOD THROUGH HOSPITALITY
Romans 15:7

In **Romans 15:5–6,** we read, *"May the God who gives endurance and encouragement give you the same attitude of mind toward each other that Christ Jesus had, so that with one mind and one voice you may glorify the God and Father of our Lord Jesus Christ."*

As faithful Christians, we try to glorify God through our worship, service, witness, and today's focus, **hospitality**.

Greece is a magical country. Googling the top reasons to visit it, you'll see articles about its hospitable people, its delicious variety of foods, its coffee culture, its glorious history and architecture, stunning islands and beaches, and the Mediterranean climate. Since 1978, I've enjoyed all these wonders, but the people's hospitality is what I hold most in my heart and often brings me back to Greece.

My primary residence is in Connecticut, United States. Immigrants like me feel like we don't belong to either the country we visit or our country of residence because we're not native to either. But that doesn't happen in Greece. Although I still struggle with the Greek language, friends and family make me feel like I'm one of them. That is why I love Greece. Likewise, God wants us to be hospitable to everyone. *"If you really keep the royal law found in Scripture, 'Love your neighbor as yourself,' you are doing right'" (James 2:8).*

There are many ways to glorify God, to show that God lives and reigns in our hearts. Our worship glorifies God within our circle of believers and congregation members. However, hospitality glorifies God in our communities, where we find people seeking to be accepted and received *"as one of our own."* It's in the community where your gift of hospitality will have the most significant impact in finding and bringing back the lost sheep who've been injured by religious practices that, instead of attracting, have alienated God's people.

My beloved, you and I were bought at a great price so that in body, soul, and spirit, we might glorify God through our hospitable love **(1 Corinthians 6:20).**

Let us pray: Dear God, thank You for allowing us to experience genuine hospitality, where we feel like one who belongs. Help us to receive one another, just as Christ accepted us. We pray in Jesus's name.

October 15
FAITHFUL FRIENDS
Revelation 17:14

When crossing unknown paths, we have confidence and security in reaching our destination if someone who knows the route accompanies us. My friend in the photo is **Γεώργιος Κεχαγίας (George),** who guided me in 2020 to the top of Mount Olympus and back home. Olympus is the highest mountain in Greece - it consists of a mountain range, in which **Mytikas** is its highest peak, at 2,917 meters high. I often hear, **"If you're going to climb Mytikas, don't go alone!"** Those who have gone up alone have failed, been injured, or have lost their lives. In 2021 we're dedicated to cycling along the safe routes known to George, free of dogs and other dangers.

Our verse says that the enemies of God *"will wage war against the Lamb, but the Lamb will triumph over them because he is Lord of lords and King of kings— and with him will be his called, 'chosen and faithful followers'"* **(Revelation 17:14).** We know the saying, *"the enemy of my friend is my enemy."* Following this logic, whoever fights against Jesus fights against us. And whoever fights against us fights against the Lamb. In any case, Jesus *"will triumph over them."*

As *'chosen'* and *'faithful'* friends of Jesus, we're confident that we will go through great tribulations before we reach our eternal rest. We'll be persecuted and accused like Jesus, tempted by Satan. We will suffer assaults, deceptions, evictions, and significant losses, including health and life. The route to heaven is full of trials and tribulations, but no matter how great and fearful they may be, we will reach our destination if accompanied by our friend Jesus. God has promised that *"nothing in all creation, will be able to separate us from the love of God that is in Christ Jesus our Lord"* **(Romans 8:39).** We can trust our guide, friend, and Lord.

> **The route to heaven is full of trials and tribulations, but no matter how great and fearful they may be, we will reach our destination if accompanied by our friend Jesus.**

Let us pray: Dear God, thank You for assuring us that whoever fights against us fights *"against the Lamb, but the Lamb will triumph over them because he is Lord of lords and King of kings."* Thank you for reminding us that we are *"chosen"* and *"faithful"* friends. Help us to transmit to the world our confidence that in everything we are *"more than conquerors through him who loved us" (Romans 8:37).* We pray in Jesus's name.

October 16
BE HUMBLE IMITATORS
1 Peter 5:5B

My mother was a humble, simple, and even innocent soul. She'd innocently strike up conversations with strangers or their babies, as you can see in today's photo. When she lived in the USA, my mom spoke to everyone in Spanish, without considering that the only thing they understood was her greeting in English. From there, she spoke only in Spanish. The other thing they understood was her beautiful, humble smile and expression of loving acceptance on her face.

Jesus said, *"Take my yoke upon you and learn from me, for I am gentle and humble in heart, and you will find rest for your souls"* **(Matthew 11:29).** Today, God echoes Jesus's words, first addressing the young: *"In the same way, you who are younger, submit yourselves to your elders. All of you, clothe yourselves with humility toward one another, because, 'God opposes the proud but shows favor to the humble. '"* (1 Peter 5:5).

Everyone is called to practice mutual respect, with humility and meekness, regardless of age and position. By humbly submitting to God's will and direction, we'll find God's favor in treating everyone with respect. Through the Bible, we learn to pray as Jesus humbly demonstrated in Gethsemane: *"My Father, if it is possible, may this cup be taken from me. Yet not as I will, but as you will"* **(Matthew 26:39,42).**

> **BY HUMBLY SUBMITTING TO GOD'S WILL AND DIRECTION, WE'LL FIND GOD'S FAVOR IN TREATING EVERYONE WITH RESPECT.**

The Lord Jesus *"humbled himself by becoming obedient to death— even death on a cross! Therefore God exalted him to the highest place and gave him the name that is above every name, that at the name of Jesus every knee should bow, in heaven and on earth and under the earth, and every tongue acknowledge that Jesus Christ is Lord, to the glory of God the Father"* **(Philippians 2:8-11).**

All things belong to Jesus Christ. Whoever trusts with all their heart that Jesus is their Lord will humbly submit all things to the Lord so that God may mend and make something beautiful out of them in due time.

Let us pray: Dear God, thank You for the example of humility in our Lord Jesus Christ. Help us to be genuine imitators of His humble love. Filled with gratitude, we pray that You increase our faith, take our lives, along with all fears and longings, and do with them according to Your good and perfect will. We pray in Jesus's name.

October 17
AS THE LORD COMMANDED
Exodus 39:43

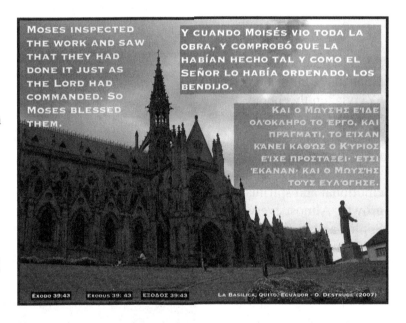

Have you heard the saying, *"you win the boss over with your work?"* Using our knowledge and skills to build, repair, or assemble things, we're resourceful, especially demonstrating our dedication and desire to do everything **just as the boss, or our beloved, likes.**

To build something **"just as"** the architect designed it, we first need the plans and the understanding to read them. Then we require the skills along with the right tools and material to execute the plan.

If God asked us to build a basilica, we'd do it even if it took us years. We wouldn't rest until it was completed. The construction of the Basilica of Quito (in today's photo) began in 1887 *and was consecrated and officially inaugurated 101 years later, on July 12, 1988.* They overcame many setbacks and limitations and completed the work **just as the architect had designed.**

Today's scriptures brought to mind the question, *"how come we don't put the same effort into building and repairing our spiritual lives?"* Hasn't God given us the strength of spirit and faith to believe and do everything the Lord commanded?

"Moses inspected the work and saw that they had done it just as the Lord had commanded. So Moses blessed them" **(Exodus 39:43).** If we do good, as God commanded, we'll be blessed. Jesus didn't say, *"Blessed are those who do things 'just as God commanded,'"* but that is the theme of the entire Bible. What He did say was, *"Not everyone who says to me, 'Lord, Lord,'*

319

will enter the kingdom of heaven, but only the one who does the will of my Father who is in heaven" **(Matthew 7:21).**

God's will is that we **do things just as God commanded**. We have the ability and means to build and mend the world's broken things. How much more beneficial would it be if we put in the same or more effort to **shape our lives according to the design and will of our Heavenly Father?** Just as Moses blessed the people, God will bless our future generations if we do this. After all, **their blessing and prosperity is our blessing.**

Let us pray: Dear God, thank You for being the architect and builder of our faith. Please **help us do everything as you command in Your Holy Word**. We pray in Your Holy Name.

October 18
GROWTH TOWARD MATURITY
Hebrews 6:1

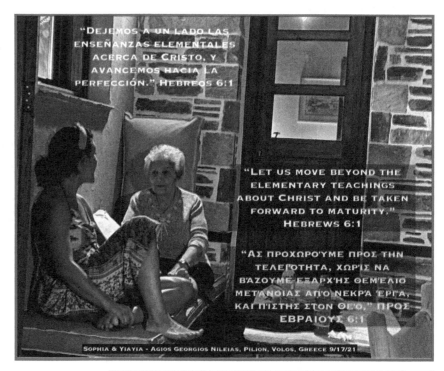

I don't know what my Sophia was talking about with "Yiayia" in this photo. Still, I thank God for her unbreakable connection with Yiayia, one that conveys energy, love, and emotional and spiritual growth. Almost every year, Sophia and Carlos visit Grandma for a couple of weeks in Greece.

God has designed spiritual growth for all adopted children. Those who have tasted the new birth must progress toward spiritual maturity. At some point, students must become teachers, and children become parents, each one transmitting the Word of Life to future generations, thus ensuring continuity of faith and maturity in Jesus Christ.

Today I share some verses that guide and encourage us to be fruitful, to grow emotionally and spiritually **toward maturity:**

> **Those who have tasted the new birth must progress toward spiritual maturity. At some point, students must become teachers, and children become parents, each one transmitting the Word of Life to future generations.**

IN FRUITFULNESS - Only by reaching maturity can we fulfill the great commission - make disciples of the whole world. Jesus said, *"This is to my Father's glory, that you bear much fruit, showing yourselves to be my disciples" (John 15:8).*

IN CHRIST - Jesus established a succession of pastors and teachers *"to equip his people for works of service, so that the body of Christ may be built up ... [so that] 15 speaking the truth in love, we will grow to become in every respect the mature body of him who is the head, that is, Christ"* (Ephesians 4:12,15A).

IN LOVE - *"May the Lord make your love increase and overflow for each other and for everyone else" (1 Thessalonians 3:12A).*

THROUGH THE WORD - *"Like newborn babies, crave pure spiritual milk, so that by it you may grow up in your salvation"* (1 Peter 2:2).

IN GRACE AND KNOWLEDGE - *"But grow in the grace and knowledge of our Lord and Savior Jesus Christ" (2 Peter 3:18A).*

BY ADDITION - *"Make every effort to add to your faith goodness; and to goodness, knowledge; and to knowledge, self-control; and to self-control, perseverance; and to perseverance, godliness" (2 Peter 1:5-6).*

Let us pray: Dear God, thank You for creating unique and intimate moments for us to get closer to You, to know and love you more each day. Help us take advantage of the time to receive the energy, love, and direction from You and achieve the emotional and spiritual growth we need to succeed in this life and glorify Your name. We pray in Jesus's name.

October 19
FAITHFULLY PATIENT PEOPLE

AND SO AFTER WAITING PATIENTLY, ABRAHAM RECEIVED WHAT WAS PROMISED. HEBREWS 6:15

Y ABRAHÁN ESPERÓ CON PACIENCIA, Y RECIBIÓ LO QUE DIOS LE HABÍA PROMETIDO. HEBREOS 6:15

ΚΑΙ ΈΤΣΙ, ΠΡΟΣΜΈΝΟΝΤΑΣ ΜΕ ΥΠΟΜΟΝΉ, ΑΠΉΛΑΥΣΕ ΤΗΝ ΥΠΌΣΧΕΣΗ. ΠΡΟΣ ΕΒΡΑΙΟΥΣ 6:15

BEAUTIFUL SANTORINI, GREECE

Hebrews 6:15

God created us to be **faithfully patient people**. We must learn to **wait with patient faith** because **God fulfills all promises in His way and time.**

IN GOD'S TIME

When Abraham was 75 years old, God said to him, *"I will surely bless you and give you many descendants. And so after waiting patiently, Abraham received what was promised"* **(Hebrews 6:14-15, Genesis 21:5).** We wonder, what kind of patience did Abraham have? Isaac, the son of the promise, was born **25 years later.** Imagine waiting that long to see its fulfillment. Some don't have the faith and patience to wait for **God's time.**

IN GOD'S WAY

Although we may never understand God's ways, the Lord's plans are always good, perfect, timely, and fair. God does things as promised but often doesn't tell us the **when** or **how** He'll fulfill it.

Meanwhile, Abraham's wife, Sarah, impatient and doubting, did things her way, offering her servant to Abraham, saying: *"The Lord has kept me from having children. Go, sleep with my slave; perhaps I can build a family through her"* **(Genesis 16:2).** Abraham was 86 years old when Hagar gave birth to Ishmael **(Genesis 16:16).**

Sometimes we're like Sarah, who initially believed but lost her faith and patience, offering her servant to accelerate God's hand in her way. When Isaac was finally born, Sarah despised Ishmael, and from there, the brothers were separated into two great nations, both blessed, but the promise to bless the whole world would be through Isaac **(Genesis 17:18-21).**

We need the faith of Abraham! Faith is a seed that, when tested, produces **faith and patience** in us. **Romans 5:3-4** says, *"We also glory in our sufferings, because we know that suffering produces perseverance; perseverance, character; and character, hope."*

Let us pray: Dear God, thank You for helping us be a **people of faith and patience** who trust in Your promises. You've done what you promised, and we believe that you'll act likewise in the future. Increase our faith to wait patiently, knowing that you keep every promise, in Your time, and in Your way. We pray in Your Holy Name.

October 20
THE LOVE OF CHRIST
John 13:1

My father, Galo Destruge, was a romantic. In his music collection, one of the old boleros is titled "Unforgettable" by Julio Gutiérrez (1944). Its lyrics say, *"In life, there are loves that can never be forgotten. Unforgettable moments that the heart always retains."* In my life, the love of Christ is incomparable and unsurpassed, even beyond the love I proclaim for my children and grandchildren. We must never forget the love of Christ, our Lord, and Savior!

322

However genuine and deep, human love is born from a heart inclined to selfishness, anger, distrust, and disappointment. Therefore, on Calvary's cross, God showed us the love of Christ as a model to imitate. Our verse says that Jesus had always loved them and *"loved them to the end."* His passion is Divine, self-sacrificing, inseparable, driving, and self-sacrificing.

DIVINE - Being Divine, Christ's love is pure, sincere, and unchanging. Jesus declared, *"As the Father has loved me, so have I loved you. Now remain in my love"* **(John 15:9).**

SELF-SACRIFICING - The love of Christ is never selfish; it doesn't seek its desires but rather the fulfillment of God's will- *"Greater love has no one than this: to lay down one's life for one's friends"* **(John 15:13).**

INSEPARABLE - The love of Christ is unconditional, unchanging, and eternal. It's not subject to human emotions or disappointments. *"Who shall separate us from the love of Christ? Shall trouble or hardship or persecution or famine or nakedness or danger or sword?" (Romans 8:35).*

COMPELLING - His love prompts us to love as Christ loved. *"For Christ's love compels us, because we are convinced that one died for all, and therefore all died"* **(2 Corinthians 5:14).**

SACRIFICIAL - Without deserving it, despite our rebellions, Jesus *"loved me and gave himself for me" (Galatians 2:20).*

Jesus Christ **MANIFESTED His love IN HIS DEATH** - *"This is how we know what love is: Jesus Christ laid down his life for us. And we ought to lay down our lives for our brothers and sisters" (1 John 3:16).*

Let us pray: *"We praise you, God, we praise you, for your Name is near"* **(Psalm 75:1).** Lord, you've manifested Your unforgettable love and presence in our lives, family, and community. Thank you because, by Your love, we're not abandoned without a shield and sustenance. Everything we need comes from you. May our children and their children praise you for eternity.

October 21
DELIVERED FROM FEARS
Psalm 34:4

Very early in the morning, together with our coffee, we seek God, who listens and delivers us from all fears.

As children, we can't understand that parents do their best to raise their children with experiences and lessons that promote socialization which helps surround them with people who demonstrate love and trust. But parents aren't perfect, and sometimes we fail.

Some children grow up learning that sometimes parents unintentionally show a preference for one of their children. Sometimes parents separate/divorce and choose which of their children to live with, thus reinforcing that love is not forever. Based on these experiences, they fear being **abandoned**, not cared for (**listened to**), and **not being loved** even as adults.

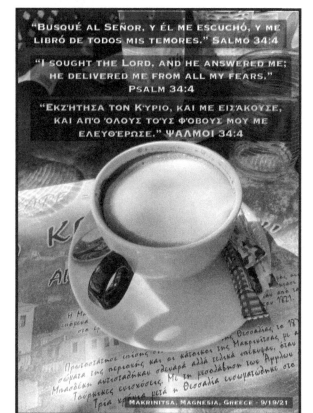

Of the fear of not being loved, traumatized individuals who seek relief from worries tend to distrust and do not expect much from people. In adolescence, they affirm that love is fleeting and sometimes feigned, that love from afar is foolish.

The fear of abandonment causes some to maintain almost every friendly or intimate relationship on the periphery. Some choose to distance themselves from meaningful relationships gradually or abruptly. Some don't have connections with any of their school or college peers.

Fear of not being heard - For half my life (up to age 35), I preferred to listen and be silent in almost every social interaction except at school or work. Religion and math always attracted me, and I was the first to raise my hand to answer questions.

In 1989, I experienced the **"unforgettable and inseparable love of Christ."** *"I sought the Lord, and he answered me; he delivered me from all my fears" (Psalm 34:4).* It was then that I learned that God loves everyone the same but pays more attention to the needy, the orphans, the widows, and the poor. The arm of God is so immense that the Lord can embrace and place a kiss on our cheeks (as my dad used to do), saying, *"This is my Son, whom I love; with him I am well pleased"* **(Matthew 3:17).**

Let us pray: Dear God, thank You for listening and *"delivering us from all our fears."* Only in You do we find true peace, love, and happiness. Your love prompts us to love like you, forgive, listen, trust and welcome others as you do. Thank you for showing us Your love, which is forever and for everyone, without preferences. We pray in Jesus's name.

✚ ✚ ✚ ✚ ✚ ✚

One of the songs of my youth I've engraved in my memory banks is *"Piensalo"* (Think about it) by Raphael. The lyrics say in part, *"Everything ends someday, even love. Nothing is forever. Think about it. Think about it; it's the truth."*

The world teaches us that **nothing lasts forever,** even in our churches. Pastors and priests come and go, we're retired, or we retire voluntarily, some leaving a great void in their communities.

Sometimes parishioners place too much importance on the charisma of the outgoing priest. They stop attending the congregations which had filled a void in their lives for many years. For decades, they continue comparing the successor pastors with their favorite pastor. This practice is not healthy for the spiritual life of the person or the church. We must keep our eyes fixed on our High Priest, Jesus.

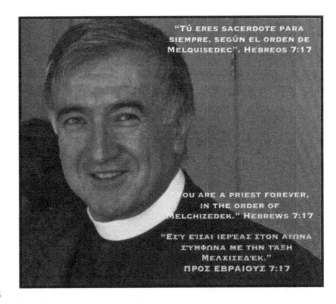

God's Word points to the **eternal Priesthood of Jesus**. *"You are a priest forever, according to the order of Melchizedek"* **(Hebrews 7:17).** Before Jesus, the priests sacrificed animals for the remission of their sins and those of the people. But those priests lived and died, requiring a line of succeeding generations of priests. However, Jesus, who lives eternally, is our **Priest forever.**

Since Jesus lives forever, *"He is able to save completely those who come to God through him, because he always lives to intercede for them" (Hebrews 7:25).* Everything ends someday in this life, but God's love and salvation are forever.

I thank God for the great privilege and honor of serving as a priest in the communities of Norwalk and Bridgeport. I often wish I hadn't retired. But life circumstances and obligations change, and God has called me to dedicate these years to my family, to care for my mother-in-law, and grandchildren, to be a guest preacher and write daily meditations. Praise God!

Let us pray: Dear God, thank You for sending Jesus to be our High Priest, who saved us forever and lives to intercede on our behalf. I pray for those who were part of El Camino and La Gracia and those who've distanced themselves from their churches; grant them the joy and happiness of assembling in the name of Jesus. To Him be all glory, honor, and power.

> **Everything ends someday in this life, but God's love and salvation are forever.**

October 23
TEACHING WITH INTEGRITY
Titus 2:7-8

We're all teachers to someone. Parents teach their children. Older siblings, through words and actions, mentor their younger siblings. Aunts and uncles teach their nieces and nephews, etc. Our example is vital. We can't say *"don't smoke, don't drink"* and do it in front of or hidden from them. Our teaching must be by example and presented with *"integrity, seriousness, and soundness of speech that cannot be condemned"* (Titus 2:7-8).

Titus was sent to Crete to establish churches and elders in each city **(Titus 1:5)** with instructions on what to teach the elders in the congregations so that *"no one will malign the word of God"* **(Titus 2:5).** Elders must be **"temperate, worthy of respect, self-controlled, and sound in faith, in love and in endurance. Likewise, teach the older women to be reverent in the way they live, not to be slanderers or addicted to much wine, but to teach what is good... 6 Similarly, encourage the young men to be self-controlled"** (Titus 2:2–3,6).

Paul highlights the behavior and commitment expected from Titus as a pastor and teacher. *"In everything set them an example by doing what is good. In your teaching show integrity, seriousness and soundness of speech that cannot be condemned, so that those who oppose you may be ashamed because they have nothing bad to say about us"* (Titus 2:7-8).

God expects nothing less of you and me as teachers and coaches to those under our care and direction. We're to teach the Word with integrity to last and produce much fruit for generations.

As a pastor, God entrusted me to deliver a triune Bible-based message: 1. **You are loved.** 2. **God is with you**, and 3. **The best is yet to come.** As parents, brothers, uncles, coaches, teachers, etc., God commissioned us to teach His sheep with integrity and seriousness, with wholesome and true words, and by the example of our life which follows the Master's teachings, **so that God's Word is not blasphemed.**

Let us pray: Dear God, you've given us a great responsibility! Lives and families depend on the integrity and truthfulness of our teachings. Grant us Your Holy Spirit to help us teach with excellence and joy so that Your Word may flow throughout the world, transforming and renewing lives, families, and communities. We pray in Your Holy Name.

October 24
ONLY JESUS SAVES
John 5:39

Moses instructed the people that God's Words *"are not just idle words for you—they are your life. By them you will live long in the land"* **(Deuteronomy 32:47).** Jesus says that the Scriptures *"testify about me"* **(John 5:39).**

Jesus addressed the religious leaders who were looking for an excuse to kill him. *"You study the Scriptures diligently because you think that in them you have eternal life. These are the very Scriptures that testify about me, yet you refuse to come to me to have life"* **(John 5:39-40).** They rejected Him, believing that the mere study of the Word would save their lives. The religious leaders didn't seek salvation through the promised Messiah but via works of study and observance of rules.

> You study the Scriptures diligently because you think that in them you have eternal life. These are the very Scriptures that testify about me. John 5:39
>
> Ustedes escudriñan las Escrituras, porque les parece que en ellas tienen la vida eterna; iy son ellas las que dan testimonio de mí! Juan 5:39
>
> "Ερευνάτε τις γραφές, επειδή εσείς νομίζετε ότι μέσα σ' αυτές έχετε αιώνια ζωή· και εκείνες είναι που δίνουν μαρτυρία για μένα." ΚΑΤΑ ΙΩΑΝΝΗΝ 5:39

Following the resurrection, Jesus appeared to the disciples and, after eating, said to them: *"This is what I told you while I was still with you: 'Everything must be fulfilled that is written about me in the Law of Moses, the Prophets and the Psalms.' Then he opened their minds so they could understand the Scriptures. He told them, 'This is what is written: The Messiah will suffer and rise from the dead on the third day, and repentance for the forgiveness of sins will be preached in his name to all nations, beginning at Jerusalem'"* **(Luke 24:44-47).**

My beloved, the Bible is the map that reveals the essence of Jesus Christ and leads us to our Holy refuge with strategically placed markers along the way. Jesus Christ is the most desired pearl in the world. Studying God's Word is useful and necessary to discover the Way. However, faith and gratitude are indispensable for God to open our *"minds so [we] could understand the Scriptures"* and receive the Grace of God through the Holy Spirit.

God *"saved us, not because of righteous things we had done, but because of his mercy. He saved us through the washing of rebirth and renewal by the Holy Spirit, whom he poured out on us generously through Jesus Christ our Savior, so that, having been justified by his grace, we might become heirs having the hope of eternal life"* **(Titus 3:5–7).**

Let us pray: Dear God, thank You for helping us understand that Your salvation is not by works but by grace and that *"Salvation is found in no one else, for there is no other name under heaven given to mankind by which we must be saved"* **(Acts 4:12).** We pray in Jesus's name.

> The religious leaders didn't seek salvation through the promised Messiah but via works of study and observance of rules.

October 25
LIVING STONES
1 Peter 2:5

Jesus changed Simon's name (which means one who listens), telling him, *"You are Simon son of John. You will be called Cephas" (which, when translated, is Peter)" (John 1:42).* **Peter** comes from the Greek; *"Pétros - G-4074 Πέτρος; a (piece of) a rock."* Peter, the first spiritual leader of the Christian church, was not the cornerstone, but a piece of THE ROCK, who is Jesus Christ. Jesus transformed him into a living stone and is doing the same with us, building the Kingdom of God and bringing hope and love to God's lost sheep.

Like Peter, God chose, rescued, and polished us like living stones to build us up as a robust, resistant, and precious spiritual house. We were created to surrender our love, devotion, worship, and praise to the Lord and hope to His people. *"Therefore, I urge you, brothers and sisters, in view of God's mercy, to offer your bodies as a living sacrifice, holy and pleasing to God—this is your true and proper worship"* **(Romans 12:1).**

God calls us to offer our lives as living stones, founded on Jesus Christ, the living, chosen, and precious stone as a living sacrifice, holy and pleasing to God, to build up the people of God. *"As you come to him, the living Stone—rejected by humans but chosen by God and precious to him— you also, like living stones, are being built into a spiritual house to be a holy priesthood, offering spiritual sacrifices acceptable to God through Jesus Christ" (1 Peter 2:4-5).*

My beloved, let us keep our eyes fixed on the author and finisher of our faith, on the cornerstone on which we must build our spiritual homes and temples of praise and honor to God. **1 Peter 2:6-7** says, *"See, I lay a stone in Zion, a chosen and precious cornerstone, and the one who trusts in him will never be put to shame. Now to you who believe, this stone is precious."*

Let us pray: Dear God, thank You for transforming us into living stones and sacrifices for You. Thank you for calling us to be *"a holy priesthood, offering spiritual sacrifices acceptable to God through Jesus Christ"* **(1 Peter 2:5).** Help us at every opportunity to bless our children, family, and friends with spiritual sacrifices that lead to Your heavenly abode. We pray in Jesus's name.

✛ ✛ ✛ ✛ ✛ ✛

October 26
FOR THE SINS OF THE PARENTS
Ezekiel 18:30

The ancient belief was that children paid for the sins of their parents. But in Ezekiel, God nullified that form of punishment. From then on, God said, *"The one who sins is the one who will die" (Ezekiel 18:4).*

Based on that belief, *"As he went along, he saw a man blind from birth. His disciples asked him, "Rabbi, who sinned, this man or his parents, that he was born blind? "Neither this man nor his parents sinned," said Jesus, "but this happened so that the works of God might be displayed in him"* **(John 9:1-3).**

"VOY A JUZGAR A CADA UNO DE USTEDES SEGÚN SUS CAMINOS, POR LO TANTO, VUÉLVANSE A MÍ Y APÁRTENSE DE TODAS SUS TRANSGRESIONES, PARA QUE SU MALDAD NO SEA LA CAUSA DE SU RUINA. PALABRA DE DIOS EL SEÑOR." EZEQUIEL 18:30

"I WILL JUDGE EACH OF YOU ACCORDING TO YOUR OWN WAYS, DECLARES THE SOVEREIGN LORD. REPENT! TURN AWAY FROM ALL YOUR OFFENSES; THEN SIN WILL NOT BE YOUR DOWNFALL." EZEKIEL 18:30

"ΘΑ ΣΑΣ ΚΡΊΝΩ, ΚΆΘΕ ΈΝΑΝ ΣΎΜΦΩΝΑ ΜΕ ΤΟΥΣ ΔΡΌΜΟΥΣ ΤΟΥ, ΛΈΕΙ Ο ΚΎΡΙΟΣ Ο ΘΕΌΣ. ΜΕΤΑΝΟΉΣΤΕ, ΚΑΙ ΕΠΙΣΤΡΈΨΤΕ ΑΠΌ ΌΛΕΣ ΤΙΣ ΑΝΟΜΊΕΣ ΣΑΣ· ΚΑΙ ΔΕΝ ΘΑ ΕΊΝΑΙ ΣΕ ΣΑΣ Η ΑΝΟΜΊΑ ΓΙΑ ΑΠΏΛΕΙΑ."
ΙΕΖΕΚΙΉΛ 18:30

God's work is evident in us receiving forgiveness and eternal life (through faith in Jesus's sacrifice) instead of punishment for our rebellions. Not being worthy of such great love and sacrifice, our hearts fill with gratitude, and with the help of the Holy Spirit, we attempt to be faithful and obedient to God, doing the good that God asks of us and avoiding evil.

The ancient belief was that children paid for the sins of their parents. But in Ezekiel, God nullified that form of punishment. From then on, God said, *"The one who sins is the one who will die" (Ezekiel 18:4).*

Under the law covenant, those who sinned deserved punishment. But God offers forgiveness to those who previously broke the law if they repented of their sins. If that person *"keeps all my decrees and does what is just and right, that person will surely live; they will not die" (Ezekiel 18:21).*

Likewise, God establishes punishment for those who previously acted justly. *"But if a righteous person turns from their righteousness and commits sin and does the same detestable things the*

329

wicked person does, will they live? None of the righteous things that person has done will be remembered. Because of the unfaithfulness, they are guilty of and because of the sins they have committed, they will die" (Ezekiel 18:24).

Thankfully, God establishes that the righteous father will not die for the injustice of his son, nor will the honest son die for the transgression of his father. *"The righteousness of the righteous will be credited to them, and the wickedness of the wicked will be charged against them" (Ezekiel 18:20).*

Let us pray: Dear God, thank You for making us recipients of Your love and mercy through the sacrifice of Jesus Christ on the Cross. Thank you that Jesus is the only one who died for our sins. Guide our thoughts, words, and actions so we may act with justice and righteousness in everything. We pray in Jesus's name.

October 27
WHAT DO YOU WANT ME TO DO FOR YOU?

"What do you want me to do for you?" Mark 10:51

"¿Qué quieres que yo haga por ti"? Marcos 10:51

"Τι θέλεις να σου κάνω;." ΚΑΤΑ ΜΑΡΚΟΝ 10:51

I love the story of blind Bartimaeus because it's my story, and I believe, with some variations, your account. Until we met the Lord, we were on the sidelines, blinded by fear, anger, lies, racial and political divisions, jealousy, denial, desires, temptations, etc.

Blind Bartimaeus wasn't on *"the road of success"* but instead on the sidelines, like many of us **begging**;
- for a stroke of luck,
- for a second opportunity,
- for a job,
- for a chance to demonstrate our skills,
- to be healed of our spiritual blindness,
- for a light to guide us out of these long quarantine tunnels.

Bartimaeus was persistent in shouting, *"Jesus, Son of David, have mercy on me!" (Mark 10:47).* The marginalized (the poor, the lame, the homeless) back then, and even now, are *"seen, but not heard."* They have no voice or vote. I'm sure that nine out of ten people ignore them. *"Many rebuked him and told him to be quiet, but he shouted all the more" (v.48).*

We often don't cry out for fear of being politically incorrect. However, the fact remains that we need a healer. So be persistent in shouting out. Jesus won't respond as the world does. He doesn't want us to remain marginalized and silent. On the contrary, His ear is attentive to the cry of His sheep.

Jesus asked the disciples to bring Bartimaeus to Him. And here's the question I love: *"What do you want me to do for you?" Jesus asked him. The blind man said, 'Rabbi, I want to see.' 'Go,' said Jesus, 'your faith has healed you.' Immediately he received his sight and followed Jesus along the road"* **(Mark 10:51-52).**

Jesus asks us today. *"What do you want me to do for you?"*

Elisha asked for a double portion of Elijah's Spirit, and his request was granted because he didn't depart from his master **(2 Kings 2:9).**

Consider: What do you want Jesus to do for you today? What part of your life needs healing, forgiveness, renewal, and restoration?

Jesus said, *"Ask and it will be given to you" (Matthew 7:7).* If we ask with faith, we'll be healed **(Mark 10:52).**

Let us pray: Dear God, we cry out as Elisha and Bartimaeus. Grant us Your Holy Spirit and increase our faith in Christ, our physician par excellence. Heal and guide us to Your light. We pray in Your Holy Name.

✛ ✛ ✛ ✛ ✛ ✛

October 28
WIDOWS, ORPHANS, AND FOREIGNERS
Psalm 146:9

God loves everyone the same but pays more attention to the needy, orphans, widows, and foreigners.

Speaking to widows, God says in *Isaiah 54:4-5, "Do not be afraid; you will not be put to shame. Do not fear disgrace; you will not be humiliated. You will forget the shame of your youth and remember no more the reproach of your widowhood. For your Maker is your husband."* The widows will never again be seen as abandoned women or sad in spirit because God will gather and show compassion to them.

331

My mom passed away in 2008, and my dad in 2012. Soon after, my brother John said, *"now we are orphans."* Although I was 58 years old, the notion of being an orphan was etched in my mind. But, thank God, who is *"A father to the fatherless, a defender of widows"* **(Psalm 68:5).** God warns us, *"Do not take advantage of the widow or the fatherless" (Exodus 22:22).* On the contrary, we're *"to look after orphans and widows in their distress"* **(James 1:27).**

About us foreigners, God's commandment says, *"do not mistreat them. The foreigner residing among you must be treated as your native-born. Love them as yourself, for you were foreigners in Egypt" (Leviticus 19:33-34).*

My beloved, we rejoice that God *"upholds the cause of the oppressed and gives food to the hungry. The Lord sets prisoners free, the Lord gives sight to the blind, the Lord lifts up those who are bowed down, the Lord loves the righteous" (Psalm 146:7-8).* In the same way that God has poured out His love, care, and protection on orphans, widows, and foreigners, God commands us to *"uphold the cause of the poor and the oppressed" (Psalm 82:3b).*

Let us pray: Dear God, thank You for Your great and inexhaustible love and care. Grant that we may renew our covenant of love daily with you and our neighbors, particularly with foreigners, orphans, widows, and the poor. Grant us eyes to see and ears to perceive the needs of Your sons and daughters, and give us the courage to receive and support them in their distress. We pray in Jesus's name.

October 29
REASON TO REJOICE

"For all have sinned and fall short of the glory of God." Romans 3:23

"por cuanto todos pecaron y están destituidos de la gloria de Dios". Romanos 3:23

"δεδομένου ότι, όλοι αμάρτησαν, και στερούνται τη δόξα τού Θεού·"
ΠΡΟΣ ΡΩΜΑΙΟΥΣ 3:23

Even though we've all sinned and fallen short of the glory of God, in Christ, we have good reason to rejoice: **God's love and grace** (unmerited favor) **are freely available to ALL!**

Regardless of our past or the magnitude of our disobedience, our life is essential to God. The proof is in the story of the harlot Rahab who helped Joshua to conquer the city of Jerico. In **Matthew 1:5**, we discover that Rahab was the great-grandmother of King David, from whom stems the line of Jesus.

Your life is of great value. God alone knows in detail the plans He has for you. God says, *"For I know the plans I have for you, 'declares the Lord, 'plans to prosper you and not to harm you, plans to give you hope and a future'" (Jeremiah 29:11).* God has provided the way for you and me to be found innocent, freed from condemnation, and adopted into God's family. This is a great reason to rejoice.

We rejoice because God's justice requires that the wages of sin be death, but instead of this punishment, God offers us the gift of eternal life through Jesus Christ our Lord **(Romans 6:23).**

Look at it this way: If you had received a speeding fine, and the judge, having video proof of Your infraction, declares you guilty, but he pays the required fine of $200, wouldn't you be jumping for joy and gratitude? We've been convicted of sinning against God, and Jesus paid our penalty. The punishment for sin was death, but Jesus paid our debt with His life. Would you agree that it's a great reason to rejoice?

Good or bad, our past doesn't determine whether God will redeem us or not. The faith that we put in Jesus's redeeming work makes God's grace effective.

Let us pray: Dear God, thank You because, despite our inability to seek you and do the good you ask of us, you don't get tired of creating ways for us to reconcile with you. Lord, I'm not worthy of Your love and grace, but say Your Word, and I will be cleansed, forgiven, and received within Your family. May my mouth and heart never tire of declaring Your grace, love, and wonders. We pray in Jesus's name.

> **GOD'S LOVE AND GRACE (UNMERITED FAVOR) ARE FREELY AVAILABLE TO ALL!**

October 30
WHO IS RAHAB?
Joshua 2:12

I'm thankful for God's goodness. On Thursday, October 29, 2020, God granted my daughter Sophia the joy and privilege of being a mother. I congratulate Carlos and Sophia for the love with which they've brought my grandson, Lázaro Elias Aristizábal, to this world. I know he will have a wonderful life because love and tenderness abound in his parents and family. I pray that the Lord continues showing kindness to all our children and families.

The prostitute Rahab's prayer was for mercy in exchange for hiding two spies Joshua sent to Jericho. She asks for this guarantee: *"Now then, please swear to me by the Lord that you will show kindness to my family, because I have shown kindness to you"* **(Joshua 2:12).**

Aside from saving the two spies, Rahab doesn't appear to be of great importance, mainly because of her profession. She was a woman, perhaps insignificant and isolated from society. But God chose her so that Jesus the Savior would be born through her lineage. In the Bible, we discover that *"Salmon the father of Boaz, whose mother was Rahab, Boaz the father of Obed, whose mother was Ruth, Obed the father of Jesse, and Jesse the father of King David"* **(Matthew 1:5-6,16).** And Jesus was born from the line of David.

It's wonderful to see God's favor working through people that the world, at some point, had discarded. **God doesn't choose by appearances, greatness, or riches to bless the world but looks** to the person's heart to measure their flexibility to be tested and refurbished into a vessel of honor and blessing.

We don't know God's plans for our children, but we trust they're good. Like Rahab, their significance might be realized generations later. From Rahab to Jesus, there were 17 generations. You may think your life doesn't make a difference, but God doesn't do anything routine. Your Architect and Builder will *"complete the good work He begun in your life"* **(Philippians 1:6).** Then *the world will know you were born for greatness;* that there's a God for whom nothing is impossible, too late, or of no use.

Let us pray: Dear God, thank You for showing us that You use simple things to bless our world. Thank you for your kindness toward our family. Bless our children and their generations. We pray in the name of Jesus.

> *The world will know you were born for greatness; that there's a God for whom nothing is impossible, too late, or of no use.*

✝ ✝ ✝ ✝ ✝ ✝

October 31
YOUR HOUSE, A HOLY REFUGE
Joshua 2:19b

When we put our hope in The Divine Architect by faith, God turns our house into a holy refuge. Today we continue exploring more details about Rahab's life and role in God's salvation plan.

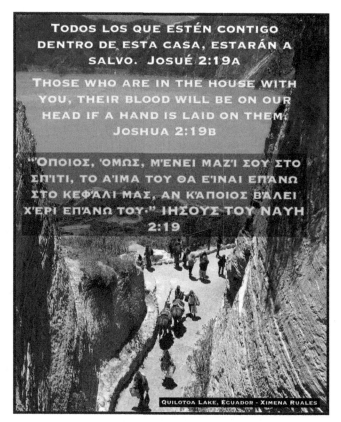

TODOS LOS QUE ESTÉN CONTIGO DENTRO DE ESTA CASA, ESTARÁN A SALVO. JOSUÉ 2:19A

THOSE WHO ARE IN THE HOUSE WITH YOU, THEIR BLOOD WILL BE ON OUR HEAD IF A HAND IS LAID ON THEM. JOSHUA 2:19B

"ΟΠΟΙΟΣ, ΌΜΩΣ, Μ'ΕΝΕΙ ΜΑΖΊ ΣΟΥ ΣΤΟ ΣΠΊΤΙ, ΤΟ Α'ΙΜΑ ΤΟΥ ΘΑ Ε'ΙΝΑΙ ΕΠΆΝΩ ΣΤΟ ΚΕΦΆΛΙ ΜΑΣ, ΑΝ ΚΆΠΟΙΟΣ ΒΆΛΕΙ ΧΈΡΙ ΕΠΆΝΩ ΤΟΥ." ΙΗΣΟΥΣ ΤΟΥ ΝΑΥΗ 2:19

QUILOTOA LAKE, ECUADOR - XIMENA RUALES

Knowing that God was with Israel, Rahab hid Joshua's spies and informed them that all of Jericho was demoralized because of them **(Joshua 2:9)**. The spies gave three conditions for her and her entire family to be spared from the destruction that awaited the city of Jericho: (1) tie the scarlet cord on the window **(v.18a)**. (2) Everyone must stay inside the house **(v.19)**, and (3) not report them to the authorities **(v.20)**.

Rahab risked her life by associating with the Israelites, but she believed that Israel's God would reward her kindness. **James 2:25** says, *"was not even Rahab the prostitute considered righteous for what she did when she gave lodging to the spies and sent them off in a different direction?"*

334

Immediately after hearing the three conditions, by faith, Rahab tied the red ribbon on the designated window. She **trusted** the messenger's promise, gathered her entire family, and everyone in her house was saved from destruction by the earthquake that shook and the fire that burned Jericho to ashes. **It was an act of faith on Rehab's part that saved her entire family.**

Staying indoors reminds us of when the angel of God passed through all of Egypt, taking the life of every firstborn **(Exodus 12:29)**. Israel was instructed to stay inside the house, celebrating the Lord's Passover. All of Egypt went into mourning that night, but not so with Israel. Everyone who remained inside the holy refuge was saved. Rahab believed Joshua's messengers, and she and her household were saved.

God invites us to trust His Divine Word, to make our home a holy refuge for this and our future generations. **Only by heeding God's conditions found in the Holy Scriptures do we have hope that God will turn our house of straw into a holy refuge and fortress for our children and family.**

Let us pray: Dear God, thank You for revealing Your salvation plan through the life and faith of Rahab, a member of Jesus's family by faith and marriage. Allow us to place our lives and homes in Your hands so that You may strengthen and turn them into sacred and consecrated temples for Your service. We pray in Your Holy Name.

> **Only by heeding each of God's conditions found in the Holy Scriptures, do we have hope that God will turn our house of straw into a holy refuge and fortress for our children and family.**

- NOVEMBER -
NEW GENERATIONS -
GLASS / ARISTIZABAL

And so, we arrive at your generation, the one we know and love the most. One that carries roots back to Europe, and South America, with surnames in your bloodline that no longer register in your birth certificates but which have shaped and determined the place and time of your birth. I pray that you won't forget these names, which are part of who I am and where you come from. That you imitate the courage and faith of our ancestors. **Destruge, Illingworth, Hunt, Villa, Cosio, Villamar, Nazíroglou (which became Xanthópoulos), Koktsidis, Sandoval, Ortega. And to these names, we joyfully add Glass and Aristizabal.**

Ségolène and Salomé Destruge-Glass - your parents met and fell in love online. Though they were on opposite sides of the United States, they overcame all obstacles to shorten the distance, much like a romantic movie. They persevered until God finally joined them together in marriage. **Ségolène, I love you, my first granddaughter, my joy and gratitude.** When you were born (April 15, 2016), your dad and I were the happiest men. I had never seen your dad happier than when he presented you to us in the hospital room. You are unique, energetic, beautiful (like your mom and dad) and so intelligent. Rocking you to sleep and napping with you are precious, unforgettable moments. The thought of you reading this journal inspires me to be a better writer and compose more songs. I love creating songs with you. I pray someday we'll publish something together.

Salomé, our second granddaughter, born September 14, 2019, you're somewhat quiet, introverted like me, but so filled with love, joy, and tenderness. COVID-19 kept us apart for nearly ten months, and we missed being part of your life then. But I'm so grateful that we're back together again and making up for the lost time. I thank God for you, my sunshine. You give the sweetest hugs and kisses!

Lázaro Elías Aristizabal Destruge, agorakimou, you arrived unexpectedly. On March 17, 2020, while quarantined in Cuenca, Ecuador, your parents called to announce that they were expecting you. What a great and long-awaited answer to prayer you are. You arrived on October 29, 2020, and changed our lives completely. Your contagious joy encourages me to *"rejoice in the Lord, always" (Philippians 4:4).* Your happiness reminds me of your uncle and God-parent Jean-Paul when he was a baby.

Our family would be incomplete if we didn't mention our dear grand-nephews (your cousins), **Harniman-Destruge** (Henry and Stella), and **Couch-Destruge** (Thalia, Nathaniel Simon, and Daphne Paloma), beloved members of our family, with whom we're blessed to share to a large degree, the same blood and history.

Henry, because you were the first of the grand-nephews, we had the joy of spending all our time and attention with you. I've always told you that we love you the longest. Thia Mery and I were incredibly blessed to be your babysitters during your first two and one-half years. It was a gift to watch you grow, take the first steps, and say your first words. As you grew and went to school, I was blessed to pick you up from school, attend spelling bees, help you with homework and explore the Norwalk parks. Although we joke about **when I love you the most**, I truly love you all the time and am grateful that you're in our life. You taught me to be a patient great-uncle and grandfather for the rest of your cousins.

To each of you, **Henry, Stelli, Thalia, Simo, and Palomita**, I can't wait to see what you and God will make of your lives, but I believe they are good and honorable and pray that you may know that you were created to achieve great things for God, family, community, and humanity. Each of you is precious and loved, and you fulfill our dreams. I speak for megaly Yiayía, Yiayía Fanny, and thia Mery in saying; We love you to the end of the world and back!

November 1
THE ANTIDOTE AGAINST EVIL
Romans 12:21

My beloved friends and family, the blood of my blood, I always thank God for you in my prayers. I pray that we are nourished and strengthened in the spirit so that love and charity may abound among us and that by doing good, we can overcome evil in our world, spreading God's love, starting with those surrounding us daily. Today's spiritual breakfast is a portion of the antidote against evil.

"NO SEAS VENCIDO POR EL MAL, SINO VENCE CON EL BIEN EL MAL."
ROMANOS 12:21

"DO NOT BE OVERCOME BY EVIL, BUT OVERCOME EVIL WITH GOOD."
ROMANS 12:21

"ΝΑ ΗΗ ΝΙΚΙΈΣΑΙ ΑΠΌ ΤΟ ΚΑΚΌ, ΑΛΛΆ ΝΑ ΝΙΚΆΣ ΤΟ ΚΑΚΌ ΔΙΑΜΈΣΟΥ ΤΟΎ ΑΓΑΘΟΎ." ΠΡΟΣ ΡΩΜΑΙΟΥΣ 12:21

MY BEAUTIFUL BRIDE AND I AT CHARLES BRIDGE, PRAGUE. 8/14/2018
MI PRECIOSA ESPOSA Y YO EN EL CHARLES BRIDGE, PRAGUE. 14 DE AGOSTO, 2018

Our body is a beautiful mechanism. It warns us when it detects a virus through our temperature. Infection or any foreign organism triggers the alarm, and the temperature rises. So, we take medicine to normalize the temperature and fight the virus until we heal entirely.

Spiritually we know that evil has infected us when the temperature of anger rises out of nowhere, and we begin to repay evil with evil. God warns us, *"Do not repay anyone evil for evil" (Romans 12:17A).* Our love for God compels us to respond peacefully to insults, slander, and contempt because love doesn't take revenge but leaves room for God to judge **(v.19).**

And yet, we're defeated by evil when we stop admiring the good God has placed in our neighbors and only observe and criticize their faults - the things that annoy us. We're overcome by evil when we selfishly seek our good, forgetting the covenant we made with God and the person that years back was deeply loved and seen as the most precious being in our world.

The enemy has convinced many people that everything comes to an end, even love. And when love dies, it is better to separate. But that is not true. Love does not die. Love never fails nor ceases to exist. As we age, we begin to understand and appreciate that love transcends trials and barriers, and over the years, it takes different and better forms of expression which fill us with gratitude. Unfortunately, some finally appreciate the nature of love only after having lost or rejected it.

Let us pray: Dear Lord, grant us the antidote to overcome everything that opposes the love you've planned for our lives and that of our children and their children. We pray in Jesus's name.

November 2
THE PROMISED LIGHT

"You, Lord, keep my lamp burning; my God turns my darkness into light." Psalm 18:28

"Señor, mi Dios, tú mantienes mi lámpara encendida; ¡tú eres la luz de mis tinieblas"!
Salmo 18:28

"Επειδή, εσύ θα φωτίσεις το λυχνάρι μου· ο Κύριος, ο Θεός μου, θα φωτίσει το σκοτάδι μου."
ΨΑΛΜΟΙ 18:28

Whatever our adversity or darkness, we trust in God's Word, which promises to light our way to victory. God won't let us fight in the dark, but will offer light to the obedient, righteous, just, benevolent followers of Jesus, who make up the future church of Christ.

THE OBEDIENT - trust fully in God's promises. They don't lose hope that God will illuminate the way at the right moment. *"What you decide on will be done, and light will shine on your ways" (Job 22:28).*

THE RIGHTEOUS AND JUST - reflect God's goodness, justice, and compassion. *"Even in darkness light dawns for the upright" (Psalm 112:4).* When we act justly and righteously, God promises to shine His light on our path even in darkness **(Psalm 97:11)**. *"The path of the righteous is like the morning sun, shining ever brighter till the full light of day" (Proverbs 4:18).*

THE BENEVOLENT - In **Isaiah 58:6-8**, God shows us the fast that is pleasing to the Lord; *"to loose the chains of injustice and untie the cords of the yoke, to set the oppressed free and break every yoke! Is it not to share your food with the hungry and to provide the poor wanderer with shelter—when you see the naked, to clothe them, and not to turn away from your own flesh and blood?"* When we do these things out of love and gratitude, *"then your light will break forth like the dawn, and your healing will quickly appear; then your righteousness will go before you, and the glory of the Lord will be your rear guard" (v.8).*

THE FOLLOWERS OF CHRIST - enjoy the light of life. Jesus said: *"I am the light of the world. Whoever follows me will never walk in darkness, but will have the light of life" (John 8:12).* Therefore, we freely and generously share this loving light with our neighbors. *"Anyone who loves their brother and sister lives in the light, and there is nothing in them to make them stumble" (1 John 2:10).*

Let us pray: Dear God, we await the day when our churches reflect Jesus's qualities, who gave His life so that it could rise again. Help us be just, righteous, benevolent, and obedient as Jesus was so that no one may say that the church is irrelevant, dead, and desolate. We pray in Your Holy Name.

November 3
LOVE - THE DISCIPLESHIP TEST
John 13:35

The first and greatest commandment is to love God above all things **(Mark 12:30).** It's essential in our lives to demonstrate our vertical love toward God.

Jesus identifies love as the test of our discipleship. The greatest wish of parents is that their children love each other. As a good parent, God's second greatest commandment is equal to the first but directed horizontally toward our neighbors. Our heavenly Father commands us to *"love our neighbor as ourselves"* (**Mark 12:33**).

An interpreter of the law asked Jesus, *"Who is my neighbor?" (Luke 10:29).* Today, we understand that we should love everyone around us, including those that aren't part of our community. This includes those passing through our neighborhoods and individuals who don't share our religious, political, or civic vision. **Loving them means treating them as we'd like them to treat our children in similar situations or us.**

> The greatest wish of parents is that their children love each other. As a good parent, God's second greatest commandment is directed horizontally toward our neighbors. Our heavenly Father commands us to *"love our neighbor as ourselves."*

We need the Holy Spirit's help to love God and others as Jesus loved us. In one of my favorite Gospel scenes, Jesus asks Peter, *"do you love me more than these?" (John 21:15)*. Jesus uses the Greek word "αγαπάς" (**agape** - love). Peter responds with the word "φιλώ (filo)," which means *"to like"* as a friend. Knowing that Peter still can't love as Christ loves, Jesus downgrades the question to *"do you like me more than these?"* Peter affirms, "yes," and Jesus entrusts him to *"feed my sheep" (v.17)*, which means "love my sheep."

My beloved, loving God and one another (**the golden rule**) is the daily nourishment that strengthens our faith. It's the compass that guides our actions, intentions, and words. Our spiritual GPS (God Positioning System) leads us on the right track, ensuring that we reach the heavenly mansion. Love is our antidote against the evil virus, but most of all, it's proof that we are Jesus's disciples.

Let us pray: Dear God, grant that the Spirit of Christ may abide in us and allow us to show agape love to other Christians and to all whom you place in our path. This way, the world will know that we are Jesus's disciples. We pray in Your Holy Name.

November 4
THE PROOF OF GOD'S LOVE
Romans 5:6

Have you ever wondered, **"How can I know God loves me?"** You can find multiple proofs of God's love for you in the Bible!

Proof # 1- HIS SACRIFICIAL LOVE- In **Romans 5:6**, we discover God's love for you and me. *"You see, at just the right time, when we were still powerless, Christ died for the ungodly."*

Proof # 2 - HIS SUBSTITUTIONARY ATONING LOVE - *"But God demonstrates his own love for us in"* that Jesus took our place and punishment on the cross *(Romans 5:8, 1 John 3:16A).*

Proof # 3 - HIS ADOPTIVE LOVE - *"See what great love the Father has lavished on us, that we should be called children of God!" (1 John 3:1A).*

Proof # 4 – HIS SAVING AND LIFE-GIVING LOVE - *"But because of his great love for us, God, who is rich in mercy, made us alive with Christ even when we were dead in transgressions—it is by grace you have been saved" (Ephesians 2:4-5).* **John 3:16**, perhaps the best-known Bible verse in the world, affirms God's universal love: *"For God so loved the world that he gave his one and only Son, that whoever believes in him shall not perish but have eternal life."*

Proof # 5 - HIS POWERFUL LOVE - In **Ephesians 3:17-19**, Saint Paul intercedes with prayer so that *"being rooted and established in love, [we] may have power, together with all the Lord's holy people, to grasp how wide and long and high and deep is the love of Christ, and to know this love that surpasses knowledge—that you may be filled to the measure of all the fullness of God."*

Proof # 6 – HIS VICTORIOUS LOVE - God's love is so great that it gives us victory over evil. *"No one who is born of God will continue to sin, because God's seed remains in them; they cannot go on sinning, because they have been born of God" (1 John 3:9).*

Let us pray: Dear God, thank You for the abundant proof of Your universal love recorded in Your Holy Bible so that we may *"grasp how wide and long and high and deep is the love of*

Christ" (Ephesians 3:18). Grant that we may trust and study Your love letter to help us discover who You are, who we are, our purpose, and the type of love that we must show to our neighbors. We pray with grateful hearts in Jesus's name.

November 5
GOD-CENTERED
Psalm 127:1

In the Hebrew tradition, building a house meant raising a family, as seen in **Ruth 4:11**. *"May the Lord make the woman who is coming into your home like Rachel and Leah, who together built up the family of Israel."*

Our verse tells us that if God is not at the center of our plans, desires, aspirations, defenses, efforts, and labors, life

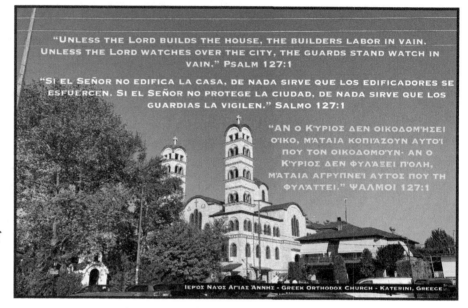

itself is in vain; or, as the psalmist said, *"vanity of vanities" (Ecclesiastes 1:2).* It's like *"chasing after the wind"* **(v.14).**

In Hebrew, the word שָׁוְא **(shav)** means *"vain, useless, misleading, false, hypocritical, lying, vanity."* We understand that nothing makes sense or purpose if God doesn't direct our home, employment, business, ministry, family, thoughts, and words. Everything is like *chasing after the wind.*

My brothers and I had a musical group called Los Monjes. We worked in bars and dance halls, encouraging the fleeting joy of couples and drinking buddies. We always dreamed of recording our music, but it never happened. However, when God became the center of my life, I joined a band (Brand New Spirit) that praised God by bringing original praise music to hospices and churches, and in two years, we recorded a cassette. **Lesson**: God blesses and prospers our efforts when we place Him at the center.

Jesus says, *"They worship me in vain; their teachings are merely human rules"* **(Mark 7:7).** If God is not at the center, everything we propose is in vain. But, if we treasure God's Word, we are saved and will not have *"believed in vain"* **(1 Corinthians 15:2).**

342

I worked for many years in the retirement savings industry, sharing that retirement planning would also be vanity if God is not in the center. I'm thankful that God was present as a powerful force helping those who sought to build a spiritual house in which the Lord would be their center and foundation.

Let us pray: Dear God, we need you to be at the center of our plans, to have the certainty that we've not *"ran or labored in vain" (Philippians 2:16)*. Thank you for making us recipients of Your grace and love. We know that our efforts are not in vain because you've built a mansion in heaven so that where You are, we may also be together with the family we've raised with tears, sacrifices, joys, and **divine inspiration**. Thank you, in Jesus's name.

> If God is not at the center, everything we propose is in vain. But, if we treasure God's Word, we are saved and will not have *"believed in vain"* **(1 Corinthians 15:2).**

November 6
JUST AS COMMANDED
Joshua 8:35

In Joshua's reading, we see the beginnings of the transition of power (from Moses to Joshua). In this ceremony, God renews His covenant with the people through Joshua's leadership.

Three things stood out for me in reading Joshua. As the new supreme commander, 1. Joshua built an altar *"as Moses had commanded"* **(v.31)**. 2. He organized the people *"just as Moses had commanded"* **(v.33),** and 3. he *"read all the words of the law"* **(v.34)**.

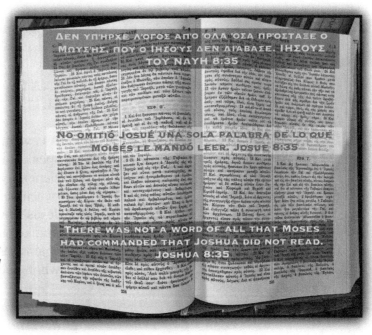

Let's look at these three points in detail:
1. Joshua built an altar just *"as Moses had commanded"* **(v.31)**.

It's natural that a new commander such as Joshua might ignore the instructions of the previous commander, in this case, Moses. Some might say, *"I'm in charge now, and things will be done as I order!"* But Joshua was a humble servant who valued the instructions received from his teacher Moses. Joshua complied with each of them, just *"as Moses had commanded"* because he knew that God verbalized all of them!

343

Joshua built the altar just *"as Moses commanded... and on the stones, he also wrote a copy of the law of Moses"* **(v.31-32).** Joshua didn't even think of writing his ordinances.

2. Joshua organized the people just *"as Moses had commanded"* **(v.33).** What caught my attention was the inclusiveness that God seeks in His people. Note that God did not renew the covenant only with the Jews but included *"foreigners"* among the people **(v.33).** Joshua organized the people, including the foreigners, just *"as Moses had commanded."*

3. He read all the words of the law **(v.34).** With all the people gathered, Jews, foreigners, women, and children, Joshua read all the words of God's covenant, just *"as Moses had commanded."*

Many times, some pastors avoid reading or preaching from certain passages of the Bible. For example, readings from Revelations, a book that, for some, has the fragrance of freedom and justice, but for others, it is terrifying. Some avoid reading passages of the Bible that are controversial. But Joshua didn't do such a thing. He read the good and the bad, *"the blessings and the curses"* God had planned for His people. Joshua did not omit a single word from what Moses commanded him to read **(Joshua 8:35).**

Let us pray: Dear God, give us humble and servant hearts to do all you command in Your Word and through Your prophets. Please help us to be inclusive like you. We pray in Your Holy Name.

✛ ✛ ✛ ✛ ✛ ✛

November 7
EVIL INCARNATE
Matthew 24:12

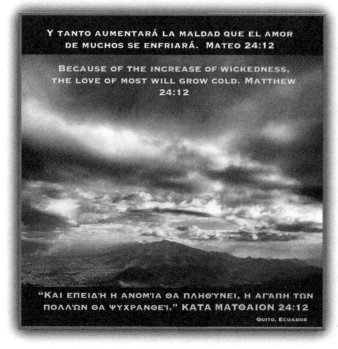

As evil spreads like a virus, **Matthew 24:12** speaks to Christians worldwide. We're experiencing a division and apparent hatred between people who, having professed faith in Jesus Christ, allow their political affiliation to invoke hateful feelings, actions, and words against neighbors of the opposite party, whom we are to love as ourselves.

"Evil is a mental state of contempt for justice, righteousness, truth, honor, and virtue ... Evil begins with a disposition of the mind, then it is externalized in acts, that mold the character of those who give themselves to it, marking their destination."[19] Evil is anything that is opposed to God's will. *The prophet Isaiah says, "Woe to those who call*

---

[19]Ventura, S. V. (1985). *Nuevo diccionario bíblico ilustrado* (p.706).

evil good and good evil, who put darkness for light and light for darkness, who put bitter for sweet and sweet for bitter" **(Isaiah 5:20).**

The enemy is deceptive, characterizing all who don't think like us as **"the devil"** and inclines us to take action against them in the name of God and the church. However, our fight is not against the flesh but the powers of darkness.

Jesus warned: *"Watch out that no one deceives you. For many will come in my name, claiming, 'I am the Messiah,' and will deceive many"* **(Matthew 24:4-5).** As to Jesus's return, the Bible says, *"Look, he is coming with the clouds,"* and *"every eye will see him"* **(Revelation 1:7).** He won't come in secret or reveal Himself exclusively to one, but to the whole world.

Jesus also warns us, saying, *"many false prophets will appear and deceive many people. Because of the increase of wickedness, the love of most will grow cold"* **(Matthew 24:11-12).** If anyone instructs us to hate or act in such a way as to cause harm or loss to another human being, they're a false prophet! We're not to obey them!

God will never command us to do or feel something His Word calls wicked or sinful. If we do, it's because we're listening to the father of lies, to evil incarnate. The defense against this is fasting and prayer!

Let us pray: Dear God, help us to be prudent. Don't allow the enemy to use us to spread evil and hatred. May Your Holy Spirit fan the fire of peace and love in our hearts and help us turn the opposition into Your disciples. We pray in Jesus's name.

> **God will never command us to do or feel something that His Word calls bad or sin. If we do, it's because we're listening to the father of lies, to Evil incarnate.**

November 8
WHY WE PRAISE
Psalm 113:3

Joshua 1:8 encourages us to meditate on God's Word day and night and do all that is written in it to succeed in life. One of the forms of meditation is **singing praises**.

As redeemed and adopted children of God, **Psalm 113:1-3** calls us to *"Praise the Lord. Praise the Lord, you his servants; praise the name of the Lord. Let the name of the Lord be praised, both now and forevermore. From the rising of the sun to the place where it sets, the name of the Lord is to be praised."*

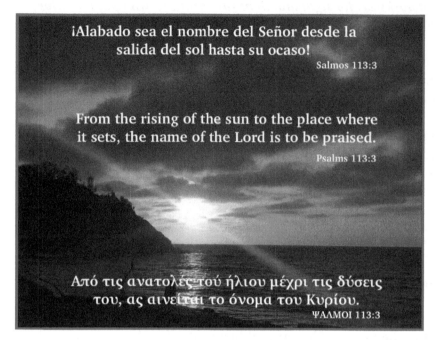

¡Alabado sea el nombre del Señor desde la salida del sol hasta su ocaso!

Salmos 113:3

From the rising of the sun to the place where it sets, the name of the Lord is to be praised.

Psalms 113:3

Από τις ανατολές του ήλιου μέχρι τις δύσεις του, ας αινείται το όνομα του Κυρίου.

ΨΑΛΜΟΙ 113:3

Throughout the generations, faithful believers have transmitted God's marvels and greatness through the praises found in the Psalms. If we fulfill our task of praising God day and night, our future generations will also praise God forever. Praise The Lord!

We praise God for His Sovereignty. *"The Lord is exalted over all the nations, his glory above the heavens. Who is like the Lord our God, the One who sits enthroned on high, who stoops down to look on the heavens and the earth?" (Vv. 4–6).*

Nothing happens in our lives without God being aware of it. God's Word says that *"God is faithful; he will not let you be tempted beyond what you can bear. But when you are tempted, he will also provide a way out so that you can endure it"* **(1 Corinthians 10:13).** The fact that the Lord is above all things prompts us to praise God day and night for generations.

We praise God for freeing us.
"He raises the poor from the dust and lifts the needy from the ash heap; He seats them with princes, with the princes of his people. He settles the childless woman in her home as a happy mother of children. Praise the Lord" (Psalm 113:7–9).

In our most challenging life moments, when there was no hope of escape, caught between the cross and the sword, God extended His right hand and rescued us from the enemy's claws. We all have a liberation testimony to share with family and friends. Do it today! Tomorrow may be too late!

Let us pray: Dear God, thank You for who you are in our lives, for rescuing us and putting a song of praise on our lips. Please encourage and touch our future generations with Your love, presence, provision, and hope through our witness and praise. We pray in Your Holy Name.

FREE OF ERRORS AND INCONSISTENCIES
Genesis 24:14

Many times, studying the Bible, we find parallel passages with significant similarities. For example, in **Exodus 2:17-21**, Moses defends some women and gives their sheep water. Their father receives him at home and offers his daughter Zipporah as his wife. In **Genesis 29:9**, Jacob meets Rachel, gives water to her sheep, and receives Rachel's promise as a wife. Today we find Rebekah by the well, offering to water the camels of Abraham's servant, who sought a wife for Isaac **(Genesis 24:19)**. Three stories with similarities and differences, all by a well where God unites lives to fulfill His promise.

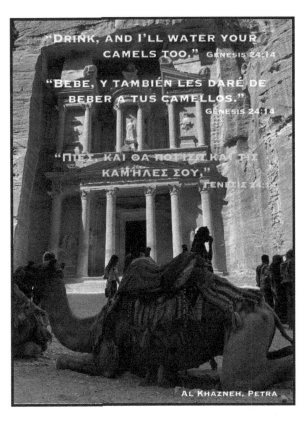

God promised Abraham, Isaac, and Jacob their seed would be as countless as the stars. It's the same story where some details are repeated. Applying these parallel images in our times, we should be courteous, kind, and subservient to women because the promise to bless our seed will come through them.

There are similarities and differences in the account of Jesus's anointing with an alabaster jar of costly perfume. In **Matthew 26:6-13**, a woman in Bethany anoints Jesus's head. The parallel verses of this same account are found in **John 12:1-8** and **Mark 14:3-13**. Mathew and Mark place this story in the house of Simon, the leper, while John puts it in the home of his friend Lazarus, whom Jesus resurrected. Matthew and Mark agree that the woman anointed Jesus's head, while John indicates Mary anointed His feet and dried them with her hair. Therefore, it's apparent that we have two parallel events and not, as some want to convince us, that the Bible contains errors.

Please don't allow the enemy to distract you by pointing to the differences in the stories to conclude that the Bible is full of inconsistencies and errors. Yes! There are some different details, but by faith, let's look at the similarities and learn what God wants to teach us.

> **Don't allow the enemy to distract you by pointing to the differences in the stories to conclude that the Bible is full of inconsistencies and errors.**

Let us pray: Dear God, thank You for this fundamental lesson. Help us always be ready to defend the Bible's truthfulness and authority, whose words were dictated by the inspiration of Your Holy Spirit, in which there are no errors or discrepancies. Don't allow wrong teachings to cause us, or our children, to doubt and turn to the world and its philosophies for answers. We pray in Your Holy Name.

November 10
SENT OUT IN JESUS 'NAME
Luke 4:18

We thank God for adopting us into His family, and for saving us from an uncertain and obscure future. This adoption engraves in our minds and hearts that the best is yet to come. That's the message of hope that we're sent to share.

At church, we sang, *"**Sent out in Jesus 's name**, our hands are ready now to make the earth the place in which the kingdom comes. The angels cannot change a world of hurt and pain into a world of love, of justice and of peace. The task is ours to do, to set it really free. O help us to obey and carry out your will."* (The Faith We Sing #2184).

God's Spirit has sent us *"to proclaim good news to the poor. He has sent me to proclaim freedom for the prisoners and recovery of sight for the blind, to set the oppressed free, to proclaim the year of the Lord 's favor"* (**Luke 4:18-19**).

God is not distant or ignores the sufferings of the people. **Acts 7:34 says,** *"I have indeed seen the oppression of my people in (INSERT YOUR COMMUNITY _____). I have heard their groaning and have come down to set them free. Now come, I will send you back to (_____)."*

God instructs us, *"Call to me and I will answer you"* (**Jeremiah 33:3**). It shouldn't surprise us that when we pray for God to send someone to heal or rescue, sometimes it pleases God to send you or me. God sends us to pray and act for all who suffer under authorities who have stolen their citizens' freedom and dignity.

Our adoption doesn't come without responsibilities. Every child has specific duties at home. Don't be afraid to call out to the Lord; you'll see splendid and marvelous things that God will do in and through your life.

Let us pray: Dear God, we pray for the freedom and dignity of Your people who suffer from hunger, violence, threats, lack of resources and medical care in different countries worldwide. Please have mercy on them and send Your angels to release the captives. Clarify our responsibilities and give us wisdom, power, and compassion to do Your will. We pray in Jesus's name.

November 11
HAPPY BIRTHDAY, SON
1 Samuel 2:27

1 Samuel 2:27 reflects the words of Hannah, thanking God for the gift of life. She had been barren, and **"Because the Lord had closed Hannah's womb, her rival kept provoking her in order to irritate her"** *(1 Samuel 1:6).* Seeing Hannah's sadness, her husband asked her, *"Hannah, why are you weeping? Why don't you eat? Why are you downhearted? Don't I mean more to you than ten sons?" (1 Samuel 1:8).*

Nothing could fill the void in her soul, not her husband's riches or flattery. Hannah went to the temple, and with tears and groans, she prayed to God, begging for a son. Having heard the content of Hannah's prayer, the priest blessed her, saying, *"Go in peace, and may the God of Israel grant you what you have asked of him" (1 Samuel 1:17).* That's how Hannah conceived and later appeared before God with the child. And she said to the priest: *"Pardon me, my lord. As surely as you live, I am the woman who stood here beside you praying to the Lord. I prayed for this child, and the Lord has granted me what I asked of him" (1 Samuel 1:26–27).*

We're often worried and sad. But God says not to worry about tomorrow, about what we will eat, drink, or wear. *"But seek first his kingdom and his righteousness, and all these things will be given to you as well" (Matthew 6:31-33).* Instead of worrying about the physical (which we can't take with us), we should worry about the soul. Trust that God will bless you with good health of your body, mind, and spirit. Trust that God hears your prayers, and you'll see that by faith, like Hannah, you can activate God's blessings in your life and those of your children.

Let us pray: Dear God, we pray for all the sterile women of the world, that you grant them the gift of life and faith that we celebrate in Jesus Christ. We place our children under Your protection; may they be yours all their days. I thank You because 42 years ago (1980), you gave Margarita and me the most wonderful gift we had ever received, our son, Jean-Paul Xanthópoulos Destruge. Thank you for his smile and kind heart, for making him a good son, father, brother, husband, and friend. Thank you for placing him in my life. We pray in Jesus's name.

November 12
ROOTED AND BUILT UP IN CHRIST
Colossians 2:6

Don't be discouraged when things don't go your way. We should anticipate that problems, divisions, and temptations will come our way, attempting to cause us to let go of our Lord's hand. But, we should always follow our Lord's way of peace and reconciliation.

How can we follow in His footsteps? **Colossians 2:7** commands us to live: *"rooted and built up in him, strengthened in the faith as you were taught, and overflowing with thankfulness."*

"Rooted" means **"to take root"** in Jesus Christ and His teachings. Trees that withstand great storms are those whose roots are deeply intertwined and whose trunks are flexible and move with the winds. They don't tear easily from their place because they have solid and deep roots.

"Built up in Him" means that we must weigh all building materials in our spiritual life against the foundation of our faith: Jesus Christ. **Verse 8** says, *"See to it that no one takes you captive through hollow and deceptive philosophy, which depends on human tradition and the elemental spiritual forces of this world rather than on Christ."*

Many will come with worldly philosophies and deceptive words, such as *"live and let live"* or *"God accepts us just as we are,"* implying that there's no need to change our lifestyle. If that were true, we'd have a complete social disorder. Imagine what our world would be like if it weren't a crime to steal, give false testimony, kill, etc. Given these conditions, we cannot say *"live and let live."* Today we see a radical change in which it has become customary to lie and give false testimony. We need to lovingly resist this type of disorder that threatens our society.

350

The Lord is a God of order who has organized everything in life so that the world can exist and subsist for a long time. But if we break God's Holy Word in favor of contradicting world philosophies, our world and our children's children won't have a chance to enjoy the fruit and presence of God in their lives.

Let us pray: Dear God, show us how we are to walk and lead our children and loved ones. Free us from accepting the philosophies and standards of this world. Give us solid and deep roots, clinging to Your Word and the example of our Lord Jesus Christ, in whose name we pray.

> **Trees that withstand great storms are those whose roots are deeply intertwined and whose trunks are flexible and move with the winds. They don't tear easily from their place because they have solid and deep roots.**

✝ ✝ ✝ ✝ ✝ ✝

November 13
ATTENTIVE TO GOD'S HANDS
Psalm 123:1

We're going through times we've never experienced; everything that was normal has been turned upside-down. COVID-19, which has claimed nearly 6.5 million lives across the planet (@8/2022), has us locked in our homes, looking in anticipation at the heavens, from where our help and relief comes.

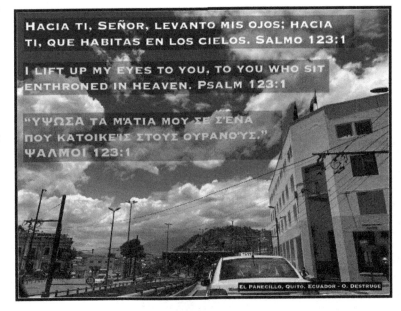

Unfortunately, for much of 2020-21, governments had disappointed us in their response to the pandemic. Unemployment and food insecurity were on the rise. Therefore, we lift our eyes to the Lord who dwells in heaven, crying out with the psalmist, *"As the eyes of servants look to the hand of their master…, so our eyes look to the Lord our God, till He shows us his mercy"* (**Psalm 123:2**).

"In the East, servants in attending on their masters are almost wholly directed by signs, which require the closest observance of the hands of the latter." As God's servants, we must look closely (1) to God's hand to assign His work to us; (2) God's supplying hand to receive our

351

portion; (3) His protecting hand, [to deliver us from evil;] and (4) His correcting hand [to straighten us out and place us in His path.][20]

I believe that *"the best is yet to come,"* but to get to the best part, we must go through the valleys of the shadow of death and dark tunnels. Jesus said that He'd return *"like a thief! Blessed is the one who stays awake and remains clothed, so as not to go naked and be shamefully exposed"* **(Revelation 16:15).** In Revelation, we find the most fearful destruction and punishment for those who haven't looked to God's hand for His portion, direction, correction, and protection. It's terrifying to envision the many different punishments that lie ahead. But the good news is that they won't touch God's faithful servants or their homes.

You've nothing to fear if you're attentive to God's hand and tuned to His voice. When the fearful day of the Lord comes, with your gaze fixed on the heavens, you and your home will be delivered from God's wrath and receive your reward; **new wedding clothes to enter the ceremony as the Lamb's bride.**

Let us pray: Dear God, *"Have mercy on us, Lord, have mercy on us."* We raise our arms and gaze toward Your throne, crying out for our people and planet, for Your creation. Lord, show us Your mercy. We have not been faithful stewards of the earth nor good neighbors with our neighbors. Forgive us, Lord, and show us Your hand that we might receive our portion, direction, correction, and protection. We pray in Your Holy Name.

November 14
DIVIDED HOUSES
Matthew 12:44

The problem with divided houses is that in the end, they're left in ruins, empty and unprotected. Yes! Some are swept up and adorned for sale, but that's not God's will nor our original plan. As for the nation and family, God wants us to prosper through unity. To protect our home and future generations, it's worth partnering with Jesus, our soul's most potent guardian, lover, and defender.

Today's verses conclude the exchange between the Pharisees and Jesus **(Matthew 12:22-45).** The Pharisees sought to kill Jesus. Seeing Him cast out demons, they accused Him of witchcraft (which was a capital offense), saying, *"It is only by Beelzebul, the prince of demons, that this fellow drives out demons"* **(Matthew 12:24).**

[20] Jamieson, R., Fausset, A. R., & Brown, D. (1997). Commentary Critical and Explanatory on the Whole Bible (Vol. 1, p. 385). Oak Harbor, WA: Logos Research Systems, Inc.

Jesus explains, *"Every kingdom divided against itself will be ruined, and every city or household divided against itself will not stand"* **(Matthew 12:25).** It's senseless that Jesus would cast out **demons** in Satan's name. Jesus demonstrates that His works of restoration and cleansing come from God. At the same time, the Pharisees' works are superficial, leaving the individual clean outside but **internally void of faith and unprotected from the enemy**.

"When an impure spirit comes out of a person, it goes through arid places seeking rest and does not find it. Then it says, 'I will return to the house I left.' When it arrives, it finds the house unoccupied, swept clean and put in order. Then it goes and takes with it seven other spirits more wicked than itself, and they go in and live there. And the final condition of that person is worse than the first. That is how it will be with this wicked generation" **(Matthew 12:43-45).** The evil generation refers to the Pharisees and their disciples.

My beloved, we can't be neutral about Jesus. Either we believe that He comes from God with the power to save, heal, cleanse, and protect, or we continue to **live divided and uncertain** about our future. Jesus says, *"Whoever is not with me is against me"* (Matthew 12:30a, Luke 11:23).

> We can't be neutral about Jesus. Either we believe that He comes from God with the power to save, heal, cleanse, and protect, or we continue to live divided and uncertain about our future.

We want our children to enjoy unity, mutual acceptance, respect, and support in their homes, communities, and nation. Not that they be divided by political, economic, or religious affiliations. Our task is not to judge or accuse, but to do God's will, to *"love our neighbor as ourselves"* **(Mark 12:33).**

Let us pray: Dear God, open the eyes and understanding of those in leadership positions over Your people, leaders who refuse to recognize Jesus's Lordship and authority. May they know You in Spirit and Truth and serve Your people with dignity and kindness. **May our children rejoice in the unity with Jesus and His people.** We pray in Your Holy Name.

November 15
HAPPY ANNIVERSARY!
Psalm 3:3

Two words in this verse require analysis: **Shield** and **glory**.

"Shield" offers the image of God surrounding the chosen people. We're bombarded by contaminants that, without God's help, we'd fail to adequately protect ourselves. That's why God promises to be our shield and anti-virus.

"Shield" (meguinná in Hebrew) means *"protector, **armor**, or a skin of thick crocodile scales."*

We have the impenetrable armor of God, who promised to protect His own. *"Do not be afraid, Abram. I am your shield, your very great reward" (Genesis 15:1).*

As believers in the Lord Jesus Christ, with eyes placed on Him, we must put on this armor daily so that no evil may cause a mortal wound. So that sin can't penetrate our lives and homes, disqualifying us from the prominent position and adoption that we have in Christ.

"Glory" - Many times in our prayers, we repeat, *"to God be the glory."* We attribute this word to the majesty of God. **Glory:** כָּבֹד **kabód**; means *"splendor, honor, majesty, nobility, power, wealth."* Without Jesus, we are nothing. Even the life we have exists in Him, by Him, and for Him **(Romans 11:36, Colossians 1:16)**. Whatever power, wealth, or nobility that people may observe in our lives flows from Jesus, the source of our existence and all that we are.

After purifying us, God will raise the previously shamed heads of His followers, placing them in high places. Today November 15, 2021, I thank God for lifting my head. Forty-six years ago, a beautiful 19-year-old young lady said, **"Yes, I will,"** becoming my wife, friend, partner, co-builder, and advocate for the home and family that God had planned for us. I humbly consider myself the winner of this sacred contract. I OWE everything I have and am to God, my shield and glory, and to Margarita, who has significantly fought to reach this glorious point in our lives. Happy Anniversary, *"agapymou" (my love.)*

Let us pray: Dear God, thank You for Your love, kindness, shield, and glory that illuminates and protects our lives and homes. Let us ensure daily to put on the armor that you offer us by faith and that you be glorified in our lives. May Your presence always be with us as a shield, guarding our hearts, lives, souls, and minds. Deliver our children and us from all evil.

November 16
BEFORE AND AFTER CHRIST
Hebrews 10:39

BEFORE CHRIST - With immense gratitude, I testify that as of August 22, 2022, it's been 33 years, five months, and 22 days since Jesus rescued me from an erratic life, full of doubts, low self-esteem, subject to drastic emotional changes, wavering between the winds of modernism.

AFTER CHRIST - With God's help, I'm no longer what I was, of those who *"shrink back and are destroyed, but to those who have faith and are saved"* **(Hebrews 10:39).** Today, I know that God is by my side, strengthening my faith, and placing my feet on a firm path and foundation. God transforms our lives so that from now on, we walk steadfastly.

FIRM IN COURAGE AND LOVE - No more fear! *"Be on your guard; stand firm in the faith; be courageous; be strong. Do everything in love" (1 Corinthians 16:13-14).*

FIRM IN PURPOSE AND WORKS - No more low self-esteem! Now, *"Therefore, my dear brothers and sisters, stand firm. Let nothing move you. Always give yourselves fully to the work of the Lord",* knowing that your work is not in vain *(1 Corinthians 15:58).*

FIRM IN FREEDOM FROM SIN - No longer subject to sin! *"Stand firm, then, and do not let yourselves be burdened again by a yoke of slavery"* **(Galatians 5:1).**

FIRM IN ONE SPIRIT - No longer blown by the four winds! God calls us to present ourselves as children of God, *"stand firm in the one Spirit, striving together as one for the faith of the gospel" (Philippians 1:27).*

FIRM IN THE LORD - Leaving idolatry behind! *"Stand firm in the Lord in this way, dear friends!" (Philippians 4:1B).*

FIRM IN FAITH - *"not to become easily unsettled or alarmed by the teaching allegedly from us" (2 Thessalonians 2:2).* God is by your side, and nothing can separate us from God's love.

FIRM IN DOCTRINE - No more without direction and guidance! *"Stand firm and hold fast to the teachings we passed on to you" (2 Thessalonians 2:15).*

355

Let us pray: Dear God, thank You for removing our doubts, fears, and hesitation. Thank you for establishing us firmly and powerfully on Jesus, the rock. For granting us courage, love, self-esteem, purpose, freedom, faith, and hope in Jesus Christ and the power of Your Holy Spirit. Help us to be useful in our mission to bring Your love and salvation to the world. We pray in Jesus's name.

November 17
OUR DIVINE HELPER
Mark 13:11

Public speaking was my weakness from childhood until 1989 when I discovered and trusted our verse; *"do not worry beforehand about what to say"* **(Mark 13:11).** The Holy Spirit is our Divine helper who reminds us of Jesus's promises and whispers **"what to say"** when words matter.

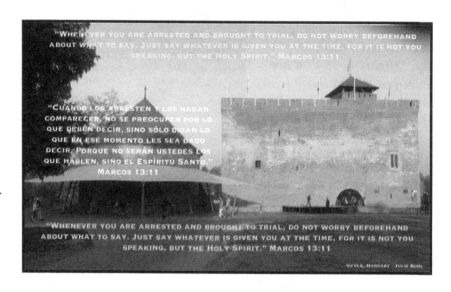

GOD TURNS OUR ISOLATION INTO PRESENCE, GUIDANCE, AND SUPPORT:
The poor and afflicted generally live isolated from society, the source of mutual physical and emotional support. However, all who trust God as their helper are freed from their afflictions because they have God's divine presence. *"But as for me, I am poor and needy; may the Lord think of me. You are my help and my deliverer; you are my God, do not delay"* **(Psalm 40:17).**

Before the invention of GPS, if we were lost, especially in the dark of night, we were prone to get discouraged. The same happens in our spiritual walk; without God, we walk in darkness, fearful and discouraged. But with the Lord as our helper, we have God's guiding light and support. *"So do not fear, for I am with you; do not be dismayed, for I am your God. I will strengthen you and help you; I will uphold you with my righteous right hand"* (Isaiah 41:10).

GOD TURNS OUR FEAR INTO STRENGTH AND JOY:
Before God came into my life, I had low self-esteem and many worries, one being public speaking. But God turned my fears into strength, confidence, and joy. *"The Lord is my strength and my shield; my heart trusts in him, and he helps me. My heart leaps for joy, and with my song I praise him." (Psalm 28:7). "So we say with confidence, 'The Lord is my helper; I will not be afraid. What can mere mortals do to me?'" (Hebrews 13:6).*

My beloved, I urge you to put all your fears in God's hands. You'll never regret it!

Let us pray: Dear God, help us to trust that by holding Your hand, nothing can separate us from Your love or change Your plans for our lives. May Your presence be a guide, sustenance, strength, and joy to those who seek Your Divine Help. We pray in Jesus's name.

November 18
PRAY FOR YOUR ENEMIES

"Lord, do not hold this sin against them." Acts 7:60

"Señor, no les tomes en cuenta este pecado". Hechos 7:60

"Κύριε, να μη τους λογαριάσεις αυτή την αμαρτία·." ΠΡΑΞΕΙΣ ΑΠΟΣΤΟΛΩΝ 7:60

Praying for our enemies is healthier than cursing them. People come into our lives who influence the rest of our lives, for better or for worse. Some leave fragrant and irreplaceable footprints; we wish they'd never left. We wish others never existed because they left seemingly irreparable wounds.

For 20 years, my soul was wounded (enraged) when my father's friend influenced the dynamics of my family. At the suggestion of that *"drinking friend,"* events occurred that impacted my brother John's mental health throughout his life. Every time I remembered that person or saw his photo, I felt the pain and anger again, wishing I'd reacted, taking a baseball bat and throwing him out of the house before the damage happened. I'd ask God to punish that man's children similarly. But those reactions made me feel worse.

Thank God, in 1990, instead of cursing him like before, I put this man in God's hands, saying, ***"Father, forgive him because he didn't know what he was doing. Perhaps this man never had a father and didn't learn a father's love."*** Since then, his memory or name has had no physical or emotional effect on me, even though we still live with the consequences.

My beloved, praying for our enemies is healthier than cursing them. We should forgive them as Christ did on the cross. *"Father, forgive them, for they do not know what they are doing,"* saying or judging **(Luke 23:34)**. Forgiveness restores our inner peace, allowing us to live in harmony with God and our neighbors.

The enemy wants us to return evil for evil, but God says, *"Do not gloat when your enemy falls; when they stumble, do not let your heart rejoice" (Proverbs 24:17)*. On the contrary, *"If your enemy is hungry, give him food to eat; if he is thirsty, give him water to drink. In doing this, you will heap burning coals on his head, and the Lord will reward you" (Proverbs 25:21-22)*.

Let us pray: Dear God, help us know the love of a father and mother so that when we advise our friends how to discipline their children, we may do so with wisdom and love. Help us to forgive as you've forgiven us and thus heal our wounds. We pray for those suffering from depression and mental health. Fill them with the peace of Jesus, in whose name we pray.

November 19
CONSOLIDATION OF THE KINGDOM
1 Corinthians 15:24

If we read **1 Corinthians 15:24** out of its historical context, we might wrongly conclude that Jesus is / will be inferior to God at the Consolidation of God's Kingdom.

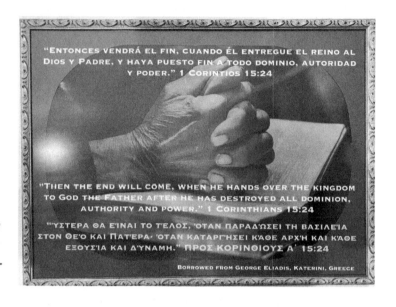

We must understand that ever since humanity's fall, when sin gained its first victim, God planned to manifest Himself in human flesh to save us. Speaking of Jesus, **1 Timothy 3:16** says, *"He appeared in the flesh, was vindicated by the Spirit, was seen by angels, was preached among the nations, was believed on in the world, was taken up in glory."*

When we accept that God came to our world in human form, that Jesus is *"Immanuel, God with us"* (**Matthew 1:23**), and that *"in Christ all the fullness of the Deity lives in bodily form"* (**Colossians 2:9**), then we can understand and explain today's text.

God will complete the Salvation Plan in the role of the Son. *"Then the end will come, when he hands over the kingdom to God the Father after he has destroyed all dominion, authority and power. For he must reign until he has put all his enemies under his feet"* (**1 Corinthians 15:24-25**).

God's work as Son, through the cross and Resurrection, still saves souls today. Jesus still has a vital role in this kingdom. God will fulfill His purpose when the last person has been saved; when God's enemies have been cast off, the dead will rise again, consolidating God's Kingdom (the dead and alive). Then, there'll no longer be a need for Jesus's salvific role, and He will return to the position He had before the world's creation. *"When he has done this, then the Son himself will be made subject to him who put everything under him, so that God may be all in all"* (*1 Corinthians 15:28).*

In God's human manifestation as the Son, Jesus has absolute authority over all things in this world. God the Father rules with love and power in the Kingdom of Heaven. On the final day, God will Consolidate the Kingdom *"so that God may be all in all."*

Let us pray: Dear God, thank You for revealing how you've manifested yourself to the world to save and lead us to Your coming kingdom. Increase our faith and understanding to testify of Your love and salvation to the world. We pray in Jesus's name.

November 20
OUR REWARD IS COMING
Isaiah 40:10 & Revelation 22:7

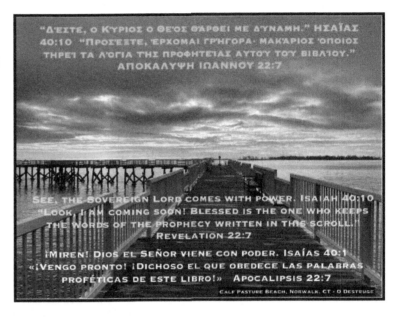

The newscasts are dark and pessimistic wherever we look, listen, or read. Just look at the politics, and it seems we're in a losing battle. Nobody's looking out for the voters' needs, for the middle and lower-class citizens. With some exceptions, politicians look out for their own pockets and security, not caring about ordinary people. Is there any hope? Yes!

What beautiful promises we find in today's verses! Glory to God! As we joyfully welcome the news of a COVID-19 vaccine, with much more joy, we anticipate the return of our Lord, who **comes with His reward** for His beloved people.

A reward is something one receives for good behavior. God will reward all who've believed and obeyed God's complete Word. My beloved, all that we've suffered, endured, and tolerated will end one day. Our justice draws near. Jesus says, *"Look, I am coming soon! Blessed is the one who keeps the words of the prophecy written in this scroll"* **(Revelation 22:7).**

The prophet Isaiah comforts us with these words, *"See, the Sovereign Lord comes with power, and he rules with a mighty arm. See, his reward is with him, and his recompense accompanies him"* **(Isaiah 40:10).**

What is the reward? Since the Garden's exile, our punishment has been to eat our daily bread through painful toil until we return to the dust from which we were created. For the woman, her punishment has been the multiplied pain of childbirth. **(Genesis 3:16-19)** These will all end when Jesus returns. There will no longer be any curse, injustice, disease, or pain. Everything will be perfect in the presence of our Great Shepherd and God.

Our reward is that God Himself *"will tend his flock like a shepherd: He gathers the lambs in his arms and carries them close to his heart; he gently leads those that have young"* **(Isaiah**

40:11). Our reward is *"the crown of righteousness… which the Lord will award to all who have longed for his appearing"* **(2 Timothy 4:8).**

Let us pray: Dear God, thank You for assuring us that our struggle is about to end, that the wages of our punishment have been paid twice over by our Lord **(Isaiah 40:2),** who returns soon with His reward. Through Your Holy Spirit, keep us faithful to Your Word and clinging to You, our hope and eternal joy. We pray in Your Holy Name.

✝ ✝ ✝ ✝ ✝

November 21
SHOWERS OF BLESSINGS
Ezequiel 34:28

Ezekiel 34 is divided like this:
1. The Prophecy against the shepherds of Israel **(Vs. 1-10),**
2. God himself will search for the lost sheep **(Vs. 11-16),**
3. God will judge between the fat and the lean sheep **(Vs. 17-24),** and
4. The covenant of peace **(Vs. 25-31).**

In these verses, God contrasts the false shepherds and His **"servant David" (v.34),** pointing to Jesus Christ, son of David, who identifies himself by saying, *"I am the good shepherd. The good shepherd lays down his life for the sheep"* **(John 10:11).**

To the false shepherds, God accuses them of taking care of themselves **(v.2),** *"You have not strengthened the weak or healed the sick or bound up the injured. You have not brought back the strays or searched for the lost. You have ruled them harshly and brutally. So they were scattered because there was no shepherd, and when they were scattered they became food for all the wild animals. My sheep wandered over all the mountains and on every high hill. They were scattered over the whole earth, and no one searched or looked for them"* **(Ezekiel 34:4-6).**

Since these shepherds neglected their work, God will judge them by removing them from their work, and they will not be able to feed themselves **(v.10).** *"I myself will search for my sheep and look after them,"* says the Lord **(v.11).**

God unilaterally establishes a **covenant of peace** with His scattered people. It's a covenant that will take place when Jesus returns for His sheep, guaranteeing that, in God's kingdom, there will no longer be *"savage beasts"* that threaten the people **(v.25).** We will live in complete security. Furthermore, God will bless the people with all their basic needs (*"showers of blessings"* - **v.26**).

360

There will be no more hunger or distinction between rich and poor. We will all share equally in God's provision.

More importantly, the people will know that *"The Lord is our God"* and He will be with us forever **(Vs. 27,30)**. There will be no confusion over who is herding the flock.

Let us pray: Dear God, in our hearts, we wouldn't want to wait for Your covenant to be realized when the Lord returns. We want Your showers of blessings to be a reality now. Yesterday! Open our understanding, touch our hearts, to bring pieces of this heavenly vision here to earth that so much needs Your peace, love, and goodness. Make us instruments of Your peace Lord. We pray in Your Holy Name.

November 22
SEEKING GOD FROM EARLY DAWN
Psalm 63:1 (NKJV)

Without God, we live thirsty, tired, susceptible to temptation, anger, irritation, hostility, selfishness, etc. The world offers temporary solutions, but only in God do we quench our thirst and find permanent peace, rest, shield, strength, and provision. When we've crossed a barren desert, struggled, and lost our spiritual energy, when life is empty of purpose, love, and light, it behooves us to come into God's presence.

Psalm 63:1 says, *"Early will I seek You; My soul thirsts for You."* We come to God with more desperation than when our cell phones are 8% charged and we don't have a recharger at hand. From early in the morning, let us seek God's unlimited power.

We were created to have intimate communion and a relationship with God. Early every morning, we need the water of life which only God offers to strengthen our souls and gain courage. Those who seek the fullness of life find their rest and strength only in God. *"As the deer pants for streams of water, so my soul pants for you, my God. My soul thirsts for God, for the living God. When can I go and meet with God?"* **(Psalm 42:1-2A).**

The apostle Paul's greatest desire was to leave this world and be with Christ. However, he needed to remain in the flesh to fulfill his mission **(Philippians 1:23-24).** The believer wants to be in God's presence, to rest from the constant fight against evil and unkindness on our battle-fields. That is why the persistent question: *"When can I go and meet with God?"* Only God knows the day and hour of our rest. But, the important thing is to know that God is OUR God.

Let us pray: O God, you are our God; we have been chosen to fulfill Your Divine plan. There-fore, we will eagerly seek you from very early in the morning. Our soul thirsts for you. We're surrounded by evil on every side. Our flesh yearns for you. Like an oasis in the desert, Your presence satisfies our soul. Please help us promote good in this life, delight in Your presence, and help us share the hope you've planted in our hearts. We pray in Your Holy Name.

November 23
WHAT IS BETTER THAN LIFE?
Psalm 63:3

What is better than life? God's mercy is better than life! Without God's mercy, goodness, and love, life is not called living but merely existing.

MERCY is to feel compassion for the evil done against others. In the Hebrew Testament, we find the word חֶסֶד **kjésed** (**H2617**); which means, among others, *"goodness, and clemency."* In the new testa-ment, merciful appears in verses like **Matthew 5:7,** *"Blessed are the merciful, for they will be shown mercy,"* or **Luke 6:36,** *"Be merci-ful, just as your Father is merci-ful."*

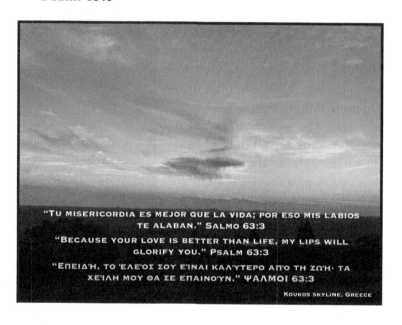

"TU MISERICORDIA ES MEJOR QUE LA VIDA; POR ESO MIS LABIOS TE ALABAN." SALMO 63:3

"BECAUSE YOUR LOVE IS BETTER THAN LIFE, MY LIPS WILL GLORIFY YOU." PSALM 63:3

"ΕΠΕΙΔΗ, ΤΟ ΕΛΕΟΣ ΣΟΥ ΕΙΝΑΙ ΚΑΛΥΤΕΡΟ ΑΠΟ ΤΗ ΖΩΗ· ΤΑ ΧΕΙΛΗ ΜΟΥ ΘΑ ΣΕ ΕΠΑΙΝΟΥΝ." ΨΑΛΜΟΙ 63:3

KOUKOS SKYLINE, GREECE

MERCY is a Divine Attribute in which God forgives our sins. It means not applying the justice (punishment) that we deserve but instead granting us the pardon (forgiveness) we do not deserve. The Bible establishes that the penalty for sin is death, that is, separation from God's presence, *"but the gift of God is eternal life in Christ Jesus our Lord"* (**Romans 6:23**).

God is merciful and cares for us. God doesn't want anyone to be lost but for everyone to come and trust Him. God calls and receives us at all times, in whatever situation we are. God's mercy is available unconditionally 24/7. Unconditionally means that it doesn't matter how far we have strayed from God or how great our rebellions have been. Nothing prevents us from drawing close to God, pleading for forgiveness and mercy. Our children and their children must be clear about this offer of mercy and reconciliation with their Creator.

Our young ones often incorrectly believe their temporary lack of judgment would be unforgivable by their parents or God. For example, a pregnancy outside of marriage. Fear can cause them to hide and end the pregnancy. They must know that nothing can make us love them less and that they can trust God and us with their greatest regrets and failures because God's Mercy is unconditional and eternal.

God has promised to extend kindness, forgiveness, and mercy to those who invoke and trust Him. Filled with gratitude for God's favor, we respond with renewed faith, hope, and acts of love toward God and our neighbor, especially for our children.

Let us pray: Dear God, thank You for Your love and mercy. Help us to love, forgive and show mercy like You. We pray in the name of Jesus.

> **Our children must know that nothing can make us love them less and that they can trust God and us with their greatest regrets and failures because God's Mercy is unconditional and eternal.**

✚ ✚ ✚ ✚ ✚ ✚

November 24
WHEN IN TROUBLE, TRUST GOD!
John 16:33

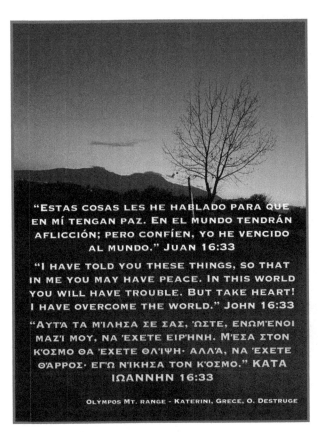

"ESTAS COSAS LES HE HABLADO PARA QUE EN MÍ TENGAN PAZ. EN EL MUNDO TENDRÁN AFLICCIÓN; PERO CONFÍEN, YO HE VENCIDO AL MUNDO." JUAN 16:33

"I HAVE TOLD YOU THESE THINGS, SO THAT IN ME YOU MAY HAVE PEACE. IN THIS WORLD YOU WILL HAVE TROUBLE. BUT TAKE HEART! I HAVE OVERCOME THE WORLD." JOHN 16:33

"ΑΥΤΆ ΤΑ Μ'ΙΛΗΣΑ ΣΕ ΣΑΣ, 'ΩΣΤΕ, ΕΝΩΜ'ΕΝΟΙ ΜΑΖ'Ι ΜΟΥ, ΝΑ 'ΕΧΕΤΕ ΕΙΡ'ΗΝΗ. Μ'ΕΣΑ ΣΤΟΝ Κ'ΟΣΜΟ ΘΑ 'ΕΧΕΤΕ ΘΛΙ'ΨΗ· ΑΛΛ'Α, ΝΑ 'ΕΧΕΤΕ Θ'ΑΡΡΟΣ· ΕΓΏ Ν'ΙΚΗΣΑ ΤΟΝ Κ'ΟΣΜΟ." ΚΑΤΑ ΙΩΑΝΝΗΝ 16:33

OLYMPOS MT. RANGE - KATERINI, GRECE, O. DESTRUGE

Being a Christian does not free us from the world's troubles, catastrophes, and trials. Jesus said, *"In this world you will have trouble. But take heart! I have overcome the world" (John 16:33).* If we face trials with our strength, it's possible that we'd be defeated, that our souls will surrender to discouragement and depression, ending up in dark places, devoid of hope and even the desire to live.

Psalm 27:13-14 says, *"I remain confident of this: I will see the goodness of the Lord in the land of the living. Wait for the Lord; be strong and take heart and wait for the Lord."*

Consider the following questions; "What would have been of me if it hadn't been for the Lord? Where would I be today if it hadn't been for the hand of God? Would I be alone, divorced, financially broke, or physically destroyed?" If I hadn't believed that the Lord is my rock and fortress, that God is the basis of my life, my soul would have fainted, and I wouldn't be here today enjoying life, my family, and God's presence.

Many are still unaware of the peace, confidence, and strength that Jesus offers through adoption into God's family. You and I discovered this treasure and power through the Holy Scriptures. *"Faith comes from hearing the message, and the message is heard through the word about Christ" (Romans 10:17)*. Thus, amid afflictions, instead of giving up, we trust that we'll overcome our troubles because Jesus promised to give us victory.

> **If we face trials with our strength, it's possible that we'd be defeated, that our souls will surrender to discouragement and depression, ending up in dark places, devoid of hope and even the desire to live.**

The world is full of people who need to know the value that God has placed in their lives. Many are unaware of God's good plans for their lives and that their present situation does not impede starting over, with renewed strength and hope, to do something good and noble with the life that God has given them. We have many souls to rescue and fill with the faith that fully trusts in God.

Let us pray: Dear God, grant us the privilege of sharing with loved ones and strangers the good plans that You have for their lives, to fill their souls with faith and hope, to see Your goodness in their lives and those of their children. Encourage our hearts to wait on You. We pray in the name of Jesus.

✛ ✛ ✛ ✛ ✛ ✛

November 25
THE DIVINE WAY
Psalm 25:4

We learn to follow the Divine way through Bible study and the example of Christian mentors and pastors. Fear and shame have no place in God's ways since *"His ways are everlasting,"* leading to abundant life. **(Habakkuk 3:6C NKJV)**. God expects and rejoices when we make His ways known.

I had been upset for several years with Johana, a co-worker. When God came into my life in '89, I went to Johana, asked her forgiveness for spurning our

"SHOW ME YOUR WAYS, LORD, TEACH ME YOUR PATHS." PSALM 25:4

"SEÑOR, DAME A CONOCER TUS CAMINOS; ¡ENSÉÑAME A SEGUIR TUS SENDAS!" SALMO 25:4

"ΔΕΙΞΕ ΜΟΥ, ΚΥΡΙΕ, ΤΟΥΣ ΔΡΟΜΟΥΣ ΣΟΥ· ΔΙΔΑΞΕ ΜΕ ΤΑ ΒΗΜΑΤΑ ΣΟΥ." ΨΑΛΜΟΙ 25:4

NOV. 2021 - CYCLING PATH TO LITHOXORO, GREECE - O. DESTRUGE

friendship, and shared my experience with the Lord. We reconciled, and I invited her to the prayer and fellowship group that we started in my office. After studying the book of Philippians, we extended an invitation, and she received the Lord with joy. Her life changed; becoming pleasant, cheerful, kind, and generous to the needy.

A few months later, Johana suffered an asthma attack and went to rest with the Lord. Suppose we hadn't shared the gospel? Who knows what would have become of her soul? This experience removed my fear about whether or not to share the gospel of Jesus Christ with friends and family.

There is no fear or suspicion in the Divine way because we are doing God's will. Although we are imperfect, God's *"way is perfect: The Lord's word is flawless; he shields all who take refuge in him" (Psalm 18:30).* In the Divine Way, the devil cannot touch us because God is our shield and refuge.

Along the Divine Way, God's guidance, direction, and inspiration, like the sun, are high and unmistakable. *"As the heavens are higher than the earth, so are my ways higher than your ways and my thoughts than your thoughts."* **(Isaiah 55:9).** *"The ways of the Lord are right"* **(Hosea 14:9b)** and **"unsearchable" (Romans 11:33).** In our limited minds, we could never understand God's mind. Still, our heart recognizes God's unmistakable voice and joyfully and gratefully submits to the Lord's direction because there is no better way than the Divine Way.

Let us pray: Dear God, *"Great and marvelous are your deeds, Lord God Almighty. Just and true are your ways, King of the nations" (Revelation 15:3).* Teach us to walk in Your truth and to seek Your face. We pray in Jesus's name.

✝ ✝ ✝ ✝ ✝ ✝

November 26
DISCIPLINED IN PRAYER
1 Thessalonians 5:17

"OREN SIN CESAR." 1 TESALONICENSES 5:17

"PRAY CONTINUALLY." 1 THESSALONIANS 5:17

"ΑΔΙΆΚΟΠΑ ΝΑ ΠΡΟΣΕΎΧΕΣΤΕ." ΠΡΟΣ ΘΕΣΣΑΛΟΝΙΚΕΙΣ Α΄ 5:17

KYRIAKI XANTHOUPOULOU'S PRAYING HANDS KITCHEN PAINTING

Creating a new discipline takes three weeks. For example, studying the Bible requires a secluded place without distractions and a separate time exclusively for studying.

At the company where I worked, I formed a fellowship and prayer group. We met every Wednesday in the same room at noon for almost ten years. I instructed my assistant not to interrupt us, even if the company's president was looking for me—this established discipline and commitment for all.

Today, God calls us to *"pray continually."* But is that possible when we have other obligations,

365

work, and chores? Yes, of course! **If we can love at all times, we can pray at all times!** Do you believe in love at first sight? Who doesn't remember the time when struck by cupid, we couldn't stop thinking about the beloved person all day? Although they weren't by our side, their presence accompanied us in all places and activities. We looked forward to returning to them as soon as possible.

In his sermon entitled, *"Pray Without Ceasing,"* Ralph Waldo Emerson said, *"It is not only when we audibly and in form, address our petitions to the Deity that we pray. We pray without ceasing. Every secret wish is a prayer. Every house is a church; the corner of every street is a closet of devotion."*[21] In love with Jesus, we are aware of His presence and remain in communion with Him at all times and places.

The Greek word **"without ceasing"** is ἀδιαλείπτως (adialeíptos); which means uninterruptedly, i.e., without omission. Just as love is constant, prayer becomes an uninterrupted communication with our Creator. We get closer to the Beloved by repeating Bible promises such as; *"I can do all things through Christ who strengthens me"* **(Philippians 4:13 NKJV)** or, *"Nothing can separate me from God's love"* **(Romans 8:39)**.

> Just as love is constant, prayer becomes an uninterrupted communication with our Creator. We get closer to the Beloved by repeating Bible promises.

Let us pray: Dear Lord, help us to develop the discipline of being in communion with you at all times. Remind us that everything that brings us into Your presence and fragrance becomes a prayer, a hymn, a verse, a blessing, a greeting to the neighbor or stranger, or even cutting the Christmas tree. Thank you because we can sing as we work and pray as we rock our granddaughter to sleep on our lap. Let our lives become a continual prayer and praise to You. We pray in the name of Jesus.

November 27
HAPPY THANKSGIVING
Revelation 14:6

Seven countries (the United States, Canada, Australia, the Netherlands, Saint Lucia, and Grenada) celebrate Thanksgiving today. We gather with family around the dining room table to thank God for His care, direction, and provision. For Christians, each day is a day of Thanksgiving to God for having rescued, bandaged our wounds, and given us a new and eternal identity as adopted sons and daughters of God, with a place reserved at His banqueting table.

The Lord's banquet is incomparable to any here on earth, not even my mother-in-law's, who prepared the most delicious Greek-American dishes for us. You and I have a place at the table, but many from *"every nation, tribe, language, and people"* are still unaware of our King's invitation and kindness. We must use the gifts that God has given us to go out through our neighborhoods,

---

[21] https://thevalueofsparrows.com/2014/02/02/sermon-pray-without-ceasing-by-ralph-waldo-emerson/.

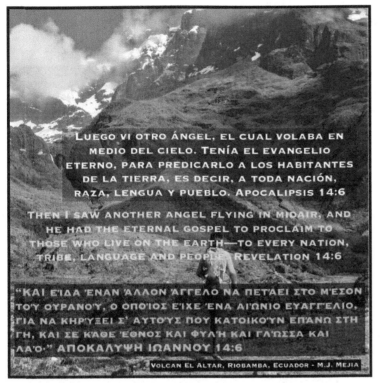

LUEGO VI OTRO ÁNGEL, EL CUAL VOLABA EN MEDIO DEL CIELO. TENÍA EL EVANGELIO ETERNO, PARA PREDICARLO A LOS HABITANTES DE LA TIERRA, ES DECIR, A TODA NACIÓN, RAZA, LENGUA Y PUEBLO. APOCALIPSIS 14:6

THEN I SAW ANOTHER ANGEL FLYING IN MIDAIR, AND HE HAD THE ETERNAL GOSPEL TO PROCLAIM TO THOSE WHO LIVE ON THE EARTH—TO EVERY NATION, TRIBE, LANGUAGE AND PEOPLE. REVELATION 14:6

"ΚΑΙ ΕΊΔΑ ΈΝΑΝ ΆΛΛΟΝ ΆΓΓΕΛΟ ΝΑ ΠΕΤΆΕΙ ΣΤΟ ΜΈΣΟΝ ΤΟΥ ΟΥΡΑΝΟΎ, Ο ΟΠΟΊΟΣ ΕΊΧΕ ΈΝΑ ΑΙΏΝΙΟ ΕΥΑΓΓΈΛΙΟ, ΓΙΑ ΝΑ ΚΗΡΎΞΕΙ Σ' ΑΥΤΟΎΣ ΠΟΥ ΚΑΤΟΙΚΟΎΝ ΕΠΆΝΩ ΣΤΗ ΓΗ, ΚΑΙ ΣΕ ΚΆΘΕ ΈΘΝΟΣ ΚΑΙ ΦΥΛΉ ΚΑΙ ΓΛΏΣΣΑ ΚΑΙ ΛΑΌ." ΑΠΟΚΑΛΥΨΗ ΙΩΑΝΝΟΥ 14:6

VOLCAN EL ALTAR, RIOBAMBA, ECUADOR - M.J. MEJIA

villages, and mountains in search of the sheep that are hungry and thirsty for justice but do not know from where their next crumbs of bread, milk, and honey will come. Our task is to invite them to the Thanksgiving feast.

Some might say, **"I can't, I'm afraid to speak in public!" "I don't know what to say!" "They won't believe me,"** and **"What if they reject me?" "Better to send someone more capable."** Others will say, **"I don't have time!"** These were my excuses at first. But let's **remember with gratitude** that you and I came to the Lord's table because someone overcame their fears and invited us. At first, it wasn't easy to ask, but little by little, it became easier. It's like climbing mountains. No novice could climb 4550 meters to El Altar Volcano without first having conquered previous peaks of 2,000 and then of 3,000 meters, as did my cousin, María José, in today's photo.

As redeemed children of God, we're entrusted with the *"eternal gospel to proclaim to those who live on the earth—to every nation, tribe, language and people"* **(Revelation 14:6).** Don't be afraid to testify about what God has done in your life. God allowed you to go through trials so you'd conquer them and give testimony of how God's hand guided, delivered, and placed you in positions of honor and hope. **Perhaps one day, around a dining room table, someone will give thanks for you, the angel who brought the gospel of peace, love, and hope into their lives and that of their home.**

Let us pray: Dear Lord, 2021 has been an incredible year, but You've been by our side, caring for, guiding, and supplying all our needs and desires. Thank you for the precious gift you've brought to our family, for our grandson, Lázaro Elías. Thank you, my Lord.

November 28
BLESS YOUR APPOINTED LEADERS
Psalm 80:17

Psalm 80 affirms the people's faith and complete trust in God to rescue and care for them as a pastor. *"Restore us, O God; make your face shine on us, that we may be saved"* **(v.3).** It's a prayer for deliverance and restoration, which depends on God's chosen leader for the work.

The appointment of a new spiritual or political leader is a significant event in people's lives as it brings hope of blessings, changes, and prosperity. In both, we ask that God's hand be on the chosen person so that with wisdom and kindness, they may guide, nurture, protect, and inspire the people to serve God and their neighbor.

When by inspiration of the Holy Spirit, the Conclave of Cardinals of the Catholic Church elects a new Pope, they announce it by crying out *"Habemus papam,"* which is Latin for, 'We have a Pope!'

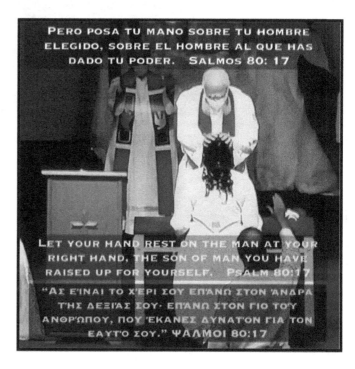

At the beginning of November, citizens went to the polls to vote for the president and other leaders in the United States. The people have elected and claimed **"Habemus president-elect."** We've already done part of the work by voting. The second and continuing part remains - to pray that God will put His hand and spirit on our elected leaders, giving them wisdom and resources to lead the people they represent.

Some Churches were also blessed with the ordination of pastors. In the Methodist Church, the church's laity and clergy affirm by vote the calling of the person to be a pastor. Then the bishop, placing his hand on the head of the elected, prays for the Holy Spirit to strengthen the *"Elder that is ordered to a ministry of Word, Sacrament, Order, and Service. This means elders preach and teach God's Word, provide pastoral care and counsel, administer the sacraments of Baptism and Holy Communion, and order the church's life for service in mission and ministry."*

Ezra 8:22 says, *"The gracious hand of our God is on everyone who looks to him, but his great anger is against all who forsake him."*

Let us pray: Dear God, we thank You for the leaders and pastors you've chosen to lead Your people. Please help them to accomplish the work you have placed on their shoulders. Help us to serve and love one another, to eliminate divisions by remembering that first of all, we are Your children and brothers in Christ. Please help us support our leaders by doing Your will. We pray in the name of Jesus.

> **We ask that the hand of God be on the chosen person so that with wisdom and kindness, they may guide, nurture, protect, and inspire the people to serve God and neighbor.**

GOD KEEPS ALL PROMISES
2 Peter 3:9a

God's promises are trust-worthy - God keeps them and will fulfill them all. Jesus said, *"For truly I tell you, until heaven and earth disappear, not the smallest letter, not the least stroke of a pen, will by any means disappear from the Law until everything is accomplished"* (Matthew 5:18).

In Noah's time, God saw the evil that existed on earth and regretted having created it. God offered to save Noah and his family from the flood through an ark God instructed Noah to build.

The first promise (covenant) that God made is this: *"But I will establish my covenant with you, and you will enter the ark—you and your sons and your wife and your sons 'wives with you. You are to bring into the ark two of all living creatures, male and female, to keep them alive with you"* (Genesis 6:18-19).

God sent rain for forty days and nights, such that the waters covered the tops of the mountains, and all living creatures that didn't enter the ark died. After the waters had receded, Noah and his family, with the animals, left the protection of the ark, and God promised not to *"destroy all living creatures, as I have done. As long as the earth endures, seedtime and harvest, cold and heat, summer and winter, day and night will never cease."* As proof of this covenant, God established the rainbow in heaven.

The Bible has many promises of kindness, patience, and blessing for you and your family. **Have you read the entire Bible to discover how many wonders God has prepared for you and your children?** If we don't know the promises, how can we claim them? Jesus said, *"Ask, and it will be given"* (Matthew 7:7).

God gets sad seeing evil spreading like a virus throughout our world. But God is also very patient, not wanting anyone to be lost, but instead that everyone would repent and return to Him in search of His love and mercy. **We have much work to be done! God is counting on us to keep our promises!**

Let us pray: Dear God, may you find us faithful and use us so that through our life and witness, Your beloved sheep may return to the fold and be saved from judgment day. We pray in Your Holy Name.

November 30
ENCOUNTERS
Psalm 90:12

Psalm 90 has lifted me from discouragement in times of trial and bitterness. During my first years walking with the Lord, having come out of a dark period, I listened daily to the reading of the Bible on the radio, which began with **verses one and two:** *"Lord, you have been our dwelling place throughout all generations. Before the mountains were born or you brought forth the whole world, from everlasting to everlasting you are God."*

My life-changing encounter with **God** was like this: Before I knew about God's love, the Lord knew me and was by my side, guarding my soul according to His good purpose. One day in 1988, feeling the weight of the world on me, I told my parents, *"'I don't want something drastic to happen to me, like death, but I wish I'd fall ill in the hospital for almost a month and have no responsibilities.' My parents responded; 'Son, don't say that even as a joke.'"*

A few months later, God orchestrated my encounter with Jesus on a spiritual retreat. They were three days of revelation, renewal, rest, and spiritual transformation. Speaking about Bible study, the speaker (Tim O'Donnell) said we need *"three weeks to create a new discipline."* The day after the retreat, I asked the Lord to give me three weeks without obligations or work to study the Bible. The following day, leaving the house for work, I slipped on the ice and broke my ankle. The Doctor gave me three weeks of recovery at home. Every day Margarita left early with the children; she went to work and the kids to school and daycare. As soon as they left, I opened the Bible and enjoyed uninterrupted time with the Lord and God's Holy Word.

The best medicine to calm our anxieties, learn to organize our lives, and prioritize our days well is by seeking encounters with the Lord through His Word. In them, we appreciate for the first time the greatness of God's love for you and me. Encounters with God give us the necessary strength and wisdom for troubled times like these.

Let us pray: Dear God, thank You because from generation to generation, you have been our refuge, wisdom, rest, and sustenance. *"May your deeds be shown to your servants, your splendor to their children"* **(Psalm 90:16).** Increase our faith so that our children and we might enjoy every daily encounter with you and Your Word. We pray in Your Holy Name.

December 1
TAKE ADVANTAGE OF THE TIME
Psalm 90:10

At the finance company, helping employees save and invest for retirement, I often presented employees with a planning paradox. Many spend days and weeks planning for an annual vacation, for their honeymoon, but don't spend an hour planning for their retirement that, beginning at 65-67, will last the rest of their lives. They see it as such a distant and low-priority event. The same happens with our spiritual life.

Christians must prepare for life, in this life, to enjoy eternal, abundant life in the presence of our Savior. Some may think that God has promised everyone a minimum of seventy years to live and that they have plenty of time to mend their ways. Others may believe that God has failed in His promise since we know that human longevity is quite varied. Some barely reach hours of life, like my twin, and others reach one hundred years.

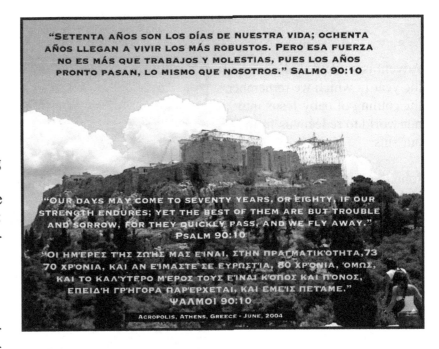

The point we see in **Psalm 90:10** is not that everyone will live to be seventy or eighty years old, nor that we have many years to repent and turn to God, but that 70-80 would be the average lifespan. For some, like Jesus, their life would be very short. But, essentially, our time is limited for all of us, and one day we'll die. How we've lived and in whom we've placed our trust will determine our eternal dwelling place, be it one of eternal rest or torment.

It is vital that our children and we answer the following question affirmatively: Have you placed your trust in Jesus Christ as your only and sufficient Savior and Lord?

As we wait for the day of our complete redemption when Jesus returns for His people, we have a vital task of being faithful witnesses who are sent in search of the lost sheep and who make good use of their time so that, whether our days are few or long, we live for God.

Let us pray: Dear God, thank You for helping us understand the brevity of life and our responsibility as Your

> **Make good use of your time so that, whether your days are few or long, you live for God.**

adopted children to rescue Your beloved people, our friends, and family. Thank you for the great privilege of being chosen as Your messengers and guides. Please help us to make good use of the little time we have. We pray in Your holy name.

December 2
ADVENT - A CELEBRATION OF LIFE
Luke 1:76-77

Advent is a wonderful season of the year in which we remember the coming of baby Jesus into our world to redeem us from our sins.

John the Baptist was chosen and sent as a messenger to prepare the way of the Lord. **Verse 80** says, *"And the child grew and became strong in spirit."* John's spiritual growth didn't occur in a vacuum but was directed, shaped, and stimulated by his father Zachariah's knowledge about his son's calling. Zachariah was committed to raising John according to God's will.

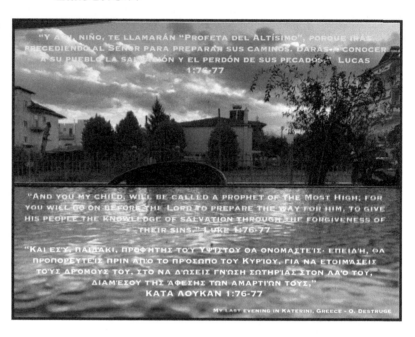

I ask myself, how different might our lives be if God had revealed to our parents what would be our mission or purpose? God no longer speaks the way He did when He was revealing His Salvation Plan, but the Holy Spirit speaks to us, inspiring and directing us when we pray to know how to raise our children. Conscious that God has a plan and purpose for every believer, we must seek divine direction and take an active role in the spiritual growth of our children.

As a new father, when my son Jean-Paul was born, I felt blessed, and proud and prayed to God, declaring that *"this child will grow up healthy, not attracted to drinking buddies, and will be the pride of the family and a model for his siblings and cousins."* With God's help and protec-

> **Conscious that God has a plan and purpose for every believer, we must seek divine direction and take an active role in the spiritual growth of our children.**

tion, we've tried to be good examples to our children. It's essential to avoid the many stumbling blocks and growingly inadequate standards accepted in modern society **(Romans 12:2).**

Advent is a beautiful season to celebrate the coming of Jesus into our world and lives and to experience again the pride, joy, and gratitude for the gift of life that God deposited in our homes through our children. Advent gives us new and better reasons to rejoice and share the reason for our faith and hope.

Let us pray: Dear Lord, thank You for the gift of life and salvation through Jesus Christ and for the immense and sometimes fearful role of being parents. Please help us to seek Your direction in raising our children in the knowledge and power of Your Word. We pray in Jesus's name.

December 3
FRIENDSHIP WITH GOD PRODUCES HUMAN FELLOWSHIP
Malachi 3:16

Enmity with God produces selfishness and strife, while friendship with God creates human fellowship. Those faithful to God need each other to receive support and encouragement amid a society adverse to the Lord. **Psalm 119:63** states that we are to be *"a friend to all who fear you, to all who follow your precepts."*

Today's Malachi reading contrasts *"between the righteous and the wicked, between those who serve God and those who do not."* God accuses those who distrusted Him as thieves and sinners, using their words and thoughts to condemn them. *"You have said, 'It is futile to serve God. What do we gain by carrying out his requirements and going about like mourners before the Lord Almighty?" (Malachi 3:14).*

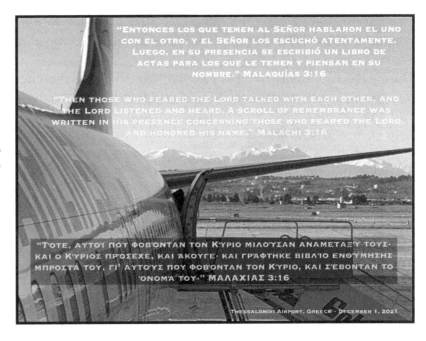

God accuses them of being thieves because they did not give full or well-measured tithes. **Verse 3:10** is perhaps the best-known and most quoted of Malachi. *'"Bring the whole tithe into the storehouse, that there may be food in my house. Test me in this,' says the Lord Almighty, 'and see if I will not throw open the floodgates of heaven and pour out so much blessing.'"*

But of the righteous, God says, *"they will be my treasured possession. I will spare them, just as a father has compassion and spares his son who serves him" (Malachi 3:17).* Friendship with God produces in us the desire to know God, to be faithful to His teachings, and encourage fellowship through prayer and the sacraments **(Acts 2:42).** Fellowship produces gratitude toward God **(Philippians 1:3).**

Friendship with God lights our way, leading us toward human fellowship and the continual cleansing of our sins **(1 John 1:7).** Today, many want to convince us that it is *"futile to serve*

God." Without companionship, we could fall victim to such lies. That is why it's vital to help each other understand that it is better to listen and serve God than man.

Let us pray: Dear God, thank You for all who accompany us on this walk through Your Word. Bless us with wisdom, ears tuned to Your voice, and hearts obedient to Your will. We pray in the name of Jesus.

December 4
TURNING HEARTS BACK TO GOD AND FAMILY

"He will turn the hearts of the parents to their children, and the hearts of the children to their parents; or else I will come and strike the land with total destruction." Malachi 4:6

"Y él hará que el corazón de los padres se vuelva hacia los hijos, y que el corazón de los hijos se vuelva hacia los padres, para que yo no venga a destruir la tierra por completo". **Malaquías 4:6**

"αυτός θα επαναφέρει την καρδιά των πατέρων προς τα παιδιά, και την καρδιά των παιδιών προς τους πατέρες τους, μήποτε έρθω και πατάξω τη γη με ανάθεμα." **ΜΑΛΑΧΙΑΣ 4:6**

During the 13 years I served as pastor of two Hispanic churches in Connecticut, the Lord gave us a vision to *"Turn hearts back to God and family."* Our motto was, *"Promote the physical, social and spiritual well-being of Hispanic families. Reconcile Families with Jesus Christ and with each other,"* taken from **Malachi 4:6.**

We addressed the physical well-being of our day laborer neighbors by offering Saturday breakfast, consisting of cream-cheese bagels/rolls, coffee, hard-boiled eggs, and bananas. As we learned their needs, we expanded into English classes and various seminars on knowing their community and their rights.

We addressed their Social well-being through monthly meals and birthday celebrations. For a while, we offered dance lessons with a professional dance instructor. Spiritual well-being was nurtured through short five-minute messages delivered before serving the meals and by handing out personalized meditations and prayers written explicitly for the day laborers.

The meditations often spoke about the Messiah, whom God sent in human form as a defenseless and humble baby to win back the hearts of the people so that all who trusted Him would fall in love again with God and family and return to the unity, harmony, and warmth of the family.

After ministering to the day laborers for a few years, it was a blessing to hear their testimonies of how they had given up drinking and were reaching out to their families back home because they had learned that the essential thing in life was to be reconciled with God and family.

Let us pray: Dear God, thank You for giving us the ministry of reconciliation. Thank you for life and family. We need Your guidance and protection, so we may continue to *promote the physical, social, and spiritual well-being of our friends and families.* Help us to listen only to

Your voice so that we do not stumble or lose our way. In Your hands, we entrust our children, family, and friends. We pray in the name of Jesus.

December 5
YOU WILL BE CLEANED
Ezekiel 36:25

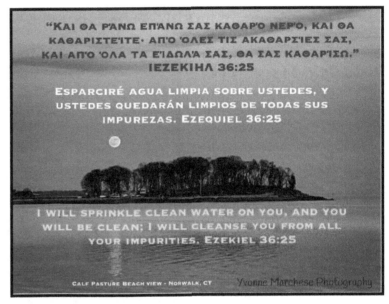

In September 2018, heavy rain flooded my tool shed. I kept some things of sentimental value there, among them my father's vinyl records. The water and mud disintegrated the cardboard and paper that covered them (the jackets), and when they dried, they became encrusted in the discs. I threw the jackets in the trash. It saddened me to think that the records would also be recycled and that I'd never listen to them again. But because of their sentimental value, I tried washing them with water, soap, and disinfectant. Although without jackets, they were clean externally, and I didn't try to play them until recently.

I spent almost the entire month of November 2020 copying the records to digital files. I've enjoyed listening to the melodies that calmed my stress and anxiety during adolescence. I also took time to erase the imperfections and scratches that tend to occur in records due to use, time, and sometimes neglect. Now the digital files sound like new, and closing my eyes, it seems that I'm sitting with my father, listening to songs of the heart.

My father's love for music attracted me to become an amateur musician. He invested a lot of time and money in his music collection. Likewise, God loves creation and today tells us that our lives are more valuable than those records. The jackets (our bodies) have no eternal value or utility. God calls us back so that He may **cleanse us from all impurity** and filth. It doesn't matter how much dirt has become encrusted in our exterior. **God values what we have stored in our hearts, and that's worth rescuing at all costs. You will be cleaned!**

"I will put my spirit in you," says the Lord **(v.27)**, so that we may continually cleanse and disinfect our lives from all evil that clings to our lives. So that we may follow *"God's decrees and be careful to keep God's laws"* **(v.27)**.

2020 has ravaged and disrupted the lives of many with tsunami-like physical and spiritual storms. Their lives and possessions have been washed away by rivers of mud. God sends us to rescue and cleanse their homes, lives, and minds so that they may be clean, saved, **better than before**, and return to the ways of the Creator and lover of their souls.

Let us pray: Dear God, thank You for cleansing us from all evil. Thank you for the value you put in each life and for keeping us focused on Your mission and purpose. Let us be useful tools to rescue, bandage, and clean Your lost sheep. We pray in Your holy name.

December 6
GUARDIANS OF THE KING'S HIGHWAY
Isaiah 40:3-4

Isaiah 40:1–2A says: *"Comfort, comfort my people, says your God. Speak tenderly to Jerusalem, and proclaim to her that her hard service has been completed, that her sin has been paid for."*

Every day that God grants us life, the Lord expects you and I to guide and comfort friends, family, and strangers who don't know the way and travel through deserts, dark tunnels, and long restless nights. How? By being **faithful guardians of the message and the King's Highway.**

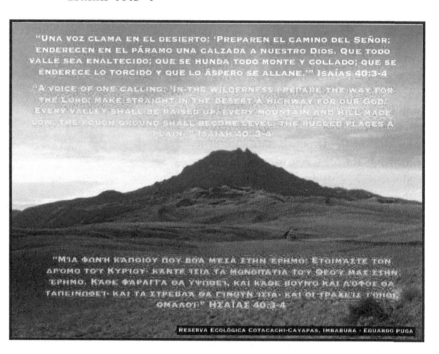

The King's Highway is paved with sacrifices, love, and promises God has recorded for His beloved people. We comfort them by making known God's mercy, whose anger doesn't last forever, pointing to the Highway God has provided so that our condemnation is nullified and our sins are forgiven. **God has paved the Highway in the deserts of our lives** so that those of us who were once exiled, set apart, and lost can return to God's house to dwell under His care, direction and protection.

The commutation of our sentence is entirely free, by God's grace, through faith in Jesus Christ. God accepts us as we are, but His love and mercy are so great that God doesn't leave us the way he found us. By God's grace, I'm no longer what I was, and if God gives me life, in five years, I won't be what I am today. Every day, God's love and Word **straighten everything crooked in our lives,** cleansing us of all impurities and making us worthy to enter into God's presence.

Once rescued and forgiven, as guides and **guardians of the King's Highway**, we're sent to comfort, prepare, and guide friends, loved ones, and strangers along the Way of the Lord. Through prayer and study of the Word, God gives us the clarity to anticipate and remove all obstacles that may arise in overturning our convictions and forgiving our iniquities.

> Every day, God's love and Word **straighten everything crooked in our lives,** cleansing us of all impurity and making us worthy to enter into God's presence.

Let us pray: Dear God, thank You for showing us the Highway to Your heavenly mansion, for commuting our sentence, and for forgiving our sins. Please help us to be faithful guardians of Your Word and lovingly guide Your sheep through the Highway back to Your fold. We pray in Your Holy Name.

December 7
EVERYTHING YOU NEED
2 Peter 1:3

We truly have everything necessary to achieve eternal life and, in this world, to lead a godly life that glorifies and pleases God.

The marvelous thing is that we don't have to labor for it nor offer any time, money, or resources to acquire these needs. This promise DOES NOT depend on our morality or social class. God has placed it within reach of EVERYONE because of His great love through Jesus Christ.

King Solomon, the wisest man in the world, extensively analyzed life, our needs, and pleasures and concluded that *"everything is vanity."* His conclusion was this: *"Fear God and keep his commandments, for this is the duty of all mankind"* (**Ecclesiastes 12:13**).

God has given us **everything necessary to know, love, and find Him through His Holy Word.** It's not a promise for the future. It's a fact. The Bible's purpose is this: the **revelation and call to believe in Jesus Christ.**

Previously we were blind and deaf to God's presence and direction. We lived unhappily with our life which didn't please God nor our families and friends. God sent Jesus Christ as a sacrificial lamb to rescue and transform us into adopted children. We didn't have to do anything except believe in Jesus and confess Him as our Lord and Savior.

But the devil wants to keep us blind and deaf. Therefore, **God has also given us faith** to believe in Jesus and His Holy Word. *"For it is by grace you have been saved, through faith—and this is not from yourselves, it is the gift of God"* (Ephesians 2:8).

If this weren't enough, God has also given us the **gift of love and hope**. Love leads us to live a godly life, which extends its hand to the needy, offering them everything they need to know and please God. Hope and faith encourage us to resist the enemy's lies and tricks.

Let us pray: Dear God, I pray for each friend and family member here. May they may know that You've given them everything necessary to live a victorious, safe, full life that causes you to smile with pleasure and complacency. I also pray that you fulfill Your precious promises of eternal life in our children and their generations through the testimony of our lives. We pray in Jesus's name.

December 8
THE WORKS OF CHRIST
Luke 7:22

God had clearly announced the works He'd do to strengthen the weak and fearful and heal His

people's diseases. In **Isaiah 35:3-7**, God prophecied about the saving work of Jesus, which also extends to our lives and time: *"Strengthen the feeble hands, steady the knees that give way; say to those with fearful hearts, 'Be strong, do not fear; your God will come, he will come with vengeance; with divine retribution he will come to save you.' Then will the eyes of the blind be opened and the ears of the deaf unstopped. Then will the lame leap like a deer, and the mute tongue shout for joy. Water will gush forth in the wilderness and streams in the desert. The burning sand will become a pool, the thirsty ground bubbling springs. In the haunts where jackals once lay, grass and reeds and papyrus will grow."*

But when Jesus arrived, bearing all these works that God promised to do for His people, the religious leaders refused to publicly believe in Him for fear of losing control over the congregation.

378

Even John the Baptist hesitated for a moment. From prison, he sent his disciples to ask Jesus, *"Are you the one who is to come, or should we expect someone else?"* **(Luke 7:20).**

It's natural to hesitate when we're between a rock and a hard place. We all doubt at some point. Jesus answered them: *"Go back and report to John what you have seen and heard: The blind receive sight, the lame walk, those who have leprosy are cleansed, the deaf hear, the dead are raised, and the good news is proclaimed to the poor"* **(Luke 7:22).**

God's prophecies rest on the fulfillment of His promises. You and I are sent to strengthen and comfort those who suffer by recounting the wonderful works that God has done in our lives. God will do the same for those who suffer today.

Let us pray: Dear God, thank You for sending Jesus Christ to fulfill Your promises to redeem, rescue, and heal our afflictions. Help us prepare our testimonies about how you've worked to bless our home and family. We pray in Jesus's name.

December 9
WHOM SHALL I FEAR?
Isaiah 12:2

Before meeting the Lord, I lived surrounded by fear and low self-esteem. But all that changed when the Lord became my light and salvation. The more I repeat, *"The Lord is the strength of my life. Whom shall I fear?"* the stronger my faith, joy, and confidence **in times of trial.**

The Gospel Choir at FCC in Norwalk used to sing:
"The Lord is my light and my Salvation. Whom shall I fear? Whom shall I fear? **The Lord is the strength of my life; whom shall I fear?** *In the time of trouble, He shall hide me. Whom shall I fear? Whom shall I fear?* **The Lord is the strength of my** *life; whom shall I fear? Wait on the Lord and be of good courage. He shall*

strengthen thy heart. Whom shall I fear// **The Lord is the strength** *of my life;* **whom shall I fear?"**

When the choir sang, the crescendo power of their voices filled the sanctuary. The repetition of ***"The Lord is the strength"*** and ***"Whom shall I fear?"*** burrowed into my heart and soul, filling me with trusting confidence that **God is my salvation; I will trust and not be afraid.**

Jesus said that **we would have times of trouble**. They will come from every corner and source, even our closest friends and family, manifested in illness, job losses, finances, arguments over inheritances, etc. The enemy will use all types of drama to divide the family, to cause you to throw in the towel on work, love, or even God. But Jesus bids us to have faith, to **trust** that the Lord is our strength and shield. Jesus has *"overcome the world"* **(John 16:33).** Our antidote to fear is to Trust in the Lord.

Let us pray: Dear God, thank You for being our shield, hope, confidence, and confidant. You've placed songs in our hearts to remind us to have faith and to always trust you, especially **in times of trouble.** You've given each of us a specific assignment in accordance with our unique gift. Help us set aside any fear of failure or pain and use our gifts of speech and song to lift the confidence of those who've lost hope, particularly during this pandemic that has turned our world upside-down. We pray in Jesus's name.

December 10
AN ABUNDANT SPIRITUAL HARVEST

"Remember this: Whoever sows sparingly will also reap sparingly, and whoever sows generously will also reap generously." 2 Corinthians 9:6

"Pero recuerden esto: El que poco siembra, poco cosecha; y el que mucho siembra, mucho cosecha". 2 Corintios 9:6

"Λέω, μάλιστα, τούτο, ότι αυτός που σπέρνει φειδωλά, φειδωλά και θα θερίσει· και αυτός που σπέρνει με αφθονία, με αφθονία και θα θερίσει."
ΠΡΟΣ ΚΟΡΙΝΘΙΟΥΣ Β΄ 9:6

We all want an **abundant spiritual harvest** in our home, family, community, church, country, and world! God promises an abundant harvest to those who know how, when, and where to sow. I've learned that planting a new ministry requires prayer, time, patience, and plenty of attention, love, and nourishment.

Everything starts with prayer. Ask God to illuminate you on the best way to nourish the seeds. If you're working with a group from a different culture, ask God to show you how to win their trust and love. **2 Corinthians 9:8** says, *"And God is able to bless you abundantly, so that in all things at all times, having all that you need, you will abound in every good work."* Having everything we need, we can become the voice of the voiceless; defend the dignity of every human being, and sow righteousness. God will supply all the needs and use all means so that we may bear fruits of unfailing love **(Hosea 10:12)** —fruit that will last **(John 15:16).**

Time, patience, attention, love, and nourishment: In 2008, with much joy and gratitude, we started a new ministry with four church members from Norwalk who lived in Bridgeport. We began with home services. For almost two years, the harvest in Bridgeport was less than ten people, but we persisted patiently. In the third year, by taking an active, caring role in the host church's food pantry, visiting clients 'homes, and praying for them individually, we saw significant growth and fruit until 2017, when I retired. *"Those who sow with tears will reap with songs of joy"* **(Psalm 126:5).**

God calls us to **sow with abundant gratitude and joy.** *"Each of you should give what you have decided in your heart to give, not reluctantly or under compulsion, for God loves a cheerful giver" (2 Corinthians 9:7).* God's Word urges us to sow so that we may have an **abundant spiritual harvest** because *"from the Spirit, we'll reap eternal life"* **(Galatians 6:8).**

Let us pray: Beloved God, grant that wherever we go, we may always sow Your seeds of love, justice, and hope. You are *"able to bless us abundantly, so that in all things at all times, having all that we need, we'll abound in every good work"* for Your Kingdom. We pray in Your Holy Name.

✚ ✚ ✚ ✚ ✚

December 11
SPIRITUALLY MINDED
Philippians 3:16

Philippians is one of my favorite books in the Bible, not because it's tiny and easy to read, but because in four chapters, we feel the love and joy of living spiritually in and for Jesus Christ.

Several verses have marked my spiritual life, such as;
1:6 *"He who has begun a good work in you will complete it until the day of Jesus Christ."*
1:21 *"For to me, to live is Christ, and to die is gain."*
3:20 *"But our citizenship is in heaven. And we eagerly await a Savior from there, the Lord Jesus Christ."*
4:4 *"Rejoice in the Lord always. I will say it again: Rejoice!"*
4:6 *"Do not be anxious about anything, but in every situation, by prayer and petition, with thanksgiving, present your requests to God."* And,
4:13 *"I can do all this through Christ who strengthens me" (NKJV).*

In whatever situation, these verses give me peace, strength, and hope because I'm confident that by the end of my days, God will complete the good work He began in me. Finally, I'll have the **spiritual mind** that God saw when He formed me in my dear mother's womb.

Meanwhile, God invites us to develop a spiritual mind, which considers all that we longed for in the material world as *"a loss because of the surpassing worth of knowing Christ Jesus my Lord, for whose sake I have lost all things. I consider them garbage, that I may gain Christ"* **(Philippians 3:8).**

God calls us to be like-minded, with one way of thinking and living, humbly like Jesus Christ, who stripped himself of His Divinity to come to this world and die as a criminal so that you and I might conquer sin and death. In reality, we haven't yet conquered sin. We live tied to a body that seeks its satisfaction. *"Those who live according to the flesh have their minds set on what the flesh desires; but those who live in accordance with the Spirit have their minds set on what the Spirit desires. The mind governed by the flesh is death, but the mind governed by the Spirit is life and peace"* **(Romans 8:5–6).**

The believer's goal is to know Jesus Christ and be His faithful imitator, reflection, and ambassador. In this race, there's only one prize, Jesus Christ. There is no consolation prize! Only the gold crown of righteousness.

Let us pray: Dear God, grant us that, as the body of Christ, we may *"walk by the same rule, and be of the same mind."* Give us spiritual minds to pursue the goal of knowing and **faithfully** imitating You. We pray in Your Holy Name.

IN THIS RACE, THERE'S ONLY ONE PRIZE, JESUS CHRIST. THERE IS NO CONSOLATION PRIZE! ONLY THE GOLD CROWN OF RIGHTEOUSNESS.

December 12
WHEN WE RETURN FROM OUR CAPTIVITY
Psalm 126:2

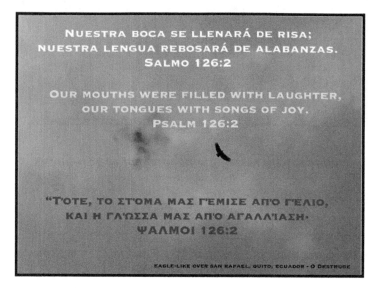

NUESTRA BOCA SE LLENARÁ DE RISA; NUESTRA LENGUA REBOSARÁ DE ALABANZAS. SALMO 126:2

OUR MOUTHS WERE FILLED WITH LAUGHTER, OUR TONGUES WITH SONGS OF JOY. PSALM 126:2

"ΤΌΤΕ, ΤΟ ΣΤΌΜΑ ΜΑΣ ΓΈΜΙΣΕ ΑΠΌ ΓΈΛΙΟ, ΚΑΙ Η ΓΛΏΣΣΑ ΜΑΣ ΑΠΌ ΑΓΑΛΛΊΑΣΗ· ΨΑΛΜΟΙ 126:2

EAGLE-LIKE OVER SAN RAFAEL, QUITO, ECUADOR - O DESTRUGE

Perhaps we wonder when will the Lord deliver us from this suffering? **Psalm 126** is a praise song by those who returned from captivity and a promise of hope for those still held captive in Babylon or any form of present-day bondage.

Regarding our verse, most Bibles speak to us in past terms, *"When the Lord brought back the captivity of Zion."* Few versions, such as the ERV (Easy To Read), speak in futuristic terms, *"It will be like a dream when the Lord comes back with the captives of Zion."* Not all of the Israelites returned from captivity. Many remained in Babylon, and even today, many remain estranged from God, so it shouldn't distract us much if the translation uses *"brought"* or *"will bring"* The result is the same. We live in the world (Babylon), but we're not of the world. Even believers who've returned positionally to the Lord's arms feel a longing to return physically to God's house, to the New Jerusalem. Therefore, *It will be like a dream when the Lord comes back with the captives of Zion. We will laugh and sing happy songs!"* **(Psalm 126:1-2 ERV).**

God offers us the key to being free of our physical-emotional captivity. We must repent, convert, and obey God to return to God's arms. Listen to God's Word: *"When all these blessings and curses I have set before you come on you and you take them to heart wherever the Lord your God disperses you among the nations, and when you and your children return to the Lord your God and obey him with all your heart and with all your soul according to everything I command you today, then the Lord your God will restore your fortunes and have compassion on you and gather you again from all the nations where he scattered you. Even if you have been banished to the most distant land under the heavens, from there the Lord your God will gather you and bring you back"* **(Deuteronomy 30:1–4).**

Beloved, when we repent wholeheartedly, returning from captivity, even at a distance, on our way to the arms of the Lord, *"It will be like a dream… We will laugh and sing happy songs!"* **(Psalm 126:1-2).** Then we'll be truly free to soar **on eagle's wings** and see our world from God's vantage point. Although physically we're still in this world, we **can** be free by returning to the Creator.

Let us pray: Dear God, thank You for showing us the way back to Your arms, where there will again be laughter, joy, and praise in our hearts. Please don't stop illumining our way back to you. We pray in Your Holy Name.

December 13
INVARIABLE AND HUMBLE

"Jesus Christ is the same yesterday and today and forever." Hebrews 13:8

"Jesucristo es el mismo ayer y hoy y por los siglos". Hebreos 13:8

"Ο Ιησούς Χριστός είναι ο ίδιος χθες και σήμερα, και στους αιώνες."
ΠΡΟΣ ΕΒΡΑΙΟΥΣ 13:8

Today's verse reminded me of a beautiful hymn we used to sing in church. (Translated from Spanish to English):
"Jesus Christ yesterday amongst my grandparents. Jesus Christ today amongst my brothers. Jesus Christ here today, presence and memory, Lord of History, Jesus The Lord.
How lovely the people who remember. Surely they also have Hope! How lovely the people who study their history. Who join to celebrate, singing their faith. How lovely this gathering of many

believers who live to create a community! How lovely is life, when together we seek Truth and Justice, Peace and Liberty."

My dad was overly sensitive and bothered by people's variability. I'm drawn to people that are always the same; who always have a smile on their face, and when they see you, whether after a week or after ten years, they give you a bear hug or a tight handshake. How lovely are such people! They make you feel welcome, loved, at home, like family!

That's why, since my mom took me to the movies to see **"King of kings,"** I fell in love with Jesus's invariable and humble character. Studying His life, we discover that He always spoke the truth (in love), that He perpetually loved (even His tormentors), that He leads His sheep through the right paths **(Psalm 23:3)**, and offers abundant life to all who believe in His name.

I appreciate His steadfastness, and through decades of abiding with Jesus and His Word, I've come to believe that He is *"the Way, the Truth, and the Life" (John 14:6),* that He is the *"King of kings and Lord of lords" (1 Timothy 6:15).* Today I'm eternally grateful knowing that Jesus gave His life so that you and I may become invariable, humble imitators of His character and life.

As leaders in our homes and God's representatives in our communities, we must be blameless in conduct and steadfast in our example so as not to be a stumbling block to the young in faith and subject to variability.

Let us pray: Dear God, we adore and bless you. Thank you for opening our ears, eyes, and hearts so we may know Your unchanging, loving character. Teach us to be invariable with our smile and affection toward Your lost sheep so that they too may discover that You are *"the Way, the Truth, and the Life,"* and together, we may establish Justice, Peace, and Freedom in our world. We pray in Jesus's name.

December 14
LED BY A CHILD
Isaiah 11:6

God has placed in humanity the desire to explore our environment, become independent from our parents, and conquer the world. We have an adventurous spirit that doesn't back down from danger. For example, mountaineers live to conquer the highest peaks, exposing their bodies to the risks of hypothermia, loss of limbs, and life, just to stand on the summit for a few minutes. They pay tons of money to guides to take them along the safest routes.

Isaiah 11:6 presents us with a child as an expert guide for ascending to heaven. *"And a little child will lead them."* Logic tells us that we can't depend on a small and weak child. How can a child know the way? Could he defend us against wild animals? Rather than help, climbing with children is an additional hazard for adults!

But faith tells us that only this child named Jesus can lead us to the entrance of the Kingdom of heaven. This child is the true incarnation of God, who came to rescue and guide us back home. Jesus said, *"I am the Way, the Truth and the Life" (John 14:6).*

AUNT GLORIA, DAD, MOM, OSCAR, TIA BLANCA, MICHELLE & RICKY

"Y UN CHIQUILLO LOS PASTOREARÁ."
ISAÍAS 11:6

"AND A LITTLE CHILD WILL LEAD THEM."
ISAIAH 11:6

"ΚΑΙ ΈΝΑ ΜΙΚΡΌ ΠΑΙΔΊ ΘΑ ΤΑ ΟΔΗΓΕΊ."
ΗΣΑΪΑΣ 11:6

BROADWAY TERRACE, NYC, CIRCA 1967

Although in our minds, we envision Him in the form of a child, especially during Christmas, even as a child, Jesus showed great intelligence. *"Everyone who heard him was amazed at his understanding and his answers"* (**Luke 2:47**). *"And Jesus grew in wisdom and stature, and in favor with God and man" (v.52).*

You and I were created in the image of God, but unlike Jesus, who was fully human and fully Divine, we are fully human, imperfect, but created and destined to live, love, and serve God and neighbor. In this world, we are to grow *"in wisdom and stature, and in favor with God and with man" (*Luke 2:52).*

We're all on the road climbing unknown routes, crossing valleys, and exploring the best way to reach the summit unscathed. The best guide is the child Jesus. He came to guide us to our eternal home along the Safe Path.

Let us pray: Dear God, thank You for giving us the faith to trust our lives and family in our Divine guide and Savior. Allow all the children of the world to come close to You. Let no one prevent them because Your Kingdom is for those like them (**Mark 10:14**). We pray in the name of Jesus.

> faith tells us that only this child named Jesus can lead us to the entrance of the Kingdom of heaven. This child is the true incarnation of God, who came to rescue and guide us back home.

December 15
SEVEN - GOD'S PERFECTION
Isaiah 11:2

The numbers in the Bible are symbolically important as they reveal God's mind and purpose.

The number seven first appears in the Bible in the seven days of creation, when God completed His creative work. From there, we relate seven to something complete, perfect, finished - God's perfection.

The text identifies seven gifts of the Holy Spirit that will rest perfectly and fully on the Messiah:

1. REST - In Hebrew, *"to rest"* (נוח *núakj - H-5117)* means **"to rest, settle down, dwell, remain."** God's Spirit permanently *"settled"* upon Jesus. *"For God was pleased to have all his fullness dwell in him" (Colossians 1:19)*. When we receive Jesus as Lord, God transforms our hearts into His permanent abode, allowing His peace and love to rest upon us.

2. SPIRIT OF WISDOM— In Jesus, *"are hidden all the treasures of wisdom and knowledge"* **(Colossians 2:3)**.

3. SPIRIT OF UNDERSTANDING - Jesus knew people's thoughts and responded with righteousness, justice, and love. *"He did not need any testimony about mankind, for he knew what was in each person" (John 2:25)*.

4. SPIRIT OF COUNSELING- *"For to us a child is born, to us a son is given, and the government will be on his shoulders. And he will be called Wonderful Counselor, Mighty God, Everlasting Father, Prince of Peace" (Isaiah 9:6)*.

5. SPIRIT OF POWER- Jesus promises to share His Divine power freely. *"I am going to send you what my Father has promised; but stay in the city until you have been clothed with power from on high" (Luke 24:49)*.

6. SPIRIT OF KNOWLEDGE of the deep things of God. Jesus promises to reveal such knowledge to His followers. *"All things have been committed to me by my Father. No one knows the Son except the Father, and no one knows the Father except the Son and those to whom the Son chooses to reveal him" (Matthew 11:27)*.

7. SPIRIT OF FEAR OF THE LORD - Reverential and obedient fear is the first step toward true *"understanding"* **(Psalm 111:10)**.

Let us pray: Dear God, thank You for each of my friends, family, and readers holding this journal. I ask that *"Your Spirit of wisdom and understanding, the Spirit of counsel and might, the*

Spirit of the knowledge and fear of the Lord rest upon us" (Isaiah 11:2). We pray in Jesus's name.

> THE NUMBER SEVEN FIRST APPEARS IN THE BIBLE IN THE SEVEN DAYS OF CREATION, WHEN GOD COMPLETED HIS CREATIVE WORK. FROM THERE, WE RELATE SEVEN TO SOMETHING COMPLETE, PERFECT, FINISHED - GOD'S PERFECTION.

December 16
BENEFICIARIES OF A NEW COVENANT
Jeremiah 31:33b

With much love, fear, and sincerity, the Israelites promised to follow and obey God in everything. Yet, soon after, particularly in good times, they forgot their promises, putting God aside in favor of other gods and the world's attractions. Despite their constant rebellion, God was good and merciful to His chosen people. Every time they disobeyed, there were consequences. God punished and then rescued them, making them **beneficiaries of a new covenant**.

"'The days are coming, 'declares the Lord, 'when I will make a new covenant with the people of Israel and with the people of Judah'" **(Jeremiah 31:31).** It won't be a covenant like the one God made with their ancestors, written on distant stones that the people couldn't see or touch; which due to the world's cares, are often forgotten, ignored, and rejected. This covenant would be different and difficult to forget, neglect, or distance oneself from it. *"I will put my law in their minds and write it on their hearts. I will be their God, and they will be my people. No longer will they teach their neighbor, or say to one another, 'Know the Lord,' because they will all know me, from the least of them to the greatest," declares the Lord. "For I will forgive their wickedness and will remember their sins no more"* **(Jeremiah 31:33-34).**

God is good, committed to forgiving and forgetting our transgressions. We're blessed to be **beneficiaries of the new covenant**. But that doesn't give us the freedom to sin freely. God is good! But punishment awaits those who intentionally reject His will, love, or abuse His friendship **(Isaiah 2:19).**

God's great love compels Him to enter into a **new covenant WITH EVERYONE**. The only way we're forgiven of our sins is by putting our complete faith and hope in the sacrifice of the Lord Jesus Christ on the cross. **God is always ready to welcome us back into His fold with outstretched arms.**

Let us pray: Dear God, allow us to be faithful **beneficiaries of this new covenant** with you. Write Your law in our hearts so that we never forget Your precepts. Help us share the good news of Your love, kindness, and friendship with all who don't know You yet, or have forgotten the fragrance and peace that Your presence and friendship offer. We pray in Your Holy Name.

> We're blessed to be **beneficiaries of the new covenant**. But that doesn't give us the freedom to sin freely.

December 17
PATIENCE

"You need to persevere so that when you have done the will of God, you will receive what he has promised." Hebrews 10:36

"Lo que ustedes necesitan es tener paciencia; para que, una vez que hayan hecho la voluntad de Dios, reciban lo que él ha prometido darnos". Hebreos 10:36

"Επειδή, έχετε ανάγκη από υπομονή, για να κάνετε το θέλημα του Θεού, και να λάβετε την υπόσχεση." ΠΡΟΣ ΕΒΡΑΙΟΥΣ 10:36

PATIENCE comes from the Greek word **G-5281 υπομονή (ipomoní)**, which means resistance or joyful endurance (or hopeful), perseverance.

Have you noticed the impact of heavy snow on tree branches? Healthy branches **bend with and resist** the weight of snow, returning to their position once the sun's rays melt the snow. On the other hand, dry, malnourished, and weakened branches break under heavy weight.

The same happens in our lives. When we feed daily on God's Word and savor it during the day, filled with faith and **patience**, we can endure the storms as a spiritual exercise whose result will strengthen our spiritual muscles , preparing us to resist the following and more massive storms.

Faith is a seed that, when tested, produces trust and **patience** in us. Today's verse tells us, *"You need to persevere so that when you have done the will of God, you will receive what he has promised."*

If we're unfit, storms have the capacity to crush our spirits, faith, hope, and love. The devil will use all means to create storms that seem too heavy to endure. If we try to support the weight alone, we'll feel excruciating pain in our spirit. **Patience,** however, helps us think clearly. Look around, and you'll find friends, family, and even strangers willing to help you withstand the stress. **You are not alone or abandoned.**

During a battle, God told Moses that the people would have victory if he kept his hands raised to heaven. But his arms grew tired. Aaron and Hur held Moises's hands up and thus defeated the enemy **(Exodus 17:12-13).** God stills our storms to a whisper **(Psalm 107:29).** Rays of light will appear with the dawn, removing all obstacles along your journey with God.

Food for thought: In what area of my life do I need to be more patient?

Let us pray: Dear God, grant us faith and patience to withstand the storms with hands raised toward You as an expression of faith and gratitude for Your faithfulness. Help us run with patience and perseverance the race that You've set before us **(Hebrews 12:1).** Incline our ears (including our children, family, and friends) toward Your Holy Scriptures; that they might be rays of light to ease the weight of our trials. We pray in Jesus's name.

> When we feed daily on God's Word and savor it during the day, filled with faith and patience, we can endure the storms as a spiritual exercise whose result will strengthen our spiritual muscles.

December 18
THE DIVINITY OF CHRIST
Hebrews 1:6

Today's keyword word ("**superior**") appears as the title of this section of Hebrews. **"The Son is superior to the angels."** In **Hebrews 1:5-14**, we find a contrast between the angels and Jesus Christ. These verses paint a picture of the Son's superiority, majesty, and divinity.

First, we find the divinity of Jesus in the word **"Son"** and the relationship with the Father. Because God never said to any of His angels: *"You are my Son."* I have begotten you today, nor *"I will be*

389

his Father, and he will be my Son" (v.5). One of the reasons the religious leaders sought to kill Jesus was because He identified himself as a *"Son of God"* **(John 10:36).**

Today's verse says, *"Let all God's angels worship him."* In the ten commandments **(Exodus 20, Deuteronomy 5),** God explicitly prohibits all creation from praising, worshiping, or bowing down to anyone other than God because God is jealous. Could this be a biblical inconsistency? No! It's not a textual contradiction because **Jesus is Eternal God**, who descended from His throne and came to Earth in human form to save and restore our relationship with our eternal Father.

We find another image of **Jesus's Divinity** in the following verse: *"But about the Son he says, 'Your throne, O God, will last for ever and ever; a scepter of justice will be the scepter of your kingdom'"* **(Hebrews 1:8).** Here God applies the title of **"God"** to the Son and points to **Jesus's throne and scepter**, both symbols of majesty. Jesus is superior to all the Earthly kings because He *"loved righteousness and hated wickedness."* That's why God anointed Him, God **(v.9).**

Verse 13 affirms Jesus's position at the right hand of the Father, one that was never granted to any of His angels. Without taking any of the merits from the angels, God says that the presence and protection of Jesus are superior because the angels obey Jesus. What a precious blessing to have direct access to the chief, King, and architect of all humanity and heavenly bodies.

Let us pray: Dear God, thank You for sending Jesus Christ to our world, explicitly to save and restore our relationship with you, King and Lord of our lives. Help us not to trust anything or anyone else for our salvation and direction, apart from Your Word and guidance from the Spirit of Jesus Christ, our Lord, in whose name we pray.

> **The presence and protection of Jesus are superior because the angels obey Jesus. What a precious blessing to have direct access to the chief, King, and architect of all humanity and heavenly bodies.**

December 19
WHEN WE'RE DIVIDED
John 7:43
When divided, we're easy prey for the enemy!

As I read today's lectionary readings, two different verses caught my attention this morning. I was divided on which of them to focus our attention on until I noticed the word *"divided"* in **John 7:43.**

The other verse was **Judges 13:12B**, *"what is to be the rule that governs the boy's life and work?"* This journal and daily meditation group exist because God put in my heart to dialogue with my children and the children of their children through these daily meditations. Therefore, Manoah's question to God's angel is one that every parent should ask God on their knees *"How should we educate and guide the child?"*

Our children's education brings us to the importance of establishing a solid foundation for our faith and hope. The Bible is our trustworthy guide leading us into the Lord's presence. The focus verse says that *"the people were divided because of Jesus"* **(John 7:43).** Some said He was a prophet, others that He was the Messiah, others didn't believe, and others wanted to apprehend Him. In **Mark 8:27,** Jesus asked His disciples, *"Who do men say I am?"* Jesus asked this question, knowing the people were **divided** because of Him. He did it so that His disciples would clarify their ideas about Him. To deepen their convictions and strengthen their faith.

THUS THE PEOPLE WERE DIVIDED BECAUSE OF JESUS. JOHN 7:43

There is still a division. For many, Jesus is one of the greatest prophets, the Teacher of teachers, but not God. Yet, for those who have felt His grace and forgiveness in their hearts, for those who upon hearing His voice were raised from their graves of despair, Jesus is the supreme being of all the universe, *"Wonderful Counselor, Mighty God, Everlasting Father, Prince of Peace"* **(Isaiah 9:6).**

My beloved, God's Word instructs us to teach our children to defend themselves against human philosophies that are ignorant of the person, power, and authority of Jesus Christ and that, by trusting God's Word, they may walk guided and grasping God's hand. Let's not allow our children to fall prey due to a lack of knowledge and guidance.

Let us pray: Dear God, thank You for Your Word and Your Holy Spirit, who guides and strengthens us daily on this walk. Remove any divisions that exist, especially between members of the same family. Let our children and their children be well instructed and be good instructors to their children. We pray in Your Holy Name.

December 20
PRAISE GOD AMID TRIALS
Psalm 113:3

Did you know that **The Lord is with you** amid any difficulty or trial you might face? God goes behind you as a tower of fire and bodyguard as He did with Moses. God goes ahead of you, opening a way in the sea and desert. He walks alongside you sharing His yoke, and above you, illuminating your soul.

Many years ago, I discovered that the best way to combat trials and frustrations is through praise and worship. God is worthy of our praise from sunrise to sunset. Praise God during trials, and you'll see God's mighty hand working in your favor.

When things go wrong, we often complain, Lord; *"Why is this happening to me? What did I do to suffer in this way?"* Instead of complaining, consider praising God in good times and bad times. Adore God in your difficulties, thank God for another opportunity to strengthen your faith, and ask God: **What do you want me to learn from this situation?**

When young King David was pastoring his sheep, he didn't see the attacks by bears or lions as a punishment but as a demonstration that God was fighting for him, giving him victory, first over bears and lions and then over the giant Goliath. Praising God increased David's trust and dependence on God, allowing him to have victory after victory even over greater giants and armies.

> Instead of complaining, consider praising God in good times and bad times. Adore God in your difficulties, thank God for another opportunity to strengthen your faith, and ask God: **What do you want me to learn from this situation?**

Maybe you're encountering some modern-day giants. Before facing them, consider praising the Lord, putting your struggle in God's hands, and He will give you the victory. He did it with ordinary people who relied upon God's providence, such as David and Moses. God has done it with me and will do it with you.

Let us pray: Dear God, today we just want to present ourselves to thank You for this new day and to praise Your Holy Name. You're lovely, beautiful, just, and majestic. You're our shield, strength, and strong tower who raises our heads in front of our enemies. You demolish every wall that stands between Your people and Your Divine purpose. Thank you for lighting our way and guiding us to Your heavenly mansion. *"From the rising of the sun to the place where it sets, may your Holy name be praised!"* **(Psalm 113:3).**

December 21
OUR CONSOLATION
Romans 8:18

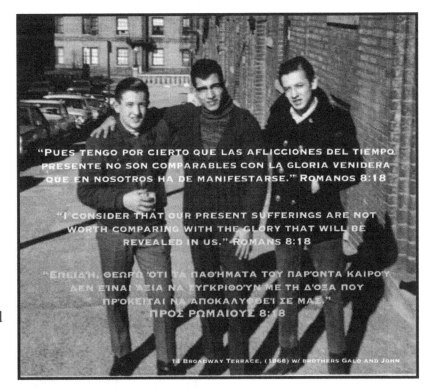

"PUES TENGO POR CIERTO QUE LAS AFLICCIONES DEL TIEMPO PRESENTE NO SON COMPARABLES CON LA GLORIA VENIDERA QUE EN NOSOTROS HA DE MANIFESTARSE." ROMANOS 8:18

"I CONSIDER THAT OUR PRESENT SUFFERINGS ARE NOT WORTH COMPARING WITH THE GLORY THAT WILL BE REVEALED IN US." ROMANS 8:18

"ΕΠΕΙΔΗ, ΘΕΩΡΩ ΌΤΙ ΤΑ ΠΑΘΗΜΑΤΑ ΤΟΥ ΠΑΡΌΝΤΑ ΚΑΙΡΟΎ ΔΕΝ ΕΊΝΑΙ ΆΞΙΑ ΝΑ ΣΥΓΚΡΙΘΟΎΝ ΜΕ ΤΗ ΔΌΞΑ ΠΟΥ ΠΡΌΚΕΙΤΑΙ ΝΑ ΑΠΟΚΑΛΥΦΘΕΊ ΣΕ ΜΑΣ." ΠΡΟΣ ΡΩΜΑΙΟΥΣ 8:18

14 BROADWAY TERRACE, (1968) W/ BROTHERS GALO AND JOHN

Jesus warned that we'd have troubles but asks us to have faith since He has *"overcome the world"* (**John 16:33**). Our verse comforts us by affirming that our momentary sufferings are incomparable to the glory and honor that we'll receive in due time.

While we remain here, God *"comforts us in all our troubles"* (**2 Corinthians 1:4**) sending us out to share with the world the comfort, strength, and hope we've found in walking hand in hand with God.

Noah was a just and noble man who walked with God. Noah in Hebrew means **"quiet"** or *"quiet, resting place, where one finds comfort."* Some of the benefits of walking with God is that God extends His hand when we;

- ✦ pass through the valleys of the shadow of death, lifting us toward life and hope.
- ✦ pass through deserts, quenching our hunger and thirst.
- ✦ pass through infinite dark tunnels, lighting our way.
- ✦ are on the edge of the precipice, lifting us from despair.

In our darkest moments, our only refuge, hope, strength, and comfort is God. After overcoming our trials, looking back, we can sing: *"You have turned my lament into dancing… you clothed me with joy"* (**Psalm 30:11**), and thus we can comfort those who suffer.

This is our consolation: *"I consider that our present sufferings are not worth comparing with the glory that will be revealed in us"* (**Romans 8:18**). Those who have come under God's protection, as Noah did by entering the ark, are called to 1. be messengers of comfort, hope, and love and 2. walk before God and the world with upright and just hearts.

Our lives bless and glorify God when we're the reflection of Christ to those who have been lost. We're the aroma of salvation and hope for those who, because of the tempter's lies, are presently blind and deaf to the pleading of the Spirit.

Let us pray: Dear and merciful God of all consolation, thank You because Your Word is faithful and Your promises are reliable. Come *"comfort all our ruined places. Come and change our desert into Eden, and our wastelands into the Lord's Garden,"* so that, in our house and those of our children, we may find thanksgiving, joy, praise, and singing **(Isaiah 51:3).** May our lives glorify Your Name. We pray in Jesus's Name.

December 22
PRINCES AND PRINCESSES OF PEACE
Micah 4:3

In **Isaiah 2:4**, we find today's parallel verse. Both point to the reign of the Messiah at His second coming. *"For to us a child is born, to us a son is given, and the government will be on his shoulders And he will be called Wonderful Counselor, Mighty God, Everlasting Father, Prince of Peace"* **(Isaiah 9:6).**

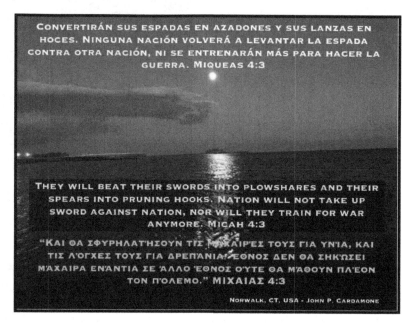

This future awaits those who've placed their trust in God, in His Sacred Word, knowing that our life belongs to God who offers us complete and everlasting peace and joy in the presence of the *"Prince of Peace."* God will bring an end to wars in the last days. Grateful for the wonders that The Lord has done to rescue and give us a place of honor in His kingdom, we must strive to be good ambassadors, creating an atmosphere of true peace here on earth. Jesus told us to *"be at peace with each other"* **(Mark 9:50).**

It's not easy to achieve the true peace that Christ offers. But it's not impossible either. As ambassadors of peace and love, we must first make peace with God through Jesus Christ. Saint Augustine said we *"can't find peace until we make peace with God."* Making peace with God means no longer resisting His will. It is *"to act justly and to love mercy and to walk humbly with Your God"* **(Micah 6:8).** It means striving to live in harmony with everyone, doing what pleases God. We're called to sow seeds of unity in the Spirit, reconciliation, forgiveness, hope, and love. *"If it is possible, as far as it depends on you, live at peace with everyone" (Romans 12:18).*

My beloved, we're the reflection of Jesus, the **Prince of Peace**. As we approach Christmas, consider; *How am I doing in my role as prince/princess of peace?*

Let us pray: Dear God, help us to create in our environment a small reflection of the peace that you will bring to the world when you return for Your church. May we be a true oasis in the desert, filling empty vessels with the water of life that flows from Your love and goodness. Let Your peace offering begin in our hearts. We pray in the name of our *Prince of Peace*.

December 23
UNCHANGING FAITH
Micah 4:6-7

God's love and mercy are unchanging! What God did with the Israelite people, God will also do with and for us who are the New Jerusalem through faith in Jesus Christ. No matter how far we might be lost, God will seek, find, rescue, and make us a strong and unchanging nation of faith.

The book of **Micah** covers the time around 740 - 680 B.C. Through the prophet Micah, God accuses political and religious leaders, saying, *"Her leaders judge for a bribe, her priests teach for a price, and her prophets tell fortunes for money" (Micah 3:11A).* Because of such leaders, the people went astray, sinning against God. Their punishment was the Babylonian captivity that lasted almost 60 years (598 - 538 B.C.) **(Micah 3:5).**

But the Lord's punishment is not forever. *"For his anger lasts only a moment, but his favor lasts a lifetime" (Psalm 30:5).* Despite the bad faith of those leaders who caused their exile, out of love and promise to Abram that his children would be as countless as the stars, God promised to gather His sheep to make them *"a remnant… and a strong nation"* **(Micah 4:6-7).**

Just as God punished and saved the Israelites, God will also do to us; The Lord will save and rescue us, no matter why or by whom we strayed from the path or how long we've been away from God. The Lord will gather us, and from *"that day and forever"* will be our King. But of those who cause stumbling blocks in faith, Jesus said, *"Things that cause people to stumble are bound to come, but woe to*

> The Lord will save and rescue us, no matter why or by whom we strayed from the path or how long we've been away from God.

anyone through whom they come" (**Matthew 18:7, Luke 17:1**).

My beloved, nothing can separate us from God's love except our unbelief!

Let us pray: Dear God, thank You that you gather us to form a strong nation that knows and obeys Your commandments despite our rebellion and straying from Your ways. During this last week of Advent, turn our hearts back to the most precious gift in the world, Your presence, and redemption through the child Jesus, who is God with us. We pray in Your Holy Name.

December 24
SEEKING THE GREAT LIGHT
Isaiah 9:2

I'm fascinated by astronomy. When my son Jean-Paul was six years old, with an amateur telescope, we looked to the night skies to see a great light, Halley's Comet, crossing our planet, and I said, *"My son (agorymou), the next time this comet crosses will be in 75 years. I'll no longer be with you, but perhaps you might see it again."*

In December 2020, my son shared with our granddaughter Ségolène almost the same experience, with the *"conjunctions between Jupiter and Saturn,"* which occur every 20 years, but not all are equal in proximity. *"The 2020 great conjunction… [was] the closest since 1623 and the closest observable since 1226! 2020's extra-close conjunction won't be matched again until March 15, 2080."* [22]

Two thousand and twenty-one years ago, a bright light, announced by the prophets (**Numbers 24:17**), guided the wise men and shepherds to the manger where Jesus, the light of the world, was born. In **Luke 1:76-79**, we read, *"And you, my child, will be called a prophet of the Most High; for you will go on before the Lord to prepare the way for him, to give his people the knowledge of salvation through the forgiveness of their sins, because of the tender mercy of our God, by which the rising sun will come to us from heaven to shine on those living in darkness and in the shadow of death, to guide our feet into the path of peace."*

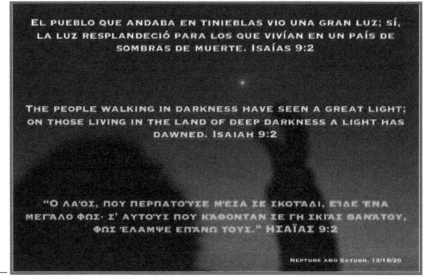

Like the wise men, shepherds, John the Baptist, and all the disciples and martyrs

---

[22] https://earthsky.org/astronomy-essentials/great-jupiter-saturn-conjunction-dec-21-2020

396

throughout the centuries, we're privileged to have found, seen, and been transformed by the great light of Christ. We're not what we were, but we won't be what we are today because each day, God's great light illuminates our minds and hearts to **transform** us into faithful witnesses of the light and guides for those who *dwell in darkness and the shadow of death,* seeking salvation and the way of peace.

Let us pray: Dear God, grant that we continue looking toward the heavens throughout generations in search of **your great light**. Have mercy on those who faint amid darkness and trials. We pray in the name of the child Jesus, our great light and Savior.

December 25
MERRY CHRISTMAS / KALÁ CHRISTOÚGENA
Luke 2:7

What joy! It's here! For weeks we've waited and prepared to receive Christmas Eve, the night when love and goodness were born in our world to combat evil, bringing light, peace, and salvation to all creation.

During this beautiful season, the traditional greeting is; "Merry Christmas." In Greek, *"Kalá Christoúgena,"* which means *"Good Birth of Christ."* On Christmas Eve, we gather with family and friends worldwide to celebrate the birth of Jesus Christ. Family traditions include dinner, reading the gospel narrating the birth of Jesus, singing hymns such as *"Silent Night,"* watching or hearing the Christmas Eve Mass or attending the Christmas Candle Service, and exchanging gifts.

By making room for Jesus in our life, we can give or receive the greatest gift of a **Good Birth of Christ (Kalá Christoúgena)** in human hearts. From Jesus's birth until now, many of us have not made room or time for Jesus because of other obligations and commitments. That's why Joseph and Mary laid baby Jesus *"in a manger, because there was no guest room available for them"* **(Luke 2:7).**

If we understood the power and new life that we acquire by opening our hearts to Jesus, we'd make room in our lives for the most significant inheritance, gift, and experience in history. None of the material gifts we give (or receive) compare to the glorious and majestic experience of becoming an adopted child of God. By accepting Jesus in our hearts by faith, we receive our citizenship and adoption papers, which make us co-heirs with Jesus in His kingdom **(Romans 8:17).**

The essence of Christmas is God's love, acceptance, and grace. God's love traversed time, space, and suffering exclusively for you. It's all about you! Therefore, let us give thanks today for the greatest Christmas gift, and let us diligently share this love with those whom God places in our space, screen, or path. **Merry Christmas! Kalá Christoúgena!**

Let us pray: Dear God, thank You for Your most significant gift that's been born in our hearts. May the peace and joy of Jesus reign in our hearts during and after this beautiful season. We pray in Your Holy Name.

December 26
BORN IN HUMBLE HEARTS

"Today in the town of David, a Savior has been born to you; he is the Messiah, the Lord." **Luke 2:11**

"Hoy, en la ciudad de David, les ha nacido un Salvador, que es Cristo el Señor". **Lucas 2:11**

"επειδή, σήμερα, στην πόλη τού Δαβίδ, γεννήθηκε σε σας σωτήρας, που είναι ο Χριστός, ο Κύριος." **ΚΑΤΑ ΛΟΥΚΑΝ 2:11**

Have you ever wondered why God chose simple shepherds with the announcement of Jesus's birth? Of all the excellent communicators that were there, why the shepherds? Indeed, they were not the best educated. They were simple shepherds in charge of animals. Why were they chosen instead of political leaders, priests, Pharisees, or scribes?

The job of tending sheep was the lowest in society. We understand that sheepherders were not trustworthy or acceptable as witnesses. Why, then, did the heavenly messengers come to the shepherds? Could it be that God, who designed and knows the human heart, saw a heart willing to believe in those poor and humble shepherds?

This question is somewhat clarified by reading **James 2:5**: *"Has not God chosen those who are poor in the eyes of the world to be rich in faith and to inherit the kingdom he promised those who love him?"* Jesus also clarifies that it's impossible for a rich person whose confidence lies in his treasures and abilities to enter the kingdom of heaven **(Matthew 19:24)**.

Jesus didn't come to save the religious or the rich who trusted in their lineage, education, or possessions. It was understood that the Messiah would come for those of Abram, Isaac, and Jacob's descent. But Jesus clarified that He came not for the healthy but for the poor, isolated and sick **(Mark 2:17)**. He made salvation available to everyone humble enough to believe.

Therefore, we can affirm that the world's Savior seeks to be born in humble hearts that fully trust in God's redemptive work. The proof is that we who once lived apart and distanced from God now have access to the throne of grace through faith in the atoning work of Jesus Christ.

Let us pray: Dear God, thank You because you didn't choose the wise or rich to spread the message of salvation throughout the world; you've chosen simple people, and this fills us with hope and courage to go where you send us to spread the good news; that today, in this place, the Savior of the world is born to us. Please give us success in spreading Your good news in our circles of influence. We pray in Your Holy Name.

December 27
SPIRITUAL EARS
Proverbs 8:34

Why is it that children cannot listen to parents' advice, but they easily heed the opinion of others? The Word tells us: *"A fool spurns a parent's discipline, but whoever heeds correction shows prudence" (Proverbs 15:5).*

Jesus said: *"But everyone who hears these words of mine and does not put them into practice is like a foolish man who built his house on sand. The rain came*

down, the streams rose, and the winds blew and beat against that house, and it fell with a great crash" (Matthew 7:26-27). God forbid our dreams and prayers for our youth be dragged into ruin by the foolish currents of this world.

Our world, family, community, and churches need men and women who have **consecrated their ears to faithfully listen to God's instruction with patience and humility**.

With patience - Congregations often impose a time limit on the preacher, especially when there are sporting events after church. In Nehemiah's days, God's Word was heard with reverence, expectation, and spiritual ears. *"They stood where they were and read from the Book of the Law of the Lord their God for a quarter of the day, and spent another quarter in confession and in worshiping the Lord their God" (Nehemiah 9:3).* Can you imagine standing for six hours, listening to the reading of God's Word, confessing, and worshiping? **We need patience and spiritual ears to receive God's correction.**

We also need **humility** to put it into practice. Our nature resists when others impose their opinion on our life. I was impressed by **Liliana's** response to my advice and correction: *"Thank you* *for correcting me."* I've never forgotten her wise humility. This is how we should respond when God corrects us through His Word or our pastor. *"Blessed are those who listen to me"* **(Proverbs 8:34).**

God's correction leads us to life and God's favor **(Proverbs 8:35).** God's Word is the good seed in search of spiritual ears that *"hear the word, retain it, and by persevering produce a crop" (Luke 8:15).*

Let us pray: Dear God, in our distress, we called Your name and cried out to You; From Your temple, You heard our voice, and we know that our cry reached Your divine ears **(2 Samuel 22:7).** Grant us ears attentive to Your Word and the patience and humility to thank You when you correct us because you do it with love. We pray in Jesus's name.

✚ ✚ ✚ ✚ ✚

December 28
FORGETTING OUR SHAMEFUL PAST
Isaiah 54:17

It's possible to take **Isaiah 54:17** out of context. That's why I invite you to read **chapter 54:1-17** to understand the depth of this promise and guarantee that God makes to His children. Two essential points appear in these verses: 1. God will cause us to forget the shame of our past **(v.4),** and 2. No weapon forged against you will prevail **(v.17).**

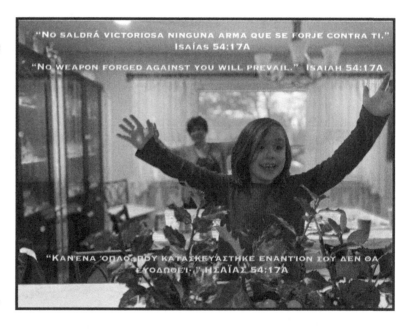

Verses 1-3 call us to rejoice in whatever our situation of defeat, weakness, or poverty might be. It invites us to extend our reach (our hope) and concludes with the promise that our *"children will dispossess nations and settle in their desolate cities."*

<u>Verses 4-8</u> invite widows not to fear loneliness because God will be their husband, and they will **forget the shame of their youth.** They will never be seen as abandoned women or sad in spirit because God Himself will pick them up and show their compassion.

<u>Verses 11-17:</u> God will adorn widows with precious stones, and your children *"will be taught by God."* There will not be a shortage of strong leadership. The peace of God will multiply among your children. God will adorn you with justice. You will no longer be oppressed nor fear any evil because all *"who conspires against you will fall."* These promises conclude in **verse 17:** *"no weapon forged against you will prevail, and you will refute every tongue that accuses you. This is the heritage of the servants of the Lord, and this is their vindication from me."*

These promises become even more important when we recognize that **Isaiah chapter 53** focuses on the suffering of Christ for His people, and **chapter 54** represents the triumph and fruit of the Messiah's suffering. God uses the widow to symbolize God's people, to show that **our past sufferings do not compare with the great blessings God has prepared for His children.**

Let us pray: Dear God, thank You for rescuing us from the great misery and estrangement in which we lived before receiving our redemption through faith in Jesus Christ. Allow us to **forget the shame of our past.** To seek forgiveness from those we've offended, but more than anything, to seek that Jesus is our guardian-redeemer. We pray in Jesus's name.

December 29
THE HOME'S FOUNDATION
1 Corinthians 3:11

In building our home and God's kingdom, we must carefully choose the construction material. As parents, we must base our lives on Christ because wolves disguised as sheep threaten the inheritance of our children and communities. Jesus Christ is the trusted foundation on which to build vibrant lives, homes, and communities.

In all the marriages that I officiated, I ensured that the couples listened, understood, and accepted the same thing that the pastor told us when Margarita

and I were planning our marriage: *"Unless the Lord builds the house, the builders labor in vain. Unless the Lord watches over the city, the guards stand watch in vain"* **(Psalm 127:1).** Marriages begin with lofty, noble, and profound dreams which the enemy will try to break down their foundation. To defend against all attacks, the Lord must be the home's foundation, protecting and directing words, actions, and thoughts.

Often, homes that start with much warmth, love, dreams, commitment, and trust become fractured for lack of protection and God's daily presence - giving way to seasons of coldness, disinterest, and mistrust. Some couples become physically and emotionally distant. We must invoke God's daily presence to mend our fractures and wounds.

The church was constituted to **reconcile** the distance separating us from God and each other. This includes spouses, parents and children, siblings, friends, etc. God has entrusted us with the ministry of reconciliation so that where there are walls, coldness, and disapproval, we'd destroy them in the name of Jesus. The Christian is anointed and commissioned to go where there are gaps, to build bridges. *"See, today I appoint you over nations and kingdoms to uproot and tear down, to destroy and overthrow, to build and to plant"* **(Jeremiah 1:10).**

The world will try to convince us that *"all roads lead to God,"* but Jesus said there is only one way. *"I am the way and the truth and the life. No one comes to the Father except through me"* **(John 14:6).**

Let us pray: Dear God, thank You for teaching us that there is only one foundation on which we must build our homes and communities; Jesus Christ. Thank you because His forgiving arms are open to everyone - no one is excluded or rejected. All who trust in Him establish an excellent foundation to raise their children and future generations. We pray in Jesus's name.

December 30
BE WATCHING, ALERT, AND PRAYING

"Take heed, watch and pray; for you do not know when the time is." **Mark 13:33 NKJV**

"Pero ustedes, presten atención y manténganse atentos, porque no saben cuándo llegará el momento". Marcos 13:33

"Προσέχετε, αγρυπνείτε, και προσεύχεστε· για τον λόγο ότι, δεν ξέρετε πότε είναι ο καιρός." ***ΚΑΤΑ ΜΑΡΚΟΝ 13:33***

Our verse implores us always to be vigilant. In **Luke 21:36,** the Lord adds, *"and pray that you may be able to escape all that is about to happen, and that you may be able to stand before the Son of Man."* Older versions say, *"Watch therefore, and pray always"* **(NKJV).** Other versions say, *"Be alert at all times" (NRSVA).* **Matthew 24:42** says, *"Therefore keep watch, because you do not know on what day your Lord will come."*

Jesus warns the disciples and us, *"Take heed, watch and pray; for you do not know when the time is"* **(Mark 13:33).** In essence, as God's children and representatives, God places us as sentries to **watch, be alert, and pray** for His flock.

GUARDING: As shepherds do, we must stand at a high point, looking carefully into the distance to identify any beasts that try to approach the flock. We can't be distracted from the mission to care, protect, and prevent the thief from robbing God's house. Unfortunately, every day we observe **salaried** sentries distracted by their cell phones instead of being the eyes of protection for the people.

ALERT: Lives and souls depend on the care of the sentry on duty. It's essential to understand our role as God's sentries and appreciate that others' lives depend on our faithfulness and preparation to remain awake. Jesus said, *"Watch and pray so that you will not fall into temptation. The spirit is willing, but the flesh is weak."* **(Mark 14:38, Matthew 26:41).**

PRAYING: In addition to guarding and being alert, Jesus instructs us to keep praying. We pray for the state of our soul, of those in our family and church, so that, even though our human defenses might fail us, God's unfailing protection may guard His flock ; so that the enemy does not find a way to pervert the instructions that we've received through God's Word.

Let us pray: Dear God, I didn't have the privilege of serving in the military as a sentry. I'm grateful for our military, our sentries around the world who've been dispatched and strategically placed in high places to care for and protect Your people. Keep them under Your mantle of protection, help them stay watchful, and return them to their homes safe and sound. Help us watch, be alert, and pray for our people and future generations. We pray in Your Holy Name.

> **We pray for the state of our soul, of those in our family and church, so that, even though our human defenses might fail us, God's unfailing protection may guard His flock.**

December 31
STARTING-OVER WISELY
1 Kings 3:9A

Today we say goodbye to 2021 and receive the new year with joy and **wise anticipation**. We don't know what 2022 brings, but we trust God's good plans. We receive the New Year with a

sense of undeserved grace coupled with immense gratitude and expectation for better days ahead.

The New Year is an excellent time to **start over with a clean slate**. Perhaps some 2021 goals weren't met. That's OK. I didn't lose the weight I wanted, but I didn't gain any and I feel healthy. I did ride my bike over 1700 miles, including a 293m hike to Lithoxoro, Greece, and accomplished the essentials: dedicated time to family, published our daily meditations and videos, and began organizing this journal.

So give your servant a discerning heart to govern your people and to distinguish between right and wrong. 1 Kings 3:9A

"Δῶσε, λοιπόν, στον δοῦλο σου νοήμονα καρδιά, στο να κρίνει τον λαό σου, για να διακρίνω ανάμεσα στο καλό και στο κακό." Α΄ Βασιλέων 3:9Α

Yo te pido que me des un corazón con mucho entendimiento para gobernar a tu pueblo y para discernir entre lo bueno y lo malo.» 1 Reyes 3:9A

SOPHIA DESTRUGE - ICELAND

As you consider 2022 goals, consider creating meaningful, **reachable** targets that will benefit your future generations. Pray that God grants you the **wisdom** and willpower to sacrifice the necessary time and effort. **Starting over wisely** is possible through our Lord and Savior, Jesus Christ. *"Therefore, if anyone is in Christ, the new creation has come"* **(2 Corinthians 5:17).**

The start of a New Year is also an excellent time to forget past failures and wait for seasons of renewal and blessing. Leave any mistake made during the past year in God's hands so that, with **hearts molded by experience and Divine wisdom**, we may seek forgiveness, reparation, and restoration. It's time to leave behind the things that are useless or inconvenient **to God and family**.

Every new day we awake is an opportunity to walk with our Savior. Yesterday's failures are unnecessary, excess baggage. The father of lies wants us to doubt God's promises and presence. He whispers in our ears, *"If God were with you, you wouldn't have failed, you wouldn't have become ill, your business or marriage wouldn't have failed, etc."*

But you know what? Let me close with this final thought of affirmation. You were created to fly high like eagles, free from yesterday's burdens. Therefore, *"Remain in Christ!"* Feed on God's Word. **Seek God's Wisdom** and the prayerful support of your brothers and sisters worldwide. **You're not alone!**

Let us pray: Dear God, we don't know what tomorrow brings, but we know you'll be with us each new dawn. Grant that during the coming year, in deeds and words, we may magnify Your name and kingdom and that Your people find heavenly hope, peace, healing, and wisdom. Thank you for the amazing joy and privilege of publishing for friends, family, and present and future generations this book, dedicated to **"The Blood of my Blood."** We pray in Your Holy Name.

CLOSING REMARKS

For much of my life I was neither a Christian nor a leader. Prior to February 28, 1989, I was a shy, introverted techie who saw an opportunity to acquire quick wealth in real estate. I went to church out of obligation but fell asleep most of the time. The sermon was the best time to close my eyes and catch a power nap. Unfortunately, real estate took a nosedive in 1987, and with it, all my dreams, hopes, and savings. Not only were we in debt, but I was also emotionally and spiritually bankrupt!

I didn't know Christ and knew nothing about trusting God's leading. God's love and Grace were unfamiliar, and the power of the Holy Spirit was in snooze mode. I'd just changed jobs and things were deteriorating, working long hours seven days a week to save my job and home. When I was at work, I wanted to be home; when I was home, I couldn't think of anything except work and debts. Anxiety filled me and led to many sleepless nights.

The Father of Lies is real and cunning! He made me believe that I was a bad provider, useless as a husband, father, employee, and investor, and pointed to my half-million-dollar life insurance policy as the answer to debt. I almost believed that everyone would be better off without me. The M*A*S*H theme song and its soothing refrain, "suicide is painless," kept buzzing around my head:

> *"That game of life is hard to play*
> *I'm gonna lose it anyway*
> *The losing card of some delay*
> *So this is all I have to say*
> *That suicide is painless."*

I almost acted on the lie, but God had better plans! My 8-year-old son, Jean-Paul, had become aware of our financial difficulties and said to me: *"Dad, its ok if we're broke, as long as we're together."* In February 1989, a friend invited me to a three-day spiritual retreat where I experienced an intimate, personal, and transforming encounter with Jesus. I had known about Jesus, but I did not know the depth of God's love through Christ, nor did I know the purpose for which I existed. I had believed in God, but only from afar, and I didn't understand what it meant to believe in Jesus Christ and His redemption. On Saturday, February 25, during an evening prayer chapel, I came to the realization that, in spite of my faults and failures, I was loved by God and my family, and began accepting and loving myself, as I was.

Since that three-day retreat in '89, my life was radically transformed. I found peace in my heart and stopped worrying about many things. I came out of my cocoon and used music as a platform to tell of God's love. My legal techie experience helped me to study the Bible with joy and purpose and as I grew in the fear and knowledge of the Lord I began to take on new responsibilities within the church.

I've been blessed to serve on many fourth-day retreats, first as a layperson (including planting a fourth-day community in Cleveland) and later as a spiritual director. Each experience has prepared me for who I am today. God is in the business of loving the unlovable, strengthening the weak, enriching the poor in spirit, and putting Humpty Dumpty together again. God did it with me, and can/will do it with you or your loved ones who are facing seemingly unbeatable Goliaths.

I encourage you to consider attending a three-day retreat, away from the pressures and distractions, to strengthen your faith and relationship with God. https://www.footsteps-sand.org

It has been an incredible journey, walking with you through the Bible and organizing these 4-minute daily meditations. You, my friends and family, were on my mind each day as I sat down to pray, meditate, write and edit this book. The following thought encouraged me daily: *"What an amazing joy and honor that God has granted me, that I should have the privilege to converse across time and space, with friends, family, and my future generations, the blood of my blood."* I've spoken through the written word, and, in whatever decade or century you exist, you've responded with your thoughts and prayers. The three of us (you, God, and I) have been in a marvelous daily dialogue across time, space, and into eternity.

Thank you for granting me the tremendous joy and privilege of sharing this space and moment to meditate on God's Word with you. I pray that your faith in God has been renewed and strengthened (as mine has) and will continue to grow as you seek to know better and follow our Creator God.

Till we meet again, same time and place tomorrow, or in heaven; *"May the Grace of our Lord Jesus Christ, the Love of God and the Communion of the Holy Spirit be with you today and always"* **(1 Corinthians 13:14).** May the Spirit of Jesus rise upon you and fill you with love, joy, peace, light, and hope.

Μέχρι να συναντηθούμε ξανά, στην ίδια ώρα και στο ίδιο μέρος αύριο μέσα από αυτό το βιβλίο, ή στον ουρανό. *"Η χάρη τού Κυρίου Ιησού Χριστού, και η αγάπη τού Θεού, και η κοινωνία τού Αγίου Πνεύματος είθε να είναι μαζί με όλους σας" (Προς Κορινθίους Β' 13:13).* Είθε το Πνεύμα του Ιησού να έρθει επάνω σας και να σας γεμίσει με αγάπη, χαρά, ειρήνη, φως και ελπίδα.

Five Truths of the Gospel of Salvation

1- The Truth About Love - God loves you and wants you to have an abundant life. *"For God so loved the world that he gave his one and only Son, that whoever believes in him shall not perish but have eternal life" (John 3:16).*

2- The Truth About Sin - Sin separates us from God, depriving us of abundant life. *"For all have sinned and fall short of the glory of God"* **(Romans 3:23).**

3- The Substitutionary Truth - Jesus Christ took your place on the cross and paid the full price of your salvation making it possible for you to reconcile with God. *"But God demonstrates his own love for us in this: While we were still sinners, Christ died for us"* **(Romans 5:8).** *"Jesus answered, "I am the way and the truth and the life. No one comes to the Father except through me" (John 14:6).*

4- The Truth About Repentance - In order to return to God, you need to repent of your sins. *"Repent, then, and turn to God, so that your sins may be wiped out" (Acts 3:19).*

5- The Truth About Faith - Eternal and abundant life is a gift that God offers you through Christ. It will be yours if you receive Him as Lord and Savior. *"For the wages of sin is death, but the gift of God is eternal life in[a] Christ Jesus our Lord" (Romans 6:23).* *"Yet to all who did receive him, to those who believed in his name, he gave the right to become children of God" (John 1:12).*

Five Reasons to Seek God

1. Matthew 6:33 - *"But seek first his kingdom and his righteousness, and all these things will be given to you as well."*

2. Colossians 3:1 - *"Since, then, you have been raised with Christ, set your hearts on things above, where Christ is, seated at the right hand of God."*

3. Amos 5:14 - *"Seek good, not evil, that you may live. Then the Lord God Almighty will be with you, just as you say he is."*

4. Psalm 70:4 - *"But may all who seek you rejoice and be glad in you; may those who long for your saving help always say, 'The Lord is great!'"*

5. Psalm 63:1 - *"You, God, are my God, earnestly I seek you; I thirst for you, my whole being longs for you, in a dry and parched land where there is no water."*

Christ Initiates the Invitation

"Here I am! I stand at the door and knock. If anyone hears my voice and opens the door, I will come in and eat with that person, and they with me" **(Revelation 3:20).**

Is there anything in your past or present that you think God won't forgive if you approach Him with a repentant heart? The Bible teaches that all sins are forgivable when we trust in Jesus's sacrifice. You can receive Christ right now, by faith, through prayer. Everyone is invited to receive forgiveness and reconcile with God. The only thing God asks is to hear our repentant attitude.

Prayer to receive Christ

The following is a suggested prayer guide:
"Lord Jesus, I need you. Thank you for dying on the cross for my sins. I open the door of my life and ask you to come in and be my Savior and Lord. Thank you for forgiving my sins and giving me a second chance at eternal life. Take control of my life. Make me the person you saw when you formed me in my mother's womb."

If this prayer expresses the desires of your heart, say it as written or in your own words.

As you pray this prayer of Salvation, God, Jesus, and the Holy Spirit will enter your life to guide your thoughts, understanding, words, and actions, from this day forward. Continue daily meditating on God's Holy Word.

INDEX - BY SCRIPTURE VERSE

VERSE	DATE	TITLE
Esther 4:16	Sep 27	PERSONAL SACRIFICE FOR SUCH A TIME AS THIS
Exodus 14:14	Jul 18	GOD FIGHTS FOR HIS PEOPLE
Exodus 14:15	Sep 11	TELL MY PEOPLE TO MARCH
Exodus 16:12	Sep 18	GOD SATISFIES HUNGER
Exodus 19:4b	Mar 4	TIRELESS
Exodus 23:12	Oct 3	REST, RECHARGE, AND REFRESH
Exodus 3:5	May 8	GOD TRANSFORMS THE ORDINARY
Exodus 3:17	Aug 28	GOD DESCENDED FROM HIS THRONE
Exodus 30:33	Jan 12	CONSECRATED FOR WORSHIP
Exodus 32:26B	Jul 29	WHEN WE FALL INTO IDOLATRY
Exodus 39:43	Oct 17	AS THE LORD COMMANDED
Ezekiel 18:30	Oct 26	FOR THE SINS OF THE PARENTS
Ezekiel 33:12	Mar 27	GOD'S RIGHTEOUSNESS
Ezekiel 34:11	May 2	LOST SHEEP
Ezekiel 36:9	Mar 28	GOD WILL TAKE CARE OF YOU
Ezekiel 36:25	Dec 5	YOU WILL BE CLEANED
Ezequiel 34:28	Nov 21	SHOWERS OF BLESSINGS
Gal 3:28	Sep 30	SPECIAL, BUT EQUALLY LOVED
Gal 5:13	Feb 4	CALLED TO BE FREE
Gal 6:9	Aug 6	THE DAY OF REST
Gen 1:27	Apr 6	CREATED IN GOD'S IMAGE
Gen 2:7	May 20	THE BREATH OF LIFE
Gen 7:6	May 15	BUILD THE ARK
Gen 11:6	May 25	UNITY IS NOT OPTIONAL
Gen 16:4	Feb 26	I WILL BLESS THOSE WHO BLESS YOU
Gen 24:14	Nov 9	FREE OF ERRORS AND INCONSISTENCIES
Gen 24:40A	Jun 13	GOD MAKE YOUR JOURNEY A SUCCESS
Gen 27:4	Jul 3	PARENTAL BLESSINGS
Gen 37:9	Aug 8	GOD STILL SPEAKS IN DREAMS AND VISIONS
Gen 41:38	Aug 14	KNOWLEDGE AND INTELLIGENCE FROM GOD
Gen 42:24a	Aug 15	JOSEPH WEPT
Heb 1:6	Dec 18	THE DIVINITY OF CHRIST
Heb 1:8	Mar 1	SCEPTER OF JUSTICE
Heb 2:1	Feb 15	PAY CAREFUL ATTENTION
Heb 2:9	Jun 10	EVERYTHING SUSTAINED BY HIS POWERFUL WORD
Heb 3:6	Mar 15	OUR GLORIOUS HOPE
Heb 4:16	Mar 19	SUSCEPTIBLE TO SIN
Heb 6:1	Oct 18	GROWTH TOWARD MATURITY
Heb 6:15	Oct 19	FAITHFULLY PATIENT PEOPLE
Heb 7:17	Oct 22	FOREVER
Heb 9:15	Mar 29	MEDIATOR OF A NEW COVENANT
Heb 10:36	Dec 17	PATIENCE
Heb 10:39	Nov 16	BEFORE AND AFTER CHRIST
Heb 11:1	Mar 2	WALK WITH THE KING
Heb 11:19	Sep 9	FAITH THAT ENSURES SALVATION
Heb 11:6	Jun 11	HOW TO PLEASE GOD
Heb 12:1	Sep 6	GET RID OF EXCESS BAGGAGE
Heb 12:11	Sep 7	DISCIPLINE HURTS, BUT HEALS
Heb 12:2	Mar 31	THE JOY OF THE LORD
Heb 13:17	Jul 19	PRAY FOR YOUR PASTORS
Heb 13:8	Dec 13	INVARIABLE AND HUMBLE

VERSE	DATE	TITLE
Hosea 6:6	Apr 20	INTIMACY WITH CHRIST
Isaiah 7:14B	Mar 25	GOD WITH US
Isaiah 9:2	Dec 24	SEEKING THE GREAT LIGHT
Isaiah 11:2	Dec 15	SEVEN - GOD'S PERFECTION
Isaiah 11:6	Dec 14	LED BY A CHILD
Isaiah 12:2	Dec 9	WHOM SHALL I FEAR?
Isaiah 26:3	Apr 14	PERFECT PEACE
Isaiah 26:3 GNT	Apr 24	FIRM IN PURPOSE
Isaiah 32:15	May 4	WHEN THE SPIRIT OF GOD COMES UPON US
Isaiah 40:3-4	Dec 6	GUARDIANS OF THE KING'S HIGHWAY
Isaiah 40:10	Nov 20	OUR REWARD IS COMING
Isaiah 41:10	Jul 31	GOD WILL NOT FAIL
Isaiah 43:10	Mar 22	ONLY GOD CAN SAVE
Isaiah 44:2	Jul 17	FORMED, CHOSEN AND HELPED
Isaiah 51: 4	Mar 7	THE EYES OF GOD ARE UPON US
Isaiah 53:12	Apr 2	OUR MEDIATOR
Isaiah 54:17	Dec 28	FORGETTING OUR SHAMEFUL PAST
Isaiah 58:4b	Feb 17	MORE THAN DUST IN THE WIND
Isaiah 60:2	Jan 6	TRANSFORMED BY GOD'S LIGHT
Isaiah 60:20	Mar 17	WHEN WILL OUR SORROWS END?
Isaiah 65:24	May 5	GOD ANSWERS PRAYER
James 1:2	Aug 26	DON'T GIVE UP!
James 1:13	Aug 27	RESISTING TEMPTATION
James 2:26	Sep 10	SAVED BY FAITH OR WORKS?
James 3:17	Jan 2	WISDOM
James 4:7	Jan 31	DIVINE SUBMISSION
James 4:7	Oct 9	IT IS WRITTEN!
James 4:8	Sep 20	WE CAN DRAW CLOSE TO GOD WITH CONFIDENCE
James 5:7	Jul 6	BE PATIENT
Jer 2:7	Mar 18	LET'S RESPECT ALL ORDINANCES
Jer 29:13	Feb 3	HOPE, TRUST, AND PRAY
Jer 31:33b	Dec 16	BENEFICIARIES OF A NEW COVENANT
Jer 33:3	Mar 26	WONDERS OF GOD
Job 14:12	Apr 11	WE'LL RISE AGAIN
Job 19:25	Feb 16	MY REDEEMER
Job 28:28	Oct 12	WISDOM IS BORN FROM FEAR
John 1: 1	Mar 21	THE WORD WAS GOD
John 1:29	Jan 13	HEAL US FROM ALL EVIL
John 4:4	Mar 14	A NECESSARY MEETING
John 5:39	Oct 24	ONLY JESUS SAVES
John 6:35	Feb 29	THE BREAD OF LIFE
John 6:35	Aug 11	SERVING WITH GREAT LOVE
John 7:34	Sep 15	THE MISUNDERSTOOD TRUTH
John 7:43	Dec 19	WHEN WE'RE DIVIDED
John 7:7	Jul 7	MIRRORS OF THE SOUL
John 8:29	May 23	THINGS THAT PLEASE GOD
John 8:32	Sep 22	I'M FREE
John 8:51	May 9	SAVED BY FAITH OR OBEDIENCE?
John 12:27	Mar 30	WHY JESUS CAME
John 12:36	Mar 3	CHILDREN OF LIGHT
John 12:46	Jul 11	BEARERS OF THE LIGHT

VERSE	DATE	TITLE
John 12:48	Mar 24	CONDEMNED BY THE WORD
John 13:1	Oct 20	THE LOVE OF CHRIST
John 13:34	Apr 1	LOVE ONE ANOTHER
John 13:35	Nov 3	LOVE - THE DISCIPLESHIP TEST
John 14:16	Jun 6	THE GREAT ADVOCATE
John 14:27	May 16	NOT AS THE WORLD GIVES
John 15:16	Aug 25	CHOSEN
John 16:20	May 19	OUR COMFORT AND HOPE
John 16:33	Nov 24	WHEN IN TROUBLE, TRUST GOD!
John 19:30	Apr 10	WHY CALL THIS A GOOD FRIDAY?
John 20:19	Apr 18	PEACE BE WITH YOU
John 20:21	May 26	SENT TO HEAL AND LOVE
John 21:15	Jan 17	FEED MY LAMBS
Jonah 3:10	Feb 27	MERCIFUL GOD
Jonah 4.4	Feb 28	IS IT RIGHT FOR YOU TO BE ANGRY?
Joshua 2:12	Oct 30	WHO IS RAHAB?
Joshua 2:19b	Oct 31	YOUR HOUSE, A HOLY REFUGE
Joshua 23:10	Jul 30	SPIRITUAL POWER
Lam 3:55-58	Apr 4	YOUR FIGHT IS OUR FIGHT
Luke 1:76-77	Dec 2	ADVENT - A CELEBRATION OF LIFE
Luke 2:11	Dec 26	BORN IN HUMBLE HEARTS
Luke 2:7	Dec 25	MERRY CHRISTMAS / KALÁ CHRISTOÚGENA
Luke 4:18-19	Nov 10	SENT OUT IN JESUS 'NAME
Luke 5:10	Jan 9	TRANSFORMATIVE INSTRUCTIONS
Luke 6:31	Jan 5	JESUS' GOLDEN RULE
Luke 6:45	Jun 16	TREASURES GAINED BY OBEDIENCE
Luke 7:22	Dec 8	THE WORKS OF CHRIST
Luke 7:32	Jul 14	DANCING IS FORBIDDEN
Luke 8:10	Jun 5	HAPPY BIRTHDAY IN HEAVEN DAD
Luke 10:16	Jan 23	SPEAKING OF REJECTION
Luke 10:23B-24	Jul 4	BLESSED ARE THOSE WHO HEAR
Luke 11:17	Jun 9	DIVISION WEAKENS
Luke 14:14	Apr 25	AT THE RESURRECTION OF THE RIGHTEOUS
Luke 16:10	Jan 30	CHARACTER
Luke 16:26	Oct 13	JESUS - OUR BRIDGE TO GOD
Luke 17:3	Jun 27	REBUKE THE SINNER. FORGIVE THE REPENTANT
Luke 18:17	Jan 20	WE MUST BELIEVE LIKE A CHILD
Luke 19:41	Feb 13	SEE JESUS IN EVERY TEAR
Luke 24:44b	May 13	FULFILLED MESSIANIC PROPHECIES
Luke 24:46 (NKJV)	May 22	NECESSARY THINGS
Mal 3:16	Dec 3	FRIENDSHIP WITH GOD PRODUCES HUMAN FELLOWSHIP
Mal 4:6	Dec 4	SATURDAY GREETING
Mark 3:10	Feb 10	EVERYONE WANTED TO TOUCH HIM
Mark 6:37	Jul 28	GIVE THEM SOMETHING TO EAT
Mark 6:51	Jun 23	GOD HAS POWER OVER STORMS
Mark 7:9	Sep 1	BETWEEN LAW AND TRADITION
Mark 9:12	Feb 21	ALL THINGS RESTORED
Mark 9:23	Jun 30	FAITH - GIFT AND COMMANDMENT
Mark 10:51	Oct 27	WHAT DO YOU WANT ME TO DO FOR YOU?
Mark 11:17B	Mar 10	GOD WORKS THROUGH PRAYER

INDEX - BY KEY WORD

KEYWORDS	DATES
CONSECRATION / CONSECRATED	
	1/12, 3/5, 5/8,10 8/3,25, 12/27
CONSEQUENCES	1/14,19, 3/18,27, 7/12,27,29, 8/27, 11/18, 12/16
COST OF REDEMPTION	1/25, 2/23, 3/23, 4/10,24, 5/16,31, 6/29, 8/18,31, 9/19, 10/14
COURAGE	1/20, 6/5,6, 8/5,12,17,26, 9/16, 10/12, 11/16
COVENANT	2/1, 3/22,29, 4/14,15,24, 6/2, 7/8,21, 9/17,30, 11/29, 12/16
CROSS / CALVARY	1/12,25, 2/4,21,25, 3/29, 4/2,15,17, 5/16, 6/14, 9/28, 10/7,
CURSED	2/1,16,26, 7/3,14, 8/31, 12/12
DEATH	1/10,11,31, 2/2,4,8,10,11,16,22,23, 3/3,30,31, 4/2,3,10,11,19,
	24,25,27,28, 5/3,9,21,22,27,30, 6/4,17,28 8/5,19,23,25,31,
	9/9,10,14,15,22,27,29, 10/1,6,7,13
DECISIONS	6/13, 7/17,25, 8/4,7,11,16, 9/1,19,20, 10/2,12,21,30, 11/2,
	12/10,29
DEFENDER	1/20, 2/23, 4/4,7, 6/18,28, 7/18,30, 10/21,24,28, 11/28
DEPRESSION	1/23, 2/2,23, 3/4, 7/19, 9/22, 11/18,24
DESIRES	1/24, 3/11,20, 4/3,6,20, 6/4, 7/1, 8/1,17, 9/2,23,29, 10/20,27,
	11/5,27, 12/11
DESOLATION	5/4, 7/28, 11/2,13, 12/28
DESPISE / DISPARAGE	1/23,25, 2/25,26,28, 5/6,29 7/14, 8/13, 9/2, 10/7, 12/25
DESTROY	1/14,26, 2/27,28, 3/11,20, 4/15,17, 7/16,22,29, 8/13,21,
	9/5,13,16,24,25, 10/6,10, 11/16,19,24,29, 12/29
DEVIL / SATAN / ENEMY	2/19,23, 3/3, 7/17,31, 8/27, 9/6,21,23,28, 10/5,6,13, 11/7,14,
	12/7,17,19
DISCIPLESHIP / DISCIPLES	
	1/9,21, 3/14, 4/1,7,9,11,18,21,29, 5/9,11,14, 6/12,17, 23,27,
	8/12,23, 9/19,26, 10/23, 11/2,3,
DISCOURAGE / DISCOURAGED	
	2/4,23,29, 3/29, 4/5,7, 7/6,19, 8/26,30, 9/21, 11/12,17, 24,30,
DISOBEDIENCE / REBELLION	
	1/13,19,21,23, 2/13,18,25, 3/4,13,24,18,20,27, 4/12,15, 5/1,4,
	6/16,17, 7/25,27, 8/9,31, 9/23,27, 10/6, 12/27,29
DIVINE CARE	2/19,20,26, 3/4,7,28, 5/2, 6/11, 7/22, 8/11,13,18,19,28,
	9/5,11,23, 10/8, 11/13,20,21,28, 12/6
DIVINE POWER	2/5,10,14,16,21, 3/3, 4/18, 5/22, 6/6,17,23, 7/16,25,26,30,31,
	8/9,11,12,13,19,21, 9/8,9,15,17,24,25,26,27, 10/12, 11/4,15,
	12/15
DIVISION	1/14,19,31, 6/9,27, 8/13, 9/21,23, 10/13, 11/7,14, 12/19
DOCTRINE	1/19, 4/23, 5/14, 8/13,16, 9/1, 11/16
DOUBT	1/22,25, 2/23, 4/11,21, 5/1, 6/9,30, 7/8,26,31, 8/12,17, 9/15,22,
	11/9, 12/8

418

KEYWORDS	DATES
GIVING	1/17,23, 2/3,4,25, 4/19,29, 7/17, 8/23,28, 9/4,19, 11/28, 12/14,20,29
GOD'S FAMILY	1/13, 2/4,7,23, 3/6,14, 4/8, 5/23, 8/6,7,22,25, 9/3,21,25,30, 10/1,4,8, 12/4
GOD'S PRESENCE	1/5,12,14,16,20,31, 2/4,8,9,10, 3/2,5, 4/3,7,19,25, 5/21,30, 6/2,6,7,13,18,23,28, 7/12,24,25,28,31, 8/10,11,12,19,21,27,31, 9/9,11,14,17,18,20,23,24,27,28, 10/20, 11/12,17,21,22,24, 12/18,20,24,29
GOD'S VOICE	1/27, 4/5,6,7, 5/25, 6/13,19,20, 7/8,28, 11/13, 12/19
GOD'S WILL	1/2,7,9,31, 2/1,13,22,23, 5/25,27, 6/11,17,19,20,29, 7/5,22,28, 8/3,23, 9/3,10,15,28,29, 10/4,5,12,16,17,19,20, 11/7,14,25, 12/2,31
GOD'S ANGER	2/28, 3/6, 4/15,28, 5/3, 6/27, 7/27,29, 9/9
GOD'S CHILDREN	1/2,18,21,23, 2/1,14,16,22, 3/1,3,4, 4/19, 5/15, 6/5, 7/5,11, 8/18,31, 9/3,28, 10/4,11, 11/27, 12/18,30
GOD'S CHOSEN	1/7, 2/1,11,17, 3/5, 4/3,15, 6/2,12, 7/17, 8/20,25, 9/28,30, 10/30, 12/26
GOD'S CORRECTION / DISCIPLINE	
	1/17,21,27, 2/18,24, 4/17, 5/7,18, 6/10,25, 7/27, 8/5,8, 9/7, 11/18, 12/27
GOD'S FAVOR	1/21, 2/23, 3/10,25,28, 4/17, 5/7,30, 6/7,18, 7/13, 10/16,30, 11/23, 12/27
GOD'S GIFT	1/2,6,11,25, 2/2,7,8,10,20, 4/10,21, 5/2,5,24, 6/3,30, 9/4, 10/8, 12/25
GOD'S GRACE	2/17,19,22,25,26, 4/17, 6/16, 7/21,31, 8/18, 9/2,10,17,23,30, 10/1,4,11,24,29, 12/14,26,25
GOD'S HOUSE	1/5,13,15, 3/10,14,15, 6/1,12,25, 10/1,12, 11/5,
GOD'S KINGDOM	1/8,20, 3/1,3, 4/23, 5/5, 6/15, 7/22, 8/5,9,12,18,24,31, 9/3,10,27, 10/6,13, 11/11,19, 12/14
GOD'S LOVE	1/2,3,5,15,16,25, 2/7,8,14,16,17,19,22, 3/4,27, 4/23, 5/9, 6/29, 7/8,21,28, 8/5,9,10,11,12,13,17,18,24,25,31, 9/7,14,23,24, 10/8,15,16,20,28,29, 11/1,4,23, 12/16,25
GOD'S MERCY	1/1, 2/8,9,23, 7/21, 8/17, 11/2,23, 12/16,23
GOD'S PEOPLE	3/31, 5/26, 6/2,21, 8/5, 10/14, 12/28
GOD'S PROMISES	1/4,18,20,21,22,28, 2/8, 3/2, 4/7,15, 5/5,28, 6/1,2,5, 7/13,30,31, 8/9,24,28, 9/9,14,15,16,17,20,24,27,28,30, 10/11, 11/29, 12/1,7,8,28
GOD'S TEMPLE	3/8,9,10,13, 6/19,21,26,29, 8/18,19,24, 9/15, 10/25,31, 11/11, 12/27

KEYWORDS	DATES

KEYWORDS **DATES**

GOD'S WORD - (THE BIBLE)

1/9,14,16,17,20,21,23,25,26,27,28,29, 2/2,3,4,5,8,13,15,19, 22,24,25, 3/3,5,7,21,28, 4/5,8,16,18,20,30, 5/9,11,12,17, 21,27,31, 6/1,3,9,12,14,17,22,25, 7/7,8,11,15,20,22,23,25, 26,30, 8/2,3,5,7,8,9,11,12,13,16,20,21,30, 9/1,2,3,4,6,9, 13,15,16,17,23, 24,26,27,28, 10/9,10,11,12,24,29, 11/6,8, 9,12,24,29, 12/6,11,19

GODLY WISDOM
1/2,27,29, 2/19, 5/22,23, 6/1,18,30, 7/22, 8/4,5,12,14,16,30, 9/1,2,3,15, 10/12, 11/19, 12/15,31

GOOD
1/2,8,9,14,16,21,23,24,26,27,29,30, 2/3,7,10,13,14,15,16, 17,19,21,22, 3/1,4,6,11,12,18,19,23,24,27, 4/3,4,7,10,11, 13,17,18,22,29,30, 5/2,6,7,10,11,17,18,20,23,24,26,30, 6/1,3,5,7,8,11,16,19,20,22,23,24,27,29,30, 7/2,3,7,20,22, 25,30, 8/3,5,6,8,13,17,21,28, 9/3,4,6,8,10,11,12,13,14,21,24,30, 10/2,3,5,6,8,10,12,13,16,17,18,19,23,26,29,30, 11/1,2,3,6,7,10,11, 13,20,21,22, 23,24,30, 12/2,8,9,10,11,15,16,19,20,22,25,26,27,31

GOSPEL / EVANGELIZE
2/5,15,17,19, 3/3, 7/10, 8/13,16, 9/8,17, 11/10,27, 12/6,8

GRATITUDE
1/1, 2/18,22,24, 4/19,24, 5/9, 6/3,5,8,10,25, 7/19,22,23, 8/23, 9/2,9,24, 10/1,3,8, 11/11, 12/2,10,12,20,31

GRIEF / AFFLICTIONS
2/10,23,25, 3/3,4,17, 4/17, 5/19,26,30, 6/26,29,30, 8/2, 9/3,7,20,

GRUMBLING / ARGUING
5/2, 6/12, 9/18,23, 10/2

GUIDANCE / CONSULT
1/27, 2/1,9,26, 3/7, 4/7, 5/15, 7/1,22, 8/8, 9/17,23,28, 10/15, 11/5,17,25,28, 12/6,14,15,19,

GUILT
1/11, 2/12, 8/27,31, 9/12, 10/7,26,29

HARMONY
1/11,13,24, 3/1, 4/8,9,16,23,28, 5/10,23,25,28, 6/1,12, 8/19,27, 10/5, 11/18, 12/4,22

HATE
1/7,13, 2/26, 3/17, 5/29, 6/22, 7/7,29, 9/23, 11/7, 12/18

HEALING / HEALER
1/15,22, 2/5,6,10,11,12,17,23,25, 3/2,4,5, 4/21, 5/3,13,26, 27, 6/7,26,30, 7/12,23, 8/1,3,29,31, 9/7,8,12,20,24,26,29, 10/10,27, 12/8

HEAVEN
1/2,3,10,15,21,22, 3/2,7,21,22, 5/2,5,10,27,31, 6/10,11, 7/2,3, 8/4,5,9,16,21,22,23,24,28,30, 9/1,3,10,13,14,18,19,24,25,26, 10/15,17,24,25, 11/3,5,8,13,21,25,29, 12/3,6,11,12,14,17,18,20, 24,26,31

HELP
2/7,17,18,26, 3/6, 4/8,14, 5/5,23, 6/27,28, 7/17,30,31, 8/16, 9/1,13,24, 10/12, 11/17, 12/17

HOLINESS
1/18,23, 3/5, 4/24, 5/8, 11, 6/15, 7/24, 8/25, 9/23,30, 10/13,25

KEYWORDS	DATES
HOLY SPIRIT	1/2,15,19,23, 2/11,12,15,17,18,22, 3/5,21,28, 4/15,16,28, 5/4,7,10,13,14,17,20,21,22,24,26,28,29, 6/1,6, 15,17, 7/5,7,16,26,30, 8/2,4,10,11,13,14,16,18,19,20,27,30, 9/3,6,8,10,15,17,20,26,28,29, 10/1,7, 11/3,9, 12/5,21
HONESTY	1/30, 9/7,16, 10/26, 12/13
HONOR / GLORIFY GOD	2/5,12, 3/10, 4/18, 5/9, 6/3,10 7/4,15, 8/4,22,23, 9/1,13, 10/3,14,25,30, 11/6, 12/21
HOPE	1/1,2,4,10,21, 2/3,8,15,22,23, 3/1,3,6,20, 4/5,9,11, 5/9,15,16,19,22,24,28, 6/7,14,16,18,22,23,25,30, 7/15, 8/5,6,16,17,19,20,27,29, 9/11,17,21,28,29, 10/1,7,8,31, 11/10, 12/7,11,12,21,31,
HOSPITALITY	5/18, 10/14,
HUMILITY	1/2,15,23, 2/9,10,14,18,23, 3/1, 4/17,29, 5/1,31, 8/17,23,25, 9/3,16,29, 10/9,16, 11/6, 12/13,22,27
IDOLATRY	1/18,23, 3/20, 4/12,13, 5/10, 6/17,20, 7/29, 8/9,13, 11/16
IMAGE OF GOD	2/28, 3/8, 4/6, 5/29, 6/16, 8/2,17, 12/14
IMITATORS	1/8,28, 4/28, 5/7,18, 8/25, 10/11,16, 12/22
IMPARTIALITY	1/2, 5/6,7, 9/30, 10/21
IMPOSSIBILITY	2/8, 4/9,12,20,27, 5/7,23,25, 6/11,30, 7/26, 8/29, 9/8,9,12,30, 10/30, 11/22,26
INHERITANCE / LEGACY	1/2,27,28, 3/1,2,20, 4/11,14, 5/16, 7/20, 9/20,28,30, 10/6
INJUSTICE / UNJUST	3/1, 5/2,29,30, 6/8,18, 8/31, 10/1,6, 12/3
INSPIRATION	1/10,27, 3/22, 4/23, 6/1, 8/5, 11/9
INSTRUCTION	1/2,8,9,13,27,29, 2/19, 3/5,7,18, 6/12 7/3,11,24, 8/5,7,8,14, 9/2,3, 10/23, 11/6, 12/19,28
INTEGRITY	1/8,30, 6/7, 10/23, 12/15
INTERCESSOR / INTERMEDIARY	
	2/27, 4/2, 5/14, 7/29, 9/27,
INTIMACY / INTIMATE	2/7, 3/28, 4/3, 6/19,20, 10/4,5,6,8,18, 11/22
JEALOUSY	1/12, 4/12,30, 6/9,19, 8/1, 10/27, 12/18
JESUS CHRIST	1/5, 2/1,5,8,10,12,13,16,19,21,22,23,24, 3/1,2,3,4,5, 4/10,15, 5/13, 6/1,22,25, 7/7,15,21,23,26,28,29, 8/5,6,11,13,15,17,19, 20,23,24,25,31, 9/1,3,6,8,9,10,14, 15,16,17,20,22,23,24,25,27,28,29, 10/1/7,13,16,12/4,13,18
JESUS 'DIVINITY	1/23, 3/21, 5/14, 11/14,19, 12/18
JOY / GLADNESS	1/1,3,4,10,11,20, 2/2,11, 3/6, 5/2,3,4,19,22,23,26,28, 6/2,7,8,14,22,23,24, 7/14,16,19,23,24,26, 8/4,12,16,17,19,20,24, 9/7,17,21,27,28, 10/18,13,29, 11/17, 12/10,11,22,31
JUDGEMENT	1/7,22,27,29, 2/14,26, 3/23,24, 4/1,10,25,26,28,29, 5/6,7,8, 6/16,21,26, 7/24,27,29 10/13, 11/21,23,29

KEYWORDS	DATES
MOURNING / SADNESS	1/10, 2/11,13, 3/17,31, 4/10,25,27,30, 5/19,29,30, 6/7, 8/15, 9/11, 11/11
NEEDS	3/14, 4/3, 5/22, 10/7,27
NEIGHBOR / NEIGHBORHOOD	
	1/5,11,17,24, 2/6,12,17,18,25,26, 3/7,27,29, 4/1,2,17, 18,20,24,28, 5/1,16,17,23, 6/6,23,26,29, 7/11,20,23,28, 9/2,13,16,23, 10/5,6,10,14,28, 11/1,2,3,4,6,13,14,18,23, 11/26,27,28, 12/14,16
NEW BIRTH / NEW LIFE	1/3, 2/8, 3/28, 4/8,25, 5/8,17,28, 6/4, 9/15,22,25,30, 10/8,18
NEW THINGS	1/3,4,21,25, 2/8,21,28, 3/3,13,15,21,22,28,29, 4/1,5,8, 11,14,16,17, 5/4,5,8,13,15,16,17,28, 6/4,5,10,17,19, 7/4,5,14,21,22, 8/6/8,16,25,29, 9/4,12,22,25,28,30, 10/3,4,8,18, 11/6,23,26,27,28,30, 12/2/10,16,20,25,31
OBEDIENCE	1/2,9,12,19,21,25,26,24,27,29, 2/1,11, 3/7,18,28, 4/12,15,20, 5/3,9,15, 6/6,11,16,17,19,20,21,30, 7/13,16,19,29, 8/9,23,24,30, 9/2,3,8,9,10,19,23,27,28, 10/12,17, 11/2,6, 12/5,12,16,27
OBSTACLES / BARRIERS	1/26, 3/4,10,16, 4/7, 7/19,24, 8/13, 9/4,6, 10/4,5, 11/1,23, 12/6,14,17,30
OFFENSE	1/11, 3/9, 10/5, 11/18
OPPORTUNITIES	1/11,25,31, 2/19, 8/1,20,23,24, 9/14,25, 10/25,27, 12/20,31
ORPHANS	1/9,22, 2/13,14,20,26, 3/1,11,15, 6/5,6,7,18,19,20, 8/16, 9/13,18, 10/21,28
PATIENCE	2/19, 3/2,4, 7/6, 8/5,19,20,25,26, 9/6,23, 10/11,19, 11/29, 12/10,17,27
PEACE	1/2,5,7,11,13,16,20,21,29, 2/2,3,11,12,15,25, 3/1,6, 4/2,14,16, 18,24,26,28, 5/4,16,23, 6/2,14,15,16,22,23, 7/13,20,23, 8/12,17,24,27,30,31, 9/8,28, 10/1,5,6,13, 11/21, 12/11,22,25,28
PENANCE	2/17, 9/12, 12/8
PERSECUTION / OPPRESSION	
	1/23, 2/11, 3/1, 4/3,11,13, 5/13,26,27,30, 6/18, 8/28, 9/8,16,19, 10/1,2,15,20,28, 11/2,10,28
PERSEVERANCE	1/24,27, 3/15,16,17,30,31, 4/13,16,23,26,30, 5/5,9, 6/9, 7/6,13, 8/20,26,31, 9/11, 10/5,19, 12/17,27
PHILOSOPHIES	1/23,28, 4/26,30, 7/25, 8/7, 9/25
PLEASING GOD	1/14,24,27, 2/19, 3/20,27, 5/23, 6/11,15,30, 7/22,27, 9/2,13,27, 10/17, 12/7

KEYWORDS	DATES
POOR / POVERTY	1/16, 2/17,26, 5/23, 6/18, 7/19,28, 9/13,27, 12/26
PRAYER / INTERCESSION	
	1/24, 2/2,3,8,9,18,23,25,26, 3/5, 4/2,13, 5/5, 6/13,26,29, 7/9,10,13,19,22,24,25, 8/1,16,22,26,30, 9/1,3,4,6,13,14,16, 10/3,4,7,8,10,11, 11/10,11,18,26, 12/2,10,30
PREJUDICE	5/6, 7/25
PRIDE	1/13, 2/12,26, 3/17, 7/17, 9/13, 10/2
PRISON / IMPRISONED	4/4, 6/19,24, 8/14,15, 9/6,8,16, 10/2,28, 11/10, 12/8
PRODIGAL CHILDREN	1/15,16, 2/25, 5/28, 7/31, 8/13, 9/20
PROPHECIES	5/11,13,24, 6/20,21, 8/15, 12/8
PROSPERITY	1/1,9,27, 3/1, 4/29, 6/13, 10/6,8
PROTECTION / SAFETY	1/6,8,14,26,28, 2/2,9,17,26, 3/2,4,7,18, 4/7,13,14,18, 5/2,4,21, 6/23,25,28, 7/3,13,16,18,23, 8/10,18,24, 9/9,20,24,28, 10/1, 11/13,15, 12/18,30
PROVIDENCE	6/13, 11/20
PROVISION	1/24, 2/9,26, 3/13,14, 4/24, 8/18, 9/18, 12/7,
PRUDENT / CAREFUL	1/8,16, 2/15,19,20, 3/7,16, 4/23, 5/1, 6/6,26, 7/10, 8/22,24,30, 9/1,5,29, 11/7, 12/5,29,30
PUNISHMENT / WRATH	2/25,27, 3/1,27, 6/26, 8/19,31, 9/23,27,29, 10/6,13,26, 11/13, 12/16,23
PURIFICATION	1/13,18, 2/18, 3/4,9,15,16, 6/10,15,20,21,25, 9/12,20,23,28, 10/6,13, 11/15, 12/3,5
PURPOSE	1/1,6,11,15,18,25, 2/10,12,17,22,23, 3/2, 4/6,24, 6/3,6, 7/4,10,15, 8/8, 9/27, 11/16, 12/15
RECONCILIATION	1/29, 2/12,25, 4/6, 5/2, 7/20, 10/13, 11/25, 12/29
REDEEMER / REDEMPTION	
	1/13,25, 2/16,20,27, 3/4,12,22,30, 4/4,5,10, 5/1,13,16,22,30, 6/20,21,25, 8/31, 9/28, 10/7,13, 12/2,26
REFRESHMENT / RENEWAL	
	1/4, 2/17, 3/4,9, 8/2,13,14, 10/1,3, 12/11
REFUGE / FORTRESS	1/21,26, 3/31, 5/4,8, 6/18,28, 7/20,23, 8/10,19,20, 9/29, 10/31, 11/25,30, 12/9,11,21
REGRETS	4/17, 7/20,23, 8/10,19,20, 9/29, 10/31, 11/25,30, 12/9,11,21
RELATIONSHIPS	1/3,5,11,16,29, 2/7,21,22, 3/6,26,27,28,29,v4/3,9,15,20, 28, 5/20, 6/2, 10/4
REPENTANCE	1/15, 2/12,17,27, 3/18,27, 4/15,17, 6/2,22,27, 7/9,27, 9/6,12,20, 10/1,7, 12/12
RESCUE	1/6,15,18,22,25, 2/3,5,10,17,23,25, 3/2,3,22,29, 4/5,13, 23,24, 5/2,3,21,24,30,31, 6/2,18,26,c8/3,10,23,28,31, 9/5,22,23,24, 11/8,16, 12/5,6,8,12,14,16,23

KEYWORDS	DATES
RESPECT / REVERENCE	1/2,7,12,27,29, 2/18,23, 3/5, 4/26, 5/7,8, 7/19, 9/13,23, 10/6,12,16
RESPONSIBILITY	1/14, 2/19, 4/16, 6/13, 7/31, 11/10, 12/1
REST / REPOSE	2/6,27, 4/14,22, 7/28, 8/6, 9/6, 10/3, 12/1,15
RESTITUTION	2/9,21, 3/1,2,26,31, 4/15, 5/3,25,26,31, 6/1,8, 12/5
RESURRECTION	1/25, 2/8,9,21,22, 4/5,10,11,18,25, 5/9,22,28, 8/6,23, 9/8,9,14, 11/19
REVEAL / MANIFEST	1/2, 2/11, 4/9, 6/1,6,14,18, 8/14, 9/2,20, 11/19
REWARD	1/21,24, 2/8, 4/24,25, 6/30, 9/13,19, 10/6, 11/20
SACRIFICE	1/3,6,23,25, 2/4,11,20 4/2,8,10,19, 5/16,30, 6/5,16, 7/29, 8/11, 19,23,29,31, 9/2,9,14,19,27,28, 10/7,20,25, 11/4, 12/8
SALVATION / SAVIOR	1/21, 2/6,11,12,15,17,22, 3/1,3,5, 4/2,3,4,5,12,13, 5/9,15,30, 6/2,20,21,26,28,30, 7/10, 8/4,5,13,14,16,24, 9/6,7,9,10,15,17,22,24,27, 10/1,11,13,22,24,30,31, 11/4,8,10,16,28,29,30, 12/14,21,23,25,28
SANCTIFICATION / PURIFICATION	
	1/18, 2/10, 3/4,9, 4/8, 5/17, 6/10,15, 7/3, 8/25
SEEK GOD	1/24, 7/24, 8/1, 9/15,20, 11/22,25,30, 12/31
SELF-ESTEEM	2/23, 7/4,17, 9/12,22, 12/9
SELFISHNESS	1/13, 2/21, 3/18, 4/8, 7/8, 8/5, 9/23,26, 10/2, 12/3
SERVANT / SERVICE	1/1,5, 2/4,20 4/3, 5/1, 6/3,8,18, 7/5,17,19,28,29, 8/2,11,23,25,31, 9/2,10,13,17, 10/1,2,14
SICKNESS	2/18, 3/4, 4/21, 5/19, 6/7, 8/5,31, 9/29, 12/26
SIN / SINNER	1/11,13,15,18,19,23,25, 2/4,11,12,16,17,18,21,22,25,27, 3/4,6,7,9,10,20,26,27, 4/1,2,10,11,15,17, 5/2,9,10,27, 6/11,17,20,21,26,27, 7/11,14,27,30, 8/9,15,25,27,29,31, 9/6,12,15,16,20,22,27, 10/1,7,10,13,26, 11/1, 12/23
SLAVERY	1/13,23,25, 2/4,11, 5/8, 9/15, 10/1
SPIRITUAL CONFLICT	5/10, 7/1, 8/28
SPIRITUAL FOOD / HUNGER	
	1/14, 2/11,24,25, 4/30, 6/18, 8/4,11,22, 9/10,18, 12/17
SPIRITUAL FREEDOM	1/13,16,21,25, 2/4,11,15,16, 3/5, 4/3,12,24, 5/1,8,9,27, 6/14,18, 7/4,12,18, 8/13,17,22,28,30, 9/8,15,22,28,29, 10/21, 11/16, 12/12,16
SPIRITUAL GIFTS	1/2, 4/9,21, 5/2, 6/3,18,30, 7/26, 8/3, 9/17,27, 10/4, 12/15
SPIRITUAL GROWTH	4/16,23, 7/22, 8/22, 9/2, 10/18, 12/2,14
SPIRITUAL MIND / MATURITY	
	4/9, 5/17, 7/1,6,18,22, 8/5,20,26,30, 9/14,21, 10/14,17,18, 12/11,15
SPIRITUAL RESTORATION	
	1/11,13,15, 2/21, 3/2,4,28, 5/3,4, 6/24, 8/3, 9/22, 10/27, 12/5

KEYWORDS	DATES
SPIRITUAL THIRST	1/8,17, 5/8, 11/22
SPIRITUAL TRANSFORMATION	
	1/6,9, 2/11,12, 3/3, 4/17,25, 5/8, 7/26, 8/12,13, 9/2,17,28,29, 10/11,25, 11/16
STEWARDSHIP	1/30, 2/6,10, 3/17,18, 4/3, 5/20,25, 6/3, 8/18, 11/13
STORMS	2/3, 4/14, 5/16, 6/23, 7/5,30, 9/28, 10/2, 11/12, 12/1,5,17
STRANGER / ALIEN / INMIGRANT	
	2/23, 3/5,22, 4/26, 9/13, 10/28
STRENGTH / POWER	1/26, 2/12,19,22,23, 3/2,4, 5/30, 6/28, 7/3,26,30, 8/2,6,10,17,20,22,26, 9/20,21,26, 10/1,3,4,5,17,
STUDY / MEDITATION	1/17, 2/24, 6/12, 8/5,7,30, 9/2,3, 10/24, 11/6,8,9,25,26
SUBMISSION	1/31, 2/26, 4/26, 6/10,17, 8/23,27, 10/9
SUCCESS	2/7, 5/26, 6/13, 8/1,26,30, 9/21, 10/27, 12/26
SUFFERING	1/6,20, 2/21,23,25, 4/11,27, 5/22,26,30, 6/24, 8/15,17,31, 10/7, 12/28
SUICIDE	2/23
SUSTENANCE / FOOD	1/1,4,8,10,17,26 2/17,19,22, 3/13,14, 4/22, 6/10,18, 7/15,16,28, 8/8,16, 9/18,28, 11/17,20,27, 12/10
TEMPTATION / TEMPTER	1/22,24,31, 2/7,25, 4/15, 5/10, 7/11,27, 8/17,27, 9/8, 10/9,12, 12/30
THANKSGIVING	2/2, 8/4, 11/27, 12/2,31
THOUGHTS	2/21,23, 3/7,26, 4/5, 5/23,30, 6/11,15,23,25, 7/17, 8/5,15, 9/8,11,22,24,29, 10/10, 11/5,25, 12/3,15,17,29
TRADITION	4/26, 9/1
TREASURES / RICHES	1/24,27, 2/1,19, 5/10,30, 6/16,22, 8/9, 9/13,17,24,27, 10/12
TRIALS / TRIBULATIONS / STUMBLING	
	1/2,27, 2/3,11, 3/2, 4/18, 5/2,9,16,21,23, 6/23,24,27
TRINITY	3/21, 4/8, 5/14, 7/22,23, 8/10,15,19,20,26,28, 9/8,25,28,29, 10/23
TRUST / TRUSTING GOD	1/3,4,26,28,31, 2/3,5,27, 3/2,4, 4/1,14,16,24,26, 6/11, 13,17,24,25,29, 7/18,22,30, 8/10,27, 9/1,9,20, 24,28, 10/1,5,6,7,12,15,31, 11/12,24,28, 12/1,9,20,21,22,26
TRUTH	1/7,16,19,23,28, 2/13,17, 3/12,21,30,31, 4/26, 5/3,9, 15,27, 6/1,12,16,17, 8/27,30, 9/15,22, 10/11, 12/13,29
UNBELIEVERS / DISBELIEF	
	1/6,18, 2/10,12, 3/26, 4/11, 7/26, 12/8,23
UNITY	1/7, 2/7, 5/25, 7/13, 8/19, 10/4, 11/14
UNITY IN CHRIST	3/13, 4/4,8, 5/29, 6/9, 7/23, 11/14
VALUABLE	1/25, 2/6, 4/24, 10/8,29, 11/24, 12/5

KEYWORDS	DATES
VICTORY / CONQUERORS	1/1, 2/11,16, 3/2, 4/4,15, 5/21,30, 6/24,30, 7/11,12,18,20, 8/12,20,26,27, 9/21,24,27,10,7,15, 11/4,20, 12/20
VIGILANT	1/22, 3/15, 5/10, 6/19,20, 12/30
WARN	2/9, 7/13, 8/20, 9/5,13, 10/10,28, 11/1,7, 12/21,30
WATCHFUL	2/20, 3/7, 4/4,18, 11/13, 12/30
WATER OF LIFE	3/18, 9/15,17, 10/1
WEAPON / ARMOR	4/9, 6/30, 11/15
WEARINESS	3/4,28, 8/2,6, 12/17
WIDOW	5/27, 6/5,19,20, 10/28, 12/28
WITNESS / TESTIFY	1/19,21,26, 2/5,19,23, 3/1, 4/23,24, 5/13,16, 7/10, 8/14,16,20,21, 9/4,6,8,21,24,28,29, 10/14, 11/8,27,30, 12/1,2,24
WOMEN IN THE BIBLE	1/31, 3/2,16,25, 4/18, 6/19, 8/27, 9/14,27, 10/6,9,30, 11/5,9,11, 12/25
WORK	2/22, 3/2, 8/5,6, 9/10,29, 10/7
WORRY	1/22, 2/2,6,24, 3/3, 4/7,22, 5/31, 11/11, 12/11
WORSHIP / PRAISE	1/1,12, 2/26, 4/10,20,27, 5/22, 6/7,10, 8/4,18,27, 9/9,17,24, 10/7,14, 11/8, 12/12,18,20

PHOTO CREDITS

DATE	Picture Location / Subject	Photo Credit
26-Jun	New Mexico Sunset	Barbara Mora
18-May	Egypt	Carlos & Sophia
21-Jun	Sphinx, Egypt	Carlos & Sophia
1-Aug	Vic I Myrdal Church, Iceland	Carlos & Sophia
8-Aug	Pyramids, Egypt	Carlos & Sophia
14-Aug	Pyramids, Egypt	Carlos & Sophia
17-Aug	Great Pyramid, Egypt	Carlos & Sophia
30-Oct	Waterfall - Iceland	Carlos & Sophia
18-Dec	Winter flowers	Carlos & Sophia
19-Dec	Hvolsvöllur Glacier, Iceland	Carlos & Sophia
31-Dec	Iceland springs	Carlos & Sophia
17-Sep	Moon	Carlos Aristizabal
3-Apr	Australian Sunset	Claudia Mejía
11-Mar	Moon over Chimborazo, Ecuador	Eduardo Puga
10-Apr	Puembo night sky, Quito, Ecuador	Eduardo Puga
29-Apr	Chimborazo Volcano, Ecuador	Eduardo Puga
2-Jun	San Francisco Church - Quito, Ecuador	Eduardo Puga
9-Jun	Moon over Chimborazo, Ecuador	Eduardo Puga
3-Jul	Cotopaxi, Ecuador	Eduardo Puga
20-Jul	Chimborazo Volcano, Ecuador	Eduardo Puga
31-Jul	Imbabura, Ecuador	Eduardo Puga
18-Sep	Chiviqui, Tumbaco, Ecuador	Eduardo Puga
11-Oct	Iliniza Volcano, Ecuador	Eduardo Puga
23-Oct	Venus seen from Quito, Ecuador	Eduardo Puga
22-Nov	Reserva Ecológica Cotacachi-Cayapas, Imbabura, Ecuador	Eduardo Puga
6-Dec	Reserva Ecológica Cotacachi-Cayapas, Imbabura, Ecuador	Eduardo Puga
16-Dec	El Chimborazo Volcano, Ecuador	Eduardo Puga
28-Nov	Ordination Rite - Laying hands, Long Island, NY	Elizabeth Abel
22-Mar	Rt 66, USA	Erika Webster
7-Apr	He is risen - written on sand	Erika Webster
11-Feb	Snow, Norwalk, CT, USA	Fanny Zamora
3-Nov	Basílica del Voto Nacional, Quito, Ecuador	Gabriela Chacón
12-Nov	Parque Nacional Antisana, Ecuador	Gabriela Chacón
16-Nov	Cuenca, Ecuador	Gabriela Chacón
8-Dec	Antisana NationalPark, Ecuador	Gabriela Chacón
19-Nov	Praying Hands - Katerini, Greece	George Iliadis
28-Aug	Thronos - Mt Olympus, Greece	George Kexagias
29-Aug	Mt. Olympus, Pieria, Greece	George Kexagias
4-Sep	Mt. Olympus descent, Pieria, Greece	Giannis Theodoridis
5-Sep	Mt. Olympus summit, Pieria, Greece	Giannis Theodoridis
1-Jun	Moon over Acropolis, Athens, Greece	Greek Gateway
25-Oct	Autumn changing colors - Canada	Jane Orfan
22-Dec	Sunset, Norwalk, CT, USA	John Cardamone
9-Apr	Quito at night, Cotopaxi, Ecuador	José Mejía R.
9-Jul	Rocky Mountains, The Flatirons, USA	Joylene Ceballos
28-Jul	Rocky Mountains, The Flatirons, USA	Joylene Ceballos
19-Jan	Volcano Tungurahua, Ecuador	Juan Illingworth
21-Jan	Sedona, AZ, USA	Julie Bohl
26-Jan	Ephesus, Turkey	Julie Bohl

DATE	Picture Location / Subject	Photo Credit
28-Jan	Clearwater, FL, USA	Julie Bohl
17-Mar	Clearwater, FL, USA	Julie Bohl
2-May	Herington farmer, Kansas, USA	Julie Bohl
27-Jun	Port Chester NY garden, NY, USA	Julie Bohl
11-Jul	Lighthouse	Julie Bohl
25-Sep	Rose	Julie Bohl
2-Oct	Kansas Farm, Kansas, USA	Julie Bohl
17-Nov	Gyula, Hungary	Julie Bohl
9-Nov	Al Khazneh, Petra, Turkey	Luna Mar
26-Feb	Snow-covered afternoon - Norwalk, CT, USA	Luz Chaux
8-Jan	USA winter snow	M. Lynne Taylor
Feb	Xanthópoulos Brothers - 1924	M. Destruge
May	Elefthérios P. Koktsidis	M. Destruge
27-Nov	El Altar Volcano, Riobamba, Ecuador	M.J. Mejía
11-Dec	El Altar Volcano, Riobamba, Ecuador	M.J. Mejía
16-Feb	Cotopaxi, Ecuador	Margarita Viteri
12-Jun	Los Chillos Valley, Quito, Ecuador	Margarita Viteri
27-Jan	Moligt Les Bains, France	Mariella Castagnet
4-Jul	El Carmen, Ecuador	Martha Rodriguez
24-Jul	Clouds reflected on the lake, Ecuador	Martha Rodriguez
25-Jul	Boat on lake	Martha Rodriguez
14-Nov	Grand Teton Ntl Park, Wyoming, USA	Martha Rodriguez
2-Jan	Salt Desert - Bolivia	Michi Niederberger
4-Jan	Palomino - La Guajira	Nora Otalvaro
23-Jan	Santorini, Greece	Nora Otalvaro
23-Mar	Sunset	Nora Otalvaro
8-Apr	Flamingos in flight	Nora Otalvaro
30-May	Red bird	Nora Otalvaro
19-Sep	Boats on the water	Nora Otalvaro
1-Jan	Statue of Liberty, NY, USA	O. Destruge
9-Jan	Puyo, Ecuador - Jan, 2010	O. Destruge
11-Jan	Kerkyra, Corfú, Greece	O. Destruge
14-Jan	USA winter snow	O. Destruge
16-Jan	Cuenca, Ecuador	O. Destruge
18-Jan	Greece Islands	O. Destruge
20-Jan	Apple picking - Danbury, CT, USA	O. Destruge
25-Jan	Washington DC, Pres. Inauguration 2021	O. Destruge
2-Feb	Cristo de la Concordia, Bolivia (2004)	O. Destruge
4-Feb	Fruit Salad - Santorini, Greece	O. Destruge
6-Feb	Sheep - Ecuador	O. Destruge
9-Feb	Norwalk Snow shadows, Norwalk, CT, USA	O. Destruge
14-Feb	Dad and me - Baños, Tungurahua, Ecuador	O. Destruge
20-Feb	Salomé Destruge	O. Destruge
22-Feb	Communion Elements	O. Destruge
23-Feb	Cochabamba, Bolivia - 2004	O. Destruge
25-Feb	Otavalo Woman - Ecuador	O. Destruge
28-Feb	Guayasamín Museum - Quito, Ecuador	O. Destruge
Feb-29	Greek Bread	O. Destruge
Mar	Collage - Inspiring women	O. Destruge
1-Mar	Uncle Jorge Ortega's funeral, Ecuador	O. Destruge
2-Mar	Cotopaxi, Ecuador	O. Destruge
5-Mar	Papoú Aristoklís Xanthópoulos	O. Destruge
6-Mar	Quito sky, San Rafael, Ecuador	O. Destruge
7-Mar	Mitad del Mundo - Quito, Ecuador	O. Destruge

DATE	Picture Location / Subject	Photo Credit
8-Mar	San Agustín, Quito, Ecuador	O. Destruge
16-Mar	Bilován Bolivar - Ecuador	O. Destruge
18-Mar	Cotopaxi, Ecuador	O. Destruge
19-Mar	Rodrigo Sandoval, Parthenon, Greece	O. Destruge
24-Mar	Adventure Bible	O. Destruge
26-Mar	Santorini Crater, Greece	O. Destruge
27-Mar	Cuenca, Ecuador	O. Destruge
29-Mar	Mass during 2020 Pandemic - Cuenca, Ecuador	O. Destruge
30-Mar	Cochabamba, Bolivia - 2004	O. Destruge
31-Mar	Quinipet Campground, NY	O. Destruge
Apr	My grandparents	O. Destruge
4-Apr	San Rafael, Quito, Ecuador	O. Destruge
6-Apr	Destruge Family reunion 2010, Cuenca, Ecuador	O. Destruge
14-Apr	Tandapi rainforest, Ecuador	O. Destruge
21-Apr	Street Musician - Quito, Ecuador	O. Destruge
1-May	San Rafael, Quito, Ecuador	O. Destruge
3-May	Flying over Swiss Alps	O. Destruge
6-May	Otavalo Market, Ecuador	O. Destruge
7-May	Family Camp, Quinipet, LI, NY, USA	O. Destruge
10-May	Over the clouds - Ecuador Andes	O. Destruge
11-May	Paralía, Katerini, Greece	O. Destruge
19-May	Litochoro, Greece	O. Destruge
21-May	Concordia Christ, Cochabamba, Bolivia	O. Destruge
22-May	Alangasí, Quito, Ecuador	O. Destruge
24-May	Paralía, Katerini, Greece	O. Destruge
25-May	Moon over Katerini, Greece	O. Destruge
27-May	Katerini Church, Greece	O. Destruge
28-May	Katerini Fields, Mt. Olympus, Greece	O. Destruge
31-May	Roses, Koukkos, Greece	O. Destruge
7-Jun	Evangelical Greek Church, Katerini, Greece	O. Destruge
8-Jun	Norwalk Day Laborer breakfast, Norwalk, CT, USA	O. Destruge
13-Jun	Flying home after 3-month lockdown, Ecuador	O. Destruge
14-Jun	Greek Daily Meditation, Katerini, Greece	O. Destruge
16-Jun	Papoú & Yiayiá gardening, Norwalk, CT	O. Destruge
18-Jun	Cochabamba, Bolivia - 2004	O. Destruge
23-Jun	Santorini Ferry, Greece	O. Destruge
24-Jun	Lavender field, Katerini, Greece	O. Destruge
25-Jun	Pastor Praying - Greek Evangelical Church, Katerini, Greece	O. Destruge
1-Jul	Oscar Destruge - Greek visa photo	O. Destruge
5-Jul	Lofos, Sevastí, Katerini, Greece	O. Destruge
6-Jul	My children, Cotopaxi, Ecuador - 2012	O. Destruge
7-Jul	Selfie - O. Destruge	O. Destruge
8-Jul	Otavalo, Ecuador	O. Destruge
14-Jul	Sergiani, Sevastí, Katerini, Greece	O. Destruge
15-Jul	Destruge-Glass Family	O. Destruge
16-Jul	San José de Chimbo, Bolívar, Ecuador	O. Destruge
18-Jul	Katerini Port, Greece	O. Destruge
21-Jul	Kings Buffet Table, Bridgeport CT, USA	O. Destruge
26-Jul	Paralía, Katerini, Greece	O. Destruge
29-Jul	San Rafael, Quito	O. Destruge
30-Jul	Shrine, Paralía, Katerini, Greece	O. Destruge
5-Aug	Ermouppolis, Greece 2004	O. Destruge
7-Aug	Church roof - Santorini, Greece	O. Destruge

DATE	Picture Location / Subject	Photo Credit
9-Aug	O. Destruge - Preaching	O. Destruge
10-Aug	Pichincha Volcano, Ecuador 2009	O. Destruge
11-Aug	Greek Bread - Katerini, Greece	O. Destruge
12-Aug	Lázaro & Fanny, Norwalk, CT	O. Destruge
13-Aug	Church - Santorini, Greece	O. Destruge
19-Aug	Church - Koukkos, Greece	O. Destruge
20-Aug	With Yiayía - Paralía, Katerini, Greece	O. Destruge
23-Aug	Greek Evangelical Church family, Katerini, Greece	O. Destruge
25-Aug	Calf Pasture sunset, Norwalk, CT	O. Destruge
26-Aug	Marco Ortega - La Ronda, Quito, Ecuador	O. Destruge
31-Aug	Chapel - Paralía, Katerini, Greece	O. Destruge
1-Sep	Paralía, Katerini, Greece	O. Destruge
6-Sep	Cycling - Litochoro, Greece	O. Destruge
7-Sep	Dinning - Korinós, Greece	O. Destruge
10-Sep	Panecillo, Quito, Ecuador	O. Destruge
11-Sep	O. Destruge - Selfie - Bicycling - Katerini, Greece	O. Destruge
12-Sep	Flying over Swiss Alps	O. Destruge
13-Sep	Cycling - Sevastí, Katerini, Greece	O. Destruge
14-Sep	Yiayía & Sophia - Katerini, Greece	O. Destruge
15-Sep	Cycling - Lofos- Sevastí, Katerini, Greece	O. Destruge
16-Sep	Jacob & Sandy's wedding June 2018, MA, USA	O. Destruge
20-Sep	Agios Georgios Nileias, Magnesia, Greece	O. Destruge
21-Sep	4 Generations - Agios Georgios Nileias, Magnesia, Greece, Sept. 2021	O. Destruge
22-Sep	Schloss Burg Castle, Solingen, Germany	O. Destruge
23-Sep	Afetes, Magnesia, Greece	O. Destruge
24-Sep	Cycling - Pierias, Greece	O. Destruge
27-Sep	Greek Evangelical Church - Sevastí, Katerini, Greece	O. Destruge
28-Sep	The Lord's Prayer - Greek Evan. Church – Sevastí, Greece	O. Destruge
29-Sep	Agios Georgios Nileias, Pilion, Greece	O. Destruge
30-Sep	Sophia & Yiayía - Paralía, Katerini, Greece	O. Destruge
1-Oct	Louxemburg Garden, Paris, France	O. Destruge
3-Oct	Yiayía knitting - Katerini, Greece	O. Destruge
4-Oct	Wedding Ceremony - Katerini, Greece	O. Destruge
5-Oct	Chalet Castelo, Neos Panteilimon, Pieria, Greece	O. Destruge
6-Oct	Dinning - Archaaia Pydna, Pieria, Greece	O. Destruge
7-Oct	Headstone Cross - Sevastí cemetery, Katerini, Greece	O. Destruge
9-Oct	Selfie Litochoro, Pieria, Greece	O. Destruge
10-Oct	Sheffield Island Harbor, Norwalk, CT	O. Destruge
12-Oct	Paralía, Katerini, Greece	O. Destruge
13-Oct	Cotopaxi, Ecuador	O. Destruge
14-Oct	Lázaro & Yiayía - Neos Panteleimonas, Pieria, Greece	O. Destruge
15-Oct	Good friend and guide, Georgios Kexagias	O. Destruge
16-Oct	Abuelita Lilia - Baños, Ecuador	O. Destruge
17-Oct	La Basílica, Quito, Ecuador	O. Destruge
18-Oct	Sophia & Yiayía, Agios Georgios, Pilion, Volos, Greece	O. Destruge
19-Oct	Santorini, Greece	O. Destruge
20-Oct	Sophia & Carlos' Wedding 11/05/2010, NY, USA	O. Destruge
21-Oct	Cappuccino, Makrinitsa, Magnesia, Volos, Greece	O. Destruge

DATE	Picture Location / Subject	Photo Credit
22-Oct	Pastor O. Destruge headshot - Norwalk, CT, USA	O. Destruge
24-Oct	John 5:39 Scripture	O. Destruge
26-Oct	Oscar's Bible	O. Destruge
28-Oct	Coffee reunion - Korinós, Greece	O. Destruge
1-Nov	Charles Bridge, Prague, Chec Republic	O. Destruge
4-Nov	Cycling - Sevastí, Koukkos, Katerini, Greece	O. Destruge
5-Nov	Greek Orthodox Church, Katerini, Greece	O. Destruge
6-Nov	Oscar's Greek Bible	O. Destruge
7-Nov	Cloudy Quito from Teleférico, Quito, Ecuador	O. Destruge
10-Nov	Oscar's Cross - used to be my ring	O. Destruge
11-Nov	Jean-Paul Destruge B'day collage	O. Destruge
13-Nov	El Panecillo, Quito, Ecuador	O. Destruge
15-Nov	Sergiani, Sevastí, Katerini, Greece	O. Destruge
20-Nov	Calf Pasture pier, Norwalk, CT, USA	O. Destruge
23-Nov	Koukkos Skyline, Greece	O. Destruge
24-Nov	Olympus Mt Range, Katerini, Greece	O. Destruge
25-Nov	Cycling - Litochoro, Greece	O. Destruge
26-Nov	Praying Hands - Katerini, Greece	O. Destruge
29-Nov	Greek Orthodox Church, Katerini, Greece	O. Destruge
30-Nov	Giannis Adamides Organist, Katerini, Greece	O. Destruge
1-Dec	Acropolis, Athens, Greece	O. Destruge
2-Dec	Katerini, Greece	O. Destruge
3-Dec	Thessaloniki Airport, Greece	O. Destruge
7-Dec	Luxembourg Garden, Paris, France	O. Destruge
12-Dec	Eagles/vultures - San Rafael, Quito, Ecuador	O. Destruge
14-Dec	Broadway Terrace - going to church, Manhattan, NY, USA	O. Destruge
21-Dec	Broadway Terr w/ my brothers, Manhattan, NY, USA	O. Destruge
23-Dec	Romerillos, Cotopaxi, Ecuador	O. Destruge
25-Dec	Rockefeller Center, NYC, USA	O. Destruge
27-Dec	Family Christmas Photo, Norwalk, CT, USA	O. Destruge
28-Dec	Granddaughter Ségolène Destruge	O. Destruge
29-Dec	Summit Mt. Olympus, Pieria, Greece	O. Destruge
12-Jul	Ark of the Covenant	Public domain
10-Jul	Marco Island, FL, USA	Rachel Castillo
15-Jan	Old sandals	Rights Reserved
22-Jan	Norwalk Lightning skies, Norwalk, CT, USA	Rights Reserved
5-Feb	Buoy	Rights Reserved
17-Feb	Campfire	Rights Reserved
16-Apr	Flowers and mountains	Rights Reserved
4-May	Mountain top desolation	Rights Reserved
4-Jun	Baños, Ecuador	Rights Reserved
8-Nov	Sunset	Rights Reserved
21-Nov	Wolve	Rights Reserved
9-Dec	Andes Refuge, Ecuador	Rights Reserved
24-Dec	Neptune & Saturn sky view	Rights Reserved
7-Jan	Constantinople, Turkey	Sophia Destruge
17-Apr	Sunset Hvar, Croatia	Sophia Destruge
18-Apr	Nisos Paros, Naousa, Cyclades Greece	Sophia Destruge
19-Apr	Carlos & Sophia	Sophia Destruge
30-Apr	Sunset, Greece	Sophia Destruge
26-May	Carlos & Lázaro	Sophia Destruge
19-Jun	Norwalk Sunset - Sophia	Sophia Destruge
8-Oct	Lázaro Elías Aristizabal Destruge	Sophia Destruge

DATE	Picture Location / Subject	Photo Credit
21-Aug	Romerillos Methodist Church, Ecuador	Tamiacurisisa Viracocha
15-Dec	Mt. Olympus, Pieria, Greece	Tania Kalcheva
20-Dec	Mt. Olympus, Pieria, Greece	Tania Kalcheva
13-Apr	Daniel in lion's den	Blackartdepot.com
1-Feb	Quilotoa Lake, Ecuador	Ximena Ruales
18-Feb	Ice-covered cross, Shelter Island, NY, USA	Ximena Ruales
31-Oct	Quilotoa Lake, Ecuador	Ximena Ruales
17-Jun	Moon over Quito, Ecuador	Yumiseva
5-Dec	Calf Pasture moon, Norwalk, CT	Yvonne Marchese Photography

Made in the USA
Monee, IL
21 March 2023

29923125R00254